My Crown Is A Secret

Volume 7

Garrick David Pattenden

Copyright © 2025 Garrick David Pattenden

All rights reserved.

ISBN: 978-1-83417-009-1

DEDICATION

For the children — and for every adult who still carries the soul of a child within their heart. And especially for Marc MK Kenzie who will turn 10 years old this June 22nd, 2026. May your heart always carry the spark of adventure, wonder, and the endless love of family.

With all my love,

Garrick

CONTENTS

	Acknowledgments	i
1	The Birthday That Came and Went	1
2	A Week Before the World Changes	32
3	The Crown in His Blood	57
4	The One Week Window	86
5	The Final Quiet Before the Storm	115
6	Thunder-farts and Diaper Bombs	145
7	Into the Water	172
8	The Leak Contained	203
9	Countdown to Disappearance	235
10	The Royal Jet to Gatwick	279
11	The King of Quiet	312
12	The Digital Ghost	333
13	The Letter to the Editor	359
14	Kendrick Speaks	496
15	Return of the King	431
16	The Final Heirs	458

PREFACE

This is not a story about kings and crowns in the way the world expects. Nor is it a tale bound by the strict borders of history, religion, or tradition. This is a story of memory — of how the past whispers through the hearts of children who carry far more than their years suggest. It is about family: not only by blood, but by choice, by love, and by the quiet covenants formed when souls recognize each other.

Some may read this through the narrow lens of adult reason, seeking explanations that fit rules they have long accepted. But children know better. They see with hearts uncluttered by fear. They understand that family is not simply who you descend from, but who holds your hand when the world grows quiet. In these pages live those truths — where adoption is not absence, where love makes room, and where crowns are not always worn upon heads, but carried in the soul.

The world may not always understand such things. That is fine. This book was never written for the world. It was written for those who already know.

— Garrick David Pattenden

CHAPTER 1: THE BIRTHDAY THAT CAME AND WENT

No one in the castle spoke of the birthday that morning. Not out of forgetfulness, nor avoidance, but because the memory had already been claimed by another place—one far quieter, far simpler. On the outskirts of Copenhagen, tucked behind a modest courthouse and past the street where only old men walked their dogs and returned home before dusk, Eli celebrated his fourth birthday with his parents: Judge Algren and Arlene. The boy wore a deep navy jumper with too-long sleeves and a golden crown stitched by hand into the shoulder seam, the same one he wore on his third birthday, and the same he would likely wear again next year. The cake was almond and strawberry. The candles bent softly to the wind of his breath, and no one interrupted. No castles. No cameras. No press. Just a boy and the people who raised him.

Ben did not go. He could not. That wasn't something that needed discussion anymore. The walls of Rosenshavn Castle had long ago absorbed the truth that some celebrations were safer at a distance. While others wrapped gifts or checked the weather for the party, Ben sat in the east window tower with his elbows on the stone ledge and his voice recorder in hand. The castle was too quiet to pretend. He cleared his throat once, then again, then pressed the red button, and whispered with all the weight a man could carry without breaking: "Happy birthday, buddy. I didn't forget."

He held the recorder for a moment longer, thumb still hovering near the stop button. Then came the words not meant for anyone's ears but his own. "I never could." His breath left him in pieces, not all at once. The kind of breath that didn't belong to sorrow, nor regret, but the hollow ache of a truth withheld for too long. In the other room, Isla shifted beneath the linen throw, still asleep. Her body bore the calm of impending labour—eight months and three weeks exactly. She would not stir unless she had to. The child inside her shifted with familiarity, as though it already understood the cadence of the house, and its father's silence.

Ben had memorized the dates, not just marked them. He'd tracked every passing month since Isla told him, quietly and without theatrics, that she was expecting twins. She had said it without blinking. There was no celebration then either—only the gravity of knowledge passed between two people who could no longer pretend they lived ordinary lives. Isla carried two children beneath her ribs, children born not only of love but of lineage, and with that came a burden she never asked for. But she accepted it. In silence. In full.

There was no need to announce royalty in the halls of Rosenshavn. The children already treated Ben and Isla with reverence, though not because of titles. It was a reverence earned from years of bedtime rituals, scraped knees cleaned without scolding, and stories told without skipping the hard parts. Those within the walls knew who Ben was. Most outside them still didn't. That had always been the point. To be a king no one saw, a ruler who did not sit on thrones or wear crests in public. To be the one they never suspected—that was the secret of survival.

Clara had passed him earlier that morning with a folded blanket and a half-smile, one that said: "Today is not about you." He appreciated that. Clara always understood the right amount of detachment required to hold a family together. Isla had not yet opened her eyes. Her lips parted with sleep as if whispering names not yet spoken. Ben rose from the tower ledge and turned down the flame on the lantern. He walked back through the narrow corridor, past the family tapestry Isla had begun embroidering when her belly first began to swell, past the small chair where Tobias used to nap after night shifts, and into the master room where everything began.

In the far drawer of the bureau, wrapped in tissue paper beside the old DNA records, was the gift Ben had intended for Eli. It wasn't extravagant—just a wooden soldier carved by hand. Ben made it in the dark hours after midnight during Isla's second month of pregnancy, when sleep was rare and meaning was hard to come by. The soldier wore no crown, but a sash, painted faint red, rested across its chest. In Ben's eyes, that sash meant everything. The quiet weight of duty. Not the kind that demanded praise, but the kind that required hiding when necessary. A soldier without armour, without weapon, but never without loyalty.

He'd never known his own father, not truly. And yet, here he was, crafting toy soldiers for a boy who wasn't biologically his, but who loved him anyway. The ache of that thought struck him deep in the chest, but he did not let it settle. He placed the soldier back in the drawer and closed it slowly, as if to delay the sound. Then he turned to Isla's side of the bed, knelt down without disturbing her, and touched her ankle just once—lightly, reverently. She did not wake. Her skin was warm. The babies were due in seven days, if not sooner.

The sun had not risen. But the castle had. In small ways. Lights blinked on in the kitchen. Clara's coffee kettle boiled, though she refused to call it coffee. "It's just boiled leaves," she always muttered. Tobias sang off-key in the nursery while changing the youngest's pyjamas. Silje hummed quietly while folding the same blanket for the third time. But none of them mentioned Eli's birthday. That belonged to another house now. Another life. And Ben respected that.

By the time Isla stirred at last, the castle clock read 6:12 a.m. She opened her eyes, placed a hand on her belly, and looked toward Ben without speaking. He nodded once. No words. Just a look that said yes, I remembered. She closed her eyes again, and the castle—still holding its breath—returned to its rhythm. Seven days. One message sent. And a secret that could no longer stay quiet much longer.

The black ink bled slightly through the paper, not enough to mark the wall behind it, but enough to show it had been pressed deliberately. Not a flourish, not a circle, not even a proper "X"—just a single diagonal stroke intersected by another, a mark of finality without sentiment. Seven days from now. That was what it meant. Ben didn't have to write the word birth, nor did he need to mark it in red. The black ink was more honest. It carried the weight of the moment without ceremony. He closed the calendar and placed it face down on the table as though to spare the rest of the castle from its quiet proclamation.

Isla hadn't seen him do it. She didn't need to. They had marked time together for months, whispering each week into the folds of each other's arms like sacred liturgies spoken in darkness. Her belly now carried not just fullness, but purpose. The twins—unnamed, unseen—moved like tides beneath her ribs. The room seemed to shift with her now. Chairs creaked differently when she passed. Floors softened. Even the kitchen smelled of gentler herbs, as if the castle itself was preparing to receive new life. Clara noticed first. Not with words, but with action. She began boiling water earlier, folding towels tighter, placing extra pillows beside Isla's side of the bed without being asked.

Clara also brought the stretch bands—those long, cloth-like slings used to ease the weight from Isla's back. She'd learned it years ago in a clinic somewhere near Skagen, taught by a midwife who refused to be called a nurse. Isla had resisted the help at first, claiming her spine would adjust on its own. It didn't. And Ben, knowing better than to argue, simply watched as Clara wrapped the bands around Isla's waist and gently pulled from behind to align her hips. Isla winced once, then sighed. Clara didn't say you're welcome. She just nodded and reached for the next sling.

Silje, ever precise, had taken to folding baby clothes in the library—claiming the long wooden tables were more suitable for symmetry. The tiny garments were mostly creams and greys, soft cottons with wooden buttons, not a single synthetic piece in sight. She folded with both reverence and restraint, never cooing or commenting on their size, never asking about names. The names, she understood, were not hers to know. Not yet. There was something unspoken in the castle: that the arrival of these twins carried a weight not to be diluted with idle joy. They were royal, yes. But more than that—they were revelations.

Tobias, who pretended nothing made him uncomfortable, had been given the task of assembling the birthing tub. He grumbled as he carried the collapsible frame up three flights of stairs, muttering about poor Danish plumbing and cursed stairwells. But he did it without complaint. His hands moved quickly, confidently. When Ben passed by the room, he caught Tobias pretending to test the temperature of the empty tub with an outstretched hand, as though the air alone could tell him something about what was to come. Ben didn't interrupt. He simply offered a slight nod, which Tobias returned, then went back to tightening a valve that didn't need tightening.

The children—those still too young to grasp time—sensed the change in atmosphere. They didn't ask. But they paused in their games more often. Thunderfart tag had been replaced with quieter pursuits. Wooden trains. Sock puppets. Whispered questions about when they would get to meet the babies. Some asked if they'd be allowed to hold them. Others just peered at Isla's stomach as if expecting to see tiny faces pressing outward. The older ones knew better. They took on extra chores without instruction. One girl volunteered to dry the dishes, unprompted. Another folded towels and placed them outside Isla's door. No one spoke of it. It simply happened.

Ben remained in the background, watching. He didn't command. He didn't instruct. That had never been his way. He watched as the house turned inward, not in fear, but in anticipation. He knew what was coming, and not only because of the date circled on the calendar. It was in the way the hallways sounded at night—quieter, deeper somehow. It was in the way the castle's draft no longer chilled him. The air was warmer. As if even the walls were holding their breath.

That evening, Ben stood in the study with a small silver key in hand. It opened the cabinet where the ancestral documents were kept—the birth records, the lineage scrolls, the maps that Isla had once traced with her fingertip to prove a point about royal descent. He pulled out a sheet, the one with his own haplogroup scribbled beside his father's in faint pencil. R1b. He traced it with his thumb, then folded it again, careful not to let the crease fall on the family name. The truth of his DNA was no longer something to hide. But it wasn't yet something to declare. Not yet.

He returned the sheet to the cabinet and locked it again. Then he turned and looked toward the hallway, where Clara's humming had stopped. The birth tub was now fully assembled. Tobias had placed a towel beside it and left the room. Silje passed by with the folded clothes, nodding toward Ben without breaking stride. Everything was in motion, even if nothing had begun. The countdown was not a metaphor. It was real. Measurable. Inescapable.

Later that night, Isla asked him softly, "Have you told them?" Ben shook his head. "No," he whispered. "They know without knowing." She nodded, eyes half-closed. "Good. Let's keep it that way." The next morning, she would begin experiencing the false contractions. Not the real ones yet. But close. The castle would not sleep the same again. Not until the twins were born. And even then—especially then—it would never go back to the way it was before.

The sky above Rosenshavn Castle did not shimmer with stars so much as it blinked with questions. Satellites blinked once, twice—then vanished. A high wind moved the tree line far below, but up here, at the peak of the castle's watchtower, the world seemed pinned in place. Ben leaned against the stone parapet, arms crossed, gaze fixed eastward. His mind wandered where no child's birthday candles could reach. The horizon, though dark and unmoving, pulsed with a quiet unease, like a page before the first word is written. He wasn't anxious. Not in the usual sense. He was listening. Waiting. Measuring patterns like the old days.

Years ago, Sørensen had taught him to observe the road before the dust rose, to mark the changes in air pressure before a drone passed overhead, to trust that silence was rarely honest. "Stillness is your enemy," Sørensen used to growl, arms folded across his chest like a storm cloud with muscles. "Nothing truly dangerous ever makes noise before it's too late." Those words had never left Ben. They belonged to his marrow now, fused deeper than birthright or throne. The air tonight was still. Too still. And that frightened him more than any approaching chaos.

Copenhagen slept to the west. The sea curled quiet at its edge. And yet, the city lights—those usual flares of movement—were dimmer than expected. A certain rhythm was missing. He could feel it. He didn't need to explain that to anyone; they wouldn't understand unless they, too, had once lived in a digital trench war at age ten, sending out pulse signals to track breach attempts. Most children played with toy trucks. Ben intercepted military-grade wireless interference and decoded it by hand. The game had always been far bigger than the adults knew.

Now, he couldn't help but see it all again. That flicker on the road wasn't a passing car. That long pause between radio beacons on the security panel below? That wasn't routine. And it wasn't just him imagining it. Not tonight. Tonight, he was watching for something real. The kind of thing that made Sørensen check locks twice without knowing why. The kind of thing Ben could smell in the silence—like smoke that hadn't quite formed yet, but whose heat was already climbing through the walls.

Below him, the castle gave no sign of disturbance. The night crew patrolled in pairs, silent, respectful, trained to avoid light and unnecessary motion. Tobias had walked the entire southern wing with Clara before she returned to Isla's side. He had heard them laugh in the hallway— Clara teasing Tobias about getting diaper duty again if the twins came early. But upstairs, in this tower, humour had no foothold. Only memory, calculation, and the weight of decisions lived here.

Ben slid his hand into the inside pocket of his overcoat. He removed a small black device, matte and smooth like river stone, marked with a single blue diode. A silent tracker, fully analog. Sørensen had given it to him the year they learned about the first breach—back when Ben wasn't a king yet, just a boy with fire in his mind and a strange destiny pressing on his shoulder blades. The device vibrated gently. Once. Then again. It wasn't picking up local traffic. It was reading a scan frequency—a low, slow ripple of data pings bouncing from somewhere outside the usual jurisdiction. Someone was scanning the area for weaknesses.

He didn't need to name them. He'd met people like that before. "Information is a drug," Sørensen once warned, tapping the side of Ben's skull. "You get a taste of the truth, and suddenly, all you want is more. Doesn't matter who it hurts. Doesn't matter what gets exposed." Ben knew exactly what the man meant. And tonight, someone was clearly jonesing for a hit.

A faint hum of cold wind brushed the glass of the upper window behind him. He didn't turn. His eyes stayed fixed on the northwestern quadrant, where the treeline folded back just enough to reveal the quiet curve of the access road. No vehicles. No trespassers. But the calm didn't feel earned. It felt forced. Or worse, orchestrated. A kind of quiet that knew it was being watched.

In the past, he might have cracked open his laptop and traced the pings himself. But tonight, he didn't need software to know he was being studied. The scent of it was in the air, in the pace of the wind, in the odd way a single owl hooted and was not answered. The silence was wrong. Not blank, but held. As though someone out there was waiting for him to blink first.

He tapped the tracker once more. The signal drifted, then steadied. Still not local. Still not safe. He slipped it back into his coat, tightened the buttons near his collar, and remained at the parapet. He would not move until the rhythm returned. Until the stars above Copenhagen blinked in their right sequence. Until whatever ghost was watching either showed its face or vanished entirely.

The stairs behind him creaked gently. It wasn't fear. It was someone's heel, cautious but not sneaky. Ben didn't flinch. "You can come up," he called, soft but clear. Sørensen emerged from the stairwell, wearing that same dark jacket he'd worn for twenty years. "You feel it too?" Ben asked without turning. Sørensen said nothing for a while. Just came to stand beside him, arms crossed, watching the same quadrant of sky. "I do now," he said. "Been off for about an hour." Ben nodded slowly. "I thought so. Something's not right in Copenhagen." "You think it's time?"

"Not yet," Ben said. "But almost. Whoever's out there, they're not guessing. They know where to look. They're just too afraid to come closer." "They won't stay afraid for long." "I know." Sørensen reached into his pocket and passed Ben a folded paper. "Map of escape routes. All updated." "I'll go over it in the morning." "We might not have until morning." Ben finally turned to look at him. "Then we'll go over it now." They stood side by side in the watchtower, father and son not by blood but by bond. Their breaths rose like steam in the cold. Below them, the castle remained still. But the wind had started to change direction.

Ben did not raise his voice. He didn't have to. The sound of parchment turning was enough to summon the room to stillness. Pancakes cooled. Bacon crisped and sat forgotten. A half-formed argument over whose turn it was to clear plates dissolved mid-sentence. One by one, the children pulled their chairs closer. Some remained standing. Others leaned over elbows and stacked plates as if forming a wall around the old brown ledger that lay opened like a book of royal secrets. But there were no crowns drawn in its margins. No swords. No castles. Just the dry marks of ancestry, printed in blocky type and speckled with faded fingerprints. Ben lifted the page. The castle was silent.

"This is not a royal book," he said, tapping the open ledger with a single knuckle. "It's not gold-leafed. It's not signed by kings. And yet, it holds more truth than most royal proclamations ever did." He looked over at Thomas, then Kristian, then Lukas, who was already squinting at the numbers like they might sprout wings and fly off the page. Peter and Max-Leo sat cross-legged beside the fireplace, each with a piece of toast, their bites slowing. Even little Freja-Marie, too young to understand, had turned toward her brother's voice, mouthing a soft sound as if she felt the gravity of the words even without meaning. Isla listened from the window bench, eyes locked on the ledger, hands still.

"This page says where I come from. But more than that, it says where you come from," Ben continued, tracing a path with his finger. "This is called a haplogroup. It's a fancy word, but all it really means is... a family of families. It's like a great tree. Each branch leads to another. This one, here, is my maternal line. It's the line of the mothers before me. It goes back thousands of years, all the way to a woman we call H5a1. She lived around 6,500 years ago, likely in southeastern Europe. Her story was almost forgotten—until now."

Thomas sat forward. "Like great-great-great-great times a million grandma?" he asked, lowering his voice in case reverence was expected. Ben nodded solemnly. "Yes. Exactly that. And her story is still written inside of me—inside of you, if you carry her blood. Her daughters crossed through ice and wind and forest. They passed through what's now Hungary, and Poland, and northern Scotland. She's not a myth. She was real. Her hands might've held clay pots or dug for roots, or maybe just held her daughter's face as she died. That's not history in a book. That's your flesh remembering itself."

He turned the page, revealing a small tree-like chart lined with letters and numbers, stretching downwards. "H5a1 came from a larger group called H5, and before that, H, and before that, R... all the way to one woman in Africa, around 150,000 years ago. She is the mother of every mother's line on Earth. This line never breaks—not through war, not through time. It is passed from mother to child like a candle lit in the dark." "And the fathers?" Kristian asked, his hand half-raised. "Is there a father's tree too?"

Ben smiled. "There is. And it runs through the Y chromosome. That's the paternal haplogroup. Mine is called R-S660. It traces to a man who lived around 3,800 years ago. That's 152 generations. Think about that. Imagine each of those men standing behind you, shoulder to shoulder, forming a line that stretches across time." He paused to let the weight of that image settle. "They were farmers, warriors, kings. Some held nothing. Others ruled empires. But they all lived. And they all carried the same strand of fire inside them."

Max-Leo scratched his head. "So... we're like made of maps?" "Exactly," Ben said, with no hesitation. "Living maps. And every step you take echoes a thousand that came before. You may think you choose your steps alone, but your blood remembers roads long vanished. That's why we don't lie to children about who they are. Because your ancestors didn't survive plagues and ice ages and war just so you'd be told you're ordinary. You're not."

He pointed to a line that veered toward Scotland. "This is Ava. A woman found in a tomb in Achavanich. She lived 4,250 years ago and shared part of this maternal DNA. She had dark eyes, dark hair, and skin like southern Europeans. And yet she lived and died in Scotland. That means our ancestors didn't stay in one place. They moved. They built. They buried their dead with beakers and flint, and when the wind blew too hard, they walked."

The children didn't fidget. They didn't interrupt. Even Tobias, who had wandered into the room under the pretence of checking the stove, remained by the door, arms crossed, listening as if hearing a sermon he didn't know he needed. Isla still said nothing. Her fingers rested on the hem of Freja-Marie's blanket, but her gaze had not moved from the ledger. She knew Ben was not simply teaching genetics. He was threading a crown into memory, word by word.

"This part," Ben continued, gesturing to the right margin, "connects to the Irish kings—the Uí Néill dynasty. You may have heard of a man named Niall of the Nine Hostages. He's more legend than history, but his blood runs through millions. They ruled parts of Ireland from the 7th to 11th centuries. My Y-DNA—my paternal haplogroup—is linked to that same tree. Not because someone made it up, but because it was always there, quietly waiting to be remembered."

Peter's toast slipped onto his lap. He didn't notice. "But what if someone says that's not real? That DNA doesn't mean royalty?"

Ben's face didn't soften. "Then they're wrong. Royalty is not about thrones. It's about inheritance. Blood doesn't lie. This isn't a story someone told me. It's the truth my bones told them. You can't fake it. You can't buy it. And once you know it... you never forget it." Lukas frowned. "So does that mean we're royal too?"

Ben's hand moved from the page and gently tapped Lukas's chest. "If your blood carries it, yes. But even if it doesn't, your love makes you family. I was adopted by Kendrick, and Annemarie is my biological mom, but this house... this family... made me a Rosenshavn in every way that counts. Royalty starts in the blood, but it lives in your choices. And every one of you was chosen."

Freja-Marie let out a soft hum, kicking her tiny foot into Isla's side. A small ripple of laughter passed through the circle, and the heaviness of history lightened just enough to let the moment breathe. Ben closed the ledger gently. "That's enough for today," he said. "The pancakes are cold. But the truth isn't. The truth doesn't need to be warm to matter. It just needs to be known."

And with that, the plates were finally cleared. But not a single child left without first glancing again at the old ledger, as if hoping to catch their own name forming in the faded ink—a name that meant something, not because it was written by kings, but because it had finally been read by one.

There were corridors in Rosenshavn Castle that did not echo. They breathed. Their silence wasn't emptiness but memory—quiet recollections folded between floorboards and stitched into drapery that had outlived entire governments. Ben walked with Clara in a hush more sacred than conversation. They did not need to speak. Their shoes made no sound against the softened oak beneath them, as if the floor itself recognized the weight of those who had learned to walk, and fall, and rise again upon it.

Clara moved ahead of him, one hand brushing the tapestry of the eastern hallway, her fingers reading it like Braille. Here had been the crawling races. The blanket forts. The one time Emil had duct-taped an entire loaf of bread to a wall, claiming it was "art." The house had not forgotten. Neither had Clara. She paused at each doorframe as though greeting the ghost of a younger version of herself—a smaller, unsure girl who used to check behind every curtain to see if her place had really come with permanence.

Ben stopped beside her at Lukas and Max-Leo's old room, where the wall still bore the pencil lines of growing limbs and ambitions. The names had been etched in shaky handwriting, first by the children, then traced again by Tobias in thicker, straighter lines. No one had ever painted over them. Not even the restoration crew had dared. Paint cannot replace presence. Ben reached out and ran a thumb across the final line on the wall, marked last summer. "He shot up two inches overnight," he whispered, smiling through the fog of change.

They moved on, passing Peter Emil's bookshelf—still slightly crooked from where he'd attempted to balance it on his own, insisting that being eight made him "almost a man." The shelf leaned forward as if bowing toward memory, still half-stocked with mismatched encyclopedias and two battered copies of The Tale of the Wooden Stag. "He used to hide sandwiches behind those," Clara murmured, not turning back. "Said he was building reserves for a castle siege." Ben laughed softly. Peter Emil had always been a strategist.

The hallway opened to the western nursery where Freja-Marie had spent her first nights—Isla asleep in the rocker, Tobias hovering like a hawk in case her blanket moved too far down. Ben remembered that room in the grain of his bones. He remembered holding her so lightly that he feared she'd vanish. He remembered Isla's voice, hoarse from sleepless songs. And he remembered Clara, then just twelve, reading bedtime stories from volumes thicker than her arms, with the poise of a scholar and the heart of a sister.

They turned down the corridor toward what had once been Kristian and Lukas's shared room, now transformed into a study nook and reading den. But the castle didn't forget who had wept beneath those bunk beds the first month—who had missed Paraguay, who had stared out the window whispering names of faraway grandmothers. The drapes were new. The furniture had changed. But the shape of grief remained faintly stamped into the air, preserved like ancient dust.

Clara stopped walking. She did not face him when she spoke. "They know something's changing," she said, the words landing with the softness of snow and the weight of stone. "Even the ones who don't understand what a birth means yet. They know." Ben looked at her—still only fifteen, yet impossibly older in this moment. He didn't ask how she knew. He had once taught her how to observe the quiet. And now, she was teaching it back to him.

Ben exhaled slowly and turned toward the central staircase, the one where Lukas had once tripped carrying a tray of breakfast, spilling orange juice and jam all over Tobias's trousers. A week later, Tobias gifted Lukas a new tray and a hand-stitched napkin that read: Try again. It hung now above the pantry. A silent memorial to both clumsiness and grace. The castle remembered it all.

"I haven't told them everything," Ben said, finally breaking the stillness. "Not yet." Clara nodded once, still facing forward. "You will," she said. "They'll ask. They always do." Her voice did not carry judgment. It carried truth. And that was heavier.

They paused again outside the double doors to the art room where Max-Leo once painted the entire floor in muddy browns and deep greens, shouting that it was "the dinosaur swamp." The paint had never fully lifted. The colour bled faintly through even after multiple cleanings. It had stayed, stubborn as childhood.

A soft creak echoed behind them, and Isla appeared at the far end of the hall, one hand on her back, the other resting lightly over her stomach. Her smile was faint, half-mooned and familiar. "Everyone's downstairs," she said gently. "Breakfast is waiting." Clara moved first. Ben hesitated. The castle was whispering too many names at once.

He turned to the wall across from the nursery and ran a hand along the panel seam. Behind that wall had once been a hiding spot—a crawlspace Tobias carved out for Kristian during his first thunderstorm. No one used it anymore. But Ben could still feel the comfort it gave—a place to retreat when the world shouted too loudly. He had one of those in Kent. He would need it again.

Clara glanced over her shoulder. "She's going to need you this week," she said. "Not just for the birth. For the silence after." Ben nodded. She was right. Clara usually was. He reached out and touched the nearest wall, just once, and said quietly, "You remember everything, don't you?" The stone did not answer. But it did not need to.

Together, they walked back toward the stairs, where waffles and bacon waited, and stories would resume. But the castle remained behind them, watching, listening, preserving every step like scripture. It was more than a building. It was witness.

She didn't need to say it aloud. Her silence had already decided it. The garden, though trimmed and proper, held a wildness she refused to tame—dandelions refusing to die, lavender that grew in stubborn clumps by the stone benches, and ivy that returned no matter how often it was pulled from the greenhouse gates. Isla sat in its midst, an immovable breath among things that refused to be managed. Her right hand rested flat against her stomach. The other tucked under her thigh, fingers curled, resisting the urge to tighten.

Silje read from the Danish birth registry as if it were a fairy tale. Her voice rose and dipped with its usual northern lilt, unafraid of pauses or mispronunciations. "Here—listen to this one," she said, laughing. "Born during a thunderstorm. They named him Torden." She pronounced it with a theatrical boom that made Isla smile, eyes closed. But the smile didn't stretch. It only hovered. Like something borrowed. She nodded but didn't speak.

The first kick came mid-sentence. The second came before Silje could finish laughing. Isla didn't flinch, but her fingers moved—reflexively. Left hand joining the right. A cradle. She exhaled through her nose and opened her eyes toward the birch trees, where wind had begun to stir the branches with a restlessness that seemed familiar. April was only days away. But it wasn't the month that bothered her. It was the knowing. The kind of knowing no one gives language to.

A chair scraped softly across the stone path behind her—Clara's doing, no doubt. She always cleared the breakfast cups and left the garden just as the birds began their mid-morning lull. She would return later with Freja-Marie and a honey biscuit in each hand. Ben would linger long enough to check Isla's eyes but not long enough to interrupt. He had learned. This was Isla's hour.

The garden was not beautiful in the royal sense. It did not bloom for photographs or yield tidy rose arches. It was honest. It grew what it wanted—what the soil insisted belonged. Wild strawberries along the base of the wall. Thorny brambles too proud to be trimmed. And a single crooked tree that leaned so far left it seemed to bow perpetually toward the castle's west wing. This is where Isla came to think—not about the crown, not about the birth, not even about the betrayal they both knew was coming. She came here to hold space for what had not yet arrived.

Silje stopped reading. She folded the paper over her knee and didn't speak. Silence between them wasn't awkward. It was a shared blanket they didn't have to stitch. When Isla finally turned toward her, it was only to say, "I think they know it's coming." Silje didn't ask what it meant. She didn't have to. Her hand reached across the stone table and touched Isla's wrist gently. "They've known longer than you think." That was all. But it was enough.

The breeze carried the faint scent of damp stone and thyme. The soil had been turned earlier that week by Emil, who'd insisted the basil needed room to "breathe properly." Isla remembered him saying it as though he were speaking about lungs rather than leaves. "Plants need space like people do," he had argued. "Too close and they choke each other." She had nodded then, and nodded again now. Emil would make a fine guardian one day.

Kendrick had walked this same garden path the night before. Not to interrupt. Just to look. He had paused at the archway and watched her for a full minute before returning indoors. He didn't wave. Didn't speak. But the respect in that pause had echoed louder than a speech. She had grown up under his watchful care. And now, as queen, she was still under it. Not ruled, not owned, but honoured.

Her fingers found the curve of her hip and pressed against it, adjusting her balance. She wasn't uncomfortable, not yet. But she was aware of time in a new way. Everything was measured now. Meals. Kicks. Breaths. The quiet between them. She knew the days were narrowing. She had seven at most. Six if the twins insisted on coming early. They were stubborn. She could feel it. The boy kicked high. The girl pressed low. One watched. One led.

Isla closed her eyes again, not to sleep but to listen inward. She didn't feel afraid. Not really. But she felt the sharpness of the edge she now walked. Birth wasn't ceremony. It wasn't royal. It was biological warfare. It was every cell of her body battling to bring forth a future. She would do it without fear. But she would not pretend it was easy. Isla was not one to lie to herself.

A bee hovered near her collarbone before deciding she wasn't a flower after all. She didn't flinch. Not even as it circled twice. She had grown used to being still under pressure. It was part of ruling. Part of motherhood. Part of surviving long enough to let the truth grow around you. She had once told Ben that her greatest strength was not endurance—it was discernment. "I know what's coming," she had said in bed one night, long before the world suspected. "I know who'll stay. And who won't."

Behind her, the greenhouse door clicked. Isla turned just enough to see Silje rising, folding the registry in half, placing it into her satchel with a deliberate grace. "I'll go prep the linens," she said. Isla nodded. "Use the lavender ones." Silje smiled. "Already did." Then she was gone, and Isla was alone again with the ivy, the tree, and the certainty inside her belly that the world was about to tilt.

Her hand drifted once more across her stomach, tracing the faint hiccup that now fluttered from within. She didn't speak to the babies. She never had. She believed they already knew everything worth saying. But she did hum. Quietly. A low, half-forgotten song from her own girlhood. She hadn't sung it in years. But it had waited. Like everything else in this castle.

Isla breathed in, held it, and exhaled long. It was the kind of breath that ended a season. That told the sky: We're ready now. A guard stood near the edge of the garden, shadowed by the stone wall. He did not move. He did not speak. She knew he was there. That was enough. She did not need words. She had her silence. She had her crown. And the castle? The castle was listening.

Ben nearly missed it. Had the morning light not angled just so across the landing, he might have stepped right past the tiny bundle of yarn. A sock. Pale cream. Hand-stitched along the ankle seam in soft grey thread. Too small for any of the children already born. Too quiet to have been left there on purpose. He bent slowly, knees groaning from too many crouches in too many hours at Isla's bedside, and lifted it between his fingers like parchment from a sacred archive. It weighed nothing. But it held everything.

He sat down on the step. Just beneath the portrait of Kendrick as a younger man—crownless, smiling, shirt sleeves rolled—and let the stair creak beneath him. The castle breathed in quiet rhythms now. Kitchen doors swaying, a broom brushing the stone, someone's kettle humming near the staff quarters. But here, on this stair, the world stood still. A sock. No wider than three fingers. Initialed with two sets of letters so personal they ached.

B.A.H.R.—he read them aloud without voice. Benedict Adrian Harvick of Rosenshavn. And beneath that, curving softer and stitched in Isla's unmistakable tilt, I.C.S.G.R.—Isla Claire Stuart-Gibb of Rosenshavn. Her name came first. Not out of vanity, but out of history. She had been the first to believe him. Not Kendrick. Not Annemarie. Not even Sorensen. Isla had believed with the certainty of a child reading a map she had drawn herself. And she had been right.

He didn't ask her why the initials were placed that way. He didn't need to. She had always known what came before what. Whose name should guard the threshold, and whose should follow in faithful strength. Even before he had proven anything. Even before the DNA, the history, the echoes from Hungary and Kent. She had known because she had chosen to know. And that kind of belief made blood look lazy.

Ben rubbed the sock between his palms. It was soft, like the threads of Clara's baby blanket, like the way Emil still leaned into his chest before bed, whispering goodnight as if it were a secret code. The sock held that same energy. Not a garment, but a prophecy. One that had slipped its drawer in the nursery and found its way into the hallway like a royal message tucked into the folds of morning.

He had not prepared a speech for the twins. Not yet. But he had thought it over. Thought about what it meant to be born into silence. To inherit a kingdom the world didn't know you ruled. To be born with titles you couldn't say aloud. "Prince" and "Princess" were only words until the world gave them meaning—and this world, he knew, liked to twist meanings into headlines.

Downstairs, he heard the quick skip of feet. Likely Lukas or Peter Emil on their way to breakfast, still too young to walk, always running. He made no move to hide the sock. If they asked, he'd tell them. If they didn't, he'd still tell the twins one day. That he had found this sock, here, on the stairs, before they were born. That it had appeared like a promise dropped from heaven—or maybe just from Isla's sewing basket.

His fingers pinched the rim where the letters curved upward. She had chosen soft grey. Not gold. Not red. Not regal. Grey, like the sky before a storm. Grey, like the spaces between childhood and responsibility. He loved her for that. For not dressing their child in colours borrowed from someone else's kingdom. She had stitched them into their own. Thread by thread.

He leaned his elbow on the step behind him and let his spine relax. The sun had reached his feet now, warming the wool of his socks. He wore mismatched ones again—Isla always noticed, always teased, never fixed it. It was her way of letting him remain flawed. He hoped the twins would grow up flawed. He hoped they would never be perfect. Perfect children never remembered where they came from.

He folded the sock and slipped it into his coat pocket, close to his chest. He didn't want it in a drawer. Not yet. It needed to stay with him for a while. Like a quiet guard. Like a flag planted before the war begins. He had work to do before the world found them. Before the headlines. Before the betrayal that he still felt shadowing him from Copenhagen.

He looked up the stairs, then down. No one was watching. No portraits blinked. No creaks from behind the curtains. But he could feel it—this was the moment. The moment a father begins to shape a memory before the child exists. The moment that memory builds a castle inside his chest and defends it against time. "I'm not ready," he whispered. But the sock disagreed.

He stood, one hand on the railing, the other guarding the fabric in his pocket. When he reached the top of the stairs, he didn't look back. The step where he had sat would be warmed now, slightly dented, marked by a moment no one else had seen. But someday, maybe, his son or daughter would sit there too. Maybe they would find something left behind—another sock, a story, a piece of him—and understand the weight of a single step. And maybe, just maybe, they would believe it was enough.

Ben sat alone in the study, though no one ever called it that. It was a corner room near the west-facing balcony, with a desk older than Denmark's last three monarchs and a window frame that cracked in winter. The shelves were stacked with both journals and crumbs—evidence of a room used by thinkers, not polished by staff. At its heart lay the genealogy book. Not just a record. Not just a tree. A living archive. An oath disguised in paper.

He did not use his regular pen. Not the one he signed birthday cards with. Not the one he doodled football brackets with beside Emil. This pen was brass, dipped in a ceramic inkwell he only refilled twice a year. The ink, deep violet, shimmered slightly when wet—almost regal, but not flashy. Regal didn't matter here. Truth did. And truth had no need for calligraphy.

His fingers gripped the edge of the page. He turned it slowly, past the name of his mother, Annemarie, etched in with both shame and grace. Past the line where Kendrick had written his own signature, claiming Ben with the firmest stroke Ben had ever seen from him. Past the names of those before him. The ones who died in silence. The ones who were never buried with crowns but carried dynasties in their DNA.

He found the next page. Blank. Waiting. It was not intimidating. It was not welcoming. It was a page, and it demanded honesty. He dipped the pen once, pressed the tip to the parchment, and began to write—not with flair, not with performance, but with reverence. The first line bore no title. No prefix. No embellishment. Just his full name, written as if spoken in truth: Benedict Adrian Harvick of Rosenshavn.

Then beneath it, the sentence: "Born with a burden too early, raised with a name too late." He let the ink dry. He did not blot it. The smudge on the lower loop of the "y" was his fingerprint now. He had lived that sentence for twenty-three years. Every year had added to its weight. Every moment in silence had carved another scar into the word "burden." But here, on the page, it was finally made visible.

He moved on. The next entry would not be for himself. It would be for the children. Not yet born. Not yet known by the world. But known to Isla. Known to him. Known to the castle walls that had already begun to echo with their presence. He wrote only: "Child of Benedict Adrian Harvick and Isla Claire Stuart-Gibb of Rosenshavn. Due to arrive within the House before the thaw of April. Name not yet given. Title not yet permitted. Legacy already present."

He left a line between the two. One for each child. Twins. The page seemed to lean into the air differently now, as if bending under the tension of the unsaid. He could not write "Prince" or "Princess." He would not lie. The world had not permitted such words—not yet. But his hand lingered where the surnames should go. He left them blank. Not out of omission. Out of protection. They did not belong to the world yet. And perhaps, they never would.

Outside the window, the branches swayed with the wind off the sea. Salt and cold and spring pollen mixed in a way only March could manage. He imagined their children hearing that wind one day, asking what it meant, asking where it came from. He would not say it came from Denmark. He would say it came from before. From the place where all things begin—the place between silence and history.

He set the pen down and reached for the edge of the desk. His knuckles brushed the drawer that held the letter. The one Isla had written the week they found out. The one she refused to give him until he'd told his truth to the children. Not the truth of crowns. The truth of weight. Of silence. Of responsibility you don't ask for but inherit anyway. He didn't open the drawer. Not yet.

The sun had risen further now. Light crept across the rug, inching toward his boot. The warmth didn't reach him, not really. The castle's study always stayed cold, even in summer. Kendrick said it helped keep the mind alert. Ben believed it simply kept the ghosts close. This room remembered too much. But today, for once, it had received something new.

He stood, leaving the book open on the desk. He knew someone—probably Clara—would close it later with that quiet reverence she always gave to papers. No child would touch it. They understood it wasn't just a book. It was the story of them. And someday, one of them might add to it. One of the twins, perhaps. A son who bore the same silence Ben had worn. A daughter who questioned it.

Ben crossed the room and placed his hand on the doorframe. Not out of habit. Out of grounding. He had felt dizzy earlier. Isla said it was from too much worry. Sorensen said it was from not enough coffee. He believed them both. But it passed. It always did. What remained was the throb in his hand from writing too carefully. Too slowly. As if every letter might bruise the page.

He looked back once. Just once. The ink shimmered faintly, still drying. Still vulnerable. And in that moment, he did not feel regal. He did not feel kingly. He felt like a father with no map. A husband with no script. A man caught between being hidden and being known. He did not know which was safer. He only knew which was true. And so he left the book open.

Tobias crouched low beside the nursery cabinet, muttering like a man preparing for battle. His right knee clicked every time he shifted, but he ignored it. The drawer in question—long, overpacked, and criminally disorganized—had reached its breaking point. "This," he announced to no one in particular, "is a disgrace to nappies everywhere." He lifted a wad of unfolded diapers that had clearly been jammed in without shame or order. "Look at this. Folded backwards. A crime." He placed them in a fresh pile, flattening each one with the precision of a royal chef plating crepes.

From behind him came the soft shuffle of tiny feet on tile, the unmistakable tiptoe of a toddler either curious or guilty. He didn't turn around. "Don't even think about it," he said, reaching for the stack of wipes. "These are not for chewing." The toddler paused. Then resumed tiptoeing toward the laundry bin. Tobias smirked. "You can throw in a sock. But if it's your sibling's, I'm not helping you later."

The drawer clacked as he slammed it open too hard. A tower of pull-ups nearly tipped. He caught them in time, balancing the bundle with one hand while nudging a pacifier away from the edge with his elbow. "If anyone ever questions my dexterity," he said through gritted teeth, "remind them of this exact moment." A silence followed that was not entirely comfortable. Not quite peace. Not quite chaos.

Then it happened.

A sound—monstrous in its audacity—erupted from somewhere near the toy bin. It was not the small whisper of a baby's sigh or the innocent puff of an adjusting cushion. It was a thunderclap wrapped in mischief. The kind of explosive resonance that could only mean one thing: a child had farted with such force it startled even the doll in the corner. Tobias froze.

"That," he said, standing slowly and turning toward the crib, "was not me."

From the hallway, a voice—quick, loud, and already defensive—shouted back, "That wasn't me!" The footsteps scrambled off before accountability could be demanded. A second voice giggled. Then a third. And then, from somewhere deeper in the castle, the unmistakable sound of Ben's laugh echoed through the corridor.

It was not a mild laugh. It was a full-throated surrender to the absurdity of the moment. The kind of laugh that didn't ask permission. Ben appeared in the doorway, holding a nearly empty mug and blinking back tears of humour. "That was a solid eleven on the Richter scale," he said, glancing at the infants as if expecting to find one of them guilty. "Do we have to evacuate?"

Tobias shrugged, returning to the drawer. "Unless you want your office to become the new nursery, I suggest we install an airlock." He handed Ben a stray diaper, already knowing it wouldn't be used. "I've seen less devastation in war zones."

Ben sat down on the edge of the bench beside the changing table, still chuckling. He picked up a sock—one of the twins'—and turned it over in his hand. "Why does every serious day end with something like this?" he asked, not expecting an answer. "One minute I'm teaching them DNA haplogroups. Next minute, someone detonates a thunderfart and the whole castle resets."

"It's balance," Tobias replied, wiping his hands. "You drop too many truths in one day, the universe sends a kid to remind you you're still mortal." He tapped the edge of the drawer shut and stood back to admire his work. It was pristine. He immediately knew it would last no longer than ten minutes.

A whimper from one of the cribs turned both their heads. The culprit, red-cheeked and blinking from sleep, stretched and reached upward. Ben stepped forward instinctively, lifting the child with a motion both practiced and loving. The baby's hair stood up at the back, one sock missing, the other barely clinging to a heel. "Was it you?" he whispered, bouncing them gently. "Was it your sonic masterpiece?"

The child blinked. Then grinned. Tobias sighed. "Guilty." Ben looked toward the hallway. "We need to install microphones. Or lie detectors." He tucked the baby close to his chest. "Or just admit this is the only place on earth where royalty and ridiculousness share the same space." "Exactly," Tobias said, stretching his arms. "You can carry the crown. I'll carry the wipes."

Another distant sound—this time clearly from an older child running—punctuated the air. A door creaked. Someone giggled from a stairwell. Life moved on. The serious moments had not left. The secrets still slept beneath layers of page and silence. But the castle itself was never still for long.

Ben exhaled. "I think we're ready." Tobias raised an eyebrow. "For what?" "For everything." They stood in the nursery, one man holding a child, the other holding nothing but a sense of duty stitched together with humour. And behind them, the diaper drawer sat—newly organised, momentarily untouched, already plotting its rebellion.

He walked with silent steps that morning, not because he feared waking anyone, but because the library itself seemed to demand a kind of reverence. There were rooms in the castle designed to impress—ceilings vaulted high like chapels, floor tiles polished to mirrorlight—but this one held something older than architecture. It was not the grandest room, nor the most photographed, but it was sacred. Modeled after the quiet one in Kent, down to the same scuffed brass pulls and heavy-lidded windows, the library wore its familiarity like a second skin. Every shelf had been touched, not just dusted. Every book had once been read for something more than entertainment. Truth had been hunted here.

Ben paused near the first shelf on the left, running his hand across the spine of a brown, cloth-bound volume. He did not need to read the title. His fingertips remembered the shape of it, the tilt of the faded label. It was the first book he had ever opened during a real search—not for fantasy or for school, but for names. Not fictional names, not invented dynasties or imagined wars, but living threads woven into his blood. He had been ten. Isla had been nine. She'd pulled the book before he did. And she was the first to say, softly and without ceremony: "This one is us."

He took the book now and moved to the small reading table under the west window, where a sunbeam was already forming a patch of warmth across the seat. The castle was still quiet—Isla still sleeping, children still nestled in rooms scented with books and lavender. Ben sat slowly, not because he was tired, but because sitting at that table always made him feel younger. Smaller. Less king. More boy. And the boy had questions the man had learned not to ask aloud. But they lived on, curled between lines and ancestral charts and coats of arms too precise to be accidental.

Opening the book, he found the same page Isla had once pointed to. Stewart–Gibb. A hyphen that carried more than grammar. A bond between families that spanned centuries, a claim whispered through generations who had stopped writing it down after the titles were stolen. Ben remembered Isla tracing her finger across it, back then. Not with excitement, but with a sort of fierce sadness. She hadn't been looking for proof. She had been looking for her place. And she had found his too.

He leaned forward now, elbow pressed against the edge of the book, palm cradling his forehead. These were the things adults forget—what it feels like to be seen for the first time. Not by a parent, not by a teacher, not by someone told to love you, but by a peer. Another child. A mirror not of resemblance, but of recognition. Isla had seen something in him back then. Not royalty. Not even intelligence. She had seen that he was asking the same question she was: Where do I come from, and why was it hidden?

Ben ran his thumb along the margins, remembering how they'd pencilled in their own notes before anyone had taught them how to cite sources. At the bottom of the page, faded but still legible, were initials that only children would write with such certainty: B.A.H. and I.C.S.G. The same initials Isla had stitched into the sock. The same ones she'd written on every secret letter during their teenage years, tucked under pillows or slipped into books. He smiled, just slightly, but it was the kind that bruised more than it lifted. Because even then, they knew something was coming. And still, they chose to remember each other.

He turned the page. It creaked—not from age, but from dignity. The kind of paper that does not bend unless it must. And there it was again: another branch of the Stewart-Gibb line, this time drawn with ink that looked older than the rest. As though someone else, long before them, had traced this line by candlelight, whispering their way back to something nearly lost. It was never just about kings and queens. It was about belonging. About finding your place in a family you were told didn't exist anymore.

Ben looked up at the stained-glass window above the shelves. The morning light passed through blue and gold panes, casting a crosshatch of colour over the floor. But there was no religious iconography here—no saints, no halos, no crosses. Just leaves. Oak and ash, gnarled and tangled, reaching upward in defiance of the cold. The Rosenshavn seal sat in the corner, barely visible. It was not new. It had always been there. Even when they didn't know it.

He closed the book gently, holding it for a moment as though it might still have more to say. Then he placed it back on the shelf, in its exact place. This room had not forgotten. It remembered who had found what, and when. It remembered Isla's voice the first time she had said, "You are not who they told you you were." It remembered the sound of chalk scratching out a family tree, of small fingers drawing crowns next to names that had none left.

The genealogy book waited in his satchel by the door. He had updated it just yesterday. A quiet entry, written without pride. He had not listed himself as king. He never did. He only wrote: "Born with a burden too early, raised with a name too late." But in this room, titles didn't matter. The truth had its own authority. And Ben, at least here, never needed to defend it.

He walked to the second row, where the foreign archives were stored. Hungarian, Danish, Scottish—all overlapping like threads in a larger weave. The Árpád lines. The ones Kendrick used to tease him about. "You've got more kingdoms in you than I've had cups of coffee," he'd once said. But Ben didn't smile at the thought. Not today. The air was shifting. The castle felt it. Isla felt it. Even the books felt it. There were no more years to prepare. There were days.

He glanced toward the door, half expecting Isla to appear, hair pulled up, hands wrapped around a mug of warm milk. But she didn't. She was resting. She needed to. The twins would arrive soon. And when they did, the library would no longer be a quiet place of study. It would become their beginning. The way it had once been his.

Ben took one final look around the room. Every corner spoke. Every shelf whispered. And he knew without needing to ask: the children would remember. Just as he had. Just as Isla always had. They would not forget where the truth began. Not because someone told them, but because someone showed them.

And when they returned years from now—taller, louder, covered in scraped knees and royal obligation—they would stand in this room and understand. This is where it started. The crown they wear was hidden not in gold, but in the pages of a library. And that, too, was no accident.

The room had already begun to darken when Ben returned, ledger in hand, and his voice barely louder than the creak of the floorboards. The younger children had gathered in a ring of pillows beneath the high beams of the reading hall—some lying on their stomachs, others curled like kittens, all waiting. Not for a fairy tale. They didn't ask for magic. They wanted to know the truth. Clara sat against the corner cushion, arms wrapped around little Søren, while Lukas fiddled with a strand of fringe from the carpet. The fire crackled low in the grate, and Silje pulled the last curtain shut. When Ben sat, there was no need to ask for attention. It was already his.

He opened the ledger not at the front, where kings often placed their crests, but near the centre, where the worn pages bore names handwritten in a language few of them could read. Ancient Hungarian. The Árpád dynasty. "Tonight," he said, "we're not learning about a king. We're learning about a man who carried a legacy in his blood long before anyone wrote it down." He paused, letting the fire cast shadows on the page. "His name was Béla. Béla the Third. He ruled not because he wanted to, but because he had to. Because responsibility runs deeper than crowns."

Kristian raised his hand, but didn't wait. "Is he why you're royal?" The question was clean, childlike, free of awe. Ben met his eyes and gave the smallest nod. "Partly. His DNA runs in my veins. Just like it might run in yours. But it's not the DNA that makes someone noble. It's what they do with it." The children shifted. Some leaned forward, others sat up straighter. This was not a bedtime story. This was a confession wrapped in biology.

Ben explained mitochondrial lines, how mothers passed markers to sons and daughters alike. He told them of paternal haplogroups, of signatures etched into their bones that spoke across centuries. He told them how science could trace more than ancestry—it could trace purpose. "DNA doesn't lie," he said, not with bravado, but with the calm certainty of someone who had been lied to often. "People might. But the code inside you… it remembers."

Frederikke leaned her cheek against her fist. "But if you come from him, that makes you a king." Ben didn't blink. He closed the ledger slowly and folded his hands on top. "It makes me a responsibility," he said, so gently that the fire itself seemed to lower its flame to listen. "It means I don't get to choose what I carry. Only how I carry it." Isla stood in the doorway then, quiet and unseen, arms crossed, the faintest smile beneath tired eyes. She had heard that answer before.

The children did not giggle or poke or wander. They sat in the hush of inherited truth. Not one of them asked about crowns or castles. Instead, Clara's voice broke the quiet. "Does it mean we have to carry it too?" Ben turned, not to answer quickly, but to measure the weight of her question. "Some of you will," he said. "Some of you already do. But not because of me. Because of you. The choices you make, the kindness you show, the strength you carry when nobody thanks you for it."

Tobias leaned against the far wall, arms folded, unreadable. But even he didn't interrupt. He had heard Ben teach before. He had seen the DNA charts, the documents, the death certificates rewritten with the truth. But this—this was different. This was legacy being handed over like a candle in a dark hall. Ben wasn't just talking about Hungary. He was talking about them. Every last one.

Ben reached into his pocket and pulled out a folded paper—his own haplogroup report. "R-S660," he said, "That's the paternal one. It means I descend from a line of kings, warriors, land-builders. Scotland, Hungary, England. I didn't ask for it. I didn't even know until I was your age. But once I did… it changed everything." He passed the paper to Lukas, who held it like something sacred. Not because of what it said, but because of who had given it to him.

Nohr asked quietly, "Did it make you sad?" Ben tilted his head. "Sometimes. Knowing who I came from… meant I had to admit who I never got to meet. Who died long before I had the chance to say their names." He looked at the wall where the family photos hung—some framed, some printed, some drawn in pencil by little hands. "But it also gave me something back. It told me I wasn't an accident. And neither are any of you."

There was a long pause, the kind that stretches without awkwardness when everyone is thinking the same thing. Then Mikkel, from the back, said, "So what do we do now?" Ben smiled. Not with teeth, not with grandeur. Just with the deep warmth of someone whose burden had finally met comprehension. "You live like it matters. You help each other. You honour the name you've been given, whether it's written in a royal book or not."

The fire had burned low by then, leaving only embers and a hush. Ben passed the ledger around, letting each child hold it if they wished. Some did. Some only looked. But none dismissed it. Because this was no story of far-off kings. This was their house. Their family. And their blood might not be Béla's—but their courage could be.

As the children filtered out in pairs—socks dragging, eyes wide—Ben folded the documents back into their pouch. Isla met him at the door. She didn't speak. She only rested her hand over his, holding it steady as he closed the latch. The fire behind them gave its last crackle. And in the silence that followed, no one spoke of crowns. Only of inheritance. And of love.

The light in the hallway had dimmed to that golden hue that only appears when the sun has given its last apology to the day. Ben moved silently past the portrait gallery, hands behind his back, not seeking conversation, only stillness. But as he approached the stairwell that led to the west corridor, he heard it—two voices in the hush, low and close, like folded pages in an unread chapter. Kendrick's tone was firm, softened only by the familiarity in it. Annemarie's voice was quieter, but not unsure. They were speaking to each other as they had done for decades—without preamble, without explanation. Just truth passed like wine between two old souls.

Ben paused—not to eavesdrop, not to pry, but because something about their tone made the air tighten. He stood still as stone beneath the archway, listening only because the walls gave him no choice. He caught one phrase, not loud, not meant for him, but unavoidably heard: "He'll have no choice soon." It was Kendrick who said it, his voice tired but absolute. There was no cruelty in the words. No manipulation. Just inevitability, the kind that grows with seasons and lineage, not with threats.

Annemarie's reply was muffled, perhaps a sigh, perhaps her hand on his shoulder. Ben didn't move. He didn't need to hear more. He already knew. That sentence was not prophecy. It was memory. It had already happened. The moment Kendrick stepped down from the throne—not publicly, not with ceremony, but quietly, over the span of years—it had begun. The weight had been handed over not with a sceptre but with silence. And Ben had carried it, unknowingly at first, then with increasing understanding. Now, there was no mistaking it. Kendrick was no longer king. He was the head of the House, the master of the castle, the heart of the family. But the crown—whether spoken aloud or hidden in whispers—belonged to Ben.

Ben stepped back from the archway without a sound, retracing his steps as though the hallway itself had turned to glass beneath him. He didn't want Kendrick to know he'd heard. Not yet. Not while the silence still preserved something sacred between them. There was no bitterness. Kendrick had been his protector, his guide, his father when the world had none to offer. But fatherhood and monarchy were different garments, and one of them had now been stitched into Ben's skin without his asking.

He entered the north corridor, his footsteps purposeful now. No child wandered here after dark—this was the corridor of ancestors, portraits, sealed doors, and journals locked in cases. Ben ran his fingers along the ridge of one panel, tracing the carved crest of House Rosenshavn, wondering if the stone beneath his fingertips had once whispered to Kendrick the same thing: You'll have no choice soon. Because kings, real kings, are not made with votes or applause. They are forged in silence, appointed by truth, and recognized only by those who already carry part of the burden themselves.

Back in the west wing, Kendrick stood at the window with Annemarie beside him. He didn't speak again. He didn't need to. They had said what had to be said. They knew their son—whether born or chosen—would rise. Not because he wanted to. Because the kingdom would call, and the world would no longer look away. That time was closer now than any of them liked to admit.

Ben sat on the stairwell near the linen cabinet and closed his eyes. The words repeated themselves—not hauntingly, not angrily, but like a heartbeat in the back of his mind. He'll have no choice soon. He exhaled, resting his arms across his knees, head bowed but not bowed in defeat. Only in the posture of someone bracing for the gust that would follow the storm's eye.

He remembered what Isla had said to him once, in Kent, before they even understood who they truly were. She had whispered, "Some of us are born with storms waiting." He hadn't understood then. But he did now. The quiet before the labour. The hush before the leak. The whisper of a crown that could no longer hide in the genealogy pages. It was all part of the storm, and it was nearly here.

In the rooms behind him, the children slept, unaware of the sentence that had just passed through the castle's lungs. Ben rose. He didn't return to his chambers. Instead, he walked the length of the east hall, where the nursery lights glowed dimly, and sat beside the cradle that waited for two names not yet written. He looked at them not as a king, but as a man who knew what it meant to carry something too heavy for anyone else.

And as he reached forward to straighten one of the blankets Isla had folded earlier, he spoke aloud, but only to the silence: "I never wanted the crown. But I won't drop it."

The wind did not howl. It murmured. A hush, almost reverent, swept against the outer stone of Rosenshavn Castle like a secret trying not to be overheard. The storm had built steadily through the night, and though thunder rolled low and persistent like a sleeping lion, not a drop of rain had touched the windows. Even the sky, it seemed, was holding something back. The castle stood firm, but the air pressed inward, dense and watching. In the observatory hall, Ben stood without a coat, hands in his trouser pockets, watching the grey horizon shiver behind the glass. He said nothing. No thoughts spoken. No prophecies dared. Just silence and stormlight.

His reflection blinked in the pane—older now than he ever expected to be at twenty-three. There were lines he hadn't earned by vanity. His shoulders, broader than when he first arrived in Denmark, no longer carried the awkwardness of youth, but the weight of unseen recognition. Yet tonight, he was neither ruler nor son. Just a man who missed a boy's birthday. Seven months ago, that boy had turned four—his only chance to do so. Ben had sent a voice message. That was all he could offer. No visit. No hug. No crown-shaped cake or paper hats. Judge Algren and Arlene had thrown Eli a modest celebration in their garden, and though the child never complained, Ben felt the ache of it still, like an invisible bruise no one could tend to.

He touched the window with one hand. It was cold, like the glass didn't quite want to let warmth through. There was a kind of poetry in it—the unfallen storm, the unreachable son. Somewhere in the countryside, the lightning flickered, but never struck. Ben whispered under his breath, not quite a prayer and not quite a memory. "You only turn four once, buddy." The words dissipated like breath on glass. He didn't say more. The walls didn't ask for it, and the thunder offered no reply.

In the east wing, a child coughed once and turned over in sleep. Ben didn't glance back. He knew every voice in the castle. Every sleeper under every quilt. The house was alive tonight, restless though quiet. Like a dog sensing a tremor beneath the earth, not barking, only alert. Something had shifted since morning. No alarm had rung. No message had arrived. But instincts don't lie. The storm outside mirrored the one within—a brewing pressure with no obvious release. He knew the signs. He'd learned them long ago. Some battles announce themselves. Others watch from the dark, waiting for the right hour.

A shutter banged against the library window. Not hard enough to crack, just enough to be heard. Ben turned from the observatory and walked toward it. He latched the frame, pressed his palm once to the wood, then let go. The castle groaned faintly under the pressure of the wind. Nothing unusual. And yet tonight, it all felt unusual. He glanced toward the stairwell that led down to the nursery and then to the storage corridor beneath the birth wing. The smell of lavender and old books lingered in the air, as if the rooms had tried to stay unchanged despite the world turning.

Ben passed the old family portrait of Kendrick and Annemarie in their younger years. He paused not because of their faces, but because someone—probably Emil or Clara—had left a pair of tiny shoes at the base of the frame. Newborn size. Soft. Wool stitched. The twins weren't even born yet, but already, the house made space for them. Already, the next generation had marked its claim. Ben knelt, not to pray, but to straighten the shoes. He lined them evenly, side by side, and adjusted the corner of the rug they sat upon. When he stood again, he didn't smile. But his eyes did something else. They held.

Outside, the thunder gave one long growl, deep and mournful, as though mourning something not yet lost. Still no rain. Still no flash. Just sound without flame. Isla had said it once: "Some storms never fall. They just stand there watching." She wasn't wrong. This one wasn't going to drop rain. It wasn't going to cleanse or shatter. It was the kind that listened, waiting for someone to make the first move. Ben knew better than to be the one to flinch.

He returned to the hallway that overlooked the eastern courtyard. A few lamps flickered—low wattage bulbs made to look like candlelight. Clara must have replaced them again. Tobias had mocked her for it. "What century are we even in?" he'd grinned. But Ben liked it. He liked the illusion that time slowed down inside these walls. That maybe thunder didn't matter, and storms stayed outside. He knew better, of course. But he let the fantasy linger a little longer.

He didn't check his phone. Not tonight. He didn't need an alert to tell him what he already felt. The world outside the castle still believed he was a rumour. A noble rumour perhaps, a whisper from old dynasties and darker archives, but a rumour nonetheless. He was content to leave it that way. At least, for now. But storms—real storms—don't ask for permission. They come when they're ready. They come when you're not.

The hallway creaked beneath his feet as he turned toward his chambers. The sock he had found yesterday still sat on the stair banister, waiting for a foot that hadn't yet entered the world. Isla had laughed when he showed it to her, pretending not to remember stitching the initials. But she had. Every thread of their life together had been sewn from things half-forgotten and wholly sacred. No tabloid, no outsider would ever understand that.

Ben opened the nursery door. The nightlight flickered gently, casting soft shapes across the wall—stars, a crown, a little fox. He exhaled and sat beside the crib, not to rest, but to anchor. The silence in this room wasn't heavy. It was holy. The storm would wait. It had to. There were things in this house more important than headlines.

Tomorrow might come with questions. It might come with noise. But tonight was not for them. Tonight was for thunder without rain. For kingdoms still in wombs. For names not yet signed. For the memory of a birthday unshared. And the whisper of a father who stayed silent—not out of fear, but because the truth was still preparing its entrance.

The room was dim, not dark. A single lamp glowed beside the hearth, its light bent low and golden across the edge of the velvet armrest. Ben sat with Isla pressed into his side, her hair damp from a recent bath, her breath slower now as the weight of the day slipped from her ribs. The castle, though not asleep, had quieted. One by one, rooms had been sealed for the night. Only their chamber remained open like a final stanza waiting to be read. A bowl of water stood on the windowsill, silver in reflection, and beside it lay the two books no child was meant to touch—the birth ledger, and the royal seal book.

They would not be used tonight. Not yet.

Isla shifted slightly, enough to press her cheek against the hollow of Ben's collarbone. Her hand rested over her stomach, cradling the curve that would soon not be a curve at all. "They already know," she whispered—not to him, but into the room, as if the walls had asked. Ben didn't answer. He hadn't answered much all day. He had watched, listened, taught, and guarded. But now, there were no more things to manage. Only this. Only the moment where names were spoken without parchment, title, or audience.

He took her hand. Not with ceremony. Not with trembling. Simply so her fingers could rest between his. Their palms fit together the same way they had when they were children sitting cross-legged on the library floor in Kent. Isla had pointed to his past before he ever had the courage to face it. Now she pointed to their future, quietly and without a trace of pride. She had chosen their names long before her belly had grown. Not for popularity. Not for approval. But because each name carried something forgotten. Something recovered.

She said the girl's name first. Soft. As if it might break if it were said aloud too forcefully. Ben didn't flinch, but something behind his eyes flickered. Isla had never spoken it outside of dream or journal. Tonight, she allowed herself to name their daughter as though calling her home. Ben pressed his lips to her hair, and for a long moment, nothing else moved. The window didn't rattle. The coals didn't shift. Even the castle seemed to pause in its sighing.

He did not repeat the name. He wouldn't. Not yet. It was hers to say. He would only carry it, and carry her, until the day that name belonged to more than the two of them. The world would not be given this gift. Not now. Not by force or curiosity. The press would wait. The people would guess. But the name belonged first to silence. To trust. To the whisper shared in secret between one who bears the crown and one who bears the child.

Isla said the second name without hesitation. The boy's name. It rang differently—firmer, weightier—but no less sacred. It belonged to no ancestor, no dynasty. It had been made new. Forged. She didn't smile when she said it. She looked straight ahead, as if seeing the child already, as if naming was no longer an act of hope, but of preparation. She placed her hand firmly over her belly. Ben watched. Still silent. Still unmoved in body—but everything in him burned.

The twins had kicked earlier that day. Once each. Then again. And again. Isla had told him, "It's not pain. It's presence." She had no poetry in her tone, only truth. Tonight, the movement had stilled. They were listening now. They always listened. Names had that power. Names made space where none existed before.

Ben closed his eyes. He thought about the books that would record them. How he would write the names with ink that did not smudge. How he would press the wax seal beside the surname. Or leave it blank. Maybe that part would wait. Maybe they would never bear the full weight of the world's label. Not until it was earned by their own footsteps.

He thought about how many names had been taken from children like him. Names erased, buried, forged into something else. He had lived as a shadow of a lineage no one believed existed. A footnote. A flicker in forgotten margins. These twins would not be shadows. Not footnotes. They would be pillars. But only when ready. Only when their names could no longer be stolen by those who had no right to them.

Isla kissed his chest—just once—and whispered the name again. He did not say it back. But he pulled her closer. And in that small motion, she knew he had memorized it. Carried it. Protected it. She rested against him like a stone set in velvet. Neither moved again for several minutes.

Across the room, the cradle sat empty, its sheets newly laid, its side rail half-lowered. Tobias had built it by hand. Clara had stitched the lining. Silje had selected the wood. Everyone had touched it, blessed it, contributed to its quiet presence. But no one had asked the names. Not once. Not even Kendrick. They knew better. This was not a matter of lineage or decorum. It was something older. A silence deeper than loyalty. Even in a castle of blood and birthrights, some things were not to be spoken aloud.

Ben turned the lamp off. Isla didn't object. The darkness took its place around them gently, the kind that comes when a fire is low but not gone. He pressed a kiss to her temple. "They'll come when they're ready," he said, finally. It was the only thing he'd said all night. Isla whispered, "They already have."

The first light broke through the east window with an unusual stillness. No birds, no bells. Just a quiet slice of dawn draped across the oak desk where Ben had fallen asleep again. He hadn't meant to. His hand was still holding the pen, uncapped, the ink dried in a tiny blot beside a number—seven. He rubbed his eyes and sat up slowly. The castle clock hadn't yet chimed six. But his body had already decided: today was the day to begin the countdown. The last one.

He rose without a sound and reached behind the desk, behind the tapestry where the map of Denmark hung, and found the smoothed-out wallboard. He had kept it hidden, not because it held a secret, but because it didn't need to be public. It wasn't for others. It wasn't royal. It was personal. Just a wall marked by fingernail scratches, pencil lines, and faint etches of days gone. He pressed the edge of a black charcoal stick into the wood and drew a small vertical mark. Not dramatic. Not even neat. Just enough to say it plainly—six days to go.

Isla stirred behind him. Her voice didn't reach out, but her breath shifted. She knew when he wasn't beside her. She always knew. Her hand slid across the blanket, touched the empty space, and then rested there. She didn't call for him. She didn't need to. Instead, she waited. A queen without crown or decree. Just a woman in her final days of carrying two children who would never be ordinary again. Not after what the world would soon find out.

He sat at the edge of the bed. Not facing her. Just close enough. "One week," he said, not quite whispering. "Then the birth. Then…" He didn't finish the sentence. He couldn't. The next part wasn't etched in any wall. It was written in instinct, in the quiet threads of consequence that had begun to tug months ago when the test results had confirmed what Isla already knew— Ben's DNA was not just noble. It was undeniable.

She looked at him without turning her head. Her eyes had a softness that only came in the final hour of sleep. But her voice was steady. "You'll need to go. When the time comes." It wasn't a question. And he didn't answer as if it was. He just nodded, once. Slow. No grief in it. No denial either. It was what it was.

The castle walls seemed to lean in around them, as if listening. This wasn't an announcement. This wasn't even a plan. It was inevitability made flesh. A truth that had waited too long to be born. Much like the twins. The hallway outside their room remained still. No laughter. No movement. The children hadn't yet begun their morning rituals. That silence, too, was a sign. Something was shifting. The building knew.

Ben stood and moved to the side table where his old ledger remained open. He had left it halfway through a sentence the night before, distracted by a Braxton Hicks contraction Isla didn't want to admit had startled her. He reread the line. It was something mundane—"Place of birth: Rosenshavn Castle"—but it stared back at him like a riddle. Place of birth. What about place of exposure? Of exile? Of escape? These children were not simply being born. They were about to become visible. Whether he wanted them to or not.

He reached for a second charcoal stick and circled the number seven, then crossed it. Six now. It felt like crossing out time itself. One less day of quiet. One less day of anonymity. Soon the windows would no longer shield them. The corridors wouldn't echo with peace. Cameras would come. Drones. Headlines. Truths twisted by strangers. And Ben, whether ready or not, would have to leave.

He didn't think of it as fleeing. Not yet. This wasn't cowardice. It was containment. A shield formed by absence. His leaving would be the only way to keep the others from harm. Kendrick had taught him that. Sørensen had reinforced it. And Isla… Isla had never once asked him to stay. She had only asked him to be safe. To return.

A knock came at the door. Clara. Always gentle. Always timed. "Your breakfast, sire," she said with just enough sarcasm to make it sound ordinary. He chuckled under his breath. "Leave it," he replied. "We'll be down soon." Clara never pushed. She never asked about marks on the wall or dark circles under Ben's eyes. But she knew. All of them did. Silje, Tobias, even the younger children—they felt the change humming beneath the floorboards.

Isla rose slowly, one hand on the mattress, one across her stomach. "You're not just counting days," she said. "You're counting peace." He helped her up without correcting her. She was right. He wasn't measuring time. He was measuring quiet. He was measuring breath. He was measuring how many seconds were left before the name Benedict Adrian Harvick no longer belonged to their family alone.

They walked to the window. From this view, the outer grounds of the castle looked like a painting. Untouched. A deer passed silently near the treeline, unbothered by the humans watching from above. The world still pretended nothing was different. But soon, that pretence would fracture.

Ben touched the glass. "It's still mine," he said softly. "Until the noise begins." Isla didn't answer. She leaned her head against his shoulder and breathed in the quiet. She had always been the stronger one. Even before the tests, before the papers, before the heralds of Europe would begin whispering about the return of an unseen king.

He had seven days. But today, he only needed to survive the first of them. And for that moment, that morning, that fraction of borrowed stillness—he would not move.

The flame was small, but steady. It sat in the brass holder by the window, just beneath the carved sill where the nursery curtains had been drawn back. No one spoke when it was lit. There was no ceremony to it. No blessing, no royal decree. Just a single candle, quietly burning its way through another Danish night, casting soft shadows on the stone wall behind it. It wasn't for a king. It wasn't for a bloodline. It was for a boy who wasn't there.

Ben stood with his arms crossed, the matches still in his hand. The candle had been lit just after ten o'clock, the moment when the castle usually fell quiet—after the final mug of coffee had been set down, after the last sock had been found in the hallway, after Isla had shifted into sleep beside her growing belly. He always lit it when the silence settled. Not because Eli was his son—because Eli was not. But because he mattered. That mattered more.

The child had not been born in this castle. He hadn't been raised inside these walls. He didn't have a bedroom upstairs, nor a name in the household ledger. But for three days—exactly three days—after his adoption by Judge Algren, he had been allowed to stay from breakfast through bedtime. And those days had etched themselves into the wood and memory of the castle like a soft thunder no one tried to hush. The laughter had been loud, the fart games legendary. Ben still found toy spoons in odd places, reminders of the meals shared and the joy uncontained.

It was Kendrick who arranged the adoption. Quietly. Deliberately. He had seen something in Eli's eyes that day in the orphanage—the same look Ben had once carried as a child, though he never spoke of it. No one objected. No paperwork had been mishandled. No feathers ruffled. It was simply done, because it was right. The Judge had taken to the child without hesitation. Eli had, by every observable instinct, chosen him. Not the other way around.

Ben had never once called him his son. He never would. That title belonged to the man who tucked Eli in each night, who read him bedtime stories, who brushed the crumbs off his collar after meals. Judge Algren had earned that name the way most fathers didn't—by being present when no one else had offered to be. Still, Eli had carved out a space in Ben's world. A space not filled with obligation, but affection. Uncle. That was the only name Ben ever answered to in the boy's company. And that was more than enough.

He watched the candle flicker once, a faint ripple in the wax pooling near the base. It reminded him of Isla's breath when she slept—steady, but occasionally stirring. The candle wouldn't last the night. It never did. It wasn't meant to. Just long enough to whisper to the darkness that Eli hadn't been forgotten, even if he was far. Even if he didn't live here. Even if the world called them unrelated.

Freja-Marie stirred in the crib across the room, making a quiet sound that reminded Ben just how little time remained before the twins would arrive. He crossed the floor, not to pick her up, but just to stand nearby. Watching her breathe. Watching the tiny hand flex in a dream. He wondered if she, too, would one day ask about Eli. About the little boy who left toy hammers in the garden and sang louder than the birds when pancakes were served.

The candle guttered slightly. Ben knelt down, inspecting the flame without touching it. He didn't blow it out. He never did. It was never extinguished by hand. It was allowed to fade on its own, as remembrance should. Forced endings never sat well with him. Not with boys like Eli, who deserved beginnings made of gentleness, not grief.

The nursery clock ticked past ten-fifteen. Still no sound from the hall. Isla was likely still asleep. The Judge, by now, would be finishing his second glass of Coffee—never a first—and likely reading Eli's favourite story aloud even though the boy had already memorized it. "Tell it again," he always said. "Even if I know it, I want to hear it in your voice." Ben smiled faintly at the memory. He hadn't even known the Judge could read in character voices until Eli brought it out of him.

He rose and looked once more at the candle. "Four years old," he murmured. "Just once in a lifetime." The child's birthday had passed seven months ago. A quiet day. No royal telegrams, no parades, no lavish cakes. Just cake and laughter and the knowledge that, for once, a child who'd had nothing now had someone. And someone was everything.

Ben returned to his chair, the one with the worn arms and the frayed cushion that Clara refused to replace. He pulled a blanket over his knees and glanced at the flickering light again. His mind wasn't on lineage tonight. It wasn't on secrets, betrayals, or DNA strands waiting to unravel. It was on a boy with a gap-toothed grin who had managed, in just three days of castle visits, to leave a legacy that candles still bowed to.

He reached over to the side table and opened a small notebook. He didn't write anything. He just opened it. The first page was a simple sketch—Eli's. Drawn in blue marker. A picture of "Uncle Ben" holding a balloon, badly proportioned, but unmistakably joyful. That page had never been scanned, digitized, or copied. It lived where it belonged. In ink. In the room where light met memory.

The candle began to shrink. The flame leaned to the right, nudged by a draft from the corridor. Ben closed the notebook gently and rested his hand on top of it. "Sleep well, kid," he whispered, the same words the Judge had once used when leaving the nursery after a castle visit. "One month," he added under his breath. "Just one more month." The candle hadn't gone out yet. And neither had the memory. Some things were too small for headlines. But not too small for love.

CHAPTER 2: A WEEK BEFORE THE WORLD CHANGES

Monday arrived with no grand ceremony, no overt mention of the calendar's creeping urgency. The sun cast its light across the eastern hall as though unaware of the week ahead, brushing lazy gold onto the polished floors where the children's bare feet would soon tiptoe in search of breakfast. In the nursery, someone coughed. In the kitchen, the smell of cinnamon overtook the kettle's rising whistle. The castle moved like a body in half-sleep—fully alive, but unwilling to stir too fast. Nothing felt rushed, yet nothing felt still either.

Ben sat at his desk, not reading but thinking, the kind of thinking that draws a man into silence more than speech. He had moved three books already—two about dynasties and one about land inheritance—and laid them aside in favour of a simple, leather-bound ledger. His hand hovered over it, then opened the cover with quiet reverence. The pages were not sacred in the religious sense, nor ceremonial. They were factual. Genetic. A record of bloodlines, yes, but more importantly, of burdens. Every line in that book had a consequence, and none of them were theoretical.

From the kitchen came the clang of a pan and the unmistakable groan of Tobias teasing someone about scrambled eggs versus omelettes. Isla, moving slower now, passed the door to Ben's study without speaking. She didn't need to. He stood the moment she reached the stairs, eyes following her ascent with a mixture of pride and calculation. Eight months and three weeks. Her gait had changed. Her eyes were quieter. But her back remained straight, and her jaw still held the unspoken strength of a woman who had already done the unthinkable more than once.

Clara passed him next. She nodded, still tying her hair back with the old green ribbon that had belonged to Isla years before. Clara was twenty-one now, though you wouldn't know it by her still-youthful posture and the quiet way she moved through the halls. She had been adopted by Ben and Isla when she was seven, under Kendrick's protection, after surviving a household that offered no love, no names worth remembering. Ben had been ten. Isla too. They had no authority, no legal claim—but Kendrick did. And with a stroke of royal endorsement, Clara became theirs. She had been their daughter ever since.

The staff moved about with an odd kind of choreography—too practiced to be spontaneous, but not so forced as to seem anxious. The birth was not yet discussed openly, but it haunted every motion. Meals were smaller. Blankets had been doubled in the guest wings. Tobias had ordered extra diapers under the pretence of reorganizing storage. Even the power grid had been quietly tested twice in the last week, just in case. Sørensen called it "a week of controlled chaos." Ben called it something else—"the last safe Monday."

Out in the courtyard, Lukas and Peter were chasing Emil, whose laughter rose like a birdcall through the morning haze. None of the boys had asked about the coming twins. Children rarely asked what adults had not yet said aloud. But their eyes were keener than most suspected.

Max-Leo had drawn a picture of two cribs just yesterday, without prompting. Kristian had placed his own blanket beside the guest bassinet, "just in case someone needs it," he'd said. Even Lukas, who typically lived somewhere between rebellion and mischief, had become gentler in Isla's presence.

Ben returned to his notes. He wasn't preparing a lesson plan. He was drafting a legacy. He had done it before—many times—but this one had weight. This wasn't about titles or castles or even his own role. This was for the children who didn't know yet that royalty was not a crown you wore, but a history you bore. He would begin with the haplogroups, move through the migration paths, and eventually share the names—Hungary, Denmark, France. Not for glory, not to impress them. But because he believed they had a right to know the story that made them.

Outside his door, Clara lingered for a moment. "Do you want me to bring them in now?" she asked, not quite whispering, not quite interrupting. Ben looked up, his expression unreadable. He gave a small nod. She disappeared down the hall. A moment later, Isla's voice floated down the stairs, calling for Emil and Kristian. The tone was motherly, but the rhythm was royal. Even when tired, even when swollen with child, Isla's words carried the weight of a woman who would defend her family until the last breath.

The castle was quiet in its acknowledgement of the day's meaning. No one spoke it aloud. But every action—every creak of wood, every softened step, every glance exchanged—betrayed a knowledge that something irreversible was near. This was the last Monday before the world shifted. Before names were signed, before legacies were spoken aloud. Before the storm without rain.

And Ben, sitting there with one hand on the edge of history and the other curled around a pencil, knew better than anyone that once the story was told, it could never be untold. Only expanded.

The kitchen smelled like home. That kind of home that isn't built in blueprints or bought with contracts, but baked into the walls by the breath of people who stayed. Warm loaves sat in their cloth-lined baskets, steam rising in quiet halos while Clara passed the butter dish from child to child. The table was fuller than usual—not crowded, not loud—just full. The kind of full that made a castle feel like a cradle, wide enough for legacies, soft enough for bedtime.

Ben stood at the head of the table, not as a lecturer, not even as a king. Just as Ben. One hand rested on the old ledger, the other tore a piece of bread and dipped it in the honey, then offered it to Emil, who took it with a grin. The children were waiting. Not fidgeting—waiting. They knew the difference. When Ben told stories, you didn't move too fast. You'd miss something.

"R-S660," Ben said, his voice low, but never forced. "It's not a robot. It's not a code from a movie. It's part of me. And part of some of you too." He let the word settle on their faces before continuing. "It's a haplogroup. That means it's a thread in the rope of our past. It came from a father. And from his father. And from his father's father's father." Max-Leo tilted his head, brow furrowed like he'd just bitten a lemon. "So… it's, like… where your people came from?"

"Yes," Ben nodded, "but not just where—who. My R-S660 line comes from Hungary. From old kings. Warriors. Builders. Men who ruled not because they wanted to—but because they had to." He didn't exaggerate. He didn't dramatize. He just told it as it was. The truth needed no crown. "And what about us?" asked Peter, licking honey from his thumb. "Do we have that?"

Ben's eyes softened. "Some of you do. Some of you don't. But the story still belongs to you. If your blood doesn't carry it, your heart still can. Royalty lives in love too. But yes, Peter—some of you do. R-S660 is still running through this table. So is H5a1. That's the maternal line. My line. The one that came from the women who survived. Crossed borders. Buried kings. Gave birth in the dark. And raised children in the light."

Isla said nothing. She didn't have to. Her hands were folded in her lap, her shoulders square, her gaze fixed on the flicker of the stove's pilot light. It was her way of listening—fully present, but not performative. Clara, seated beside her, leaned forward. "So what does mine say, Daddy?"

Ben smiled at the name. Daddy. Not "Ben." Not "Sir." Just the word that had stuck since she was seven and scared of thunder. "Yours says Árpád," he answered quietly. "It says Gibb. It says Nielsen. And it says Harvick. Because the day we chose you—Isla and I—you took us all into your blood. You were never borrowed. You were never temporary. You were claimed." Clara leaned her head against his shoulder and closed her eyes. "Then I want my babies to have that too someday." "They will," Ben said, brushing her hair back gently. "Because you'll tell them. Just like I'm telling you."

Tobias passed another slice of bread to Lukas, who was still trying to pronounce "haplogroup" under his breath. The kitchen had gone quiet again, not because the story was over, but because it had landed. The way only true stories do—straight into the chest. No one said bedtime yet. No one needed to. The story itself had tucked them in. And Ben, with one hand still holding the ledger, kissed Clara's forehead and whispered, "Goodnight, Baby Girl."

Ben didn't use a projector. He didn't need one. The castle's great table had become his chalkboard, and the children his scholars. On a parchment the size of a pillowcase, his handwriting stretched like roots: names, dates, lines of blood trailing across borders long forgotten by modern maps. Hungary was not just a dot. It was a pulse. A heartbeat. A path. And Ben followed it with the calm certainty of someone who had walked it in dreams.

He pointed to a name the children had begun to pronounce correctly now—Béla. "This man," he said, "was a king. But don't let the title fool you. He wasn't made of gold or carried on pillows. He got sick. He got old. He raised children and buried family. He made mistakes. His crown didn't make him better than you. His blood made him responsible." The pencils continued scratching. Each child had their own parchment now, sketching what Ben called "The Line That Remembers." Clara tilted her paper sideways, tracing the branch that veered through Transdanubia. Her eyes narrowed with focus, but her voice stayed casual. "So if we come from Hungary, how come we live in Denmark?" she asked.

"Because Hungary didn't own us," Ben answered. "We came through Hungary. Through kings and mothers and fishermen and soldiers who crossed into Denmark, into France, into England. Blood doesn't stay in one land. It keeps moving until it finds a home." He tapped the parchment again. "And our home is here."

From the far end of the table, Annemarie stepped into the room without shoes, her robe gathered at the waist, curls slightly undone from sleep. She didn't interrupt, but her question came the moment Ben paused. "Why Hungary?" she asked gently. "I remember you speaking it once, years ago. You were just a boy. You called it Magyar. I never forgot the sound of it. But I forgot the story."

Ben didn't look up right away. His hand rested on the edge of the map, steady. "I died once, remember?" he said plainly. "One of the three times. And when I did, I heard a voice. He spoke in a language I didn't know. At least, not then. It was Magyar. Hungarian. And I understood it like I was born to it." He looked up now, meeting her gaze. "That voice saved me. Pulled me back." Annemarie nodded. No wide eyes. No gasps. Just the smallest frown of memory pulling at her mouth. "That was nearly twenty years ago." Her voice was soft. "I remember now. You told me he said you weren't done yet." Ben smiled without warmth. "He was right."

Clara looked between them but didn't interrupt. She had stopped sketching and folded her hands instead. Her pencil rolled off the table. No one retrieved it. Alex Nielsen, her biological father, had once said Clara didn't need to speak when the truth was being told—only to listen. And she listened now, chin resting on her folded arms, brown curls falling into her eyes, the same eyes Isla wiped when Clara was seven and had arrived afraid of storms.

Peter held up his map. "So… King Béla is kind of like your grandfather?" Ben nodded. "Yes. A thousand years back, but yes. A real one. No fiction, no fairy tale. DNA doesn't lie. And neither do bones buried with royal seals." Max-Leo grinned. "So what does that make you?" Ben gave no answer. He turned the page of the ledger instead. But his smile—quiet, tired, and faint—was all the answer they needed.

The morning light entered sideways, curling like steam across the surface of the parchment spread across the long kitchen table. There were jam jars near the edge, half-used, lids forgotten, as if the family had paused their breakfast not out of hunger but revelation. Isla leaned closer, her hand hovering just above the names, not yet touching. Her fingers were clean, her sleeves rolled, and her question came with no urgency, only curiosity. "Where do I fit?"

Ben didn't rush the answer. He looked at her with a gaze reserved not for his wife, but for the keeper of a flame. There was something about lineage that demanded reverence, and he gave it now, reaching for the red pencil. "Here," he said, circling her name with careful pressure. "Not at the end. Not in the margins. You're not an offshoot, Isla. You're a centre point. The maternal lines anchor the forest."

She lowered her hand to the page. Her thumb landed beside a name long faded by time—Stuart. A name she had heard whispered in libraries, tucked into letters, mentioned in royal circles with either envy or resentment. Her family had always known. But no one had ever mapped it like this. Denmark. Scotland. France. They crowded together like neighbours on the same old street, none of them asking who arrived first. Clara leaned forward too, eyes narrowing. "Do the roots always cross?" she asked.

Ben gave a soft laugh. "Of course they do. Family trees don't grow like ladders. They twist. They merge. They curl under each other like vines." He pointed to the red thread Isla had followed earlier. "Some roots come from kings. Some from farmers. Some from war. Some from silence. But they all lead here. This house. This moment."

From the end of the table, Alex Nielsen's voice drifted in—more grunt than sentence, as he passed by carrying a crate of trimmed lavender. He didn't need to be part of the lesson to know where his daughter stood. "Don't let 'em confuse you, Clara. Blood matters, sure—but not half as much as showing up."

Clara rolled her eyes affectionately but said nothing. She had lived enough years between names to understand what her father meant. Adopted at seven by Ben and Isla, she had never needed to be told she belonged. Her name was stitched into her pyjamas before she knew how to read it. Nielsen by blood. Harvick by vow. Rosenshavn by decree.

Ben marked two new names on the maternal side. One, a line from Burgundy. The other, faint and Celtic, tracing to the old houses of Galloway. He wrote slowly, pressing the pencil deeper than necessary. "Every child in this castle," he said, "comes from somewhere. And every one of you leads to somewhere else." Isla looked down again. "We're messy." Ben nodded. "Beautifully so." Outside the window, the garden breathed in quiet rows of green. Trees didn't grow in lines. They reached for light. And so did the people of this house.

The door remained closed. Not locked. Not forgotten. Just... closed. It had been that way since morning. Ben didn't knock. He didn't call through. He didn't need to. Some doors held more meaning when left untouched. Annemarie's silence wasn't distance—it was her inheritance. The walls between them, thick with castle stone and the weight of legacy, carried more than sound. They carried memory.

She had heard every word from the family table. The maternal lines. The red circle around Isla's name. The root drawn from Hungary to the lowlands of France. She had heard Clara's laugh, and the delicate hush Isla gave when the pencil stopped moving. And she had heard Ben's voice steady as a rope across water, always guiding, never drifting. But she did not join them. Not yet. Some mothers showed love with noise. Hers had always arrived through presence, even when her presence was made of silence.

Ben glanced once toward her door. Nothing moved. No creak. No breath. But he felt her there. His mother. By blood. The one who carried him, named him, and—when the world unravelled—followed him into it again. He remembered Kent not as a village, but as a before. A time before the loss. Before Alan disappeared. Before the kitchen tiles cooled without footsteps. Before he asked no questions because the answers were always blank.

Alan had left when Ben was seven. Not just out of the house—but out of the story. His name wasn't erased. It was ignored. Vanished in the way that cowards vanish: cleanly, completely, without the courtesy of a door left ajar. Ben never asked where he went. He only remembered the sound of the front latch clicking on a Monday morning and never hearing it again. His mother never spoke poorly of him. She didn't have to. The silence was louder.

By ten, Ben's feet no longer recognized English ground. He and Isla had boarded a plane to Denmark, hands still sticky from airport sweets, their parents chatting in low tones that pretended everything was an adventure. Robert and Claire Gibb had arranged it carefully. Isla had been born one day before Ben—August 1st and 2nd, same year, same hospital, three doors apart in Kent. They had met in the library at seven years old, tracing back family trees for a school project neither of them remembered finishing. But they remembered the map. They remembered Scotland and Hungary and something about the word "Stewart" that made Isla pause.

The castle in Denmark wasn't home at first. But then Kendrick stepped forward—not as a king, but as a father. At twelve, Ben was no longer a visitor. Kendrick didn't just adopt him; he gave him a seat, a name, a place to rest. And Ben—quiet, careful, already carrying too much—gave him permission to marry his mother. With dignity. With pride. Annemarie hadn't asked for it. But Kendrick had. Ben had said yes without blinking. Because Kendrick had never been silent. He had shown up.

Now, thirteen years later, the boy who once circled names in a Kent library was the man who circled bloodlines in a Danish castle. His fingers rested on Isla's shoulder as she traced lines that connected France to the Uí Néill of Ireland. But still—Ben's eyes flickered back toward the closed door. Because no matter how many kingdoms rose beneath his hands, no matter how many titles were carved into stone or birth ledgers stitched in gold, he was still Annemarie's boy. Her son. By blood. And her silence still meant more than a room full of applause.

Isla noticed his shift but said nothing. Clara glanced toward the hallway and nodded once—barely. Even Emil looked up from his drawing of a family tree shaped like a dragon. They all understood. The castle ran on more than lineage. It ran on knowing who had shown up, and who hadn't. Kendrick had stepped in. Alan had stepped out. One man stayed. One did not.

The door never opened that morning. But Ben didn't need it to. He had already been let in, long ago, when his mother chose him. Chose Denmark. Chose to raise him in a house where silence didn't mean absence. It meant something sacred, protected, and—above all—understood.

The castle was quieter than usual that afternoon, the kind of stillness that arrives before thunder or truth. Ben sat in the alcove just outside the nursery, sorting a stack of folded muslins and trying to remember if he'd already double-washed the pale blue ones with stars. There was a comfort in busywork. It made time feel slower—less determined. But his phone buzzed. Once. That gentle vibration he'd come to expect only from two people: Isla or the Judge.

He didn't rush to check it. He knew. Some messages don't call attention to themselves. They don't arrive with alarms or alerts. They hum. They whisper. He wiped his hands, turned the screen over, and there it was. A message from Judge Algren. Just one photo. No caption. It didn't need one.

Eli's face filled the frame. Chocolate moustache smeared confidently across his upper lip like it was earned in battle. A toy knight clutched in his hand—the toy knight. The one Ben had given him the last day he visited, the one with the missing sword tip and the oversized helmet. Eli grinned like the world had never betrayed a single soul. That kind of grin only a child untouched by burden could give. Or maybe a child who had been saved just in time.

Ben stopped folding. The muslin in his lap fell beside him, unnoticed. For a moment, the entire room became Eli's face. The sunlight angled through the high panes of glass and rested across Ben's cheek as if to soften whatever was coming next. He opened his voice messages. Pressed play. It was his own recording. One he had sent a day earlier.

"I miss you, buddy. You'll always be my favourite knight."

The tone was warm, playful. But now, replaying it, he heard something else. Something behind it. A hush between syllables. A weight. He hadn't known if Eli would hear it right away—if the Judge would show it to him. But Judge Algren never held back what was true. And Eli, despite being only four, knew how to receive things with the gravity of a boy much older.

Ben smiled, then lost the shape of it. His lip trembled before he even noticed it moving. He blinked, hard. Once. Twice. Then let the tears fall. Not hidden. Not turned away. He didn't believe in hiding what was real. Eli had seen him cry before. That night on the castle stairs when he gave him the toy knight and whispered, "Your name means something to me." And again, when Eli had said, "You're like my uncle but better, 'cause you tell the truth even when it's sad."

Ben never claimed Eli. He never tried to. The boy was Judge Algren's son. Adopted legally, raised with a dignity no courtroom could fabricate. But love, when unforced, makes its own declarations. Eli was Ben's nephew. And Ben—without title, decree, or legal string—was something softer. Something children don't always name. Something they feel and remember.

The nursery walls held their own memories. A week from now, they'd hold more. The twins would arrive, and the castle would shift again. But for now, it held the image of one child whose footsteps never echoed in its halls past sunset, but whose laughter was still stitched into the furniture.

Isla walked in briefly and saw the screen. She didn't speak. She just placed her hand on Ben's shoulder and nodded. Then left. It didn't need explaining. Nothing did. When something is real, it doesn't require defence. It just waits until it's seen.

Ben reached into the drawer beside him and pulled out a small wooden box. Inside, folded and faded, was the tissue Eli had used to wipe Ben's cheek the first time he saw him cry. "Don't worry," the boy had said. "You can still be strong even if your face leaks." It wasn't a joke. Not then. It was gospel—but without religion. A child's truth that bore no shame.

He placed the photo on the desk. Printed it. Framed it. Not to hang. Just to hold. Sometimes, memory needed to be touchable. He knew he'd see Eli again. That wasn't in question. But the ache of waiting was its own companion. One he didn't silence. One he let sit beside him, without apology.

The room had already begun to dim by the time the plates were cleared. Dusk settled with a kind of gentleness that made even the castle seem smaller, more tender in its breath. Isla, quiet as she often was in the evenings, did not give instructions. She didn't call the children by name. She simply took her seat on the large, fur-lined reading rug beside the hearth and opened the worn book resting in her lap. The children came on their own. They always did.

Her voice never rose above the crackling logs. She didn't dramatize the lines. She didn't perform. Isla read history the way a surgeon handles skin—steady, reverent, deliberate. The children sat in a half-moon around her, the youngest curled under their blankets, the older ones cross-legged with elbows on knees. Ben leaned in the doorway, arms folded, but he said nothing. Tonight was hers.

In her hands lay the story of Princess Élisabeth Charlotte of Lorraine. A child not much older than Clara had once been when she first came into their care. Born into high blood, royal halls, and the expectations of a title that never got the chance to be worn. Élisabeth had been promised to a life within the Abbey of Remiremont, her future cloistered but gilded, a path lined with reverence and marble. But promise doesn't argue with plague. It never has.

"May 4th, 1711," Isla read, the flicker of flashlight resting against her cheek. "Élisabeth was ten years old. She died at the Château de Lunéville, followed by her younger siblings—three children gone within a single week." She paused for just a second. Not for effect. For breath. The kind of breath one must take before reading grief aloud.

Silje tucked a blanket over Peter, who had stilled beside her. Tobias shifted his weight but didn't interrupt. Even he, the shameless mocker of diaper explosions and pancake fumbles, knew better than to break Isla's tone. Clara leaned her chin on her knees, watching Isla more than listening to the page. It wasn't the facts she followed—it was the flame.

Ben listened from the shadows. He already knew the story. He had traced that family line back more than once, had mapped it across walls and digital trees, had whispered it to himself in the cold Kent library where the truth of Isla's bloodline first appeared between bindings. But hearing it now, here, from her lips, was different. It wasn't a tale of royalty. It was a mother's voice remembering children who were never held long enough.

Isla continued, reading slowly now, her voice catching on the words "buried in the Ducal Crypt at the Church of Saint-François-des-Cordeliers." She did not flinch as she read the names of Élisabeth's mother, her grandmother, the line that tied her to Elizabeth Stuart and, further back, to King James. No need to say "royal." No need to whisper "dynasty." The children already understood. They felt it in her breath.

There was no need to embellish. The names stood tall on their own: Elizabeth Stuart, Charles I Louis, Élisabeth Charlotte d'Orléans. Each generation a scaffold of names, a bridge of blood reaching through Europe. But the story was not about who ruled. It was about who was lost. The tale of Élisabeth Charlotte was not one of reign but of remembrance. A portrait of a girl who never lived long enough to know what her crown would feel like.

Isla held the flashlight low now, letting it skim the pages without glare. It wasn't just a tool to read—it had become a symbol in the room. To the children, that lamp was more than light. It was her presence, steady and unbreakable. They leaned toward it without realizing. They listened not because they were told to—but because Isla made silence feel safe. "She was buried among her ancestors," Isla whispered now, the final line falling like snow across a field. "Not because of her title, but because she was loved."

A breath passed. The children didn't applaud. They didn't speak. For one long moment, they simply sat with it. With her. With the story of a girl whose gown had never gathered dust because she had never lived long enough to dance. Ben stepped closer, not to speak, but to stand behind Isla. He rested his hand on her shoulder as she closed the book and placed it beside her. The flashlight remained lit, flickering against the pages like a candle at a vigil.

Max-Leo broke the stillness. "She was only ten?" His voice was small. Isla nodded once, eyes never leaving the fire. "Only ten." "But she matters," Clara said firmly, eyes set with quiet conviction. "She always did," Isla replied. "Even when the world forgot." And with that, she turned off the flashlight—not to end the story, but to seal it. Not everything ends in flame. Sometimes, it rests in memory. And tonight, a ten-year-old girl long gone was remembered in the castle where children still lived.

Ben lifted the last wooden box from the shelf beside the nursery door. Its lid was older than the others, sanded smooth by use but not neglect, and when he eased it open, the hinges gave a soft groan, like a grandfather clearing his throat before saying something important. Inside lay a cradle—folded down to its bones, joints fitted with brass pins, hinges darkened by age. And beneath it, tightly wrapped and pressed like a pressed flower between history books, was the Danish flag. The red was still deep, the cross still cream against it, not white. Worn in places. Touched by hands that had meant every stitch. Kendrick had sewn it himself, that day thirteen years ago when Ben was still a boy in the eyes of the world, but not to the man who had crowned him.

The cradle didn't belong to anyone yet. It hadn't held the twins. Not yet. But it would. And the flag that lay beneath it wasn't draped in ceremony, nor held hostage in glass. It was fabric made sacred by sweat and silence. A crown never needed to be placed on a head to matter. Some were sewn thread by thread into the folds of memory. That's where Ben found his title. In the quiet.

The room around him was filled with the gentle hum of children's footsteps coming and going, of whispers that didn't ask questions but still wondered everything. Emil, who never tiptoed, entered without knocking. He stood in the doorway a moment, saw the cradle before seeing the flag, and then stepped closer. His eyes flicked from the folded wood to the red cloth. His fingers hesitated—then, with a softness rare for a boy of eight, he reached out and touched the edge.

"Is this yours?" he asked, not reverently, not fearfully. Just plainly. Because to Emil, things only mattered if they were shared. Ben looked down at the boy, then back to the flag. He knelt and smoothed the fold, then held Emil's hand to it. "It's ours," he said. "It's always been ours."

That moment hung in the air longer than expected. Long enough that the children entering behind Emil paused. Max-Leo stood to the left. Peter leaned against the doorframe. Clara, ever watchful, didn't ask why Ben had brought the cradle out. She just sat on the low bench, hands in her lap. She already knew.

Downstairs, Isla's voice carried up faintly. She was reading again. The story of Queen Ava of Scotland. The same one she had shared last spring. She never read it the same way twice. Her voice changed with the room, with the moment, with the air in the castle. She didn't recite. She didn't perform. She simply remembered. And when Isla remembered, everyone else did too.

Ben folded the flag with both hands and laid it inside the cradle. He didn't fold it military-style. This wasn't a ceremony. This was a home. He touched the corners gently, as if the cloth had breath. And when he finished, he placed the cradle in the corner of the nursery and didn't speak again.

The children sat in a half-circle before the fireplace. Tobias had made space between the baskets of clean laundry and the stacks of folded nappies. He didn't need to ask what was going on. He just adjusted the cushions so the children could see Isla clearly. She held no book this time. Just her voice.

Her story tonight was not a bedtime tale. It was about the daughter of King Kenneth III, about the Scotland before maps, when Ava walked the glens and wrote her own endings to history's harsh beginnings. Isla didn't lift her tone for drama. She didn't cry at the sad parts. Her voice was steady, her hands resting over her belly. The twins moved. The castle listened. Even the youngest of the children stayed still. It wasn't discipline. It was awe. They didn't need to know the facts to feel the truth. Ava wasn't a legend in Isla's mouth. She was family. She had always been family.

Ben stood at the arch between rooms. From his place, he could see the cradle, the flag, the circle, the glow of the hearth. His eyes drifted from child to child—Clara's steady posture, Max's tilted head, Emil's still hands—and something in his chest shifted. Not pride. Not even sorrow. Just a quiet responsibility. The kind that didn't begin when you were crowned—but when you realized the crown was never meant to be worn alone.

Clara raised her hand at the end of Isla's story. Not to ask a question. Just to speak. "She was ours too, wasn't she?" she said softly. Isla nodded, brushing her hand over her skirt. "She still is." The flashlight near the cradle flickered again, catching on the brass of the joints. The room seemed to breathe. And when Isla closed her eyes, the silence that followed wasn't empty. It was filled with everything they now knew and everything they had always known but didn't yet have words for.

The cradle, untouched by time. The flag, untouched by fame. The children, untouched by doubt. In that room, they didn't need the world's permission. They had their own. And tomorrow, they would learn more. Because a legacy, like a cradle, must always be made ready before it is needed.

The flashlight clicked once as Ben adjusted its beam across the old ledger's page, the warm yellow cone of light illuminating the names he had already traced with his fingertip a hundred times. He sat cross-legged on the nursery rug, with the children half-wrapped in blankets and curiosity, their eyes fixed not on him, but on the shapes of names that sounded nothing like Denmark or Scotland. Names with hyphens. Names that ended in "de" or "le." France had always whispered. It never shouted. Clara curled beside him with her knees tucked up, not as the twenty-one-year-old she was, but as the little girl who had first crawled into his lap years ago with a head full of questions. She leaned slightly, brushing her arm against his, but said nothing. Her presence was enough. It always was.

Ben didn't start the story like a king. He didn't speak with grandeur. He flipped the page, paused, and looked down at the surname La Fontaine. "This one," he said, "wasn't a soldier. He wrote about water. Made drawings of rivers. Said his family came from a village that doesn't exist anymore." The children looked at the page but didn't interrupt. They waited. He turned the page again. Moreau. Charbonneau. Delacroix. Not all noble. Not all pure. Some were only remembered because they signed the back of a land record or were listed in someone's birth registry, written in ink that had faded long ago. "We don't keep them because they were famous," Ben said. "We keep them because no one else will."

Max-Leo asked, "Were they kings too?" His voice was half-hopeful, half-skeptical. Max had never trusted the idea of thrones, only people. Ben shook his head. "Some were stewards. Some were poor. Some were soldiers who never got to speak again." He lifted his finger and pointed to the margin. "One of them carried a message in his coat, but he died before delivering it. They only found it years later. The message just said: I did my part. That's all." The room stilled. The only sound was the slow, rhythmic turning of the pages. Freja-Marie shifted in her bassinet, letting out the softest squeak, barely more than a sigh. Isla, from the armchair, leaned forward slightly. She said nothing. Her gaze was steady.

Peter sat with a piece of yarn wrapped around his fingers. He pulled it tight between each hand and said, "Why do we keep their names if no one else remembers them?" He wasn't challenging Ben. He was just trying to understand the point of remembering shadows. Ben didn't rush the answer. He set the book on the floor and looked around the room at each face. "Because legacy isn't about who sees it. It's about who holds it. You don't carry something because it's valuable to others. You carry it because it was passed to you with care."

Kristian added, "Like a flashlight." He held up the small one Isla had let him borrow earlier. "Someone gives it to you, and you don't drop it." Ben smiled at that. "Exactly." Silje brought in a small tray of coffee for the adults and warm milk for the children, setting it down without comment. She gave Isla a glance that said everything without words. The castle was leaning in now, not physically, but with presence. Even the air felt like it was listening.

Ben opened the folded page tucked in the back of the ledger—handwritten notes, rough sketches, translated lines from French archives. He pointed to one. "This man," he said, "stood in courtrooms and defended families who didn't have anyone else. He was a count's cousin, but he never used the title. He said he'd rather be useful than recognized." The children nodded. They understood that.

Outside, a soft wind ran past the window frames, tapping at the shutters but never strong enough to get in. Tobias leaned against the hallway door, not participating, but keeping watch as he always did. His eyes scanned the room, making sure every child had a blanket, every cup had a handle. Clara reached out and gently closed the ledger. "We'll remember them," she said. It wasn't a question. It wasn't even a promise. It was a fact. Ben leaned back, flashlight dimmed now, casting only a faint halo on the ceiling. "They weren't royal," he said. "Not most of them. But they carried something sacred. Like a whisper that never wanted to be loud, just heard."

The room began to shift toward bedtime, but no one stood yet. Not right away. They were still sitting with the weight of what had been said. The kind of weight that wasn't heavy, but solid. In the cradle beside the wall, the Danish flag still rested beneath its fitted sheet. The French names wouldn't be stitched into banners or raised above towers. But they would live in this room. In this castle. In these children. Because someone had said them out loud. And someone would again.

Clara pulled the scrapbook from the chest at the foot of her bed with the kind of reverence reserved for memory, not paper. The pages no longer lay flat—they arched slightly, swollen from years of warmth, humidity, and quiet retellings. She laid it open on her lap and sat with her knees folded beneath her, smoothing the spine with one hand while the other rested lightly on the page. A drawing stared back at her—three stick figures holding hands. The smallest one in the middle wore a paper crown. She traced the crooked crayon lines, the soft edges of childhood still pulsing within her fingertips.

Ben entered quietly, not because he was trying to be unnoticed, but because he always respected Clara's moments of reflection. She didn't turn around to greet him. She knew the sound of his walk before she ever saw his face. When he sat beside her, she leaned in, resting her temple against his shoulder without a word. The page didn't move, but her voice did. "Daddy," she said, gently. "You were my first history lesson. You didn't just tell me where I came from. You showed me I mattered."

Ben didn't speak right away. He looked down at the drawing and smiled the way only a father can—one corner of his mouth lifting in quiet disbelief that so much time had passed, and yet it still felt like yesterday. "I wasn't trying to teach," he finally said. "I just wanted you to know you were home." Clara nodded. She never called him by his name. Not once. Not since the day he became her father. She had always said it clearly—Daddy—and he had never asked her to say it differently.

She turned the page, revealing a pressed drawing of Isla at a library desk, her hair sketched in sweeping loops, her hand pointing to a family tree. "I remember this one," Clara whispered. "You told me how you met Mommy at the library in Kent. You were both seven. But even then, you already knew." Ben gave a faint laugh. "She was reading about her own family. I was pretending to read about mine." Clara didn't laugh. She looked up at him seriously. "You weren't pretending. You were finding her."

The next page was blank, except for a folded paper taped in the centre. She peeled it open carefully, revealing a note written in smudged pencil: 'Clara is allergic to mustard. Do not give her any. Love, Daddy.' Ben stared at it and blinked twice. "You kept that?" Clara chuckled. "You wrote it after I threw up on the duvet, remember? It was mustard. My first time ever having it. The Castle Doctor had to come and check me. You were the one who figured it out." She looked at him with solemn eyes. "You held my forehead, Daddy. You stayed beside me the whole night."

Ben's hand slowly closed over hers, not to stop the memory, but to anchor it. "I remember," he whispered. "You were burning up. You were so brave. You didn't even cry. You just looked at me and asked if I could sing." Clara smiled softly. "You did. Off-key, too." He grinned. "Still do." That day had stayed etched in his mind—not for the panic, but for the trust in her eyes. It was mustard, just mustard, but that was the day she chose him not just as her protector, but as her forever.

She reached into the back of the scrapbook and pulled out a strip of photos from a downtown photo booth. "DNA Day," she said proudly. "You took me to get tested when I turned eight. You and Mommy were eleven. You made it sound like we were going on a royal mission." Ben nodded. "You wanted to know where you came from. I wanted you to know you were part of something ancient and alive. You never needed a throne, Baby Girl. You already had a name."

Clara turned to him then, her voice low but full. "You always called me Baby Girl. You still do. Even when I'm grumpy or tired or twenty-one." He tucked a strand of her hair behind her ear and kissed her forehead. "Especially then." She leaned forward and gave him a soft kiss on the lips, just as she had done every night since she was seven. It wasn't habit. It was heritage—the kind of unshakable affection that outlives paperwork, courtrooms, and time.

Ben adjusted the hem of her sleeve and folded the scrapbook closed. "You know, I never thought I'd be a father. Not really. Not in any of the ways that counted on a form. But the moment you looked up at me in that courtyard and said, 'Are you my new Daddy?'—well, that changed everything." Clara's smile widened. "You said yes before you even asked Kendrick." Ben nodded. "That's because I already knew. And Kendrick did too. He was just waiting for me to catch up."

The room fell quiet for a moment as Clara rested her head against his chest. He smelled like cedar and coffee—same as always. The sound of the wind tapping against the window didn't disturb them. Nothing did. She was twenty-one now, grown in the eyes of the world, but still his little girl in every way that mattered. He wrapped his arms around her and whispered, "I'm proud of you, Clara. You've never forgotten where you came from. And you never let me forget who I became."

She closed her eyes, letting the weight of his words settle into her bones. "You're not just my Daddy. You're my beginning. My history. My proof." He didn't reply with words. He just held her tighter.

Later, as the castle lights dimmed, and the halls fell quiet, the scrapbook sat on the nightstand—closed, but still alive. Inside it, between the pages, were more than drawings and notes. There were echoes, memories, anchors to a time when love had to be louder than uncertainty. And in the centre of it all was Clara, still calling him Daddy. Still kissed goodnight. Still chosen.

Tobias had a habit of making light where silence threatened to stretch too long, and tonight was no exception. As dinner wound down and the last of the roast vegetables were being cleared from the children's plates, he lifted his glass of sparkling grape juice with mock pomp and jested, "Well, I suppose we'll need celebratory wine and a tray of devilled eggs when the twins arrive." He didn't expect the table to go quiet. He didn't expect Ben to stop mid-chew and look up— not angry, not amused. Just flat and unwavering.

"No alcohol," Ben said, wiping the corner of his mouth with the cloth napkin as if nothing more needed saying. "Not now. Not ever. Not in this castle." His tone had not changed volume, but the walls heard it. Even the fire in the hearth settled back a little. "And no eggs either. Kendrick hates them. Always has. And so do I."

Clara blinked slowly. Emil stared. Lise stopped her fork in mid-air. No one laughed. This wasn't a joke. Ben didn't explain rules without a reason. "Yogurt's off the table, too," he added, quieter now but not less certain. "Because of Lise. Tobias, you know that." Tobias's smile faded into a wince of recognition. He nodded, rubbing the back of his neck with one hand.

"I didn't think—" he began, but Ben cut him off—not rudely, but with a look that said he'd rather not revisit the memory in too much colour. "She was seven. Now she's eight. But you know what happened. That white sauce in the bowl? She thought it was ranch or cream cheese or something like that. It was yogurt. Full of bacterial culture. She dipped her carrots into it like any child would. Five minutes later—well, you remember the rest."

Tobias did remember. In fact, everyone at the table remembered. It wasn't the kind of thing that vanished from a person's memory with time. She had thrown up so hard and so fast it had erupted like a fountain of warning right down the front of his shirt, staining it from collar to bootlaces. They'd had to peel the socks off his feet and toss the whole outfit. The smell lingered longer than his pride.

"Same goes for vinegar," Ben said, shifting in his seat slightly. "Thomas. He's eleven now, but when he was eight, he had a salad that Kendrick didn't know had vinegar in the dressing. It was just a drizzle. Barely noticeable. Didn't matter. Twenty minutes later, he was bent over in the garden throwing up in the soil while Kendrick held his hair back."

Ben didn't speak with malice. He wasn't scolding. He was protecting. That castle had rules, and every one of them had been written in the stomachs of children. "We're not here to debate what's reasonable," he continued, calmly but firmly. "We're here to prevent a repeat of the vomit volcano that claimed your uniform last spring."

Clara smirked behind her water glass but didn't laugh aloud. Tobias gave a small grunt of submission and held both hands up. "Noted. Loud and clear. Never again. Eggs, yogurt, vinegar, alcohol. They don't belong. They're banished." Ben gave a short nod. Not because he needed the acknowledgement—but because it meant the lesson had landed.

Kendrick, who had been quietly folding a napkin into a square for Freja-Marie, didn't even raise a brow. He simply hummed his agreement, as if to say, Some rules write themselves. No one in the room questioned it. No one made jokes after that. Even the toddlers sensed the seriousness—Peter looked suspiciously at his plate, then slid it an inch to the left without touching anything that might look creamy.

Tobias leaned toward Lise and gave her a gentle side-hug. "You still owe me a new t-shirt," he whispered playfully. She grinned and whispered back, "You shouldn't have fed me yogurt, then." The moment passed with that brief flicker of levity, but the rule remained etched into castle law. There were no printed signs. There didn't need to be.

By the end of the evening, the kitchen staff had already revised the week's meal plans. Sauces were double-checked. Dressings were labelled in bold. The fridge had an entire shelf cleared and marked for allergy-safe items. Kendrick took a marker and wrote "NO EGGS. NO EXCUSES." on the dry-erase board beside the pantry. Someone had drawn a cartoon egg with a red X over its face. Ben walked past the board with a glance, nodded once, and kept walking. It didn't need to be beautiful. It just needed to be followed.

Isla later tucked Freja-Marie in and whispered, "No yogurt dreams, sweet girl." She kissed her daughter's cheek and turned off the nightlight. Downstairs, Tobias cleaned the dining table in silence. He didn't mind the reminder. He had learned more about fatherhood by watching Ben enforce one rule than he had in a year of trial-and-error parenting. Rules at Rosenshavn were not written in anger. They were written in consequence. And consequence, as Tobias well knew, often came wearing the scent of sour milk and regret.

The courtyard was quiet except for the metallic rasp of stone on steel. Sørensen sat beneath the archway near the east well, sharpening a row of long-forgotten blades—not for any real defence, but to remember what once was. His hands moved with a practised rhythm, not as a soldier, but as a steward of stories too dangerous for the record books. Ben watched him from a low stone bench, the evening light catching the edges of the folder Sørensen eventually handed him. It was leather-bound, creased at the corners, with a single label pressed into the front in black ink. SHIELD: STINK BOMB CLASSIFIED. Ben laughed the moment he saw it. "Did you keep them all?" he asked, already knowing the answer. Sørensen's eyes barely flicked up as he replied, "You don't throw out royalty."

Inside the folder were schematics, screenshots, and pieces of code only two people in the castle could understand. Ben flipped through the pages slowly, his fingers brushing the old data trails like a composer revisiting a forgotten score. "I was ten," he muttered. "Just ten. And they tried to track me—through school records, back-channel birth registries, global DNA databanks. I didn't know what they were looking for back then, but I knew what they were after. Me." He closed the folder gently, like a priest sealing a relic. "So I gave them something else to look at."

What Ben had done thirteen years earlier was never called war. It had no casualties, no battlefields, and no news coverage. But it was a strike—swift, precise, and untraceable. He used a battered tablet—technically a kids' device—but equipped with custom software that had outwitted adult systems. He didn't learn that from Sørensen. The reverse was true. Sørensen had watched in disbelief as Ben, crouched on the floor in pyjamas, ran three concurrent breaches on encrypted systems across three continents. Kendrick had nearly fallen off his chair laughing—not because it was funny, but because he couldn't believe it. "The kid's a ghost," Kendrick had said. "A royal ghost. They'll never catch him."

They never did. Ben froze assets in Amsterdam. Disrupted inheritance chains in southern France. Slashed emergency backup nodes belonging to a private royal council in Austria. He didn't just hide. He reversed the search. He put them on the defensive. They didn't know where the attack came from, and when they finally traced the ping, it rerouted through a pizza parlour in Newfoundland. By the time they realised it was a dead end, Ben had already vanished behind thirty layers of camouflage, his true location buried beneath meaningless digital trails.

The operation, later dubbed Operation Sovereign Burn, was launched with no announcement. There was no press. No whistleblower. Just silence. But the damage was real. Kings and queens, dukes and heirs, woke up to find their titles under investigation, their names flagged, their holdings frozen. Calls were made. Lawyers panicked. Several aristocrats tried to bribe their way into the silence, but no reply came. They knew. They didn't know how, or when, or even where the attack came from. But they knew who. And they understood one thing clearly: the boy was still alive.

Inside the leather folder, Sørensen had printed and kept Ben's final embedded message—planted in the corrupted archive of one particularly arrogant European house. "Mess with this family again and the stink bomb won't be a warning next time." That was it. One sentence. And it worked. Thirteen years later, no retaliation had come. No kingdom had tried to re-ignite the search. Whatever had scared them back then was still working now.

Ben didn't smile as he remembered it. Not because it wasn't funny, but because it wasn't over. "They'll come again," he said, handing the folder back. "They always do. The ones who believe in power by bloodline alone—they think I'm just a rumour. A myth to silence. But the moment I surface, they'll try again. The stink bomb was never the end. It was the scent. It's still in their noses." Sørensen nodded. "And if they do?" "They'll find out I've grown up," Ben replied. "And this time, I don't need a tablet. I've got names, codes, vault maps. I've got legitimacy."

It hadn't been just about him. Ben did it to protect the castle—Isla's safety, Kendrick's trust, the future of the twins who hadn't yet been born. Even Clara, whom he wouldn't meet for another few months, was in his mind somehow. It was as if he knew she'd arrive, and when she did, she'd be safe because of what he'd already done.

Back in the courtyard, Sørensen rolled the whetstone between his palms. "I thought you were going to tell me why you used the word stink bomb." Ben smirked. "Because it wasn't permanent. Just... unbearable. Just enough to make them run. Just enough to warn them." He looked up at the sky, now nearly dark. "The next one won't be a warning."

Nothing in the castle had ever been touched. Not the financial records, not the registry of Rosenshavn, not even the utility logs. It was as if Ben had thrown a global tantrum but spared his own room. "They called it an act of cyber terrorism," Sørensen recalled aloud. "But I called it good parenting." Ben laughed at that. "You always were a fan of teaching the hard way."

The two sat in silence for a while longer. Then Sørensen handed him a small chip drive, newer than the others. "You'll want this next time," he said. "I've been working on upgrades." Ben tucked it into his coat without looking at it. "Next time, they'll need more than a firewall to keep me out." He stood and left the courtyard slowly, folder in hand, not triumphant—but ready. The blades were sharp, the files backed up, and the shield in place. It wasn't just memory now. It was preparation. The storm hadn't come yet. But they both knew it would.

The note was small. Folded into quarters and slipped between pages of an old gardening book that Isla hadn't touched in years. Silje had only pulled it from the shelf because of its green cover—hoping to find the section on edible wildflowers for a coffee substitute. But as the book opened, the note fluttered to the floor like a leaf too shy to fall. It landed near her foot, curling at the edges. She bent down, picked it up with care, and opened it slowly. A single name stared back at her in Isla's unmistakable cursive. No title. No explanation. Just one name.

She had only read the first syllable when Isla's voice crossed the room like a thread pulled taut. "That's mine." Her words weren't sharp, but they weren't casual either. Silje froze, then turned. Isla wasn't angry. She didn't reach for the paper. She didn't scold. Instead, she took two slow steps forward and reached out her hand—not to Silje, but to the note itself. As she took it gently from Silje's fingers, she added, quieter now, "This one's mine."

The room, suddenly, felt smaller. Not from tension—but from reverence. Silje nodded once, then turned away, giving Isla the gift of silence. Everyone in the castle knew by now not to ask questions when names were being written. Especially these names. They weren't for discussion, nor opinion. They weren't for cooing or joking or accidental slips on intercom systems. These names belonged to the stars first—not the newspapers.

Isla folded the note again, tighter this time, as if folding it would press the meaning deeper into the parchment. She didn't put it back in the book. She held it against her chest, fingers curled like she was carrying something warm. "It's just one," she said to no one in particular. "But it's real. And it's safe with me." There was no one in the room but Silje now, but the air had shifted—as though the walls themselves understood the importance of what had been almost revealed.

This wasn't the first time a name had come close to escaping. Months earlier, one of the castle children had overheard Ben muttering a phrase in his sleep, something that sounded like a name, and repeated it during breakfast. The entire room had gone quiet. Kendrick had cleared his throat, and Ben had calmly said, "That was the name of a street in Kent. Not a baby name." No one believed him. But no one asked again.

For Isla, names were more than syllables. They were codes. Keys. And sometimes, shields. The right name could build a legacy. The wrong one could open doors better left closed. In her mind, names were shaped by constellations, carved by the wind across meadows only she and Ben knew. They didn't choose names for trend or tradition. They chose them because they fit, the way shoes fit the feet of a child not yet born.

The note, now folded into a near-perfect square, disappeared into Isla's back pocket. She didn't speak about it again. Not to Ben, not to the staff, not even to herself. Some names were sacred in ways that had nothing to do with ceremony and everything to do with identity. She'd wait. Wait until the birth. Until the moment when stars blinked their approval. Until the child's eyes opened and the name fit like it had always belonged.

Later that evening, Silje passed Ben in the hallway. He looked at her curiously, as if something invisible had shifted. "Everything alright?" he asked. She smiled. "Perfect." There was no need to say more. He'd seen the folded note before. He'd written a few himself. All of them sealed, stored in the red leather box marked For the Right Hour.

Downstairs, the other staff whispered about the moment, trying to guess the name. Someone suggested Ava. Another said Charlotte. But each was met with a quiet shake of the head by Tobias, who simply muttered, "If it was meant to be said, she'd have said it." And that was the end of the game.

Even the youngest of the castle children knew better than to repeat anything they overheard involving the twins. They'd been warned gently but clearly. "If you say a name before the child is born, it floats away," Clara once told little Elias. "And then it won't come back." Elias had gasped and covered his mouth with both hands. He never guessed again.

Isla didn't hide the note out of fear. She hid it because it wasn't ready. Names, in her world, had to be born at the same time as the child—not earlier, not by accident. They weren't gifts. They were destinies. And once spoken aloud, there was no taking them back.

She spent the rest of the evening in the nursery, brushing the lint off the folded muslin cloths, checking the temperature gauge near the window, adjusting the pillows in the rocker. But the name stayed sealed in her pocket, like a promise not yet made.

Ben never asked. He trusted her with the naming in a way few kings could have. Because he knew she didn't name for power or pageantry. She named for truth. And that truth—whatever it would be—had to be hers first.

By midnight, the castle had returned to its quiet hum. The name had not escaped. The stars had not yet claimed it. But in the stillness of that hour, Isla stood by the window, hand against her belly, whispering it softly into the dark. Just once. So it would know it was not forgotten.

Ben never raised his voice. He didn't need to. When he picked up the chalk and dragged it slowly across the board in the study room, the sound alone was enough to still the group. The older children, a mix of those biologically and honourably part of the castle, leaned in without asking what the line meant. They had been here long enough to know Ben's lessons were never just about knowledge. They were about survival. At one end, he wrote one word in crisp, straight letters: Stories. On the other end, he paused before writing the second word: Truth. He underlined both. Then, turning around, he waited.

Silje, seated with her legs crossed beneath her, whispered something to Tobias. She was only twenty-one, but wise beyond the softness of her smile. Tobias, just a year older, leaned back in his chair and gave a slight nod.

He was always the first to catch on, but never the first to speak. The others watched Ben. They could tell by his posture that this wasn't a night for bedtime tales. This was something else. Something real. And Ben's version of truth never arrived as a lecture—it arrived as memory.

"I need you to know," Ben began, his voice steady, "that we didn't end up here by coincidence. You live in a castle. You eat because someone made sure you would. You're safe because someone paid a price. And you're told the truth—because we decided not to keep lying." The air shifted slightly, like the room itself had inhaled.

He tapped the word Stories. "These," he said, "are what the world tells to keep things simple. Royal stories. Family stories. The kind that make bedtime easier." He tapped Truth. "This is what no one will tell you unless you ask. And when you do ask, people will say you're too young to hear it. But not in this house. Not anymore." His eyes swept the room.

Silje raised her hand, but Ben gestured for her to speak freely. "Is it dangerous to know the truth?" she asked. Her voice wasn't timid. It was layered with a caution that came from knowing danger had always lived just outside the gates. Ben didn't flinch. "It's dangerous not to know it," he answered. "Because then you'll believe whatever version someone else writes about you. And that's how legacies are lost."

Tobias leaned forward, elbows on his knees. "But what if someone uses the truth to hurt us?" Ben let the question settle. "Then you know where to stand," he said. "Right here." He struck the middle of the line with the chalk and left a dot. "You learn when to speak, when to wait, and when to blur it—just enough to keep yourself safe, but never so much that you forget who you are."

One of the younger teens asked quietly, "Is that what you did when you sent the Stink Bombs?" The room tightened. Ben took a breath. "Yes," he said. "That was truth delivered like a story. I made it sound funny so people wouldn't panic. But I wasn't playing." No one interrupted. No one laughed.

He walked to the window and looked out toward the northern fields where the lights of Rosenshavn barely flickered. "When you grow up hidden, you get used to people writing things about you. Stories to erase you. Stories to replace you. But I had to write back. I had to freeze their stories in their own data centres and leave a stink that wouldn't wash off. That was me saying, 'You don't get to lie about this family anymore.'"

They sat with that. Not a single child looked away. Not even Silje, who usually blinked when things got too real. Tobias reached for a piece of chalk and without asking, drew a circle around the dot in the centre of the board. "That's where we live now," he said. "Between what they tell and what we know."

Ben turned back, smiling—not with amusement, but with approval. "That's exactly right. We live in that space. We defend it. And when the time comes, you'll be the ones to teach others how." He placed the chalk down carefully, never breaking eye contact. "Just remember—truth isn't the same as facts. Facts are small. Truth is who you become when no one's watching."

The lesson ended without a bell. They stood together, not by routine but by recognition. The room had shifted. They weren't just students now. They were heirs to a history that required silence, strength, and storytelling in equal parts. Silje stayed back, as she always did, to walk out last. Tobias waited for her. And Ben, before extinguishing the overhead light, looked once more at the board. The words remained: Stories on the left, Truth on the right, and in the centre, a single mark. It wasn't a scar. It was a birthmark. One they all shared, whether they liked it or not.

It was nearly midnight when Ben stepped out into the northern courtyard. The fog had thickened across the castle grounds, silencing even the wind. Lamps glowed faintly along the perimeter wall, casting long shadows across the flagstones. Uncle Sørensen stood alone beneath the archway, wiping the condensation from a polished shield as though time hadn't passed at all since the last war. Ben didn't speak at first. He waited until the shield was set down, until Sørensen's eyes rose to meet his without question. Only then did he whisper, "I'm heir to seven royal houses. Maybe eight."

Sørensen didn't blink. Not at the number. Not at the implication. He only adjusted his weight, stepped forward once, and said, "And?" Ben let out a breath that had held for years. "If the world finds out," he continued, "they'll burn it all down. Everything we've done. Everything we've kept quiet. Everything Kendrick protected." His voice didn't tremble, but there was a pressure behind it—one of scale, of inheritance too large for one man to carry without crushing his chest.

The older man didn't argue. He placed a hand on Ben's shoulder and tightened his grip with just enough force to say what words couldn't. "Then we build from the ashes," Sørensen said quietly. "Again." It wasn't a threat. It wasn't even comfort. It was confirmation. That the truth had already survived once, and if needed, it would survive again. Ben turned slightly, eyes scanning the walls of the old castle that had become both cradle and fortress. "I didn't ask for any of this," he said.

"No king ever does," Sørensen replied, "but it finds them anyway." He walked with Ben across the courtyard, their boots scuffing quietly against damp stone. "You carry the lines of England, Denmark, Hungary, France, Ireland, Spain—and one more we've never confirmed on paper. But it doesn't matter. Blood knows. And power always finds its way home."

Ben stopped beside the old battlement wall, his hands tucked deep into his coat. "It's not the crown I'm afraid of," he said. "It's what they'll do when they find out it belongs to someone who won't play their game." Sørensen laughed once—short, dry. "Let them play. We're not in the game. We're the end of it." He picked up a flat stone and tossed it into the courtyard fountain where it skipped once and sank.

"You were ten when you cracked open a dozen royal servers and froze their lines," Sørensen said. "You didn't do that to play king. You did it because they started hunting you. They'll do it again. And next time, you'll be ready with more than just an iPad." Ben smiled slightly at that, the ghost of a smirk in the corner of his mouth. "It was a tablet," he corrected. "Second-hand. Cracked screen. No one even knew I was watching them until I locked the last gate."

"And then you signed the attack 'Stink Bomb,'" Sørensen added, shaking his head. "They thought it was a prank until the Swiss banks froze. Idiots." Ben leaned against the stone ledge. "They still don't know it was me. Not really." Sørensen lifted a brow. "You think they're done guessing? You're twenty-three now. They're not guessing anymore. They're waiting."

The torchlight—no, the flashlight now, because Ben had insisted—flickered as Sørensen adjusted its beam across the gravel path. "You've got one week left," he said. "After that, the twins are born. You'll be a father. Again. You don't get to hesitate after that." Ben nodded, jaw tight. "And if they come?" he asked.

Sørensen didn't hesitate. "Then they'll find every gate shut. Every archive sealed. And you? You'll be gone before their satellites even reload." He turned to him fully. "You were hidden for thirteen years. You were protected by more than blood. You were guarded by love, silence, and a house that remembered what kingship meant before the cameras ever arrived."

Ben looked up to the high tower where Isla now rested. "I don't want the twins growing up in a war." Sørensen joined him in that gaze. "Then teach them how to win it before it starts." The silence between them wasn't empty. It was layered with history, names, losses neither of them had spoken aloud. Kingships never came with warning. But Ben had been preparing since the day Kendrick pulled him from the edge of anonymity and declared him a sovereign son.

And now? Now the names of seven houses lived in his marrow. Not just titles—but legacies. Lineages that stretched from the Scottish highlands to the fields of Aquitaine, from the towers of Madrid to the northern coasts of Denmark. Sørensen clapped him once on the back, solid and grounding. "If the world burns," he said again, "we build. You know we will." Ben nodded. "Seven houses," he repeated. "Maybe eight." Then, quieter still, "But only one crown." Not the kind worn. The kind born. The kind no one could take. Not now. Not ever.

The morning was slower than usual. Not because the castle had slept in, but because Isla hadn't yet stirred. She lay on her left side with the pillows tucked tightly behind her back, one arm stretched beneath her head, the other curved gently across the arch of her stomach. Light filtered in through the tall windows, soft and golden, catching strands of her hair in a quiet halo she didn't ask for. She wasn't asleep, but she wasn't fully awake either. Her breath was even, her face calm, her legs curled slightly to ease the weight she'd been carrying. At 8 months and 3 weeks, her time was nearly here.

She did not cry. She did not make a sound. She placed both hands on the curve of her belly and whispered something too quiet for the guards outside to hear. "We're almost there," she said, not as a promise but as a fact. Her voice was warm, level, spoken directly to the lives inside her. The twins had been moving more lately, especially at night. Isla felt it all—every twist, every stretch, every strange little rhythm of feet or elbows pressing against her ribs. She never flinched. She welcomed it. It meant they were strong.

Ben stood in the doorway, leaning lightly against the frame, arms folded. He didn't enter. He didn't speak. He had already learned that moments like this weren't meant for sharing—they were meant for witnessing. Isla didn't see him at first, or if she did, she chose not to acknowledge him just yet. Her fingers traced the same circle across her belly three times, then stilled. There was nothing mystical about it. It was instinct. She knew where they were. One resting higher than the other. One with a quicker kick. They were already different, and she had already memorized them.

There were charts in the hallway drawer—precisely folded medical notes, names of nurses on-call, silent agreements between Kendrick and the private midwife team flown in from Kent. None of that mattered to Isla in this moment. She was charting her own course, one heartbeat at a time. Her belly had dropped slightly overnight, not much, but enough for her to feel it. Her lower back ached, the kind of ache that meant everything was getting ready, pulling downward, loosening the earth for something ancient and real to arrive.

Ben's eyes didn't move. He stood there for what might've been ten minutes, saying nothing. He was holding a clipboard earlier, something about logistics, but it now sat abandoned on the floor outside the room. There was no paperwork that could prepare a man for this. Not for the quiet strength of watching someone you love get ready to split herself in two. Not for the grace with which she breathed through it.

Isla shifted then, carefully rolling onto her back. Her breath caught for just a moment as she adjusted the weight of her belly, then settled again. She didn't groan. She didn't complain. She exhaled slowly and opened her eyes. Her gaze drifted up toward the canopy of the bed, where Ben had once, weeks ago, taped glow-in-the-dark stars at Clara's suggestion. Some were peeling. She smiled faintly. The kind of smile reserved for private jokes and exhausted victories.

She turned her head, finally meeting Ben's eyes. No words were exchanged. There didn't need to be any. Her eyes said everything. I'm fine. Don't worry. Stay with me. And Ben understood. He stepped forward only when she gave a slight nod, lowering himself into the chair beside her. Not on the bed. That space was sacred now. It belonged to her and the twins. He respected that boundary, even as he stayed close enough to count the freckles on her arm.

She reached out and touched his hand, palm to palm, warm and certain. "They know your voice," she said, barely above a whisper. "They settle when they hear you." Ben swallowed but didn't look away. "They're listening," he replied. "You're doing all the work, and they still want me?" Isla chuckled softly, then winced slightly—her belly tightening with a mild contraction. Practice. Nothing serious. But real enough to remind her it was soon.

He leaned closer then, placing one hand lightly over hers and the other over her belly. One of the twins kicked. He laughed, a real, soft laugh, like it caught him by surprise. "That one's mine," he said. "He's stubborn already." Isla shook her head. "No," she murmured, "that's the girl. She takes after you." Another kick followed, this time lower. Isla didn't flinch. "And that," she said, "is the boy. He's quieter. But he means business."

They sat there like that for a long while. No one interrupted. The castle moved around them with respectful slowness, as if everyone sensed what this week meant. Clara brought coffee but left it at the door. Sørensen passed by once with an old map under his arm and gave a quiet nod before vanishing again. Even Tobias knew better than to knock. The stillness in the room was its own declaration. This was not a waiting room. It was the calm before everything changed.

Ben finally broke the silence. "A week," he said, voice low. Isla nodded. "Maybe less," she replied. "Maybe tonight." He didn't argue. He knew better than to question her timing. Her body had never lied to her before. And besides, she was right. They were almost there. Not just to the birth, but to something much larger—something that would shape the next chapter of the castle, the family, and the line.

He didn't promise her rest. He didn't promise that the world would stay quiet. But he did promise to be there. For every breath. Every step. Every push. And when the time came, he would be the first to catch what came next. Not a prince. Not a princess. But two small, wriggling truths that would carry all of them forward.

Isla closed her eyes again, hands steady, heart certain. Ben reached for the clipboard, then thought better of it. He stayed beside her, fingers laced, listening to the quiet thud of two small lives getting ready. And outside the castle, the world continued turning, unaware that its future had just taken a breath.

CHAPTER 3: THE CROWN IN HIS BLOOD

The corridor behind the library shelf did not creak when the latch turned. It clicked with purpose, like it had been waiting. Ben stepped through first, barefoot and silent, and the children followed close behind, each holding the shoulder of the one before them. The light above flickered only once before settling into a steady hum, casting a dim glow on the steps carved deep into the rock. No sound travelled back up the hallway. No laughter, no breath, not even the rustle of a sleeve could bounce off those limestone walls. It was a room that didn't echo because it wasn't built for noise. It was built for containment.

The walls had been lined with lead back in the sixties, when lead was still allowed and secrets were still handwritten. Kendrick once said it was meant to store classified government tapes from a war nobody won. But Ben knew better. This room was older than the Cold War. Older than the politics that pretended to guard it. The shelves were thick oak, the kind that would split the blade of a weak axe, and the air tasted like paper that had been breathing for generations. A thick leather-bound volume sat on the centre table, its edges darkened from the oils of those who had touched it in fear, in reverence, or both.

Ben said nothing at first. He let the children look. Some stared at the markings on the floor—symbols burned into the tile by hands no longer alive. Others noticed the fingerprints etched into the brass handles of the locked drawers. Clara didn't need to ask. She already understood that what was kept here was not meant to be explained with a single story or simplified into a bedtime tale. Emil tilted his head, squinting at a family seal too worn to read. "Is this where the bloodline's kept?" he asked. Ben didn't answer. He simply walked toward the far cabinet, placed his hand on a sensor no one else could see, and waited for the magnetic lock to yield.

When the door swung open, it made no sound. Inside was the case. The one no one but Ben had touched in thirteen years. It was not large. In fact, it was smaller than the violin box Clara once kept under her bed. But it was heavier. That weight wasn't metal. It was truth. He pulled it out and placed it on the table without ceremony, then lifted the lid as if unveiling the bones of an ancestor. Rows of envelopes sat stacked, each one marked in his handwriting—some dated, some not, all sealed with wax. The oldest record was marked in bold red ink: Isla. Traced. He didn't look up.

The children gathered around him. No one reached for the documents. They didn't need to. The weight of the air told them this was not a space for touching. This was a space for absorbing. Ben took one folder, opened it slowly, and spread its contents with exactness. DNA records, bloodline trees, migration patterns, and the forensic trail of royal descent spanning not just centuries—but continents. He pointed to a line traced in gold: Harvick–Stuart–Gibb. Then, with a second finger, he dragged another line intersecting it: Rosenshavn–Árpád. The centre of the Venn diagram was marked not with names, but with two simple stars. No names. Just stars.

"These," he said, tapping the stars, "are not your future. They're your past. Yours to keep. Yours to protect. Yours to honour." His voice didn't rise. He spoke as one does in museums, or burial sites, or at the edge of some impossible truth. They listened. No one interrupted. Tobias's hand tensed at his side, but he did not speak. Even Silje, ever the question-asker, stayed quiet. Isla stood in the doorway, one hand on her hip, the other against her belly. She had known these documents existed. She had never asked to see them.

Ben reached into the case and pulled out a map, unrolling it across the table with two brass weights shaped like ravens. The map had been drawn by hand, decades before he was born, but it told the story clearer than any modern database could. Lines crossed oceans. Arrows circled kingdoms. Crowns were placed beside names that had been erased from public record but never from blood. "We never needed a throne to be royal," Ben said. "But the crown's in our blood. In yours. And no one will ever take that from you."

He turned to Emil and nodded. "The silence of this room protects what the world would destroy if it knew too soon." Then to Clara, "And your memories, baby girl, protect what no document ever could." She didn't blush. She nodded once. She knew he meant the night she found her family here—not by birth, but by truth. Isla finally stepped forward, one hand still on her stomach. "They'll ask questions," she said softly. "One day. About where they came from." Ben didn't blink. "Then we'll answer with a mirror. And a map."

Tobias spoke first. "Does anyone outside this room know?" Ben looked at him, hard, then shook his head. "Only Kendrick. And Sørensen. And even they don't know everything." He gestured to the far wall, where a locked cabinet stood with no visible handle. "What's behind that?" Silje asked. He didn't reply. He wouldn't. That wall was for another time. Another telling. The silence wrapped itself around the group again. Not cold. Not cruel. Just full. Weighted. Earned.

They stood like that for several minutes. No one wanted to break the moment. No one wanted to be the one who made a sound that might bounce off the limestone and carry something out of the room. Eventually, Ben closed the case. Slowly. Respectfully. Like one folds a flag or lowers a body into the ground. He latched it. Locked it. And returned it to its place. When he stood upright, the children were already facing the door. They knew. There was nothing left to say here. Not out loud.

As they exited, one by one, Ben stayed back for a moment and looked at the sealed case. Then at the map. Then at the faint outline of two stars. "They're not born yet," he whispered, "but they already carry the crown." He ran a hand over the table. No dust. Not in here. Not in the room that doesn't echo. And with that, he turned off the light.

There was a lock behind the third cabinet on the eastern wall—flanked by limestone shelves and encased in a structure no child had ever even noticed before. It sat flush against the grain, brushed into invisibility, invisible until Isla ran her fingers across the smooth inner bevel and paused. She tilted her head, just slightly. "Here." Her voice was not loud, not proud.

She spoke like someone answering an ancestral summons. Beside her, Ben remained still. His hand hovered near the panel but did not press. It was Isla who reached forward with a quiet finality, and then tapped six digits into a brass keypad disguised within the woodwork. A sound like softened gravel whispered through the room, followed by the smallest hiss of hydraulics. The panel released. The cabinet opened inward.

The room was already quiet before. But the silence that followed the opening of that hidden cabinet felt different—thicker, older, bound by something deeper than stone. The space behind it had not seen breath nor daylight in over a decade. No light flickered. No alarm rang. Just breathless stillness, and the scent of polished cedar, preserved ink, and age. Inside the compartment, the shelves were made not of wood, but of old brass and blackened steel—cold to the touch, heat resistant, sealed by design. Ben reached in first, retrieving a flat archival folder sealed with royal red wax and stamped with the Harvick family crest. Then came the DNA charts—layered and framed beneath tempered glass, edges aligned so perfectly it seemed unnatural. Isla reached next.

Her fingers touched the edge of a frosted glass case. She slid it forward. Inside rested a single vial. Thin, amber-glass. Cork-sealed. Wax-dipped. Labelled in hand: King Benedict Adrian Harvick of House Rosenshavn – Blood Sample. No date. No lab signature. Just his full title and name, written in Isla's handwriting from five years ago. She stared at it for a moment—not as one in awe, but as one in recognition. Her thumb ran along the wax seal. "We agreed not to freeze it," she said quietly. "To keep it as it was. Living. Witnessing." Ben nodded. "Because lineage should never be preserved in theory alone. It should live in trust."

There was no crown in the cabinet. Not the physical kind. The actual royal diadems remained on display in the ceremonial throne room, atop their velvet pillows—one gilded, one silvered, neither worn. That had been their decision long before the twins were conceived. Isla had said it first: "We were born royal. We do not need a band of gold to confirm it." And Ben had smiled, kissed her temple, and placed the crowns on the thrones themselves, saying, "Then let the thrones wear them. They hold more weight than our heads." Since then, the crowns had remained untouched. Symbols only. Legacy, not leverage.

Isla moved to the chair in the corner of the room—the one lined with sheep's wool and stitched in soft burgundy thread. She lowered herself slowly, almost reverently, resting the glass vial in her palm. The silence didn't fade. It expanded. Ben stood across from her, hands in the pockets of his dark coat, his gaze fixed not on the vial, but on her. He had loved her since before either of them knew what it meant. And now, at twenty-three, with twins about to enter the world, he knew that love was no longer private. It was recorded in blood. "Do you remember what we said the day this was taken?" Isla asked, voice like fog across glass.

"I said it was just a backup," Ben replied. "And you said there's no such thing as just a backup—not when it comes to legacy." Isla gave a small nod. "And now we have children who will never wonder where they come from." She didn't mean biologically. She meant spiritually.

They had built this archive room beneath the castle not to preserve royalty, but to protect memory. Not everything would be passed on through genetics. Most of it would pass through silence, story, sacrifice. The kind of truths that cannot be decoded by science, only honoured through presence.

Outside the thick limestone walls, no echo could reach them. That was the point. The room had been designed that way. Lead-lined. Signal-blocked. Earth-anchored. It was a womb for remembrance. A sanctuary for what must never be distorted by public curiosity or political translation. Here, the family's truth could breathe without translation. Here, no voice had to defend itself against misunderstanding. Isla placed the vial into a recessed holder inside the cabinet's deepest shelf and closed the frosted glass over it. Then, without looking away, she whispered, "I want them to know who we were. Not just who they are."

Ben crossed to her side and knelt, one knee against the marble. "They'll know," he said. "They'll know because we've never hidden it. We've only protected it." Isla turned toward him, her eyes catching the faint glow of the brass sconces above. "And Freja-Marie?" she asked. "Will she understand she was here first?" Ben's mouth curved into a smile. "She'll be the only one who remembers the castle before the twins arrived. She'll know she was their aunt before they knew how to cry." Isla laughed softly at that. "An aunt at not even a year old. We really do rewrite every rule, don't we?"

He leaned closer and kissed her knuckles. "We don't rewrite them. We remember the ones they tried to erase." That had always been their philosophy. House Rosenshavn didn't invent heritage. It resurrected it. They restored what others buried. The crown in Ben's blood wasn't new. It was ancient. The crown in Isla's hands wasn't decoration. It was declaration. And together, the two of them didn't just rule—they remembered. They honoured. They preserved the blood, not to elevate themselves, but to protect every child who would one day need proof that love built this house long before anyone ever moved in.

Ben stood slowly, the weight of the past never making him heavy, only certain. He pulled Isla to her feet and led her to the far wall where the ancestral maps hung in silence. Each frame was etched with glass-etched timelines, linking kings and queens, cousins and sons, scattered lines reunited beneath one name: House Rosenshavn. Ben traced a finger along the southern route that connected Hungary to Denmark all the way to the house of Windsor in England, past the inked names of Árpáds and Harvicks and Stuart-Gibbs. Isla followed his hand, her own resting just beneath. "One day," she murmured, "they'll ask us who we were before we were parents."

"And we'll tell them we were protectors first," Ben said. "Not of thrones. Of truth." The maps gleamed behind the glass. The room, though underground, felt no less alive than the nursery upstairs. They stayed for another moment, not speaking, simply standing before the quiet archive of their own becoming. There was no need for ceremony. This was the ritual: two souls, twenty-three years old, guardians of a legacy older than memory, staring at a vial of blood not because it made them powerful, but because it made them accountable.

As they turned to leave, Isla touched the cabinet one final time. The door sealed itself silently. The room didn't echo. But if it had, the sound would have been reverent. No crowns had to be worn that day. They had already been inherited—in love, in lineage, in the lock no one else even knew existed.

Ben unfolded the folio on the centre table, a long walnut surface set into the archival room's southern wall. The hinges groaned slightly from age, but the leather held strong. The folder was over two inches thick—well-fed with paper, sealed reports, hand-written transcriptions, and forensic printouts layered beneath one another like the veins of a living document. No dust clung to the corners. Isla cleaned it monthly, though she'd never admitted it aloud. The children were still gathered nearby, most of them sitting cross-legged or kneeling, reverent in their curiosity but silent under the weight of what they were about to see.

He began with the chart everyone knew best: the Rosenshavn bloodline tree. It wasn't decorative, and it wasn't romantic. It was clinical—sequenced from the National Archives of Denmark and backed by third-party DNA reports collected and stored in sealed vials upstairs in the black freezer, keyed to Isla's fingerprint only. "This is where I come from," Ben said plainly, his index finger tracing from Árpád, down through Béla III, into the minor Hungarian cadet branches that twisted their way into southern England and Denmark. "That's the royal line," he said. "But that's not the only one."

He turned the page—meticulously—and revealed Isla's chart. Stuart. Gibb. Plantagenet. Connected through three generational veins that had been diluted through marriage but never broken. Her side wasn't archived in Danish libraries. Hers required British clearances, closed file requests, and one specific data breach he'd committed before he turned fourteen. Isla had been shocked when he presented it to her three years ago. Now, she stared at it the way one looks into a mirror. "The children," Ben murmured, "won't just be born into legacy. They'll be legacy themselves. No crown placed on their heads will ever match what's in their blood."

The evidence was irrefutable. Not a single date out of sequence. Not a single name without documentation. Every connection came with corresponding timestamps from registries, scanned microfilm from churches and census rolls, even the odd immigration stamp from pre-war passports. These weren't myths strung together by hopeful historians. These were data-verified lineages, cross-matched with forensic timestamps and mitochondrial sequencing. He showed them one envelope marked "Isla – 2024 DNA Re-Verification." The children didn't understand the specifics, but they saw the seriousness in his posture and the tight precision in his words.

"Every family tells stories," Ben said after a pause. "But not every family has proof." Then he smiled—just slightly—and added, "But proof alone doesn't make it real. It's what you do with it that matters." He stepped away from the table and let the children lean closer. Max-Leo pointed to a looping signature in blue ink and asked who it belonged to.

"That," Ben said, "is the last signature my grandfather left before he died." The room went quiet. It wasn't grief. It was gravity. These weren't just papers. They were bodies, breath, and blood written down and bound together.

He opened a small envelope from the bottom of the stack. Inside were photographs—copies, not originals, but clear enough. One showed Isla's great-grandmother with a young girl in a dress identical to the one that now hung in the wardrobe upstairs. Another showed a man seated on a step with a crown half off his head, grinning. "He hated rules," Isla said, peering over Ben's shoulder. "Sound familiar?" Ben laughed quietly but didn't argue. He knew who she meant. He had that same grin whenever he bent protocol to protect truth. "Most crowns weren't earned," he said. "They were inherited. But you can still live in a way that earns it all over again."

As he spoke, his hand swept across a newer chart—one he had updated just last week. This one had two names that hadn't been there before. He didn't even notice he was saying it until it slipped out. "And this is where Hannah's and Frederik's lines will begin." He froze. Silence hit the room like the drop of a stone in a pool. Isla turned her head. Her brow lifted—not in anger, but amusement. "Excuse me?" she said, as casually as possible. Ben coughed once. "I mean—hypothetically." But the children had already caught it. Tobias let out a quiet whistle. Clara smirked. Lukas grinned.

Isla tilted her head, folding her arms. "So we're naming them without discussing it first?" Ben tried, valiantly, to appear unfazed. "It was a placeholder. You know. Just… for formatting." She took two steps forward, lifting the corner of the paper with one finger. "Hannah and Frederik?" she read aloud. "Not, say, Elise and Thomas? Or Freja and James?" Ben sighed. "It just felt right." Isla paused, then smiled. "It does, actually." The children murmured. A name, once spoken aloud, never really disappears. It lodges itself into memory, into rooms like this, where truth is honoured more than ceremony.

"No one outside this room repeats those names," Isla said, scanning the children. "Not yet. Not until they're ready to meet the world." Heads nodded. Ben folded the page again with care, but the secret had already been released. The names had taken root. Not because he declared them—but because he said them like a father. And everyone heard the difference. Kendrick once told him that royal names weren't picked—they were remembered. And Ben, in that small slip, had remembered what hadn't yet been spoken.

He turned the pages again, slower now, closing the folio with both palms as if pressing history into silence. "We are not royal because someone says we are," he told them. "We are royal because we kept the truth when others buried it. Because we bled for it. Because we recorded it in places like this. And one day, when people say the names of your children, they won't be asking if they deserve the crown. They'll be asking how they carried it."

No crown rested on the table. No sceptre leaned in the corner. But the evidence—rows upon rows of verified bloodlines, court records, heir logs, and DNA confirmation—sat heavier than either. Isla walked to his side, rested her hand on his, and together they stood as the children looked on. Some would carry the name. Others would protect it. And all of them now knew that what ran through the unborn twins' veins wasn't borrowed power. It was ancestral proof. Built not by fantasy, but by paper, blood, and the absolute permanence of truth.

Ben held the second folder like it was thinner only in appearance. It held less weight by volume, but not by consequence. He laid it flat beside his own, careful not to let the edges touch. "This," he said with a reverence that didn't require volume, "is Isla's line." The children leaned in, even though they'd already sensed that whatever came next would not be about battles or kings with armies. Isla's heritage was different. It moved like underground rivers—quiet, constant, and too deeply rooted to ever dry out.

The top page bore no fanfare. No insignia. No royal crests or grand Latin mottos. Instead, it opened with the name of Isla's grandmother, handwritten in soft ink, accompanied by a photograph so faint it looked like memory itself. The children watched as Ben lifted the photo gently, revealing a single-page excerpt beneath: a registry from 1923, linking the family name to a lesser-known Scottish branch of House Stuart. "Not all rulers sat on thrones," Ben said. "Some stood behind them and made the harder decisions in silence."

Isla stepped forward now, her gaze not defensive but protective. "My family never wanted the front page," she said. "But they were there. Every treaty signed, every land preserved, every war that didn't happen—my blood remembers those too." She pointed to a name three generations above hers, a woman listed only as 'E. Stuart, Keeper of the Northwood Holdings.' "She never called herself queen. But Parliament deferred to her." Tobias blinked. "That's allowed?" Isla smiled. "It wasn't about being allowed. It was about being undeniable."

Ben opened the next page and turned it sideways to show a string of notary seals from three different countries—each one validating Isla's maternal line back to the days of Mary of Guise. "She didn't inherit the drama," he said, almost teasing. "She inherited the quiet strategy." The children didn't laugh. They understood it already. The ones who speak least are often the ones who see most. Clara nodded quietly. Jasmin folded her arms, watching Isla now with something approaching awe.

"They didn't parade titles," Isla continued. "They protected land. They preserved records. They raised children who could think for themselves." She paused, her fingers tracing the edge of one folded map. "My mother told me that our legacy wasn't to rule with iron—but to hold the paper when no one else remembered where the signatures were." Ben touched her hand. "That's what kings forget," he murmured. "It's the people who hold the paper who make the throne possible."

The document listing Isla's full maternal bloodline was only twelve names long. But each name came with corroboration—birth and death certificates, land registry records, war exemption documentation, and, most remarkably, three signed testimonies from regional magistrates declaring that her family line had functionally ruled territory in all but name. "That's what makes it powerful," Ben said. "They didn't need the crown. It was always in the way they moved." Isla said nothing in response. She didn't need to.

Max-Leo pointed to a passage written in Gaelic. Isla translated without needing to look it up. "Those who are silent will be remembered when the shouting ends." She didn't explain the context. The phrase hung in the air like a forgotten anthem. Even the smallest children felt it. Because even without fully grasping the intricacies of monarchy and inheritance, they understood legacy. And they knew there was more than one way to wear power.

Ben slid out one last sheet from beneath the others—a sealed document, stamped with both a notary seal and the emblem of a defunct British archive. He held it up, unopened. "This one," he said, "was recovered only last year. It confirms what no one else wanted confirmed—that Isla's line qualifies for succession. But she chose not to claim it. She chose instead to live here." He looked at her. She didn't flinch. "You can't rule what you don't understand," she said. "And I never needed to prove myself to people who never asked the right questions."

The room was still. There were no flags, no music, no parchment scrolls proclaiming her as queen. But something deeper settled over the children. A kind of knowing. A recognition that Isla's restraint was her power. That what she carried was heavier than a title. She carried the memory of peace. The kind that wasn't written in wars, but in quiet decisions made in rooms like this, by people like her—un-thanked, unremembered, but always there.

Ben closed the file and placed his hand atop hers. "Theirs was the legacy of silence. But this generation—" he glanced toward the children "—will not be silent when truth is needed." No one responded. Not because they disagreed. But because they understood that silence, when chosen, is the most powerful voice of all. The kind Isla carried in every glance, every choice, every name she would someday give her children.

And when those children came, with their dual heritage and their undeniable names, it wouldn't be just Ben's fire they carried. It would be Isla's stillness. Her steadiness. The unshakeable weight of truth passed down without ceremony. Because the blood that runs the deepest is the one that doesn't demand to be seen. It simply moves—quiet, dignified, unyielding—and leaves behind a line that never forgets.

Ben didn't pace. He never did in rooms like this. He stood anchored, one hand resting on the old carved table as if he drew stillness from it. The children had grown quiet again. Not out of boredom—but reverence. The kind that comes when something long buried is about to surface. He didn't need to raise his voice. "There were names," he began, "that were removed not because they disappeared—but because they no longer served someone else's power." His eyes didn't blink. "But the blood didn't forget. And it never will."

He lifted the next document—an unbound parchment folded so many times it looked creased into muscle memory. It was brittle, fragile even, but the ink was stubborn. "This," he said, "was my great-grandmother's birth record. Issued once. Buried twice. And still it found its way to me." He unfolded it like a secret confession. "Her name was omitted from succession logs before she could walk. Not because she wasn't of royal blood—but because she was born to a union that threatened too many alliances."

Jasmina shifted in her seat, her eyes flickering toward the names at the top of the family tree. "So she didn't count?" Ben didn't hesitate. "She counted more than most. That's why they erased her. Not because she was weak—but because she was strong enough to change the order." Isla, seated quietly near the bookshelves, nodded without needing to say a word. They had both grown up understanding that power was not always inherited—it was often taken, and taken quietly.

Ben moved to the side and unrolled a longer map. It showed routes—not of armies or treaties—but of blood. Crossed lines, marriages off-record, adoptions, and closed registries. "The official crown histories won't show these," he said. "But these people built nations, brokered peace, saved cities, and raised monarchs. They just weren't born at the right dinner table." Tobias leaned forward. "Then who decides what gets remembered?" Ben looked straight at him. "That's the real war."

A document near the bottom of the pile had no name at all. Just a date. A royal decree from the early 1800s that had redacted a full branch of the line due to what was described as "conflict of noble interests." Ben didn't flinch. "That meant someone married someone they weren't supposed to. And their children vanished from the scrolls. Not from life. Just from history." He tapped the margin of the decree. "But blood keeps its own records."

The younger ones didn't speak. They didn't have to. They were watching Ben's face now, not the paper. There was something in his jaw, tight but controlled. Not anger exactly—but justice simmering at a low boil. "The kingdom believed it could write its own version of truth," he continued. "And for a long time, it did. But truth doesn't care about ink. It lives in blood." He picked up a vial—not labelled, just etched faintly with a single initial. "And blood never lies."

Freja, from where she sat cross-legged, tilted her head. "So... who was erased that we don't know about?" Ben looked down at the table. "You won't find their names in books. But you will find their traits in us. In the way we lead. The way we forgive. The way we remember even when we're told to forget." He set the vial down and opened a velvet-lined case. Inside was an old brooch, inscribed in a language none of them could read. "She wore this to her deathbed. Her name was never spoken in the palace again. Until now."

Isla stepped forward, placing her palm on the table. "We don't restore people by rewriting history. We restore them by remembering the truth they carried." She looked at Ben, who nodded once—sharp, final. "And that's why we keep these records down here. Not for show. Not for ceremony. But because someone has to carry what the crown forgot."

Ben didn't close the files right away. He let the silence wrap around them. The kind of silence that comes when a secret finds air for the first time in generations. "The world above calls this history," he said quietly. "But down here, we call it family." The children sat a little straighter now. As though they, too, were part of something hidden and enduring. Something that wouldn't be erased.

He moved to the wall and unlatched a concealed drawer. Inside was a letter—faded, torn at the edge, but sealed. "This is from the last unacknowledged heir of a European throne. She died in a house that never called her by her title. But she passed her name to her daughter. And that daughter passed it to me." He didn't open it. He didn't need to. Its power was in its presence.

And as the lights flickered just slightly, as if sensing the weight of memory in the air, Ben looked around at the faces before him. "We don't carry these stories because they are comfortable. We carry them because they are ours. And we don't let go of our own." The children didn't clap. They didn't cheer. They simply understood. What the crown forgot, the blood had kept warm. And now, it had a voice again.

Ben ran his thumb along the creases of the old ledger as though it might flinch. It didn't. It simply opened, slow and stubborn, as though even the paper knew it had waited too long to be seen again. The spine cracked faintly as he laid it flat upon the table. Its edges were brown with time and secrecy. No embossed crests, no seals of recognition. Only names. Dozens of them. Some crossed out. Some underlined. A few smeared with water damage—whether from rain or tears, he couldn't say.

He uncapped the red pen. Not to grade or correct, but to remember. He circled the first name without a word. Then the second. Then the third. "These," he said finally, "were ours." His voice was quiet, not from sorrow but from intent. "They still are." The children leaned forward, drawn by the power of seeing names they'd never heard spoken aloud. Names that belonged to no textbooks, no royal registries, no genealogical scrolls. But they lived. Once. And maybe still.

Isla stood just behind him, reading over his shoulder. "Who decided to strike them?" she asked. Ben didn't look up. "Someone who wanted to clean a story for history books. But truth doesn't wash that way." He pointed to one name—Anselma C. of Westmark—struck through with an inky slash that left a jagged scar across the parchment. "She had three sons. None of them were acknowledged. All of them changed the kingdoms around them."

Freja knelt near the corner of the room, where a thin drawer had been pulled from the wall. It contained index cards, handwritten with the same urgent script. "Why hide these down here?" she asked. Ben did glance up then. "Because up there, the world thinks silence equals shame. But down here, we know better. Down here, silence means memory held close." He paused. "This isn't a vault. It's a graveyard of erased blood. And it's our job to speak the names again."

Kristian reached out and traced one signature with the back of his finger. "This one looks like mine," he murmured. Ben's hand stilled. "That's because you carry his line," he said softly. "They never knew he had descendants. But he did. And you're the proof they can't delete." The boy didn't speak again. He didn't need to. The connection had already rooted itself deep within him.

Isla tapped a folder that hadn't yet been opened. "This one's sealed." Ben nodded. "For a reason. That name was considered treason to even whisper. But we will." He unfastened the string and unfolded the final page. It was a confession letter. Not of guilt—but of parentage. A prince who had chosen love over duty. His children were scattered across Europe, their names stripped, their bloodline denied. But not anymore.

"This one here," Ben said, tapping a name smudged near the edge, "was exiled because he chose the wrong bride. And this one—" he circled another—"because she spoke out when a crown sat badly on the wrong head. The system didn't protect them. It erased them." His voice was clear now. Not soft. Not sentimental. Just certain. "But we don't."

He pulled out a faded envelope from beneath the table—one no one had touched in decades. It held only initials: E.H.V. The handwriting looked hurried, cornered. "This was the last signature of a girl whose only crime was surviving a betrayal in the court." He placed the envelope in front of Lukas. "Her blood reaches you. Whether you asked for it or not." Lukas swallowed, visibly. "So that makes me what?" Ben didn't blink. "It makes you unignorable."

The chalkboard had been erased, but Ben picked up the chalk again. He drew no diagrams. Just a list. Each of the ghost signatures now transcribed in bold, looping letters. "You are old enough to carry these now," he told them. "Because you understand the weight of silence. And you understand what it means when history tries to forget you on purpose."

Jasmina stepped forward and placed her hand over one of the names. "So what do we do with them?" Ben smiled for the first time. "We speak them. We remember them. And when the time comes, we stand where they never got to." His words landed like heirlooms. Heavy but meant to be passed on.

He turned to the children one by one, naming each erased ancestor by name, by region, by impact. None of them were just entries on a page. They were actions, legacies, unresolved reckonings. The children felt it—not as guilt, but as inheritance. One they never asked for, but one they wouldn't trade back.

When the lights dimmed at the end of the hour, Ben closed the ledger gently, not in dismissal—but in reverence. "They thought erasing names would erase consequences. They were wrong." He looked once more at the chalkboard. "The ghost signatures never left. They just needed someone brave enough to bring them back."

Ben held the test results as if they were a crown in paper form—creased, well-worn, kept in a folder so plain no one would suspect its power. He set them down gently on the table, then smoothed the corners with his palm. "We did these tests on our tenth birthday," he said, not to boast, but to root the children in the facts before them. "Isla and I asked for them. We didn't know what we were looking for. We just wanted to know who we were. And then… we found out."

The room was still, lit only by the soft golden sconces carved into the stone. No one interrupted. Not even Freja, whose head tilted curiously, already sensing this was the kind of story that shifted things in a family. "We thought it would say something simple," Ben continued. "A country, a region, some traits, maybe a famous ancestor. What it gave us instead was a map so big, we needed time to see it all." He handed the papers to Emil first, trusting the boy's quiet focus.

The top of the report showed a tree with too many branches. Royals from opposing kingdoms. Nobility traced through wars, treaties, and betrayals. "That's not a family tree," Lukas whispered. "That's a battlefield." Ben smiled faintly. "Exactly." He tapped one section—traced from his father's side through Danish lines, and another from Isla's maternal side that looped around to British sovereign blood. "We didn't expect it to overlap. We didn't expect it to connect. But it did. Twice."

Silje leaned forward, noting the dates printed along the bottom margins of the results. "These are from 2024." Ben nodded. "Our tenth birthday. Kendrick planned a celebration so big we could hear the fireworks echo off the fjords." He paused. "That was the night the world celebrated something it didn't understand." His eyes dropped to the table again. "And it was the last time I pretended to be ordinary."

The silence thickened. No one moved, and even the children's breathing had slowed. "I didn't tell anyone then, not even Sørensen. But I knew someone would come looking." His voice was steady but edged. "Because if this kind of bloodline was found—twice, no less—it would change everything. It would scare the people who'd spent generations hiding things like us." He placed his finger on a sequence ID stamped in red ink. "This is the part that got flagged in the database. Someone tried to trace it."

Kristian frowned. "What do you mean traced?" Isla finally spoke then. "It means someone noticed the pattern before we did. Someone watching the same systems we thought were just for fun. They ran surveillance on children. They looked for heirs." Her tone wasn't shaken. It was sharpened by the truth. "And we lit up their radar like a house fire in the dark."

Ben leaned back against the stone archway, folding his arms. "So I hacked them. I went into their backend through what looked like a gaming app. They didn't expect a ten-year-old to know how. But I knew." He looked at Tobias, then Silje. "You all think I've only ever carried truth. But I've carried weapons too—digital ones. I used a tablet, not a sword. But it cut through just the same."

The children watched him differently now. Not in fear, not in awe—but with a growing understanding of what it meant to be royal in secret. "That's when the Stink Bombs started," Ben added. "Phase one was just a test. Phase two made them nervous. Phase three shut down the registries in Europe for six days. They thought it was a bug." He tapped his own temple. "It wasn't."

Isla walked to the board and picked up the red marker Ben had used earlier. She drew a circle—then drew two crowns within it, one larger than the other. "This was never about claiming thrones," she said. "It was about surviving. Our blood made us targets. But our minds made us dangerous." She held the marker up to the light, then quietly capped it.

"Why didn't you tell anyone then?" Freja asked gently. Ben didn't hesitate. "Because I needed time to grow into it. I needed time to figure out what kind of king I'd need to be. Not for a country—but for a family like this." He looked across the room at each of them. "And now you're old enough to understand what it means. Power doesn't ask if you're ready. It just shows up."

Kristoffer muttered something under his breath—something like respect, but shaped through confusion. "So the war started when you were ten." Ben's eyes met his. "Yes. And I won. But that doesn't mean it's over." He glanced at the DNA charts again. "Because we're still here. And the people who once tried to erase us? They know now. They failed."

The test results were left open, visible to every child in the room. Not to shock them. Not to scare them. But to inform them. Isla stepped beside Ben and took his hand. "The only way to keep peace," she said softly, "is to know what you're defending." Ben nodded. "And who you're protecting." As the group began to rise, papers in hand, minds awake, Ben said one last thing. "This DNA didn't crown us. It warned us." He pointed to the red sequence again. "And now it warns them too. So when they come—and they will—we'll be ready."

Ben held the test results as if they were a crown in paper form—creased, well-worn, kept in a folder so plain no one would suspect its power. He set them down gently on the table, then smoothed the corners with his palm. "We did these tests on our tenth birthday," he said, not to boast, but to root the children in the facts before them. "Isla and I asked for them. We didn't know what we were looking for. We just wanted to know who we were. And then… we found out."

The room was still, lit only by the soft golden sconces carved into the stone. No one interrupted. Not even Freja, whose head tilted curiously, already sensing this was the kind of story that shifted things in a family. "We thought it would say something simple," Ben continued. "A country, a region, some traits, maybe a famous ancestor. What it gave us instead was a map so big, we needed time to see it all." He handed the papers to Emil first, trusting the boy's quiet focus.

The top of the report showed a tree with too many branches. Royals from opposing kingdoms. Nobility traced through wars, treaties, and betrayals. "That's not a family tree," Lukas whispered. "That's a battlefield." Ben smiled faintly. "Exactly." He tapped one section—traced from his father's side through Danish lines, and another from Isla's maternal side that looped around to British sovereign blood. "We didn't expect it to overlap. We didn't expect it to connect. But it did. Twice."

Silje leaned forward, noting the dates printed along the bottom margins of the results. "These are from 2024." Ben nodded. "Our tenth birthday. Kendrick planned a celebration so big we could hear the fireworks echo off the fjords." He paused. "That was the night the world celebrated something it didn't understand." His eyes dropped to the table again. "And it was the last time I pretended to be ordinary."

The silence thickened. No one moved, and even the children's breathing had slowed. "I didn't tell anyone then, not even the government. But I knew someone would come looking." His voice was steady but edged. "Because if this kind of bloodline was found—twice, no less—it would change everything. It would scare the people who'd spent generations hiding things like us." He placed his finger on a sequence ID stamped in red ink. "This is the part that got flagged in the database. Someone tried to trace it."

Kristian frowned. "What do you mean traced?" Isla finally spoke then. "It means someone noticed the pattern before we did. Someone watching the same systems we thought were just for fun. They ran surveillance on children. They looked for heirs." Her tone wasn't shaken. It was sharpened by the truth. "And we lit up their radar like a house fire in the dark."

Ben leaned back against the stone archway, folding his arms. "So I hacked them all. I went into their backend through what looked like a gaming app of Chess. They didn't expect a ten-year-old to know how. But I knew." He looked at Tobias, then Silje. "You all think I've only ever carried truth. But I've carried weapons too—digital ones. I used a tablet, not a sword. But it cut through just the same."

The children watched him differently now. Not in fear, not in awe—but with a growing understanding of what it meant to be royal in secret. "That's when the Stink Bombs started," Ben added. "Phase one was just a test. Phase two made them nervous. Phase three shut down the registries in Europe for six days. They thought it was a bug." He tapped his own temple. "It wasn't."

Isla walked to the board and picked up the red marker Ben had used earlier. She drew a circle—then drew two crowns within it, one larger than the other. "This was never about claiming thrones," she said. "It was about surviving. Our blood made us targets. But our minds made us dangerous." She held the marker up to the light, then quietly capped it.

"Why didn't you tell anyone then?" Freja (Oliver's mom) asked gently. Ben didn't hesitate. "Because I needed time to grow into it. I needed time to figure out what kind of king I'd need to be. Not for a country—but for a family like this." He looked across the room at each of them. "And now you're old enough to understand what it means. Power doesn't ask if you're ready. It just shows up."

Kristoffer muttered something under his breath—something like respect, but shaped through confusion. "So the war started when you were ten." Ben's eyes met his. "Yes. And I won. But that doesn't mean it's over." He glanced at the DNA charts again. "Because we're still here. And the people who once tried to erase us? They know now. They failed."

The test results were left open, visible to every child in the room. Not to shock them. Not to scare them. But to inform them. Isla stepped beside Ben and took his hand. "The only way to keep peace," she said softly, "is to know what you're defending." Ben nodded. "And who you're protecting." As the group began to rise, papers in hand, minds awake, Ben said one last thing. "This DNA didn't crown us. It warned us." He pointed to the red sequence again. "And now it warns them too. So when they come—and they will—we'll be ready."

The air had been heavy the day they left England—not with storm, but with the quiet pressure of change. Isla remembered Kent in flashes: the tall grass behind the school, the curve of the garden wall near her mother's kitchen, the old bicycle left rusting near the back fence. Nothing about it screamed farewell. But somehow, even as a child, she'd known they were not coming back. The luggage was packed too precisely. Her mother's voice had been too steady. And Ben—he hadn't said a word the entire ride to the airport.

She sat now, older and heavy with life inside her, on the bench carved into the south alcove of the underground room. The memory came back all at once, not just as image but as weight. "We thought we were running from something," she said, eyes cast toward the stone floor. "But we were running to something. Our place. Our bloodline. Our family. Here, to Kendrick. To our parents." The word tasted truer now than it ever had in Kent.

Ben stood across the room, adjusting the edges of the map that had curled from age and humidity. He didn't look up. "I knew the moment we landed in Copenhagen," he said, "that we weren't just guests anymore. I don't think I could explain it then. But I felt it." Isla smiled softly. "I felt it too. The quiet under the air. The way the walls didn't echo. The way no one asked questions."

There were no photos from that day—not in any family album, not in Kendrick's vaults. But the moment was etched into Isla's spine like a fingerprint. She could still feel the way her mother's hand had pressed gently on her shoulder as they walked through passport control. Could still hear the way the Danish agent mispronounced her last name and then quickly waved her through, as if he knew not to ask. As if someone had warned him not to.

"We were children," Isla whispered, not with shame, but disbelief. "Children with royal blood in a country that wasn't looking for us—yet." Ben finally turned, meeting her eyes. "But they would have. Eventually. If we hadn't moved when we did. If Kendrick hadn't set the plan in motion when he did." His tone was matter-of-fact, but not cold. It was just the truth, sharpened by time and memory.

The children gathered around them listened with a silence that was not usual for their age. They sensed what was being said was not for storytelling. It was for remembering. Lukas leaned against the stone archway, his small hand curled tightly around the fold of his shirt. Clara placed a hand on his back without words. Even Emil stayed quiet, his head tilted with attention.

"There was no parade," Isla added. "No banner. No welcome signs at the airport. We were met by one man. Sørensen." The name alone drew a shift in posture from a few of the children. "He gave us two things: an envelope with a castle address… and a toy bear I haven't seen since." She smiled faintly at the memory. "I think he still keeps it. Somewhere."

Ben picked up one of the sealed cases and handed it to Isla. "This wasn't about hiding behind walls," he said. "It was about protecting what had been forgotten. What they forgot, because it didn't serve their paperwork." His fingers traced the old emblem burned into the leather. "We didn't belong in Kent. We never really did. It was a holding space. A waiting room."

"But the island…" Isla looked upward, as if through the stone. "This place remembered us. Before we even stepped foot in it." She tapped the seal of Rosenshavn with her thumb. "It remembered me."

Ben opened one of the drawers and pulled out the old passport pages from their arrival. The ink had faded, but the stamps remained. "We were documented. But not revealed." He laid them flat on the table. "There's a difference. And Kendrick knew how to walk that line better than anyone." Isla nodded. "He didn't bring us here to crown us. He brought us here to keep us."

The way she said keep was not possessive—it was sacred. The kind of word that comes from being chosen, not collected. "We grew up in the echo of something bigger than us," she said, glancing at the children now seated on the stone steps. "And now, it's your turn to carry that without letting it crush you."

Freja shifted her weight and asked softly, "Did you ever want to go back?" Isla paused. Then answered without hesitation. "No. Because going back would have meant forgetting. And we were never raised to forget."

Ben folded the old documents and returned them to the drawer. "The world we came from asked us to be quiet. This one asked us to remember. That's why we stayed. That's why we raised the crown here." As the light from the torches dimmed with the hour, Isla looked once more toward the stairs. "We didn't move to Denmark to hide. We came here to belong." And for the first time in years, she felt the truth of that not just in her words, but in her bones.

The folder wasn't dusty, nor old. It was marked in Ben's modern handwriting with a simple label: SEARCH PROTOCOL – TRUTH ARCHIVE. Inside were not royal scrolls or coats of arms—but printouts, screenshots, and raw data strings. To anyone else, it would look like a madman's binder of online ancestry research. But to Ben, it was the final puzzle piece that proved the legacy no kingdom ever meant to admit.

"They didn't want us to know," he said, tapping a page that showed a crude DNA match chart with over thirty flagged markers. "But I made the data speak." The children leaned closer, expecting secrets from some grand laboratory. But the logo at the bottom of the page said something much simpler: Ancestry.com. Lukas squinted. "You used… that site?" Ben smiled. "That site has more power than they'll ever admit. Because it connects blood to names. And names to history. And that's where the real battle lives."

He reached for the tablet lying beside the old files and pulled up the saved archives—threads of connections, surnames that appeared and reappeared over centuries. "These aren't guesses," he said. "They're confirmations. Their system wasn't built to expose royalty. It was built to sell family trees. But it couldn't help itself. The truth bleeds through." His fingers slid across the screen with familiarity. Isla watched with admiration, but also wariness. This part of Ben—the part that hunted through data instead of landscapes—was the part she knew never stopped working.

"When I was twelve," he continued, "I figured out how to crack their source layers. Not to steal anything. Not even to hide. But to cross-reference. To stitch together what they kept apart on purpose." He tapped two surnames. "These names belonged to two lines that were said to have died out centuries ago. But here they are—on Isla's side and mine. Repeated. Hidden. But traceable."

Clara stepped forward. "But wouldn't they just delete the records if they found out?" Ben nodded. "They tried. Some data points were removed. But data leaves shadows. If you know where to look, you find the gaps—and the gaps tell the story." His tone wasn't smug. It was steady, patient. Like a historian who no longer cared about applause, only accuracy.

"This is what governments missed," Ben said. "This is what royal registrars never accounted for. Not rebellion. Not revolution. But revelation." He held up a laminated sheet. "Algorithms don't bow to thrones. They just calculate. And I made them calculate the truth." Isla turned to the children. "He's not exaggerating. Every connection he made, he backed up three times. We didn't go to them. We made the truth come to us."

Freja pointed to a redacted name on one of the charts. "What's that one?" Ben raised a brow. "That's the one they tried hardest to bury. A line that traces to Isla's father's mother—someone erased from three registries. But not from the database backup." Lukas exhaled. "So even when they hide it, it's still there?" Ben's voice was firm. "Especially when they hide it."

He placed the documents into a fireproof folder and sealed it again. "This isn't about digital victory," he said. "It's about giving our children the truth—not a legend, not a crown passed down by ceremony. But a name backed by proof." Tobias ran his hand over the old chart. "So we're not just royal because they said so." Ben knelt beside him. "You're royal because the blood remembers. And the paper finally caught up."

Isla walked over and placed her hand on Ben's shoulder. "You built an empire without touching a single throne." He shook his head. "I didn't build it. I uncovered it. It was always there. It just needed the right eyes to see." His eyes drifted toward the children once more. "I was never supposed to find it. But they underestimated one thing: a boy who was willing to look."

The room fell silent. Not from awe, but from understanding. This wasn't just a digital discovery. It was a restoration. A reconstruction of truth long buried by history and hidden in plain sight by cowardice. "They called it a family tree," Ben muttered. "But they forgot—roots run deeper than paper."

He closed the folder and leaned back against the stone wall. "Ancestry is more than lineage. It's memory. It's warning. And now, it's weapon." Isla smiled faintly. "And you've already used it." Ben nodded once. "I didn't start a war. I made sure the right names were impossible to forget."

It took them time to realise what they were looking at. At first, the children saw names, maps, and markers. A forest of paper and charts that seemed too complicated to matter. But as Ben pointed to each branch—his finger hovering over one bloodline, then tracing it into another— they began to see it. Not symbols. Not history. But themselves. Not just a crown inherited, but a future defined by the blood already running in their veins.

"They kept saying we were the next generation," Tobias whispered. "But this is different." Ben gave no dramatic speech. No rallying cry. He simply said, "You're not next. You're now." That silence—honest, heavy, irreversible—hung in the air as Isla stepped forward, her hands resting lightly on the swell of her belly. She didn't need to say anything. The meaning was already there.

Two lines. Once separate, now converged. Hers and his. Stuart and Harvick. Quiet and commanding. Peaceful and defensive. A convergence not drawn in ink, but in inheritance. In legacy. "These twins," Isla said softly, "won't be raised to be royals. They already are." Clara nodded with a calm that felt ancient. "They don't need the coronation. They are the coronation."

Ben knelt and unfolded a small vellum sheet, older than any of them in the room, but still legible. It showed two crests, one atop the other. "They tried to keep the lines apart," he said. "To stop the merging. To prevent too much power in one family." He smiled, a little bitter, a little amused. "But blood doesn't care about politics. It remembers what the mind forgets."

Lukas asked what everyone else was thinking. "Does this mean the twins outrank the rest of us?" Isla shook her head firmly. "No one outranks anyone. Not here. Not in this house. But they will carry both legacies. And because of that, they may have to protect it all." It wasn't said as a prophecy. It was said as a preparation. And that changed everything.

The crown, in this castle, did not sit on a cushion. It moved in footsteps. It laughed in hallways. It lived in the way Ben walked beside Isla, never in front of her. It breathed in the way Isla taught without raising her voice, and led without seeking a stage. These were not rulers who claimed power. They were power—because they never needed to prove it.

Kristian looked at the twin crests again. "So that means their last names are both?" Isla nodded. "They will carry both. Because to deny one is to split the truth. And we will not do that." She looked at Ben, who stood with his hands folded in front of him, not a king posing for attention, but a man finally at peace with what he was born into.

"We've spent years hiding," Ben said. "Not because we were ashamed, but because we were unfinished." He looked down at the bump beneath Isla's dress. "This—this completes the line. Two threads become one. And not one of them will be broken." The weight of it was more than noble. It was eternal.

Max-Leo raised his hand hesitantly. "What happens when other royal houses find out?" Ben exhaled slowly. "Then they'll do what they've always done. Plot, panic, pretend." He smiled. "But it won't matter. Because it's already too late. The line is set. The blood is sealed. And no crown in Europe can unmake what has already been made."

There was no need for ceremony. No oath or anthem. Just truth. Quiet, dignified, immovable truth. The kind that doesn't blink when challenged. The kind that sits in silence because it doesn't need to shout. The kind that grows in children who do not know fear, because they were raised by people who taught them how to lead without cruelty.

Isla placed her hand on her stomach again, more protective than before. "They won't grow up with titles," she said. "But they'll grow up knowing exactly who they are. No confusion. No rewriting. No borrowed history." Ben added, "And if anyone ever tries to erase them, they'll find themselves facing all of us. Together."

There was a reason the lines had converged in secret. A reason the papers had been kept hidden. Because this wasn't meant to be used for power grabs or property. It was for something far more dangerous to the old world: clarity. The world of crowns depended on confusion. This family depended on none.

As the children circled the table again, looking at the symbols with new eyes, it was no longer a lesson in bloodlines. It was a confirmation of what they had always felt. The order was not in the titles or the records—it was in the way Isla stood with one hand on her unborn children, and Ben with one hand resting on hers.

The line wasn't political. It wasn't legal. It was human. It was spiritual without religion. It was honour without decree. And it had just been made real in the simplest way: through truth passed down, without fear, without shame, and without the need for permission.

There are truths that shine too brightly to be worn in public. And Ben knew this one could blind the world. He didn't raise his voice when he said it, didn't pace or gesture with fire in his hands. He simply stood before the children with one file closed, one hand over it, and said, "We don't speak of this. Not out loud. Not even in celebration." It wasn't shame. It was strategy.

"This truth isn't pretty," he continued. "It's dangerous. It unsettles people who've built entire kingdoms on lies." The room was heavy. Even Lukas and Kristian stood still, arms crossed, eyes focused—not because they understood all the politics, but because they felt the pulse of something ancient. Something that was not meant to be turned into headlines or ballads.

He tapped the name at the top of the sealed file: King Kendrick X of House Rosenshavn. "He's not just King by position," Ben said. "He's King by blood. And I am, too. And so is your Aunt Isla." The silence that followed was full of motion—eyes darting between faces, minds racing to connect names and events.

"True royal lines don't flaunt their blood," Ben said. "They protect it. They don't tattoo it on their foreheads. They engrave it in legacy, in silence, and in children who walk in rooms without needing to announce who they are." It wasn't pride. It was precision. He wasn't there to convince them. He was there to prepare them.

Ben leaned forward slightly. "The world has crowned people who never had the right. Who silenced the ones who did. If they knew this family still carried the real claim... they'd come for it. Not through diplomacy. Not with flowers. They'd come with fire." Isla stood beside him without flinching. This was her blood too, and her silence was agreement.

Tobias looked down at the folded pages on the table and asked the only question that mattered. "So why keep the records?" Ben gave the softest reply of the day: "Because truth doesn't expire. And someday, if the world collapses again, the next ones will need to rebuild. We won't hand them stories. We'll hand them proof."

He nodded slowly toward the five names listed, carved now not only in the file but in the minds of those present. Kendrick. Benedict. Isla. Thomas. Freja-Marie. No added titles. No embellishments. Just a bloodline, traced through time and silence. Protected in rooms like this one, and never spoken of beyond these walls.

"We don't hide this because we're afraid," Ben added. "We hide this because people get greedy when they think power is up for grabs." His tone never broke. It didn't need to. This wasn't a lesson. It was an initiation. A reminder that the crown lives not in coronation, but in knowledge carefully guarded.

Even the youngest of them—Max-Leo, Peter Emil—stood a little straighter. The weight of lineage isn't in knowing you descend from kings. It's in knowing what it costs to protect that truth when the world would rather you bury it beneath someone else's version of history. The burden was never loud. It was always dignified.

Kristian opened his mouth to ask if the public would ever know. But Ben answered before the question left his lips. "No. Not unless they try to erase us." That was the only condition. The only circumstance under which silence would become declaration. And even then, it wouldn't be with speeches. It would be with records. With timelines. With the blood itself.

"Some of the royal houses still holding crowns today," Isla said softly, "hold them through deception. Through marriages designed to overwrite bloodlines that should have survived." Her voice was steady. Her eyes were steel. She wasn't just the mother of future monarchs. She was already one in her own right.

"And that," Ben concluded, "is why this room exists. Why you were brought here. So you'd know the difference between a name and a legacy. Between a story and a sovereign." His hand remained on the folder. Not guarding it. Just holding it. As if the file itself trusted no one else to bear its weight.

He walked to the edge of the table and ran his hand along the polished wood. "People will tell you to celebrate your lineage," he said. "But real heirs don't need applause. They need courage. Silence takes more strength than shouting ever will."

When the group filed out of the room, no one joked. No one whispered. The absence of noise was not uncomfortable—it was reverent. As if each child understood that they had been given not just a secret, but a crown wrapped in silence. Not one to wear. One to protect.

And as the door closed behind them, Isla looked at Ben, then back at the sealed folder. "Do you ever wish we could speak it out loud?" she asked. Ben smiled faintly. "One day," he said. "But not yet. Not until the world stops fearing the ones who carry truth in their blood."

The courtyard was quiet, the type of quiet you only find in stone-walled places that have survived too many winters and not enough betrayals. Sørensen leaned against the archway with his arms crossed, watching the children file past him in small groups, their faces still tight with thought after what they had just seen below. He waited until the last child—Max-Leo—passed, then stepped into the hall where Ben stood alone, his hand still resting on the edge of the heavy wooden door.

"You've given them something dangerous," Sørensen said, voice low, but not scolding. It was the tone he used when handing over live weapons—steady, respectful, without drama. Ben didn't look at him. His eyes stayed on the carving at the top of the door, a crown etched in iron and stained with time. "I gave them truth," he replied. "And truth doesn't owe anyone safety."

Sørensen stepped closer, until his boots clicked softly against the ancient tile. "A throne," he said, "can be usurped. But not a bloodline." Ben turned to face him. "That's the point," he answered. "They can't steal what they can't fake. Not anymore." He opened his palm and revealed a small, laminated strip—an identical copy of the mitochondrial DNA chain stored in the royal files below. "This is the real crown."

They stood there for a long minute, two men whose lives had been shaped by things unspoken. Sørensen remembered the files from years ago—the first time Kendrick showed them to him, and the quiet fury in his gut when he saw how many names had been erased. Not by time. By choice. Because truth didn't serve the lie of the moment.

The children had not been told to believe. They had been shown the lineage, the records, the science that underpinned monarchy not by fiction, but by forensic fact. Sørensen rubbed his jaw and said, "You know they won't forget this. Once seen, it stays." Ben nodded. "That's the hope."

He paused before adding, "They don't need to prove anything to anyone. That's the difference now. This house doesn't survive on public favour. It survives on blood that matches the files. On names written in ink and bone." Sørensen placed one hand on the back of Ben's neck, a gesture he'd only used with his own daughter before. "Then they're safe. As long as they remember."

In the upstairs parlour, Lukas and Peter Emil were already talking about what they'd seen—not loudly, but with an intensity that made it clear the crown had shifted from storybook to skin. Jasmina sat at the window, her arms folded, repeating the names under her breath like an oath. Even the youngest understood: this wasn't pageantry. This was inheritance.

Ben walked into the parlour and addressed them plainly. "It doesn't matter if the world calls you princes or peasants," he said. "What matters is that your blood matches the truth. That no one can rewrite your name just because it's inconvenient to their narrative." His tone was calm, not dramatic. He wasn't trying to inspire. He was trying to equip.

Sørensen remained in the hallway, listening. The silence in the room was reverent, not fearful. These weren't secrets now. They were shields. And for once, the shield didn't come in the form of a blade or a guard at the gate. It came in the form of a test result, a lineage chart, a name scratched out by history but revived by science.

Ben stepped aside and let Isla enter. She carried nothing, said nothing at first, but stood beside her husband with her head held high. The children didn't rise, didn't bow. They didn't need to. She was their blood. That was enough. "One day," she said, "the world might challenge this again. And when they do, you won't need to argue. You'll show them the files. You'll show them your face."

Tobias, quiet but always alert, asked the question they were all circling. "So we don't talk about it outside?" Ben shook his head. "We don't deny it. But we don't perform it, either. This crown doesn't need a stage. It needs guardians."

Lise, hands folded in her lap, added softly, "But what if someone tries to take it?" Ben smiled faintly. "They can take medals. They can take robes. They can even take thrones. But they can't take what flows through your veins. That's the part they'll never own."

And with that, the room shifted. Not in drama or celebration—but in understanding. The children didn't see themselves as royals. They saw themselves as something rarer. Un-stealable. Un-fakeable. Sovereigns by sequence.

Sørensen, listening still, finally turned back toward the main hall, muttering just loud enough for himself: "Truth doesn't ask for loyalty. It only waits to be proven." And in that moment, beneath the weight of files and blood and silence, the castle held its breath—not for fear, but for reverence. They would speak of this again, but only in places where the echoes stayed within stone. Because this wasn't a family secret. This was a sovereign code. And it was written in the only language that couldn't be forged: blood.

Isla stood by the stone-framed window, her hands resting at the slope of her stomach, where life moved in soft, rhythmic patterns she could feel but not yet explain. The morning light had not yet pierced the clouds over Rosenshavn, and the castle was quiet in that sacred way only found before breakfast. She was still. Not because she lacked energy, but because her thoughts had grown heavy enough to keep her rooted in place. She wasn't staring out the window. She was staring inward.

Ben entered without knocking. He knew that threshold well, and respected it without fuss. He crossed the room with steady steps, saying nothing at first. Isla didn't turn to him, not right away. She waited until he stood beside her, until the silence had stretched long enough to become something shared. Then she spoke, almost a whisper. "What if this is it?" Her voice didn't tremble. It settled like dust. "What if the line ends with us?"

Ben didn't answer immediately. He took her hand gently and ran his thumb along the bone just above her wrist. The pulse there beat soft but strong. "Then we leave enough behind," he said, "that they'll never forget we existed." Isla closed her eyes. It wasn't enough to have children. It had to mean something. Blood alone wasn't survival—it was memory, passed on deliberately, not by accident. And memory, left unguarded, could be rewritten.

She turned toward him, her hands now framing the curve of her belly. "Do you think it's enough? A boy and a girl?" Ben nodded. "It has to be. This line requires both. If one is missing, the code breaks. It dies with us." She breathed in slowly, as if she could feel the weight of centuries behind her ribs. "And if the world erases us again?" Ben met her eyes. "They won't. Not this time. The paper trail is iron. The files are backed up in five countries. And if all else fails, the children will carry the truth in their own veins."

Isla pressed her forehead against his chest, not for comfort, but for grounding. "But what if one of them doesn't want it?" she asked. "What if they walk away from the name, the proof, the weight of it all?" Ben exhaled carefully. "Then we've done our job. Because real legacy isn't forced. It's offered. If they refuse it, it's because they're strong enough to live without it."

The fire had not yet been lit in the room, and the cold crawled up through the floor tiles like a reminder. Even castles could be brittle in the morning. Isla took a slow step back and placed both palms over her belly again. "I dreamed last night that one of them was taken," she said. "Not killed. Just erased. As if she'd never existed." Ben closed the distance between them in two steps and wrapped her in his arms. "That won't happen. Because you'll make her unforgettable."

She didn't cry. Neither of them did. They had moved beyond tears. What they felt now lived in the bones—something ancestral, something old. Isla thought of the names they hadn't spoken aloud, the ones still folded in her pocket like a secret prayer. Not to the sky. To the blood. Names didn't save people. But they remembered them.

Ben led her to the small table beneath the window, where a stack of folders still sat from the night before. He opened the top one and pointed. "See this line?" he said, tracing the bloodline like a river with his finger. "It almost ended twice. Here and here. Both times, it survived because one woman said, 'Not yet.'" Isla looked at the dates. 1643. 1881. The line had been fragile before. But not broken.

"We're not fragile," she said. Ben smiled faintly. "No. But we're finite." That was the difference. A kingdom could be rebuilt. A house could be restored. But a bloodline—once lost—was gone. The idea that a royal name could vanish from the earth without a single enemy lifting a sword—that terrified Isla more than any war.

In the hallway, one of the children laughed. It sounded like Lukas. The sound bounced, light and unaware. Isla leaned her head against Ben's shoulder. "Promise me," she said, "if something happens to me—if the line is at risk—you'll protect it. Even if it means breaking every rule." Ben didn't flinch. "I've broken worse for less."

They sat together in silence as the light began to move across the stone floor. Outside, the castle walls held firm. Inside, the bloodline whispered quietly through Isla's pulse, through the twins yet to be born, through the man beside her who would rather burn down the world than let them be forgotten.

If this was the end, it would not be a quiet one. It would be marked. Proven. Etched into files, memory, and the breath of every child who still carried the Harvick name. Because a line doesn't end with silence. It ends when no one remembers it existed. And that, they had already vowed, would never happen here.

Clara didn't raise her hand when the children began asking questions. She waited, as she always did—listening, observing, collecting silence before offering her voice. Her feet were flat against the old stone floor, and her hands were folded carefully in her lap. She didn't fidget. But she didn't breathe easily, either. Her eyes were locked on Ben as he moved through the room, answering each question with patient certainty and quiet fire.

When the others quieted, and the air stilled again, Clara finally spoke—not loudly, but clearly. "If you're royal..." she began, her voice steady but not sharp, "then what does that make me?" The pause that followed was brief, but deliberate. Ben turned. He didn't blink. He crossed to her slowly, not like a king answering a subject, but like a brother approaching the keeper of something too sacred to name.

He crouched down so they were eye-level, and his smile was quiet, real, grounded in something deeper than lineage. "You're the one I chose to carry it forward," he said. His voice didn't rise. He wasn't correcting her. He was restoring something. "And the crown doesn't argue with a choice like that."

Clara's lips parted, but she said nothing. She didn't need to. Her question hadn't come from insecurity. It had come from a place even deeper than blood. It had come from the centuries-old doubt that asks whether belonging can be earned if it wasn't inherited. And Ben had answered her without condition.

There were no gasps in the room. No dramatic reactions. The others knew what she meant. They had asked the same question in different forms—through glances, through posture, through hesitation at the door of the archival room. Ben hadn't answered a question about royalty. He had answered a question about identity.

Kendrick had once said that the true measure of a royal house wasn't its vault of crowns or scrolls—it was how it protected the ones it didn't have to protect. Clara was chosen. Not claimed out of obligation. Not adopted for appearance. She was woven into the house's future because her character, her loyalty, her sense of justice, had demanded a place no bloodline could deny.

Ben stood slowly, not because the conversation was over, but because it had reached its truth. He looked across the room, then back at Clara. "A bloodline is a map," he said. "But family—that's where you decide to stay."

Clara felt her shoulders ease. Her posture shifted—not into pride, but into peace. She had always known she was loved. But now, it was something else. She was recognized. The history on the walls didn't include her name yet. But she knew now, without needing ink or seal, that it would.

Ben walked to the far table and picked up the file he had once feared opening too soon. He held it out—not to Clara directly, but to the space between them. An offering. "Your name's not in this because of when you were born," he said. "It's going in because of who you are."

Clara took the file. She didn't need to open it. Not yet. What she held was more than paper. It was proof that family was not limited by ancestry. The crown itself—so often mistaken as a thing worn on the head—was something Ben had just placed in her hands, weightless but unshakable.

Behind her, Astrid shifted quietly, and Silje folded her arms across her chest with an approving nod. They understood. The royal family of Rosenshavn was not bound solely by what passed through blood. It was defined by what survived in spirit. In loyalty. In intention.

Isla, standing beside the window, had watched the whole exchange without a word. When Clara turned toward her, she simply nodded. Nothing more was needed. Isla had known the answer to that question long before Clara asked it.

Ben stepped beside his wife. "Some crowns are inherited," he said. "Some are earned. The ones you earn never fall off." Clara heard every word. But it was the way he said them—not like a speech, but like a vow—that made them stick.

The room didn't erupt. There were no loud declarations, no celebratory cheers. But the quiet that followed was fuller than it had been before. A silence not of absence, but of confirmation. In that moment, Clara understood her role not as a page in someone else's story, but as a chapter of her own. Her question had not been weakness. It had been strength in disguise. And Ben had met it with truth. The crown in his blood had made him king. The crown in her heart had made her family.

Ben's hands moved with the certainty of someone who had waited too long to be misunderstood. He pinned each document one by one to the board—bloodline graphs, political fragments, intercepted messages, DNA lineage charts, and something handwritten in charcoal that looked older than anything else in the room. It wasn't a map in the traditional sense. No coastlines. No landmarks. Just names, blood connections, arrows, and a red thread running through it all—starting with him.

He stepped back slowly, arms crossed, and surveyed the board like a strategist studying a battlefield. His silence was deliberate. He wanted the children to look. Not glance, not skim, but look. To see not just what had come before them, but what was already turning its gaze toward them. "This," he said finally, tapping the centre point of the red thread with his index finger, "is not history. It's a warning."

The youngest children were too small to grasp it, but the older ones leaned forward instinctively. Clara's breath caught before she even realized she had been holding it. Emil stood slightly straighter. Freja-Marie didn't blink. The air in the hidden room shifted, not with fear—but with readiness.

Ben continued. "The houses will come. Not because we've provoked them. But because they know we exist. And that, alone, threatens the lie they've built their power on." His tone didn't rise. There was no anger. Only truth delivered like iron.

The line on the board that connected his name to Isla's was drawn in gold ink, slightly raised on the parchment. It shimmered faintly in the dim light of the lead-lined room. Below it, two new names had been added just hours before—Hannah and Frederik. Their birth had not yet happened, but already the world was reshaping itself to reckon with them.

Silje stepped forward, her eyes narrowing on one of the older names near the bottom. "They've erased people before," she said quietly. "Will they try again?" Ben nodded, slowly. "They might. But not from this house. Not again. Because we've turned the silence into strategy."

There was a reason this room was hidden. A reason nothing echoed here. Secrets didn't echo when they were protected. They waited. And the children, adopted or not, bore names that would one day be impossible to erase. Ben had made sure of it.

He looked at Lukas, then at Clara, then at the others in quiet succession. "Many of you weren't born here. But you belong here. Blood makes you traceable. But love makes you permanent." The words weren't poetic. They were policy. The policy of a royal house that refused to define family by biology alone.

At the base of the board, small framed photos had been added beneath each family name. Not just the biological lineages, but the adopted ones. Ben had insisted on it. So had Kendrick. Every child under the Rosenshavn roof was listed, protected, and traced—not to preserve an image, but to declare an unbreakable record. If anyone tried to erase them again, there would be evidence. Proof. Witnesses.

Clara turned to Isla. "So we're on the map now?" Isla smiled faintly. "We are the map now." There was no more running. No more hiding. Every choice made in silence had now been pinned, labelled, and documented.

Ben tapped another page—one that showed alliances between European houses still active today. "They will test our story. They'll test the chain of names. They'll ask how a boy with a tablet outsmarted their vaults. But they won't be able to undo it." He held up a small vial. "Because even if they burn this map, they can't burn what's inside here."

The vial contained nothing more than a preserved sample of his own blood—sealed, timestamped, and documented alongside the rest. Not for science. Not even for proof. But for inheritance. For the day someone demanded a test that he'd already passed. Emil stepped beside Ben. "What happens if they come here?" Ben met his eyes. "Then they'll find a house ready for them. One that doesn't need a throne to prove who we are."

There were no swords drawn. No trumpets. No dramatic speeches. Just quiet nods from children who were not raised in ignorance, but in awareness. The board remained where it was—uncovered, untitled, unmissable. The map wasn't just a collection of lines and names. It was a declaration. The children of Rosenshavn—biological, adopted, or chosen—would not be hidden. They would be counted. They would be ready. And they would be remembered.

Isla sat back in the cushioned chair built only for this room, where the limestone cooled the floor and the light came not from the sun but from the deliberate glow of old glass bulbs strung overhead. Her hand rested against her belly, fingers spread lightly, as though listening through skin. She didn't need anyone to tell her what they were. She could feel them. The movement wasn't chaotic anymore. It was rhythm. It was choreography. One was pushing upward, the other pressing outward, as if they'd already begun speaking in their own quiet language.

Ben stood just behind her—not close enough to crowd, not far enough to retreat. He had his hands clasped behind his back, but he was watching. Every slight shift of her palm. Every small breath that caught in her throat. Every faint smile she gave when she felt one of them roll beneath her ribs. He didn't interrupt. He just waited. Let it play out. Let it be sacred.

"They're not just our children," he said finally, his voice low, steady. "They're the answer to every erased name that came before us." He didn't mean it in poetry. He meant it in policy. In consequence. In defiance of every royal historian who thought the crown could be gatekept by parchment and ceremony alone. These children were not created for the spectacle. They were created for continuity.

Isla didn't reply at first. She just let her fingers trace a figure-eight over the curve of her belly, something instinctive, something ancient. "They already know," she said softly. "I can feel it. They're not afraid of what's waiting for them. Not one bit." And she believed that. Not out of hope, but because of something deeper. Something stitched into their blood.

The room was still. There was no hum of machines. No sound of footsteps overhead. The children had all left hours ago. Sørensen had locked the outer doors. Kendrick had nodded once and turned away, as if to say, this part belongs to you. There was no performance here. Just two sovereigns. Two bones. Two bloodlines converging in one body, already preparing to stretch into two.

Ben stepped forward, finally, and knelt down in front of her—not to speak to Isla, but to them. "Hannah," he said quietly, testing the sound of the name as though it were a spell. "Frederik." Isla exhaled in surprise, laughing through her nose. "You just said them out loud." Ben blinked, and the corner of his mouth lifted. "I suppose I did."

She reached for him, placing his hand over hers, guiding it to the strongest part of the movement. He didn't pull away. "You've said a lot of things in here," Isla whispered. "But that might be the one that changes everything." He didn't argue. He just pressed his hand more firmly against her and nodded.

The name Frederik had belonged to a grandfather on Kendrick's side, a name that had once been blacked out in a registry. Hannah came from Isla's grandmother, who had died without ever revealing who her royal cousin had been. Both names had been forgotten in court records. Both now lived again. Not as homage. As warning.

"They'll carry everything," Ben murmured. "Not just our names. Not just the crown. The decisions we make now will live in their bones." Isla didn't flinch. "Then let's make good ones." And for a second, there was no castle, no thrones, no royal seals. Just two people kneeling in silence over the greatest truth they'd ever helped bring into the world.

The board still stood behind them. The map. The red thread. The names. But for now, they faced only each other. It wasn't about proving anything to the outside world. It was about making sure these two would never have to prove who they were to anyone.

Ben reached into his coat pocket and pulled out two polished acorns—tokens he had carved months ago, one etched with an H, the other with an F. He set them beside Isla, not as decoration, but as placeholders. He believed in the power of symbols, yes. But only when they were earned. "They won't wear their crowns," he said. "Not at first. But they'll be crowns. And no one will be able to take that from them." Isla nodded. "They don't need a coronation. They've already been born into it. They just haven't arrived yet."

The light above flickered slightly, just once. Ben turned off the switch before it could burn out completely. "Let them rest," he said. "There's enough war waiting for them outside the womb." Isla closed her eyes, still smiling, still tracing. The last words spoken in that room that night were not written down. They weren't shouted. They weren't announced. They were breathed. One name at a time. Hannah and Frederik. And the crown passed into bone.

CHAPTER 4: THE ONE WEEK WINDOW

The calendar in the kitchen had never been more important. It was not a decoration. It was not for birthdays or meal plans or holiday memories. It was a warning. Ben held the marker without breathing. He didn't need to count the days. He had done so a dozen times already. He uncapped the faded red and drew the final circle around the square marked Saturday. Seven days. No more. That was the line. That was the limit. He would not allow it to extend beyond that.

He capped the marker, returned it to its drawer, and shut it gently. Everything had to be gentle now. Even the floorboards seemed to creak softer under his weight. Isla was in the sunroom, stretched on the chaise with both hands cradling her belly. She had not asked what Ben was planning. She didn't need to. Her eyes—tired, calm, wide with something deeper than fear—already knew. Their unspoken language had become fluent. And Ben had stopped trying to offer reassurance she didn't need. She knew what was coming. He knew too.

Down the hall, the children's voices rose and fell like waves against the shore. It was their laughter he was trying to protect. The echo of it. The weightlessness. The ease of knowing nothing dark waited around the corner. But Ben had heard something different that morning. It wasn't what the children said. It was the pause between. The flicker of a shadow outside the west-facing windows. Sørensen had seen it too. That made it real. Sørensen's instincts were never wrong. And when he didn't speak, Ben listened harder.

In the back room, Sørensen sat with three screens arranged in a crescent before him. His face was as expressionless as the cold blue monitors. The feed looped from camera to camera every four seconds. Each rotation showed nothing unusual—until it did. Ben watched over his shoulder as the same figure appeared twice. Two days apart. Different coat. Same gait. Same tilt of the head. A walker who didn't walk for exercise. A man who looked, but didn't admire. A presence. Not a passerby.

Ben didn't ask questions. He didn't need to. Sørensen reached across the table and picked up the old secure-line phone. The one that hadn't rung since last year. He pressed the speed dial, and Kendrick answered before the second tone. No pleasantries. No delay. Kendrick's voice came cold and clipped. "They're sniffing around. Be ready." Then the line went silent. Sørensen didn't move for another twelve seconds. Then he said only this: "Time to lock the doors."

Ben left him there, but not because he doubted Sørensen's judgement. If anything, he trusted it too much. It frightened him to know the man had activated security level three without speaking to anyone. No announcement. No conversation. Just a shift in presence. Sørensen didn't blink much when danger crept close. He simply watched harder. The old soldier never truly retired. Not in spirit. And not in this house. Not when Ben was still here. Not with Isla expecting. Not now.

Walking back through the main hall, Ben paused at the long gallery windows and looked out toward the south wall. It was a clear afternoon. No wind. No footprints in the lower garden. But he could feel something that didn't belong. Something too still. The dogs hadn't barked in two days. The neighbour's curtains hadn't fluttered. And someone had stolen the extra copy of the village newspaper from the bakery—again. Harmless details until they added up. And they were adding.

Inside the sunroom, Isla had drifted off. Not deeply. Not soundly. Just enough to rest her eyelids. One hand had slipped off her stomach and now curled under her chin. Ben didn't dare wake her. Not with a week left. Not with everything quietly tightening around them. He sat near her, not touching, not moving, just watching. Her breathing was steady. The babies moved now and then. Kicks against skin. Reminders that even the smallest hearts beat loud when the world gets too quiet.

Thomas passed the doorframe, paused, and looked at Ben. He said nothing, but his eyes lingered. The boy was eleven. Still small in frame, but not in perception. Ben had already begun speaking to him like a man. Not with lectures, but with truths. The kind that fathers pass to sons, even if the relation is twisted by time and titles. Thomas stepped in and sat beside Ben on the rug. Together, they listened to Isla sleep. The silence was their teacher.

"I'll protect her," Thomas whispered, voice low but sure. "I'll protect them all." Ben didn't speak. He placed a hand on his little brother's shoulder, held it there for a moment, then released. Promises didn't need to be dramatic. They needed to be kept. And Ben trusted Thomas more than most men twice his age. Perhaps it was because Thomas had never been taught to hide emotion. Or perhaps it was because he had seen what fear looked like in someone else's eyes— and chose never to cause it.

As evening drew closer, the walls of the house seemed to lean inward. Not physically. But spiritually. Even Tobias lowered his usual volume. Clara walked softer. Silje lit one extra candle in each hallway. No one had declared a state of alert, but the mood had declared it for them. This was the calm before something unnamed. Ben didn't know what form it would take— journalists, drones, cameras, whispers, rumours, or worse. But it was coming. And the countdown had already begun.

Later that night, after Isla had gone to bed, and Sørensen had resumed his post in the surveillance room, Ben walked to the calendar once more. The red circle looked louder now. It felt final. Not like a goal—but a deadline. He ran one thumb over the ink. Still dry. Still sharp. Then, without reason, he whispered aloud to no one, "Seven days. Not one more." And in the dark kitchen, those words carried more weight than a royal decree.

Sørensen would call it preparedness. Kendrick would call it strategy. Isla would call it instinct. But for Ben, it was something far more ancient. Something encoded in the blood. A sense passed down from one crowned head to the next. The quiet before revolution. The stillness before exposure. A birth was coming. So was betrayal. But first, there would be seven days. Not one more. And Ben had no intention of wasting them.

The rhythm of the monitors never changes. Four seconds per frame. One camera after the other, like a seasoned heartbeat that refuses to stutter. Sørensen sits still, hands folded on the desk but never fully relaxed. His chair doesn't creak. His breath is shallow. His posture has not shifted in nearly thirty minutes. Some men train their eyes to move quickly. Sørensen trained his to move slowly—and with intent. No blink. No twitch. Just calculation.

There are twelve cameras positioned along the estate perimeter. Five of them are set on motion-triggered alerts. The other five roll continuously, their lenses trained on the lesser-watched approaches—the hill beyond the orchard, the service road where the mail comes once a week, the corner near the compost bins where kids sometimes drop soccer balls and pretend they didn't mean to climb back in. Sørensen knows every blind spot. He designed them that way.

But today, he spots something that was not there yesterday. At the east gate, a man appears, then vanishes off the edge of the frame before the loop resets. It isn't enough to raise an alarm, not yet. People walk. The world doesn't freeze for royalty. Still, something curls at the back of Sørensen's neck like static. He rewinds slowly. Four seconds again. The same man—hesitant step, slouched posture, hands behind his back like he's just out for air. But that gait. That lean. That pause at the gate before moving on. Not a walk for exercise. A reconnaissance drift.

Sørensen doesn't move his mouth when he speaks. "Second sighting. Not the same coat. Same man." Ben steps in behind him and doesn't need to ask who he means. He already knows. "Two days in a row?" he asks, his voice quiet. Sørensen nods once, then returns to the screen. His fingers tap a code into the side panel. Kendrick's number is called—not his mobile, but the encrypted line. One ring. Then Kendrick answers. No questions. Just breath. Then one phrase: "Be ready."

That was all it took. Sørensen doesn't bother writing it down. He never records calls that matter. He turns to Ben. "He knows." Ben nods. "Then so do we." Neither man mentions Isla. She doesn't need to be disturbed unless there is a reason. Right now, suspicion is not yet evidence. But it is enough to switch protocol from monitoring to containment. Sørensen gets up only long enough to secure the back window locks. Then returns.

The weight of that moment doesn't settle like fear. It settles like a plan. Sørensen never gets frightened. Not even when the castle was breached six years ago. Not when Benedict was ten years old and had crawled into a hidden passage to reroute the surveillance wires after a storm surge fried the grid. Sørensen had found him under the generator with a flashlight in his mouth and grease all over his face. He didn't yell then. He didn't blink. He just handed Ben a wrench.

From that day forward, something shifted between them. A man who had guarded kings his whole life looked at a boy and saw a different kind of future. Not one dictated by gold-threaded robes or empty thrones, but by intellect and awareness. Sørensen began teaching Ben things no royal tutor could. Pressure points. Silent signals. Code names. Systems of redundancy. When Ben turned fourteen, he taught Sørensen how to clone a motion sensor into a child's toy and build a fail-safe alarm system through a window latch. Neither of them ever mentioned it aloud.

Now, at twenty-three, Ben still watches Sørensen with the same respect. Not fear. Never fear. But reverence. Not for his strength, though Sørensen had that in spades, but for his precision. The old man didn't waste movement. He didn't bark orders. He simply acted. And when he said "they're close," you didn't ask "who?" You asked "how long do we have?"

On the screen again, the man appears. Four seconds. Then gone. Sørensen doesn't write it down. He logs it in memory. His hand moves to the second panel beneath the main console. From it, he pulls a small binder. Not a file. A manual. One of only four copies. He flips to the back page and slides a tab from yellow to red. No alarm sounds. But the house knows. Lights shift subtly. Perimeter motion sensitivity recalibrates. From this moment forward, all vehicles entering the outer court are scanned for metallic anomalies. Silent protocol. Elegant. Invisible. Very Danish.

Ben doesn't need to ask what comes next. He has already memorized the order of operations. Sørensen trained him too well. "I'll talk to Thomas," Ben says. Sørensen nods. "Let him know I'll be watching the monitors until shift change. He's old enough to know what vigilance means." Sørensen doesn't add sentiment to his words. It isn't his way. But Ben sees the flicker in his expression—a slight softening. That boy matters. All the children do. Because if they fall, the legacy falls with them.

Ben walks to the far window, hands behind his back. "You think this one's a freelancer?" he asks. Sørensen doesn't respond right away. He waits for the fourth rotation of the cameras. When the face doesn't appear again, he finally says, "No. Too controlled. No lens. No notes. Just presence. That's professional." Ben exhales slowly. "Paparazzi don't walk like that." "No," Sørensen confirms. "Spies do."

They let the words sit in the room for a while. No rush to fill the silence. No panic. Just recognition. It was only a matter of time. Secrets never stay buried forever. And this family, as much as they guarded it, still lived under the shadow of its own truth. A truth no one wanted to speak of—but many had begun to suspect. The child king. The hidden prince. The lie that became law.

Isla hadn't been told about the figure yet. Not because she couldn't handle it—but because Ben wouldn't let her worry when her body was already working hard enough. One more week. That was the deal. She would give birth, and he would disappear for a while.

Sørensen had agreed to escort him. Not just as security. Not as an old guard. But as family. The screens blink again. The man does not return. Sørensen doesn't blink either. "He's not gone," he says softly. "He's just waiting." Ben nods. "So are we."

The curtains were drawn but the light found its way in. That pale, milky wash of late spring that makes every shadow look thinner than it is. Isla lay with her eyes closed, though no part of her was asleep. Her hand rested lightly across her belly—firm but not pressing. She counted the days the way only a mother in her ninth month could. Eight months, three weeks, two days. Not one more. The twins had shifted again. One lower. One higher. Like they were keeping watch already, taking turns with her ribcage. One foot pushed gently against her hand. A response. A whisper.

The room smelled faintly of lavender oil and fresh linen. Ben had replaced the pillowcases that morning. She didn't need to ask. He was always moving, always preparing, as if order might stave off the inevitable. But Isla knew better. The calm wasn't comfort. It was warning. The castle never stayed this quiet, not even in sleep. There was always a voice, a step, a laugh somewhere down the hall. But today, the silence wasn't peaceful. It was padded. Carefully arranged. There were things she wasn't being told.

She heard him before he spoke. That breath he takes when he's trying to steady his heart before it reaches his throat. Ben leaned against the frame of the bedroom door, careful not to cross the threshold. He knew better than to disturb the stillness she had fought so hard to claim. "You doing alright in there?" he asked, his voice barely above the hum of the wall heater. She didn't open her eyes. "I'm resting," she answered. It wasn't a lie. But it wasn't sleep.

Ben stayed in the doorway. "One more week," he said. "Then it's done. I'll be with you every second." But Isla heard the flicker behind the words. The hesitation in the rhythm. She knew her husband too well. He was already preparing to go. He hadn't said it. He wouldn't. Not yet. But the energy in the house had changed. Sørensen's voice had lost its playful rasp. The guards along the south wall had doubled. Even Clara had spoken more softly when she came to bring lunch, as if the castle itself was holding its breath.

Isla turned onto her side with effort, the weight of the twins a living wall beneath her ribs. "Ben," she said, "you need to leave." She heard his breath catch. "Don't say that," he replied. "You know I can't go before…" She cut him off. "You can. And you must. But not yet. After they're born. When everything's quiet. Then you go. You don't look back. I'll be fine. You know that." Her voice didn't rise. It didn't tremble. It simply stood.

He stepped into the room then. Just enough to kneel beside the edge of the couch where she lay. "I can't leave you." "You must," she whispered. "For them." Her hand returned to her belly, the slight shift of a heel pressing outward like punctuation. "You think I don't feel it?" she asked. "Something's coming. I don't need cameras to know that. I can feel it in your shoulders. In Sørensen's eyes. Even in the children. They're quieter. They know something's different."

Ben rested his forehead against the back of her hand. "I promised you I'd be the one here. The one who stayed." "And you will," she said, "but not by being in the room. By being alive." The word hit him differently than she expected. He didn't flinch. But he exhaled like someone who'd been holding a stone in his chest for too long. She brushed a curl from his forehead. "I know what it costs you. Hiding. Running. Pretending you're not a king." She paused. "But I also know what it costs when you don't."

The clock ticked once. Then twice. The babies rolled slightly beneath her skin. One hiccupped. Isla smiled without laughing. "They don't know the world they're being born into. But I do. And I won't let it take you from them. Not now. Not ever." Ben stood slowly. His knees cracked from the crouch. She watched him walk to the window, then stop. "Kent," he said, barely audible. "The cottage. I could go there. Just for a while. No one would suspect it." She nodded. "Exactly. Sørensen will go with you. He's already halfway packed."

Ben turned. "You planned this?" "No," she said. "But I knew it would come." She shifted again, pulling a knit throw tighter across her legs. "You think I don't hear the hushed voices? I've carried two children through nine months of fear and love and legacy. I feel the temperature drop when the wrong person walks past my door. I'm not a fool." Her voice hardened slightly. "I am a queen. By blood."

He smiled, barely. "I still remember the day you said that for the first time. You were twelve. You kicked the library desk when they told you your family history project had too many footnotes." She allowed a breath of amusement to slip. "You were the only boy I knew who found footnotes exciting." "Still do," he admitted. They shared that rare silence again. The one that meant everything was spoken, even when the air stayed still.

Isla winced as a sharp movement gripped her side. Just a Braxton-Hicks, she told herself, but her hand tightened reflexively. Ben was at her side before she said a word. "You alright?" She nodded slowly. "They're just stretching. Reminding me who's boss." He rubbed her back once, then stopped himself from saying too much. He always tried to protect her from his worry. But she never needed him to. She just needed him to listen.

"After they're born," she said again, her voice low but sure. "You leave. I'll be alright. You know how strong they've made me." Ben didn't disagree. He simply kissed her forehead and whispered, "I'll make sure they never find us. Not this time." And Isla, without opening her eyes again, said quietly, "They already have. Now we control the story. Not them."

As Ben stepped out of the room and closed the door gently behind him, Isla opened her eyes for the first time in an hour. She stared at the ceiling. The quiet returned. But it was not empty. It was filled with the hum of strategy. The breath of lineage. The weight of something older than both of them. And in that stillness, Isla did not sleep. She waited.

The garden behind the castle still smelled of rosemary and thyme, though most of the season's bloom had already passed. The stone path, still damp from the morning's watering, curled behind the herb boxes and ended at the low bench under the pine. Ben chose that spot on purpose. No windows could see it. No walls could overhear it. Thomas followed behind, hands in his hoodie pockets, kicking a bit of loose gravel with every step. He didn't speak, but his eyes were watching—always watching. Just like Ben used to, at that age.

When they reached the bench, Ben sat first. Then stood. Then sat again. Finally, he knelt in front of his little brother, the same way their father had once knelt before him. Except this time, Ben knew what had to be said. He placed both hands on Thomas's shoulders, steady but not heavy. "You're going to be a great father one day," Ben said, his voice clear but warm. Thomas blinked, his brows drawing down the way they did when something didn't make sense. "I'm eleven," he replied. There was no sarcasm. Just fact.

Ben smiled faintly. "So was I once. Now I'm king." Thomas's eyes narrowed slightly, like he was weighing whether or not that counted as logic. "That doesn't mean I'm ready." "You won't be," Ben replied. "Not when it matters. No one ever is. That's how you know it's real." He gave his brother's shoulders a small squeeze, not firm enough to hurt, just enough to plant the weight of the moment there. "But I need something from you. A promise."

Thomas looked up. There were no birds chirping this time, no laughter from the windows. Just that low, ambient hum of a garden too still for comfort. "You want me to protect Isla." Ben nodded. "And the babies." "I can't protect two babies." "Yes," Ben said gently, "you can. You won't be alone. Mama will be here. Clara. Tobias. Silje. Even Sørensen. But when I'm gone—when I leave for a little while—I need to know you won't panic. You'll stay strong. You'll remind them what I'd say, if I were here."

Thomas shifted his feet. "What would you say?" Ben looked him straight in the eye. "That they're not alone. That they were born into strength. That they are not to be pitied or hidden. That this family stands tall no matter what the world throws at us." Thomas chewed on that like a boy who both believed it and didn't quite want to. "What if I mess up?" he asked. "You will," Ben said. "So did I. So does everyone. But you keep your head up. And you keep going. And you don't let fear decide who you become."

Thomas kicked a bit more gravel. "Is this about the men outside?" Ben didn't answer immediately. He glanced toward the hedge, then back. "It's about legacy. And safety. And the fact that people outside these walls think they have a right to know who I am. What I am. But you know what's more important?" Thomas waited. "That the people inside these walls know how to protect what matters when I'm not here."

At that moment, Sørensen approached from the south gate with a slow, measured walk. His jacket was zipped to the collar, hands behind his back like he always did when trying not to interrupt. Ben stood and met him halfway. "She packed already?" Ben asked quietly. Sørensen gave a single nod. "Maria knows we're leaving once the twins arrive. She doesn't understand why. But she trusts me. She always does." Ben nodded in return. "She's only nine. This shouldn't be her story to carry."

Sørensen's face didn't change, but his eyes did. "Then let's make sure it doesn't become one." Ben turned toward Thomas. "You remember Maria, don't you?" Thomas nodded. "She's the one who beat me at chess with her eyes closed." Ben chuckled softly. "That's her." "She's weird," Thomas added. "She's smart," Sørensen corrected. "And she's coming with us. Kent will be quiet. Safer for her. Safer for Ben."

Thomas crossed his arms. "Then why do I have to stay?" Ben stepped forward. "Because you belong here. This is your home. Your family. This is where your strength matters most." He paused. "Thomas, do you understand what I'm asking you?" There was a long silence. Then the boy nodded. "You want me to protect Isla. The twins. And our secret." "Yes," Ben said. "But not just that. I want you to promise me that one day, you'll have children too. You'll carry it forward. You'll never let the line be broken."

Thomas scrunched his nose. "Ew." Ben laughed. "Not now. Someday. When it's right." "Okay," Thomas said, still unsure but willing. "I promise. But only if I get to name them." "Deal," Ben replied. "Just don't name them Thunderfart and Cheesebrain." "You can't stop me," Thomas grinned. Ben leaned in. "Oh, but I can."

As Sørensen gently motioned for Ben to join him by the garden gate, Thomas lingered by the bench. He looked down at the gravel path where their conversation had fallen like invisible stones. Then he looked up at the sky, muttered something too soft to hear, and walked back toward the castle with his hands no longer in his pockets.

Ben followed Sørensen, the two men exchanging no more than a glance. There was no need. The plan was in motion. Kent was waiting. Maria would be ready. And Thomas—young, wide-eyed, uncertain Thomas—had just accepted the weight of a crown he couldn't see.

The drawer in the west corridor had been sticking for three weeks. Everyone kept forgetting to report it, until Tobias passed by and heard the screech of the track again. That sound always bothered him, like a scream that nobody took seriously. He dropped his satchel by the doorframe and pulled out his tools with the steady rhythm of someone who fixed things not just because they broke—but because he could not bear to leave them broken. It wasn't just wood or metal. It was trust.

He had the drawer halfway dismantled when the voice caught him. Sørensen's boots passed the hallway first, soft but unmistakable, followed by the low warble of his private radio call. Tobias didn't lean out. He didn't flinch. He just froze—listening, tools motionless in hand. Kendrick's voice came through the other side of the receiver like static sewn with urgency. "They've got scent," Kendrick said. That was all. But Tobias knew what it meant. That wasn't metaphor. That was warning.

He didn't interrupt. He wouldn't dare. Sørensen had likely forgotten Tobias was even working that wing. But the message—short as it was—crawled under Tobias's skin and made camp there. He closed the drawer slowly, gently, without even tightening the final hinge. He left the hammer on the floor, walked toward the nursery wing, and started checking every screw in every hinge. One by one. With care. With silence.

The first room had two cribs. Still empty, still waiting. Tobias checked the latches on the window. Then the bolts on the interior shutters. Then the tiny locks on the upper cabinetry where Isla's birth supplies were neatly folded and stacked. Nothing was loose. Nothing rattled. But Tobias checked again. And again. Not because he thought they were vulnerable—but because they couldn't be.

In the hallway, he knelt beside the low runner carpet that always slid when someone walked too fast. He re-secured the corners, tucked them back under the baseboard moulding the way he'd taught Thomas to do it. The boy always forgot. But boys should forget things like that. Boys shouldn't be thinking about threat patterns and blind spots. Tobias did the thinking for them. And he always would.

At the third room down, he paused. This one would be for the twins, once they arrived. Tobias didn't enter. He stood in the doorway, staring at the double cradle that had only been moved in three days ago. The light from the window fell just across the foot of each bassinet, as if even the sun was choosing not to touch the pillows. He stepped in, counted the boards beneath his feet. Still seven. Always seven. No creaks. No gaps.

He tightened the doorknob. It didn't need it. He did it anyway. He tested the fire alarm. Then replaced the battery. He measured the curtain tiebacks to make sure the cords wouldn't dangle within reach of newborn fingers, not now, not in a few months. He walked the perimeter again. Nothing out of place. But still, something in his gut churned. Kendrick's voice echoed again in his mind. "They've got scent." That meant time was short.

Hours passed. He didn't notice the dusk. He didn't stop for dinner. Sørensen passed by again at one point, heading toward the control room, but neither man spoke. They didn't need to. Sørensen gave a slight nod. Tobias gave nothing. His hands were full of a childproof drawer latch he didn't remember installing. His back hurt, but he didn't straighten. His knees ached, but he didn't rise. He wasn't tired—until he was.

Somewhere between the second and third door checks, he sat down. The hallway light dimmed to its nighttime setting. The tiles were cold. He didn't move. He leaned back against the wall, crossed his arms, and rested his head against the cool plaster. The toolbelt dug into his hip. He didn't care. He was still listening. Just in case.

That was how Ben found him. Past midnight, barefoot, having just returned from checking on Isla for the fourth time. He didn't speak at first. Just stood at the edge of the corridor, staring at his old friend sleeping upright like a soldier without a command. The man who had raised Clara, changed diapers in the dark, mopped vomit from every imaginable surface, and never once asked for thanks.

Maria came padding softly down the corridor from the opposite side. She rubbed her eyes, holding a fraying blue bunny in one hand, and blinked at the sight of Tobias. "Is he okay?" she whispered. Ben crouched next to her and looked toward the man slouched under the window. The screwdriver in his pocket was still gripped between two fingers. His glasses were skewed slightly off his nose.

"He's okay," Ben whispered back. "Just tired." Maria hugged her bunny tighter. "He doesn't look tired. He looks like a tree." Ben smiled faintly. "He is a tree. The kind that keeps houses standing when storms hit." Maria yawned and leaned into Ben's side. "Did a storm come?" "Not yet," Ben said. "But he heard the thunder."

They let Tobias sleep. He needed it. No one woke him. When morning came, and he found himself still against the wall, with a crick in his neck and the imprint of the toolbelt buckle on his arm, he didn't make a sound. He stood. Straightened his glasses. Picked up the hammer. Then walked toward the kitchen as if nothing had happened. And when Maria passed him on the stairs and asked again, "Are you okay?" he gave a small shrug of his shoulders, just enough to mean yes, maybe, or not really—but he'd still be there. Because Tobias heard everything. And sometimes, that was enough.

Clara sat at the long kitchen table, feet tucked under her chair, a steaming cup of raspberry mint tea untouched beside her elbow. Her hand moved slowly across the page, the pencil lead whispering against the grain of the notepad. She had written Prince first, then beneath it, Princess. No names yet. Just the titles. The crowns they were born with, even before breath. She stared at them, lips pressed tight, eyes steady. There would be names. Not borrowed ones. Not family hand-me-downs. Names that no one had ever worn before. Names meant for royalty that would never be mistaken for anything else.

The kitchen light was warm, falling in soft gold across the polished counter. Morning had faded into noon without anyone noticing. Maria sat across from Clara, her elbows on the table, reading a slim hardbound book titled The Villages of Kent: From Cottages to Crownlands. She read aloud every third line to herself, whispering the names of hamlets as if they were spells: Westerham, Edenbridge, Goudhurst. She liked the sound of them, old and round and honest. Her small finger slid down the map printed inside the back cover, pausing over the edge of a forest not far from Ben's childhood town.

Isla entered slowly, her steps quieter than they'd been the day before, one hand cradling her belly as if balancing two lives inside her took more care than usual. She wore a pale cotton robe, no slippers, her hair loosely braided down her back. She moved like a woman who was almost ready. Clara didn't look up until Isla's hand brushed her shoulder. "No ideas yet?" Isla asked, her voice lower than a whisper, softer than light. Clara smiled and turned the pad slightly, showing the two words without speaking.

Isla leaned in. "They'll have names fit for stories," she said. "Not like mine. I was named after a woman who burned her life down." Clara shook her head, eyes sharp, lips curled into something sly. "You lit ours up." Maria looked up at that, lowering her book. "Was she really named after someone who burned things?" Isla grinned. "No. I just didn't like her much." They all laughed. It wasn't loud. But it was real.

The laughter, however, didn't last. It stopped at the exact moment Clara's eyes moved past Isla's shoulder and toward the window above the sink. She didn't flinch. She didn't gasp. She simply blinked, then narrowed her eyes. Maria followed her gaze and froze. There had been someone. A shadow. A movement. A man standing just beyond the edge of the eastern orchard—near enough to see, far enough to doubt. And then, he was gone.

Clara rose first. She didn't speak. She walked to the window and stared for a full twenty seconds, counting them aloud in her head, eyes focused on the edge of the tree line. Maria stood next to her. "You saw him too, right?" she whispered. Clara nodded once. "Same coat as before?" Clara shook her head. "Different. But the way he turned—it was the same." Isla reached the window last. She didn't need to ask what they were looking at. She already knew.

Sørensen had said someone was sniffing. Kendrick confirmed it. Now they were sure. The castle grounds were too vast for comfort. Too open in places. The old trees that once made the land feel private now made it feel exposed. Isla's hand found the latch. Locked. Of course. But she checked anyway. Then closed the curtain gently, as if drawing a line between inside and out might actually stop what was coming.

Back at the table, Clara picked up the notepad again. She stared at the two titles. Prince. Princess. The pencil hovered over the blank space beneath each one. "We need to name them before they arrive," she said, not looking up. "Names aren't just names. They're protection. They're shields." Isla eased herself into the seat beside her. "Then we choose names that can't be stolen," she whispered. "Names that don't bow."

Maria folded her book and laid it flat. She looked toward Clara, her voice barely audible. "Do you think he was taking pictures?" Clara nodded slowly. "If he wasn't, someone else will." Isla didn't speak. But her fingers tightened around her teacup. She hated tea. But it was warm. And in that moment, she needed something to hold.

A long minute passed before any of them moved again. Clara tapped the pencil once, twice, three times. She wrote a single letter beneath Prince, then stopped. She didn't want to finish it. Not yet. Not while the outside world still hovered at the edge of the trees like a thief waiting for nightfall. Isla touched her hand. "Tomorrow," she said. "Not today."

The window stayed closed. But Clara's eyes returned to it again and again. And when Tobias passed the corridor and glanced in, he saw them sitting at the table—not laughing, not speaking, just watching. And he knew. He didn't ask what happened. He didn't need to. He turned back down the hallway and reached for the hammer again.

Outside, the wind shifted. Nothing moved at the edge of the trees. But the air felt different. Watched. Not by ghosts. Not by memory. But by eyes that didn't belong. Clara wrote one more line on the notepad before folding it closed and pressing it to her chest. She whispered it into her own shirt. You don't get to win.

The wind changed first. Not its direction, but its scent. It crept in through the chimney flues and under the door seams, drifting across polished floors and old wool rugs as if it had walked in uninvited. Sørensen noticed it before anyone else. He stepped out from the surveillance wing just after dawn, narrowed his eyes toward the orchard, and sniffed once. The smell had arrived—storm salt, he called it. Not sea breeze, not brine, not the pleasant tang of ocean air after rain. This was different. It was the smell of ships crashing, steel groaning, and something deeper below—disturbance.

In the kitchen, the chef ruined the risotto. He blamed it on the heat, the pan, the rice. But Clara had seen him stir it five seconds too long, distracted by the way the breeze slid down the exhaust hood and over his shoulders. "What's that smell?" Maria asked. "It smells like the harbour when the cranes fall silent." Nobody answered. It wasn't the kind of question that invited comfort.

The guards doubled their rounds without needing orders. The outer circuit closed in a tighter figure-eight. Boots echoed down hallways with more weight than usual. One guard stood longer at the window in the east corridor. Another, positioned near the nursery wing, tapped twice on the earpiece before saying nothing at all. They didn't speak. They moved. Like a dance they'd rehearsed but hoped never to perform.

Ben stood alone near the north wing landing, staring out a narrow casement window that faced the southern sea. The wind pushed in hard against the panes, whistling at the edges. The latch had been left loose. Not open, not wide—but not secure. Ben turned the handle tight, sealing it, then held his palm against the glass. Cold. Too cold for early spring. The sea was speaking. And it wasn't whispering anymore.

He didn't flinch, didn't shout. He turned on his heel and found Sørensen already behind him. "The wind," Ben said. Sørensen nodded once. "Storm salt." Ben exhaled through his nose, then spoke quieter. "We should tint the windows. All of them." Sørensen tilted his head. "Every pane?" "Not stained glass. The flat glass. Like the ones in the cars. Keeps drones out. Stops long lenses. We can't have one slip." Sørensen rubbed his chin, already calculating.

Later that afternoon, Sørensen approached Kendrick and Annemarie in the small sitting room adjacent to the gallery. Annemarie held a book in her lap but hadn't turned a page in twenty minutes. Kendrick listened with arms folded. No argument came. No questions. He simply said, "Do it." Annemarie closed her book. "I want it done before nightfall."

In the nursery, Clara moved the curtains closed without being asked. Not out of fear, but duty. She tucked one panel behind the radiator and adjusted the hem so it wouldn't drag. Even the children were quieter. Maria and Thomas whispered while drawing castles and clouds, unaware of the full weight their silence held. Isla remained in the sunroom, her eyes closed, pretending to sleep—but her breath was too alert for dreams.

Back in the dining hall, Ben reviewed the architectural map of the estate with Sørensen. They circled every exposed panel, every potential angle of view from a drone or a telescopic lens. "The east hallway, by the gallery—ninth window," Ben said. "It's not shaded." Sørensen marked it. "You always were good at noticing what everyone else missed," he muttered. Ben grinned faintly. "Blame the stink bomb years."

Downstairs, a contractor had already arrived. No questions asked. A Royal Services silent-call protocol, only enacted under security shadow level four. Within the hour, rolls of film, neutral tints, and sealing adhesives were unpacked and labeled. The glass would not be replaced—it would be obscured. Not so dark as to alert suspicion, but dark enough to blur the line between inside and out. Enough to let a family breathe again.

The scent remained, though. Lingering like a memory that refused to leave the room. Sørensen said it would pass, but Ben knew better. The salt didn't mean the sea was angry. It meant someone near the shore was. Someone who shouldn't be. Someone who hadn't earned the right to stand that close.

At dinner, conversation tried to return. Tobias said something mildly funny about a dream involving exploding diapers and flying spoons. Maria laughed. Thomas rolled his eyes. Isla didn't smile, but her hand found Ben's under the table and held it. He looked at her and nodded once, enough for her to know: he wouldn't leave until the twins were safe. That promise hadn't changed.

Outside, the storm hadn't started. But the air shifted again. A small branch snapped on the west side of the orchard. A drone hummed past the hedges before cutting upward and vanishing into cloud. Sørensen didn't run for it. He just marked it on the log, then clicked the timer. "Ten seconds visible," he wrote. "No markings. Pattern irregular. Altitude 400 feet."

Ben reread the note, then tucked it into his coat. "We may have less time than we thought," he said. Sørensen didn't blink. "Then we act faster." He checked his watch. "Window film should be done by nightfall. After that, we blackout all ground floor lighting." "Agreed." "Ben?" Sørensen stopped him before he turned to leave. "You taught me a lot when you were ten. Don't let me forget it now." Ben smiled. "Only if you let me tint the nursery windows myself." "Deal." It was the kind of conversation that meant nothing to anyone else. But in that castle, on that day, it meant everything.

Ben didn't choose the heavy parchment because it was formal. He chose it because it wouldn't smear. The pen he used was old—inked manually, dark, unrelenting. He uncapped it slowly and stared at the blank sheet for longer than he wrote on it. The light above the desk buzzed slightly, flickering once. But he didn't move. His eyes tracked the words as they appeared in silence, never read aloud. It wasn't a letter to a nation. It wasn't a command. It was a contingency. A goodbye he hoped would never be opened.

He began with Kendrick's name, nothing more. Not "Dear." Not "To." Just Kendrick. Then, below it, he wrote one sentence: "If I do not return, raise them like they're yours." The pen hovered. He didn't write Isla's name next. He didn't need to. The entire letter was for her, even if addressed elsewhere. He tried again. "Tell them who I was only when they're old enough to understand why I kept them hidden." Then he stopped. His hand went still. Something inside him recoiled. He read the sentence back, once. Then he tore the parchment in half.

He didn't crumple it. He didn't toss it. He folded the torn pieces in deliberate symmetry and slid them into the fireplace. There was no ceremony. No spark of regret. Only the strike of a match, the kind used to light oil lanterns, and the slow lean of his wrist as the fire caught and consumed the page. Ben sat back in the chair and watched the flame do what he could not— finish what was started.

The ashes curled tight like dead leaves in autumn. He didn't scatter them. He didn't even move. But Sørensen saw them later. He entered the room under the guise of checking on window tints and caught the scent of scorched ink and silence. He didn't ask. He didn't comment. He glanced at the hearth, then back at Ben, and simply nodded once. That was enough. They both understood. Letters were written for the living, not for the ones left behind.

That night, Sørensen installed a second bolt on the inside of Ben and Isla's bedroom door. It was thick, industrial-grade, but quiet when it locked. It wasn't there to keep Ben in. It was to keep others out. No announcement was made. Sørensen didn't even tell Kendrick. He just stood at the door, ran his thumb along the grain of the frame, and mounted the bolt cleanly in under twenty minutes. He said nothing. But when Ben returned to the room, he noticed. And he understood.

Later, Ben walked to the nursery where the cribs waited, empty but not lifeless. He placed his palm on the edge of one, ran a finger along the rim. Hannah and Frederik. Their names had weight now. They weren't ideas anymore. They were children, nearly here, pressing against the barrier between womb and world. He exhaled once, deeply, and turned to check the new blackout curtains. Sørensen had installed those too. And the soundproofing panels. And the extra latch on the balcony door.

In the back hallway, Sørensen checked his notes. Not digital. Not logged. Just paper. Paper couldn't be hacked. He recorded every security update, every lock, every code reset. A red pen marked the items that mattered most—nursery perimeter, Isla's bathroom window, upper library skylight. He checked the hinges himself. He didn't delegate. That was the old way. The true way. The royal way. Trust meant doing the work yourself.

Meanwhile, Ben paced. Not from fear. From memory. He was trying to remember if he had forgotten anything. The way his mother used to hum before bed. The way Isla tilted her head when she thought too hard. The sound of Maria's laugh. The tone of Thomas's voice when he asked serious questions. It all mattered. Because if something happened to him—and only if—they would need to remember who he was by the pieces he left behind, not the headlines.

Clara found him later that night. She brought him a hot drink. Not tea. Never tea. It was cocoa, dark and bitter, no sugar. He accepted it, nodded, and said nothing. Clara stayed for a moment longer than necessary, then turned to leave. "They'll be safe," she said without turning around. Ben didn't answer. But when the door closed behind her, he whispered, "Not if I'm here."

At the far end of the hall, Maria peeked around the corner. She didn't speak. She simply watched her father—the only one she'd ever known—staring out the window toward the orchard, silhouetted by firelight. She didn't know what was coming, but she knew it wasn't small. Even children can smell a shift in the air when the grown-ups don't smile enough.

Ben spent the rest of the night checking old notebooks. Not for plans. For memories. For drawings. For things he'd written when he was young, when being royal was a secret even he didn't know. He read a note from himself at age ten: "If I ever have a family, I'll do it right." He folded it and slipped it in his coat pocket. That one, he wouldn't burn.

Morning came slow. The smell of ash still lingered, but breakfast carried on. Tobias made pancakes because they were easy to reheat. Sørensen skipped breakfast. He was already up, checking the eastern garden sensors. Clara wrote in her journal. Maria sat beside her, drawing trees. Isla rested, the bump of her belly rising gently beneath a wool blanket. Seven days remained. Not one more.

And Ben? He stood in the hallway holding no paper, no speech. Just a decision. No more letters. No more goodbyes. Not unless it was absolutely necessary. There were things to prepare, yes. But not for death. For life. For the kind of life they had all bled to build—and would again if they had to.

Clara entered with quiet hands, the way nurses used to walk in old hospitals. Balanced between duty and care. She didn't knock. She didn't need to. The door had been left open, half on purpose, half by exhaustion. Isla hadn't spoken in over an hour. Not to Ben. Not to Maria. Not even to herself. Her eyes were red—not from pain, but from everything else. Clara had seen that look before, on women forced to wait while the world asked more of their husbands than it ever should have.

She placed the glass down on the nightstand with a soft clink, not loud enough to make Isla flinch. The juice was homemade—apple, with a touch of lime, the way Isla liked it. Cold but not sharp. Clara stepped back and waited. She never forced comfort. Isla turned her head slightly, acknowledged her without words. Then her chin dropped. Her shoulders folded. One hand moved to her stomach. The other wiped at a tear that wasn't trying to hide.

"He always protects us," Isla whispered. Her voice had that edge of salt and shame that comes from knowing you're strong, but tired of proving it. "But who protects him?" She didn't expect an answer. It wasn't a real question. Not the kind meant to be answered. It was an ache in sentence form. Clara knew the difference. She crossed the room slowly, lifted the corner of the blanket, and sat beside her.

"I do," Clara said plainly. No royalty in her voice. No titles. Just truth. "And so does Sørensen. And Maria. And Thomas. And Kendrick. And Annemarie. And even Tobias, even if he doesn't say it. We all do." Her hand found Isla's and squeezed it, not hard, but enough. Enough to mean something. Isla didn't answer. But she squeezed back. That was enough, too.

They sat like that for several minutes. No tears. No words. Just breath and shadow and the slow, quiet rhythm of the moon shifting higher in the sky. The light that filtered through the curtains wasn't strong. It was gentle. As if the moon knew not to be too loud tonight. Clara looked at Isla, then at the growing shape beneath her skin. "You're doing so well," she said, not because she had to, but because it was true.

Isla finally leaned her head against Clara's shoulder. It wasn't something she did often, even when they were younger. Isla didn't collapse. She didn't lean. She stood. But tonight was different. Tonight she was allowed to melt. "He wants to go," she said, eyes tracing the grain of the wooden floor. "To Kent. After they're born. To keep them safe." Her voice didn't tremble, but her hands did. Slightly. Almost invisible.

"He will," Clara replied. "And when he comes back, they'll be here waiting." She didn't offer hope as a substitute for truth. She offered it as a companion. The kind that didn't deny the pain but sat with it. Clara always knew how to sit with it. It was something she learned from watching her own mother disappear and return in fragments. She wouldn't let that happen to Isla. Not now. Not ever.

Clara stood and walked to the windowsill. Her fingers brushed the curtain aside. The courtyard below was quiet. Too quiet. She didn't say that aloud. Instead, she asked, "Do you want me to stay here tonight?" Isla nodded. Just once. Clara grabbed the extra blanket from the rocker and laid it across the small sofa under the window. She would sleep there. Lightly. Just in case.

Maria peeked into the room and whispered, "Is Mama okay?" Clara nodded gently and motioned her in. Maria tiptoed toward the bed and kissed Isla's hand. Then, satisfied with the silence, she turned and left. Children had a way of reading the room even when no one spoke. Especially Maria. She was Sørensen's daughter, but she had Clara's heart. That's what Ben always said.

The night stretched longer than usual. Clara didn't sleep. She rested, but her eyes remained half-lidded, always watching the door, listening for the sound of steps too heavy or voices too low. Isla shifted once, breathing deeply, finally sliding into something close to sleep. The kind that doesn't rest the body but gives the mind a small reprieve. Clara didn't wake her.

In the corner of the room sat a leather-bound book, unopened. Clara glanced at it, debated reading, but chose not to. Instead, she wrote a line in her own journal: "He protects. She weeps. And we all hold the line until he returns." She closed the book softly, as if sound could disturb the delicate balance Isla had finally found.

Later that night, the wind pressed gently against the windowpane, not enough to startle, just enough to remind them that the world was still moving. Clara leaned her head back and exhaled. "We are ready," she whispered to herself. Not because she was. But because they had to be. And sometimes saying it first made it true.

The castle never spoke, but tonight it refused to sleep. The kind of night where floorboards breathed. Doors whispered. Even the air thinned itself, quieting so that the smallest sound might be heard. Sørensen's boots made no echo on the stone. He'd oiled the soles for nights like this. He knew every hall by memory, every turn by instinct. The east wing smelled of salt and linen. The west carried a faint scent of varnish and lavender. His flashlight never flickered. His hand never trembled.

In the corridor by the nursery, Tobias checked the taps again. The plumbing had never failed, but that wasn't the point. The point was to make sure it wouldn't tonight. He tapped each pipe with the flat of his wrench and listened for resistance, like a doctor checking bones. When he reached the last room, he didn't turn the knob. He leaned against the doorframe and sighed. He hadn't slept the night before either. He didn't expect to tonight.

Down the main staircase, Ben moved slowly. Not with fear, but with purpose. He stopped at every bedroom. Jasmin's. Elia's. Maria's. Thomas's. Even the nursery they'd set aside for the twins. He didn't say their names, not yet. But he thought them. He kissed each forehead, careful not to wake them. Even Thomas, though older, still slept with one sock on and the other kicked off sometime during the night. Ben chuckled silently. That hadn't changed in years.

He passed the old grandfather clock on his way to the sunroom. It read 2:48. He thought about adjusting it, then didn't. Time didn't matter tonight. The castle had its own clock, and it ran on worry and watchfulness. He reached the window overlooking the long hill below the property and saw nothing—until he saw something. Two cars. Moving too slow for lost tourists. Too smooth for delivery. The kind of slow that carried intention. His jaw set.

Ben didn't move for several minutes. He simply watched. The cars passed. No lights flashed. No brakes tested. But the feeling stayed behind, like the scent of rain after it's gone. He stepped away from the glass and closed the curtain. He didn't say anything aloud, but his hand rested on the sill for longer than necessary. Then he turned and walked back toward the bedrooms. Nothing would come tonight, he told himself. But still—he checked each lock again.

In their shared room, Isla stared at the ceiling. One hand under the blanket pressed against the left side of her belly. The other cupped the right. She felt each movement. One strong. One softer. They kicked together, but never at the same time. She whispered to them, not in words, but in feelings. Her eyes didn't close. Her breath stayed shallow. She hadn't cried since earlier, but now her eyes welled again. Not from pain. From pressure.

She thought about Kent. About the idea of Ben leaving. About how she told him to go, and how she already regretted it. But she knew he had to. And she knew he would come back. Still, her mind danced with images of empty rooms, of curtains pulled too tightly, of silence that lasted longer than it should. She rolled onto her side and exhaled through her teeth. The pain wasn't physical. It was mental. Emotional. A readiness she didn't want but accepted.

In the security office, Sørensen leaned forward. His elbows rested on the edge of the desk, fingers pressed into his temples. The cameras showed nothing. That made him more anxious than if they had shown something. "Too quiet," he muttered. Then louder, as if the walls might hear, "It's always too quiet before it's not." He scribbled a note: Tints. Drone barriers. Recheck south fence. He tapped it twice with the back of his pen and moved to camera seven.

At the outer garage, Tobias locked the last side door and tested it twice. He noticed a rust stain that hadn't been there yesterday. He'd clean it tomorrow. Maybe. If tomorrow wasn't chaos. On his way back in, he passed Sørensen and gave him a single nod. Sørensen returned it. Neither man spoke. They didn't need to. They both knew the smell of something coming. And it wasn't just the salt in the wind.

Thomas sat upright in bed. Not from a nightmare, but from intuition. He didn't know why he woke. He just did. He climbed out of bed quietly, found his socks, and tiptoed to the door. He opened it and found Ben standing there. Neither spoke. Ben just crouched, hugged him once, and nodded. Thomas nodded back. Then returned to bed. But he didn't sleep either.

Maria lay curled in her small bed with the book on Kent still open beside her. She hadn't turned the page in over an hour. She stared at the same photo of the seaside cliffs, the same paragraph about chalk and wind and rain. The words blurred. She blinked them back into place. Then she closed the book. "Not yet," she whispered. "Not yet."

In the kitchen, Clara made a cup of coffee she wouldn't drink. She just wanted the smell. She lit a candle instead of turning on the light. It flickered blue for a moment, then steadied to amber. She looked out the back window and saw Sørensen standing near the tree line. Just watching. Like a shadow that had finally grown tired of hiding. She didn't wave. He wouldn't have waved back.

The castle didn't sleep. Not tonight. Not while too much moved beneath the surface. Not while engines hummed down hills too slow to be innocent. Not while a king kissed the brows of children who did not yet understand the weight of silence. Not while a queen lay awake between two heartbeats that kicked in different rhythms. Not while guardians checked locks and left nothing to chance. When morning came, no one said "good morning." They simply carried on—awake, alert, and ready.

Ben found her in the hallway again, sitting against the radiator with her knees to her chest and her hands tucked inside the sleeves of her sweatshirt. Maria Anika Sørensen wasn't the sort of girl to fidget or complain. She simply folded inward when something was too big to name. The quiet ones were the ones who carried the most, and Ben knew that. He didn't ask what was wrong. He just sat down beside her, one hand resting on his knee, waiting.

Sørensen watched from the end of the hall, arms crossed but eyes soft. He didn't step forward. He knew when to stay back. Ben had always had that ability—to see where others were blind, to kneel when others stood tall, and to listen before deciding what needed to be said. After a moment, Maria uncurled just enough to lean into his side. She didn't cry. Not yet. But her head found his shoulder, and that was enough to begin.

"I know we have to leave," she said, not looking up. "I know it's not forever. But it feels like I'm leaving everyone behind. Again." Her voice didn't shake, but her fingers gripped the sleeve fabric tighter. Ben didn't interrupt. He waited until her breath evened out, then wrapped his arm around her shoulder with quiet steadiness. She didn't pull away.

"You won't be bored in Kent," he said finally, with that slight humour only she could detect. "There's this one tea shop that serves cocoa instead. I only go there for the biscuits. And the library still smells like dust and mystery. You'd like it. You'll see." She didn't answer, but her chin dipped slightly, the way it did when she was weighing something important. That was always a sign.

He continued, his voice softening. "One day you'll understand. It's not about power. It's about safety. This crown isn't mine because I want it. It's mine because I was born with it. That's different. That's heavier." His words didn't carry bitterness, only burden. The kind of weight one accepts rather than curses. He didn't look down at her when he spoke. He looked forward, as if seeing the road he'd have to walk before she did.

Maria sat up then, straightened her back, and turned to face him fully. Her dark eyes didn't blink. "I'll protect us too, always. I swear." Her voice held no hesitation, only truth. It wasn't dramatic. It wasn't loud. But Ben felt the promise in it. As if something ancient had passed between them—unspoken, but binding. He nodded slowly. "I believe you."

He reached for her hand and felt how cold it had gone, despite the warmth of the house. That's how she was when she held things in too long. He turned her palm upward and pressed his own into it. "You don't have to keep it inside, you know. Crying doesn't make you weak. Not crying doesn't make you strong. It just makes you hurt longer." He glanced toward the hallway window. "Even the strongest dam cracks if no one releases the pressure."

She looked away, her lips pinched together. Her throat bobbed as she swallowed hard, but no tears came. Not yet. Not still. Ben watched her try to hold everything behind her eyes, and it broke his heart more than if she'd wailed. He brought her into a full hug then, tucking her under his chin, holding her the way only someone who knew what hiding felt like could.

"I don't want Isla to see me cry," she whispered into his chest. "She's already scared." Her words came out like fabric being torn quietly. Ben held her tighter. "Isla knows. She sees more than anyone. She won't think less of you. None of us will." He paused. "I've cried more times than I can count. Not just as a boy. Even now. You think I don't cry just because I wear a title?"

That made her finally laugh, just a little. It cracked the edge of the dam. Her shoulders trembled once. Not a sob, not yet. But the pressure shifted. He felt it. Sørensen finally stepped closer, but still didn't speak. His eyes met Ben's. Ben nodded. It was time. They'd leave soon. But not without making sure Maria's heart didn't split from silence.

When Sørensen kneeled beside them, Maria turned and crawled into his lap like she was four again. She hadn't done that in years. He didn't question it. He simply wrapped both arms around her and closed his eyes. "You're my girl," he whispered into her hair. "And you're his girl too. That means you don't carry this alone. Ever."

The hallway light flickered slightly, the bulb buzzing just enough to remind them that even castles get tired. But no one moved. Ben leaned back against the radiator, folded his arms, and watched his two shadows beside him. Maria, the girl who couldn't cry, was slowly learning that sometimes not crying hurt more than letting go.

She wouldn't break. That wasn't the fear. The fear was that she'd go too long without bending, and something inside her would crack in silence. But not tonight. Not under this roof. Not with the people who loved her more than blood or title could measure. Ben rose after a while, kissed her forehead gently, and stepped down the hall. He didn't need to look back. He knew she'd be okay now. For tonight.

The envelope came wrapped in black waxed linen, sealed without a crest, coded without return. Sørensen had been waiting at the south gate an hour early, arms crossed, pacing just once between every gust of wind. The moment the courier arrived, he took the package, offered no words, and burned the cloth wrapping in the old steel pail he kept under the porch. Fire erased evidence. Smoke told no tales. Then he brought the parcel inside like it held the only heartbeat left in Denmark.

Ben sat at the long oak table beneath the old pendant lamp. The light flickered slightly, but he didn't blink. He ran a thumb across the edge of the envelope and caught the faintest imprint of pen pressure beneath the surface. Kendrick had written something—but not words. Lines. Directional lines. Instructions that only Ben would recognize. He slid a finger beneath the seal and unfolded the contents with reverence, not hesitation.

The map was old, at least forty years by the look of it. Yellowing around the borders, crease lines worn like battle scars, corners soft from handling. But it had been updated. Hand-drawn corrections appeared in blue and red ink, freshly traced. Kendrick's script was unmistakable. There were dotted lines through the forests near Roskilde. Arrows pointing toward abandoned roadways, footpaths known only to hunters, smugglers, and royals with reason to vanish.

Sørensen stood behind him, arms folded, reading every inch without needing to speak. This was no suggestion. This was a command in graphite and ink. The exits were mapped. So were the threats. In a neat box in the top left corner, Kendrick had written just three words: Not If—When.

Ben didn't look up right away. His eyes moved from path to marker to the tiny X just outside of Kent—the cottage. His old one. He hadn't told Kendrick where it was. But Kendrick knew. Of course he did. He'd never been just a step ahead. He'd been watching the board since Ben was a boy. Sørensen leaned in slightly and traced a finger down the east corridor exit route. "That one. Middle of the night. Fog only."

Ben nodded. He took the paper like a final exam—one mistake, and the whole castle would be breached. It wasn't paranoia. It was preparation. He'd lived without it before, and it nearly cost him everything. Now he studied it like the parchment held his future children's breath in its folds. Because it did.

Sørensen reached into the cupboard and brought out an old thermos and a bag of boiled eggs. He laid them on the counter without comment, then returned to the table with a leather case. Inside were four signal blockers, a burner phone, and a ceramic utility knife. Ben didn't ask when he'd packed it. He just took it as a sign: war doesn't start with an explosion. It starts with preparation.

Then Ben got up, walked into the south corridor, and returned with his slingshot. Not the plastic toy of a child, but the polished oak weapon built by Sorenson himself when Ben was ten. Custom-fitted. Weighted properly. No one but him could shoot it straight. He'd taken down drones before. He could do it again. The new pellets weren't rocks. They were steel. Sørensen smiled when he saw it.

"You going to practice?" he asked, gruff but amused.

Ben just loaded a pellet and walked to the back doors. A drone passed thirty feet overhead. The sound of its engine barely more than a whisper. Ben's arm lifted, elbow bent, eyes narrowed. The projectile flew faster than the sound. The drone flickered. Then dropped like a stone. Sørensen raised his eyebrows and muttered, "Still got it."

The guards retrieved the wreckage. It had no markings. Freelance, probably. Or worse—freelance pretending not to be state-funded. Either way, it was a test. And Ben had passed. Sørensen carried the map into the panic room where only fingerprints and blood access would open the doors. Kendrick's handwriting couldn't fall into the wrong hands. Not while the children were still inside the womb.

Ben returned to the table and set the slingshot down, pressing his palm against the polished handle as if grounding himself. He didn't speak for a while. When he finally did, it was quiet. "This isn't retreat. It's repositioning." Sørensen didn't answer. He just folded the signal blockers into the go-bag and adjusted the shoulder strap to Ben's frame. He'd measured him years ago. Nothing had changed.

Later, Clara brought down a notebook with a list of emergency codes. Tobias checked the cellar doors again. Isla hadn't been told about the drone—not yet. She needed peace. Peace, even if manufactured, even if borrowed, was still worth preserving. Ben rolled the map back into a tight scroll and bound it with a leather cord. It would not leave his hand again until they were gone. And if it had to burn, it would burn in his hand. Outside, the sky cleared, but no one trusted the stars.

The castle had fallen into its quiet hum. Not sleep. Not silence. Just the hush of things too cautious to rest. Somewhere down the south corridor, a guard's boot clicked on tile. From the old staircase, a warm creak passed through the bannister like a house trying not to wake itself. But eleven-year-old Thomas moved like a ghost. He didn't use a flashlight. He didn't carry a toy or a reason. He just walked, barefoot, down the hall toward the room where light flickered under the door. It wasn't candlelight. It was softer. A lamp on low.

He stood outside her room, waited exactly five seconds, and then tapped once on the doorframe. Not the door itself. Not loud. Just enough. Just the polite way he had been taught by Ben. Inside, Isla's voice came gently through the stillness. "Come in, sweetheart." No one else spoke to him quite that way. No one else called him sweetheart and meant it like a trust.

The door opened with its usual catch, and he slipped in without a sound. The lamp near the bed cast a soft pool of amber across the sheets. Isla was propped up with two pillows, a warm knitted blanket pulled to her waist. Her hands rested on the great roundness of her belly, like a mother securing treasure. She smiled when she saw him, her voice barely above a hush. "You couldn't sleep either?"

Thomas shook his head, then crept closer to the edge of the bed where the shadows shifted gently with the rise and fall of Isla's breathing. He didn't ask permission to sit. He didn't need to. She moved the blanket slightly, turned sideways just enough for him to see what he came for. The skin on her belly tightened suddenly—two small shapes pressed outward in perfect defiance of physics. One heel. Then another. The skin stretched with a gentleness that somehow made him stare harder.

Thomas's eyes widened. "They're fighting," he whispered. Isla smiled, closing her eyes just for a moment. "They're dancing." "They're trying to escape," Thomas said, grinning now, the nervousness gone. "Just like someone I know," Isla murmured, rubbing a circle around the most stubborn kick.

Thomas didn't ask who. He already knew. She meant Ben. Of course, she meant Ben. There were things Thomas didn't need explained—he could feel them in the way Isla said them. Not with bitterness. Not even with worry. But with something like pride. As if escape wasn't cowardice, but legacy.

He reached out slowly, and she guided his hand to the curve where the heel had been. Just beneath the surface, a slow shift happened again. The girl. Then the boy. One of them seemed to respond to Thomas's hand. He felt it clearly—firm, certain, a nudge back. His whole body lit up. "That one's mine," he whispered.

Isla laughed softly. "She'll let you believe that for now." His mouth opened in mock offence. "She?" "She. And he." Her hand joined his, warming the space between them. "It's nearly time."

He didn't know what to say to that. So he sat still. Not afraid. Just full of thought. He had promised Ben earlier in the week. Promised that he would look after Isla and the babies. He thought it had just been something people said. But now, staring at the tiny kicks from inside a world he couldn't see, Thomas understood something differently. This wasn't a story anymore. These weren't just the twins. They were real. They were alive. And they were going to need him.

He looked up at Isla. "They're going to be loud." She nodded, smiling. "Oh yes." "And messy." "Very." "But they'll be ours," he said, and he meant it. Isla didn't respond with words. She simply reached for his hand again, squeezed it, and let it rest on her stomach where the next kick was waiting. There was no music playing, but Thomas thought he could hear something anyway. Like the rhythm of change. Like the sound a new life makes just before it arrives.

He stayed there longer than he meant to. Maybe half an hour. Maybe more. She didn't make him leave. And when the smallest of yawns cracked across his face, Isla gently eased him onto the couch in the corner of the room, pulled a warm blanket up to his chin, and whispered something into his hair he didn't quite catch. Maybe it was a blessing. Maybe it was a promise. Whatever it was, he believed it. As the night deepened and the castle held its breath, Thomas slept—his arm still curled over his chest as if he were still cradling the moment. And down in the womb, the girl and the boy nudged each other once more, already taking turns being the bold one.

Ben moved slowly, deliberately, as if speed would damage something fragile inside the room. He didn't turn on the overhead light. Only the desk lamp, muted and yellow, gave off a glow that pooled like secrecy over the polished wood. His fingers brushed across the row of books until they found what didn't belong—an old laptop, black, not sleek, not modern. Its hinges creaked when opened, like a memory folding back into place. The screen flickered, the startup sound silenced long ago. Ben didn't need fanfare. He needed silence.

The drawer below the shelf held what he was looking for. A small, square black case with a zipper so tight it took both hands to undo. Inside lay the drive. Not the kind children used for school assignments or downloaded games. This one had been shielded, encrypted, and registered through at least four international jurisdictions. The initials etched into the top weren't his. They belonged to a man who died three years earlier, one of the last who ever spoke the truth aloud. Ben plugged it in anyway.

The screen lit gently. No logos. No apps. Just command lines and folders with names like "Witness_Ledger" and "Pattenden_Seedline." He knew what they meant. He had written them. But now, with less than a week before everything changed, he had to finalize the archive. Not for vanity. Not even for defense. This was the bloodline itself. The map to what made him who he was—not through memory, but through DNA. Through documents the world wasn't supposed to see. Through voices long gone but recorded anyway. Each folder held a truth someone had once tried to erase.

Sørensen entered the room without a knock. He never knocked when it was about security. His eyes scanned the screen. Then the door behind him. Then the corners of the room. "How much of it is ready?" he asked, voice low, almost buried beneath the hum of the old processor. Ben didn't answer with numbers. He simply said, "Enough." Sørensen nodded once and pulled a second device from his coat pocket—a newer drive, same encryption, same fireproof shell.

Ben handed him the master copy. It weighed next to nothing but carried centuries. "One goes to Harrison. No detours. No deviations. He'll know what to do." Sørensen didn't question it. He slipped the drive into a velvet pouch, sealed it with wax—not just any wax, but the family crest seal. A mark Harrison would recognize, and so would anyone foolish enough to break it. The second copy would go to Kendrick by hand. Sørensen himself would deliver it if necessary.

Ben's hand hovered over the delete button for the local files, but he didn't press it. Not yet. Instead, he created a shadow copy on a hidden partition and renamed it something no one would ever guess: "LegacyDraftFinal." He then powered down the machine, disconnected the drive, and wrapped the cord tightly around it like a ritual. "No cloud," he reminded Sørensen. "Ever." And Sørensen, always old-school, gave him a half-smile. "Wouldn't trust it with a grocery list."

Outside, the wind was picking up. Ben could hear the faint clatter of something metal shift against the windowpane—maybe the latch on the south tower. Maybe something else. But he didn't look up. His eyes were fixed on the closed laptop now resting inside a hollowed-out dictionary. The casing would fool anyone who wasn't looking for it. And those who were, he figured, would never think to read.

Sørensen sealed the courier package. Not with a stamp. With a thread of code embedded on a microchip taped inside the case. Harrison's system would scan it, verify the signature, and auto-purge the contents if tampered with. Precaution, always. But this time, it felt heavier. "What about Isla?" Sørensen asked, almost without meaning to.

"She already knows," Ben said, voice brittle, hands steady. "She told me not to wait."

"Smart woman."

"She married me."

"Point proven."

The room fell still again. The only sound was the soft whir of the processor winding down. Ben reached for a fountain pen on the desk and wrote one word on a folded piece of paper: If. Then he slipped it between the pages of the dictionary beside the laptop. Just in case. Not because he expected to fail. But because history has a habit of forgetting those who don't write themselves into it.

When Sørensen left, he didn't look back. And when the lock clicked behind him, Ben closed his eyes—not to rest, but to remember the password. Not the one that opened the files. The one that started it all. The first name that ever mattered to him. The one Isla spoke when she said yes.

The clocks in the west corridor had all stopped at different times, as if refusing to agree on how late it truly was. But Sørensen didn't need a clock to know it was 2:47 a.m. The hallway lights were on their lowest dim, casting long shadows that moved when he didn't. His boots made no sound on the flagstone. His pistol wasn't drawn, but it could be. Something in his stomach—the old knot, the old pull—had woken him a minute before. He hadn't even made it to the surveillance room. He didn't need to.

He moved like a memory—silent, fast, unforgettable. The southern corridor smelled faintly of varnish and salt. It had rained earlier. He felt it in the base of his spine, in the joints that reminded him he wasn't twenty anymore. Still, he moved like he was. When he reached the narrow gate door beneath the old ivy wall, he paused. His left hand hovered just above the panel. But it wasn't locked. It was cracked. Barely.

He drew his sidearm. It wasn't for show. It was a tool. The kind only gets drawn when something's wrong. He pushed the gate open just wide enough to slip through and immediately crouched low to the hedge line. His eyes swept left, then right. The only sound was the light drip of moisture from the branches above. No scent of sweat. No sound of breathing. No idiot smoking too close to a camera. No tracks. Just one thing. Right at the base of the gate.

It was a cream envelope. No stamp. No writing on the outside. But it was placed there with such surgical precision that Sørensen didn't touch it at first. He scanned the area twice again. Checked every visible angle. No lights flicked from the trees. No rustle in the branches. Whoever had been here was gone, and they'd been gone long enough to leave only intention behind.

Sørensen used gloves. Latex, not leather. He didn't disturb the edges as he lifted it. The paper was still cool. Left within ten minutes. Inside was not a note, but a photograph. A single photograph printed on matte paper—thick, archival. No watermark. No message. Just an image of Ben. Sitting in the library. Yesterday. Lower West Wing. Third window from the corner. Untinted. The photograph had been taken from an elevation above the outer wall. Which meant one thing. Drone.

Sørensen didn't waste a breath. He memorized the details, refolded the envelope, and tucked it into the inside pocket of his vest. He left the gate exactly as he found it—ajar. But this time, a motion sensor beam crossed the space just above the soil. One hair-trigger alert. One missed shadow. One warning. No sound. But anyone who came through again would trigger a cascade of red across every monitor in the tower. Sørensen liked quiet. But he wasn't afraid of alarms.

When he returned inside, he didn't say a word. But by the time the sun was up, the castle's west-facing windows had changed. A new film coated the glass. It wasn't ordinary tint. It was reflective, thermal-resistant, and drone-invisible. The technicians were flown in before dawn. Only four people even saw them arrive. Sørensen made certain Ben was one of them.

Ben studied the photograph for a long time. He didn't ask who had delivered it. He didn't raise his voice. He didn't pace. He simply stood by the fireplace, turning the image in his hands like it had weight. "They missed the first time," he said. "They won't miss again." Sørensen nodded. "Not if they never see again."

The guard roster changed that morning. No names. Just rotations. Doubled at the gates, tripled at the eastern slope, and drones of their own sent out under royal security clearance. Every drone tagged. Every camera accounted for. Every sweep archived. Sørensen installed two new infrared beams at the corridor arch. No one else knew the frequency. Not even Kendrick. Sørensen didn't like risks. But more than that, he didn't like being watched.

Maria asked Ben later what had happened. Ben kissed the top of her head and said, "Someone forgot we don't play games here." Maria didn't ask again. But she checked every latch on every window in the playroom before she went to bed.

Clara noticed the change in Isla. She didn't say much, but the way Isla tucked a pillow beneath her back now had more intention. The windows in her room had been tinted too. But she still kept the curtains drawn. She said it was for the light. But everyone knew it was for the dark.

When Sørensen returned to his quarters, the photo had already been scanned, re-encrypted, and sent to Harrison under the codename "Missing Curtain." Harrison would understand. That was the name of the file Ben had once used when they were twelve. Back when the threat wasn't public. Back when secrets were safe behind bookshelves and quiet villages. Now, there were no bookshelves deep enough. No corners quiet enough. And Sørensen had no intention of sleeping until they were gone.

Ben didn't make the announcement during a meeting. He didn't summon anyone. He waited until Sørensen had just sat down for tea—which, of course, he didn't drink. The mug was there only as a decoy, something to keep his hands from looking suspicious. Sørensen never trusted idle fingers. But Ben sat across from him now, arms folded loosely, gaze sharp. "Time for another chess match," he said, voice light. But Sørensen heard the deeper timbre, the signal underneath. The boy he once trained had grown teeth. Sharp ones.

"Another game?" Sørensen asked, arching a brow. "Didn't we run out of opponents last year?" Ben didn't laugh. "Not the game itself. The architecture." He leaned forward, slow, deliberate. "I want you to craft it this time." Sørensen blinked once, then tilted his head. "Me?" The man had built out royal security vaults, planned digital redirections across three continents, but misinformation was not his usual sport. Until now. "Yes," Ben said simply. "Consider it your first sovereign assignment in misinformation architecture."

It wasn't the challenge that startled Sørensen—it was the title. "Sovereign assignment?" he repeated. "You're invoking that now?" Ben nodded. "If they want to provoke a king, let them play against one." Sørensen set down the cup. Empty, as always. "And what are the rules?" Ben smiled. "There are none. We don't give them rules. We give them a scent. And we let the dogs chase until they're winded."

Sørensen's face didn't change, but something inside him lit like iron on coals. "You want me to build something they'll believe?" "No," Ben replied quietly. "Something they'll chase. Too believable. Too personal. Just enough to fracture the factions that believe they already have the truth. I want them to argue amongst themselves." Sørensen nodded slowly. "And what flavour of bait are you imagining?" Ben paused for effect. "Genealogy."

That was the moment Sørensen sat back, the full shape of the plan settling into his bones. "You want to suggest a shadow heir narrative." Ben nodded. "Let them wonder if I'm being secretly groomed to inherit one of the defunct houses. Maybe Hungarian. Maybe Austrian. Give them enough that it doesn't look fake—but not enough to prove." He stood and began pacing slowly, hands behind his back. "We can float papers. An old seal here, a birth registration there. Link me to three thrones. Hungary. Denmark. Norway. Undisputed, unclaimed. Just enough to make them sweat."

Sørensen looked up. "They'll bite." "Of course they will," Ben said, already halfway to the wall. "And while they're too busy arguing about which dynasty I supposedly belong to, we secure the real one." The truth didn't need to shout. It only needed room to breathe. "The chessboard is set. But this time, we don't give them pieces. We give them rumours dressed in royal silk."

By now Sørensen had pulled his old black notebook from his inner pocket. Pages were already filling with symbols, names, fictional timelines that could be made to look convincing under a forensic audit—but fall apart upon deeper examination. "We'll need signatures," he muttered. "Stamps. Registry copies. A whisper planted in an embassy lunchroom." Ben nodded. "And a historian or two who's willing to remember a house that never quite went extinct."

"You want this done before they get to the gate again?" Sørensen asked, already flipping pages. "Before the babies are born," Ben answered. "I want the world too busy spinning their own theories to notice the real ones arriving." Sørensen didn't flinch. "We'll keep them in check. Kings and queens are born every day. But decoys? Decoys are crafted."

Ben stepped to the window, one that had only recently been tinted. Outside, the wind whipped the leaves into a spiral that danced without care. "They think they've cornered us," he murmured. "But all they've done is surround a door we never walked through." Sørensen raised his eyes. "What do we name the file?" Ben didn't even turn around. "Call it Stinkbomb-22. Just for old time's sake."

There was no laughter in the room. Only memory. The name of a ten-year-old hacker operation that had once rerouted an entire intelligence firm's servers to rerun episodes of vintage British sitcoms for six hours straight. Uncle Sorenson had found the boy that night, barefoot on the library floor, sipping juice from a mason jar and smiling like a ghost had told him a secret. Now, the man across from him was no longer ten. And the secret was no longer harmless.

That evening, a ghost file appeared on a shared drive deep in a dark part of the net. No name. No metadata. Just enough breadcrumbs to spark a firestorm. Within six hours, whispers began. By midnight, three intelligence freelancers had already drafted internal notes suggesting the emergence of a lost heir to House Árpád, with connective lineage threading toward a line of Norwegian nobles. Ben's name was not mentioned. But everyone knew anyway.

Sørensen signed off for the night, but not before locking the Stinkbomb partition behind four layers of rotating encryption. Ben kissed Isla's forehead, whispered to the twins through her skin, and said one last thing to Sørensen as the man passed him on the stairs. "Keep them busy until they forget what they came for." Sørensen nodded once. "They're already lost." And the castle went to sleep—knowing that the real war had not yet come. But when it did, they would not be caught sitting at someone else's table. They'd already built their own.

CHAPTER 5: THE FINAL QUIET BEFORE THE STORM

The castle was never truly silent. Even in the deepest hours of the night, when the halls stood empty and the portraits seemed to sleep, there was always the gentle hum of life. The creak of stone under wind, the faint shifting of old wooden beams, the quiet tapping of boots from a guard changing post. But tonight, even those sounds faded, as though the walls themselves were holding their breath. Clara noticed it first, pausing mid-step in the north hallway as a cold shiver ran up her back. The candle she carried flickered, not with wind, but with warning. Something had changed.

Ben felt it the moment he opened the library door. He had returned to the same place he had first met Isla all those years ago, the same place where the truth of his blood had first been uncovered. Tonight, it did not welcome him. The windows rattled, but not with force—there was no storm. And yet the wind curled against the stone as though whispering of something unseen. He closed the door without entering, sensing that whatever he had once sought there had already been found. There was no more hiding.

Tobias stopped in the hallway outside the east wing. He had been humming to himself—one of those made-up melodies he often sang when no one else was around. But the moment he passed beneath the portrait of Frederik the Silent, the notes caught in his throat. It wasn't fear. It was reverence. It was the kind of silence that wrapped around you like velvet and told you to hush. He stood there, blinking, until Clara appeared at the other end of the corridor and gave a single nod. She felt it too.

In the west room, where Isla had fallen asleep beside the warm glow of the hearth, her breathing grew deeper. Not troubled, not pained—but heavier. Her hand, resting on her rounded stomach, twitched slightly as one of the twins shifted. Ben moved toward her without making a sound. He knelt beside the chair, resting his hand gently over hers. Isla didn't wake. She didn't need to. Her body already knew. The babies were listening. Something in the air was speaking to them.

Outside, the leaves did not rustle. The wind did not howl. And yet the trees bent just slightly, as if bracing for something they could not name. The moonlight had a different cast to it—paler, yet sharper. Clara stepped out to check the supplies on the veranda and found herself staring skyward, unable to explain the tightness in her chest. She had been calm for weeks. But tonight, something inside her whispered, prepare.

Ben left Isla sleeping and passed down the eastern hallway, his fingers brushing along the stone walls as he walked. He had done this hundreds of times. It was a ritual of sorts—an old habit from childhood when he had first arrived at Rosenshavn and found himself lost in a home that was never meant to know him. But tonight, the walls no longer felt like stone. They felt like memory. Like names. Like voices calling softly from long ago, telling him that nothing was accidental.

Silje appeared like a ghost at the end of the corridor. She did not speak. She simply stood, arms crossed, hair tied back, a soft arch to her brow that warned against questions. Ben didn't ask. He didn't need to. Silje had the same look Tobias had worn earlier, the same sense of awareness, like an animal knowing a storm was coming long before the clouds appeared. She glanced toward Isla's room, then turned away. Her station for the night was chosen.

In the nursery, Clara folded the last of the baby clothes. The drawers were labelled. The bottles had been sterilized. Everything was in place. But she lingered longer than usual, smoothing the edge of a soft blue blanket again and again, as if unsure if it was soft enough. She had been through this once before—when she was brought to the castle, her arms empty, her voice trembling. Now she stood ready to receive someone else's child, with steady hands and an open heart. And still, something about tonight felt different.

Kendrick stood alone on the south balcony, hands behind his back, eyes fixed on the horizon. The stars were clear, the clouds sparse. There was no logical reason for his unease. But he had long stopped relying on logic. He trusted feeling. He trusted the pull in his bones that told him the tides were about to change. He had ruled silently for years, but even silence had its seasons. His silence was nearing its end.

Inside the master chamber, Isla stirred again. Ben had returned, settling into the armchair beside her. He hadn't spoken in nearly an hour, not since Clara had placed a gentle hand on his shoulder and whispered, not yet. He watched Isla as one of the twins pressed outward, causing the blanket to rise slightly. His heart caught in his chest. He knew it wasn't labour. But he also knew it wasn't far.

The castle cat, a sleek grey creature named Saffron, padded noiselessly across the floor, stopping just beside Ben. She had never taken to him. She was Isla's cat, through and through. But tonight, she pressed against Ben's leg and purred—low and deliberate. He glanced down, surprised. Animals knew before humans did. He took it as a sign.

In the servant's quarters, Tobias lit the last lantern. He didn't speak to anyone. He simply placed his tools beside the door, washed his hands at the basin, and waited. He wasn't a midwife. He wasn't a doctor. But he had caught more children in this castle than anyone else. Not physically—but emotionally. He held them all, when they screamed, when they fell, when they needed someone to stay calm. Tonight, he knew, he might have to hold Ben.

Elsewhere in the building, clocks ticked slower. Or perhaps they only seemed to. Every hallway felt like it stretched longer than before. Every echo sounded louder. Even the fire in the hearth crackled without warmth, as if it too had gone into waiting. The castle had never been so awake while pretending to sleep.

Ben stood again, this time walking to the window. He placed his palm flat against the glass. The sky was unchanged. But in his chest, something had shifted. A line had been crossed—not by Isla, not by the babies, but by time itself. This was no longer waiting. This was the breath before a shout. The silence before thunder. The final calm before history turned its next page. He whispered to no one. "It's nearly time." And the castle, in its breathless hush, agreed.

Isla shifted beneath the covers with a sharp breath, her hand pressing instinctively to the firm swell of her stomach. The room was dim, only the early hour's grey light sneaking in past the curtains, but her eyes opened immediately. She didn't cry out. She didn't sit up. She lay still, waiting for the sensation to pass. It didn't. It deepened. Not pain—tightness. As though the muscles inside her body had remembered something important all at once and clenched around the truth.

Ben had already been half-awake, seated upright beside the bed with a notebook open and pen resting against his knee. He had not slept. Not really. His mind had danced all night between the history lessons he meant to teach the children and the whispered memory of Kendrick's words. Now, at Isla's smallest exhale, he closed the book without a sound. He watched her hand move across her abdomen again. Her brow furrowed, but she wasn't frightened. Not Isla.

Another breath. Shorter. This time, her eyes glanced to Ben's without lifting her head. She didn't need to speak. He was already reaching into the drawer for his watch. "How long?" he asked, voice low, words rounded by habit. Isla gave a faint shrug, smiling despite the tension. "I don't know. A while, maybe." Ben started timing. He wouldn't call it a contraction. Not yet. Not without certainty. But the weight behind her stillness had changed.

Five minutes passed. Then ten. Another wave came, and this time Isla winced—not from pain, but from annoyance. "Still not rhythmic," she muttered, tossing her head back against the pillow. "Just enough to ruin a dream about waffles." Ben gave her a small look of amusement and scribbled something in the notebook. "That dream again?" he said. She nodded. "I was winning at a waffle-eating contest against Tobias. And Tobias was crying." She grinned. Ben smirked, but didn't laugh aloud. His eyes stayed fixed on her face, watching for signs of escalation.

He stood and walked toward the wall intercom, pressing the button gently before speaking. "Clara, we'll need the doctor." His voice remained steady, but the message carried. Clara's reply came seconds later: "Already on the way." Of course she was. Clara knew the pattern of his tone. She had been waiting for it. In the hallway, footsteps quickened. The Castle Doctor, a seasoned woman named Helene Møller, was already on her second cup of coffee. She didn't rush. She never did. But her coat was on before the echo reached the base stairs.

Helene entered with her usual expression—focused, unsentimental, deeply competent. "Braxton Hicks again?" she asked without greeting, gesturing for Ben to step aside. Isla answered before he could. "Feels like the cousins of the ones from yesterday." Helene raised an eyebrow. "Persistent family, aren't they?" She placed her cool fingers along the base of Isla's belly and waited. The moment the next wave of tension passed through, Isla's breath caught again, this time a little deeper. "Not labour," Helene said, already checking her notes. "Not yet. But you're close."

Clara arrived with warm towels and fresh linens, placing them without a word near the basin. Tobias hovered at the door, arms folded, not entering until Helene waved him in. "Prepare the room," she said. "We'll keep her comfortable here until further notice. But no bath yet. Too soon." Isla watched them moving about, then turned to Ben with a sly smile. "I could still beat you in soccer," she said. Her voice was light. Ben didn't answer right away. Then he laughed. The kind of short, crooked laugh that only Isla could pull from him when everything felt too sharp.

Only Ben laughed. Clara blinked, but didn't smile. Tobias tilted his head as if trying to decide whether the joke was permitted. Helene didn't react at all. Isla looked around, rolled her eyes, and said, "Tough crowd." She shifted upright with Ben's help, resting against the mound of cushions Clara had stacked earlier that morning. Her hand stayed protectively on her abdomen. The twins weren't moving much yet, but she knew they would. Soon. When it was time. But not yet.

Helene sat on the edge of the chair across from her. "Any unusual pressure? Back pain?" Isla shook her head. "Nope. Just the usual tightness. Feels like someone squeezing me from the inside, trying to remind me who's in charge." Helene nodded. "Your body's gearing up. You're probably within forty-eight hours. But every woman's rhythm is different. The twins might decide to linger." Ben glanced at his notebook again, then at Isla. She had stopped smiling.

The room settled into a kind of quiet preparation—not panic, not anticipation, just readiness. Ben knew this rhythm well. He had felt it once before, when Clara was first brought into their lives, when she had cried for hours until he finally whispered the right words. He had felt it when he first kissed Isla, back in the rows of dusty genealogy books, neither of them understanding yet that destiny wasn't something written in stone—it was written in blood.

"Should I cancel today's lessons?" Clara asked, already halfway to the door. Isla waved a hand lazily. "Let them learn. They're more interested in Ben's family tree than I am." Then she paused. "Actually, that's not true. Tell them we'll all be doing some 'genetic gymnastics' later. I want to know who I'm giving birth to." Tobias groaned dramatically. "Please don't say the word 'genetic' before breakfast." That earned a faint smile from Helene. Isla beamed. "Then eat faster."

Ben remained beside her, still not laughing much, though the smile touched his eyes. He could see how the others moved differently now. Clara stepped softer. Tobias spoke quieter. Even Saffron the cat had curled up unusually close to Isla's feet. The castle had adjusted its rhythm. The quiet had grown heavier. The air was thick with time. Isla rested her head against Ben's shoulder, whispering, "Not yet, but almost." He didn't answer. He only kissed the top of her head and whispered, "I know."

Helene stood, nodded to Ben, and added, "I'll be downstairs. Page me if she feels anything sharper, stronger, or too close together. For now, she's in pre-labour. Rest is more important than pacing. The real thing isn't far off." Isla nodded, eyes already closing again. Ben eased her back down, pulling the blanket gently over her legs. The twins had quieted. Or perhaps they were simply listening.

Outside the window, the light shifted. It wasn't quite dawn—but it wasn't dark either. That uncertain in-between space where morning was promised but not delivered. Ben stayed beside Isla, notebook resting forgotten on the floor. He no longer needed to time anything. He knew exactly where they were. They were on the edge.

The castle may have worn its stones like a relic, but behind its broad walls lay the comforts of modern life—floor heating, two-person showers, flush controls built into the wall, and a whirlpool tub big enough to seat four. The room was nothing opulent. Just an en suite tucked off the eastern side of the master bedroom. Acrylic tub. No gold. No porcelain filigree. Just clean lines and a tub that had only ever known ordinary evenings, not royal births. No one in Rosenshavn spoke of it as anything ceremonial. No one addressed it like a shrine. It was simply where Isla had chosen to give birth, and everyone understood. The walls were painted a soft grey-blue, the floors white-tiled, and the ceiling sloped downward from the tall wooden beams that hadn't been painted in over sixty years. There was nothing sacred about it—only familiar.

Tobias knelt first, crouching down to inspect the drain valve beneath the tub's lip. His fingers ran along the edge, checking not for flaw, but simply for rust or wear. None. He stood again and removed the panel from the base, inspecting the intake motor, made sure the pipes were warm, not calcified. Beside him, Clara had brought in two clean buckets, a new bottle of vinegar, and a soft cloth. No bleaches. No sterile gloves. Just vinegar and cloth. "Same as last time," Tobias said under his breath. Clara didn't answer. She'd already poured the vinegar and begun wiping the tub's rim with one long continuous stroke. Once. That was all it took. The smell wasn't strong. It simply belonged.

Silje stood at the door with her arms crossed, holding a stack of folded bath towels, all white. She didn't look bothered. Not nervous. Not rigid. She leaned against the frame the same way she always did when waiting for something to finish. She turned her head and glanced at the hallway, watching for motion. There was none. Everything stayed quiet. Tobias and Clara finished in under ten minutes. There was no endless scrubbing, no need for repeated sprays. It wasn't obsessive. It was just careful. No one repeated anything. No one second-guessed the work. Clara handed Tobias the cloth, which he dropped into the corner pail. Done.

Ben stood in the corner by the open window, looking not outside, but down. His arms were folded across his chest, his mouth still. He hadn't moved in five minutes. No pacing. No restlessness. His hands stayed still, but his head had gone elsewhere. Isla wasn't in the room—she was lying on the bed in the next room over, stretching her legs beneath a thick blanket, counting breaths and closing her eyes every few minutes. Ben had checked in on her twice. She waved him off both times. "Go get it ready," she'd said. And so he did. But standing there now, staring down at the polished white acrylic, he wasn't thinking about Isla. Not exactly. He was thinking about the past.

Clara was seven when she arrived. Ben remembered it too clearly—almost strangely so. The castle lawn that morning had dew on it, and the soccer ball they'd kicked around left tracks in the wet blades. Clara was good at soccer. He'd told her that. She smiled and shrugged. Her father stood awkwardly near the fence, talking with Kendrick, who was still in his gardening gloves. Ben didn't know why they were there at first. He only knew that Isla had insisted they come. Isla knew Clara from playing soccer. Not closely. Just enough to know she wasn't getting much at home. Clean, yes. Well-kept. But something was missing.

The job came swiftly. Kendrick didn't wait. He brought Alex Nielsen into the castle within forty-eight hours. Groundskeeper. Full-time. No interview needed. Clara came with him every day. Then she stayed the night. Then stayed another. Then moved in. It wasn't slow. It was swift and kind and without pomp. Clara didn't ask for anything. She ate what was served, helped with dinner cleanup, didn't complain once. And one night, when Ben had been doing drawings at the kitchen table, Isla sat down beside him and whispered, "We should keep her." Ben didn't respond. He just looked up. She wasn't joking.

Two weeks later, Kendrick had completed the paperwork. Legally. Not just guardianship. Adoption. The judge—someone who had once played cards with Ken's father—approved it without fanfare. Clara was theirs. Not in a pretend way. Not in some temporary stopgap way. Ben and Isla were only ten. It didn't matter. They weren't pretending to be grownups. They were already grown up enough. And Kendrick knew it. He told them later, "You did more for her than adults do in a lifetime." That stuck.

Now Clara stood in the hallway holding another folded towel. Taller. Older. Her hair tied up in a loose knot, half-damp from earlier. Ben looked at her and didn't see a child anymore. But he also didn't see a grownup. He saw Clara. The same girl who once curled up in the corner with her shoes still on. The same girl who never asked for seconds, but always made sure others had theirs. She was family. Not by blood. But by choice. And that mattered just as much.

She had become Princess Clara Ann Nielsen Harvick of House Rosenshavn thirteen years ago. The title was official, though no one used it aloud. Just once. There were crowns in the castle. Tiaras. Ceremonial garb locked behind the mirror doors of the long chamber room. They did see the daylight. Four Times in Ben's lifetime. Isla had worn one too, and she'd been Queen since the day they married. The children didn't play with them. Not once. They weren't toys. They weren't symbols. They were simply there—historical things, long untouched, only by Kendrick, Ben and Isla.

Ben didn't care for titles. He never had. Even as a pre-teen, when Kendrick first told him who he is, Ben brushed it off sort of. He didn't want it. Not the throne. Not the recognition. Not even the trappings. The he had to accept it. Isla once asked if he ever played with rubber ducks. He didn't. Not once. No toy had ever drawn his attention. Books had. Paper. Pens and Pencils. The things that make sense and had meaning. He'd rather spend hours tracing ink than pretending to be something he wasn't. Still true now.

The water system made a low hum behind the wall. Silje stepped forward to flick the digital tap once, testing the temperature. The first heat kicked in slowly. Then the jets clicked. Tobias nodded. "It's good." No one cheered. No one smiled with glee. It wasn't a party. It wasn't solemn either. It was preparation. Normal. Quiet. Steady. And when Clara knelt to finish wiping the handles of the tub, she did it once, then stood. The towels were hung. The vinegar bottle was returned to the cleaning cupboard. Nothing smelled like lemon or bleach. Just stone, water, and light. Ben turned toward the hallway as if coming back from a long distance. He said nothing. He didn't need to. His eyes fell on Clara. She glanced up, then smiled. Only then did Ben speak. "We're ready." And they were.

Clara walked into the room with steady steps, her arms full of fresh linens, her eyes already scanning the floor for anything out of place. She didn't speak as she moved. The air didn't call for words, only attentiveness. The castle lights were dimmed, not for mood, but for focus. She set the linens down neatly on the dresser bench and moved to Isla's bedside without waiting for instruction. Isla was resting, her legs pulled slightly in, hands resting low on her belly. She was breathing deeply, rhythmically, not asleep, but not quite alert. Clara leaned in gently, adjusting the blanket to sit higher over her chest, then sat beside her and counted the breaths. Twelve in one minute. Good. Calm. No irregularity.

She stood again, smoothing the edge of the duvet as she moved to the window. The pane had been left slightly ajar to let in the sea air. It smelled clean, no moisture, no wind. Clara pressed her palm flat to the windowframe, checking for draughts. None. She stepped back, hands brushing the skirt of her cotton tunic. The room temperature was comfortable, just as the doctor had advised: not too warm to overheat the body, not too cool to shock it during transfer. Seventy-one degrees Fahrenheit. Tobias had checked earlier, but Clara checked again—not from doubt, but from instinct. Then she walked to the tub.

It stood dry and waiting, gleaming beneath the soft overhead light. There was no water in it yet. There wouldn't be for two more days, unless Isla's contractions changed. Clara didn't care about the water levels. She crouched down and checked the height of the rim, mentally picturing how Isla would enter. One step, turn, ease in backwards. Ben would hold her elbow. Silje would support her shoulders. She would sit without pressure. Clara stood up and crossed to the towel rack. All six were present. Folded square. Cotton, not microfibre. The birth doctor had approved them last week.

There was no clipboard. No notebook. Clara didn't need one. She had memorized everything—the spacing of the bathmats, the drawstring on the curtain, the angle of the heat lamp. None of it was ritual. It wasn't clinical. It was just life happening in the castle, and she would see it done right. Because this wasn't just any birth. This was her brother and her sister coming into the world. And she would be ready for them. Clara stepped back toward the bed and checked Isla's position again. Her head had shifted to the left. She was still breathing deeply. The expression on her face told her she was calm—but tired. Tired in a good way.

Then Clara pulled the fitted sheet from the linen bench and began the careful process of changing the bedding. Not because it was dirty. Not because it had to be sterile. But because it was what she wanted for her mom. Her mom. She still said the word that way. She was twenty years old, but nothing about it had changed. From the moment Isla first wrapped a blanket around her shoulders at age seven, Clara had called her "Mommy." Not with any hesitation. Not with any teasing. She just did. And Kendrick never corrected it. Ben never flinched when she called him "Daddy." It was accepted from the beginning. Because she meant it. And they did too.

Clara lifted the pillows and folded the old sheet back, her hands working methodically. She didn't rush. She didn't linger. The new sheet stretched over the mattress perfectly, and she tucked it beneath the corners with a single sweeping motion. Each side smoothed. No wrinkles. The pillowcases were next. Ben had already fluffed the pillows earlier that morning, something he did every day for Isla, ever since her belly grew too large to bend properly. Clara smiled briefly at the thought, but didn't allow herself to pause. She placed the pillows back and fluffed them once more, for her own satisfaction.

There was a folded cotton robe lying over the footboard. Clara picked it up, shook it once, and folded it tighter. She placed it at the head of the bed, within Isla's reach. Then she turned to check the basket of supplies they had placed on the sideboard: herbal lotion, extra cloths, clean water bottle, an unopened bar of goat's milk soap. She sniffed it. Plain. No perfume. Just the way Isla preferred it. Everything in its place. She opened the cabinet drawer and placed a small notepad inside—blank, not for writing, just in case someone needed paper. Then she shut the drawer and turned to the door.

From the hallway, she could hear someone speaking softly—Tobias's voice, and Silje's laughter. The sound was warm. The castle always had these sounds, just tucked into the walls like old echoes. Clara didn't smile, but her shoulders loosened. She stepped out into the corridor and motioned for Tobias to come in. "Done," she said simply. He nodded and followed her in without question. She didn't give him instructions. He didn't ask for any. He had watched her clean the tub. He had watched her measure the towels. He had no doubt the room was as it needed to be. When she handed him the spare cloth, he took it and left again.

Ben hadn't returned to the room. He was still somewhere near the main sitting room, Clara assumed, deep in his thoughts. But she hadn't asked him to come back. He needed that time, and she gave it to him. She walked back to Isla's bedside and sat again. Isla turned toward her, opening her eyes slowly. "Everything ready?" she asked, voice a little dry. Clara nodded. "Everything," she said. Isla reached for her hand, and Clara took it. No need for thanks. No ceremonial words. Just fingers wrapped around fingers.

Clara sat for a long time that way, letting Isla's hand rest against her palm. Her eyes scanned the room one last time. She hadn't forgotten anything. The tub was ready. The air was still. The towels were warm. The bed was clean. And she was ready. Not just to help—but to witness. To stand in that room when the twins arrived, and to know—without question—that her place in the family had always been exactly where she stood.

Ben left the bedroom not to pace, but to observe. The heavy oak door clicked shut behind him, and for a moment, he stood still at the top of the stairwell, listening. The castle had many ways of whispering. He had learned to hear them over the years—not in words, but in how the walls held breath, how the floorboards paused before they creaked. Tonight, something was different. Not wrong. But disturbed. He stepped slowly into the corridor, one hand brushing the edge of the railing, eyes tracking nothing and everything. His footsteps were muffled by the thick woven runner that led toward the southern wing. No one had disturbed it. Not yet.

The leak hadn't come from within. He was sure of that now. Every person under that roof had bled to keep the secret. It was the city—Copenhagen—his old home, his forever home, and now the city that betrayed him. The name that spilled was not casual. Someone sold it. That part was clear. Ben had narrowed it down earlier in the week, just before Isla's last appointment. The rumours in the papers hadn't written themselves. It wasn't the Palace Watch or the Danish Royal News. No—this came from a smaller freelance outlet, the kind that lurks at ferry terminals and trains with a phone held sideways. Someone gave them the name. Not Kendrick. Not the castle staff. Not even the regulars from the café where he and Isla used to sneak their scones on Tuesdays.

He passed through the archway by the old stone alcove where the long gallery started. His hand brushed the top of the carved banister. The stain had worn off over the decades, but no one ever refinished it. They liked it that way—lived in.

Honest. He stopped near the window, tilted his head, and looked out. The town was asleep, but he knew the news cycle wouldn't be. By morning, more headlines would appear. Maybe even something international. Something with teeth. That's what made it dangerous. The truth wasn't what hurt. It was the timing. Two days before Isla gave birth, and someone had chosen now of all moments.

The name hit him harder than expected—Oscar. The name alone burned hotter than the betrayal. Ben had known him since they were nine. They played soccer almost every evening in the back fields, scuffed knees and hand-slapped goals. They'd shared chocolate bars, comic books, stupid summer plans. Oscar had slept over at the castle when storms rolled in. He'd helped Ben build that ridiculous wooden ramp out near the stream that nearly sent them both tumbling. He was the one who'd taught Ben how to elbow-check during a throw-in. Eleven years of friendship. And now this. Two years ago, Oscar had to move. His family left for northern Zealand. He said they'd keep in touch, but things went quiet. Ben didn't press. Now he knew why.

Oscar had lost his job. The company folded. Rumour said they gave no severance. He was desperate. But that didn't excuse it. Ben stared out the window until his jaw clenched too tight. It wasn't about being found out. It was about who did the finding. Oscar hadn't just leaked the truth. He had broken something deeper. Trust wasn't currency at Rosenshavn Castle. It was oxygen. Without it, you suffocated. Kendrick had taught Ben that early on. Kendrick—who had protected Ben's identity since the day he came to Denmark. Who made sure not even state officials breathed his title unless necessary.

Ben turned sharply and began walking. Not fast. Deliberate. He passed the blue parlour and made his way toward the rear corridor that overlooked the west courtyard. The scent of rosemary came through the vents—Silje had been tending to the garden again. Somewhere, a clock chimed once. He stopped near the staff corridor where Kendrick usually emerged after night checks. Sure enough, a moment later, the man himself appeared. No words. Just a nod. Ben met his eyes, and Kendrick returned the look with silent affirmation. They both knew. There was no need to speak Oscar's name aloud. It would be dealt with.

Ben exhaled slowly and looked down at his hands. He wasn't trembling. But the weight of it all had set into his bones. He wasn't worried for himself. He was worried for Isla. For Clara. For the babies that hadn't even arrived yet. Every rumour, every slip, every headline would follow them, like wind through open shutters. He hated that thought. Not the exposure. The permanence. Once it's out, it's out. And there was no putting it back. His job now was to hold steady. Kendrick would handle the legal implications—he always did. But Ben would need to face Oscar himself. Not out of vengeance. Out of principle.

He returned down the corridor slowly, taking one last scan of the hall. Nothing stirred. No whispers. No cracked doors. The castle was asleep, even as his thoughts refused to rest. Back in the east wing, he passed the corner where Isla kept the old wall art Clara had drawn at age eight—stick figures with crooked crowns. He smiled. For a moment. Then the smell hit him. Coffee. Fresh. From the kitchen. He didn't need to guess. Isla was awake again. Her cravings were back. She was predictable in that way. But not just predictable—strong. In the face of everything, she was craving coffee.

He stepped into the kitchen, where Silje was already handing Isla a steaming cup. She gave Ben a look that said, Don't you dare protest. Ben lifted both hands in surrender and smiled. "Doctor didn't say she couldn't," Isla said dryly, taking a careful sip. Ben chuckled, kissed the top of her head, and pulled out the chair beside her. He didn't mention Oscar. Not yet. She would find out soon enough. For now, they sat in quiet. Two sips. Three. Then Ben said softly, "Everything's quiet in the hallways." Isla nodded. "Good. Because in two days, nothing will be."

Silje didn't announce herself when she positioned her chair just outside the birthing room. She didn't have to. She placed it neatly beneath the wall sconce where the hallway split between the royal family's quarters and the staff staircase. The stone was cold, but she didn't mind. She folded her arms across her chest and leaned back slightly, boots planted flat on the rug, shoulders steady, head upright. Her job wasn't to stop an army—it was to stop foolishness. And she was exceedingly good at it. Those who had tried in years past to push past her learned swiftly not to try again. A door was a door. A hall was a hall. But Silje was Silje. And she didn't budge.

It wasn't that she didn't trust the household. She did. Implicitly. But in the last week, trust had become a luxury they could no longer give away for free. One man in Copenhagen had broken it—just one—and now every knock, every unexpected delivery, every external contact brought with it the twinge of caution. Silje wasn't interested in dramatic speeches or shouting accusations. She wasn't like Tobias, who sometimes spoke before thinking, or like Kendrick, who could control a room with silence. She preferred stillness. The weight of her presence was enough. And that presence now sat in the very heart of the hallway where she could see everything.

Isla was resting two rooms down. Clara remained in the adjacent washroom, collecting towels and setting up the warming lamp Kendrick had rigged from the old studio lightboxes. The whirlpool tub had been cleaned and sterilized. The room no longer smelled like bath soap but like eucalyptus and cotton. It calmed Isla, and it seemed to calm the staff. Not Silje. Her nerves weren't soothed by scent or by idle reassurances. She needed eyes. She needed a hallway she could see clearly, without clutter or company. She needed to do what she did best—watch.

The first knock came at ten past two. The hallway was quiet, but the sound carried. Not sharp. Not rushed. A standard knock. But Silje stood immediately and moved to the front vestibule. It was a courier—one of the usual types they'd seen before. Blue jacket. Clean boots. Familiar Danish accent. She didn't open the door immediately. Instead, she pressed the intercom first. "Name and delivery?" she asked, the crispness in her voice cutting through the receiver. "Medical crates," the man replied, holding up a scan tag. "From NordMed. Replacements for back-ordered items. Signed off by Dr. Karlsen."

She didn't let him in.

Instead, she retrieved the clipboard Isla had given her earlier that morning. It had the list of approved items, notated in Clara's handwriting. Ten thermal blankets. Three packs of absorbent pads. One spare IV line. Two saline drips. Gloves. Gauze. Cooling gel. A fresh fetal monitor wand. Silje read each aloud, made the courier confirm every item aloud, then stood silent for a moment more. "Where did you pick up from?" she asked. The man answered precisely. "Nørrebro. Main warehouse." That was correct. She opened the door exactly four inches, received the crates, signed nothing, and closed the door with the same force she always did. Clean. Quiet. Absolute.

She carried the boxes herself. They weren't heavy, just awkward. She brought them to the secondary prep room beside the linen chamber and set them down without ceremony. No need for congratulations. She unpacked the contents, compared them to the list again, then placed the empty containers to the side. Clara would check them again before storage, but Silje didn't need a second opinion. She trusted her own judgment. Always had. If anything was off—even the smell of the box, even a dent in the side—she would have known. But this time, everything passed. That didn't make her relax.

Returning to her seat outside the room, she glanced once toward the stairwell. Tobias had just finished wiping down the door handles. He gave her a short, sideways smile. She didn't return it. Not because she was rude. But because smiles had a time and place, and this hallway wasn't it. Not today. She looked at the camera above the ceiling beam. Kendrick's design, years ago. Just for internal use. No recordings stored. Just a silent loop that let staff see who walked where. Silje didn't need the monitor. She had her own eyes. And they had never failed her.

Clara came into view briefly. She nodded respectfully, carrying the fresh towels into the birthing room. Her steps were careful, balanced, deliberate. Silje respected her for that. She had grown well—not into a child pretending at adulthood, but into someone who understood her weight in the world. A daughter to Ben and Isla, yes. But more than that. She had a centre. And Silje trusted people with centres. Not many others.

She heard movement in the bedroom across the corridor. Isla, perhaps stirring again. Or perhaps Ben, returning from the kitchen. His footsteps were lighter now, less burdened. Or perhaps just better hidden. Either way, he passed behind her with no words, only a pat on her shoulder. She let it happen. He didn't speak. Neither did she. That was enough.

Another hour passed. Still, she didn't leave her post. Clara brought her a sandwich. She ate it cold. A little mustard, some ham. Nothing fancy. She finished it in three bites and returned the plate to Clara's tray without comment. Someone offered her a blanket. She waved it off. Cold didn't touch her anymore. It hadn't for years.

This was her station. She would stay. Not until relieved. Not until told. Until the twins were born. Until Isla had screamed her final scream. Until Ben had held both children in his arms. Until the door had been opened and closed again with the right people inside. Only then. And not before.

Kendrick didn't knock. He never did when it came to Annemarie. She had long since stopped requiring such formalities from him, even if the rest of the Castle still moved with a kind of reverent hesitation around her. He carried a single cup of coffee in each hand—hers dark and rich, without sugar, the way she liked it, the way she had always taken it. His was growing cold by the minute, untouched, forgotten somewhere between worry and obligation. She was sitting at the small reading table beside the eastern window of the study, not reading, not pretending to. Her fingers curled softly around the rim of the coffee saucer, steady, unshaking.

He set her cup down first, then leaned against the nearby wall with the kind of casual posture that didn't suit a man who had spent most of his adult life standing at full attention. The quiet between them didn't last long. "This is it," he said simply, and she didn't ask what he meant. She didn't need to. The weight of everything that had led to this moment had long since been accounted for in the shared silences between them. They knew each other's thoughts before they spoke them, and had for years. "He's already taken your place," she said gently. Not mocking. Not bitter. Just truthful. Kendrick nodded once. "I know."

She sipped her coffee. No sugar, no cream, just the taste of heat and earth and memory. Kendrick didn't sit. He stayed upright, his back to the frame of the bookshelf. From there he could see the hallway bend and the curve of light where the stairwell ended, just out of reach of the doorway. He wasn't watching for anything in particular—he was simply keeping count of time by light. "They'll come for him," he said eventually. "Maybe not today. Maybe not next week. But the leak's already made its way into four inboxes across Europe. At least four. I traced them myself." She looked at him finally, but only with her eyes. "Oscar?"

He didn't answer with words. The way his mouth pulled tight across his jaw was enough. Annemarie lowered her eyes again, not with shame, but with grief. "He played in this castle for eleven years," she whispered. "Every summer. Every weekend. He helped Clara build that blasted soccer net out of string and broom handles. He was here, Kendrick." Her voice didn't waver, but the emotion was closer to the surface than he had seen in her for years. "He was family," she finished. Kendrick gave a shallow nod. "That's what makes it worse," he said. "He knew exactly what he was doing."

The coffee had cooled in his hand. He set it on the edge of the cabinet and crossed to the window. Outside, the clouds hovered low, not menacing but steady, unmoved by the rush inside the Castle. "The castle's not a castle anymore," he said, and this time it wasn't a metaphor. "It's a shelter. It's a strategy. We have crowned Ben in silence. Not with metals or titles, but with time. With trust. With every decision we didn't make for him." He turned to look at her. "And now we step back." Annemarie didn't argue. "Yes," she said. "We do."

He sat finally. The chair creaked, not from age but from weight. The weight of someone who had carried power for too long, not just for Denmark, but for the sake of his family. "You know," he said, his voice quieter now, "I don't think Ben even realises what kind of crown he's wearing." Annemarie smiled, not warmly, but knowingly. "That's why he wears it well," she said. "The ones who look for the crown are never worthy of it." She took another sip, then added, "And he never wanted it in the first place." Kendrick stared at his untouched cup. "Neither did I."

They sat in stillness. The air carried the distant sound of Silje's footsteps as she returned to her post by the hall. Clara's voice echoed faintly from the water room—sharp, directive, focused. Tobias's laugh followed briefly, then silence again. Everything was in motion. Every person in the castle moved around Ben and Isla like gears in a machine that refused to rust. Kendrick folded his hands together. "The moment those babies are born, everything changes. We both know it. Two new heirs. It's not just a family milestone. It's a shift in legacy."

Annemarie stared out the window again. "And yet," she said, "we're still here. Quietly watching, quietly moving. We're not kings or queens, Kendrick. We're the bricks. The foundation." Kendrick leaned forward. "But someone's chipped at the wall," he said sharply. "And it wasn't one of us." She didn't reply. She didn't have to. They both knew what Oscar had done. And what it meant. It wasn't just betrayal. It was treason. Not in some poetic, overblown way, but by the legal statutes of the Danish Monarchy. Oscar had outed a reigning monarch in hiding. In Danish law, there was no ambiguity there.

"Soccer's not played in the castle," Kendrick said suddenly, eyes narrowing with memory. "Not once. Not ever." Annemarie raised a brow. "What brought that on?" He shook his head. "Just a line Ben always repeated. This place isn't for games. The game stays on the pitch." His tone turned. "Oscar broke that line. He brought the game into the house." Annemarie stared into her mug. "And now we don't get to be anonymous anymore."

Kendrick pushed back his chair and stood again. "They're going to want a statement. They're going to hound him. But we won't let them through." Annemarie remained seated. "He'll speak when it's time." Kendrick gave a firm nod. "And until then," he said, "we watch the walls."

She stood and followed him to the door. "The real shift won't come when the twins are born," she said as he turned the handle. "It'll come when Ben decides he's done being quiet." Kendrick didn't speak. He just looked at her, steady and serious. Then opened the door, and walked out into the hallway.

The Castle Doctor entered with quiet precision, her notes folded neatly into the sleeve of her coat. She never brought a clipboard anymore—Isla once called it a medieval slab. Instead, she carried everything in memory, smooth and crisp, like her voice. The medical bay had long been replaced with a private room beside the en suite bath, a room never marked with a sign or brass plate. She didn't ask to enter the bedroom. She knew this was the hour the Queen—Isla—was still resting. Her heels barely touched the tile, and when she looked at Ben, she offered nothing but a nod. Not every moment needed commentary. She walked straight to Isla's bedside, laid her hand gently on the curve of her abdomen, and waited for the next flutter.

Outside the room, Ben stood at the doorframe. He didn't fidget. He didn't pace. He simply watched. He had learned from Sørensen how to keep still in times like this. How to breathe from the diaphragm, not the chest, and how to listen beyond walls. Isla's breath was steady. The doctor checked her blood pressure. Normal. Slight elevation from yesterday, but nothing unordinary for a woman in her final week. The babies were still. No rolling, no kicking—only subtle movement that told the doctor exactly what she needed to know. Two heartbeats. Rhythmic, full, unwavering. She turned slightly toward Ben and gave the smallest of smirks.

"They're ready," she said, her voice like the snap of a curtain cord. "We just wait."

Ben gave one single nod in return. He didn't speak. The doctor understood that the quiet meant he was calculating, measuring, waiting for the variables to move into place. Not fear. Not nerves. Simply strategy. She always respected that about him. Kendrick had told her once, long ago, "Ben doesn't panic. He builds."

In the hallway beyond, the soft click of tinted windows settling into place gave off a faint mechanical hum. The new installation had been completed that morning. Sørensen had insisted on it. Already, two drones had been spotted, and one—unlucky, but deserved—was taken out with the same handmade slingshot Sørensen had received from Ben two days ago. Sørensen didn't need technology. He needed a vantage point and silence. His preferred post was the tower window just off the northwest corridor. He didn't crouch. He leaned, always in full view of the open pane, never afraid to be seen. One drone tried twice. It wouldn't try again.

Inside the room, the Castle Doctor returned to her corner. She picked up the last of her medical kit, sterilized a new thermometer, and recorded the current temperature of the birthing suite. It had been requested that no water be poured until the contractions began. The tub sat in perfect readiness, dry, polished, and clean, not exaggerated in its preparation. Just clean. Not sterile like a hospital, but ready like a home. Tobias had handled it once, then left it alone. No scrubbing twice, no obsessive cloths. This was Denmark, not Western neurosis.

Kendrick walked down the hallway at a slow clip, coffee in hand. He hadn't spoken much that morning, not even to Annemarie. The last words from the outer city still rang in his ears— Oscar's betrayal. A name once called in childhood play. Oscar had been close to Ben. Not just close—family by default, the kind of kin made by soccer nets and late-night pizza orders in the city square. Oscar had known everything. He was never meant to tell. But the world outside offered desperation and quick cash. And for some, that was enough to commit treason.

Ben didn't dwell on Oscar. Not now. His focus stayed with Isla. But Kendrick's mind lingered. He had spoken to Oscar's father. There was guilt in his voice. There always was when fathers failed to teach loyalty. And in this castle, loyalty wasn't something requested—it was required. Oscar would never be allowed back through the gates. Not now. Not ever.

The doctor placed her last instrument on the tray. Her coat folded neatly again at her elbow. She looked once more at Isla, then back at Ben. "She's strong. So are they," she said. "I'll return in twelve hours."

Ben didn't move. His eyes followed her as she left the room. Then he turned toward the window. The clouds were gathering above the city—those low-lying ones that looked like they had stories to tell. Clara had once drawn clouds like that. He still had the sketch in one of his books.

From the hallway, Clara's voice could be heard giving instructions. She wasn't barking orders. She was gently correcting the placement of linens, ensuring no towels would be in reach of accidental spills. She wasn't obsessive. She was ready. Like everyone in the Castle. Ben turned once more toward Isla, and for a moment, allowed himself the smallest breath of relief. One week ago, everything had been quiet. One week from now, everything would be different. But tonight, it was still. And in that stillness, he stood watch.

There was a mild clatter just outside the bedroom door, not loud enough to cause alarm, but enough to make Ben glance sideways. Clara pushed the door open with her back, hands occupied by a small wooden tray that carried a plate of toast, a dish of soft apple slices, and a cup of lukewarm milk that had been stirred, not steamed. She said nothing at first, just looked at Isla with a smile that held too much weight for a girl her age. She crossed the room, set the tray on Isla's lap, and gently pulled the blankets higher around her waist. Isla gave her a tired nod, though her eyes were clear, watchful, and slightly amused.

Tobias followed closely behind, balancing a ceramic bowl in one hand and waving the other in front of his face as though regretting the decision to bring it. The smell arrived before he did—garlic, onion, and something else no one could identify. He raised the bowl like a cursed offering and announced, "My soup is here. It's a taste of culinary brilliance. You'll weep for joy or other reasons, I suppose."

Isla stared at the bowl and didn't even attempt politeness. Her brow furrowed, and her nose crinkled like a reflex from childhood. "Tobias," she said slowly, "is it breathing?" Ben didn't laugh, not audibly, but his face twitched, and his mouth pressed together in the way it always did when he was holding back. Clara had no such restraint; her laughter came in a rush, gentle but sincere, the kind that only people raised together could share without explanation.

As the bowl approached her bedside, Isla snatched a pillow and threw it directly at Tobias's chest, catching him mid-step. The soup wobbled dangerously but held. He caught the pillow without flinching and said, "I take that as a vote of confidence," setting the bowl down with theatrical reverence before withdrawing toward the hallway. "If you change your mind," he added, "you'll find me not far. Possibly crying."

Clara shook her head and slid the bowl further away from Isla. She picked up a slice of toast and handed it over without a word. Isla accepted it, her fingers curling around the edge more gently than expected. "Thanks, Clara," she said, her voice even. "This is the only thing in this room that doesn't smell like regret."

Ben stepped forward then, not from obligation but instinct. He reached across the tray, pulled the glass of milk toward Isla's side, and adjusted the napkin that had begun to slip. His silence wasn't heavy—just necessary. There were no declarations to be made, not here. This wasn't a political moment. It was domestic, and it was real. And it was his favourite kind of moment.

"Eat slow," Ben said finally, his voice low, rough from not speaking for a while. "But eat." Isla nodded. She knew better than to argue. If he had said it, it wasn't a suggestion. He never forced, but he never backed down either. She bit into the toast, and the room went quiet for just long enough to feel like safety was possible.

From the hallway came a faint murmur, likely Sørensen speaking to someone near the entrance. No sharp voices. No surprises. Clara glanced at the door, then at Ben, then back at Isla. She stayed close. She didn't ask questions. She'd already lived through enough years in this castle to understand the rhythms of silence.

Tobias returned five minutes later with a bowl of chicken soup that had more promise. He didn't announce it. He didn't need to. He simply replaced the cursed garlic concoction with the newer version and raised both eyebrows at Isla. She sniffed it cautiously and didn't throw another pillow. That was progress. "This one smells edible," she admitted. "Better."

"I'll take that as a Michelin star," Tobias replied, folding his arms and pretending to take a bow. Then he turned to Ben and added, "You'll thank me later. Or never. Either works." Ben nodded once, only slightly, then resumed his quiet observation of Isla, his gaze drifting only occasionally toward the window, where the tinted glass reflected nothing but the room's warm light.

There was something about this room—about the way it held them all—that made even the simplest meal feel like ritual. Every movement was softened by the awareness that things would not be this still again. Every sip and every bite was held longer in the mouth, not because it tasted better, but because it mattered.

Isla managed a few spoonfuls before setting the bowl aside. She wasn't weak, just full of thought. The children within her shifted, and she reached for Ben's hand without looking up. He took it, folded her fingers into his, and said nothing. Clara pulled the blanket over Isla's knees again, tucking the corner with almost maternal precision.

From outside came a whistle—one of Sørensen's signals. Not urgent, not alarming. Just a mark of movement beyond the gates. Kendrick would handle it. Everyone knew their place. Everyone trusted the rest to do their part. It was strange to eat toast and soup in such conditions, but here, in this castle, nothing had ever been normal. And no one minded.

Clara picked up the tray and excused herself, not needing permission. Tobias winked at Isla, then disappeared behind her. Ben remained by the bedside. He wasn't moving until Isla slept. Even then, he wouldn't go far. His appetite was gone, but not for food—only for the silence that followed the fall of peace. He hated the wait. He always had.

When the door clicked softly behind Clara, Isla turned to him and asked, "Do you think they'll remember any of this?" Her voice was quiet, nearly drowned by the wind pressing faintly against the windows. "The babies?" he asked. She nodded. "I hope not," he said. "But I hope we do."

The quiet outside Isla's room wasn't suspicious, just strange. It was the kind of stillness that carried intent—childlike, clumsy, and doomed to fail. Ben noticed it first. His eyes flicked to the door, where the faintest of shadows betrayed the presence of several small feet. He said nothing. Nor did Isla. She tilted her head toward the wall as though listening to a story only the Castle could tell. The air was thick with something not quite tension, but certainly not stillness.

Then came the first sound—a long, high-pitched note that began in defiance and ended in shame. It echoed too perfectly through the hallway and bounced off the bedroom door like a confession. It was unmistakably a fart, and not the timid kind. A declaration, bold and haunting. From outside came a flurry of shuffling, the distinct sound of socks on polished wood, and the muffled gasp of children attempting to hide their joy.

There was a pause, just long enough to create the illusion that maybe that was the end of it. It wasn't. A second fart arrived with less grace but more power. It cut through the hallway like a blade of embarrassment, followed by one small voice whispering, "That wasn't me." Another child hissed, "Yes, it was," and then a third voice broke in, "Stop blaming me!" They were unraveling.

Tobias, who had been seated at the foot of the hallway bench with a tray of stacked towels, didn't move his head. His voice came flat, dry, and perfectly timed. "That's two. Don't go for a third." It wasn't a warning. It was prophecy. Every child froze. Ben glanced at Isla, whose eyes had already narrowed with suppressed laughter. She covered her mouth and turned her face to the side, her shoulders shaking in silence. Clara, just outside the room, closed her eyes and sighed as though bargaining with a higher power that children simply wouldn't listen to.

Then came the unmistakable scent—the slow, creeping wave that confirmed what they all feared. Tobias stood, not hurried, just resigned, and followed the trail to the smallest among them. One of the twins in training pants had gone from mischievous accomplice to biological hazard. It wasn't just gas. It was the real thing, and it had arrived with force. Tobias crouched, inspected the evidence, and said only, "Pull-Up Bomb." His voice was flat. "Fully armed. Fully deployed."

The rest of the children scattered like leaves caught in a windstorm. Their shrieks were stifled, feet slapping against the hallway tiles, slipping over each other in their hurry to flee. None wanted to be caught near the blast zone. Tobias, meanwhile, had already removed the offending Pull-Up and was performing the royal change with quiet dignity and the same precision he would've used to clean a clock. There was no gagging. No commentary. He'd done this before, and worse.

Ben exhaled slowly and turned back toward Isla. "There it is," he said. "The calm didn't last." Isla was laughing now, out loud, unashamed. Her head rested against the pillows, her face red with the effort of holding it back. She didn't try to stop it. Clara returned to the doorway, waved a hand in front of her face, and muttered something about needing a gas mask.

"Don't light a candle," Isla warned. "We'll all go down with the Castle." Even Ben had to laugh at that. It wasn't dignified. It wasn't regal. But it was right. These moments were the ones that stuck. The ones no crown could overshadow. They weren't raising heirs. They were raising children—real, unpredictable, gloriously imperfect children.

Tobias returned to the room five minutes later, fresh gloves in hand, a rag tucked into his waistband, and a bottle of citrus spray tucked beneath his arm. "All clear," he announced. "Stink, Stank, and Stunk have been eradicated. Peace is restored, for now." "Define 'peace,'" Ben said dryly.

Tobias pointed to the window. "As in, not in here." Then he dropped the rag into the bin and sat down, wiping his brow with theatrical flair. "One day," he muttered, "I'll write a memoir. 'Diapers and Diplomacy: My Life Behind the Wipes.' Bestseller, guaranteed." Clara tossed him a damp towel. "Call it 'Pull-Up Protocol.' Subtitle: When You're Outnumbered, Outwitted, and Outworn."

Outside, the children had returned to whispering. Whether it was strategy or simple joy was unclear. But the giggles were real, and the worst of the smell had faded. Isla rested her head back and closed her eyes, a smile still playing at the edge of her lips. "They don't stop, do they?" she asked softly.

Ben answered with a kiss to her forehead. "Not until they sleep. And even then, only sometimes." She opened one eye. "So what you're saying is... we'll be hearing fart jokes at our children's coronation?" He thought about it, nodded. "Probably. And I'm fine with that." So was she.

The room had settled into a warm quiet, where only the faint hum of castle air vents and the distant shuffling of feet outside the door marked the passage of time. Isla sat propped with a firm pillow tucked behind her lower back, her palms resting gently over the swell of her abdomen. The tension in her shoulders had lessened from earlier, the early tightening no longer pressing against her spine. Ben stood beside her, not hovering but near enough to reach out, always steady in his silent observance. The atmosphere felt almost sacred, as if they were waiting for something they could not quite name—something inevitable and approaching, but for now, mercifully still.

Then it came—not a jolt, not the sharp jab of a restless foot or elbow—but a slow, deliberate turn. Isla inhaled softly, not from discomfort, but from the strange elegance of the sensation. A gentle undulation followed, like one twin stretching from shoulder to toe while the other adjusted in response. It was no longer movement for movement's sake. This had intention. This was language. Ben placed his hand upon her belly and felt it, the liquid resistance of the womb shifting beneath his palm. He didn't speak. He didn't have to. The smile that tugged at his mouth, quiet and full, said everything he needed to say.

For a moment, neither of them moved. No one entered. No voices broke through. Even Clara, who had been setting fresh towels near the tub earlier, remained just outside the line of sight. The silence was not absence, but presence—filled with breath and meaning and the intangible weight of knowing. The twins were aware. They were listening. Somehow, it seemed that they, too, were taking stock of what lay ahead. Ben drew a deeper breath and left his hand where it was, cupping the shape of his children, as though promising them something wordless and true.

Then, down the hallway, a sound cracked through the stillness like a sneeze at a funeral—loud, sudden, and followed by an unmistakable groan. Tobias was shouting something, but it was too muffled to understand at first. Footsteps scrambled. Someone—not one of the staff—was running, and then a small yelp was heard just outside the bedroom. Ben didn't flinch. He waited until the chaos settled before glancing sideways, his expression equal parts curiosity and dread.

The bedroom door opened cautiously. Clara peeked in but didn't enter. "It's Linus," she said, her voice dry. "Too many cupcakes. Too much milk. It's everywhere." She didn't elaborate. She didn't need to. Isla sighed, gently, and Ben raised one brow before turning back to her with a kind of resigned amusement. "We should've stopped him after cupcake number four," he muttered under his breath, shaking his head.

From the far end of the corridor, a louder grumble echoed—Tobias, clearly not impressed, calling for extra towels and muttering something about hazard pay. The distinct sloshing of a mop bucket followed. Linus had managed not only to vomit down the hall but also directly onto Tobias's favourite socks. The ones with the tiny whales on them. Isla chuckled despite herself. "That poor man," she whispered, her eyes watery from laughing too hard without trying. "He's changed more pull-up disasters and cleaned more child-related fluids than most field medics."

Ben smiled without humour. "He says it builds character. I say it builds immunity," he replied, finally stepping away from the bed to shut the door quietly behind Clara. When he returned, Isla's eyes were still fixed on her stomach. Another small movement passed beneath her skin, and she blinked slowly as though blinking away a dream. "They're going to come soon, aren't they?" she asked, not really looking for an answer.

"They're preparing," Ben said, carefully choosing his words, resting one hand again on her belly. "The same way we are. They know something's changing. They're trying to make space." Isla nodded but said nothing, closing her eyes for a moment, letting the motion fade before speaking again. "I wonder what they'll look like." Her voice was soft now, uncertain, the quiet musing of a mother suspended in the between.

Ben leaned closer. "Like you," he said simply, and kissed her forehead. She smiled weakly, touched by the gentleness, though her breathing hinted at an internal tightness. Not contractions. Not yet. Just nerves. The kind that built in quiet corners before storms. She knew the signs now. Her body was giving them time. But not much.

Down the hall, Tobias's voice rang out again—sarcastic, gruff, but amused. "I've been hit, Isla. Direct contact. Centre mass. Milk and cupcakes. Who even lets kids mix dairy with sugar?!" Clara was laughing now too, barely hiding it behind a sleeve. Isla couldn't help herself. She laughed again. Short, careful breaths. But full. Full of life. Full of motherhood. Ben's shoulders relaxed slightly.

Back on the bed, Isla shifted and looked around the room. Everything was prepared, but no one was rushing. No one panicked. This was the lull before the sprint, the drawing of breath before the plunge. It was a small chapter, held in warmth and worry, stitched together by steady hands and dumb jokes, and the absolute certainty that what came next could not be undone.

Isla looked again at her husband, then out toward the hallway. "We need to buy Tobias new socks," she said, her voice still cracking with laughter. "He's going to need more than character if that happens again." Ben nodded slowly. "We'll get him armour," he said. "Or an umbrella. Whichever is cheaper." They both smiled, but the weight hadn't left the room. They were ready. Almost. Almost.

Tobias had always been the type who never really clocked out. Not in his mind, not with his hands. Even when the lights were low and the castle had grown quiet in its expectant hush, he moved through the rooms like a mechanic in a silent hangar, checking systems, tightening lids, adjusting levers no one else noticed. While most would've taken the night to rest—perhaps on a chair, or in a cot just outside the water room—he remained awake, his hands busied with a small blade and a row of half-carved wooden blocks that had once belonged to the storage shed beneath the back stairs. He'd smoothed them first. Then measured them. Then whittled them, one by one, into something he called 'comfort creatures' though no one had asked him to.

The shape was peculiar. A duck, sort of. The beak was too short. The tail too square. But in his mind, they were waterfowl nonetheless. One for the girl. One for the boy. One for when one duck gets lost in the blankets and must be found again. Tobias didn't overthink the symbolism. He didn't say a word, actually, until Ben found him seated at the kitchen table with wood shavings caught in the cuffs of his sleeves and a line of half-finished birds fanned out like soldiers awaiting inspection. Ben didn't speak at first either. He simply leaned against the doorframe and watched his friend working beneath the lamplight.

"Why ducks?" he finally asked, more curious than anything. "They're water babies," Tobias replied without looking up. "They need ducks." That was all. He wiped the blade on a folded rag and kept carving, as though the logic required no further elaboration. Ben almost said something in return, but decided against it. The moment was simple, honest. It didn't need dressing.

What Tobias didn't mention—what no one outside of Isla perhaps truly understood—was that the carving kept him steady. These things, this kind of preparation, this vigilance—these were how he stayed calm. Because that night, like so many before it, had turned sour in ways only a veteran of domestic combat would understand. He had changed eight diapers before midnight. Three of them belonged to his own children. The others were shared across the Castle's extended little crew—nieces, nephews, honorary cousins. And two of them, as he had warned Ben with deadpan gravity, were not of this world.

"Chemical warfare," he whispered to himself after the second catastrophe, nose half-buried in a damp towel soaked in peppermint oil. "Weapon-grade." He even drew the hazard symbol on the diaper bin with a black marker, as if future historians would need reference. He never named the culprit. Not because he didn't know. But because certain crimes deserve discretion. And because he still had a small shred of mercy left in him—though barely.

Isla, when she'd heard him muttering under his breath while carrying the offensive nappies to the laundry chute, had offered a smirk of solidarity and a simple word of thanks. He shrugged it off, of course. That's what Tobias did. He shrugged off gratitude like it was lint on a sleeve. But it stayed with him, that moment. The way she looked at him not just as a helper, but as a fixture in this household. Someone dependable. Someone who could handle the mess.

Ben wandered into the kitchen again an hour later and found that Tobias had added paint to the ducks. Pale yellow for one. Seafoam blue for the other. And eyes. Big, sleepy eyes. The kind that made a child believe the duck could blink if only you looked long enough. He didn't say much this time either, just gave a nod and stood silently for a moment as Tobias rinsed his brush in a shallow bowl of warm water. There was something deeply satisfying in these quiet exchanges. No one trying to be impressive. Just necessary.

He took a breath, wiped his hands, and set the last duck on the ledge above the sink. Outside, the moon was drifting higher, inching over the castle roofline in a shy crawl. Clara passed through once with fresh pillowcases. Silje gave a status report from her hallway post without raising her voice. Kendrick had checked in briefly. Sørensen was still on roof patrol with his slingshot—having taken down two drones before dinner and reportedly swearing at a third. Everyone had their role. And Tobias, for all his aversion to sentimentality, found comfort in that.

As he made his way to the nursery to stack the ducklings on the windowsill, he stopped in front of the mirror in the hall. He looked at his reflection for a long while—eyelids heavy, shirt wrinkled, the faint smudge of garlic soup near his collarbone from the incident earlier. And then he laughed. Not loudly. Just a single, short exhale. The kind you let out when you've survived something ridiculous and lived to tell about it.

Back in the kitchen, the wood scraps were swept up. The rag had been folded neatly. Everything was in order. But Tobias didn't sleep. Not that night. He sat in a chair near the end of the corridor, back straight, hands clasped, and listened to the hum of the castle breathe around him. Parenthood, he thought—not just the babies, but all of it. The farts, the fevers, the art projects and projectile soup. This was it. This was the job. He'd signed up without knowing it. And he wouldn't trade it for anything. Not even a night off.

In the gentle dark of early morning, with the castle hushed and the halls fallen into their long silence, Isla's breathing slowed into a deeper rhythm. Her head shifted slightly against the pillow, one hand resting on her belly where the twins lay still. In the quiet between contractions, her body took the reprieve it needed, and her mind wandered somewhere older than pain—somewhere remembered. Ben sat nearby, watching her features soften. Then came a whisper, the kind that wasn't meant for anyone's ears but fate's. "Dewey... 929.1," she murmured. "British genealogy, Kent archives... shelf fourteen." Ben straightened, his brow furrowed gently. Her lips moved again. "Gibb... Islay... Latin registers..." Her voice trailed back into breath.

It caught him off guard. Not the dreaming—she often whispered when in deep rest—but the precision of it. Names of authors. Shelf numbers. Catalogue codes only the most seasoned researchers or secret-keepers would recite in sleep. His memory reached back without hesitation. The old reading room in Kent. The long oak tables. The tall windows that threw long shadows across their notes. He remembered how small her glasses had been on her face, and how impossibly fast she had found the Hungarian cross-reference in the third ledger of migration maps. That was the day. The day the map began.

Ben leaned forward, brushing a stray strand of hair from her forehead. "Do you still remember that day?" he asked softly, unsure if she'd respond. Her eyes fluttered, and though still caught in half-sleep, she smiled. "That was the day everything began," she said. The words were not grand or rehearsed. They came like a page from an old volume long overdue to be opened again. Ben nodded once, quietly. He knew it too.

The memory came back in colour. Not just the place, but the feeling. That first day at the Kent Archives—how small he had felt at the time, yet how certain he was that he belonged among the names written on parchment. His father, Jeff, had taken him there, encouraging him to trace the whispers of his family line through brittle documents and long-forgotten seals. Ben had found a rhythm in the turning of pages, the stacking of scrolls, the silent reverence of old names nearly erased. He had felt the weight of it all even then.

She had appeared just as the light changed in the room, her sneakers soft against the marble floor, her arms full of books, her hair not yet braided as it often was in later years. Isla had announced herself without introduction, her tone curious but not sharp. "You're in the genealogical register section," she'd said. "Most people don't look at those unless they're trying to prove something really old." He'd stared, blinking, not knowing whether to be impressed or intimidated. She'd seemed to know everything already. But it wasn't arrogance. It was clarity. Isla had always been like that—clear.

Ben had been drawn to her instantly, but he couldn't name it at the time. It wasn't love, not then. It was alignment. As though someone had placed the two of them on the same line in a ledger and drawn it forward without asking permission. She'd asked what they were researching. He'd told her. Family names. The kind that didn't always appear in the places you'd expect. Her eyes lit up then, the same way they did now when the twins kicked, or when Clara solved something without being prompted. That was Isla. She had always understood what wasn't said.

Jeff had watched the exchange carefully. Later, he would admit that he noticed something even then. A moment forming. A map widening. Not just of lineage, but of purpose. Isla hadn't just read names—she translated patterns. She spotted migratory logic buried in four-hundred-year-old pages. And when she found the Gibb line crossing into Harvick blood in the 1800s, she didn't flinch. She pointed. "That's where I fit," she had said. And Ben, though unsure at the time, nodded without hesitation. It made sense. Even then.

Isla stirred now, shifting in the bed. Her eyes opened slowly. "I was there," she whispered. "Back at the table." Ben reached for her hand, clasping it gently. "I know." Her voice was soft, but certain. "I never forgot the ledger with the seal from Kilnaish. It was worn along the top. The gold leaf had started to flake." Ben nodded again. "And the librarian who kept sneezing from the dust." Isla smiled faintly. "She said we were the youngest researchers she'd ever seen take a scroll seriously."

Outside the bedroom, the corridor remained still. Clara had stepped away to fold the last of the towels. Tobias was likely in the kitchen preparing something strange. And Kendrick, with Sørensen somewhere above, stood facing the moonlit windows, watching for movement, or shadows. But in here, in the room where the mother of the next heirs now remembered her first beginning, history folded itself inward. The line between past and present wove together without confusion.

Ben reached into the drawer beside the bed and removed a single photograph, folded twice but preserved. It was the one Isla had taken during their third visit to the library—a wide shot of the archival chamber with her notebook sprawled open across the table and Ben half-hidden behind a column of bound folios. She had written in the margin: "Where maps begin." He placed the photo beside her water glass and leaned closer. "You still believe we were meant to find each other?" he asked. Isla blinked slowly. "I don't believe it, Ben. I know it."

The air thickened just slightly, as it had all those years ago. A shift not in temperature but in recognition. The kind that settles over a home when something permanent has been named. Isla closed her eyes again and whispered into the dark, "They'll be readers, our children." Ben smiled. "And mapmakers." The castle didn't answer. It didn't need to. It had always known.

It started sometime around four in the morning, long before the city had stirred, long before Clara's second breath caught against Isla's shoulder. A light tapping against the glass window was the only hint at first, as though someone outside had gently tossed the petals of spring roses across the castle's tall panes. Ben heard it before he saw it. It wasn't a thunderstorm, nor the kind of coastal gale that made the gutter lines roar. This was different. This was the sound of something soft, slow, and relentless. Rain, endless and even, falling like an ancient lullaby across the rooftops of Rosenshavn.

He stood by the window, arms folded against his chest, not for warmth, but for containment. The room behind him was layered in breath: Isla's slower now, Clara's steadier, and somewhere deeper in the corridor, the sound of Tobias cursing gently under his breath as another diaper gave way to what he would later refer to as "biological warfare." But here, at the window, Ben stood alone. The rain was not something he feared. It was something he welcomed. It meant the noise of the world was quieted. It meant the world outside the castle would stay home. It meant time—if only for a moment—might stretch longer than it truly was.

Behind him, Isla shifted once, adjusting her blanket, her hand still resting atop her belly where the twins had grown restless through the night. No sharp kicks. No sudden turns. Just movement—soft and slow, like the weather. Clara lay beside her, knees tucked close, breathing quietly. She had offered to stay until daylight. Ben hadn't objected. Neither had Isla. The three of them had fallen into a rhythm that didn't require speaking. Clara was their daughter in every way but biology. And now, she would become the eldest of a new line. It wasn't something anyone in the room said aloud—but they all knew it.

Tobias passed the doorway without saying a word. He didn't need to. He had a look about him—half warrior, half martyr, holding what could only be described as a disaster wrapped in a small blanket. The expression on his face was familiar now. A mix of fatigue, disbelief, and comic resignation. Moments later, the soft click of a door closing down the hall told Ben everything he needed to know. Another one. Likely Linus again. Cupcakes had not been a wise choice. And milk on top of sugar had never been a known peacemaker in the war of digestive truce.

Ben didn't smile, but the corner of his mouth tilted. Parenthood, he thought, wasn't a role—they were born into it by small, sticky, unavoidable incidents. Tobias had become something of a soldier in this nightly battle. He called it "Diaper Doody," a name Ben had at first rolled his eyes at, but which Clara now used regularly and with a quiet smirk that suggested she understood how few people in the world could wear that title with the same worn pride Tobias did. And tonight, from the sound of it, there had been no clean victories.

The rain strengthened slightly, tapping in quicker rhythm now. Ben pressed two fingers lightly against the windowpane. Cold glass met warm skin. He didn't flinch. His mind was elsewhere. Not in worry, but in preparation. These were the hours that built the memory. These were the hours people later forgot in the retelling, when everyone wanted the highlights—the names, the titles, the photos, the crying. But this? This was the real story. Soft rain before dawn. Quiet breathing in a warm room. A castle stilled not by decree, but by love.

He glanced back. Isla was awake now, though only barely. Her eyes were open, but not fully focused. He could tell from the way her fingers moved across the blanket, tracing invisible lines. She was likely dreaming still, or remembering again. She'd said something about the library earlier—Kent, the ledgers, her grandfather. Ben hadn't asked for more. He didn't need to. Their beginnings were folded neatly inside one another's. The details were all still there, tucked between their breaths.

A low thud from downstairs—nothing urgent, likely a cupboard door closing—reminded him the castle was still alive. It was always alive. The rain may have softened the mood, but life still pushed forward. Somewhere on the lower level, someone was warming a bottle. On the second floor, Sørensen would be loading another slingshot pellet for the next drone to try its luck. And just past the servant stairs, Kendrick was likely reading the quiet riot act to someone on his phone about Oscar's betrayal. But none of that mattered here.

Ben let the curtains fall gently back across the window and returned to Isla's side. She didn't say anything. She didn't need to. Her eyes followed him as he lowered himself back onto the edge of the bed. "It's raining," he said softly. She nodded. "I know." Clara didn't stir, but her hand reached lightly for Isla's. Ben watched the way their fingers folded together, and for a brief, beautiful second, he saw it—the full circle beginning. Not in ceremony. Not in royal decree. But in this room, with these hands, and this child waiting just beneath the surface of time. "Think they'll like the rain?" Ben asked. Isla smiled, eyes closing again. "I think they'll remember it."

The Castle Doctor arrived without ceremony, her coat damp from the walk between the staff wing and the main corridor. She didn't knock. She didn't need to. Tobias had already opened the door for her and nodded once before stepping aside. The hallway outside had quieted to little more than a shadow. Rain still traced soft lines down the windowpanes, and somewhere far off, a child's laughter faded into a sigh. Inside, however, the silence was tight, waiting, bound like thread through the seams of an unfinished garment. The room felt poised.

Isla turned her head slightly on the pillow as the doctor entered. She didn't sit up. She didn't need to. The doctor crouched near her side with a softness more reverent than clinical. The blood pressure cuff was already coiled in her bag, her stethoscope warm from the coat pocket. She worked in practiced silence, not interrupting Isla's breathing rhythm, not asking too many questions. This wasn't her first visit tonight. Nor her last. She had the face of someone who understood birth for what it truly was—not just a beginning, but a battleground.

Ben stood against the wall, arms folded, but no longer rigid. His eyes flicked once to the hallway, then back to Isla, then back to the doctor. "They've slowed," he said quietly, not as a question. The doctor nodded, tightening the strap gently around Isla's arm. "Not today," she said with absolute certainty. There was no disappointment in her tone. No drama. Just the plain truth. The contractions had shifted, but not opened. The twins were waiting. The storm had not yet landed.

Clara didn't speak. She stood near the window again, watching the drops race each other toward the sill. She'd taken off her socks earlier, preferring to feel the cool wood floor beneath her feet. It grounded her. Every few moments, she glanced back to Isla's face, then to the doctor's hands. Her trust in the adults was full, but not blind. She needed to see it for herself—the pulse lines, the colour of Isla's lips, the steady rise of her chest. It wasn't worry. It was instinct.

The doctor packed slowly, methodically. Every item had its place. She left the cuff on the side table, clean and ready for tomorrow. "You should sleep," she said to Ben. "Both of you." Ben didn't answer. Neither did Isla. The doctor gave one final glance toward the monitor—nothing irregular, nothing urgent—then gave Clara a nod as she passed. A quiet message transferred silently between them. The girl would keep watch. She always did. Clara returned the nod and shifted her stance near the foot of the bed.

But Ben didn't move toward the bed. Not yet. His phone buzzed once in his coat pocket, the sound unusually loud against the hush. He pulled it out, checked the screen, then pressed the device to his ear without leaving the room. "Yes," he said flatly. He listened. His hand dropped slowly to his side. "Are you certain?" Another pause. "And you're sure it wasn't someone else?" A longer silence followed. Then, quietly but with no hesitation, "All right. I understand."

He didn't need to say the name aloud. Clara had already turned to him, eyes narrowed, understanding blooming across her face before the words were spoken. The doctor had stepped into the corridor now, her silhouette framed by the soft wall sconces. "It was Oscar," Ben said finally, not bitter, not loud. Just true. Isla closed her eyes. Not in pain. But in comprehension. She knew what that meant. So did Clara.

Ben stepped toward the hallway. The call had already ended, but the decision was not yet made. Or perhaps it had been long ago. His steps were quiet, nearly soundless on the hardwood. He dialled again. This time to the local Copenhagen police liaison—a direct contact maintained quietly by the House of Rosenshavn for matters like this. Not royal matters. Legal ones. The conversation was brief. Professional. Oscar's name was submitted. The evidence confirmed. The leak was no longer speculation.

"He's in custody," Ben said upon returning. His voice hadn't changed. His posture hadn't shifted. But something beneath his skin seemed to settle. Not in triumph. In resolution. Kendrick had warned him this day would come. Sørensen had prepared him. Tobias had made jokes about it for years. But none of it had stopped the sting from landing where it hurt most: betrayal by someone who had once known his laugh. Oscar had been more than a teammate. He'd been a fixture in the landscape of Ben's childhood. Now he was a footnote in a courtroom transcript.

Isla opened her eyes again. "Do they know why?" she asked softly. Ben didn't answer right away. Clara moved first, pulling the blanket slightly higher over Isla's shoulder, then turned toward the doorway. "They will," Ben said at last. "He was laid off. Needed money. Sold the story to a reporter who didn't know what they were holding." Tobias stepped into the room again, now free of any immediate diaper disaster. "And now?" he asked.

Ben exhaled, slowly. "Now it's done. And we move forward." The castle didn't breathe easier. It simply exhaled through the bones of its walls. The rain continued. Soft. Relentless. Clara checked the water room again without being asked. Tobias dimmed the hall lights and muttered something about needing sleep, but knowing full well he'd never get it. And Isla, tucked between dreams, turned toward Ben once more, her hand finding his in the dark. The castle did not sleep that night. Not fully. But it waited. Quietly. Firmly. The way it always had.

The official charge came just after midnight. High treason under Danish Royal Law—formally filed, witnessed, and confirmed by court authorities. Oscar had not resisted. In truth, there was little left of him to resist with. He had sat quietly when questioned. He had offered no denial when asked. The bank transaction was there. The transfer to a known media outlet. The conversation caught on tape. The silence that followed was not one of shame—it was exhaustion. Oscar knew what he had done. He had done it willingly. And now he would pay for it. The papers would not be kind. Neither would the court.

Ben did not ask to speak with him. There would be no confrontation. No private moment. No tearful reckoning between once-friends. That part of their story had ended two years ago when Oscar left the city and chose ambition over loyalty. Ben stayed where he was—on the bed beside Isla, one hand resting lightly over her belly as the smallest of the twins pressed against his palm. A flutter, not a kick. Just enough to say, I'm here. Isla exhaled slowly. Her breath, even in sleep, was steady. Ben watched her chest rise and fall, counting each rise as if it might teach him something he didn't yet know.

The castle breathed too, but not in the obvious way. It was in the steady click of the radiator near the foot of the wall, the shift of wood in the beams above, the faint hum of the wireless system syncing with the security servers two floors down. Everything was in place. Locked. Protected. Ben had made sure of that. Sørensen had verified it again before slipping out for his final perimeter check. There were no more drones. The tinted windows held. Nothing moved outside except for the branches of the elms in the garden. And even they were gentle tonight.

Tobias had fallen asleep half-upright in a chair pulled too close to the changing table. His arms were folded. His mouth hung slightly open. A damp towel sat over one leg. The man had changed six diapers since dinner—four of which had been categorized as "biological hazard events" by his own sarcastic classification system. No one had disputed the language. Not even Silje, who had offered him gloves and refused to make eye contact. He earned his sleep. Even if it came sitting up.

Clara lay curled at the foot of the bed, not quite a child anymore, but not yet willing to leave her post. Her head rested against the woodwork, eyes closed, blanket wrapped tightly around her shoulders. She'd helped Isla into a more comfortable position hours earlier. She'd fetched extra socks. She'd warmed a heat pad with the old rice sack in the microwave off the main hall. She hadn't spoken in almost forty minutes. Not because she was asleep—but because she didn't want to break the spell. There was something sacred here. Not religious. Just true.

Silje stood by the door as she always did. Her hands were not folded. She didn't lean. She stood as one who had already decided where her place would be, and found peace in standing still. Her eyes watched the hall without blinking, her focus intact. She had cleared every staff person hours earlier. No one unfamiliar had entered the wing. No packages remained unopened. No paper uninspected. When Tobias snored once, she did not flinch. When Clara stirred, she did not turn. She was the castle's final lock.

The Castle Doctor sat on a bench near the eastern wall, legs crossed, notes open. She held a steaming mug of tea in one hand—black, no sugar—and her pen in the other. Every once in a while, she'd glance up at Isla's face, then to Ben, then back to the charts. Her expression never changed. It was not clinical. It was not sentimental. It was a look of quiet knowing. She had been through sixty-two births in her professional life. This one, she knew, would mark her sixty-third. But she did not rush it. Births are not trains. They do not arrive on time. They arrive when called.

Ben shifted slightly, not wanting to wake Isla, but needing to check the time. The clock read 2:16 a.m. The rain had grown softer now, not harder. It hadn't stopped—it rarely did in Copenhagen this time of year—but it came in whispers instead of drumming now. The sound reminded him of the library where he first met Isla, where raindrops against stone arches made the air feel charged with electricity and mystery. It had rained that day too. Just like this. A book had fallen from the stack. She had caught it mid-air. Of course she had. That was who she was.

He wondered briefly if the world outside still believed he was no one. If the news had reached the other houses yet—the other royal lines scattered across the continent who pretended he was a rumour and not a reality. He wondered if they knew what Oscar had done. If they would watch now. Wait. React. The charge of high treason was not a whisper. It was a warning. One that did not disappear in the morning.

The files had already been sent to the Royal Legal Archives. Kendrick had reviewed them himself. The proof was clean. No trial was necessary. But one would be granted anyway. Because in Denmark, even betrayal earned its day in court. Ben respected that. Even if it hurt.

Isla stirred, murmured something too soft to catch. Her hand tightened over his. He didn't speak. He didn't need to. The castle held them. The breath of it was everywhere. In the way the doctor sipped her tea. In the way Silje did not blink. In the way Tobias had drooled just slightly down his chin. In the way Clara had curled like she did when she was seven, the day she called them Mommy and Daddy for the very first time.

And above all of it—the twins. Still not born. Still not ready. But moving. Waiting. Listening. They knew the rhythm of Isla's heartbeat by now. They knew the pressure of Ben's hand. They knew Tobias's voice. Clara's scent. Silje's silence. They knew the castle. Already. And two days from now, they would be here for good. But for tonight, they were still tucked within the stillness. And the storm had not yet come.

CHAPTER 6: THUNDERFARTS AND DIAPER BOMBS

"Even kings need air. And sometimes, all they get is the kind that's already been digested."

The air over Rosenshavn Castle carried a chill that smelled faintly of baked rye and lilacs. Ben stood behind the bedroom window, brushing the steam from the inside glass with the edge of his sleeve, watching Isla as she circled the courtyard garden. Her steps were slow, hands resting on her hips, chin tucked slightly downward in a meditative rhythm. She was not yet doubled over, not yet panting or screaming or clutching at railings. But she had entered the final week, and her womb—like the moon before a tide—was drawing its last swell toward arrival. She walked without complaint, arms swaying slightly. Her long hair had been tied up in a hurried plait that began to loosen near her shoulders. He loved her this way: quiet, observant, letting her body do what it knew how to do. She had done the math last night—eight months, three weeks exactly. Her time was near.

From behind the window glass, the distant sound of children's laughter rose up and rippled across the courtyard. A soccer ball flew through the morning like a comet, striking a rose bush near the north trellis, scattering petals like a brief flurry of pink snow. Ben blinked, rubbed the corner of his eye, and muttered something about trimming those branches before summer. Lukas was already barefoot, chasing the rebound with a triumphant yell. Emil Søren ran behind him, one sock missing, the other half folded down like a crumpled flag. The twins—Max-Leo and Peter Emil—shoved each other and shouted about cheating. No one knew the rules. No one ever did. They just ran, kicked, fell, shouted, and got grass stains they wouldn't scrub out for a week. Childhood, Ben thought, was loud—but honest.

Down below, Isla's pacing came to a halt near the tulip bed. Her hands slid to the small of her back, and she bent her knees slightly, then straightened again. It was not a cry or a groan that followed—but a single, unmistakable sound. A long, drawn-out, belly-deep rip that echoed off the stone courtyard walls and then bounced again off the east wing. There was no mistaking it. It was loud. Bold. Commanding. The fart had landed. The soccer game paused. Five heads turned. Even Lukas stopped mid-dribble, one toe frozen above the ball like a monument. No one spoke for two seconds. Then the giggles began.

Ben pulled open the window sash, leaned out with a hand to his mouth like a royal herald, and announced with theatrical grandeur, "Ladies and gentlemen, allow me to present—Her Royal Highness, Queen of the Stench!" The courtyard erupted. Children fell over each other. Lukas tumbled into the bushes. Emil Søren dropped to one knee like he'd been shot in the stomach. One of the neighbour boys coughed and pointed. Peter Emil shouted, "That was Mamma?" Isla stood perfectly still, hands on hips, a sly smile bending one corner of her mouth. "You're welcome," she said, and kept walking. Tobias, coming around the corner with a basket of freshly folded towels, laughed so hard he lost his balance and went down sideways behind the bench. The towels flew like pigeons.

"Down goes diaper duty!" shouted Axel Nielsen, who hadn't even been part of the match but arrived just in time to see Tobias flat on his back, clutching his ribs, crying with laughter. "Man down!" shouted someone else. A chorus of whooping and mocking declarations followed, each child trying to one-up the next with interpretations of the sound. "That was the Castle ghost!" "No, that was a dragon!" "No, it was the Queen's warning shot!" The children moved quickly from disbelief to mythology. It was as if a thunderclap had issued from their monarch and rewritten the laws of indoor etiquette forever. They would speak of this for years.

Ben leaned against the window ledge, shoulders shaking with laughter, trying to keep composure. He could barely hold his breath from the hilarity of it all. Every time he exhaled, another child mimicked the sound again. It had taken only seconds for Isla's bodily honesty to become the stuff of legend. He smiled down at her, beaming with pride. This was what made her a queen—not silence, not poise, not tip-toeing around bodily truths, but living out loud, even when your stomach gurgled and the world stopped spinning for a moment to hear you blow apart tradition. This family, he thought, was unlike any other.

Frederikke Andersen had appeared with her usual sketchpad, already drawing stick figures with jagged lines around Isla and comic-strip "toot" clouds drawn from the back of her skirt. She handed it to Lise Ava, who screamed with delight and fell into the grass with her knees pulled to her chest. "I'm keeping this forever," she declared. Vigga Gibb, never one to miss a chance to add commentary, said, "That was the best sound I've ever heard come out of a human." Even little Rasmus Mikkelsen was grinning, one hand pinched over his nose while he waved the other like a white flag. "She needs a gas station, not a hospital," he muttered.

Isla, unfazed, returned to her gentle pacing. She adjusted her plait as if nothing had happened, ignoring the full-volume uproar behind her. There was something sacred about it all—about living life without apology, about letting your body speak when it needed to, even if it sounded like a backfiring tractor. Tobias groaned from the gravel where he still lay, wheezing through his belly-laughs. "And I thought diaper bombs were the worst of it," he managed to say, wiping his eyes. "Now even the queen's involved? I quit." A soccer ball rolled past him and tapped his shoe.

Uncle Sørensen appeared near the eastern archway, leaning against a pillar with one eyebrow lifted and a cup of black coffee in his hand. He had heard everything. He said nothing. His silence was not judgment, only acknowledgement. Sørensen never commented on body humour. He considered it beneath his tactical training. Still, Ben saw the corner of his moustache twitch slightly. That was as close to a belly-laugh as the man allowed himself. He sipped his coffee and walked away without a word, leaving the children to their battle cries.

Astrid Elina peeked out from the parlour doors, holding a broom far too large for her. "Should I clean the air?" she asked with seriousness. Nobody answered. She walked into the centre of the courtyard, raised the broom like a ceremonial sceptre, and shouted, "I banish the fart ghost from these sacred lands!" The children screamed. Someone farted again. It was unclear who. It didn't matter anymore.

Ben returned inside, shaking his head and grabbing a towel to wipe the window sill. "One day," he said aloud to himself, "someone will write about this castle and never believe it." But that was the beauty of it. These were the stories no royal historian would dare record. These were the truths that made monarchy worth something.

And so, April fourteenth dawned in Rosenshavn with laughter, with bodily honesty, with farts that echoed against the arches and echoed still in the hearts of children. Isla's contractions had begun. Life would change tomorrow. But today—today was all thunderfarts and diaper bombs. And no one would ever forget who started it.

The soccer match resumed with all the seriousness of a World Cup final—until Max-Leo made one fatal misstep. He pivoted too hard on one foot while dodging a flying shirt (used as a goalpost), then twisted into an exaggerated wind-up to impress the neighbours. He launched his leg. The ball curved. His cheeks clenched. And then, a thunderous report split the spring air, ringing out like a ceremonial cannon from the Tower of London. Silence reigned for two heartbeats. Then chaos exploded. "Thunderfart!" screamed Lukas. "Thunderfart Champion!" echoed two more. Max-Leo fell to his knees, arms wide, eyes to the sky like he'd scored the golden goal of history.

From a second-floor window, someone tossed down an old plastic trophy from last year's family games—duct-taped, glittered, and clearly marked in Sharpie: "FART KING 2024." It hit the ground with a clunk beside Max-Leo, who claimed it with pride. Emil Søren, watching from the sidelines with a mouthful of cherry Danish, burst out with the loudest protest anyone had heard all morning. "That's not fair!" he yelled, crumbs flying. "I had one at breakfast! Nobody heard it because Freja-Marie was crying!" His complaint was met with laughter and a sympathetic pat on the back from Vigga Gibb. "Unheard farts don't count," she said sagely. "Ask the judges."

Ben stepped out into the courtyard at precisely the wrong moment. He had intended to breathe deeply, stretch his legs, maybe enjoy the slight warmth of early sun against the stone. What he entered instead was a battlefield of fart crowns, overturned juice cups, half-eaten breadsticks, and shrieking children. A shoeless Axel came sprinting past him, dragging a blanket like a cape. "Gas in the north wing!" he screamed. Peter Emil coughed theatrically into a glove and staggered sideways like a mortally wounded soldier. "Tell my mother... she was always right..." he wheezed, and collapsed into a rose bush. Ben ducked instinctively, avoiding a flying croissant. The peace he had sought was gone.

From across the field, Silje Emilie Mikkelsen Larsen—Tobias's wife and legend in her own right—stepped into the courtyard like a general returning from exile. She was not in soccer attire. She was not even supposed to be outside. She had been reading a report on vitamin shortages and baby rash balms. But something in the air had summoned her. Something deep. Something ancestral. "Who said Thunderfart?" she called, squinting toward the crowd. Tobias, who was halfway into a folding chair and already sipping orange juice, choked slightly. "Oh no," he whispered. "They've awakened her."

The children parted instinctively as Silje approached, like disciples awaiting a demonstration from a master. Even Uncle Sørensen, seated near the hedges pretending to read a newspaper, raised an eyebrow above the fold. No one needed to explain what was coming. Every child over six had heard the stories. Silje and Tobias had been together since they were barely older than these children were now—since the age of scraped knees and chalked sidewalks, of shared hot chocolate and mismatched mittens. They'd been married nearly a decade, and long before the vows, there were competitions. Weekly competitions. Unwritten. Sacred. And Silje, by all accounts, had never lost one.

Ben stepped back, warily adjusting the collar of his sweater as the wind shifted. He knew the protocols. When the Fart Queen arrived, you cleared the zone. "She's gonna do it," whispered little Ida Josefine Falkenberg, squeezing Mikkel's arm. "You'll see. No one ever wins against her." Tobias tried to interject, holding up a finger as if to reclaim his reputation. "I beat her once," he said faintly. Silence. Then a child's voice shouted from the grass: "No you didn't!" It was Lise Ava, grinning ear to ear. "She said that was only because you had the flu!"

Silje bent at the waist, not in pain, not in labour—but in full preparation. The crowd grew still. Her children, Nina and Kristian, stood beside her like heralds beside a queen. Tobias buried his face in both hands and muttered something about plausible deniability. A moment passed. Then two. Then, like a drumroll from the netherworld, a sound erupted that no mouth could mimic. Low, resonant, perfectly timed, and vibrational enough to rattle the old tin pail near the chicken coop. The children screamed. A goose took flight. One of the neighbour boys collapsed in the grass, rolling. "That wasn't a fart," said Jonas Hansen, slack-jawed. "That was a language."

In the aftermath, no one dared speak until Vigga finally whispered, "All hail the Fart King." And someone corrected her, rightly, "Queen." A slow clap began near the benches. Then it spread. The older children stood to their feet. The younger ones bowed dramatically. Even Ben, shaking his head, offered a half-smile and slow applause. "Just... incredible," he said to no one in particular. "Denmark's finest."

Tobias stood, juice glass abandoned, hands in pockets. "This is why I married her," he said, chest puffed. "You think royalty's about crowns and castles? It's about who's still funny after eleven years and four diaper explosions." Silje took a modest bow, curtsied once, and walked back inside without another word. A hush followed her departure, a strange reverence. No one knew how to follow that act.

Emil Søren, still upset about being overlooked, tried to mimic the sound, pushing from his seat until he nearly toppled over. "No," said Vigga. "You can't copy greatness." Peter Emil waved the trophy in the air but didn't offer it to Max-Leo anymore. "It's hers," he said. "She earned it."

Ben wandered toward the edge of the yard, inhaling slowly now that the storm had passed. The air still vibrated faintly, like aftershock. He glanced up at the clouds and shook his head. "Thunderfart Queen of Denmark," he murmured, "and no one saw it coming." And deep within the Castle, someone began writing it down.

There was a bowl on the patio table. It had been there since breakfast, filled once with firm, glistening cherries handpicked from the market crates in Copenhagen. Half of them were gone by midmorning. The other half—dark, syrupy, overripe—waited silently for someone foolish enough to finish them. Kristian Anton Rask, grinning ear to ear and bubbling with mischief, leaned across the table and waved a cherry on its stem like it was a prize. "Twelve," he said, eyes daring. "Bet you can't do twelve, Lukas." Lukas looked up, hands sticky from jam and juice already, and without hesitating, nodded.

The first five cherries went down with delight. His friends chanted the count with every chew. By the eighth, the grin had faded, and Lukas was rocking slightly on his heels. "Keep going!" someone shouted. "Nine! Ten!" A slow hush fell as Lukas lifted the eleventh, paused, and slipped it into his mouth with exaggerated dread. Kristian Anton, arms folded like a smug banker in a suit, tapped a foot with theatrical boredom. "You promised twelve," he said, not unkindly, but with undeniable firmness. The twelfth cherry followed, whole. Lukas chewed twice, blinked once, and stopped.

It happened slowly at first. His eyes widened, then narrowed. His knees buckled—not from drama, but from physiology. The castle lawn had never felt so silent. Somewhere across the yard, a dog barked. Lukas turned, gagged once, then twice, and then the cherries launched themselves back to freedom with all the violence and vengeance of a wronged battalion. Clara Ann Árpád-Harvick Jensen, who had just stepped out with a fresh plate of lemon bars, walked directly into the arc of splash radius. It caught her square across the skirt and down one bare leg. The sound alone would have earned applause. The smell, however, cleared a five-foot radius.

A moment passed. Lukas coughed. Clara didn't speak. She just blinked, frozen in what could only be described as elegant paralysis. She turned her head slowly toward Tobias, who had arrived a second too late with a jug of cold water. "Rookie mistake," he whispered, and handed her a towel. Clara accepted it with the stiff grace of someone who had spent ten years among children and still never saw this coming. "You'd think I'd learn," she murmured. "But no. Every year I forget about the cherries." She dabbed her arm and handed the towel back.

Meanwhile, Lukas had taken on the pale, guilt-stricken expression of a prince who had accidentally set fire to the heirloom tapestries. Tobias crouched, scooped him into his arms, and began the solemn walk toward the east washroom with the weary grace of a father carrying a live grenade. Lukas whimpered against his shirt, muttering apologies. "I didn't mean it, I swear." Tobias nodded, pressing a hand to his back. "Nobody ever means it. It's the cherries. They choose you." He was halfway down the corridor when Lukas jerked, let out a wail, and delivered round two.

The sound was wetter this time. The cherry stain spread across Tobias's favourite shirt like a red Rorschach. He stopped mid-step, looked down, and said nothing for several beats. Then he exhaled. "Of course. Of course it had to be the blue one," he said to no one in particular. "The one shirt I actually like." Lukas groaned again. "I'm sorry, I didn't know—" Tobias lifted a finger. "Say no more. You've said enough. It's in my hair." Lukas sobbed softly into his shoulder. Tobias changed direction toward the laundry instead.

Back in the courtyard, Ben had returned with a mop and a brave face. The stain on the grass would fade, eventually. The story would not. Clara sat on the edge of a bench, wearing one of Freja's emergency jumpers, sipping lemon water. "This is why I told them no fruit before noon," she muttered. "No fruit before noon and no dares before noon. But does anyone listen to me?" Kennit appeared beside her with a fresh towel. "Never," he said gently. "You're the queen of ignored wisdom." She took the towel without a smile but leaned into him nonetheless.

Inside, Tobias had stripped the boy down to his underclothes and was now hosing both of them with a detachable showerhead. "You smell like cherry soda," Tobias muttered. "But make it war crime." Lukas sniffled. "Am I going to die?" Tobias snorted. "Not today. But I'm going to send a formal complaint to the tree that grew those cherries." He turned the tap again. "Don't worry. It happens to all of us. The twins haven't even been born yet and they've ruined half the Castle." Lukas gave a feeble chuckle and wiped his nose.

As he toweled the boy dry, Tobias found a second shirt. "This one's red. Just in case," he said. "And for the record—Kristian Anton is banned from issuing fruit dares for the rest of the day." Lukas nodded gravely. "I think I'm going to stick to crackers." Tobias smiled. "Smart lad. Next time someone dares you to eat twelve cherries, ask them how many they've eaten first. If it's none, it's a trap." Lukas pulled the shirt over his head, then turned back. "I liked that blue shirt." Tobias winced. "So did I."

When they re-emerged in the courtyard, all eyes turned. The grass had been cleaned. The air was less fragrant. But the memory lingered in every glance. Max-Leo bowed. "Welcome back." Lukas bowed back. "Never again." Tobias offered a tired grin and raised both hands. "Let the record show that cherries are now classified as a Class Three Hazard."

Emil Søren approached with a juice box. "You want this?" he asked Lukas. Lukas shook his head so violently it startled a pigeon. "No. No more fruit. No more liquids. I'm going dry for the rest of the day." Someone muttered something about cracker diets. Someone else began chanting "Cherry boy" under their breath. Ben whistled sharply to shut it down. "Let's show a little dignity," he called. "At least until someone else throws up." And with that, the match resumed. But every child kept a wary eye on the cherries.

Tobias had just finished disinfecting the mop handle from the cherry catastrophe when he caught a scent so sinister it stopped him mid-step. He stood in the corridor, rubber gloves clinging to his wrists, nostrils flaring like a seasoned hound, head tilted in dismay. This wasn't the sour splash of fruit gone rogue. This was deeper. Earthier. Familiar. And mobile. His eyes narrowed. Somewhere down the hall, something squished. It was the kind of squish no floorboard should ever hear. He sighed, cracked his neck to one side, and muttered to himself: "It's time."

The trail began in the east wing, marked not by footprints but by scent. It clung to the baseboards and rose like fog from the carpet. Tobias adjusted his gloves and reached for the emergency diaper toolkit—an old navy satchel full of wipes, gloves, baking soda, disposable hazmat-grade smocks, and one half-used can of deodorizing spray that had long since given up. He took one step forward and nearly retched. "Okay," he whispered, "we're going in." The hall curved slightly. Around the bend stood his first suspect.

It was Theodor Anker Holst Nielsen, aged six, perched silently on the edge of a bench, legs stiff, back straight, face blanched with shame. A single streak of evidence leaked ominously from the waistband of his Pull-Up. Tobias nodded once. "We've got one." But before he could reach for a glove, a blur of motion caught his eye. Down the corridor—nine others. Children. Running. Scampering. The scent trailed behind them like a war banner. Some laughed, oblivious. Others clutched their bottoms in horror. A few simply cried. The Pull-Up Patrol had broken formation.

Tobias turned, clicked the intercom, and called for backup. "This is not a drill. We've got multiple bogeys, full biohazard protocol. East wing, corridor three. Bring the powder." He hung up before anyone could ask questions. By then, the children had dispersed. The scent, however, remained. He caught glimpses—Selma darting left, Linus sprinting under a bench, Alma pretending to be invisible against the wallpaper. He called out names like a PE teacher at roll call, only half expecting them to stop. Most didn't. One did—Rikke, holding her stomach like a philosopher in pain.

As he corralled them one by one, the worst struck. Kristian Anton had wandered in, face already pale from too many close-range incidents. He opened his mouth to speak, but instead gagged, leaned forward, and expelled the full contents of his lunch—grilled cheese and apple slices—directly onto the antique rug beside Tobias's foot. The impact splattered up the leg of his trousers. Tobias blinked. "Right. Now it's a double shift." Kristian moaned, wiped his mouth on his sleeve, and whispered, "I didn't mean to." Tobias didn't flinch. "Nobody ever does."

Reinforcements arrived in the form of Clara and Silje, each wearing old choir robes and armed with buckets. Clara handed Tobias a fresh set of gloves while Silje wordlessly began tossing baking soda onto the rug like she was salting icy steps. "How many?" Clara asked, nose pinched beneath a handkerchief. "Ten," Tobias replied. "Well, technically eleven now." Silje crouched beside Selma, who had surrendered on the floor with a red face and tearful confession. "I was dancing," she said, "and then it happened." Clara nodded. "The rhythm will betray you."

The cleanup turned into a full-blown military operation. Wipes flew. Smocks were handed out like riot shields. The youngest children were herded toward the bathing chamber, where Adele was already filling the oversized stone tub with warm water and a bottle of something lemon-scented and suspiciously unlabelled. One by one, soiled socks were flung across the tile. Tobias stood beside the linen bin, catching them midair with the focus of a goalkeeper. "This one's a size six," he called. "Someone claim it before it mutates."

Meanwhile, Peter Emil Rosenshavn had fashioned a clothespin for his nose and was taking witness statements. "Who farted first?" he asked. "Who set it off?" Lise Ava raised a hand. "It was Selma. She sneezed and then said, 'Oops.'" Selma turned pink. "That wasn't me. That was Freja." In response, Freja let out a satisfied bubble from beneath the bathwater. Tobias didn't look back. "One more accusation and I start assigning mop duty by volume of output." The silence that followed was total.

Eventually, the smell began to fade, if only because every child had either been washed, wrapped in towels, or relocated to the castle courtyard. The corridor still bore evidence of their journey. Tobias eyed the carpet, sighed, and rolled it up without ceremony. "It's beyond redemption," he told Clara. "This goes in the history books as a casualty." She nodded solemnly. "I'll have it framed and titled 'The Battle of the Bottoms.'" Tobias gave her a look. "Please don't."

Outside, the sun was still shining. Ben sat on the steps, blinking into the distance, holding a cup of coffee that had long gone cold. "That bad?" he asked without turning. Tobias joined him, now in a borrowed shirt, sleeves rolled to the elbow, smelling faintly of citrus and defeat. "We lost two rugs, three towels, and half my dignity." Ben nodded. "So… not the worst day, then." Tobias cracked a smile. "No, not the worst. But I need a raise."

Ben gestured vaguely toward the pantry. "There's chocolate cake." Tobias didn't move. "That won't be enough." They sat in silence for a beat, just long enough for a faint noise to echo from the hallway—another squish. Tobias stood. "No. Nope. I'm done. Someone else gets this one." He tossed his gloves onto the steps and walked away without looking back. Ben watched him go, then muttered, "That's going in the book."

The shout echoed through the parlour like a trumpet blast. "I did a whopper!" Astrid bellowed, grinning like a fox with feathers in her teeth. She stood atop the plush green couch, arms raised in triumph. The declaration brought half the room to a halt. Emil Søren froze mid-sip from his juice box. Max-Leo's dribble stalled beneath the table. Even little Maja Johansen blinked in mid-bounce. All eyes went to Astrid, who looked ready for applause.

"What do you mean, a whopper?" asked Tobias warily from the threshold. He'd heard that phrase before, and rarely did it end well. Astrid stomped once on the cushion and waited. Nothing happened. "There!" she said. "Did you hear that?" The couch springs gave a half-hearted squeak. Lukas laughed nervously. Emil Søren raised a hand. "That's just the couch." Astrid frowned. "Well, it sounded real earlier." She stomped again. This time, silence. The room exhaled.

"False alarm," muttered Clara, who had just emerged from the hall with a laundry bin nearly as tall as she was. "Praise be." She stopped. Sniffed. Turned slowly to face the twins' playpen. A smell hung in the air—not vicious, but determined. Something that came not from effort, but from inevitability. Clara narrowed her eyes. "Astrid, was that you?" Astrid shrugged. "I dunno. I think it was Jasmina."

At that moment, Jasmina turned around slowly, as if emerging from a dream. Her eyes were wide. Her bottom lip quivered. She said nothing. A second later, a sound emerged—not from the couch this time—but from Jasmina herself. Low. Rumbling. And wet. A second wave followed, this one less ambiguous. Tobias, who had just sat down, shot up like he'd been pinched. "Oh no," he said. "No, no, no. We just finished!"

Sorensen, crossing through the corridor on his late afternoon patrol, caught the scent mid-stride. His boots paused on the tile for a fraction of a second, just enough to register the danger. Then, without changing expression, he turned his head, leaned over the castle's largest rose bush, and retched once with quiet dignity. He wiped his mouth with a cloth, exhaled through his nose, and kept walking. Not a word. Not a complaint. Just the cold resolve of a man who'd seen worse and lived.

Maria Sørensen followed her father at a dutiful distance, nine years old and stone-faced. She did not flinch at the sound, the smell, or the sight of her father purging into royal shrubbery. She had been trained in the ways of battle since toddlerhood. "It's a biological attack," she said flatly to Peter Emil, who had just joined her at the foot of the steps. He nodded. "We're calling this one a Level Four." Maria adjusted her rubber boots. "It's not our first."

Back inside, Tobias had already activated the extraction code. Jasmina was gently lifted under her arms and placed upon a makeshift changing mat made of two thick towels and a poncho from last year's forest hike. Silje entered the room like a cavalry sergeant, tossed a cloth diaper into the air, and caught it without looking. "Status?" she asked. Tobias pointed. "Mid-stage rupture. Limited to pants. Shoes are clean. Socks questionable."

Silje nodded, crouched beside Jasmina, and began her work with the practiced hands of a woman who had changed more diapers than had seen hot meals. "Honey," she whispered, "you gotta warn us." Jasmina blinked. "I thought it was air." Silje didn't laugh. "It always is." Clara came around the other side with a bowl of warm water. "Isla's going to hear about this, you know," she muttered. "We should give her a full-day report."

Ben, overhearing from the dining hall, leaned his head in. "If we do that, she'll never come downstairs again." He smiled to himself, then added, "Tell her I'm taking the upstairs bath hostage until the situation stabilizes." He turned back before they could reply, shaking his head and muttering something about cherries and upholstery.

Meanwhile, Emil Søren had turned the incident into a science experiment. He held up a pencil and announced, "If you fart hard enough, you can bend the air. Like a soundwave." Freja looked impressed. "Can we see it?" "No," Emil said, "because it's invisible. But I can feel it in my leg hairs." Tilde gagged and threw a pillow at him. "You're disgusting." Emil shrugged. "So's the couch. That's why I'm not sitting."

Tobias had just finished re-fastening the final strap on Jasmina's fresh Pull-Up when she looked at him with wide, watery eyes and asked, "Am I in trouble?" He shook his head. "Not at all. You're just part of the club now." She sniffled. "What club?" He smiled. "The survivors." At that, Sorensen's voice echoed down the hall. "Do NOT use the east bathroom. It's compromised." Maria nodded in approval.

Later, when the windows were cracked and the room had returned to something resembling breathable, Tobias sank into the armchair with a towel draped over his shoulder and his shoes off. "Every time," he whispered. "Every time I think we're done, another backside makes a liar of me." Silje handed him a mug of warm juice. "You wanted this life." He nodded. "I just didn't know it would smell like this."

Outside, the cherry trees bloomed in delicate pink. Inside, the air swirled with lemon spray and stories. No one would remember the couch in ten years. But they would remember Jasmina's initiation, Sorensen's rose bush reflex, and Maria's cold, unwavering stare of fart-stained battlefield experience. And they would laugh. Not now. But one day. When the smell had faded.

Peter Emil announced the challenge with his chest puffed and his fingers sticky from the first half-eaten slice. "I can beat Max-Leo," he declared, licking a crimson streak of cherry syrup off his wrist as if it were a badge of honour. Max-Leo raised an eyebrow but didn't speak. Instead, he calmly peeled the paper off another slice and began to eat with slow, calculated precision, the way one handles explosives or defuses bombs. "It's not about speed," Max-Leo finally said. "It's about focus." Peter Emil scoffed. "It's about stomach."

Clara didn't intervene. She was too busy wiping down the juice-stained cushions from the Jasmina incident, humming under her breath in that tone that mothers and medics share when they've seen too much to argue anymore. Isla, seated upright on the sofa with her hands splayed over her tightened belly, watched the cheesecake standoff with detached curiosity. "Let them," she whispered to Ben, who had just opened a window. "This is your circus. I'm merely the womb." Ben chuckled, cautiously. "Please don't go into labour over cheesecake." Isla grinned. "Too late."

Two more slices disappeared between the competitors. Max-Leo sat calmly, chewing like a monk. Peter Emil, on the other hand, had the manic energy of a contestant on borrowed time. He inhaled the cherry-soaked crust of slice number two, dropped the paper onto the polished floor, and stood up with a theatrical flourish. "Victory!" he shouted. The room barely had time to process it. His eyes widened. His mouth opened again—but not to speak.

The sound that followed was not a word, nor a belch. It was a primal eruption—equal parts cheesecake, cherry, and regret—launched with ungodly force across the dining room tiles. Max-Leo dove under the table. Clara did not scream. She simply walked to the linen closet, pulled out the mop with a calmness reserved for hurricanes and toddlers, and returned without commentary. "I warned you," she muttered, plugging her nose with two fingers and stepping into the splash zone.

Peter Emil stood, knees shaking, hands extended like a tragic Shakespearean actor whose soliloquy had gone terribly wrong. "I didn't feel it coming," he moaned. Isla, still on the sofa, rolled her eyes with mild amusement. "You never do," she said through a small wince. Another contraction had begun. She kept breathing, one hand braced on the armrest, the other gripping Ben's wrist until her knuckles turned white.

Ben looked torn between laughter and emergency response. "Do you need anything?" he whispered. Isla shook her head. "Just keep the floor clear." Ben looked over at Clara, who had now donned plastic gloves and was mopping in slow, angry circles. "I'll grab the air freshener," he said, already heading for the cabinet where four cans—lavender, eucalyptus, lemon burst, and one ominously labelled "Mountain Breeze"—waited like weapons.

Silje entered the room just as Ben sprayed a full blast of "Mountain Breeze" over the site. She coughed twice and batted the air like it owed her money. "What the hell is that?" she asked. Ben didn't blink. "The smell of denial." Peter Emil, now sitting on the floor and wiping his lips with a castle linen napkin, looked up at Silje. "Is this what regret smells like?" She looked him dead in the eye. "No. This is what consequences smell like."

Freja-Marie, ten months old and completely oblivious to the chaos, gurgled in delight from her playpen. She smacked her hands on the plastic bars, laughing like an amused goblin at the madness unfolding around her. Tobias peeked in, still wearing a spot of cherry-stained shirt from earlier. "Did he win the challenge?" he asked. Max-Leo, from under the table, shouted, "Technically, yes. But spiritually, no."

Emil Søren entered just in time to witness Peter Emil's second wave. He turned around and left immediately. "Nope," he said. "I'm not cleaning that." Clara pointed at him with her mop. "Then find me someone who will." Tobias was already climbing the stairs. "I'll get Sørensen." "He's in the rose garden," came a voice from the hallway. "Still recovering from Jasmina."

Ben returned with lemon burst this time and layered it directly into the curtain fibres. "We'll have to burn these," he muttered. Isla's contraction faded, and she took a slow, purposeful breath. "Ben." He turned. "Yes?" "If I go into labour right now," she said, "you are not telling the doctor it was caused by cherry cheesecake." Ben raised a hand. "Scouts' honour."

Kristian Anton tiptoed in and whispered to Lukas, "Did you see it fly?" Lukas nodded. "Like a firework, but wet." They both shuddered. Tilde, who had just entered for a snack, stopped mid-step and walked right back out. "Nope," she said, echoing Emil. "Still nope."

Sorensen returned ten minutes later with a bar of soap and a bottle of rubbing alcohol. "I've cleaned up royal funerals with less drama," he muttered, stepping over a mop bucket. Maria followed behind, nose plugged with two tissues and sunglasses on like a chemical warfare expert. "This is bad," she whispered. "This is next-level bad."

As the air cleared and Clara changed her third mop head, the castle began to fall back into something resembling peace. Peter Emil, now wrapped in a towel and sipping weak coffee, had stopped shaking. Isla dozed slightly on the couch. Ben, finally seated beside her, sighed and stared at the ceiling. "You think they'll remember this day?" he asked. Isla smiled. "Only if they find the stain under the rug."

The pantry had gone quiet—too quiet for a house normally filled with the thumping footsteps of sugar-fueled children and the low hum of distant castle chatter. It was Clara who first noticed it. The moment the hallway filled with children holding their noses and whispering in scandalous tones, she stepped aside and raised her brow. "One of you," she said, "has committed culinary treason." They stood in a line: Astrid, Emil Søren, Peter Emil, Lukas, and Valdemar—all with sleeves pulled over their noses, eyes watering, and one finger pointing toward the kitchen.

No one screamed. They were too polite for that. But the expressions on their faces told the entire story. Something had escaped containment. Something deep, silent, and unapologetically vile. Rikke, youngest in the room, stood with a wooden spoon in hand and whispered, "It came from behind the flour sacks." Kristoffer turned red. "I didn't do it," he barked. "It wasn't me!" Emil Søren crouched low, sniffed the floorboards with scientific detachment, and announced, "It's not fresh. It's stuck to something."

The pantry had become a courtroom. The castle's honour was on the line. Whoever had released the infamous SBD—silent but deadly—had done so with mastery. No audible clues, no prelude squeak, no betrayal of shifting feet. Just the ghost of methane and baked bread hanging in the air like a guilty memory. And that's when Clara saw her. Backing into the garden like a cat who had tipped over a vase, Freja Christensen—Oliver's mother—slid through the servants' door with her head down, eyes averted, and the hem of her dress fluttering suspiciously in her wake.

Ben, standing in the hallway with a fresh towel for Isla, caught the odd exit. "What's going on in there?" he asked, raising an eyebrow as a gust of air met him in the chest. He took a step back. "Oh, for heaven's sake." Isla, leaning in from the parlour doorway, squinted. "Was that a war crime?" Tobias arrived, still in gloves, and sniffed the air once. "That's not natural. That's… Freja." Clara didn't need confirmation. She stormed past the children, out the side entrance, and caught Freja just as she reached the garden gate.

"You left a trail," Clara said. Freja froze. "I beg your pardon?" Clara pointed to the back of her skirt. "It's following you." Freja gasped. "It was the onion drawer." "Onions don't do that," Ben shouted from inside. "Not without backup." The children, now pouring into the hallway with hands over noses and a kind of gleeful horror on their faces, began the traditional chant: "Who cut the castle? Who cut the castle?" Tobias held up a finger. "We'll need an inquest."

Freja turned to face them all, cheeks blazing. "I said nothing because I thought it would pass!" Kristian Anton collapsed on the stairs, laughing. "It passed all right." Lukas elbowed Emil Søren. "You owe me five kroner. I said it was her." "I thought it was Peter Emil again," Emil replied, arms crossed. "He always farts when he's nervous." Peter Emil, indignantly, snapped, "Not in public!"

The Castle had declared martial law over one rogue cloud. Clara returned with air freshener in one hand and a bar of lye soap in the other. "Next time you feel something creeping up," she told Freja firmly, "you pull the pin and you warn someone." Freja folded her arms. "In my defence, I was reaching for cumin." "That wasn't cumin," Ben muttered. "That was mustard gas."

The children took the investigation seriously. Nina led the charge, clipboard in hand, interviewing all present witnesses. "Where were you when the smell hit?" she asked Silje, who had just entered with a bowl of strawberries. Silje answered without flinching. "In the laundry room. I had to evacuate." "Confirmed alibi," said Lukas. "Proceed." Jasmina walked in late and took one breath before collapsing backwards. "Tell me it's over."

Maria Sørensen, undeterred by the chaos, entered with a clothespin on her nose and a detective's cap borrowed from a costume box. "The scent particles are clinging to fabric," she explained, examining the pantry doorframe. "That means the perp stood here for at least twenty seconds." Everyone turned to Freja. "I was picking out lentils," she defended. "That's not a crime!" Maria took a sniff. "Tell that to the curtains."

The formal declaration came before lunch. Kristian stood on the back steps with Ben's old rugby whistle and blew once for order. "Freja Christensen," he said in his best judge voice, "you are hereby named today's Thunderfart Queen of Rosenshavn." Freja bowed dramatically. "I accept this honour with great shame." Clara handed her the apron of shame—a floral disaster from the 1980s—and Freja wore it with a sense of reluctant pride.

As the children returned to their game of soccer, and the pantry was aired out with all available fans, the castle resumed its rhythm. The laughter didn't die down. It only grew louder as Freja passed every room like a haunted memory. "You think the smell's gone," someone whispered, "but it's just hiding." Isla, watching from the window, chuckled and rubbed her swollen belly. "They're going to tell this story to the twins," she said. Ben nodded. "The day the air betrayed us." He leaned closer to her shoulder and smiled. "And they'll swear it wasn't them."

The lawn behind the east courtyard had mostly dried since the last rain, which made it ideal terrain for a renewed match. A battered orange ball was retrieved from beneath the tool shed, its surface sticky with something Tobias refused to identify. Ben, ever the optimist, brushed it off and called the game back to order. Children swarmed the field, already jostling and screeching. The air still bore traces of recent warfare—diaper gas and cherry vomit did not retire quietly—but no one was willing to admit defeat. Ben declared himself referee, armed with nothing but a whistle made from a pen cap and his natural gift for commanding chaos. He raised his voice like a schoolmaster and bellowed, "No tackling your own team this time!"

Lukas, who'd already tried to wrestle the ball from Peter Emil, claimed it was an accident. Axel Nielsen accused Max-Leo of unfair blocking, and Maja Johansen shouted from the sidelines that no one knew the rules. Tobias, standing near the compost bins where he'd dragged two soiled bags earlier, tried to stay neutral, but neutrality was never an option in the sport of castle soccer. The first real goal was scored by Emil Søren—by kicking the ball directly into Ben's back. "Point to me!" Emil cried. "Goalie wasn't even looking!" Ben turned, narrowed his eyes, and handed the ball back. "Fine," he muttered, brushing grass off his coat. "But that counts as treason."

Then, as Axel sprinted past with heroic speed, he froze mid-step and sniffed the air. He gagged theatrically, pointed an accusing finger toward Ben, and cried out, "He's standing right by the compost! Check his shoes!" The other players followed suit, noses twitching, suspicion rising like fog on the pitch. Ben lifted one shoe, then the other, examining the soles with mock solemnity. "I am clean," he proclaimed. "My honour is intact." Freja Christensen, walking by with a tray of sandwiches, covered her face with her sleeve and said nothing. She had learned better than to challenge methane monarchs in mid-game.

The blame was passed to Tobias, who raised both hands in surrender. "I swear it wasn't me this time," he said. "I've been innocent all morning—ask anyone!" Nobody believed him. "That's what a guilty man would say," muttered Jonas Hansen, trying to stay upwind. Ben, now fully enjoying the spectacle, took two confident steps forward, clapped twice, and said with authority, "Children. You don't know stink until you've smelled a royal detonation." A pause swept the field. The twins had gone inside for juice, Clara had taken Lukas to change his shirt, and even Silje had disappeared into the kitchen. That left only the unsuspecting, naïve, and dangerously curious on the field.

He stood still, let the silence hang, then summoned every ounce of strategic power his stomach would allow. The release was slow at first—silent, like a snake uncoiling—but then came the sound: a thick, low rumble that echoed off the greenhouse wall. It lasted seven seconds. Maybe more. The children looked stunned. A few mouths dropped open. Axel stared at the trees as if questioning the wind. Then it hit them. All at once. Like rotten eggs had been boiled inside a sock and left in a fish tank. The smell crept through the game like fog across a battlefield.

Vigga Gibb was the first to squeal. "He did it! Ben farted! That wasn't compost!" The others panicked. Emil Søren ran in circles, screaming, "I'm being poisoned!" Max-Leo and Peter Emil collapsed in theatrical agony. Kristian Anton dropped to his knees and wailed, "My eyes are melting!" Ben simply stood there, arms folded, proud as a general watching fireworks from the safety of a balcony. Silje, returning from inside, paused just long enough to catch a whiff and muttered, "Amateur," before walking away again.

Isla, observing from the window, pressed her hand to her belly and whispered to herself, "And that's the father of my children." Clara, overhearing, chuckled and replied, "He's trying to clear the air—by poisoning it." Sorensen, seated on the stone bench beside the herb pots, didn't even flinch. He took a sip of lukewarm coffee and said, without turning his head, "That's nothing. You should've heard him in Kent. Blew out a fireplace once."

The game, hilariously enough, did not stop. After gagging and running in wide arcs, the children returned to their teams, albeit with pinched noses and suspicious glances. "Let's keep playing," Tobias called out, holding his nose. "But if anyone else detonates, we call a timeout." Agnete Andersen insisted they wear clothespins, and Ben agreed. He passed out laundry pins from his pocket as if they were war medals. Rikke Andersen clipped hers to her earlobe by mistake but refused to admit it.

Eventually, the match found rhythm again. Though the field was still fogged by suspicion and stink, the tension began to lift. Children forgot their outrage as goals were scored and shins were bruised. Ben resumed his post as referee but made no promises about future emissions. "Consider it a tactical weapon," he joked. "To be used only when absolutely necessary—or funny."

By the end of the match, Tobias had scored twice, both accidental. Emil Søren tackled Clara by mistake, and Peter Emil bit his tongue trying to yell "Goal!" with his mouth full of crackers. As for Ben, he remained undefeated—if not in sport, then certainly in scent. The children, flushed and dirty, collapsed on the grass in giggling heaps. "Best match ever," Axel declared. "Even if it stank." Ben nodded, laying flat among them. "That," he said, "is what I call stink diplomacy."

Mikkel Jensen had not intended to nap. He had merely wandered out to the west lounge chair under the trellis after promising Maren he'd only rest his eyes for five minutes. The chair creaked familiarly beneath him, worn by years of elbows and sun-drenched days, and within moments, Mikkel's head leaned back at just the right angle to forget the afternoon's thunderous chaos.

Soccer echoes faded behind the hedge. A cherry-stained breeze wafted through the shrubbery. For the first time that day, all was still—until it wasn't. A sudden blurt—a wet, unmistakable release of intestinal protest—slapped the air like a protest march in a porcelain museum. Mikkel shot upright.

He stared ahead. His eyes darted. His legs stayed frozen. It hadn't come from him. Of that, he was certain. He reached under the cushion, half-expecting to find a whoopee cushion or perhaps a small, laughing child. Nothing. Then came the sound again, shorter this time, as if the Castle itself was reacting to his disbelief. A fit of giggles erupted behind the greenhouse wall. Mikkel turned just in time to see Valdemar Jensen sprint behind the hydrangeas with his shirt over his face, shouting something about "rogue winds" and "that wasn't mine!"

"What was that?" Mikkel called out. "Is there a dog?" He sniffed the air cautiously. No dog. They didn't own a dog. Not one. Not even a borrowed one. He looked around, betrayed. The smell began to spread, like an airborne warning that settled first in the nostrils and then deep into the soul. Mikkel cursed under his breath and stood. Behind him, Jasmina Bækgaard was already crying. "My nose can taste it," she sobbed, clutching her stuffed rabbit against her face. "It's in my tongue now!"

Tobias arrived seconds later, armed with a feather duster and the kind of dead-eyed focus only diaper duty could instil. He moved past Jasmina gently, told her to breathe through her mouth, and threw open the nearest window with a grunt. "We are under attack," he said. "Operation Gas Leak is in full effect." He spun on his heel, inspecting curtains, rugs, vents—anything that might have absorbed the offence. "Where is it hiding?" he muttered. "Where's the epicentre?"

Silje appeared from the kitchen with a basket of clean laundry and instantly knew. "Mikkel," she said. "You farted so hard the Castle flinched." "I didn't!" he retorted. "I was asleep! Valdemar did it and blamed the dog—except there's no dog!" Silje sniffed once, paused, and walked out. "You smell like guilt, Mikkel." "I smell like betrayal!" he yelled after her, waving his hands like a man falsely condemned. Meanwhile, Valdemar had reappeared beside the window Tobias had opened, still giggling under his breath.

Maria Sørensen, toughened by years of second-hand exposure to her father's survival training, approached the zone calmly. "I've smelt worse," she declared, then handed Jasmina a cloth soaked in peppermint oil. "Breathe this. We keep these ready in the greenhouse. My dad says it resets your brain." Jasmina nodded, sniffling. "Do you think my brain is broken?" "No," said Maria, with the stone-faced certainty of a seasoned scout. "But your sinuses might be."

The children resumed their war council near the pantry, debating which adult had created the incident and whether crop dusting counted as a stealth offence or a war crime. Filippa Andersen drew a map of the Castle on a napkin and circled every known "gas zone" since breakfast. "If we connect the dots," she whispered, "we can triangulate the source." "Like an earthquake?" asked Theodor Nielsen. "Worse," said Filippa. "A buttquake."

From inside, Clara opened another window, shouting, "Whatever you're all doing out there, do it downwind! The twins are kicking harder every time the air changes!" Isla, now seated in the parlour with a warm compress against her lower back, muttered, "It's not contractions. It's castle emissions." Ben poked his head in. "Should I apologise to the royal lungs?" "Apologise to the furniture," she snapped back. "They didn't sign up for this."

Kristoffer Kristoffersen wandered by with a plate of leftover cherry cake, took one sniff of the tainted air, and turned around without taking a bite. "Not worth it," he muttered. Even the birds seemed to fly lower that afternoon, swooping across the back garden as if trying to flee a scentwave of unnatural power. Inside the Castle, linen was being changed for the third time that day. Outside, Tobias gave orders like a general manning the trenches of a stink war.

Axel Nielsen tried to nap under the sandbox tarp but was ratted out by Nina Larsen, who claimed she saw him lift one cheek just moments before a suspicious hiss. "That was a dry shoe," Axel defended. "It squeaked." "Your shoe needs a plumber," she replied. Maren Søllested arrived then and declared a full ceasefire until further notice. "Everyone under twelve," she said, "must stay six feet away from the nap chairs and eat only bland foods for two hours."

The lounge chair that had once been Mikkel's sanctuary was now roped off with spare clotheslines and marked with a handwritten warning: "Tactical Fart Zone. Do Not Disturb." Children passed by reverently, noses covered, whispering the name of the phantom farter like a legend. Jasmina finally stopped crying. "I think it's fading," she said. "Or I'm losing my sense of smell." Maria nodded. "Either way, it's better."

By sundown, Tobias had declared the Castle "clear," though he kept the windows open and the peppermint cloths on standby. Mikkel refused to sit again for the rest of the day. Valdemar insisted he had nothing to do with it but laughed every time someone said "nap." Jasmina returned to her quiet corner, now convinced her nose had a sixth sense. And Tobias? Tobias resumed diaper patrol with the grim confidence of a man who had seen too much—and smelt worse.

By the time Tobias had folded his second pair of rubber gloves and chucked them into the bin with that same resigned flick he used to swat away sympathy, the third call came from down the hall. He stood still for a full breath. The kind of breath that only a man deep in diaper warfare dared take—full and heavy, like he knew the air he pulled in might betray him again. From the nursery door, Astrid poked her head out. "Um... she laughed too hard," she said. "She needs help." No name. No detail. Just the grim admission of comedy turned casualty.

Tobias didn't even ask who. At this point, it didn't matter. He reached for the same kit he'd been carrying since morning—wipes, gloves, clean Pull-Ups, air spray, lavender balm for the brave, mint oil for the sensitive. His back cracked as he straightened. "Third blowout before noon," he mumbled. "That's a castle record." He stepped into the room and saw her—Lise Ava Larsen, crouched in her panda onesie with a sheepish grin and a very clear loss of bodily control. She didn't cry. That was rare. She just looked up and said, "I forgot to clench."

"You forgot to clench?" Tobias echoed, kneeling down beside her. "That's your defence?" "I was laughing," she explained. "Like, belly-laughing. The kind that shakes stuff loose." Tobias nodded like a priest receiving confession. "Well," he said, "consider yourself absolved." He got to work, never flinching, never pausing. The smell struck mid-wipe. Nina Sofie ran past the doorway at that exact moment and gagged so hard she stumbled into the wall. "I'm fine!" she shouted before vanishing around the corner. "I'm okay!"

"You're a legend, Tobias," said Kristoffer Kristoffersen, walking past with a pastry in hand. "A man of honour." "Tell that to my shirt," Tobias replied. "This is number two. It's not going to survive number four." Clara brought in clean laundry, already pegging him as a lost cause. "Don't bother changing," she said. "By the time you do, another one will hit." Tobias didn't argue. Lise was finally clean, smiling, and hugging his leg. "Thanks," she whispered. "You're not grossed out." "Grossed out?" he said. "Sweetheart, I've changed thirty-eight diapers in the last two weeks. I've seen horrors."

Maria Sørensen offered him a medal made from foil and string. "You survived the stink," it read. He accepted it solemnly, then turned to see a trail of footprints—wet, but not muddy—leading out of the hallway and into the sitting room. "Kristian Anton?" he called out, not asking but declaring. From the other room came a long pause, then, "No comment!" Tobias swore under his breath and followed the trail. It ended at a sock. Unattended. Still warm.

Max-Leo appeared beside him. "Want help?" "You offering or confessing?" Tobias asked. "Just offering," Max said quickly. "But if you need a suspect... I heard Lukas had seconds at dessert." "Lukas is banned from dairy," Tobias reminded him. "He knows that." "Yeah, but the cheesecake was small," Max shrugged. "He said two small ones equal one normal. So it's fine." Tobias closed his eyes. "That's not how digestion works, kid." "Tell that to Lukas's pants."

He returned to the original site of Blowout Three, where Lise was now calmly drawing fart clouds on the chalkboard wall. "I named this one Hurricane Poo-Poo," she said proudly. "And this is Windy McBumstorm." "You're a poet," Tobias said, deadpan. "Never change." Isla walked by slowly, one hand on her lower belly, eyes tired but smiling. "Is it bad?" she asked. "It's been worse," Tobias said honestly. "You still good?" "They're practicing their exit," she said, grimacing. "Like digging their way out with forks."

Ben stuck his head around the doorframe. "Need backup?" "You have a hazmat suit?" Tobias replied. "No, but I've got mints and emotional detachment." "You'll do." Ben stepped in, sniffed, then recoiled. "Wow. Okay. That's personal." "Tell me about it," Tobias said. "This is my third for the day." "Third what?" "Third total collapse of digestive dignity." "And you're still standing?" "I'm not sure," Tobias said. "I might just be floating at this point."

Clara returned with a new shirt for him, folded and blessed. "Try not to ruin this one before dinner," she warned. "No promises," he said. "But I'll try." He changed right there behind a privacy screen, keeping his voice light enough not to alarm the kids. Lise waved at him from the other side. "Can you help me draw the next fart monster?" she asked. "I think it needs a diaper cape." "Only if it has a gas mask," Tobias replied. "Safety first."

As he stepped out, fresh shirt barely wrinkled, the hallway rumbled with another round of laughter—and one unmistakable sound. He didn't even flinch. He just turned, reached for the wipes again, and walked toward the noise like a man walking into battle. Behind him, the foil medal swung from his neck like a badge of unyielding honour. And if he had to earn a fourth by sundown, he would do it with the stoicism of a soldier who had seen—and smelt—it all.

Ben had been promised a reprieve. Isla, pressing one hand to her lower belly, had told him with a faint smirk that perhaps he should "get a little air." The phrasing had been deliberate, and yet he had taken it at face value. He stepped out into the backyard with the quiet hope of escaping the din, the chaos, and the relentless echo of squeaky shoes across the stone floors. But what met him was not fresh air at all. It was a wall—thick, pungent, and entirely inescapable—creeping across the lawn like a gas laid in wait for its victim.

Emil Søren appeared beside him without announcement, his expression a mixture of sympathy and mischief. From his pocket, the boy produced a single wooden clothespin, holding it out as though bestowing a royal insignia. "You'll need it," Emil said simply. Ben took it, clipped it to his shirt for a moment, and then, after a brief hesitation, fastened it across the bridge of his nose. It made him look ridiculous, and he didn't care. No amount of pride was worth breathing whatever this was.

From the patio, Sorensen gave a slow nod of approval, the kind of nod given only to those who understood survival in its purest form. He had trained Ben in many arts—security, observation, tactical withdrawal—but nothing quite like this. Ben didn't need to ask where the source was. That knowledge carried itself on the wind. He looked toward the far end of the garden, where Isla sat in a chair under the pear tree, her posture deceptively relaxed, her face turned slightly toward the spring sun.

Ben had known her long enough to recognise the tell-tale signs. That subtle shifting in her seat. The faint narrowing of her eyes. And then it came—a slow build to a blast so abrupt that it startled the starlings from the hedge. He said nothing. Isla, of course, said nothing. Words, in this context, were wholly unnecessary. The deed had been done, the damage irreparable. Ben could only stand there, clothespin secured, and accept his place in the line of fire.

Tobias, crossing the yard on some errand, halted mid-stride. The impact hit him first in the nostrils, then visibly in the knees. "Good heavens," he muttered, though his voice lacked conviction. Silje, trailing just behind, didn't fare much better.

She froze, her expression twisting from casual amusement into an open-mouthed realisation that they had walked into an ambush. The two of them stood together like survivors in the immediate aftermath of a battlefield shelling—unmoving, processing, trying not to inhale.

Ben almost felt bad for them. Almost. Tobias had been on diaper duty all morning; his sense of smell was already a casualty. Silje, on the other hand, had been riding the victorious glow of her earlier morning detonation, a victory that now paled against the sheer audacity of Isla's strike. The look she gave Ben was one part admiration, two parts horror. "Did you hear that?" she asked. "I didn't have to," he replied, adjusting his clothespin. "It came to me."

Max-Leo, having witnessed the scene from a safe distance near the garden gate, shouted something about "the queen reclaiming her crown," which sent half the children into another round of snickering and groaning. The other half, those within range, simply clutched their stomachs and tried to flee upwind. The tactical retreat created chaos, with Peter Emil colliding into Axel Nielsen, who fell sideways into the hedge. Ben, watching it unfold, thought briefly of ordering an evacuation drill.

Isla, meanwhile, sipped from her glass of water as though nothing at all had happened. There was no satisfaction in her expression, no smug declaration of victory—just that calm, almost meditative composure that suggested she knew exactly what she had done and didn't require applause. Ben found that composure admirable, if slightly terrifying. It was the same composure she had during tense chess matches, when she lured her opponent into thinking they had the advantage before dismantling them in three moves.

Tobias attempted to recover by waving his hands in front of his face, as though fanning the air might break its hold. "No use," Silje said grimly. "This isn't wind. This is a statement." She wasn't wrong. The potency lingered, stubborn and unapologetic, defying the usual dispersal of open space. Even the early April breeze seemed reluctant to take it away, as though unwilling to shoulder responsibility for its delivery.

Ben considered removing the clothespin but decided against it. Emil Søren had been right—this was not a battle to be fought unarmed. Instead, he walked forward slowly, careful not to disturb the air more than necessary. The trick, he had learned, was to move without creating turbulence. Sorensen called this "ghost walking" when applied to stealth operations. Here, it was a matter of survival. Tobias and Silje, less disciplined, had already stirred the air enough to regret every step they took.

Freja Christensen emerged from the kitchen door, carrying a tray of lemonade, only to freeze as the first wave reached her. "What in the—?" she began, before stopping herself and returning the tray inside. She would wait, clearly, for safer conditions. Sorensen, leaning against the wall, looked mildly amused. "You get used to it," he told her. Freja shot him a look that said she doubted that very much.

Emil Søren had taken up position near the hedge, where he was sketching something on a scrap of paper. When Ben asked, the boy revealed a crude but surprisingly accurate diagram titled "Stink Radius," complete with arrows indicating safe zones and danger points. Ben admired the detail. "This is good work," he said. "You've got the mind for security planning." Emil grinned. "I learned from the best," he said, gesturing toward Sorensen, who gave a slight bow.

Eventually, the air began to shift—not enough to be called fresh, but enough to allow movement without flinching. Ben unclipped the clothespin and handed it back to Emil, who tucked it away for "next time." There would, inevitably, be a next time. Isla rose from her chair, stretching carefully, her expression unreadable. "Better?" she asked him. "Not exactly," he said truthfully, "but I survived." She smiled faintly, the kind of smile that said she knew survival was all that mattered.

There were no cameras to catch the moment, no court-appointed scribe to dress it in polished words. This was not the kind of afternoon destined for the gilded pages of royal history. It was the sort of day kingdoms forgot and families never lived down. Ben found himself weaving between the blur of soccer balls, shrieking children, and the occasional airborne cup of apple juice. Tobias's voice rose above the din, somewhere between a command and a plea: "More wipes! We need more wipes!" His words carried the urgency of a man under siege.

Ben ducked to avoid a ball kicked wildly in his direction, narrowly sidestepping a stream of juice arcing through the air from a tipped cup. It splattered against the cobblestone with a sticky insistence. He wondered, in the moment, whether this was what monarchies were reduced to in the modern age—dodging projectiles of fruit-based drinks rather than political scandals. He doubted any royal historian would find it worth chronicling, though in his view it was the truest depiction of rule: chaos management without applause.

In the far corner of the courtyard, Isla sat watching, her face calm but her hands resting protectively on her belly. She knew well enough to remain outside the blast range of both soccer balls and small disasters. Sorensen, posted near the archway, looked like a general overseeing an unpredictable battlefield. His eyes followed each movement, not with alarm, but with the quiet readiness of a man who had seen far worse and lived to tell about it—though he never did tell.

Ben's path took him closer to the fountain, where two younger boys were arguing about whose fault it was that the juice had been spilled. The argument dissolved into laughter, then dissolved further into a race across the lawn that sent one child tumbling into the flowerbeds. A shriek went up, followed by more laughter. Ben could only shake his head. Royal dignity was a fragile concept in such an environment, crumbling the moment sticky shoes hit ancient stone.

The next ball came low, skimming the grass like a determined hound. Ben leaned back to avoid it, his heel catching on the stem of a discarded banana peel someone had thoughtlessly left behind. His balance wavered for a breathless instant, arms flailing in a gesture far from regal, before gravity claimed him. Down he went, the world tilting, the sky swinging overhead. He landed on his back with a thud that sent the nearby children into gasps, then into irrepressible giggles.

For a moment, he lay there, staring up at the shifting clouds, debating whether to get up or remain in dignified defeat. The sounds of the courtyard pressed in—shouts, splashes, the clatter of a mop bucket Tobias had kicked over in haste. Ben let the thought settle: perhaps this was simply his lot in life, to serve as both ruler and jester in equal measure. The two roles had always been closer cousins than people cared to admit.

Then, in the spirit of surrender, he released a slow, deliberate blast that echoed faintly against the courtyard walls. It was not the playful trumpeting of a victory lap, nor the accidental release of an unguarded moment—it was the sigh of a man who understood that dignity was sometimes best left unpursued. The sound drew silence for the briefest of seconds, then a chorus of groans, laughter, and shouts from every corner.

Tobias, pausing mid-cleanup, turned with narrowed eyes. "Was that…?" he began, but the truth was already written across Ben's expression. "Despair," Ben confirmed solemnly, as though confessing to a crime of state. Silje doubled over in laughter nearby, unable to hold her composure. Even Sorensen's mouth twitched in something perilously close to a smile, though he quickly turned it into a cough.

The children wasted no time in creating a new game of speculation. Some claimed Ben's contribution had surpassed Isla's earlier effort; others argued it lacked the raw force of Silje's morning display. Axel Nielsen appointed himself judge, though no one took his verdict seriously. The debate, absurd as it was, became the centre of activity, pulling everyone into its orbit.

Ben eventually rolled to his side and pushed himself to his feet, brushing bits of grass and grit from his jacket. There was no recovering the image of composure, so he didn't try. Instead, he walked back into the thick of the game, daring another ball to challenge him. "Back to work," he muttered, though whether he meant the game or the monarchy was unclear even to him.

The peel lay where it had claimed him, a quiet reminder of his fall. Sorensen, seeing it, strolled over and nudged it toward the compost bin with the toe of his boot. "Hazard cleared," he announced dryly. Ben tipped his head in mock gratitude. They both knew it was a temporary reprieve—there would always be another peel, another spill, another airborne cup waiting in the wings.

From the terrace, Isla watched the renewed game with a knowing smile. She had seen Ben fall before—not always physically, but in the sense of letting go, of loosening the impossible grip on royal expectation. Those were the moments when he looked most like himself, stripped of title and dressed in grass stains. She knew he would not thank her for pointing it out, but it pleased her all the same.

Tobias returned to his duties, armed now with a roll of wipes in each hand like weapons at the ready. The man was a marvel of endurance, able to cross the courtyard at speed while dodging both children and incoming liquids. His muttered commentary to Silje, barely audible above the noise, suggested he was keeping count of the day's disasters, perhaps for later retelling over supper.

By the time the sun shifted behind a bank of pale clouds, the courtyard had regained some rhythm. The children's laughter rose and fell like waves, the game moving across the grass with bursts of speed and sudden collapses into giggles. Ben, still marked by his tumble, found himself laughing along with them, even when the jokes landed at his expense. In the end, it was not a day for cameras, nor for the annals of history. It was a day for living—and that, unrecorded as it was, might be the rarest crown of all.

Isla sat propped against a mound of cushions on the drawing-room chaise, her feet stretched out toward the warmth of the low afternoon sun. A notebook lay open beside her, its purpose forgotten, replaced by the gentle rhythm of her breathing as she timed the tightening across her belly. From the west courtyard came the unmistakable sound of children in full battle—shouts, squeals, and the low, resonant echoes of what could only be described as deliberate detonations. She smiled faintly, recognising the pitch and cadence of her family's mischief. This was not a day for silk gloves and polite restraint.

The door to the room opened just wide enough for Silje to lean in, her hair slightly windblown from the fray outside. "It's getting worse," she announced, as though reporting enemy troop movement. "Do you want me to clear the yard?" Isla raised one brow, the faintest crease of humour in her eyes. "Clear it? No. Let them fart. It's the one honest thing left in the world." Silje's answering laugh was quick, bright, and appreciative before she vanished again into the hall, leaving Isla with the distant chorus of giggles and outrage drifting up from below.

Her gaze moved to the tall windows, the light shifting across the pane in slow golden streaks. Somewhere beneath that same sunlight, her husband was likely at the centre of the nonsense, attempting to referee and probably failing. She pictured him standing, hands on hips, in that resigned pose he adopted when the situation had long outstripped his authority. The thought was oddly comforting. She felt the familiar pull of another contraction building, low and insistent, and closed her eyes to meet it head-on.

The pain pressed in like a tightening belt, drawing her focus inward. Her breath deepened in measured counts—inhale, hold, release—an old rhythm learned in calmer hours and put to use now in these early stages. No one had officially called it labour yet, but she knew her body's signs. It would be tomorrow, perhaps, but already the air had shifted in some unspoken way. Between each wave, she allowed herself to listen again to the courtyard's disorder, clinging to the ordinary as the extraordinary drew closer.

A sharp peal of laughter rose above the rest, followed by a chorus of theatrical gagging. She could guess the cause without needing the details. It seemed to her that children were born knowing the comedy of such things, needing no tutor in its appreciation. Adults might dress it up as crude or inappropriate, but Isla believed in calling life what it was, and this—however absurd—was honest. It was joy unpolished, without ceremony. She winced as the next contraction arrived, longer than the last, forcing her hand to grip the armrest until the pressure eased.

She did not cry out, though her breath caught for an instant. Pain was no stranger here, only a reminder of what was coming. In the quiet spaces between the cramps, she thought of how tomorrow would rewrite the shape of their lives again. Two more voices would join the chaos; two more sets of feet would claim their share of the courtyard's grass. And perhaps, if the family's peculiar traditions held true, two more candidates for the annual Thunderfart crown would be born into competition.

The sound of footsteps in the corridor broke her reverie. Clara appeared briefly with a tray—fresh water, sliced pears, and a folded cloth for her forehead. She set it down without comment, her eyes catching the faint flush in Isla's cheeks. "You're breathing deeper," Clara observed. Isla's answer was a small, knowing smile. "It's starting to work." Clara glanced toward the window at the racket outside and shook her head. "They're in rare form today." Isla replied, "They should be. Tomorrow we'll be too tired to laugh."

Left alone again, she sipped the water and let the pear's sweetness cut through the dryness in her mouth. Outside, the courtyard's noise swelled and dipped like the tide. Every so often there was a thud or a splatter, followed by uproarious laughter or a cry for towels. She imagined the neighbour children among them now, widening the circle, adding new fuel to the chaos that Ben had likely been trying to escape when he first stepped out there. The thought amused her—his attempt at fresh air now thick with the scent of the family's favourite sport.

A shadow crossed the sunlight as a cloud passed overhead. The room cooled slightly, and with it came a moment of stillness. Isla closed her eyes again, hearing in her mind the layered life of Rosenshavn Castle: the thump of running feet, the slam of a distant door, the muted clink of crockery from the kitchens, the occasional bark of a laugh that could only be Tobias. These were the sounds she had come to love most, not the formal silences of ceremony, but the imperfect noise of people entirely at home.

She felt the next tightening rise, slower this time but heavier, as though the baby—both babies—were testing the boundaries of the space they would soon leave behind. Her hand went instinctively to her side, pressing in gentle counterpoint to the ache. She breathed through it without opening her eyes, trusting the rhythm, letting it crest and fade. Only when it was gone did she exhale fully, a whisper of relief slipping out with the breath.

From somewhere in the courtyard came a cry of triumph—someone had scored a goal, though whether in soccer or in the less savoury competitions of the day, she couldn't tell. The thought made her chuckle, which in turn made her belly tense again, reminding her not to overindulge in laughter just now. Still, she refused to retreat from it completely. The humour in life, she believed, was worth defending even in the shadow of great change.

Her mind wandered briefly to the birth ahead: the careful choreography of midwives, the pacing of contractions, the moment when everything else would fade into the background. She was not afraid—wary, perhaps, but not afraid. These walls had seen her grow from the girl she had once been into the woman she was now, and they would see her through this as well. That, too, was honest. And honesty, she reminded herself, was worth more than appearances.

Another cheer rose, this time followed by groans. She pictured the aftermath, someone doubled over in laughter while another sought a clothespin for their nose. "Let them fart," she murmured again to herself, tasting the truth of it. It was a thing beyond etiquette, beyond any courtly rulebook—a reminder that no matter the crown, the bloodline, or the ceremony, the human part remained unbroken.

The light shifted once more, the cloud passing to reveal the late-afternoon sun pouring back into the room. Isla leaned her head against the cushion, her body easing into the quiet between contractions. The racket outside would continue without her, as it always had, as it always would. She closed her eyes and let the sounds carry her, half-listening, half-dreaming, knowing that tomorrow, the courtyard would be louder still.

The hedge along the courtyard's far edge swayed just enough to betray a hidden presence. Ben, pausing mid-step after sidestepping a rolling soccer ball, caught the brief glint of sunlight off something metallic. It wasn't a weapon—thankfully—it was the corner binding of a notebook. He stepped closer, careful not to draw the attention of the children on the pitch, and found Casper kneeling in the cool shade, his pencil racing across the page with the intensity of a war correspondent. The boy glanced up only when he realised he'd been spotted, his cheeks flushed from both the excitement and the unmistakable odour that still lingered over the yard.

Ben crouched to meet him at eye level, one hand braced on his knee. "Keeping a record, are you?" he asked, his voice low enough that it wouldn't carry to the others. Casper nodded, his eyes alight with the satisfaction of having caught every absurd detail. In neat, deliberate strokes, he'd sketched the moment Tobias had tripped over the laundry basket, the explosion of wipes spilling like snow across the flagstones. Even the faint plume of artistic 'smell lines' curled above the figures—a detail Ben privately admired. "Write it well, Casper," he said, a smile pulling at the corner of his mouth.

The boy's pencil stilled at the sound of his name, the weight of the King's attention settling on him like a secret badge of honour. "But don't name names, okay buddy?" Ben added, tapping a finger against the open page.

Casper gave a solemn nod, though the sparkle in his eyes suggested he already knew how to disguise the guilty parties with the most paper-thin of pseudonyms. They both understood that some stories were too good to erase, but they could be told without dragging reputations into the mud—especially when those reputations belonged to people who could ground you from dessert for a week.

From the courtyard came another eruption—laughter, shouts, and a sound that suggested at least one chair had not survived the day intact. Casper's pencil twitched in response, itching to catch every scrap before the memory faded. Ben leaned back on his heels, watching the boy's hand fly over the paper, sketching not just shapes but the essence of the afternoon: the wild arcs of kicked soccer balls, the unflinching faces of those on wipe duty, the exaggerated reactions of those caught in the stink radius. It was, in its own way, a living archive of Rosenshavn mischief.

"If you need clarity on the day's events," Ben murmured, glancing toward the gaggle of children sprinting across the lawn, "just ask Tobias." The advice carried its own mischief, for Tobias's version of events was rarely factual but always entertaining. Casper grinned at that, his pencil pressing harder into the page as if to underline the name for future reference. In truth, Ben suspected Tobias's account would be even less filtered than his own memory—a version where the Thunderfart Championship had rules, judges, and a trophy worth stealing.

Casper looked up once more, his face open and curious. "Is it… okay to write this?" The question was not about permission to draw, but about recording what many would deem 'unfit for polite company.' Ben's reply came without hesitation. "It's more than okay," he said. "It's okay to fart, too. Let them rip without being ashamed of it. Just tell it honestly." The boy's expression shifted into something steadier, the quiet confidence of someone whose work had been legitimised by an authority far greater than the playground hierarchy.

The hedge rustled again as a breeze passed through, bringing with it the mingled scents of cut grass, spring blossoms, and the stubborn haze of the morning's contests. Casper wrinkled his nose, then smirked, knowing it only added authenticity to his narrative. Ben straightened, brushing off his hands, and cast a glance back toward the courtyard where Isla now watched from the balcony, one hand resting on her belly. She gave him a look that said, without words, Don't get dragged into the next round.

Casper's pencil scratched out one last scene before he flipped the notebook shut, tucking it into the canvas satchel at his side. He stood, brushing leaves from his knees, and adjusted his cap with a composure beyond his years. "You'll finish it later?" Ben asked. Casper nodded once, then turned toward the garden gate that led to the lane, his steps quiet, almost conspiratorial, as though carrying classified intelligence out of enemy territory.

Ben watched him go, feeling oddly reassured. There was something in knowing that the day's chaos wouldn't be lost to the fog of memory. It would live on—not in official records, which would never dare mention such things—but in the private archives of a boy who understood that history was not always grand speeches and golden crowns. Sometimes, it was the sound of laughter ringing over the smell of compost, recorded by someone who saw the value in it.

The hedge stilled behind him, the boy's presence gone, replaced by the return of the courtyard's noise. Ben took a long breath, instantly regretted it, and exhaled with a shake of his head. Somewhere in that yard, Tobias had struck again, and the survivors were rallying their noses for the next assault. The King of Denmark, disguised as a weary father in a cardigan, turned back toward the fray with the air of a man stepping into battle for the third time in a single day.

If anything, he thought, perhaps the boy's record would one day remind the world that dignity had its place—but so did nonsense. Both were needed to keep life in balance. And if Casper's little chronicle outlived them all, at least the truth would survive in the pages of a notebook that smelled faintly of spring, paper, and the remnants of a day nobody could forget.

CHAPTER 7: INTO THE WATER

The castle seemed to understand the weight of the night without needing to be told. Its corridors, usually alive with the echo of quick footsteps and laughter, had quieted to a deep, watchful stillness. The air carried a soft tension, not from fear, but from the shared awareness that something rare and irreversible was about to happen. Isla sat propped on the wide bed in their chamber, her hair unbound, her skin pale with the effort of the day. Each breath she drew was slow, measured, as though she were counting the seconds to hold the pain at bay. Beside her, Ben remained seated, elbows resting on his knees, his eyes fixed on her face, watching every change in expression as if they were signals only he could read. When her brows drew together, he reached for her hand without a word, the contact enough to ground them both.

Beyond the chamber walls, the younger children slept in the upper rooms, unaware of how close they were to waking in a new world. Their laughter from earlier still seemed to hum faintly in the stones, a reminder of the life that pulsed in these walls. For them, tomorrow would bring nothing but joy and wonder—news of new siblings, more faces at the breakfast table, more stories to be told at night. In the minds of children, birth was simple: a baby appeared, wrapped and waiting to be loved. But here, in the dim-lit room where Isla laboured quietly, the truth was measured in breath, heartbeat, and the passing of hours. Ben had counted every single one.

Isla's pains had been arriving for hours, but never sharply enough to pull her from composure. She breathed through each wave with the discipline of someone who understood her body's rhythm and trusted it to lead the way. Ben, though outwardly calm, felt his chest tighten each time she closed her eyes against the pull of another contraction. He would not allow himself to show strain—not tonight. He had seen her do impossible things before, but this felt different. This was not just about bringing life into the world. This was about bringing their life forward, with all the weight of their history resting on it.

In the adjoining room, a faint clink of porcelain marked the return of fresh tea, carried in by Adele, who moved without sound, her years of service having taught her how to pass through moments without intruding. She set the tray on the low table, her eyes meeting Ben's just long enough to convey the unspoken: everything is ready. He nodded once, not taking his hand from Isla's. The warmth of her fingers was reassuring, but the occasional tremor beneath the surface reminded him of the work still to come. He adjusted her blanket, tucking it around her shoulders, the small act grounding him as much as it comforted her.

Somewhere farther down the corridor, a door closed softly. The sound carried in the stillness, the kind of sound that would normally be forgotten in a heartbeat but tonight was sharpened into memory. Ben listened without lifting his head, his senses tuned to every detail. It might have been Kendrick moving through his own quarters, restless as the hours crawled. It could just as easily have been Sørensen making his final patrol before settling in near the main stairwell. Every soul in the castle seemed to be keeping vigil in their own way.

The night outside was clouded, the moon obscured, so that the only light in their chamber came from the soft golden lamps near the bed. It painted the walls in warm tones, softening the sharpness of the carved wood and stone. Isla's eyes, half-closed between contractions, caught the light now and then, and Ben found himself studying the glint as though it were a map to the hours ahead. When she stirred, he leaned closer, ready to listen if she spoke, but she only breathed, deep and steady. It was a rhythm he could have matched in his sleep, and for a fleeting moment, he imagined himself decades older, sitting just like this, waiting for something beyond his control but holding onto it all the same.

He thought briefly of the others—Clara, Tobias, Silje—how each of them would rally when the time came. It was not just him and Isla in this moment, though they were the centre of it. The entire household was an unspoken part of this birth, each person a thread in the web that held them safe. Even the children, though unaware, would carry the memory of this night in some quiet way, sensing its importance long before they could name it. It was a truth Ben had learned early in life: some events were remembered not because of what was seen, but because of what was felt in the air.

The clock on the mantel gave a low, steady tick, measuring the minutes in a language older than their lives here. Ben glanced at it, not because he cared about the hour but because it anchored him in something tangible. Isla shifted again, and he adjusted the cushion at her back, careful not to break the calm she had found. Her breathing deepened, not in distress, but in readiness. He brushed his thumb over the back of her hand, the gesture quiet but deliberate. In moments like this, words were too heavy to carry, so he let touch do the work.

Kendrick's presence hovered in his thoughts. Somewhere in the castle, his adoptive father was pacing, not because of worry alone but because of the weight of what this birth meant for the family line. The twins were more than children—they were heirs, and with that came both pride and the quiet, relentless need to protect them. Ben understood it now in a way he never had before. Every instinct in him was fixed on guarding Isla and the lives she carried, and though the night was long, he welcomed every drawn-out minute if it meant they would arrive safely.

As the hours pressed on, the air seemed thicker, as though the castle itself was holding its breath. Isla's shoulders rose and fell with the grace of someone meeting a challenge without fear. Ben had seen warriors stand before greater dangers and falter. Isla did not falter. Each moment she endured became part of an unspoken legacy that the children would inherit, not in blood alone, but in the example set before their first breath. He could already imagine telling them of this night—not for glory, but so they would understand the strength they came from.

The younger children, still deep in sleep, had no idea they would wake to the news that their family had grown. Tomorrow morning would be a rush of running feet, wide eyes, and questions tumbling over one another. Ben smiled faintly at the thought, though it was quickly swallowed by the need to remain in the present. For now, it was enough to sit in the quiet, to feel the steady rise and fall of Isla's breathing and the occasional press of her fingers around his.

The warm scent of the tea on the table mixed with the faint mineral tang of the water being prepared in the next room. The birthing pool was nearly ready. Ben could hear the quiet movements of Adele and Silje, making certain everything was in place without disturbing the room's fragile calm. Isla's eyes opened for a brief moment, meeting his, and though no words passed between them, it was enough. The look told him she was ready, in her own time, on her own terms.

When another contraction passed, Isla exhaled slowly and let her head rest back against the pillow. Ben adjusted the blanket again, his motions instinctive. He felt the night stretch around them, not threatening but protective, as though time itself had slowed to allow them these final hours before everything changed. The castle might have been built for kings, but in this moment, it was nothing more than the quietest, safest place they could be.

The low hiss of the tap filled the room like a muted heartbeat, steady and unhurried. Ben crouched beside the birthing pool, his hand submerged, measuring the temperature not by any device but by instinct, comparing it to the warmth of Isla's skin. Too cool, and the muscles would tense against the work ahead. Too warm, and it would drain her energy. He adjusted the tap with the care of someone tuning an instrument, seeking that exact point where comfort and strength met. Behind him, Adele moved soundlessly, laying fresh towels across the chair backs, folding each with precision, her eyes sweeping the space for anything out of place. The air was warm, the light low, and the castle seemed to close its arms around the room.

Isla remained in the bed for now, her eyes closed, her breathing deliberate and quiet. She had always carried herself with a kind of unshakable grace, and even now, in the quiet throes of early labour, she was in command of her own body. Ben watched her from across the room, reading the subtle shifts in her posture: the way her shoulders lowered after an exhale, the faint furrow in her brow when a contraction held on longer than expected. He kept his voice low when he spoke, as if the very air might break if disturbed too loudly. "Almost ready," he murmured, not for reassurance—Isla did not need it—but to anchor himself in the task.

Sørensen appeared briefly in the doorway, his broad frame blocking the hall light before he stepped inside. His eyes swept over the scene, taking in the calm, the order, and the readiness of the staff. He gave a small nod, a soldier's approval, then moved to check the outer corridor. There would be no disturbance tonight. The outside world could wait; in here, only the moment mattered. Ben returned his focus to the water, swirling it once with his hand to ensure an even temperature. The heat radiated upward, dampening his skin and softening the tension in his own shoulders.

The soft splash of water accompanied the sound of Silje's quiet steps as she entered with a fresh jug, steam curling from its spout. She tipped it into the pool, and Ben stirred again, feeling the slight change in warmth. It was almost there. He had imagined this moment for months, not in the abstract way fathers sometimes do, but with the precision of a man who knew every choice tonight mattered. The water would carry Isla through the sharpest hours; it had to be perfect. He tested again, and this time the heat met his skin in a way that matched the memory of holding her hands earlier in the evening.

Adele crossed the room with a basin of cool cloths, placing them within Ben's reach. "For her face, when she wants them," she said in a voice barely above a whisper. It was not an instruction but a simple offering. He acknowledged her with a quiet "thank you" and set them near the pool. Even in this, there was an unspoken choreography: everyone moving in sync without stepping over one another's purpose. Years in the castle had taught them all how to read the room without words.

From the bed, Isla shifted, drawing one knee upward as another contraction passed. She made no sound, only lengthened her breathing until the tension eased. Ben's eyes followed her hands as they smoothed the blanket over her legs, her movements deliberate, almost ritualistic. She had prepared herself for this in ways he couldn't fully grasp. She was not bracing against the pain—she was working with it, inviting it to do its necessary work. He felt a swell of quiet admiration, the kind that pressed against the ribs and left no room for anything else.

Outside, the faint creak of a stair tread signalled Kendrick's slow approach. He did not enter, but Ben knew he was there, listening, holding the moment from a respectful distance. Kendrick had never been one to pace without cause, but tonight his steps came and went like a shadow making its rounds. Ben welcomed it; there was comfort in knowing the castle's head was awake, guarding the family from beyond the door. It freed him to give his full attention to Isla.

The final adjustment to the water was made with a careful twist of the tap, cutting it off with precision. The ripples eased, leaving the surface smooth and reflective under the low lamplight. Ben leaned back on his heels, satisfied at last. He could see the faint mist rising in the air, curling toward the ceiling beams before disappearing into the warm night. The room smelled faintly of lavender from the oil Silje had added earlier, subtle enough not to overpower but enough to soften the edges of the moment.

Isla opened her eyes then, their calmness startling in its clarity. She looked toward the pool and then at Ben, the faintest curve of a smile touching her lips. No words passed, but he read the message as clearly as if she had spoken: I am ready. He rose, moving to her side, offering his arm to help her stand when she chose. She did not move yet, but her hand in his was answer enough.

Adele and Silje exchanged a glance, and without needing to be told, they began to ready the final details: a folded blanket at the pool's edge, a low stool beside it, the towels arranged in order of use. Sørensen returned to the doorway briefly, scanning the hall again before disappearing back into the quiet. Every layer of preparation was in place now. There was nothing left but to begin.

Ben knelt beside Isla once more, his hand resting lightly against her arm as another contraction came and went. He could feel the change in its rhythm, deeper and more insistent than before. The water waited, still and warm, a silent witness to what was about to unfold. In that moment, the world narrowed to the four walls of the chamber, the steady rise and fall of Isla's chest, and the weight of the hours yet to pass.

The soft knock at the door was barely more than a breath, yet it carried through the room with a clarity that made Ben turn his head. Sørensen opened it just wide enough to admit Dr. Helene Møller, her presence quiet but certain, as though the air shifted to make space for her. She removed her coat in one smooth motion, placing her bag near the low table without disturbing the rhythm already in motion. There was no rush in her movements, no unnecessary noise, only the muted authority of someone who had attended more births than she could count. Ben felt an immediate calm settle at her arrival, not because she took over, but because she stepped into the moment without altering its shape.

Isla did not lift her head when the doctor entered. Her focus remained on the warm water, her breathing slow and measured, each exhale rippling the surface in faint concentric circles. She was deep in her own space now, eyes half-lidded, her hands resting on the pool's edge. Ben recognised the change in her face, the way the muscles around her eyes softened even as the rest of her body engaged with each wave of effort. Dr. Møller crouched beside the pool, speaking in a low voice, asking nothing more than if Isla was comfortable. Isla's response was a small nod, her attention already drawn inward again.

The doctor placed her hands lightly on Isla's forearm, checking her pulse, then shifted to measure the rhythm of the contractions without a single interruption to their flow. There was a respect in her touch—unhurried, deliberate, never forcing. Ben observed this with a quiet gratitude, knowing that here, there would be no orders barked, no intrusion of unnecessary instruction. This was Isla's moment, and everyone around her was here to protect it.

Ben remained near her shoulder, one hand resting lightly against her back, steadying her as she adjusted her position. The lamplight cast a golden hue across her skin, and for a fleeting second, he was struck by the thought that this strength had always been there. He had seen it in small acts over the years—in the way she handled the children when they were sick, in the way she confronted challenges without flinching—but now it was unfiltered, entirely present, and utterly undeniable. He could not take his eyes from her.

Dr. Møller gave a quiet update to Ben without looking away from her work. "Progress is strong. She knows exactly what to do." Her voice carried no hint of surprise, as though Isla's composure was expected, perhaps even common among the women she attended. But to Ben, it was nothing short of extraordinary. He nodded, more to himself than in reply, and glanced toward the towels Adele had laid out earlier, noting their perfect order as though they too stood ready for what was to come.

Another contraction passed, and Isla's breathing remained steady. The pool's surface trembled with each deep exhale, but there was no grimace, no cry. Only the slow, deliberate control of someone entirely in tune with the process. Ben found himself matching his own breaths to hers, an unconscious tether that anchored him in the present. He didn't realise until later that the sound of the water and the rhythm of their breathing had merged into one unbroken cadence, a shared language without words.

Silje stepped forward with a cool cloth, handing it to Ben without needing to be asked. He placed it gently along Isla's hairline, feeling the heat beneath her skin. She gave the faintest sigh, and though her eyes remained closed, he knew she felt his presence. He brushed a damp strand of hair from her face, the gesture small but grounding for them both. Around them, the staff moved with quiet efficiency, their steps muted against the floorboards, their voices kept low enough to be absorbed by the warm air.

Dr. Møller checked the time, then shifted her position slightly to observe Isla from a different angle. Her expression gave nothing away, but her hands moved with a practiced certainty that told Ben everything was as it should be. She did not rush the process; she allowed it to unfold at Isla's own pace, her role more guardian than conductor. Ben appreciated that. There was nothing clinical here, nothing stripped of humanity.

Another wave came, deeper this time, and Ben felt Isla's grip tighten briefly on the edge of the pool. She didn't make a sound, only drew in more air and let it out slowly, her shoulders lowering in the release. He leaned closer, his voice low and steady. "You're doing perfectly." She didn't reply, but her breathing did not falter, and he took that as answer enough. The water glinted faintly under the light, reflecting their faces in blurred fragments.

Sørensen appeared again in the doorway, only for a moment, his eyes scanning the scene. Ben caught his gaze, and in that silent exchange there was a shared acknowledgement: all was well, for now. Sørensen gave the smallest nod and stepped back into the hall, his presence a reminder that the outside world was kept firmly at bay. The walls of the castle, for this night, were an unbreachable line.

Dr. Møller leaned closer to Isla, speaking just above a whisper. "When you're ready, we'll shift slightly in the water. No rush." Isla's head tilted in the barest acknowledgment, but she remained still, waiting for the next contraction to guide her. Ben watched the exchange, struck again by how much power could exist in stillness. It was not the absence of action—it was the holding of it, the deliberate choice to move only when the body asked.

The warmth of the room deepened, both from the air and from the steady work taking place. Ben adjusted his position, keeping one knee on the folded blanket beside the pool, his other foot grounded as though ready to rise if she needed him to lift her. Every muscle in his body was alert, but none of them tense. He had been waiting for this moment for months, yet he felt no impatience—only the steady pull forward, like a tide moving toward the shore.

Dr. Møller's eyes flicked to Ben briefly, a silent reminder to keep himself steady as well. He understood. Isla was not the only one in this room whose focus mattered. He tightened his hand over hers, grounding himself in the same rhythm that anchored her. The water lapped quietly against the pool's sides, the only sound aside from their shared breathing.

The shift in the room was almost imperceptible at first—a deepening of the water's movement, the faintest catch in Isla's breath—and then, with a quiet murmur from Dr. Møller, the air itself seemed to hold still. Ben leaned closer, his eyes fixed on Isla's face as another contraction drew her inward, her grip tightening on the pool's edge. There was no panic in her expression, only focus so complete that it silenced everything else. The surface of the water trembled, and for a moment it seemed the whole world balanced on that delicate ripple.

Dr. Møller's voice was low but certain. "Almost here." She adjusted her position with measured ease, hands poised beneath the surface, her eyes never leaving the point where new life pressed forward. Isla exhaled slowly, and the water's gentle swaying became something more—a rhythm shifting toward conclusion. Ben could feel it in his own body, an instinctive tightening in his chest as if bracing for impact, though his hand on her shoulder remained steady. The room's warmth closed in, drawing everyone present into the same narrow circle of anticipation.

Then, with one final, smooth surge, the first cry tore through the quiet—a sound raw and defiant, at once fragile and unyielding. Dr. Møller lifted the child carefully through the water, cradling the slippery form with hands that had done this countless times, yet still moved with reverence. A boy. Small, flushed, and fierce from the first breath. She did not rush to cut the cord, instead placing him gently into Ben's waiting arms, letting the bond form in those first, irreplaceable seconds.

The warmth of the child's skin against his forearms was unlike anything Ben had known. He stared down at the tiny face, eyes still sealed, mouth open from the effort of claiming his place in the world. Water beaded along his cheeks, clinging for a heartbeat before rolling away. Ben's throat tightened, his breath uneven now in a way it hadn't been through the entire labour. There was no preparation for this—no quiet conversation in the months before could match the immediacy of holding his son for the first time.

The cord still linked them, a living thread binding three hearts in the same steady rhythm. Dr. Møller glanced at Ben, her tone warm but practical. "Let him rest here a moment. He knows your heartbeat already." Ben nodded, lowering his voice to a whisper that only the child could hear, though he doubted words mattered; it was the sound that would carry. The boy shifted faintly, a small fist curling against Ben's wrist, and the world seemed to still again, holding them in that fragile pause before the next wave came.

At the doorway, Kendrick's broad frame caught the light for a moment. He had remained back through the entire birth, respecting the space without needing to be told. Now, his hand rested against the frame as though steadying himself. His eyes, normally so clear and guarded, glistened with the weight of seeing his first grandchild take breath. He did not speak, did not step forward—this was Ben's moment—but the way he lingered was its own kind of presence, one that would be remembered long after the night passed.

Isla leaned back in the water, her breathing still deep but easier now, the effort of bringing him forth giving way to quiet release. Her eyes opened to find Ben holding the child, and in that glance there was no need for language. He moved closer so she could see him fully, lowering their son toward her so the water once again touched his skin. She pressed her cheek to his damp head, closing her eyes in a moment of fierce, silent joy.

Around them, the castle felt alive in a way it rarely did at night. It was not from sound—the corridors remained hushed—but from a pulse that seemed to move through the walls themselves. Those within the old stone knew without being told that something had changed. Perhaps it was the subtle difference in the air, perhaps a shared instinct among those who had called this place home for generations, but the birth of a prince, even one hidden from the world beyond Denmark, could not pass without marking the place that sheltered it.

Dr. Møller worked quietly, preparing for the next arrival while allowing this first bond to unfold undisturbed. She moved with the certainty of someone who knew the pace of twins—there would be no rushing, but neither would there be long to wait. Ben, aware of this, adjusted his hold so the boy's weight rested more securely in his arms, his other hand still linked with Isla's. The three of them formed a single, unbroken line, anchored by the sound of water and the faint, rhythmic breathing of the child between them.

Kendrick stepped back from the doorway then, unwilling to intrude further but not yet ready to leave. His retreat was slow, deliberate, the way one might step away from a sacred space without breaking its hold. In the hallway beyond, the light fell softer, and his shadow stretched long across the floor before disappearing into the turn of the corridor. Within the room, Ben hardly noticed; the world had narrowed entirely to the child in his arms and the woman beside him, the rest of the castle held at bay by that small, perfect circle of warmth.

The moment between the births felt like a held breath, the air inside the room taut yet calm. Ben still cradled his son, feeling the small chest rise and fall against his arm, when Dr. Møller glanced toward Isla with a nod that spoke of the next arrival. The water rippled gently around her, the surface catching the soft light from the lamps above. Isla's focus remained unbroken; she shifted slightly, the warmth of the pool wrapping her like a steadying embrace. Ben kept close, torn between holding the first child and reaching for the second, knowing he could do neither fully until she was ready.

The second contraction was stronger, more insistent. Isla's breath deepened, and her hands gripped the sides of the birthing pool with quiet determination. There was no sound from her save the rhythm of inhalation and exhalation, the kind that spoke not of struggle but of surrender to what must come. The castle seemed to lean in closer, its ancient stones absorbing the moment in silence. Water lapped softly at Isla's arms, the sound a counterpoint to the slow, steady cadence of her labour.

Dr. Møller's hands moved beneath the water again, her posture attentive but unhurried. She murmured something low—perhaps a measure of encouragement, perhaps just the rhythm of her own breathing—but her eyes stayed on Isla, reading every shift in her body as if following a language long learned. Ben adjusted his stance, holding his son securely while leaning just enough to see, his heart thudding with a double awareness: the wonder in his arms and the wonder about to join it.

Then, with the grace of inevitability, the second child emerged into the water, her small form drawn gently into Dr. Møller's hands. The difference in her cry was immediate—higher, lighter, like a thread of sound carried on air rather than pushed through stone. She kicked faintly, her limbs flexing as though testing the shape of this new place. Ben's breath caught; she was perfect in her fragility, perfect in the same way her brother was strong.

Dr. Møller lifted the child slowly from the pool, allowing the water to stream away before passing her toward Ben. For an instant he stood motionless, his arms already full with the boy, until instinct guided him to shift his hold. The movement was clumsy only in thought; in practice it was natural, his body creating space for both as if it had been preparing for this moment all along. The boy nestled deeper into the crook of one arm while the girl settled against the other, her cheek finding the warmth above his heart.

Isla leaned forward in the pool, her eyes searching for both children at once. Ben bent toward her, lowering them so that her hands could touch each small head, her fingertips tracing their damp crowns. The faint smile that touched her lips was both exhausted and fierce, the expression of someone who had carried not just the weight of life but the certainty of its arrival. Her gaze met Ben's, and though no words passed, the connection was complete.

The twins lay quiet now, their brief cries replaced by soft breaths and small movements. The boy's hand flexed against Ben's shirt, while the girl's tiny foot pressed lightly against her brother's leg, as though anchoring herself to him even here. They were bound already—not just by the minutes between their births, but by something older, a symmetry written before they had faces or names. Ben could feel it in their stillness, the way they seemed to breathe in time with one another.

Dr. Møller worked quietly again, tending to the necessary tasks with the precision of someone who understood the sanctity of the moment. She made no effort to hurry the separation of cords, allowing the final pulses to pass from mother to child. The water around Isla was calm again, disturbed only by the faint ripples from her shifting legs. In her eyes, there was no trace of pain now—only a watchfulness that was almost regal in its poise.

Kendrick had not left. He stood just beyond the doorway, his hand still on the frame, though his stance had changed. His head was bowed slightly, not in deference but in the quiet acknowledgment of something he could never fully put into words. The sight of both children in Ben's arms seemed to weigh on him differently than the first had—a doubling not just of life, but of responsibility, of what this night meant for the family and the House they all carried.

Ben shifted again, holding the children closer to his chest. Their warmth seeped through the fabric of his shirt, their combined weight grounding him in a way nothing else could. He lowered his head to breathe in the scent of them—water, skin, the faintest trace of something he could only think of as newness. It was a scent he knew would fade in days, replaced by others, but tonight it was unspoiled, untouched by anything beyond this room.

Isla reached for them, her arms trembling slightly from effort, and Ben leaned forward until both children were within her embrace. The three of them formed a quiet tableau, the twins resting between them as if the world had always been this small, this contained. Ben's cheek brushed Isla's hair, damp and warm against his skin, and for a moment, neither of them breathed deeply, as though fearing the spell might break.

The names came without hesitation—Hannah and Frederik—spoken softly but firmly, each name settling over its bearer like a promise. The boy stirred faintly at the sound, and the girl's hand opened against Ben's chest, her fingers splayed in what could have been chance, but felt instead like claim. Isla's smile deepened, her eyes closing as though sealing the moment behind them.

The castle seemed to exhale then, a subtle release in the walls, as though acknowledging the completion of what had begun hours before. Outside, the night held its quiet, but within these stone boundaries, two new heartbeats had joined the rhythm that had pulsed here for centuries. The twins would be known in Denmark, their arrival whispered in corners and shared in the warmth of trusted kitchens, but beyond these borders, silence would hold. For now.

Kendrick stood with his back against the cold stone, the chill seeping through the fabric of his jacket as though the castle itself wished to steady him. He had positioned himself just far enough from the birthing room so as not to intrude, yet close enough to feel every shift in the air. The muffled sounds of water, low voices, and the faintest newborn cries reached him through the heavy door, and each one carried a weight he could not set down. The moment had unfolded without spectacle—no trumpets, no public display—but its significance resonated through every stone of Rosenshavn. Kendrick knew history was being made within that room, even if the world beyond Denmark would not know it tonight.

Annemarie stood beside him, her hand resting lightly on the curve of his arm, her presence a steadying anchor against the flood of emotion that threatened to undo him. She said nothing, her silence not from lack of words but from an understanding that speech would fracture the fragile stillness they were holding. Her gaze was fixed on the closed door, yet Kendrick knew she was seeing more than what was before her. They had guarded many secrets in their lives—some heavy, some necessary—but this one felt different, not because it was dangerous, but because it was precious beyond measure.

A faint, watery cry drifted through again, softer this time, and Kendrick closed his eyes. It struck him with sudden force that the sound was not just new—it was a continuation, a voice added to a chorus that stretched back centuries. These children were not only Ben and Isla's, they were Rosenshavn's, and by extension, Denmark's. The thought swelled in him until his throat tightened, and before he could stop it, a tear escaped. It traced a slow line down his cheek, unnoticed until Annemarie's thumb brushed it away with the same tenderness she might show their own children.

She did not look at him as she did it, sparing him the weight of acknowledgment. Kendrick was grateful. His strength had been measured all his life in how well he could stand without faltering, how resolutely he could protect what mattered. Yet tonight, he understood that strength could be quiet, could bend without breaking. The tears did not lessen him; they were a testament to what he valued, to the truth that some moments demanded surrender rather than stoicism.

The corridor stretched long in both directions, lit only by the muted glow of wall sconces. The air carried the faint scent of polished oak and the lingering aroma of the evening's meal, yet it all seemed distant now, background to the heartbeat of the room beyond the door. Kendrick had walked these halls thousands of times, had known them in light and shadow, in times of celebration and in times of loss. Yet tonight they felt transformed, as though the walls themselves had drawn closer to witness the birth, to hold the secret until it could be safely shared.

Annemarie's hand shifted to his, fingers lacing without force, the gesture speaking more than any whispered reassurance could. She, too, understood the magnitude of what they were safeguarding. The public might one day demand to know the truth, might clamor for images, details, proclamations, but not tonight. Tonight belonged to Ben and Isla alone. Their first hours as parents to both a son and a daughter were to be untouched by the noise of the outside world.

Kendrick could picture them inside, Ben holding both children, Isla's damp hair curling at her temples, her eyes fixed on the new life she had brought into being. He could imagine the way the twins would fit against Ben's chest, one hand resting protectively on each small back, his own eyes betraying the emotions he might try to contain. Kendrick's chest ached with the thought—not from sadness, but from the fierce pride that came with seeing the boy he had helped guide into manhood now standing fully in his own place.

Another faint sound reached them, this time the rustle of movement rather than a cry. Kendrick angled his head slightly, as though it might bring the scene into clearer focus. He did not need to see to know what was happening—he had been there when Thomas was born, had heard the same careful shifts, the same gentle voices working together to keep the mother comfortable. He knew Ben's gratitude would be wordless but deep, his quiet nature making every glance, every nod, every small touch mean more than any speech.

The longer Kendrick stood there, the more the moment settled into him, as though it were imprinting itself in his bones. He thought of how the children would grow within these walls, of the games they would play, the lessons they would learn, the unspoken expectations they would inherit. He thought, too, of how Ben and Isla would balance the public and private halves of their lives, how carefully they would have to guard the parts that could never be given to the world. And Kendrick knew, without question, that he and Annemarie would be there for all of it, as steady as the stones beneath their feet.

Annemarie's voice came at last, low and measured. "They're safe," she said, not as if to reassure him, but as a statement of fact. Kendrick gave a slight nod, the truth of it warming him against the chill of the wall at his back. He did not need to ask how she knew. There were some things that could be felt without being seen, and tonight, safety was one of them.

He shifted slightly, his shoulder brushing hers, the movement subtle but deliberate. It was not a moment for grand gestures; it was a moment for presence, for the kind of companionship that did not need to be named. Together, they stood guard—not in the sense of watching for threats, but in holding the space sacred until it could be returned to its keepers.

Kendrick's thoughts drifted to the future, to the day when the world might finally learn the truth of Ben's position. He wondered if Hannah and Frederik would ever know a life without scrutiny, without expectation. He hoped they might, even as he doubted it. But here, now, he could give them one thing—time. Time to be held, to be known first by the people who loved them most, before anyone else could claim a piece of them.

The quiet stretched between him and Annemarie, not uncomfortable but deep. It was the kind of silence that carried weight, that spoke of years spent walking side by side through joy and difficulty alike. They had learned long ago that some of the most important moments happened in this kind of stillness, where nothing needed to be said because everything was already understood.

Another tear slipped free before Kendrick could catch it, but he made no move to hide it. Annemarie's hand tightened briefly on his, a reminder that vulnerability was not weakness, not here, not with her. The sound of soft voices in the birthing room rose and fell again, and Kendrick breathed it in, letting the moment brand itself into his memory.

The hallway felt both endless and enclosed, a liminal space between the past and the future. Kendrick knew that when the door opened, something would have shifted irrevocably—not just for Ben and Isla, but for all of them. Until then, he would remain here, keeping vigil, the silent witness to a night that would live in the quiet places of his heart for as long as he drew breath.

In Denmark, news travelled not with the sharp crack of headlines but with the soft certainty of shared knowledge. By morning, the birth of a prince and princess had already threaded itself through Copenhagen's streets. It would not be printed in garish type on the front of any international paper—not yet—but in the cafés, bakeries, and small harbour shops, people spoke of it in hushed tones that carried pride rather than gossip. Denmark, after all, was used to guarding its own. There was no rush to force the moment into the hands of outsiders who would only trample it.

Inside Rosenshavn Castle, that knowledge settled like a warm blanket over its inhabitants. The staff moved with a lightness that belied the gravity of the event, each one understanding that the twins' arrival was something to be cherished quietly. They had all seen the storms that could follow the scent of royal blood, the hunger of a world that cared little for the sanctity of a family's first hours together. What existed here was a kind of unspoken covenant: protect the children, protect the parents, protect the truth for as long as possible.

The city itself had no need for spectacle. In Copenhagen, royalty did not exist as distant figures framed in polished portraits—they lived among the people, woven into the fabric of the streets. Ben could walk the length of Nyhavn without needing an entourage, though more often than not, someone would greet him with a nod or a quiet word of respect. That respect now extended to his children, unseen though they were, as if the entire city understood that some moments demanded discretion.

Ben had considered what would happen when the wider world learned the truth. He knew it was inevitable—secrets had a way of slipping free, no matter how carefully they were held. Yet for now, he allowed himself to rest in the knowledge that this day belonged to Denmark alone. The people outside his gates knew what had happened, but their silence was not born of fear; it was born of loyalty. That loyalty was worth more to him than any title, any ceremony.

Isla, still resting in their private chambers, understood this as well. She had grown up in a quieter rhythm, away from the demands of a public crown, yet she knew enough to recognise the gift she had been given. There were no photographers outside the windows, no reporters pressing for statements. She could hold her children without thinking of angles or appearances. She could memorise their faces without feeling the weight of an audience.

Kendrick had spoken of it often—how Denmark had its own way of protecting what mattered. In other countries, the birth of royal heirs would have been met with pageantry so loud it drowned out the cries of the newborns themselves. Here, the moment was allowed to breathe. The only announcements came in the form of shared glances, the kind of subtle nods exchanged between neighbours who had seen the castle's windows lit late into the night.

Still, the knowledge of how fragile this peace could be lingered like a shadow in the back of Ben's mind. He had seen what happened when the press found a thread to pull. One loose detail could unravel years of careful privacy. He thought of Kent, of England's relentless tabloids, of how quickly kindness could be replaced with intrusion. That was why he clung to these hours with such intensity—they were finite.

Even the youngest members of the household seemed to sense it. The children, though curious, were kept at a gentle distance from the newborns, their excitement tempered by a respect they might not have been able to articulate. They whispered to each other in the hallways, inventing theories about which twin was older, about who they might grow up to be. Their laughter was soft, their footsteps careful, as though they understood they were walking through something delicate.

The kitchen bustled, though no trays left its doors for strangers. Meals were prepared only for those within the castle walls, each dish sent up with a quiet knock rather than a fanfare. Even the cooks, who loved nothing more than sharing their work, understood the importance of containment. This was a celebration meant to be savoured privately, without the distortion that came when too many hands reached for it.

Ben stepped briefly into one of the upper corridors, looking out over the city below. The lights of Copenhagen blinked against the dark, steady and unhurried. He knew that behind some of those windows, people were speaking his children's names already, not because they had been officially announced, but because in Denmark, news could spread without malice. That difference mattered. It was what allowed him to stand there without tightening his guard.

There was a quiet satisfaction in knowing that the world beyond Denmark remained in the dark. Not because he wished to deceive them, but because he wanted to protect his family from the inevitable noise that would come. The day the truth left these borders would be the day the silence ended. But today was not that day. Today, the castle stood as both home and shield.

Annemarie had said earlier that morning, "We do not owe them this yet." She had been right. The world would take when it was ready, and when it did, it would not ask permission. Until then, they owed the truth only to themselves and to the city that already held it. The people of Copenhagen would not betray them lightly; they had too much history with Rosenshavn to squander that trust.

Even Uncle Sørensen, never one for sentiment, kept his voice low as he moved about the halls. He understood that keeping outsiders at bay required more than locked gates. It required discipline—no stray calls to friends abroad, no casual slips in conversation. The smallest fracture could let the outside in. They had all seen it happen before, and the consequences were not something any of them wished to revisit.

Ben returned to Isla's side before long, easing himself into the chair beside her bed. She was holding both twins, their faces turned toward her heartbeat as if they had always known it would be there. He thought again of the city beyond their walls, the way it carried this knowledge without pressing against them. That, he realised, was the truest kind of loyalty—one that did not demand to be seen.

As the hours passed, the castle's heartbeat slowed to match that of the sleeping newborns. Outside, the night carried on as it always did, unhurried, respectful, and silent. Within Denmark, the birth of Hannah and Frederik was public knowledge. But beyond its borders, the truth remained folded away, as carefully guarded as any crown. And for now, that was exactly how it needed to be.

The castle had quieted again, the kind of hush that comes only after a day of great change. Isla slept in the adjoining chamber, her breathing steady, the twins tucked close to her in their cradles. Ben stood at the tall window, looking out at the courtyard where the evening light washed the cobblestones in gold. His mind, however, was not on the view. It was on a boy with quick sketches, a sly smile that didn't last long, and eyes that seemed too old for his face.

Casper. The name had lingered in his thoughts since yesterday, when the boy's notebook had been filled with illustrated chaos—lopsided footballs, wild handwriting about thunderfarts, and comical arrows pointing to "the exact moment Tobias realised the smell wasn't from the dog." Yet behind all that humour had been something quieter, almost hidden, that Ben had not named at the time. It was only now, with the day's weight behind him, that he began to see it more clearly.

He found himself in the kitchen late in the evening, the place where loose conversations often began. Adele was there, tidying mugs from the long line of tea and coffee served to the family earlier in the day. She looked up when he entered, her hands never pausing in their work. There was something in her face that told him she already knew why he had come.

"You're thinking about the boy," she said softly, without preamble.

Ben didn't deny it. "Casper Arthur Bille," he replied, speaking the name as though saying it aloud might unlock some hidden door. "Tell me."

Adele set the last mug on the drying rack and leaned against the counter, folding her arms. Her voice stayed low, respectful of the castle's sleeping chambers above. "His mother was Kathinka. She used to work in the harbour market, selling bread in the mornings, mending fishing nets in the afternoons. Strong woman. Proud. She raised him alone after his father died—Casper was barely a year old when it happened."

Ben's brow furrowed. "And her?"

Adele hesitated, her gaze slipping briefly to the window as though the answer might be easier if she didn't have to look at him. "Two years ago. Fever that took her in less than a week. The neighbours tried to help, but she wouldn't leave the flat. By the time anyone convinced her, it was too late."

The words landed with more weight than Ben had expected. He had asked out of curiosity, perhaps even a quiet sense of responsibility toward a child who had drifted into their world. But now there was a pull in his chest that went beyond duty.

"Who took him in?" Ben asked.

"No one for long," Adele replied. "He's been passed between relatives, but none kept him more than a few months. Some say he's difficult. I say he's too smart for the adults he's been given. He knows when people are pretending."

Ben thought of the boy's sketches again—not just the humour, but the details, the way he had captured movement and expression in quick, sure lines. That was not the work of a child untouched by observation. That was the work of someone who had learned to watch quietly, because watching was safer than speaking.

"He lives here now?" Ben asked.

"Stays here sometimes," Adele said. "Uncle Sørensen makes sure he has a place when it's needed. But Casper doesn't ask for much. Never has. He's the sort who'd rather make himself small than risk being sent away again."

The image of the boy, hunched slightly as he drew in the corner of the courtyard, returned with sharp clarity. Ben realised then why the thought of him had stayed all day. It wasn't just pity—it was recognition. He knew what it was to carry truths quietly, to make himself small in a room until he was sure of the people in it.

Adele's voice softened further. "His birthday's in three weeks. He'll be nine. Never had more than a cupcake and a candle."

Ben stayed silent for a long moment, his jaw tightening. He could picture that small celebration—one light in the dark, a wish spoken over sugar before it was blown out. He wondered if the boy had ever wished for something that lasted beyond the moment the candle died.

"I want to speak with him," Ben said finally. "Not tonight. Tomorrow. But I'll see him."

Adele nodded, as though she had been expecting this. "You'll find him in the east garden in the morning. He likes it there. Says it's the only place where the air feels like it belongs to him."

Ben left the kitchen quietly, his footsteps muted against the stone. As he passed the nursery, he paused at the door, looking in on Isla and the twins. They slept in a peace he knew Casper had not felt in years, perhaps ever. It struck him, in that stillness, that the boy's story was not finished—and perhaps, if he had anything to say about it, it would not end as it had begun.

When he finally returned to his own room, the image of the boy's eyes stayed with him. Not the humour of the sketches, not the cherry-stained grin from yesterday's games, but the moment between—the unguarded flicker of someone who had learned too early how fragile a home could be.

The first pale light of morning crept into the chamber, casting soft gold over the curve of Isla's cheek. She stirred slowly, as though surfacing from a dream she was reluctant to leave. Ben was already there, seated at her side with the stillness of someone who had been awake for hours, watching, thinking. Between them, the twins slept without a sound, swaddled in light cotton, their tiny breaths rising and falling in a rhythm that seemed older than the castle itself.

Isla opened her eyes fully and found his gaze fixed on her, his hand resting lightly on the edge of the bassinet. "You didn't sleep," she said softly, though it was not a question. Her voice held that quiet certainty that comes from knowing the truth before it is spoken.

Ben smiled faintly, not to reassure her, but to acknowledge she was right. "I've been thinking about someone," he said. His tone carried the weight of a name before it was spoken. "Casper."

Isla's brow softened, the corners of her mouth tilting into the barest suggestion of a smile. She had seen the boy yesterday, laughing in the courtyard, his hands moving swiftly over paper. She had noticed how he looked at the others—always watching before joining in. "The one with the sketches," she said.

Ben nodded. "He's an orphan. His father died when he was a baby. His mother—Kathinka—two years ago. Since then, he's been moved from one place to another. No one keeps him for long." Isla's gaze did not leave his. She did not rush to fill the silence or to soften the truth. "And you want to change that," she said, not as a question but as fact.

Ben's hand moved to rest over hers, their fingers meeting with an ease that spoke of years rather than months of marriage. "He's bright, Isla. Clever in ways you don't see until you really look. And he's been… overlooked. I can see it in his eyes. He watches like someone who's waiting for the ground to shift under his feet."

She turned her head toward the twins, her hand brushing their blankets as though to draw strength from their nearness. "And what will you do?" "Tomorrow morning, I'll speak with him in the east garden," Ben said. "Adele told me that's where he feels the air belongs to him. I want to hear his story from him—not from someone else's memory."

Isla's eyes softened further, though her expression held its steadiness. "You already know what you'll do. This is just the part where you tell me, so you won't be accused of acting without warning." He laughed under his breath, the sound low and warm. "You've always known me too well."

"I've known you since the library," she said, her smile deepening slightly. "Since the boy who thought he was just looking for answers and instead found the truth that would change everything. You've never been able to leave a story unfinished. Not then, not now."

Ben's gaze returned to the twins. "If someone had stepped in for me when I was his age, maybe things would have been different. But I had to wait until I was old enough to act for myself. I don't want him to wait that long."

The twins stirred faintly, their faces turning toward each other as if drawn by some shared instinct. Isla watched them a moment before speaking again. "Then speak to him. And if you decide he belongs here, we'll make room. We always do."

Ben reached for her hand again, his thumb brushing over her knuckles. "It's not just about belonging. It's about giving him something solid—something that doesn't vanish because someone decides it's inconvenient."

She tilted her head, studying him as she had when they were younger, when he would come to her with ideas too big for the space they lived in. "Then you'd better make sure he knows you mean it. That you're not just passing through his life like the others." Ben nodded, the thought already etched into his mind like a promise. "I will."

They sat in silence for a time, the only sound the gentle shift of water in the birthing pool as it cooled, the faint creak of the castle's bones waking to the day. Ben could feel the shape of what was coming—not only the conversation with Casper, but the change it would bring.

When the twins settled again, their small fists curled in sleep, Isla's gaze found his once more. "Go to him in the morning," she said. "And when you come back, don't just tell me what he said. Tell me what you saw."

Ben smiled, though his eyes remained serious. "You'll know before I say it." And in that quiet moment, with the warmth of their children between them, they both understood that tomorrow's meeting would mark the beginning of something neither had planned, but both had already accepted.

The east garden carried a stillness unlike any other part of the castle, as though the air itself wished to keep secrets. The morning sunlight filtered through the ivy-clad arches, laying golden shapes across the gravel path where Ben walked slowly, his hands deep in his pockets. Ahead, on the low stone bench near the fountain, sat Casper, a small figure with knees drawn up, sketchbook balanced against them, and his pencil moving with an urgency that suggested the paper might vanish if he paused. The boy's strokes were quick and deliberate, capturing something only he could see, as though the garden spoke a language in lines and shadows. Ben stopped a short distance away, his gaze following the movement of that pencil, already reading the story without needing words. He stood quietly for a moment, letting the sound of water and the scratch of graphite bridge the gap between them, before stepping closer.

"That's fine work," Ben said at last, his voice carrying easily through the quiet without breaking it. The boy looked up briefly, his eyes squinting against the sunlight, before returning to his page as if unwilling to lose the moment caught beneath his hands. Ben did not push. Instead, he stepped to the side of the bench, close enough to see the shapes taking form—each line firm and sure, without hesitation. "Do you always come out here this early?" Ben asked, watching the steady movement of the pencil. Casper shrugged, the gesture small but telling. "It's quiet here," the boy replied after a pause, his voice carrying neither shyness nor defiance, simply stating the truth. "No one bothers me."

"That's why I came," Ben answered, lowering himself onto the bench with the careful measure of someone who did not wish to intrude. He left a space between them, not out of coldness, but to let the boy keep the control he clearly valued. "I wanted to speak with you. Not about yesterday's game, or the sketches, though those were both remarkable. I wanted to talk about something that will matter for the rest of your life." He kept his tone steady, not allowing urgency to crowd the words. Casper's pencil stopped moving, resting against the page, but he did not close the book. His small hands flattened over the drawing, holding it in place as he asked quietly, "Bigger how?"

Ben studied the boy's profile for a moment before answering. "You've had places to sleep, but not a home that's yours. You've had people nearby, but not people who are yours. And there's a difference." The boy's gaze did not leave the fountain ahead of them, its water folding endlessly over itself. "People don't keep me," he said, the statement offered like a weather report—fact, without drama. The simplicity of it tightened something in Ben's chest.

"That's what I want to change," Ben told him, leaning forward with his elbows on his knees. "If I could give you a place to belong—not for a season, not for a trial, but forever—would you believe me?" Casper's head turned slightly at that, his eyes flicking toward Ben's face for the first time. They were sharp eyes, not mistrusting, but measuring. "Forever's a long time," the boy said, as though weighing the word in his mind.

"It is," Ben agreed, "which is why I'm not saying this lightly. If I bring you into my family, it's not a test. It's not to see how it works out. It's because I mean to make you my son, with my name and my home, and to give you the certainty that you'll never have to wonder where you belong again." The boy's hands tightened on the sketchbook just slightly, the knuckles paling. "You mean… you'd be my dad?"

"Yes," Ben said without hesitation. "And not just in title, not in a way that leaves you questioning. In every sense of the word that matters, I would be your father. You would be part of this family as surely as if you had been here since the day you were born." The boy's eyes searched his face again, not in suspicion, but in hope that needed confirmation. "Would it be… one hundred percent? Not until something changes? Not until it's hard?"

"One hundred percent," Ben said firmly, his voice as unyielding as stone. "And there is nothing in this world that could make me take that back." The boy was silent for a long moment, his gaze returning to the fountain as though thinking over the promise. Then, with a certainty that did not waver, he said, "Then yes. Of course yes."

The answer did not surprise Ben—he had read it in the boy's eyes before the words came—but the sound of it settled deep in him, sealing something neither of them would ever take lightly. "Can I… can I have a hug?" Casper asked then, his voice softer, not unsure, but carrying the weight of a request he did not make often. Ben's arm went around him without hesitation, drawing the boy close, his small frame pressing against him with a force that spoke of more than gratitude.

It was not the cautious touch of strangers, nor the quick embrace of politeness. This was the grip of someone who had been holding on alone for too long and had finally found something he dared not lose. Ben closed his eyes against the warmth of it, feeling the boy's heartbeat against his own, and in that moment titles, thrones, and the burdens of kingdoms faded into something smaller than the promise they had just made.

When they drew back, Casper's eyes were brighter but free of the guarded look they had carried before. Ben rested his hand on the boy's shoulder, turning them both toward the path that led back to the great oak doors. "Come on," he said. "There's a family inside who's going to want to meet their new brother." They began walking, the crunch of gravel underfoot sounding less like an end to the conversation and more like the first steps of something neither of them had yet imagined fully, but both already knew had begun.

The afternoon sun slanted through the tall windows of the registry room, striking the polished oak table where the great leather-bound ledger lay open. Its pages, thick and edged in gold, carried centuries of history in ink and script—names of children born into the House, marriages sworn, alliances marked. Ben sat at the head of the table, the quill poised between his fingers, his hand steady though his chest felt impossibly full. He looked at the blank line before him, at the space waiting to hold the first written record of his son and daughter's names, and felt the quiet weight of the act. Ink was not just ink here—it was permanence, binding past to present, present to future. He dipped the nib into the deep black well, lifting it without a single drop spilling, and began to write in slow, deliberate strokes.

Hannah Elise Amalie Harvick–Rosenshavn. The letters curved in a rhythm that felt almost ceremonial, the name stretching gracefully across the page as if it had always belonged there. He paused only to draw a careful dash before beginning the next, the quill gliding without hesitation. Frederik Adrian Søren Harvick–Rosenshavn. The second name sat beneath the first like a steady pillar, the two bound together not just by blood but by this inked declaration. Ben read the names again, silently, before placing a final dot that marked the end of the entry. He slid the quill slightly to the side, letting his palm rest against the cool page as if to hold the moment in place. Across the table, Kendrick stood in quiet attention, his eyes following each motion with the seriousness of a man who understood the depth of what was being set down.

When Ben pushed the ledger forward, Kendrick stepped into place without a word. His hand, broader and heavier, took the quill and scrawled his own name with the authority of both witness and protector. Kendrick Rosenshavn. The signature slanted forward, purposeful and unyielding, like a blade point set into the page. He set the quill down gently, its tip resting against the silver stand, and closed the ink pot with a firm turn. Ben felt the stillness between them then—the shared knowledge that this was more than formality. These names would outlast their own voices, their own hands. They would stand in that ledger long after footsteps no longer echoed in these halls.

From the doorway, Isla watched, her arms full of the twins, their tiny faces turned toward her chest. She said nothing, letting the sound of the pen scratch be the only interruption to the silence. When Ben rose, he crossed to her and brushed a hand over Hannah's head, then Frederik's, as if blessing the names he had just set down. "It's done," he said quietly, not as an announcement but as a promise. Isla nodded, her eyes warm, the weight of the moment reflected in the softness of her expression. Ben held her gaze for only a breath before turning to Kendrick. "There's someone else who needs to be named here, in a way that's not ink but just as lasting."

They found Casper in the east corridor, crouched beside one of the narrow windows, sketching the curve of the courtyard wall. The boy looked up at the sound of footsteps, his eyes flicking between Ben and Kendrick as though gauging whether this was a summons or an interruption.

Ben crouched so they were eye level, his tone gentle but clear. "There's a family inside these walls," he began, "and I'd like you to meet them. Not as a visitor, but as someone who belongs." Casper tilted his head slightly, his hands still clutching his pencil and book. "Belongs?" he asked, the word heavy with meaning for someone who had spent years without a place to claim as his own.

"Yes," Ben said simply. "This morning I told you what I wanted—that I'd make you my son if you wanted that. You said yes. Now it's time to show everyone else what that means." Casper hesitated for only a moment before pushing himself to his feet, tucking the pencil behind his ear. He followed as Ben led him down the corridor, Kendrick's steps heavy but reassuring behind them. The closer they drew to the family wing, the louder the sound of children's voices became—a mix of laughter, shouted challenges, and the kind of noise that only came from people entirely certain they were safe.

They stepped into the main hall where the younger children had gathered in a loose cluster, playing some half-formed game that seemed to involve chasing a ball around without rules. Conversations stilled when they saw Ben enter with a boy they did not yet know, their curiosity pulling them forward in a wave. Ben rested a hand lightly on Casper's shoulder, anchoring him as much as introducing him. "Everyone," he said, his voice carrying just enough for all to hear, "this is Casper Arthur Bille. He's joining our family. You'll treat him as you'd treat any of your brothers." There was no need to add "and sisters"—the truth of it was understood.

The initial pause lasted only a breath before the crowd broke into motion. A ball was abandoned mid-bounce. Questions spilled over each other—where was he from, how old was he, could he play football, did he like cake. One of the smaller children, not waiting for permission, threw their arms around him in a hug that nearly toppled him backwards. Casper stiffened for a moment, clearly unused to such unfiltered warmth, then allowed himself to lean into it. Ben stepped back slightly, letting the children close the circle around their new brother, the sound of laughter and overlapping voices filling the air again.

From the far side of the hall, Isla appeared with the twins, moving slowly but steadily, her smile reaching even the edges of her tired eyes. She stopped beside Ben, her gaze resting on the sight of Casper surrounded by children as if he had always been part of the picture. "Looks like he's home already," she murmured. Ben glanced at her, then back at the boy, a small smile touching his own face. "That's the point," he replied quietly, knowing the truth of it would hold just as firmly as the names written in the registry upstairs.

By the time evening settled over Rosenshavn Castle, the long shadows had softened into warm pools of lamplight, and the air itself seemed to exhale. The tension of the day—the labour, the birth, the hushed movement of staff through the corridors—began to dissolve into something gentler.

Dinner was not called in the grand dining hall that night. Instead, trays were carried quietly to private chambers, the clink of cutlery muffled beneath folded napkins. Footsteps moved with unspoken awareness, slowing near doorways where the twins slept, quickening only when called to fetch something warm or needed. Somewhere in the west wing, muted laughter could be heard, as if the castle itself was allowing joy to return in measured breaths.

In the nursery, the twins lay in their bassinets, their chests rising and falling with the steady rhythm of dreamless sleep. Hannah's tiny fist rested near her cheek, her fingers curled as though still holding the memory of her father's hand. Frederik's mouth moved faintly, some instinctive echo of the first moments when he had taken his place in the world. The room was lit softly, the kind of light that never startled, and its stillness carried an unspoken truth—their presence had altered the course of more than just their parents' lives. Beyond the closed door, the household moved differently now, each step, each word tempered by the knowledge of what had been gained.

Casper stood outside the nursery for a moment, his hands tucked into the pockets of the clean sweater one of the staff had found for him. He wasn't looking at the twins so much as trying to understand the strange feeling that seemed to pull at him from inside the room. The idea that these two, barely hours old, could already have an effect on his own life was something he couldn't quite put into words. When Ben appeared beside him, Casper shifted his weight, unsure whether to speak. Ben only gestured with a small tilt of his head, the kind that meant come along.

The supper had been set in a smaller dining room in the east wing, one usually reserved for evenings when formality wasn't required. A long table of dark oak stretched the length of the room, but only the centre was set for use, plates and bowls arranged so conversation could pass easily across. The air was filled with the mingled scents of roasted chicken, warm bread, and the sharp sweetness of stewed apples. Several children were already seated, their chatter lowering to murmurs when Ben entered with Casper in tow. It wasn't an awkward silence—more the natural pause of curiosity, the way a room tilts slightly when something new enters.

Ben rested a hand on Casper's shoulder before guiding him toward an empty seat between Emil and Lukas. "This is Casper," Ben said, his tone neither formal nor casual, just steady. "He's joining us for supper tonight—and from now on, as part of the family." The words landed without ceremony, but they carried weight all the same. Emil grinned immediately, offering a quiet "Hi" while sliding a plate toward him. Lukas nudged a basket of bread in his direction, and that seemed to break whatever unspoken barrier had lingered in the air.

Plates were filled, and conversation resumed, this time with Casper drawn into its current. Questions came easily—where had he lived before, did he play any games, what was the strangest thing he'd ever eaten. Some of the younger children asked without waiting for answers, their words tumbling over each other, while the older ones listened with an attentiveness that wasn't forced. Casper found himself speaking more than he expected, his voice steadying with each response, the knot in his stomach loosening. Ben, seated across from him, caught the shift and allowed himself the smallest of smiles before returning to his own plate.

As the meal went on, the table seemed to gather its own momentum. Emil challenged Casper to a football match "as soon as the weather's good," and Peter promised to show him the best hiding places in the castle's south wing. Even the more reserved children leaned in to hear his replies, offering bits of their own stories in return. Casper ate slowly at first, cautious not to spill or draw attention, but the warmth around him began to wear away that reserve. By the time the apple compote was passed down, he was laughing—quietly, but enough that the others noticed.

Ben watched him without intruding, letting the boy navigate this first supper in his own way. He knew trust couldn't be rushed, but he also knew the signs when someone began to believe they might be safe. Across the table, Isla sat with a small plate untouched before her, content to listen, her gaze moving between her husband and the newest child at the table. Every so often her eyes softened, the look of someone who understood exactly how important it was for this moment to happen quietly, without the weight of formality pressing on it.

By the time the last of the bread was gone and the plates were cleared, the room carried a different kind of quiet than it had at the start. It was no longer the hush of uncertainty but the low hum that follows a shared meal, the unspoken agreement that everyone belongs at the table. Casper lingered in his seat, almost reluctant to leave, his eyes following the others as they drifted into small groups or wandered toward the corridor. Ben stood, waiting until the boy looked up, and simply said, "Come on. There's more to see before the night's done."

They left the dining room together, the sounds of the evening—footsteps, muffled laughter, the distant creak of an opening door—folding in behind them. Somewhere in the west wing, the twins stirred in their sleep, unaware that while their arrival had made the castle quieter in some ways, it had also filled it with a kind of breath it hadn't known for some time. The castle was alive again, its walls carrying not just the sound of life, but the weight of it. And in the midst of it all, a boy who had walked in as a guest was now walking out as part of its story.

The corridors were different at night. The light from the sconces softened to amber, casting slow-moving shadows that followed Ben and Casper as they walked side by side. The boy kept to Ben's left, his steps measured, his eyes flicking toward every archway as though committing the castle's shape to memory.

Supper had left him quieter, but not withdrawn—rather, there was a thoughtfulness in the way he matched Ben's pace, as if he knew this walk meant something more than a simple tour. They passed a closed nursery door where the twins slept, the faintest hint of warm milk lingering in the air, and Ben felt his chest tighten with a mix of pride and something heavier. His family had grown today, not only by two newborns, but by the boy now at his side.

They reached the long gallery, where tall windows faced the inner courtyard. Ben stopped at the centre, resting a hand against the cold stone of the sill. Outside, the last of the daylight was draining from the sky, the edges of the courtyard already claimed by shadow. The flag above the east tower stirred in the evening breeze, slow and deliberate. He had stood here many times before, but tonight the view seemed changed—not by the buildings or the weather, but by the weight of what was now his to protect. He could feel Casper's presence beside him, the boy leaning slightly to see what he saw. The courtyard lay still, yet Ben knew the stillness was fragile, easily shattered by a knock at the gate or the wrong voice on the wind.

For a long moment he said nothing, letting the quiet speak. Then he turned toward Casper. "Do you like it here?" he asked, not as a courtesy but as something he needed to know. Casper nodded once, his expression unreadable. "It's big," the boy replied after a pause, "but it doesn't feel… bad big." Ben allowed a brief smile at the choice of words. It was exactly the sort of thing he might have said at that age, before he learned that size meant more than stone and timber—it meant responsibility, vigilance, and the quiet ache of knowing you couldn't protect everything at once.

Ben's gaze returned to the courtyard, and his voice lowered without softening. "There's something you need to know. Soon, we'll be going away for a while. You and I." The boy's head tilted slightly, curiosity sharpening his features. "Where?" Ben kept his eyes forward, tracing the line of the wall as if it were a map. "Kent, England. A place I've known since I was younger than you. It's… quieter there, in some ways." He didn't explain the other ways—the ones where eyes followed you even in silence, where history pressed against your back like an uninvited shadow.

Casper studied him for a moment, then asked with the bluntness only a child could carry, "Does it have something to do with those weird photographers? The ones always sticking their ugly faces into the castle?" Ben turned to him fully, surprised at how neatly the boy had cut through to the truth. "Yes," he said simply. "It does." He didn't bother to dress the answer in softer language. The intrusion had been growing worse, not yet spilling into the courtyard itself but close enough that every walk in the gardens came with the risk of a lens catching what was not theirs to take. And now, with the twins' birth, the risk had doubled.

The boy's brows drew together, but not in fear. "So… we're going so they can't find us?" His tone was more practical than worried, as though weighing the problem for its solution rather than its danger. Ben's respect for him deepened. "In part," he said. "It's also so I can take care of something there. Something I can't do from here. But you'll be with me the whole time." He let the words settle, watching for any sign of hesitation. There was none. Instead, Casper's mouth pulled into a faint smile, small but steady. "Okay. Just… don't leave me behind."

The simplicity of the request struck harder than Ben expected. He crouched down so they were eye level, the distance between them closing to nothing. "I won't," he said, each word deliberate. "When I said you're part of the family now, I meant it. That means where I go, you go. Always." Casper's shoulders eased, and after a moment, he stepped forward. "Then can I have a hug?" The question was not shy, only certain in its need. Ben answered without words, drawing the boy into a full embrace, the kind that said more than any vow could. Casper's arms wrapped tightly around him, the warmth and weight of trust settling in as if it had been there all along.

They stayed like that longer than either had intended, the quiet of the gallery wrapping around them. Ben could hear the slow tick of the grandfather clock down the hall, marking time they didn't feel the need to rush. When they finally stepped apart, the boy's expression had changed—less guarded, more anchored. Without speaking, they resumed their walk, their footsteps finding a shared rhythm that carried them down the corridor.

By the time they reached the end of the wing, the last of the daylight had gone, replaced by the faint shimmer of moonlight through the high windows. The courtyard lay silver and still, yet Ben knew the peace was temporary. Outside these walls, questions were waiting, voices were sharpening, and the truth of who he was would not stay hidden forever. But here, in this moment, he allowed himself the rare luxury of believing that he could hold back the tide, at least long enough for the boy beside him to feel the ground settle beneath his feet.

When they turned toward the stairs, Ben's hand rested briefly on Casper's shoulder again, the gesture unspoken but understood. This was no longer a walk between a man and a guest—it was the quiet beginning of a promise already in motion. And in the hush of the castle's sleeping halls, that promise felt unbreakable.

The April night rested over Copenhagen with a patience that felt deliberate, as though the sky itself understood the need for calm. Beyond the castle gates, the city carried on in its quiet evening rhythm—streetlamps throwing gold across cobblestone, bicycles leaning against railings, windows lit in scattered constellations. No one beyond these walls knew of the two new lives who had entered the world mere hours ago, their cries still echoing softly in the memory of those present. The old stones of Rosenshavn seemed warmer than usual, holding a subtle heat that rose from within, as though centuries of duty and celebration had prepared them for this night. It was not the warmth of the hearth, but the warmth of history embracing the living.

From the upper nursery windows, the garden paths below curved in pale outlines, their gravel catching what little light the moon spared. The fountain at the centre murmured in a steady trickle, a sound so constant that it seemed part of the castle's own breathing. Ben stood at one of these windows, his palm resting against the sill, his gaze steady on the darkened grounds. He had seen this courtyard under snow, under rain, under the green swell of summer, but never with the awareness that the future—his children's future—would one day walk its stones. The air carried the faint scent of rain, not yet fallen but close enough to taste, and it mingled with the faint sweetness of the blooming lilacs along the east wall.

Inside, the corridors moved more softly than usual. Staff passed in measured steps, their voices lowered not from fear but from reverence. Meals were taken quietly in chambers rather than in the great dining hall, and the clinking of cutlery seemed almost too loud for the hour. In the nursery, the twins lay in their bassinets, their small forms rising and falling with the rhythm of newborn breath. Isla slept nearby, her head turned toward them even in rest, as if instinct could keep watch better than sight. A small lamp burned low, casting a steady glow that reached no further than the walls, creating a pocket of peace untouched by the restless pace of the world outside.

Kendrick made his way through the upper hall, his steps slow, a hand grazing the carved railing as he passed the grand staircase. He paused only once, glancing toward the window where Ben still stood. No words passed between them, but there was a brief meeting of eyes—one brother to another—before Kendrick moved on, the soft weight of the moment following him. Annemarie, too, walked the upper hall, checking that doors were secured and that the last of the lamps were turned down. She moved with the quiet assurance of someone who understood that safety was not in grand gestures but in the sum of small, constant actions.

Beyond the gates, the city's own pulse was steady. A tram passed in the distance, its windows briefly catching the light from a streetlamp before vanishing into the night. Somewhere, a lone bicycle bell chimed, its sound delicate and far away. These were the unknowing witnesses to the births within the castle—anonymous, unseeing, and yet part of the fabric of the night. The rain held off, though the air thickened with its promise. The scent was stronger now, mingling with the coolness that seeped into the stones. It would come before morning, perhaps in the slow hours before dawn, when the city slept and the castle's dreams were deep.

Ben's mind wandered over the day's events in fragments—the first cry, the second, the moment Isla's eyes met his as he held both children, the weight of them new and yet instantly familiar. He thought, too, of Casper, whose place here was still so new, yet already certain in Ben's mind. The boy's acceptance of what lay ahead had been simple, but its meaning ran deep. In that acceptance was trust, and in that trust was the foundation for everything Ben now intended to protect. The twins were his heirs; Casper was his choice. All three were his to keep safe, and that vow sat heavier than any crown.

The old stones beneath his feet seemed to listen, as if they could feel the vow being made. Rosenshavn had stood through storms, through wars, through celebrations and losses alike. It had seen children born and grown, seen them leave, seen them return. And tonight, it would begin again. The castle did not speak, but its warmth was answer enough. Outside, the April sky held steady, the stars pale behind a thin veil of cloud. In that stillness, Ben knew the truth: peace like this was rare, and therefore all the more worth guarding.

He stayed at the window until the moon slipped behind the clouds, the first faint drops of rain beginning to kiss the glass. Only then did he turn away, letting the sound follow him down the hall, its rhythm a quiet reminder that no matter how great the changes inside these walls, the world beyond would keep moving, unaware, until the time came to tell them. And when that time came, he would be ready.

The house had quieted into the kind of stillness that only arrived after an extraordinary day. Upstairs, Isla slept with one hand resting on the edge of the bassinet, as though to tether herself to the twins even in dreams. Ben lay close, his arm draped protectively over Casper, who occupied a small cot beside their bed for the night. There had been no time to prepare a proper room for him, and none of them had wanted to send him down the hall alone. That would be tomorrow's task—measured, deliberate, and done properly after breakfast. For tonight, proximity was the truest form of welcome.

Far below, in the quiet of his study, Kendrick set a porcelain cup onto the desk without a sound. He poured the coffee slowly, black and without sugar, the steam curling upward into the lamplight. The cup warmed his hand, but the heat that filled him was not from the drink. His thoughts sharpened, narrowing around a single, immovable conviction: these children—Hannah, Frederik, and now Casper—would never know fear, not while he breathed. It was not a hope or a wish. It was an oath carved into the very grain of his being, as unbreakable as the stone beneath Rosenshavn.

On the desk before him lay a spread of papers, half in order, half waiting for his hand. At the top of the nearest stack was a folder bearing the name that had occupied the darker edges of their lives for weeks—Oscar. The man's betrayal had been deliberate, ugly in its swiftness. He had known Ben, Isla, Kendrick, and Annemarie for years, shared meals, laughter, and confidences. And yet, when money whispered louder than loyalty, he had sold the truth to the lowest of buyers—freelance photographers, journalists eager to trade integrity for the chance at a headline. That headline had been avoided only by the quick precision of Kendrick and Ben, acting in unison.

One week ago, Oscar had been charged with treason. The weight of the word still rang in Kendrick's mind, its meaning clear and cold. It was not a term given lightly, nor was it one a man could recover from. He was already in custody, the trial's formalities yet to follow, but Kendrick knew the damage had been stopped just in time. The leak had been contained before it could swell into the tidal wave the press had been hoping for. Even so, the scent of danger still lingered at the edges of the castle walls.

Kendrick lifted the cup and drank slowly, his eyes narrowing toward the window. Even with tinted glass across every pane of the upper floors, the intrusion of photographers and journalists remained a constant threat. They prowled the gates, hoping for the smallest gap in security, their long lenses pointed like spears toward any sliver of movement. He had seen them before—faces pressed against the limits of legality, trying to peer into a world they could never enter. And he would see to it that they never did.

His mind began to sort itself into lists. Extra patrols at the east and south gates. Coordination with Sørensen to expand the inner perimeter sweeps. More staff trained to recognize false credentials. Communication lines tightened so nothing left these walls unless he approved it. This was not paranoia; it was the maintenance of peace. The twins' first days must be free of disturbance, and Casper's first nights in this family must be untouched by the shadows of the past week.

Kendrick leaned back, setting the cup down with care, his gaze falling to the map of Copenhagen on the far wall. He traced the streets leading to the castle in his mind, considering the choke points, the areas where security could be made invisible yet absolute. He knew the routes the journalists used, the alleys they thought were theirs alone, the vantage points from rooftops they assumed were unmonitored. He had anticipated these tactics before; now, with three children under direct protection, he would refine them until the press might as well have been staring at a wall of fog.

The memory of Oscar's arrest was still fresh—his shock, his indignation, the rapid shift when he realised who had ordered the charge. Kendrick did not relish that moment, but neither did he regret it. Betrayal carried its own punishment, and it was his duty to see it delivered. The stain of treachery had to be erased before it could touch the next generation. In that, he saw no room for hesitation.

Beyond the study door, the castle breathed in its deep, steady rhythm. Kendrick imagined the quiet of the nursery upstairs—the twins' soft breathing, Isla's hand still resting on the bassinet, Ben sleeping lightly with an ear tuned to any change in sound. And beside them, Casper, likely curled into the blankets, unaware that a man downstairs had just sworn a lifetime's protection over him.

Kendrick closed the folder on Oscar, sliding it to the far side of the desk. That chapter was over. What lay ahead was the work of ensuring no such threat could ever breach their walls again. His vow was not spoken aloud, but it did not need to be. The walls of Rosenshavn had heard it, and they would keep it as faithfully as he would.

He stood, the cup empty, the lamplight throwing his shadow tall across the study floor. Outside, the April night was still holding, the promise of rain hovering just beyond the horizon. Kendrick looked once toward the darkened city before turning out the light, the vow still settled deep in his chest, unshakable and final.

The castle lay wrapped in a profound stillness, the kind that seemed to honour the events of the day just passed. In the dim light of their chamber, Ben remained awake, his eyes fixed not on the ceiling, but on the two small forms resting against him. One arm curved protectively around his son, the other around his daughter, his body a bridge of warmth between them. Their breathing was delicate, uneven in its newborn rhythm, but each soft exhale was an anchor to the present moment. Life before this—before their arrival, before the ripple of change they brought—was already receding into memory. He did not mourn it. He was grateful for its passing.

Isla slept beside him, her hair spilling across the pillow, the faint rise and fall of her chest steady as the tide. Even in her rest, her presence grounded him. He could still feel the lingering warmth of the birthing pool in his skin, the memory of her calm strength etched into the hours before midnight. There had been no panic, no chaos, just the quiet discipline of two people moving through a moment that would define them for the rest of their lives. He thought of how her hands had reached for the twins with such certainty, as though she had known them for years before they came into being.

Beyond the chamber, the corridors lay in darkness. Somewhere down the hall, Kendrick's steady stride had long since faded, his vow sealed in private. Further still, in a cot tucked beside their bed, Casper slept in the same deep quiet as the twins. Ben had insisted on this arrangement for the night—not out of necessity, but out of instinct. Casper had already known too many nights in which the dark felt like a warning. Tonight, it would be something else entirely. Tonight, it would be a shelter.

Ben closed his eyes for a moment, listening. There was no sound beyond the layered breathing of those around him, no creak of the old timbers, no restless steps in the courtyard. The security team was at their posts, invisible yet absolute. Sørensen would have been through twice already, ensuring no movement near the gates. The knowledge was a comfort, not because Ben feared intrusion tonight, but because he understood that their safety was not luck—it was the result of vigilance earned and maintained.

An hour passed in this silent vigil, his arms stiff from holding both children but unwilling to shift. He knew that years from now, the details of this night might fade—the way the moonlight slanted through the curtains, the muted glow from the embers in the hearth—but the weight of them in his arms would remain. That was the measure of fatherhood: not the number of days one counted, but the moments that refused to be forgotten.

When sleep finally came to him, it was thin and restless. Dawn edged its way through the curtains far too soon, carrying with it the muted hum of the castle's waking. The staff moved with the quiet precision that followed a momentous night, breakfast preparations already underway in the kitchen. The scent of warm bread drifted upward, mingling with the faint aroma of coffee from Kendrick's study.

Ben rose carefully, settling the twins in their bassinets before stepping into the morning's light. Casper, still rubbing the sleep from his eyes, followed him down to breakfast. The boy's hair was tousled, his expression a mixture of curiosity and caution—still unsure of how much space he was allowed to occupy in this new life. Ben made sure his presence in the room was noticed, introducing him with quiet authority to those gathered, not as a guest, but as someone who now belonged here.

It was Emil Søren Ravn Harvick who bridged the last gap. Halfway through the meal, he turned to Casper with the ease of an older brother making an offer that required no preamble. "You can share my room," Emil said, his tone plain but warm. "Just so you're not alone." It was not charity; it was kinship, spoken in the simple language of children. There was no pause, no glance toward Ben for approval. It was an unprompted gift.

Casper's eyes widened, and for a moment his reply caught in his throat. Then he nodded, his voice barely above the sound of clinking cutlery. "I'd like that. Thank you." The gratitude was plain, but so was the relief—relief that someone his own age had claimed him without hesitation, that his place here was not provisional but fixed. The shift in his shoulders was subtle, but Ben saw it: the loosening of tension that had been there since the boy first stepped inside these walls.

The meal moved on, but Ben held the moment close. This was how families were formed—not by decree, not by ceremony, but in the quiet exchanges over breakfast, in the willingness of one child to make space for another. The twins would grow into their place here in time, but Casper's place had been secured in an instant by an act that asked for nothing in return.

After breakfast, plans were made to ready a proper room for Casper, though Ben suspected the arrangement with Emil would last far longer than anyone predicted. Children were not bound by formality when loyalty had been established. The cot from last night would be moved, new bedding brought in, and books chosen for the shelves, but the choice of sleeping space would remain theirs to decide.

As the castle resumed its rhythm, Ben paused at the window in the corridor, the April sky pale and untroubled. The day ahead would be full—there were visitors to be managed, security to be checked, and quiet moments with the twins to be guarded from the outside world. Yet the shift in the air was undeniable. They were no longer simply holding the future; the future was walking beside them, eating breakfast at their table, and finding a bed in a brother's room. He turned from the window, the echo of the night still warm in his chest. Life before this moment was gone, and he would not trade it back. This was the shape of the family now, and it was his to protect. Forever.

CHAPTER 8: THE LEAK CONTAINED

The study felt smaller than usual, as though the air itself had grown heavier in the hours since the court delivered its sentence. The fire in the grate had burned low, leaving more shadow than light, and the rain beyond the tall windows drew silver lines across the glass. Every now and then, a droplet would gather its courage and race down in a sudden dash, only to vanish into the sill. The family had gathered as they always did in such moments, not for ceremony, but for the quiet solidarity that had kept them together through storms of many kinds. The chairs were full, the corners occupied, yet there was no sound beyond the muted hiss of the fire. Not a soul spoke of forgiveness. No one in this room was ready for that, nor did they expect to be.

Casper sat cross-legged on the rug beside the low table, his fingers tracing the carved edges as though trying to memorise the grooves. Do not be deceived by his age—there was nothing naïve in his gaze. He listened to the unspoken words in the room as easily as others might listen to rain. He was still a boy in height and limb, but the sharpness of his mind carried the quiet weight of someone older. Since the day the papers had been signed and his name had changed, he had called Benedict "Dad" without hesitation, and with that word came a loyalty that was unshakable.

Oscar's betrayal was no abstraction to him. It was not something whispered about and hidden from the children. Casper had been told plainly, as was the way in this household. And when he finally spoke, it was not with the trembling uncertainty of a child, but with the clear, measured tone of one who understands the cost of truth. "They could be charged for invasion of privacy," he said, looking directly at Ben. "And for telling lies about you." His words, though simple, struck with a precision that made even Sørensen glance over from his seat by the wall.

Benedict's lips pressed into a faint smile—part pride, part sorrow. "You're right, son," he said, his voice soft but steady. "That is exactly what they could be charged with." The truth was, it went deeper than charges. In another time, in another era, there would have been a reckoning that left no question about where the line was drawn. But in this age, battles were fought with law and patience, not with iron. Still, hearing Casper speak with such conviction reminded him that some instincts—such as defending one's own—were timeless.

Without another word, Ben reached out, pulling the boy close into a firm embrace. It was not the kind of half-hearted gesture that adults sometimes give children when their minds are elsewhere. This was a father's hold—solid, grounding, absolute. He kissed Casper not on the forehead, nor on the crown of his head like one might do out of habit, but on the cheek, where the boy could feel the full sincerity of it. It was a kiss that carried both thanks and promise, the kind that said without words that whatever storms came next, they would face them together.

Across the room, Kendrick shifted in his chair, his hands clasped loosely in his lap. His gaze lingered on the pair, noting the way Ben's posture had changed since Casper entered his life. There was a deeper steadiness in him now, as though fatherhood—this fatherhood—had anchored something that had once drifted. Kendrick had known Ben as a son, a confidant, and a king in hiding, but seeing him as a father to a boy who was not of his blood reminded him of the quiet power in chosen bonds.

The rain intensified against the glass, its rhythm filling the spaces between breaths. Sørensen leaned forward, resting his elbows on his knees, his eyes narrowing slightly as though measuring the storm outside against the one within. He had seen Ben in battle—not with swords, but with sharper weapons: wit, cunning, and the kind of strategic mind that could dismantle an opponent without raising his voice. This latest trial, however, had pressed on something more personal. The danger had not been to Ben's throne or his life, but to his family's peace, and that was a different kind of wound altogether.

Casper, still tucked against Ben's side, tilted his head slightly to look out at the rain. "It's funny," he said, in the way children speak of things that are not funny at all, "how people you don't even know can think they own your life." His tone held neither anger nor confusion—just a cool, matter-of-fact understanding of how the world sometimes worked. Sørensen's eyes flicked to Ben, silently acknowledging the truth in the boy's observation.

Ben's gaze followed the lines of water down the glass, his thoughts caught in the narrowing space between past and future. It would have taken very little for this to end differently. One wrong step, one moment of hesitation, and the walls of Rosenshavn would have been nothing more than a backdrop for the feeding frenzy of cameras and headlines. That it hadn't come to that was due in no small part to the people in this room, and to the city beyond these walls that had closed ranks around him.

The silence between them was not empty—it was the kind that holds weight, that speaks without sound. Each person in the room carried their own version of the same thought: Oscar's act had been a betrayal not just of Ben, but of the family, the Castle, and the unspoken trust that bound them all. In the outside world, betrayal could be spun into redemption. Here, it would never be unwritten.

Kendrick rose first, pacing slowly toward the far window. He paused before it, his reflection barely visible against the darkened glass. "It's strange," he said at last, his voice low, "how a single name in the wrong mouth can set the whole world leaning forward." Ben looked up at him, their eyes meeting in the briefest flicker of shared understanding. Neither needed to say what they both knew—that the name had been spoken now, and there was no taking it back.

Casper's fingers tightened slightly on the sleeve of Ben's shirt, and without thinking, Ben placed a reassuring hand over them. The boy didn't flinch, didn't look away. It was a silent exchange, one of those small, invisible moments that spoke louder than any vow. The storm outside rolled on, its low rumble threading through the quiet like a warning. Yet in the heart of the Castle, the walls held firm. And for now, that was enough.

The conversation began the way such matters always did in the Castle—quietly, measured, without theatrics. There was no need for raised voices when the facts themselves carried their own weight. The elders sat in the great room where the fire was allowed to burn high, the flicker of its light throwing deep shadows along the carved beams overhead. Oscar's sentence hung between them like an iron chain—thirty-five years, perhaps forty if the board saw fit to let him serve every last day. Outside, the rain persisted, the sound a low counterpoint to the deliberate cadence of the discussion.

Benedict sat with Casper close to his side, one arm resting along the back of the boy's chair. He listened more than he spoke, his eyes steady on the elders as they picked apart the ruling with the precision of surgeons. Casper sat contently, leaning ever so slightly toward his father, not from fatigue but from a quiet satisfaction in being allowed to stay. It was not lost on him that many boys his age would have been sent out of the room. But here, in this family, truth was not hidden behind closed doors.

Kendrick leaned forward, elbows on his knees, his voice calm but firm. "The measure of a sentence is not just in the years," he said, glancing from Sørensen to Ben. "It's in what those years mean to the man who serves them. Thirty-five years for theft might be harsh. For treason? It's a mercy." The word landed heavy, but there was no disagreement. Even Sørensen, who rarely gave nods of agreement, inclined his head slightly.

Casper's gaze shifted between the speakers, absorbing the way they weighed justice without flinching. He didn't pretend to understand every detail of law or sentencing, but he understood betrayal. It had a shape and a taste, and it never quite left once it settled in. This was not some abstract discussion about a distant figure; Oscar had been here, part of the air they breathed. Now he was gone, and the absence had its own sharp edges.

Ben's voice entered the discussion at last, steady and without heat. "Forty years gives a man time to think," he said. "But not time enough to undo." The remark drew a low murmur of agreement from the elders. Sørensen, sitting as he often did in the armchair nearest the door, allowed the corner of his mouth to curve just slightly—his way of showing that a point had been well made.

"Thinking won't change a man like that," Kendrick countered, not out of argument but for the sake of clarity. "Once you've sold loyalty, it doesn't grow back. It's gone. Like a rope cut in two—no knot will make it whole again." He turned slightly, his gaze passing over the younger faces in the room. "Remember that. A man may regret, but regret is not the same as loyalty."

Casper caught his father's glance, and in that silent exchange understood more than words could have taught him. This was not merely about Oscar; it was a lesson in the way the world worked. The bonds you choose, the promises you keep—those are the foundations. Once you break them, you're building on sand. He kept his expression still, but inwardly he was memorising the weight of this truth.

The fire cracked sharply, drawing eyes toward it for a moment. Outside, the rain slowed, as though even the sky had tired of its own persistence. In the shifting light, the faces of the elders looked carved from older times, their expressions unmoved by the softness of the present age. This was not cruelty—it was the memory of what betrayal could cost when a throne or a family's safety hung in the balance.

Sørensen spoke next, his voice low and deliberate. "The court spared him the sentence others in his place might have faced a hundred years ago." He did not elaborate, but the implication was clear. In another era, treason had not been measured in years behind bars, but in the swiftness of a blade or the closing of a cell from which there was no return. Casper felt a small chill at the thought, but he did not look away.

Ben rested his hand on the arm of Casper's chair, grounding him in the moment. "This is the world we live in now," he said, more to the room than to anyone in particular. "But mercy does not mean forgetting. We keep the lesson, and we guard against it happening again." His tone carried no boast, only the matter-of-fact assurance of someone who had been tested before and would be tested again.

One of the elder cousins cleared his throat. "You've done what you could to protect this family, Ben. The rest of us will keep our eyes open. It's not just your fight—it's ours." There was no ceremony to the words, but they had the weight of an oath all the same. Around the room, small nods confirmed it.

Casper shifted in his seat, leaning closer to his father. "Does that mean they won't try again?" The question was simple, but it silenced the room for a beat. Ben answered honestly, as he always did. "It means they'll think twice before they do. And if they don't, they'll find the walls harder to climb."

The rain had stopped entirely now, leaving only the quiet creak of the fire settling in its grate. Kendrick sat back, crossing his arms loosely. "Forty years is a long time," he said at last. "Long enough for the world to change, and for him to realise no one's waiting for him when he comes out." It was not said with malice—only the unvarnished truth of consequence.

Sørensen's eyes met Ben's over the top of the boy's head, and in that glance was the silent acknowledgement of what they both knew. Betrayal had many forms, but the most dangerous was the kind that came from inside the walls. Now that it had been cut out, they would do everything in their power to ensure it never returned.

The meeting broke without formality, the elders drifting into smaller conversations, the younger ones trailing after them, still piecing together what they had heard. Ben remained seated for a moment longer, his hand resting on Casper's shoulder. He didn't need to tell the boy to remember this day—it would stay with him. And years from now, he would understand the full measure of what had been spoken in this room.

It began with a single sentence from Sørensen, spoken without embellishment, as if he were reporting the weather. "He was drowning in debts." The words settled into the room, neither shouted nor softened, their weight needing no flourish. The elders knew immediately what this meant. Debt is not merely a matter of owing money—it is a chain that wraps tighter with each missed payment, each whispered threat, each knock at the door. Oscar had found himself bound by more than the law could see, and in reaching for air, he had clawed his way into betrayal.

Casper was sitting beside Ben at first, his small frame upright, listening to the conversation with an intentness beyond his years. But when Sørensen continued, explaining how Oscar had sought a quick fix—how he had traded his father's trust for cash—Casper's chest tightened in a way he had never felt before. It was a pain without a wound, a hurt without a bruise, and he found himself leaning toward his father without even thinking. Ben noticed at once and without a word reached down, lifting him into his lap so the boy could curl into his chest, where the steady beat of his heart could drown out the rest.

"Some men rob banks," Sørensen said after a long pause, "others sell secrets. Both are thefts, but one is colder." His gaze moved slowly around the room, his tone without judgement yet leaving no doubt as to the gravity. "When you take a man's coin, you wound his fortune. When you take his trust, you wound his life. And in our world, the second is deadlier." His eyes settled briefly on Ben, then on Kendrick, then back to the fire. No one argued. There was nothing to argue with.

Kendrick leaned back in his chair, his arms folding slowly as if containing his own thoughts. "Money can be earned again," he said quietly. "But trust—once broken—has no market value. You can't buy it back. You can't sell a promise twice." His words were aimed partly at the younger members of the room, a caution disguised as conversation. The flicker of the firelight caught in his eyes, and for a moment the air seemed to still around his voice.

Ben kept one hand on Casper's back, the slow rhythm of his touch meant as much for himself as for his son. He knew the feeling of trust torn away—knew it too well—and he would not let the boy carry more than he had to. But he would not lie to him either. When Casper's small voice finally rose against his chest, asking, "Why would he do that to you?" Ben's answer was quiet but certain. "Because fear makes people think short, not far. And desperation makes them sell things they can never get back."

The room was silent save for the shifting of wood in the fire. Sørensen, who had been part of more confessions than he cared to count in his time as chief of security, spoke again, each word measured. "When a man is desperate, he will take the shortest path to relief, even if it leads him through fire. Oscar saw that path in a tabloid's offer. And he stepped into the flames." His eyes were on no one in particular, yet the truth reached all of them.

One of the elder cousins stirred in his seat. "He thought it would be quick money," the man muttered, as if testing the excuse for himself. Sørensen's reply came without delay. "Quick money always runs out before the trouble it caused does." A faint murmur of agreement rippled through the room. Even those who had never known such stakes could feel the truth of it.

Casper shifted slightly in Ben's lap, his ear pressed against his father's chest. He wasn't just listening to the conversation; he was listening to the man himself—the steady calm of him, the way his voice never rose in anger even when speaking of betrayal. It was something Casper wanted to remember. His small hands curled into the fabric of Ben's shirt as if holding on to more than just the man, but to the certainty he represented.

Kendrick leaned forward, elbows on his knees again. "There's a difference between need and greed," he said, his voice a shade harder now. "Need can make you desperate, yes. But greed makes you blind. He might have started in need, but by the time he took their coin, greed had already bought his judgement." His words landed like stones on still water, spreading ripples that touched each face in turn.

Ben looked down at Casper, meeting his eyes for a moment before speaking again. "You can't always stop people from making bad choices," he said, more to the boy than to the room. "But you can make sure you don't follow them down the same road. That's how you keep your own steps clean." The boy nodded, his expression serious, as if tucking the words into a place he would keep safe.

The fire popped sharply, and the smell of the burning logs drifted through the air. Sørensen eased back in his chair, the stiffness in his shoulders loosening just enough to show that the hardest part of the truth had been said. "Oscar traded years of his life for days of someone else's profit. That's the math of desperation." His tone was almost flat, but there was a quiet sadness beneath it, the kind that only those who have seen too many losses can carry.

The elders let the silence hold for a time, respecting the weight of what had been shared. Outside, the rain had started again, softer now, as though the sky itself were unwilling to let the matter rest without its own commentary. The room felt smaller in that moment, closer, the walls holding in the heat of the fire and the gravity of the truth alike.

Ben kissed the top of Casper's head—not a ceremonial gesture, but a father's way of keeping the boy anchored in something warmer than the story being told. "You're safe," he said softly. "That's what matters now." And though the words were meant for Casper, the whole room heard them and seemed to take them as their own.

Kendrick straightened in his seat, his tone shifting just slightly toward closure. "Debts and desperation are a poison," he said. "Once they get into a man, they change him. But they don't have to change the rest of us. That's the difference between their story and ours." His eyes met Ben's, and there was the smallest flicker of agreement between them—an unspoken promise to guard the family from any such fate again.

As the conversation thinned, Ben rose with Casper still in his arms, carrying him toward the doorway with the quiet authority of a man who knew when enough had been said. The boy's head rested against his father's shoulder, his eyes closing as if the words of the room had woven themselves into dreams already. The rest of the family stayed by the fire, but in the stillness that followed, there was no mistaking it: the price of desperation had been counted, and the tally would not be forgotten.

It began, as such revelations often do, not with a trumpet of announcement but with the quiet rustle of newspapers sliding onto breakfast tables thousands of miles away. Benedict's name, once sheltered behind the everyday ease of "Ben," now appeared in print with an unshakable crown upon it. Not Kendrick. Not ceremonial. Real. "King Benedict of Denmark," the headlines declared, as if they had been waiting years to fasten those words together. In the span of a morning, his identity was no longer a carefully guarded truth but an international headline translated into tongues he would never speak.

The sound of it in foreign voices was strange to him. In Danish, the word "Konge" had always been something shared only in history lessons, whispers among trusted friends, or in the safety of stone corridors. Now, in English, French, German, and others, it felt at once too loud and too careless, as if strangers had been invited to rummage through the drawers of his private life. The name was no longer his alone to carry—it had been taken, dressed up, and sent parading down streets he had never walked.

Inside Rosenshavn Castle, the reaction was immediate but not chaotic. The tinted windows and stone barriers had done their work; cameras had nothing to capture but walls and roofs. Yet the sense of intrusion seeped in all the same. Sørensen read aloud fragments of foreign broadcasts, his voice neutral but his eyes alert. Kendrick's jaw tightened with each repetition of the word "King," as though the constant ringing of it was designed to chip away at their normal life. Ben sat listening, his expression unreadable, weighing each headline not for accuracy but for intent.

What caught him off guard was not the exposure itself—he had always known that possibility lurked in the shadows—but the sudden memory of someone who had once understood him without title or pretense. It was Sørensen who brought the news, hesitating in a way that was rare for him. "Ben… there's something else," he said, the weight in his tone heavier than the stories in the press. "Jeff Phillips is gone." The words landed harder than any headline could.

Jeff had been more than a friend. He had been a fixture in Ben's life back in Kent, the kind of friend who did not ask for explanations, who could read silence as easily as words. Ben's mind leapt across the years—shared pints, quiet talks by the shore, the knowing smile Jeff wore when Ben had to slip away without reason. And now, that entire history had been cut short, not by time or distance, but by something infinitely colder. "How?" Ben asked, his voice sharper than he intended.

The answer was a blade in itself. Sørensen did not look away as he spoke. "Annemarie." There was no need to elaborate further—Ben's biological mother's name was all the explanation needed for a death that would never feel accidental. The silence in the room was immediate and complete. Even Kendrick, who could argue with the wind if it tried to change direction, said nothing.

Ben rose from his chair, pacing the length of the room as if motion might keep grief from settling in his chest. Annemarie had been a ghost in his life for years, surfacing only to harm, never to heal. Now she had reached back into the one place he thought was beyond her grasp. That she had taken Jeff—a man entirely outside her world—was a wound layered with insult. It was a message, whether she meant it as such or not.

Casper, who had been playing with a carved wooden horse near the hearth, looked up at his father's sudden change in movement. "Who's Jeff?" he asked softly. Ben stopped, turning toward his son with the deliberation of a man who knows the truth will cost him something to share. "He was my friend," he said, his voice steady but lower. "One of the best I ever had." Casper nodded, sensing enough from the tone alone to leave the rest unasked.

Sørensen broke the stillness with the crispness of a soldier pulling them back to the matter at hand. "The leak has been contained here, but internationally, the fire's still burning. They'll keep running the story until something newer pushes it aside." Ben understood. Titles sell papers. Deaths make them linger longer. And now, the two stories were bound together, whether he wanted it or not.

Kendrick spoke from the far side of the room, his voice deliberate. "You need to decide how much of yourself you'll let them take. They've already taken the name. Don't give them the man as well." Ben didn't answer immediately. He was thinking of Jeff, of the kind of man he had been—private, grounded, unwilling to perform for anyone. There was something in that worth holding on to.

Outside, the faint hum of a distant drone was quickly silenced by the snap of Sørensen's slingshot—a sound now as routine as the chiming of the Castle clock. Ben glanced toward the window, satisfied that at least some lines could still be defended. The rest, he knew, would require more than tinted glass and quick aim.

He walked back toward the hearth, his eyes on the flames but his thoughts elsewhere. The world now knew his name, his station, and perhaps enough to begin guessing at more. But they would never know Jeff—the way he laughed without showing his teeth, the way he always ordered tea for Ben before he even sat down, the way he never once asked for proof of who Ben really was. That part of his life was his alone, and Annemarie could not take that from him, even in death.

Casper climbed into his father's lap without invitation, sensing the need for closeness. Ben wrapped his arms around him, grounding himself in the one truth that still belonged entirely to him: his family, here, within these walls. The outside world could have its headlines. Inside, they would write their own.

The fire burned low as the evening closed in, shadows stretching across the study. Sørensen remained standing, eyes occasionally drifting to the window, guarding more than just the perimeter. Kendrick poured himself another measure of brandy, his thoughts unreadable. Ben stayed silent, his gaze fixed on the flames, letting them consume the noise of the day. The name was out. The truth was out. But the man—King or not—was still his own.

The moment had always been a possibility, but never a certainty—until now. The news was no longer confined to the city that loved him, no longer whispered in narrow lanes or traded in the confidence of neighbours. Beyond Denmark's borders, beyond its coastlines, the truth had been unleashed. Not Kendrick. Not ceremonial. Not a borrowed crown for pageantry's sake. Benedict Rosenshavn—King of Denmark—written in print, broadcast with emphasis, translated into tongues he had never learned and likely never would. The walls of Rosenshavn Castle, built to keep the world at a distance, could not hold back the swell of words carried on foreign airwaves.

What once had been a private truth, known and protected by the people of Copenhagen, was now stamped on headlines in cities where his name had never before been spoken. He was no longer the neighbour who shared coffee in the square, the man who coached children in the park, the quiet figure who walked the waterfront at dusk. He was a monarch to strangers—an icon, an opportunity, a target. It was not the title that weighed on him; it was the intrusion, the knowledge that the moment the word "King" fused itself to his name, the rest of the world began to believe they had a claim on him.

The announcement had not come from the palace nor the Castle's own channels. It had erupted from the same polluted source as the betrayal—the tabloid that had bought its truth from Oscar. One sentence, stripped of context, printed in bold: "Benedict Rosenshavn is the King of Denmark." It did not need proof for the claim to spread; the world did not wait for verification when a crown was in question. It was copied, reshaped, and spun into every possible angle—some told with awe, others with venom, all with the same inevitable reach.

Ben stood at the wide window of the upper study, staring out at the slate-grey clouds moving low over the city. Sørensen had already swept the grounds twice that morning. Kendrick had made three calls to trusted contacts to gauge the temperature abroad. The atmosphere inside the Castle had shifted overnight—tighter, more watchful, like a family home bracing for uninvited guests. Yet in the middle of that growing tension, another piece of news had found him, quieter but cutting far deeper.

The message had arrived not by phone call, but in the form of Kendrick himself, stepping into the study with a folded letter in hand. His eyes, always direct, carried the kind of heaviness that made words unnecessary. Ben took the paper, though his fingers hesitated before unfolding it. In the lines that followed, the world outside the Castle ceased to matter. Jeff Phillips—his closest friend from Kent—is dead. Cancer. Type unknown. The letter said little more, but it didn't need to. The finality was enough.

Jeff had been the kind of friend who asked nothing of him, who did not care about titles, lineage, or the delicate machinery of secrecy. He had been a constant from boyhood—steady, loyal, and in his own way, a guard of Ben's truest self. That such a man could vanish from the world without Ben there to stand beside him in the final hours was an ache unlike any other. It was not the loss of a public ally. It was the loss of a part of himself that had existed long before the Castle, long before the crown.

Casper, who had been lingering in the doorway, saw his father's shoulders sink in a way they never did in public. Without hesitation, the boy crossed the room, climbing into his father's arms without asking. He pressed his cheek to Ben's chest, arms wrapping around him with a gentleness that only a child could give—a kind of touch that carried no questions, no explanations, only understanding. Ben's hand came up to rest on the back of his son's head, his eyes closing as if the boy's presence alone could steady the ground beneath him.

"I'm sorry, Dad," Casper whispered, his voice small but certain. He didn't say more, because there was nothing more to say. The kiss he pressed against his father's cheek was light, uncalculated, exactly the way a child gives love—without measure, without reserve, without needing to know the full size of the hurt it's meant to heal. Ben let the moment last, drawing in the quiet comfort that came from holding something the world could never take from him.

The storm outside pressed itself against the glass, the wind rising and falling as though in rhythm with the unspoken grief in the room. Kendrick stood a little apart, his hands clasped in front of him, knowing the silence was not to be broken. He had known Jeff as well—though never as deeply—and respected him enough to let the loss stand unencumbered by platitudes. Sørensen, too, had taken the news with a wordless nod, as though he understood that some things, even for a king, could not be shielded from.

And yet, in the same breath, the intrusion of the world outside returned. Another knock at the Castle gates. Another drone felled by the sling Sørensen carried like an extension of his own arm. Another headline pinged to Kendrick's phone, this one showing a photo of Ben taken years ago, matched now to the title "His Majesty." They were relentless in their timing, as if the world conspired to strike at both heart and crown in the same hour.

Ben did not voice his anger. He rarely did. Instead, he stood, still holding Casper, and moved toward the heavy oak desk where the letter lay open. He read it again, slower this time, as if the act itself could pull him closer to the friend who had already slipped away. In the quiet, Casper shifted only enough to meet his father's eyes. "He must have been really special," the boy said softly. Ben nodded, a small, steady motion. "He was," he answered. "And he still is."

Kendrick cleared his throat gently, his voice a low murmur meant to bridge the moment without breaking it. "We'll handle the noise outside," he said. "You see to the things that matter." The look he gave was one Ben had seen before—a reminder that crowns could wait, but hearts could not. Ben gave the smallest nod in return.

The Castle would continue to defend itself from the tide beyond its walls. The media would keep chasing their pictures and their soundbites. But for the span of that afternoon, Ben let the world shrink to the space of one room, one boy, and the quiet memory of a man who had known him without needing to know the king. The title was loud now, uncontainable in its reach. But here, in the shadow of grief, it meant nothing at all.

They came with lenses longer than a man's forearm, crowding the cobblestones like scavengers drawn to a fresh carcass. Their voices rose above the wind, pitched for provocation, questions flung in half a dozen languages, none of which belonged here. They shouted Benedict's name as though it were theirs to claim, as though they had earned the right to haul it into the open air. Their cameras clicked in a feverish staccato, hungry for a glimpse they had no right to take. They were not subtle, and they were not local.

From the high windows of Rosenshavn Castle, the family could see them cluster like gulls on the docks, adjusting their tripods, wiping the drizzle from their lenses. The Castle's tinted glass returned only their own reflection, and that frustrated them more than the cold wind snapping down the street. They aimed upward, certain that somewhere behind the darkened panes, a crown waited to be captured. They did not see the quiet figures watching from the alleys and corners below.

Copenhagen is a city that does not warm easily to outsiders, but when it accepts you, it defends you with a quiet ferocity. Benedict was not merely accepted—he was one of them. To see him hounded by strangers was an affront the city would not abide. The shopkeepers near the Castle began it first, stepping out onto their thresholds, arms folded, their eyes following every movement of the foreign journalists. They did not shout; they did not need to.

When the photographers leaned too close to windows, someone's hand would appear from a doorway, blocking the view, or a body would shift into the path of a camera. The air grew heavier with the unspoken message: This is not your hunt. By afternoon, the first verbal warnings came, low and direct, in Danish sharp enough to slice the pretense from the intruders' faces. Still, the outsiders persisted, convinced that persistence would be rewarded.

It was not. By the next day, the city's patience had thinned to nothing. The morning rain had barely lifted before a group of locals moved together toward the knot of reporters at the Castle gates. Their steps were deliberate, their expressions unyielding. The journalists tried to sidestep, to hold their ground, to keep their equipment steady, but the Danes pressed forward, closing the space between them. Words came now, clear and unambiguous: "Pack your things. Go. Do not come back."

Some hesitated, scoffing at the idea that they could be moved without official authority. That was their mistake. The crowd did not touch them at first, but they made sure every path toward a shot or a question was blocked. Each time a camera was lifted, a hand or a shoulder moved into frame. Each time a microphone was extended, the air between it and its target was filled with a voice that was not Benedict's. The photographers found their perfect angles spoiled before they could be taken.

A few tried to retreat to the side streets, hoping for a quieter vantage point. They found themselves followed, the same unyielding presence keeping them in motion. It was not loud, it was not theatrical, but it was absolute. The message deepened with every step: Leave now, while you can choose to walk away.

By mid-afternoon, the warnings sharpened. Those who lingered were given no mistaking the seriousness of the command. A man who had been leaning against a lamppost with his telephoto lens found himself nose to nose with a dockworker built like the piers themselves. The worker did not raise his voice, but his words carried enough weight to make the journalist lower his camera and step back. "I said go," he repeated, and there was nothing in his tone to suggest it was a negotiation.

The Castle's security did not need to intervene; the city had taken the role for itself. Sørensen watched from the outer courtyard, one hand resting on the sling that had already brought down six drones in as many days. He knew he would not need it now. The media had underestimated the quiet loyalty of Copenhagen. They had mistaken friendliness for weakness, and now they were discovering their error.

By evening, the exodus had begun. Vans were loaded with cases of gear, reporters muttering to one another as they checked their departure routes. Those who had been most persistent were given one last escort to the train station by a pair of fishermen whose expressions left no doubt that a second visit would not be tolerated. There was no public announcement, no formal expulsion—just the firm closing of a door that would not open again.

Inside the Castle, Benedict was told only the briefest version: that the city had handled it. He did not ask for details. He knew his people, and he knew they would have given the media every opportunity to walk away with their dignity intact. If that dignity was not taken, it was because the intruders had chosen arrogance over sense. The result was their own making.

Casper listened intently as Sørensen recounted the events in his clipped, factual way. The boy's eyes lit with pride, not at the confrontation itself, but at what it meant—that his father was protected not just by stone walls, but by the living will of the people. "They know you're one of them," Casper said, his voice carrying the same certainty as if he were stating the weather. Ben only nodded, a small, grateful smile tugging at his mouth.

The storm outside had begun to break, a thin band of pale light slipping between the clouds as evening settled over the city. From the upper balcony, the streets looked emptier now, the last of the journalists gone, the cobblestones returned to their usual rhythm. The quiet felt earned. Copenhagen had spoken in the only way it needed to, and the message was final: the King was theirs, not the world's. And here, within these streets, he would never be hunted.

The Castle stood as it had for centuries, but its greatest armour was no longer its stone. It was the glass—every pane cut, treated, and set with precision to allow only one truth: that you could see out, but never in. From the street, the windows gave back nothing but the world outside, a perfect mirror that swallowed any attempt to look beyond. Photographers raised their cameras and saw only themselves staring back, their own eyes caught in the darkened reflection.

Benedict moved along the upper corridor, his footfalls absorbed by the carpets, the city below unaware that its King was watching from just beyond the glass. He paused at the corner window, where the curve of the street was visible, and saw the absence that had replaced the earlier siege. Where there had been clusters of cameras and restless bodies, now there was only the slow passage of bicycles, the distant sound of voices that belonged to locals and locals alone.

The protection was not simply a matter of technology; it was the way the Castle's design invited the outside world to underestimate it. To those who did not belong here, the darkened glass seemed like arrogance, a barrier to keep them away. To those who lived within, it was reassurance—proof that whatever storm raged beyond the walls, they would not be its spectacle.

Sørensen had overseen the installation himself a week ago, long before the first whisper of a leak. He had insisted on military-grade tinting, the sort used to shield sensitive operations from prying eyes and aerial surveillance. It had been dismissed by some as excessive, but now, as the drones lay dismantled in a storage bin and the last journalists nursed their bruised pride, its value was beyond question.

The cameras had tried every angle. Some crouched low, hoping to catch a shadow through the narrowest seam of glass. Others stood on ladders, aiming their lenses into upper windows. All had failed. Even the most expensive equipment could not outmatch the density of the film layered into the panes. Light entered easily; images did not leave.

Inside, Benedict felt the subtle shift in his own posture. The weight that had settled on his shoulders when the first headlines hit was still there, but it no longer bent him forward. Here, behind the walls and their glass shields, the siege felt less personal. The journalists had been denied the satisfaction of capturing his face in this moment, and that denial was its own quiet victory.

Casper followed his father down the hall, small fingers brushing the smooth, cool surface of the window. "They can't see us, can they?" he asked, voice pitched low as though the glass might still let sound through. Ben shook his head, his answer calm and certain. "Not now. Not ever, if we choose." That word—choose—seemed to ease something in the boy. In a world where so much had been taken from them in the last weeks, the idea of control mattered.

From the kitchen, the muted clatter of plates and the hum of casual conversation drifted upward. Life within the Castle had not stopped for the siege; it had simply folded itself tighter, keeping its warmth where it could not be stolen. The younger children played in the main hall, their voices echoing against the high ceilings, as far removed from the chaos outside as though it had never happened.

The tinted glass was not the only deterrent. Sorensen's slingshot—a marvel of precision and patience—remained at the ready, a silent promise that anything airborne and uninvited would be met with swift gravity. Six drones had already been taken from the sky, each one reduced from an instrument of intrusion to a heap of plastic and bent metal. Those who had sent them received their answer in the most undeniable way possible.

Benedict passed through the west wing, where the windows overlooked the courtyard gardens. Here, the view was pure—just the slow sway of the hedges in the wind, the fountain's arc catching the dim light. The peace of the scene was in sharp contrast to the frenzy that had tried to breach it. He took a moment there, letting the sound of the water steady him, the reflection in the glass offering only his own face back to him.

The people of Copenhagen had done their part, and it had not gone unnoticed. The absence of foreign media in the streets was not coincidence; it was enforcement. Those who had tested the city's patience had been warned, in terms clear enough that no translation was needed. The Castle's defenders were not only within these walls—they moved through the city, unseen until needed.

Casper lingered at one of the corner windows, looking down at the quiet street. "They won't come back," he said, the certainty in his voice far older than his years. Ben studied him for a moment, recognising the truth in it. The boy was right. Those who had been sent away would not return. Not after the way they had been met. Not after realising the King was not alone in his defence.

In the library, Benedict paused before one of the tall windows, its deep frame casting the glass into a darker shade. He could see the faint outlines of his own reflection, the steadiness in his expression, the set of his shoulders. For all the noise of the past weeks, this space felt untouched. That was the strength of the Fortress of Glass—it did not merely keep the world out; it preserved what was inside.

The day outside faded into evening, the city's lights beginning to bloom in the distance. From the highest window in the Castle, Benedict watched them spark to life, one by one, each a small assertion of place and belonging. The siege was over. The glass had held. The King and his family remained unseen, and in that invisibility, they had won something the media could never take—privacy by design, and safety by will.

The courtyard was quiet now, its calm broken only by the gentle hiss of wind against the hedges and the low rustle of leaves. Sørensen stood near the parapet, the slingshot resting loosely in his hand, its polished wood catching the last light of day. It was a simple instrument in appearance, but there was nothing simple about the way it had been made. Ben had commissioned it years ago from a master craftsman, not for sport, but for the kind of work that called for precision when nothing else would do. The bands were of high-grade elastic, the frame shaped perfectly to fit Sørensen's palm, balanced for accuracy at distance. It was a gift, yes, but also a trust—a tool to be used only when the need was great enough to warrant it.

Six times that need had come. Six times the air had filled with the faint, insect-like whine of approaching drones. And six times Sørensen had raised the slingshot, loaded it with a perfectly weighted steel ball, drawn the band to his jawline, and let the shot fly. Each time, the result was the same—a sharp metallic crack in the distance, a sudden shift in the pitch of the drone's engine, and then silence as the machine dropped from the sky. It was an act of defence, not sport, carried out without triumph, yet not without satisfaction.

Ben had watched the first of them fall from the upper terrace, his hand resting lightly on the stone railing. He said nothing, but when Sørensen glanced his way, there was a faint smile—approval tempered by the knowledge of what these intrusions represented. They were not toys; they were eyes, uninvited and without mercy. To allow them to remain in the air would have been to grant the outside world a view it had no right to claim. Sørensen's arm never wavered, his breath steady each time he took aim.

By the third drone, word had spread quietly through the neighbourhood. The people of Copenhagen, never ones to stand idle when the Castle was threatened, began to take their own measures. It started with watchful glances skyward, then with quiet murmurs exchanged in shop doorways. And then, almost without planning, slingshots of all sizes appeared in the hands of men, women, and even the older children. They were not the finely balanced weapon that Sørensen carried, but they did not need to be. Numbers made up for craftsmanship, and a stone launched from the right angle could do the same job as a steel ball.

The city adapted quickly. Café owners kept a bowl of small stones near their back doors. Shopkeepers positioned themselves where they could step outside at the first sign of a hovering lens. In one case, a florist stepped into the street and sent a pebble arcing into the propeller of a low-flying intruder, the crash of its landing greeted with applause from her customers. The message spread faster than any news bulletin: the sky over Copenhagen was not free to be trespassed.

Sørensen continued his work methodically. He was not swayed by the rising laughter from the streets when another drone came down, nor by the muttered curses of those who had hoped to pilot unseen. His focus was absolute, his movements measured. He had learned long ago that precision was born of patience, and in this, there was no room for haste. Each drone that fell was one less threat to the sanctity of the Castle's walls.

On the fifth shot of the day, a glint of sunlight flashed across the drone's camera lens before it disappeared from the sky. Sørensen followed its arc until it vanished behind the rooftops, his fingers already reaching for the next ball. But it never came. The hum in the air faded entirely, replaced by the distant sound of bicycle wheels on cobblestones. For the first time in days, the air above the Castle felt truly empty.

The stillness that followed was almost startling. Sørensen lowered the slingshot and glanced toward the city. The rooftops stretched outward like a map, each chimney and spire familiar. Somewhere out there, the people who had once only watched now stood ready, united in a cause that had nothing to do with ceremony and everything to do with protection. They were defending a man they knew as a neighbour, not a figure from a title.

Ben joined him at the parapet, hands clasped behind his back. "I take it that's the last of them," he said, his voice low enough not to carry to the courtyard below. Sørensen nodded, his gaze still fixed outward. "For now." The words carried no promise that the sky would remain clear forever, only that today's battle was done.

In the streets, there was a sense of accomplishment, though no one lingered on it too long. Life in Copenhagen had its rhythm, and though defending the Castle had become part of it for a time, there was bread to bake, coffee to brew, and goods to sell. The siege, in its aerial form at least, had ended not with grand declarations, but with the quiet, coordinated act of a city deciding that its own would not be hunted.

Sørensen returned the slingshot to its case, laying it down with the same care one might give a fine instrument after a performance. The leather straps were still taut, the frame unmarred despite the tension of the day. He closed the case and slid it into its place among other tools of defence, each one maintained not out of fear, but out of readiness.

From his window, Casper had watched each launch, his eyes wide with the kind of admiration reserved for heroes. When Sørensen came inside, the boy was waiting. "Did they all fall?" he asked. The answer was simple. "Every one." Casper smiled then, the kind of smile that knew safety had been earned, not assumed.

The last light of day lingered on the rooftops, and for a moment, the Castle seemed to breathe easier. The hum of the city returned to its ordinary pitch, no longer threaded with the sharp mechanical whine of surveillance. Above Rosenshavn, the sky was empty once more, save for the drifting clouds that had no interest in the affairs of kings.

It had been obvious for days now, to anyone with eyes in their head, that the people swarming around Rosenshavn Castle did not belong to Copenhagen. Their movements were different, their stares too sharp, their questions too loud. They carried themselves like they had a right to be here, yet every step they took had the jagged air of intrusion. To the Castle's residents, these strangers were not just foreign in nationality—they were foreign in purpose, the kind of people who had come not to see, but to take. There was no familiarity in their faces, no hint of the warm exchanges that passed daily between neighbours in this city. They were here for the scent of a story, not the truth of a man's life.

Inside the Castle, the atmosphere had been kept calm by design. Sørensen's precision with the slingshot had seen to it that the skies were quiet, and the tinted windows allowed life to carry on without the constant sting of being watched. Still, everyone knew the siege was not yet fully over. The ground outside the walls was not theirs to control—not entirely. And so the family carried on with their day, aware that the world beyond the gates was not yet ready to let go.

The knock came mid-afternoon—a distinct, deliberate pattern against the wood of the special visitors' door. Three short, two long, one short. It was a rhythm known only to a handful of people, and to hear it now was like a bell that rang only for them. The nearest guard moved to the panel, sliding open the small viewing slit. On the other side was Danny, his smile filling the narrow frame, the familiar creases around his eyes proof that he was carrying something worth hearing.

The door opened, and Danny stepped inside with the easy confidence of a man who belonged. The first thing he did was glance toward the smallest security camera mounted above the entry, giving it a playful salute before walking down the short corridor toward the sitting room. Ben was there already, drawn by the sound of the knock, and when he saw Danny, his shoulders eased just slightly. Sørensen followed from the far side of the hall, one brow raised in question.

Danny didn't make them wait. "They're leaving," he said, his voice warm but edged with satisfaction. "Or rather—they're being made to leave." He went on to explain, the words tumbling out with an energy that matched the news.

The people of Copenhagen had decided, quite firmly, that the outsiders had worn out their welcome. It had started small—shop doors closing early when the unfamiliar reporters came in, conversations dying the moment they walked into cafés. But it had grown quickly into something far less subtle.

Ben listened without interrupting as Danny painted the picture. Café owners who knew Ben personally had begun refusing service outright, their expressions cool, their tone clipped. Locals were standing in front of camera lenses during street interviews, blocking the shot entirely, or in some cases walking directly into frame to force the crews to cut. More than once, the sound of equipment being packed into vans had been followed by the hum of those same vans leaving the district altogether.

One particularly stubborn group of photographers had tried to set up on a corner near the bakery Ben often visited. By the time they returned from adjusting their gear, they found a wall of bicycles parked in front of them, handlebars jutting at odd angles, leaving no clear line of sight toward the Castle. According to Danny, the bikes' owners had no particular interest in moving them, not until the photographers packed up and went elsewhere. The message was simple: there would be no vantage points here.

Ben felt the corners of his mouth pull upward—not in amusement, but in gratitude. He had always known Copenhageners to be protective of their own, but this was different. This was not the quiet defence of a community minding its own affairs; this was active resistance. They were not waiting for the outsiders to grow bored. They were showing them, day by day, that there was nothing here for them to gain.

Danny leaned forward, his elbows on his knees, the enthusiasm in his voice steady as he described the scene outside. "It's not just about keeping them away from you," he said. "It's about letting them know they don't get to treat our city like a hunting ground. They're learning fast that there's a difference between visiting and invading." His eyes flicked to Casper, who had wandered in quietly and was now leaning against his father's arm. "Your friends out there are making sure you can walk into town again without feeling eyes on the back of your neck."

The thought of it brought Ben a kind of relief he hadn't let himself feel in days. His shoulders, so often squared against the weight of being watched, seemed to loosen just a fraction. He reached for Casper, pulling him closer, and the boy responded instinctively, tucking himself against his father's side. Outside, the city was fighting a battle they didn't have to fight—but they were doing it anyway.

Kendrick, who had been leaning silently against the doorframe, finally spoke. "They'll be gone soon enough," he said, his voice measured. "Not because they want to be, but because they can't stand the cold." Ben knew he was right—not the weather, but the coldness of being unwelcome in a place where warmth was usually given freely. It was a punishment far sharper than any shouted threat.

The image lingered in Ben's mind—outsiders standing awkwardly at café counters, met with blank stares and folded arms; cameras lowered not out of politeness, but out of futility. It was the kind of quiet rebellion that left no doubt about the will of the people. They weren't breaking laws or raising voices—they were closing ranks.

Danny stayed long enough to answer questions, his tone never losing its brightness, though it carried the weight of what the city had done. "They're not afraid to make it uncomfortable for them," he said finally. "And that's why it's working." With that, he stood, clasping Ben's shoulder before making his way back toward the door.

The sound of the lock sliding home behind him was not the closing off of the outside world, but the quiet assurance that it was being held at bay. Ben sat for a long moment afterward, his gaze on the window, knowing that beyond its glass lay a city that was not simply his home, but his shield. Casper looked up at him then, his expression calm but sure. "They like you too much to let anyone hurt you," he said matter-of-factly. Ben smiled at that—not because it was flattering, but because it was true. And in that truth, there was safety.

The city had always known Ben as more than the man in the Castle. To the shopkeepers, he was the polite customer who lingered long enough to ask after their families. To the neighbours, he was the quiet presence who never treated his title—whatever it might be—as something that set him apart. To the vendors who worked the market stalls, he was the man who remembered faces and paid in full without haggling. In their eyes, he was not a subject to be ruled over, nor a curiosity to be displayed, but a friend. That truth had settled deep in the bones of Copenhagen, and in times like this, it was that bond—not tinted glass or high walls—that kept him safe.

Danny's updates had become part of the Castle's rhythm. Some mornings it was the chime of the special line, the old landline tucked in the corner of the study, ringing with a deliberate patience that suggested no rush but demanded to be answered. Other times, Ben would invite him over for coffee, the sort that filled the small kitchen with a warmth that could not be staged. Sørensen and Kendrick were usually there too, leaning in around the table, their hands cradling mugs as they listened to every detail.

On the phone, Danny's voice carried with it the sounds of the city—the hiss of passing bicycles, the low murmur of people on cobblestones. In person, it came with the sharp scent of the outside air and the faint chill of wind off the harbour. His reports were never just lists of sightings or incidents; they were snapshots of a city refusing to cooperate with the outsiders. Café doors shut early. Shop blinds drawn the moment an unfamiliar camera appeared. Conversations that died mid-sentence when a stranger leaned in too close.

"It's not even angry anymore," Danny said during one such visit, the steam from his coffee curling between them. "It's cold. Colder than I've ever seen them be. You know how hard it is to get Copenhageners to turn their backs on someone? Well, they've turned their backs. And they're keeping them turned." Kendrick listened with an approving tilt of his head, his fingers drumming idly on the handle of his mug.

Ben knew exactly what Danny meant. Anger burned hot and quickly; coldness, though—coldness could last for weeks, even months. The outsiders could stay as long as they liked, but every day they did was another day without warmth, without cooperation, without any scrap of help from the people they had come to prod. It was a siege of the most Danish sort: unhurried, polite on the surface, but relentless beneath.

Casper, who had taken to sitting in on these updates, listened more closely than most grown men would have. Sometimes he asked questions—direct ones, the kind that made Danny smile at his bluntness. Other times he simply sat back, his eyes fixed on Ben, absorbing not only the words but the way his father responded. The boy could read the room as easily as any adult, and he knew that this unity, this wall of quiet refusal from the city, mattered as much as any legal defence or security detail.

Still, as much as they appreciated the solidarity, everyone at the table knew the siege was not over. The Castle might be shielded by glass and guarded by allies, but the leak itself—the root of the problem—had not yet been closed. Danny leaned forward then, his tone shifting from report to proposal. "I've been thinking," he said slowly, glancing at each of them in turn. "We can't just wait them out. You want this gone, you've got to choke it at the source. I've got a few ideas."

Ben's gaze sharpened. Sørensen set down his mug with a quiet clink, his body angling toward Danny. Kendrick's brows drew together, not in disapproval, but in a readiness to hear something worth considering. Outside, the world might think they were simply hunkering down, weathering the attention. Inside, however, there was no appetite for passive endurance. Containment required action, and action required a plan that could stand on more than hope.

Danny began outlining his thoughts, his voice even but edged with strategy. He spoke of narrowing points of access, of controlling not just the physical space but the flow of information itself. He suggested ways to cut off the story at its international source, to make it unprofitable for anyone to pursue further. Kendrick interrupted now and then with practical concerns, Sørensen with the occasional dry observation. Ben sat back, weighing each idea, testing it against his own knowledge of how such storms built—and how they could be dismantled.

Casper stayed quiet, his head against Ben's arm, his small hands curled in his lap. He didn't understand every detail of what was being discussed, but he understood the stakes. His father's safety wasn't just about what happened inside the Castle—it was about what the city could hold at bay, and what they themselves could shut down. The boy's trust in the adults around him was unshaken, but his eyes were alert, following the thread of the conversation as if it might offer him something to do.

The coffee grew cold before the discussion began to wind down. By then, they had the skeleton of a containment plan, something that could be refined in the days ahead. Danny promised to bring more details the next time they met, whether by phone or in person.

The men stood, stretching the stiffness from their limbs, each carrying the weight of the conversation differently—Kendrick with a measured patience, Sørensen with the faint satisfaction of having a target to aim at, Ben with the quiet relief of knowing that the city's shield was matched now by a plan of their own.

When Danny left, the knock of the front door closing echoed briefly in the hall. Ben stood for a moment, his hand resting on Casper's shoulder, both of them watching the space where their friend had just been. Outside, beyond the tinted glass and the guarded gates, Copenhagen continued to stand with them—not in grand declarations, but in the steady, stubborn way that mattered most. And for Ben, that was enough to carry them into the next stage.

The study doors were closed, the curtains drawn despite the daylight pressing against the glass. This was not a conversation for wandering ears or idle interruption. Ben stood at the head of the long oak table, his fingertips resting lightly on its polished surface. To his right sat Sørensen, the veteran of a hundred quiet battles no history book would ever record. To his left was Danny, his mind always turning over solutions before the problems had even fully taken shape. The three of them formed the core of the Castle's response, and this was where that response would take its final form.

Sørensen began with the hard truths. The leak had already spread to places no legal writ could easily reach—foreign presses, online outlets, and shadowed corners of the web where stories multiplied like weeds. Direct suppression was impossible; selective suffocation, however, was not. "We can't put the fire out everywhere," he said evenly, "but we can starve it here until it burns itself out." His eyes flicked to Ben, waiting for the nod that came without hesitation.

Danny leaned forward, unrolling a sheet of paper covered in his quick, neat handwriting. His plan broke the problem into three fronts: access, narrative, and deterrence. Access would be the easiest—tighten entry points to the Castle, enforce stricter boundaries with anyone seeking contact, and ensure that no unvetted person could get close enough for fresh photographs or offhand quotes. It was work the city was already helping with, but the Castle would formalise it, making it part of a visible and consistent policy.

The narrative was trickier. "If we say nothing, the story is whatever they want it to be," Danny pointed out. "If we say too much, we're feeding it." Ben listened in silence, weighing the balance between absence and overexposure. In the end, they agreed on a strategy of selective engagement: one brief statement to confirm only what was already undeniable, followed by absolute silence on every other detail. A story without fuel could not stay alight for long.

Deterrence, Sørensen's favourite subject, was where the quiet intimidation came in. It would not be threats—those could backfire—but subtle demonstrations of reach and readiness. Certain editors would find themselves served with polite but firm notices from lawyers who specialised in international privacy law. Persistent intruders would discover how very closely the Castle could monitor their movements without ever breaking a law. The point was not to punish, but to plant the seed that pursuing this story was more trouble than it was worth.

Ben's role in all of this was both central and invisible. He would be the calm face inside the Castle, going about daily life as though the outside chaos barely brushed him. In private, he would approve every legal filing, review each line of the carefully worded statement, and oversee the final tightening of security. It was a performance, but a necessary one—if the public saw panic, they would smell blood.

Casper, sitting cross-legged on the couch at the far side of the room, listened with the same intent focus he had shown during Danny's last visit. He said nothing, but his eyes followed every shift in tone, every moment when Ben leaned in or Sørensen's voice sharpened. He understood, in his own way, that this was how you fought without drawing swords—by making the battlefield so inhospitable that the enemy had nowhere to stand.

The meeting moved steadily from broad strokes to fine details. They discussed timing: the statement would be released in exactly forty-eight hours, giving them room to complete the legal groundwork without leaving the media in suspense too long. They reviewed the wording line by line, stripping away anything that might be misinterpreted or used against them. The final draft was so precise it could have been carved in stone.

Sørensen's contacts in the city were tasked with the less official side of the plan—ensuring that no "accidental" encounters with journalists could yield anything useful. Friendly shopkeepers would turn cameras away. Neighbours would steer strangers down the wrong streets. It was a campaign fought with courtesy on the surface and absolute resolve underneath.

Danny would handle the monitoring. His small network of trusted friends would keep eyes on online chatter, noting where the story was growing and where it was dying. They would track who was still trying to push it and identify any weak points the Castle could exploit. Ben trusted him in this role; Danny's patience was matched only by his ability to spot patterns others missed.

As the plan solidified, a quiet sense of control returned to the room. The storm outside had not lessened, but they now knew exactly how to weather it. This was not blind endurance—it was calculated resistance, built to last until the noise died of its own futility. For the first time since the leak broke, there was a shared understanding that they could turn the tide.

Ben closed the meeting with a simple directive: "We don't react to them—they react to us." It was a line that carried the weight of strategy, not ego. Every person in the room understood that it was not about dominance, but survival. And survival, in their world, required a patience sharper than any weapon.

When the doors finally opened and they stepped out into the hall, the air felt lighter, though the pressure beyond the walls had not changed. They carried the plan with them like armour, each man knowing his role and his boundaries. The Castle would not be a fortress of panic, but of deliberate, unshakable calm.

Casper followed Ben out, his small hand slipping into his father's without a word. He did not need to speak to know that something important had been decided. Whatever the world outside thought it knew, it would find that the man they sought to corner was already far beyond their reach.

The first thing people noticed about Judge Algren was not his height or his grey hair, but the way silence followed him into a room. He carried it like a robe, a stillness that settled over every conversation until all that remained was the sound of his footsteps. When he stepped into the Castle's study, he did not knock—he had been invited, and in this house, his arrival was never treated as a formality. Ben rose to greet him, a small gesture of respect between men who did not waste such courtesies on anyone they did not trust.

Algren's eyes scanned the room without haste, pausing on Danny, whose posture betrayed both readiness and a faint undercurrent of urgency. Sørensen sat just beyond him, leaning back as though this meeting was merely an extension of the planning sessions they had already conducted. Casper was curled on the armchair near the fireplace, an island of quiet observation. The judge took in the whole picture before setting his hat on the side table. "I hear there has been movement," he said, his voice neither curious nor dramatic—just a statement of fact.

Danny was the first to answer, stepping forward as though presenting a case in open court. He laid out the events with surgical precision: the foreign reporters, the long lenses trained on the Castle, the drones swatted from the sky, the steady resistance of Copenhagen's people. He did not linger on sentiment; he spoke in the language of cause and effect, of violations and responses. "Every citizen within reach has made it clear they will not permit further intrusion," Danny concluded, his tone a mixture of pride and steel.

Algren listened without interruption, his eyes narrowing slightly at certain points, though whether in disapproval or approval was impossible to read. When Danny finished, the judge gave a slow nod. "Then it appears your city understands the law as well as it understands loyalty." He turned his gaze to Ben, and something in the weight of it was both judicial and personal. "And yet, you called me."

Ben's reply was steady. "Because this cannot remain only in the streets, Judge. I need the law written into the shield they've already built for me." It was a plain sentence, but it carried the weight of their mutual understanding—that street loyalty, while unshakable, needed the permanence of legal authority to endure beyond the moment.

The judge moved toward the centre of the table, resting his hands on the edge as if claiming it for his own deliberations. "Then you shall have it. My trust in you is not a recent matter, Benedict, and I have no patience for those who try to carve their advantage from another man's life. The adoption paperwork will be completed without delay. It will carry the full weight of my court, and no man will challenge it without finding me already waiting for him."

Casper's eyes brightened at the mention of the adoption, though he said nothing. The word "court" was not one he feared when spoken by Judge Algren; it meant safety, finality, the sort of protection that even the strongest arms could not always provide. Ben caught his son's expression and gave the smallest nod, a silent promise that the day was coming soon.

Danny, encouraged by the judge's clarity, continued to outline the broader picture. He described how citizens had positioned themselves between cameras and Castle walls, how café owners had refused service to anyone suspected of being press, how neighbours had blocked alleyways without being asked. "They've turned the city into a filter," Danny said. "Nothing gets through without their permission."

Algren's lips curved almost imperceptibly—a rare expression for a man whose public face was carved in the stone of impartiality. "It is a fine thing," he said quietly, "when the people understand the value of what they protect." His gaze shifted once more to Ben. "But you know as well as I do that goodwill must be defended before it fades. Your enemies will tire before your friends do, but only if you keep the fight within your walls and your laws."

Sørensen, who had remained silent until now, spoke up in his measured tone. "That is exactly why the plan is built for patience, Judge. No grand strikes, no shouting. Just constant pressure until they lose interest." The judge inclined his head, acknowledging the merit of the strategy without needing to praise it aloud.

Ben could feel the room tightening into alignment—the law, the city, and the Castle itself, all moving toward the same objective. This was not a desperate gathering anymore; it was the assembly of a united front. With Algren's authority added to the balance, their containment plan no longer felt like a defence—it felt like a closing of the last gap in their armour.

The judge retrieved a slim folder from the leather case he carried, placing it on the table in front of Ben. "These are the preliminary documents," he said. "Sign them, and I will see the rest through personally. It will be as though it was always so, in the eyes of the law." Ben did not need to ask whether the matter would be kept discreet; Algren's reputation was built on precision and privacy.

Danny exhaled, the tension in his shoulders easing just slightly. "That will send a message as much as anything else we've done," he said. "If they can't even shake the foundations of your family, they'll have nothing left to chase." The judge gave a single, slow nod of agreement.

When the meeting broke, Algren remained a moment longer, speaking quietly with Ben near the doorway. Whatever was said stayed between them, but the expression on Ben's face as they parted told the others all they needed to know—this was not just a legal ally, but a man who understood what was at stake on every level.

As the judge departed, his presence seemed to linger in the air like a seal pressed into wax. Outside, the storm of cameras and questions might still circle, but inside these walls, the law itself had taken a seat at the table. And for Benedict, that was as valuable as any fortress of stone.

The table was cleared of everything except the folder Judge Algren had brought. The pale cream paper within seemed almost too plain for the weight it carried. Ben sat at the head of the long oak table, the soft light from the shaded lamps catching the edge of the pages. Casper sat beside him, close enough to feel the warmth of his father's arm, though the boy's eyes never left the documents. To him, this was more than paper—it was the moment his place in the world became unshakable.

Judge Algren slid the first page forward with deliberate care, his gaze steady on Ben. "This is the final draft," he said. "Once signed, it will be entered into the record immediately. There will be no appeals, no delays, no further permissions needed." The words carried the same calm force as a courtroom verdict. Sørensen, leaning against the far wall, folded his arms and allowed himself the smallest smile. He had been present for battles far more dangerous than this, but none so quietly decisive.

Danny, seated across from Ben, glanced toward Casper with the faintest nod of reassurance. "It's done before it's done," he said softly, the phrase meaning more to the boy than it might have to anyone else. Casper's hands tightened in his lap, his eyes shining but unblinking. Ben caught the movement and rested a hand on his son's shoulder, steadying him.

The judge uncapped his pen—an instrument of heavy silver, well-worn yet polished—and placed it on the page before Ben. The sound of the nib touching paper was soft, but in the stillness of the room, it might as well have been a drumbeat. Ben wrote his name in the same hand he had used to sign military orders, personal letters, and confidential agreements—but this was different. This was not a command; it was a promise.

Casper leaned closer, watching each stroke as though memorising it. He would remember the curve of the "B" and the way the pen lifted before the final flourish. When Ben set the pen down, Judge Algren immediately moved the second page forward. "For the court's witness," he said simply, signing beneath Ben's name with a swift, sure motion.

The final sheet required both of them—Ben's signature alongside Casper's small but determined script. The boy's hand trembled at first, but his father's hand covered his gently, guiding the pen without forcing it. Together, they drew the lines that bound them not just by love, but by law. When Casper finished, he looked up at Ben with a smile so wide it forced the corners of Ben's own mouth to lift.

Sørensen stepped forward then, retrieving the signed pages and stacking them neatly before passing them back to the judge. "There," he said, his voice carrying quiet satisfaction. "One less thing the world can question." His eyes met Ben's, and in that look was the unspoken truth—they had fortified more than the Castle's walls today.

The judge gathered the documents into his case, fastening the locks with precise clicks. "These will be filed within the hour," he said. "From this day forward, there will be no distinction in the eyes of the law. Casper Arthur Bille–Rosenshavn is your son in every way." He turned to Casper, and the rare warmth in his expression was unmistakable. "Congratulations, young man."

Casper sat up straighter, as though the words had added an inch to his height. "Thank you, sir," he said, the formality unforced. He knew enough to understand that gratitude was not just for the papers, but for the shield they now represented.

Outside the Castle, the siege of cameras and questions still churned, but in the study, the air had shifted. The weight that had hung over the family for months seemed to lift, replaced by a quiet strength. Ben could feel it in the way Casper leaned against him now—not as a child seeking shelter, but as a son who knew where he belonged.

Danny leaned forward, resting his elbows on the table. "We should mark the moment," he said. "Not publicly, not while the vultures are circling—but here, in our own way." Ben nodded, already picturing the simplest of celebrations, something that would not pierce the fortress of their privacy but would still anchor the memory.

Sørensen chuckled under his breath. "A cake, then. And not one from the kitchen—they'll insist on making it too proper. We'll bring one in from outside, from somewhere no one would expect." Ben raised an eyebrow at him, the corners of his mouth twitching upward. "You just want an excuse to leave the Castle," he said. Sørensen didn't deny it.

Judge Algren closed his case and straightened. "Enjoy your moment," he said, his tone neither indulgent nor distant. "The law has done its part. The rest belongs to you." And with that, he turned for the door, his exit as unhurried as his entrance.

As the door closed behind him, Ben looked around the room. This was not the victory the outside world would ever see in headlines or broadcasts, but it was one of the most important they would ever claim. No matter what storms came, Casper's place here could never be touched. The siege outside could howl as loud as it liked—inside, the foundation had just been set in stone.

Ben lowered himself slowly, the weight of the day still pressing on his shoulders, until he was kneeling on the polished floor in front of his son. His eyes locked with Casper's, and in that still moment there were no titles, no news headlines, no watchful eyes from the outside world—just father and son. The quiet between them was not emptiness, but fullness, heavy with the unspoken understanding that no matter what storms raged beyond these walls, nothing could reach the place they stood in now.

Casper's breathing came faster, his small hands clenching at his sides before he took one unsteady step forward. His eyes shimmered in the warm light, tears pooling but not yet falling. Ben reached out with both hands, resting them gently on Casper's shoulders, his touch steady and grounding. He could feel the faint tremor running through the boy, a mix of joy, relief, and something far older than his years.

"I love you, Daddy," Casper said, the words breaking the silence like the first crack of sunlight after a long storm. His voice was neither timid nor rehearsed; it was a truth spoken without hesitation, without the need for proof. Ben's heart clenched at the sound, the phrase cutting through every other thought that had filled his mind over the past weeks.

Casper stepped closer, his small frame leaning into his father's chest. The movement was instinctive, as though drawn by the pull of something that had always been there, even before the papers and signatures made it official. Ben's arms wrapped around him fully now, pulling him in with a protective strength that promised never to let go.

The tears finally came, hot against Ben's neck, each one carrying away a fragment of the weight Casper had been carrying. Ben pressed his cheek into his son's hair, inhaling the faint scent of soap and the outdoors, a grounding reminder of how real and present this moment was. The world outside could call him king or stranger or scandal—it meant nothing here.

Casper tilted his head up suddenly, his small hands coming to rest against his father's jaw. Without a word, he leaned in and kissed Ben on the lips—a first, unprompted, unashamed act of pure affection. It was the kind of love that needed no explanation, only acceptance. Ben held still, letting the boy lead, allowing that singular moment to stand untouched by the noise of everything else.

When the kiss broke, Casper's tears returned, but these were different—tears not of sadness but of joy so intense it spilled over. His lips curved into a trembling smile, and he let out a small, almost embarrassed laugh at himself. Ben smiled back, brushing a thumb across the wetness on his son's cheek. "That," Ben murmured, "is worth more than anything the world could ever give me."

The boy pressed his face into Ben's shoulder again, this time not to hide his tears but simply to rest there, as though that spot had always belonged to him. Ben's arms tightened once more, his fingers splaying against the boy's back in a way that wordlessly told him he was safe, that nothing—no camera, no drone, no headline—could take this away.

Behind them, Sørensen watched from a respectful distance, his usual sharp gaze softened. He understood the power of such moments, though he would never speak of it aloud. Danny, too, stood quietly, sensing that this was not a time to intrude with words or movement. This was not just a father embracing his son—it was a man claiming his rightful place as protector, guide, and anchor.

Ben leaned back just enough to meet Casper's gaze again. "You're mine," he said, his voice low but firm, the syllables wrapped in certainty. "Not because of a judge, not because of papers—but because we belong to each other." Casper nodded quickly, his tears catching in the light, and he whispered, "Always."

The boy's small fingers curled into the fabric of Ben's shirt, holding on as though he could anchor himself there forever. Ben kissed the top of his head, slow and deliberate, before resting his forehead against Casper's. Their breathing synced, the outside world falling further away until it felt like nothing existed beyond the space between them.

For a long moment, they stayed that way—silent, still, and entirely present. Then Ben shifted slightly, lifting his son into his arms as though he weighed nothing. Casper settled in against him, one arm wrapped loosely around his father's neck, his eyes half-closing in the comfort of knowing that no one could take this away now.

As Ben stood, the creak of the floorboards under his weight felt like an anchor pulling them both back into the present. But this time, the present felt unshakable. The Castle's walls were high, the windows shielded, and the people outside were loyal—but this, this bond, was the true fortress.

Sørensen gave a single nod, not of approval—Ben needed none—but of acknowledgment. Some things were stronger than law, stronger than title, stronger than any force that might try to breach them. In this moment, father and son had built something no one could dismantle.

Ben carried Casper from the study toward the heart of the Castle, their shadows stretching along the corridor walls. Whatever battles lay ahead, they would face them together—not because they had to, but because they wanted to. And in that truth, both of them knew, they had already won.

The Castle stood silent in the late afternoon light, its presence steady against the encroaching weight of a changed world. Outside, the streets had grown still; the last of the cameras and foreign tongues had vanished from sight. The drones, once a persistent buzz in the skies above Rosenshavn, were now gone entirely, their mechanical persistence replaced by the distant rhythm of city life returning to normal. The air, though crisp and clean, carried the faint scent of rain—fresh, but edged with the memory of the storm that had passed.

Ben moved through the corridor with the deliberate calm of a man who understood that victory was only temporary. His steps were steady, yet his mind traced the truth he could not avoid: a name, once spoken aloud, could never be taken back. It would live now beyond these walls, in whispers, in records, in places where even the most loyal ally could not reach to silence it. He did not fear what they knew, but he did not welcome it either.

In the heart of the Castle, the great sitting room glowed with the soft warmth of afternoon firelight. The heavy curtains had been drawn back, their tinted glass shielding them from outside eyes yet letting in the full breadth of the day's fading glow. Ben stood by the hearth, Casper still in his arms, the boy's head resting lightly on his father's shoulder. They had been together like this for what felt like hours, neither rushing to move nor speaking much at all.

The creak of the door announced Maria's arrival before her small figure stepped into view. At nine years old, she carried herself with the same quiet composure as her father—measured, assured, and unshaken by the chaos that had passed. She did not hesitate as she crossed the room, her small shoes barely making a sound on the polished floorboards. Her pace was neither hurried nor hesitant; it was the walk of someone who already knew where they belonged.

Maria came to stand directly before Ben and Casper, her hands still at her sides for a moment before she reached forward. Without a word, she wrapped her arms around both of them, her embrace somehow managing to be both gentle and unyielding. Ben felt the sincerity in the way her arms held them, her frame small but her presence filling the space around them completely.

Casper turned slightly in his father's arms so that he could return her embrace. His head rested against her shoulder, and for a brief moment, the three of them stood as if the rest of the world no longer existed. Ben felt the weight of that gesture—not for its grandeur, but for its simplicity. It was love given without condition, and in the unshakable honesty only children seemed to master.

Maria's words were few, but the truth of her presence was loud enough. She did not speak in grand declarations, nor did she feel the need to assure them with promises. She simply stayed there, her silence saying more than a hundred speeches ever could. It was the same kind of silence her father carried—a stillness that was not empty, but full.

Ben looked down at her, his hand coming to rest gently on her back. "Thank you," he said softly, the words carrying far more meaning than the simple syllables suggested. Maria looked up briefly, her eyes meeting his with the kind of sincerity that could not be faked, and then she simply nodded. She did not smile, but her presence radiated the same warmth as if she had.

The moment stretched on without discomfort. They did not feel the need to move quickly, as though they all understood that this was a moment to be held, not hurried. The fire cracked quietly in the grate, the scent of woodsmoke threading through the air, and outside the faint call of a distant gull drifted through the walls. Life continued beyond the Castle, but here, in this room, time seemed to stand still.

When Maria stepped back, it was only by an inch, her arms still loosely around them both. Her head tilted just slightly, studying Ben with an expression that seemed far older than her years. It was as though she knew—without needing to be told—that this day had changed something in ways they could not yet measure. And still, she stood without fear.

Casper rested his head back against his father's chest, glancing at Maria as if to confirm that the connection was mutual. There was no doubt in his expression—he knew she was family, not by blood or law, but by choice. That kind of bond was harder to break than any legal decree.

Ben tightened his hold on both children for a final moment before letting them stand on their own. His eyes flicked to the high windows, the tinted glass still showing nothing but the pale blue of the late afternoon sky. The world could watch all it wanted; it would not see what was in here.

Maria lingered a moment longer, her hands falling back to her sides, before she stepped back fully. She gave no parting words, but she did not need to. The strength of her gesture lingered long after she left the room. Ben and Casper stood together, still feeling the echo of her embrace as though it had woven itself into the very walls.

The Castle remained un-breached—not by ladders, not by cameras, not by whispered lies. But Ben knew the true strength was not in the tinted glass or the ancient stone. It was in moments like this, where the walls held because the people inside them did. And in that knowledge, he found the calm he had been searching for all day.

The sun had long since slipped past the rooftops when Ben and Sørensen stepped out onto the eastern battlements. The city of Copenhagen stretched below them in a patchwork of rooftops, chimneys, and winding streets, the faint glimmer of streetlamps already beginning to glow against the soft blue-grey of approaching evening. The air carried the bite of the sea, tinged with the scent of wet stone after the day's rain. It was quiet now—eerily so compared to the chaos that had surrounded the Castle only days ago. The wind, moving gently across the high walls, brought with it the hum of life from below: the clink of a shop door closing, the faint rumble of a cart on cobblestones, the low murmur of neighbours greeting one another in the street.

Ben stood with his gloved hands resting on the cold stone edge, his eyes moving over the familiar cityscape. Sørensen lingered a pace behind, arms crossed, his stance both relaxed and alert. The two men did not need to speak to share the same thought—that the danger had not passed entirely, but had only retreated. They both knew storms of this kind never truly ended. They broke apart, regrouped, and returned when least expected.

For now, the leak was contained. The headlines had dulled, the reporters had vanished, and the skies above Rosenshavn were free of drones. But Ben understood that this was not victory in the way the public might imagine. It was simply a pause. A gathering of strength before the next attempt to breach what should have remained untouchable. In that pause, however, there was time to fortify—not just the Castle, but the people who lived within its walls and those who called this city their own.

Sørensen shifted his weight, leaning on the stone, his eyes scanning the rooftops. "They'll be back," he said at last, his voice low and steady, not a prediction but a certainty. Ben nodded once, his gaze never leaving the horizon. "And when they are," he replied, "we'll be ready." It was not a boast; it was a promise. One that extended beyond the battlements, beyond the walls, into the homes and hearts of everyone who had stood by him in the past weeks.

Below, in the sheltered courtyard, the sound of light footsteps drifted upward. Casper and Maria were there, weaving around one another in slow, deliberate play. They were not chasing, not shrieking, not demanding attention—just moving with the quiet joy of two children who understood that this place was safe, at least for tonight. Ben watched them for a long moment, the corners of his mouth softening. He saw no difference between them—no hierarchy, no imbalance. In his eyes, they were equals, bound not by blood but by the deliberate choice to stand side by side.

Casper darted around a pillar and Maria followed, her laugh more a breath than a sound. They touched the edges of the gardens, stepping carefully so as not to disturb the flowers, their movements unhurried. It was as though they both understood the value of stillness now, the importance of preserving this rare quiet. They did not need noise to feel alive; their connection was the activity, the unspoken understanding that they belonged here and to each other.

Ben's gaze followed them until they disappeared behind the great oak at the far end of the courtyard. Sørensen glanced down as well, the faintest smile ghosting over his otherwise guarded expression. "They'll remember this," he murmured. "Not the headlines. Not the trouble. This." Ben said nothing, but he knew it to be true. Children's memories are shaped as much by the moments of peace as by the storms they survive.

The light above the city deepened to amber, shadows stretching long across the streets. In the distance, church bells marked the hour—not in intrusion, but as part of the city's heartbeat. From up here, the Castle and Copenhagen seemed indivisible, two parts of the same whole. That unity had been tested in recent days and had proven itself unbreakable. The walls held not because of their height, but because of the people who defended them, inside and out.

Ben straightened, stepping back from the battlement to survey the entire courtyard below. He thought of Danny, already on high alert even in the absence of visible threat. Danny's role was as vital as any stone in the Castle's foundation; he was the quiet watcher, the one who caught the first whisper of trouble before it became a roar. Knowing he was there allowed Ben to focus on more than defence—to think ahead, to be ready for the next move.

Sørensen's presence beside him was its own kind of shield. The man had been there through the smallest skirmishes and the largest storms, his loyalty unshaken. Together, they had turned away intruders not just with force, but with unshakable resolve. That, more than any weapon or wall, was the reason they were still standing.

A gull wheeled overhead, its cry sharp against the quiet. The city's lights bloomed brighter, scattered like fireflies across the darkening streets. Somewhere in the distance, a carriage moved, its wheels echoing faintly. The world was still moving, still breathing, even if for the moment it kept its distance from Rosenshavn.

Ben took one last look over the city before turning toward the stairs. "Come on," he said quietly to Sørensen. "Let's not waste this peace while we have it." His voice was calm, measured, but there was an undercurrent of readiness—of someone who knew exactly how temporary such peace could be.

As they descended the steps, the sounds of the courtyard grew louder. Casper and Maria had reappeared, moving in a slow circle around one another, exchanging glances that spoke of unspoken games only they understood. Ben paused at the bottom of the stairs to watch them for a brief moment more. Whatever storms lay ahead, these moments—this stillness—were worth defending at any cost.

The Castle's great doors closed behind them with a deep, resonant thud. It was not the sound of shutting the world out entirely, but of drawing a boundary that would not be crossed without consequence. Inside, the light was warm, the air steady, and the quiet resolve of those within matched the strength of the stone around them. The storm was gone for now, but the watch had only just begun.

CHAPTER 9: COUNTDOWN TO DISAPPEARANCE

Four days had slipped by since the twins' quiet arrival into the world, carried into breath and warmth beneath the still water of the birthing pool, and the corridors of Rosenshavn Castle had not yet settled from the echo of their first cries. The scent of clean linen and lavender still clung to the rooms that Isla had rested in, and every sound within the walls carried a heightened weight, as though the building itself were reluctant to disturb this fragile new chapter.

Ben walked those corridors without speaking, the tread of his steps unhurried, his gaze fixed on the small details that he knew would soon be pressed into memory rather than daily sight. His ears caught the faint creak of polished wood beneath his heels, the muted shuffle of staff moving about their work, and, most precious of all, the gentle stirrings of his children somewhere beyond the next door. He was aware with every passing moment that the day would come, sooner than he wanted, when he would hear those sounds only in recollection. The inevitability of that truth settled over him like the chill of a northern wind, familiar yet never welcome.

Outside the high walls, the air had changed since the birth. The loyal citizens who had always regarded the castle as a fixture of their own lives now stood more visibly in its defence. Neighbours lingered near their fences, pretending to prune hedges or sweep paths while keeping their eyes trained on approaching roads.

Children played along the pavement, their games as much a ruse as an innocent pastime, concealing the quiet network of watchful eyes that Danny had organised with an efficiency that rivalled the castle's own guard. From his vantage at a library window, Ben could see the subtle ways in which the city had closed ranks around him, not out of duty to a crown, but from the simple fact that he was theirs to protect. It was a loyalty that humbled him, even as it reminded him of the limits of such protection. No devotion could stop the reach of a camera lens. No fence, however high, could block the passage of a rumour already in flight.

The events of the previous night still lingered in his thoughts. Kendrick's counsel had been delivered without flourish, without any attempt to comfort. That was not Kendrick's way. He had spoken plainly in the low light of the study, his voice level and his words stripped of anything but the truth. There would be no hesitation when the time came to leave, Kendrick had said.

Plans were in place, the path was already set, and hesitation would turn planning into failure. Ben had nodded, not because he agreed blindly, but because he understood the nature of what was being asked of him. To leave now was not an act of retreat; it was an act of preservation. Yet the knowledge did not soften the thought of what he would be walking away from, if only for a time.

The castle itself seemed to know something was shifting. The staff moved with a certain unspoken efficiency, as though they were aware of the clock already ticking down. Even the children who normally filled the hallways with unrestrained noise had become quieter in his presence, their laughter carrying in shorter bursts before returning to the subdued shuffle of footsteps.

It was not fear that kept them hushed, but something closer to instinct — the way animals grow still before the break of a storm. Ben noticed it in the way Clara guided the little ones toward their lessons, and in the way Tobias carried a bundle of laundry without his usual habit of stopping to chat. Everything was in motion, yet all of it seemed to happen beneath the surface, as though the castle itself were holding its breath.

Ben's own breath came slower as he reached the door to the nursery. He stood outside it for a long moment, listening. The twins were asleep, the small rustle of their blankets a softer sound than the faint hum of the corridor. He pushed the door open and stepped inside, the quiet wrapping around him like a familiar cloak.

Their faces were turned toward one another in the bassinet, their features still marked by that delicate newness that made him marvel at how quickly life could enter and reshape a world. He placed a hand lightly on the edge of the cradle, not daring to disturb them, but needing the contact. It was a gesture as much for himself as for them — proof that they were real, that they were here, and that they would remain safe in the days ahead, no matter where he had to go.

He did not speak to Isla when she came in behind him, but her presence filled the space just the same. She moved to his side without hesitation, her arm brushing his lightly as she leaned over to check on the children. There was no need for conversation in that moment; both of them knew the same truth. The days they had now were counted. The hours were precious not because they might be lost forever, but because they would soon belong to memory rather than to life as it unfolded. Her eyes met his briefly, and in them he saw neither fear nor doubt, only the steady acceptance of a woman who had already decided what needed to be done.

When they left the nursery together, Ben noticed the way Isla glanced down the corridor before turning toward their rooms. She had become attuned to every movement within the castle, every sound that did not belong. Her vigilance was no less sharp than Sørensen's, though her focus was on the comfort of those within rather than the threat of those without. It was another reason why he trusted her word when she said she would be fine in his absence. She was no stranger to holding ground while others moved beyond the walls.

The thought of Sørensen brought a brief measure of reassurance. Somewhere within the castle, the man was likely making his own preparations, each one executed with the same precision that had once made him an unshakable chief of security. Ben had never seen him rattled, not in all the years they had known each other. Even when the world beyond the gates had seemed bent on pressing its way in, Sørensen had stood like stone, unyielding and immovable. That was the kind of presence Ben needed now, and knowing it would be at his side for the journey to Kent eased the sharp edge of what lay ahead.

He crossed into the west wing, where the windows overlooked the gardens. The sight of them in spring bloom should have brought a sense of renewal, but instead it carried a bittersweet note. The petals would fall, the season would turn, and when he returned, it would be different. Gardens had a way of marking the passage of time without ceremony, just as people did. The thought brought his mind back to the citizens beyond the gates — their steadfast watch, their quiet unity — and he wondered how many of them understood just how much their loyalty meant.

The sound of distant laughter broke into his thoughts. Somewhere below, children were chasing one another through the grass, their voices high and unguarded. For a moment, the normalcy of it eased the weight on his chest. It was proof that life within these walls still had its own rhythm, even when the larger world threatened to intrude. He lingered by the window, letting the sound settle into his mind like a fragment of something worth carrying with him.

As he made his way back toward his study, Ben thought again of Kendrick's words. There would be no hesitation. The truth of that instruction lay not just in its practicality, but in its demand for a certain kind of resolve. To leave was to protect, but also to trust — trust in the people who remained, trust in the walls that had sheltered them, trust in the bonds that distance could not break. It was a trust that had been earned over years, and one he would not take lightly.

The study itself was as he had left it, papers in neat stacks and the map of Kent still rolled on the desk. He sat down for a moment, allowing himself the small comfort of the leather chair that had borne witness to so many of his decisions. The quiet here was different from the nursery's; it was heavier, more deliberate. In this room, silence meant contemplation, and contemplation now meant the final weighing of what he could take with him — not in luggage, but in memory.

Evening settled slowly over the castle, the light slipping into gold as it stretched across the wooden floors. Ben rose and moved toward the shelves, running his hand along the spines of books whose weight and stories had shaped him. He paused on a worn volume of maps, pulling it free to glance at the familiar lines of Kent's countryside. The sight stirred a complicated mix of longing and resolve. This was where he would go, not because he wished to, but because he must.

The day ended as it had begun — with quiet steps and watchful eyes. Ben walked once more through the corridors, passing portraits that had become so familiar they no longer seemed to look back at him. Yet tonight, they seemed to follow his movements with an awareness that mirrored his own. History had a way of doing that, of watching as the present made decisions that would one day be called inevitable.

When he finally returned to their rooms, Isla was already seated by the window, the twins sleeping soundly beside her. She looked up as he entered, and in that simple exchange, no words were needed. They both knew the clock had begun its slow count toward departure. Each moment now was not just lived — it was held. And neither of them intended to let it slip unnoticed.

Casper had not strayed more than a step from his father all morning, his small frame shadowing Ben's as though proximity alone might alter the course of what had already been decided. The boy's eyes moved constantly, not in fear but in quiet calculation, taking in the people, the maps, and the hushed conversations with an attention far older than his years. When they reached the war room, the heavy oak table no longer bore the familiar outline of Denmark's coastline; the map had been folded away, its purpose served. In its place lay a new drawing, painstakingly inked and creased from repeated handling — a route that began at the castle gates and ended in the countryside of Kent, England.

Sørensen stood at the head of the table, his broad shoulders hunched slightly as he leaned over the map. His finger traced the planned path from Copenhagen to Gatwick, pausing at each waypoint as though committing every detail to muscle memory. He was not a man given to excess movement or wasted breath, and in moments like this, his presence filled the room without the need for words. To Sørensen, politics was a nuisance he had never learned to tolerate, but keeping Ben alive was an obligation as unshakable as the foundations beneath Rosenshavn Castle. He did not measure success by speeches or decrees — only by the safe return of the people entrusted to him.

Maria stood near the corner, watching her father's precision with a mixture of respect and inherited instinct. She had grown up learning the value of quiet readiness, and now, with the twins sleeping against Isla's chest, her role was to ensure nothing distracted from the plan. Ben stood at her side, answering questions only when necessary, his own focus fixed on the thin black lines that would soon become reality.

Isla, seated with the twins resting peacefully in her arms, spoke each step of the plan aloud. Her voice was calm, but beneath its steadiness lay the unyielding insistence of someone who would not allow a single detail to be overlooked. She repeated the departure time, the taxi route to the airstrip, the sequence of checks before boarding, and the order in which the group would disembark at Gatwick. Her eyes flicked to each face in turn, confirming their understanding before moving on. There was no room for changes once the wheels left the runway — the path had been chosen, and deviation would mean risk.

Casper edged closer to her, glancing first at Ben, then at Isla, before leaning in to press a soft kiss to her cheek. "I love you," he said quietly, though the words carried in the stillness of the room. Isla smiled faintly, shifting the twins just enough for him to lean over again and kiss each of them in turn. The moment was brief, but it anchored something inside Ben — a reminder that while routes and runways mattered, it was these small acts that gave them their reason.

Sørensen straightened from the map, rolling his shoulders as though preparing for a march. His gaze moved to Ben, a silent exchange passing between them — the kind that needed no language. Sørensen's nod was not one of farewell but of commitment. He would see this through, from the first step out of the castle to the last step into the cottage. His record spoke for itself; once he took a task into his hands, it was finished with precision.

Kendrick entered without announcement, his presence pulling the room into even sharper focus. He looked over the map briefly, not to question it, but to acknowledge its completeness. "Five days," he said simply, his tone making it clear that the number was not up for debate. His gaze lingered on Ben, not in warning, but in recognition of the weight that those days would carry. Then, with the same unceremonious efficiency with which he had entered, he left the room, his part in the planning already done.

Maria moved to stand beside her father, pointing to the final leg of the route — the narrow, unmarked lane that led to the cottage. "It's hidden enough," she remarked, her voice low. "You could walk past it three times and never notice." Sørensen's only response was a satisfied grunt, his mind already running through the list of what would need to be secured upon arrival.

Isla adjusted her hold on the twins, rocking them gently as she continued speaking. "We'll stay here until the departure," she said, her tone leaving no doubt that this part of the plan was as important as the rest. "No last-minute errands, no visitors who don't need to be here. If they can't come through the gates now, they'll have to wait until after." Her eyes met Ben's, and he gave a single, measured nod. This was her way of protecting him before he had even left — by tightening the space around them until nothing unnecessary could reach inside.

Casper climbed onto the bench beside Ben, his hand curling around his father's arm. "Will there be anyone to play with?" he asked, his voice carrying the hesitant hope of a child who knew the world was about to change. Ben looked down at him, then across to Maria, whose answer came without hesitation. "I'll be there," she said. "Every day. We'll play, and you can share my room at the cottage." The certainty in her tone drew the corners of Ben's mouth into the smallest of smiles. She understood that the promise was worth more than its words — it was a lifeline across the uncertainty ahead.

The map was rolled up and placed into a leather case, the snap of its buckle signalling the end of discussion. Plans were now set in ink and intention; the next time it was unrolled, it would be to follow its lines in motion. Ben glanced around the room one last time, noting the faces that had shaped this moment. They were not generals or courtiers, yet each carried the same weight of purpose.

As the meeting dissolved, Isla remained seated, her gaze following Ben as he crossed to her. He reached out, brushing the back of his hand against the twins' cheeks. They stirred faintly at the touch, but did not wake. The warmth of that moment sat with him as the room emptied, the sound of footsteps fading into the hall.

Outside the war room, the air felt cooler, sharper, as though the walls had absorbed the intensity of what had just been decided. Ben did not speak to anyone as he walked, but in his mind, the route was already unfolding. The castle, the gates, the runway, the flight, the landing, and finally the turn into a narrow lane that would hide them from view. Each step was locked in place, unchanging.

Five days. It was both an eternity and an instant. Every look, every sound, every breath inside the castle would be counted against that measure. Ben knew that when the time came, there would be no speeches, no farewells. Only movement — deliberate, quiet, and without hesitation. The plan was in motion, and there would be no turning back.

Danny's house stood so close to the castle that its hedge seemed to blend with the old fence line, the two boundaries sharing the same wind and rain as though they had been planted together generations ago. It was a vantage point he had never thought of as anything but ordinary — until now. Since the first whisper of trouble reached the neighbourhood, his home had become an unspoken watchpoint, a quiet post from which eyes and ears would shield Rosenshavn as fiercely as its walls ever could. The citizens had organised themselves without fanfare, relying on the same trust that had carried them through storms, celebrations, and the ordinary rhythms of shared life.

From the library's tall, arched window, Ben could see them moving about in ways that looked casual to anyone who did not know better. Children kicked a worn ball back and forth near the gates, their laughter carrying across the gravel drive. A handful of adults leaned on fence posts or sat at café tables placed just so, coffee cups in hand, their eyes following every passerby without appearing to do so. It was the kind of defence that could never be rehearsed in military drills — it was born of belonging, of the unshakable certainty that this castle and its family belonged to them as much as to the ones who lived inside.

Danny moved easily among them, speaking in low tones that travelled no further than the person he was addressing. He had always been the type to know everyone by name, from the schoolchildren racing along the cobblestones to the shopkeepers sweeping their front steps. Now, that familiarity had turned into quiet authority, and when he spoke, people listened. His instructions were simple — watch, remember, and never let an unfamiliar face pass unmarked.

Ben leaned one shoulder against the window frame, watching a pair of men pause at the edge of the square. They held their cups too long after the coffee was gone, eyes fixed in the direction of the street. One of them shifted, speaking without moving his lips, and moments later Danny was there, his approach as natural as if he had simply wandered over to comment on the weather. The men nodded, their conversation folding neatly into the day's ordinary movements, but the message was clear — the pattern had been noticed, and the watch continued.

Isla had joined him at the window now, the twins drowsing in her arms. She followed his gaze outward, taking in the sight of neighbours leaning on bicycles, sweeping their steps, or chatting over hedges, all while maintaining an unbroken awareness of the gates. "They love you," she said quietly, her voice carrying no hint of sentimentality, only truth. "Not because of what you are. Because of who you are. You're family to them."

He did not answer at once. His eyes tracked a group of older children who had set up a chalk game near the corner, their hopping patterns and shouted numbers providing a cover for glances that flicked toward every passing stranger. "It's rare," he said finally. "And you don't get to ask for it twice." The words held a weight beyond the moment, a recognition that trust, once spent, could not be borrowed again.

The morning light shifted, spilling through the glass and cutting across the spines of books behind him. Ben's thoughts moved between the comfort of this vigilance and the reality that it would end the moment he stepped onto that jet. The citizens could guard the castle and the family within, but the shield would not extend beyond the runway. In Kent, he would have to rely on other protections — ones that had nothing to do with garden hedges and watchful neighbours.

Outside, Danny was speaking to a woman carrying a basket of rolls from the bakery. She paused, glancing toward the gates before continuing on, her steps slow enough to let her take in the faces of two men walking past. Ben could almost feel the threads of communication weaving through the square, a net cast without rope or knots, yet strong enough to catch what needed catching.

Maria entered quietly, holding a folded note in her hand. "From Danny," she said, passing it to Ben. It was brief — two lines noting a car seen twice that morning, idling near the far corner before pulling away. The licence plate had been memorised, the driver's face described. Ben folded the paper and set it in his pocket without comment. No alarm, no rush — just another piece of the watch put in place.

Casper came in behind her, holding a small flag he had been given by one of the neighbours. "For the gate," he explained, climbing onto the bench to place it near the window. The fabric was worn but clean, the castle crest stitched in thread that had faded to the colour of autumn leaves. Ben rested a hand on his son's shoulder, the simple gesture holding all the unspoken acknowledgement of what that flag meant — not just loyalty to the crown, but loyalty to the man behind it.

The hours passed in a rhythm that was neither rushed nor idle. People came and went in measured patterns, never leaving the gates unwatched for more than a few breaths. Ben knew there was no official roster, no written order, yet the coverage was constant, as if some unseen clock shifted the watch from hand to hand without ever losing time. It was the sort of coordination that could not be bought or demanded; it had to be earned.

Isla left the window to settle the twins, and Ben remained there alone for a time, his thoughts following the lines of the hedge, the fence, and the square beyond. Every face he saw out there was one he trusted, yet he could not forget that trust had already been broken once — not here, but close enough to wound. That betrayal had set all of this in motion, and it was the reason a departure was being planned instead of a celebration.

Danny looked up toward the library, catching Ben's gaze through the glass. He raised his hand in a gesture that was neither salute nor wave, but something between the two — a sign that all was well for now. Ben returned it, a brief tilt of the head, before stepping back from the window. The day's watch would continue, with or without him there to observe it.

When he finally left the library, the sound of the citizens' quiet vigilance seemed to follow him — the scrape of chairs on cobblestone, the muted thud of a ball against the gate, the murmur of voices that could turn sharp in an instant. It was the soundtrack of a place that understood protection not as duty, but as kinship. And though he would soon be gone from it, the knowledge that it existed would travel with him.

The smell of warm bread and soft cheese drifted across the breakfast table, mingling with the faint scent of coffee that clung to the morning air. Casper sat forward on his elbows, chin resting on his hands, his gaze fixed on Ben with an intensity that could only belong to a child with questions ready to spill. His plate was untouched, the crust of toast resting in butter that had begun to melt into golden pools. The others at the table spoke in low tones, but Casper's eyes didn't leave his father's face, waiting for the exact moment to begin. When it came, his voice was quiet but eager. "Will there be fields?"

Ben set down his cup and gave the question the pause it deserved, looking not only at Casper but through the window beyond him, as if searching the memory itself before offering it. "There will be fields," he said, "wide enough for a ball to roll forever before you have to chase it, and green enough to make your eyes ache in the first days of spring." He leaned back slightly, letting the words settle into the boy's mind. "And the grass there smells different. The sea air mixes with it, and when the wind moves, you can almost taste the salt." Casper's mouth curved in a small, thoughtful smile, the kind that meant he was already halfway there in his imagination.

"Will there be a soccer pitch?" came the next question, quicker now, with the edge of excitement in his voice. Ben nodded, recalling the worn corner of the village green where the older boys had marked their own goal lines in chalk and stubborn will. "There will," he replied. "But it's not marked like the ones here. No painted lines. Just the shape you remember from last time you played, and the ball that refuses to behave when the ground's too soft from rain." Casper tilted his head, considering this. "That's better," he said after a moment, as though it was a judgement on the matter.

Maria, sitting across from him, reached over to nudge the butter dish closer. "You'll like it there," she said, her tone carrying the certainty of someone who had already decided it would be so. "We'll have the orchard right behind the cottage. Apples in autumn, pears before the frost. We can make juice in the mornings." Her words softened something in Casper's expression; the thought of shared mornings and sweet fruit seemed to anchor the imagined place in a way that made it more real. "And you'll be there?" he asked, though it was hardly a question.

"Always," she replied, not glancing away. "We're brother and sister by choice, not by blood. And I don't change my mind about things like that." Ben smiled faintly at her phrasing — the same kind of quiet certainty that made Sørensen trustworthy enough to hold a plan together in the face of real danger. It wasn't just reassurance for Casper; it was a reminder to everyone at the table that whatever waited in Kent would be met together, not alone.

Ben let the moment stretch, then answered the question that hadn't yet been spoken. "Yes, there will be other children," he said, breaking off a piece of bread as he spoke. "Some will speak only English, some will speak both. You'll hear their voices at the market, or when they're riding past on their bikes. And you'll learn the rhythm of it — when to listen, when to speak, when to run alongside them until you all forget whose turn it is to chase the ball." Casper grinned at that, his fingers drumming lightly against the table.

The boy's eyes lit further when Ben described the cottage itself. "It's small, but every stone has been there longer than I've been alive. The roof tilts just enough to let the rain slide off without soaking the steps, and the garden wall is low enough for you to look over into the orchard without climbing." He described the worn stone path leading from the cottage door to the back gate, each slab uneven from years of boots, bare feet, and bicycles crossing it in every season. "You'll know it by sound," Ben said. "Every step you take will be its own voice."

Isla, holding the twins nearby, listened with a faint smile, though her eyes stayed on Ben. She knew what he was doing — building Kent into a place of safety for Casper before they ever set foot there, making it more than just a hiding place. It was a piece of Ben's past being offered as a gift, wrapped in memory and softened by time. She said nothing to interrupt, allowing the flow between father and son to remain unbroken.

Casper leaned forward now, completely absorbed. "What about the library?" he asked, his tone carrying the reverence he reserved for places that seemed to belong to other worlds. Ben's voice lowered slightly, as though matching that reverence. "The library is at the far end of the high street. The windows are tall and narrow, and they make the light fall like water over the tables. The smell inside — books and dust and sea wind — never changes. And the librarian will know you the moment you walk in. She knew me before I knew myself."

That last line lingered for a moment, its weight not lost even on a child. Casper glanced toward Maria, who gave him a small nod, as if to say that what he had just heard was not a thing to be forgotten. Ben reached for his coffee again, the steam curling between them like another thread in the conversation. "There's a corner seat by the window where you can see the whole street," he added. "On market days, you'll hear the chatter through the glass and smell the bread before it reaches the door."

The boy's appetite for detail seemed insatiable now. "What about the markets?" he asked. "Do they sell the same things?" Ben shook his head slowly. "No. Some stalls are the same — bread, cheese, baskets of vegetables — but others bring things you won't see here. Wool scarves made by hand, jars of honey so thick they take all winter to finish, carved toys that look like they could walk off the table if you turned away." His voice carried a rhythm that matched the scene he was painting, and Casper's fingers curled slightly, as if holding something invisible yet tangible.

"Will it be loud?" came the next question, softer now, betraying the edge of uncertainty that always followed excitement. Ben leaned forward, resting his forearms on the table. "It will be loud when you want it to be. And quiet when you need it. You'll learn where the edges are." It was an answer that worked for more than just markets, and Isla caught the flicker of that deeper meaning, though she kept her gaze on the twins.

Maria reached for her cup, glancing at Ben over its rim. "We'll show him the orchard first," she said, as though this had already been decided. "Before anything else. That way he'll know what's ours before he sees what's theirs." Ben gave a small nod, agreeing without words. It was an instinct he recognised — to lay claim to the safe ground first, so it could serve as a base for everything that came after.

Casper sat back finally, his questions satisfied for the moment, though his eyes still held the light of imagined fields and stone paths. His toast had cooled completely, but he picked it up without complaint, chewing slowly as though the taste might carry him a step closer to the place he had just built in his mind. Around him, the quiet hum of breakfast resumed, but in the space between each sound was the pulse of something steady — a promise wrapped in the details of a village far away, yet already becoming his.

Maria set her cup down with deliberate care, the soft clink on the table drawing Casper's gaze as much as the gentle tap of her fingers against his hand. The boy looked up, crumbs still clinging to the corner of his mouth, and found her eyes fixed on his with a steadiness that allowed no distraction. Around them, the breakfast conversation continued in low murmurs, the faint clatter of cutlery marking the ordinary rhythm of the meal, but Maria's voice cut through in a quiet that demanded attention. "Brothers and sisters," she began, "are not always born in the same house or from the same parents. Sometimes they are chosen."

Casper tilted his head, the thought settling into his mind like a new piece of a puzzle. Maria did not rush to explain further. She let the weight of her words rest there for a moment, then continued. "When they are chosen, it's because something stronger than blood has decided it should be so. It's because they've already stood beside you in the hard parts and stayed for the good parts, and they don't walk away when things change." Her fingers tightened slightly on his, not in warning, but in promise.

"You and I," she said, "are that kind of family." Casper glanced toward Ben, who was listening but not interfering, understanding that Maria's words carried a different kind of truth than his own. Ben could give the boy maps, descriptions, and memories, but Maria was giving him the thing he didn't know how to ask for — the assurance that the journey ahead would not make him lose what mattered most.

"In Kent," Maria went on, "we will share the same room at the cottage. Same walls, same window, same space for the things we want to keep close. I'll be there every night, even if the wind is loud or the shadows are long. You won't wake up and wonder if I've gone." She spoke it as fact, not comfort, though the comfort in it was undeniable. Casper's shoulders eased, his hands relaxing under hers.

She leaned back slightly, but her eyes did not leave his. "And I will read to you every night. Even if I'm tired, even if the day has been long. The kind of stories that remind you who you are and where you belong." She gave a faint smile, one corner of her mouth curving up. "Not the ones that end in the middle or skip the good parts. The kind that finish the way they're meant to."

Casper's lips curved into something between a smile and a sigh, as though relief had stolen the urgency from his questions. Maria reached for her cup again, taking a slow sip before adding, "No one — not even a king — can take that away. Kings can change the rules for everyone else, but not for us. Our rules are ours alone." She said it plainly, without drama, but with the kind of conviction that left no room for doubt.

Ben's gaze flickered briefly from Maria to Casper, catching the shift in the boy's posture. The restless lean forward that had driven his earlier questions was gone, replaced by a quiet ease. It was not the kind of calm a father's reassurance could always bring. This was the kind that came when someone promised to stand in the same place you stood, no matter how far from home you were.

"I will always love you," Maria said, her voice lower now, meant for him alone. "No matter what happens, no matter where we are, no matter what anyone says. That doesn't change in Kent. That doesn't change anywhere." She let the silence after those words stretch, trusting him to carry them without needing to fill the space with more.

Casper's hand turned under hers, fingers curling slightly as if holding on to the promise itself. "Always?" he asked, though the word came out more as confirmation than doubt. Maria nodded once. "Always." No grand gestures, no raised voices — just the steady certainty of someone who had already chosen, long ago, to stay.

Outside the window, a shift in the light marked the sun's climb, the garden hedge casting longer shadows against the fence. Danny's quiet figure moved in the distance, and the sight reminded Ben of the layered defences that surrounded them. Inside, however, it was Maria's words that had built the stronger wall — one that could follow Casper all the way to Kent and beyond.

Casper sat back in his chair now, the tension gone from his small frame. He reached for his toast again, this time with genuine appetite, breaking off a piece and chewing slowly. Maria watched him for a moment, then let her attention drift toward the twins in Isla's arms, her promise already made and sealed without the need for repetition.

Ben lifted his coffee, taking a slow sip as he met Maria's gaze over the rim of the cup. There was no need for thanks between them. She knew what she had just done for his son, and he knew it was something even his own voice couldn't have managed alone. Sørensen, seated further down the table, caught the exchange and gave a small nod, as if to say that some bonds were forged in ways even the most careful planning could not design.

In the stillness that followed, the castle seemed momentarily smaller, warmer, as though the stone walls themselves had listened in. Casper, now content, reached for the butter knife and spread a thin layer across the rest of his toast. The conversation around him carried on, but his eyes no longer sought answers. Maria had given him the one that mattered.

Later, when the day's preparations pulled them all into different corners of the castle, Maria's promise lingered in the space between them. It was a thread woven quietly into the fabric of their departure — invisible to anyone outside, but strong enough to hold when the distance between Copenhagen and Kent became more than just a line on Sørensen's map.

The study was quieter than the rest of the castle, its heavy door shutting out the footsteps and voices that moved through the halls. Ben crossed to his desk without turning on the overhead light, letting the dim glow from the desk lamp cast a narrow circle across the polished wood. From the bottom drawer, beneath neat stacks of correspondence and folded maps, he pulled out a photo album wrapped in the soft wear of its years. The leather cover had darkened with age, the corners rounded from use, the spine showing faint lines where it had been opened and closed too many times to count.

Casper stood at his side before the book was even set on the desk, Maria following with the quiet curiosity of someone who understood this was not an album that was taken out for just anyone. Ben laid it flat, his fingers brushing the cover once before opening it to the first page. The photographs inside were glossy with the kind of finish no longer common, their colours softened by time, their edges curling slightly from years in their plastic sleeves.

"These were taken before we came to Denmark," Ben said, his voice even, but low enough that the words seemed meant for this room alone. "This was Kent." His finger tapped the corner of a photograph showing a narrow lane lined with stone cottages, ivy climbing the walls in thick, stubborn growth. "I lived just there, in the one with the chimney that leans a little to the left. My mother used to say it gave the house character."

Casper leaned closer, tracing the outline of the crooked chimney in the picture without actually touching it. Maria tilted her head, studying the small front garden, the low stone wall that marked its boundary. "It's smaller than I imagined," she said. Ben nodded. "Small, yes, but every inch of it felt like it belonged to us. The winters made the roof heavy with snow, and in the mornings I'd clear the path with my boots before school. That was before I knew anything about Denmark. Before I knew there was a place for me somewhere else entirely."

He turned the page carefully, revealing a photograph of himself in a dark green school uniform, the collar too stiff, the tie slightly crooked. A boy's grin — half mischief, half nerves — was fixed in place. "I was ten here," Ben said. "This was the year we left. The year the letter came that changed everything. The move wasn't just an address change; it was…" He paused, fingers pressing lightly against the edge of the page. "It was a turning point I didn't see coming. I thought I'd finish school here. I thought I'd grow up kicking a soccer in that field you see there."

Casper's eyes found the field in the background of another photograph — rough grass, a pair of goalposts that looked like they'd been hammered into the ground by hand. "Was that your team?" he asked, pointing to a group shot on the next page. Ben smiled faintly. "My first team. We played more in the mud than on grass, but we thought we were brilliant. I still remember the smell of the pitch after a hard rain. The way the air felt sharper there, especially in the early mornings."

Maria studied a photograph of a small brick library, its doorway framed by hanging baskets of flowers. "Is this where you…" She trailed off, knowing the answer. Ben's gaze softened. "Yes. This is the library where I spent most of my afternoons. It was where I learned the truth about myself, though I didn't understand all of it then. And it's where I met Isla for the first time." His hand lingered on the picture as though the memory was still within reach, as though the old bricks might carry the sound of their first conversation if he stared long enough.

He turned another page and paused over a photograph of the cottage, taken from the back garden. The roof sagged gently under the weight of years and winters, the chimney still leaning, the windows framed in white paint that had begun to flake. "This," Ben said quietly, "is where you'll stay with me. This room here," he pointed to the upper left window, "will be yours, Casper. And Maria — the one beside it will be yours. The orchard behind it is small, but the apples are the sweetest you'll ever taste."

Casper's face brightened. "Can we play there?" Ben's lips curved into a faint smile. "Every day if you like. And in the spring, the markets in the village will set up stalls along the high street. You'll see things you won't find anywhere else. Hand-carved toys, fresh bread so warm you'll burn your fingers if you're not careful, jars of jam from berries picked that morning."

Maria traced the outline of the path in the photograph, her expression thoughtful. "It's different from here," she said. "Smaller. Quieter." Ben nodded. "Yes. That's why it's safe. People there don't ask questions they don't need answered. They've known me since I was younger than you two, and they don't need reminding of it." His voice held a note of certainty that seemed to settle the air in the room.

Casper glanced at the next page, where the photographs shifted from buildings and landscapes to faces. There were neighbours leaning against fence posts, children sitting cross-legged in the grass, a shopkeeper with flour dusting his sleeves. "Will they remember you?" he asked. Ben's answer came without hesitation. "They will. And they'll know to keep it quiet. Just as they always have."

The boy studied the images, as if memorising the faces he might soon see in person. Maria rested her chin on her hand, her gaze moving between Ben and the photographs. She understood now why he had brought them here — not just to show them where they were going, but to let them see the pieces of himself that had existed long before the castle, before the title, before the secret became a burden he had to carry.

Ben closed the album slowly, his hand resting on the cover for a moment longer than necessary. "It's been waiting there for years," he said, almost to himself. "And it will be there waiting still when we arrive." He slid it back into the drawer, the soft scrape of leather against wood marking the end of the moment. But the images — and the truths they carried — lingered in the minds of both children, as vivid as if they'd stepped through the photographs themselves.

Outside, the muted hum of castle life went on, but in the study, the air felt changed — heavier with the weight of memory, lighter with the comfort of knowing where they would land. Ben rose from his chair, gesturing for Casper and Maria to follow, the album's unspoken promise locked away for now, ready to be fulfilled in the days to come.

The corridor outside the nursery was lit only by the low wall sconces, their amber glow casting a quiet warmth over the evening stillness. Ben followed Isla toward the sitting room without speaking, the hush between them shaped not by discomfort but by the weight of a conversation they had been circling for weeks. Inside, the fire was low, the curtains drawn against the cool April night. She gestured for him to sit, but remained standing, her hands resting on the back of the chair opposite him, the posture of someone ready to say something final.

"You have to go," she said, her voice steady in its first breath, though Ben caught the faint catch of emotion that followed. She had been saying these words for days, almost word for word, but now they carried the closeness of a deadline. "You know what will happen if you stay. You know how this will turn." She leaned forward slightly, her eyes fixed on his. "And I will be fine. I've told you that."

Ben's instinct was to argue — to say that leaving so soon after the twins' birth would make him feel less like a protector and more like a deserter. But as he looked at her, the protest felt hollow before it even reached his lips. Isla was not speaking from fear. She was speaking from a clear-eyed calculation of what had to be done. Her calm was not a softness; it was armour.

She moved around the chair and sat opposite him, her knees close to his, her posture forward and intent. "This isn't about wanting you gone," she said. "It's about making sure you can come back. If you stay, you make yourself a target. If you leave, you give the city — and the press — time to choke on their own rumours until they're tired of the taste." She folded her hands together, the firelight catching the ring on her finger, and let the words settle.

The sound of the twins stirring drifted faintly from down the hall — the soft, unpatterned rustle of newborns shifting in their sleep. The noise reached both of them, and Ben felt the same quiet ache he saw in Isla's eyes. They both knew that in leaving, he would miss the smallest milestones — the ones that happened without warning. The first time a child turned their head toward his voice. The first unsteady smile. The first syllables that could almost be called words.

But Isla did not let that thought anchor the conversation. She straightened, drawing in a slow breath. "You will be here for their first steps," she said, as though willing it into fact. "You will be here for their first games outside in the garden. You will be here to teach them the things only you can teach. But for now, you have to be somewhere they cannot reach you."

Ben's gaze dropped to the floor for a moment, following the grain of the wood as if it could offer another way out. When he lifted his eyes again, she was still watching him, unblinking, waiting for the shape of his agreement. He saw the set of her shoulders, the way they held their line even under the pull of exhaustion. She was not wavering, and that steadiness told him more than any plea could have.

He leaned back slightly, exhaling in a way that made the decision real in the air between them. "Five days," he said quietly. "Then we go." He did not miss the faint drop of her shoulders — the smallest release of breath — before she nodded. "Five days," she repeated, sealing the commitment.

Casper's quiet footsteps entered the edge of the moment. The boy had been lingering near the doorway, pretending to read a book on the hall bench while their voices carried. He stepped closer, clutching the book to his chest, and looked up at his father with a seriousness that did not match his age. "I'll remember for you," he said. Ben tilted his head, puzzled. "Remember what?"

"When they talk," Casper replied, his voice low but certain. "When the twins say their first words. I'll tell you exactly how they said it. And I'll make sure you know it right." The boy's determination was so earnest it caught Ben off guard. Isla smiled faintly, reaching out to touch Casper's shoulder. "See? Even he understands why you have to go."

The promise from his son lodged itself deep in Ben's mind, carrying more comfort than he expected. He reached out and pulled Casper closer, resting a hand on the boy's back. "Then I'll count on you," he said, holding him there for a moment before letting him go.

Isla rose first, crossing to the window and drawing the curtain back just enough to look out at the dim outlines of the garden. Beyond it, faintly lit by streetlamps, were the silhouettes of neighbours keeping their quiet vigil. She let the curtain fall again and turned back to him. "They'll keep watch here. Sørensen will keep watch there. And I'll keep watch over the children. That's the plan. No changes."

Ben stood and crossed to her, his presence at her side less an embrace and more an unspoken understanding. "You've already decided," he said. She nodded. "I decided the day we knew the twins were coming. And nothing since has made me think I was wrong."

For a long moment, they stood without speaking, the sound of the fire and the faint creak of the castle around them filling the space. Ben knew she was right. He also knew that every mile between them would feel heavier than it should. But this was not a choice between comfort and discomfort — it was a choice between danger and survival. Isla had already chosen. Now he had to match her resolve.

The clock in the corner struck softly, marking another hour gone. Isla touched his hand lightly before stepping past him toward the nursery. "Five days," she said again, not as a reminder, but as a final word on the matter. Ben remained by the fire for a moment longer, listening to the sound of her footsteps fading down the corridor, the resolve in her voice still hanging in the air like a drawn line he would not cross.

The private hangar lay beyond the outer gardens, concealed behind reinforced gates that only a handful of people could open without question. Its wide steel doors were rolled back against the early morning light, revealing the sleek form of the royal jet resting in readiness. Sørensen stood just inside the threshold, clipboard in hand, his eyes sweeping over every detail of the aircraft as though any flaw, however small, would be a personal insult. A mechanic signalled that the fuelling had begun, the slow hiss of aviation fuel filling the space like the quiet breath of a beast preparing to wake.

Every bolt along the landing gear was checked twice, each hinge on the cargo hatch tested with a precise rhythm that spoke of habit built over decades. Sørensen moved between the engineers without needing to raise his voice; his presence alone carried the weight of expectation. One hand remained on the clipboard, the other trailing along the cool metal skin of the fuselage as if listening for imperfections through his fingertips.

Ben arrived quietly, choosing not to announce himself, and watched from the shadow of the doorway. The smell of fuel, the distant hum of the generators, the clipped voices of the crew — it was a scene he had witnessed before, but never with such urgency in the air. This was not the routine maintenance of a ceremonial flight. This was preparation for departure without margin for error.

The flight crew, dressed in discreet navy uniforms, moved with the kind of precision that only comes from years of loyalty. Each of them had served the Royal Family for over fifteen years, and not one had ever broken the vow of silence that was as much a part of their service as their piloting skills. Sørensen spoke to them one by one, his tone low but firm, delivering instructions that were not to be written down.

There would be no public flight plan filed, no casual mentions in pilot lounges, no chatter over radio frequencies that could be overheard. The pilots nodded at each instruction, their expressions as impassive as stone. These were men who understood the value of secrecy, and the cost of breaking it. Sørensen did not threaten them — he did not have to. His reputation was the warning.

A final checklist was passed from mechanic to engineer to Sørensen, each signature marking another completed inspection. He flipped through the pages, his eyes scanning the lines with the precision of a man who could spot a misplaced comma and know it meant something was wrong. Every figure, every pressure reading, every clearance number was measured against what he already knew should be there.

Ben stepped forward then, his hands tucked loosely behind his back, his gaze following the slow movement of Sørensen's pen as it ticked the final box. "You'd know if something was off without even looking," Ben said quietly, and Sørensen glanced up, his expression softening only by a fraction. "Knowing is my job," he replied, "but checking is my duty. I don't trust the safety of this flight to memory alone."

They moved together toward the cockpit, where the pilots stood waiting for final instructions. Sørensen leaned in, his voice pitched low enough that even Ben could not catch every word. The captain, a man with lines at the corners of his eyes from years of staring into clouded horizons, listened without interruption, then gave a single nod. The co-pilot did the same.

Outside, a second crew secured the luggage compartment, each case marked only with the most basic of identifiers. There would be no royal crests, no monograms, nothing that could tie these bags to the Castle if seen in transit. Sørensen had stripped the trip of every hint of spectacle. This was not a royal procession. It was an extraction.

Ben watched as Sørensen moved from one side of the jet to the other, checking the hydraulics, inspecting the wing flaps, running his palm along the trailing edge as if reading a language only he understood. There was a comfort in that vigilance, a reassurance in knowing that if Sørensen found the smallest fault, he would stop the entire operation until it was fixed.

The fuelling completed, a soft chime sounded from the truck, and the crew began coiling the heavy hoses away. Sørensen checked the fuel logs, compared them against his own figures, and only then signed the release. "No substitutions. No last-minute swaps," he told the fuel chief. The man nodded, almost in relief, as if being trusted with this job under Sørensen's gaze was as much a burden as it was an honour.

Inside the cabin, a steward moved quietly through the aisle, ensuring every latch was secured, every safety kit stocked, every seatbelt functional. Sørensen followed behind, his eyes scanning not for comfort but for anything that could fail mid-flight. He adjusted the angle of a panel, tested the seal of a storage hatch, and examined the galley's fire suppression unit without a word.

Ben stepped up beside him as they reached the forward bulkhead. "There's no one else I'd trust with this," he said, and it was not a casual remark. Sørensen met his gaze for a moment before looking back toward the cockpit. "And there's no one else I'd stand beside for it," he answered simply.

By the time they left the hangar, the sun was higher, throwing long shadows across the tarmac. The jet gleamed under the light, every surface clean, every component ready. Sørensen paused at the threshold, giving one final look over his shoulder. It was not sentiment — it was certainty. The next time they stood here, the mission would either have succeeded, or it would not have been worth returning at all.

Ben followed him out, the faint sound of the hangar doors beginning to roll shut behind them. The preparations were finished. The plan was set. And with Sørensen at his side, he felt — for the first time in days — that leaving might be possible without looking back at every step.

The bedroom was quiet except for the soft rustle of fabric and the faint click of a suitcase latch. Ben stood at the foot of the bed, folding a plain grey jumper with deliberate precision before placing it into the weathered leather suitcase that had travelled more countries than most people visited in a lifetime. Each garment he chose was intentionally unremarkable — muted colours, no embroidery, no crests stitched along the cuffs. In Kent, he needed to be a man among men, the sort who could walk through a shop without drawing even a second glance.

Maria sat cross-legged on her own bed, a smaller case open in front of her. She placed a stuffed bear neatly against the side, then tucked a slim book of riddles and bedtime stories beside it. The bear's fabric was worn at the edges, its button eyes slightly dulled from years of being carried and hugged, but its place in the case was non-negotiable. She smoothed the book's cover with her palm as if sealing the promise she had made to Casper — that no matter where they went, the stories would follow.

Casper's bag remained open on the dresser, its contents a careful blend of necessities and comforts. Ben had taken it upon himself to pack it rather than leaving the boy to wrestle with the choice of what to bring and what to leave behind. A few shirts, a pair of sturdy trousers, and his favourite wool socks were folded in tight, deliberate layers. Between them, Ben slipped in a small leather-bound sketchbook and a handful of coloured pencils, knowing the boy would find solace in filling its pages during quiet afternoons at the cottage.

Every item was chosen with the same principle in mind — invisibility. There were no gleaming belt buckles, no tailored jackets cut to royal proportions, nothing that whispered privilege or authority. Even the luggage itself was stripped of any marker that could betray its owner's identity. The cases looked like they belonged to travellers who had saved for the journey, not to people fleeing the flashbulbs of the world's press.

Ben's hands moved with steady rhythm, but his eyes shifted often to the window. Beyond it, the gardens lay still, but he knew that beyond that stillness, the citizens of Copenhagen were already keeping watch. They could defend the Castle as fiercely as they wished, yet the threat was no longer something that could be kept at bay by gates and loyalty. This departure was not about leaving danger behind — it was about drawing danger away from the ones who could not follow.

Maria zipped her case halfway, then paused to check its contents again, her fingers brushing the bear's fur before closing the lid. She glanced toward Casper's bag and smiled faintly, noting how neatly Ben had packed it. The boy himself sat at the edge of the bed, swinging his feet, pretending not to watch the process while keeping a close eye on every move. When Ben slipped the sketchbook in, Casper's gaze softened, though he said nothing.

The absence of royal emblems was as much a statement as it was a precaution. Every thread of gold, every embroidered crest, every fine leather trim had been left behind without hesitation. These cases were packed to pass unnoticed through airport corridors, to blend into the sea of travellers moving through Gatwick without anyone looking twice. Even the shoes were practical — worn enough to suggest a life that did not need polishing.

Ben closed his suitcase with a firm click, pressing his palm against the lid for a moment as though sealing more than just clothing inside. He knew the journey ahead would not be measured in miles but in the distance between who they were at Rosenshavn and who they had to be in Kent. The clothes, the toys, the books — all of it was armour of a different kind, the kind that did not look like protection until it was needed.

Casper hopped down from the bed and padded over to his father's side, slipping his small hand into Ben's without a word. The gesture was enough to remind Ben why every precaution mattered, why even the smallest detail — a plain shirt over a tailored coat, a faded bag over a polished case — could mean the difference between recognition and anonymity. He squeezed the boy's hand gently before letting go.

Maria slid her case shut and stood, lifting it with both hands to test its weight. She set it beside the door, next to Ben's suitcase and the smaller one for Casper. Three cases, unremarkable and unmarked, stood ready for a departure that no one outside these walls should suspect. The sight of them lined up was sobering — a family distilled into luggage.

In the corner of the room, the cradle stirred softly as one of the twins shifted in sleep. Isla's voice came from the hallway, low and calm, asking if the packing was finished. Ben answered without turning from the cases, his tone even, though his eyes lingered on the quiet cradle. Packing was done, yes. But readiness — that was something different.

He stepped away from the bed, giving the room one last sweep with his gaze, checking for anything that could be left behind that might identify them. There was nothing. Not a single emblem, not a single letterhead or seal. They would leave as travellers, not as royalty, and in Kent, they would live as shadows until the noise faded.

When the door closed behind him, the room felt lighter, but only in the way a room does after something essential has been taken from it. The cases waited by the door, silent and unremarkable — exactly as they needed to be. The quiet in the room was not peace. It was the sound of preparation, the pause before movement, the stillness before flight.

The room was wrapped in the kind of darkness that only came when the castle's outer lights had been dimmed to their lowest, leaving just enough glow for a watchman to see his post. The twins lay in the bassinet at the foot of the bed, their tiny chests rising and falling in perfect rhythm, undisturbed by the faint sigh of the wind outside. Ben leaned over each one in turn, his hand hovering just above their blankets, as though even the brush of his fingers might wake them. He studied their faces as if committing them to memory — the curve of a cheek, the faint outline of a brow, the soft way their lips parted in sleep. Every detail mattered now, because he knew that soon, these quiet moments would be relived only in thought.

Isla watched him from her side of the bed, her head resting against the pillows but her eyes alert. She could see what he was doing without him having to explain it. He was marking them in his mind, storing every feature like a photograph he could never misplace. There was an unspoken understanding between them — that when distance came, they would both survive it by holding onto these small fragments of the present. No promises were exchanged, no reassurances offered. Silence, in this moment, was its own form of trust.

Across the hall, Maria was already preparing herself for what the next week would bring. She had decided early in the evening that she would spend the night in Casper's room, so that he would grow accustomed to her being close before they left for Kent. For a nine-year-old, she possessed a rare instinct for easing another's worries, and she acted on it without hesitation. When the time came for bedtime, she led Casper by the hand to his room and settled beside him on the king-size bed as though it were the most natural thing in the world.

The room itself was more than generous, with its deep-toned furniture, heavy curtains, and the faint scent of lavender drifting from a vase on the dresser. A full en-suite bathroom opened to one side, its marble counters reflecting the muted light from a wall sconce. Beyond the sliding glass doors, the balcony stretched an impressive fifteen feet by eight, its railing wrapped in ivy that had been trained to grow with precision. Even in the dimness, the garden below could be glimpsed, a reminder of the life they were about to step away from.

Maria didn't simply tuck herself in beside Casper; she took on the role of storyteller with deliberate care. She opened the book she had brought from her own shelf and began reading aloud in a clear, confident voice that carried through the room like a soft current. Every word was pronounced with care, the kind of care that came from knowing a story was not just a way to pass time but a way to bind people together. Her pacing was perfect — slow enough to savour, yet steady enough to carry Casper into the edges of sleep without him noticing.

Casper listened without interrupting, lying on his side with one arm tucked under the pillow, his gaze fixed on the pages as if they were windows into another place entirely. His breathing slowed with each paragraph, but his eyes remained open, following the words as Maria turned each page with quiet precision. She was not just reading for him; she was laying down a rhythm of comfort that he could carry with him across the sea to Kent. In her mind, this was the beginning of their shared life there — a habit formed now that would follow them to the cottage.

Back in the master bedroom, Ben finally straightened from the bassinet, his hands slipping into his pockets as he took a slow step backward. He glanced toward Isla, whose eyes had softened with fatigue, though her watchfulness had not faded. The twins shifted slightly in their sleep, one hand twitching toward the other, as though even in rest they sought each other's presence. Ben knew that leaving them, even for a short time, would be the most difficult thing he had ever done. He also knew it was necessary.

The balcony doors stood slightly ajar, letting in a faint current of night air that moved the curtains in lazy sways. Ben stepped toward them, sliding the glass further open to look out over the darkened grounds. Somewhere out there, beyond the trimmed hedges and guarded gates, was a city waiting for a story it should never have been told. Inside, within these walls, was the only truth that mattered — the quiet breathing of his children, the stillness of his wife, the knowledge that for tonight, they were all under one roof.

Isla's voice broke the silence just enough to draw him back from the balcony. "They'll remember you," she said softly, not as a question, but as a statement. Ben turned toward her and gave the faintest nod, the kind that confirmed he would do everything in his power to make sure of it. She didn't need to hear the words; she had always known how to read the space between what he said and what he held back.

In Casper's room, Maria closed the book and set it on the nightstand, her fingers lingering on the cover as though sealing the end of the evening. She shifted slightly, making sure the blankets covered them both evenly. Casper's eyes were now closed, his breathing deep and steady, though she suspected he was not yet fully asleep. She leaned over to whisper something only he could hear — a reminder that no matter where they went, she would always be beside him. His fingers tightened slightly around hers, and that was enough.

Ben returned to his place beside Isla, lowering himself onto the bed without a sound. He did not close his eyes immediately. Instead, he lay still, listening for the soft breaths from the bassinet. Each rise and fall of those tiny chests was a thread in the fabric of the night, and he was unwilling to let even one pass unnoticed. Only when he was certain that the sound would stay with him, no matter how far he went, did he allow himself to close his eyes.

The night stretched on in quiet layers — the muted hum of the castle, the distant murmur of the city, the occasional shift of the wind against the balcony doors. Within those layers, the family lay scattered across rooms but bound by the same stillness, each one holding onto their own way of preparing for what was to come. Tomorrow would bring movement, decisions, and departures. Tonight was only for breathing, for remembering, and for making the kind of memories that could withstand an ocean's width.

The nursery was warm, its faint lamplight spilling over the curved edges of the bassinets, catching on the pale fabric of the curtains that hung low against the windows. Tobias moved into the room with the care of someone stepping into sacred ground. He had done this many times before — walked into a quiet space where new life slept — but it was different now. These were Ben and Isla's twins, the firstborn prince and princess, even if Tobias refused to let such titles carry any weight in his heart. To him, they were simply family, and family was worth guarding with a fierceness that had nothing to do with protocol.

Ben was there, leaning lightly against the side of the bassinet, his gaze fixed on the slow, even breathing of his children. He did not turn when Tobias entered, but there was no need. Tobias's presence was not one that required announcement. It was the sort of presence that had always been understood, as reliable as the sound of boots on the stone corridor when a watchman passed in the night. He came to stand beside Ben, folding his arms as he surveyed the tiny figures beneath the blankets.

"I'll take the midnight shifts when you're gone," Tobias said, his voice pitched low but firm. "Feedings, changes, all of it. You won't have to worry." The words were offered without embellishment, but there was something beneath them — a promise that went deeper than the surface task. Ben knew Tobias well enough to hear it, the unspoken assurance that nothing and no one would disturb the children while he was away.

Ben gave the faintest nod, still looking down at the twins. "You sure you want to volunteer for that? Could be dangerous work." His tone carried the shadow of a smile, but Tobias met it without flinching.

"I've survived worse," Tobias said, letting the humour sit just long enough before it shifted. "You forget how many blowouts I've cleaned up. I've seen horrors that would put grown men on the floor." The corner of his mouth twitched, but the lightness faded almost as quickly as it had appeared. His expression tightened, his gaze sharpening into something far more serious.

"They won't get past me," Tobias said, his voice dropping into a tone meant for war, not for conversation. "The press, the photographers, the gossipmongers — they won't cross this threshold. I don't care how many ladders they bring or how fast they run. They won't take a single shot that you don't want them to."

Ben finally turned to look at him, studying the lines of his friend's face. Tobias was not a man given to dramatic statements, which meant that when he made one, it carried weight. There was no mistaking the conviction in his eyes — this was not about duty to a king, nor even to the crown. It was about loyalty forged through years of standing side by side, weathering every storm that had tried to breach these walls.

"You've always been stubborn," Ben said quietly, though the words lacked any criticism. If anything, there was gratitude woven into them.

"Stubborn keeps people alive," Tobias replied. His gaze shifted briefly back to the twins, softening only slightly. "They don't know yet what's coming. They shouldn't have to. And I'm going to make sure they don't feel it. Not now. Not when they're still small enough to fit in the crook of an arm."

The stillness between them held for a few moments, broken only by the faint creak of the floor as Tobias adjusted his stance. In the quiet, the twins stirred, one letting out a soft sigh before settling again. It was a fragile kind of peace, the kind that needed guarding as much as the gates themselves.

"I don't do this for titles," Tobias said suddenly, as if needing to make the truth plain. "Not for crowns, not for formalities. I do this because you're family. You've always been family. And when family's under threat, you don't ask if it's convenient. You just do the job."

Ben let out a slow breath, feeling the truth of it settle into him like a stone in still water. There was no arguing with Tobias when he spoke like that. It was the same certainty Ben had relied on in the past — the same voice that had stood with him when choices were difficult, when outcomes were uncertain. "I'll hold you to that," Ben said, though they both knew there was no need. Tobias was a man whose word was as fixed as the castle walls. "You don't have to," Tobias replied. "It's already done."

They stood together for another moment, two figures framed in the low lamplight, the air around them thick with the understanding that departure was no longer a distant plan but an approaching certainty. In the hall beyond, the faint sound of a watchman's steps echoed toward the staircase, marking the hour.

When Tobias finally stepped back toward the door, he glanced over his shoulder. "Get some rest while you can," he said, his voice returning to the lighter tone he used when matters were less heavy. "I'll be back in the morning to start my shift early. Might as well get used to the job now."

Ben nodded once more, his eyes returning to the twins. "Goodnight, Tobias." "Goodnight," came the reply, followed by the quiet sound of the door closing. The nursery fell silent again, save for the soft breathing of its smallest inhabitants and the steady hum of the castle that sheltered them.

The sitting room was lit with the soft, amber glow of the wall sconces, the kind of light that softened the sharp edges of the evening and made the world seem smaller, more contained. Isla sat on the long-backed sofa with one of the twins in her arms, the other resting in the bassinet beside her. The gentle weight of the infant was a comfort, though it did not dull the awareness of what the coming days would bring. Clara entered quietly, closing the door behind her with the deliberate care of someone who meant to stay for more than a passing visit.

She crossed the room without hesitation, her steps sure and her face calm. In her hand was a folded sheet of paper, its corners worn from being opened and closed repeatedly. She set it down on the table beside Isla, the edge of her hand brushing the polished wood. "Everything they will need for the next month," Clara said simply, her voice steady. "I've written it all down — clothes, feedings, bath times, everything."

Isla glanced at the list but did not pick it up right away. She knew what it was without reading it in detail, and she knew Clara would have accounted for far more than she herself might have thought to note. "You didn't have to do all that," Isla said, though there was no trace of dismissal in her tone.

"I did," Clara replied, settling into the chair opposite. "Because when he's gone, the only thing you should have to think about is breathing and holding them. I can handle the rest." There was a firmness to her words that left no room for polite protest.

For a moment, neither woman spoke. The quiet was not empty; it was the kind of stillness that carried meaning, a shared understanding built from years of knowing when to speak and when to simply be present. The twins' small, rhythmic breaths filled the space between them, grounding them both in the here and now.

Clara's eyes rested briefly on the bassinet, softening at the sight of the second child stirring but not waking. "They're perfect," she said quietly. "And they're going to stay that way, no matter what noise comes from outside." It was a promise as much as it was an observation.

Isla shifted slightly, adjusting the infant in her arms. "It's the space I'm worried about," she admitted, her voice low. "The space in the bed. The space in the mornings. You can fill the hours, but you can't fill that."

Clara didn't argue. Instead, she leaned forward, her elbows resting on her knees, and met Isla's eyes directly. "No, I can't fill it. But I can make sure you don't fall into it. Every time it feels too wide, I'll be there. We'll keep busy. We'll take walks, we'll sit in here and talk, we'll watch them change day by day. There won't be time to sink into missing him."

The honesty in her words carried more comfort than any hollow assurance could. Isla knew Clara well enough to believe her. She had been a steady presence for more than a decade, the kind of person who didn't drift in and out of loyalty depending on the weather. Clara stayed — through the arguments, through the silences, through the seasons when the castle felt like a fortress under siege.

The list on the table became a symbol of that commitment. It was not just a record of feedings and bedtime routines; it was a declaration that every detail would be managed, every need anticipated. Isla reached out and laid her fingers lightly on the folded paper, as if to anchor herself to that certainty.

"They'll be all right," Clara said again, more softly this time. "And so will you. Because you're not alone in this. You never have been." Isla's lips curved into the faintest smile, not of joy but of recognition. "We'll manage," she said, repeating the words they both knew were true. Clara nodded once, the conversation closing without ceremony. There was no need to drag it out or to circle around the same fears again. They had named them, faced them, and put them back in their place. That was enough.

The twins shifted again, one letting out a tiny sigh that drew both women's gazes downward. Clara reached over to adjust the blanket, her hand moving with the same care she might give to a fragile piece of glass. The gesture, small as it was, carried the weight of her promise more than words could.

They stayed like that for a while, the room quiet save for the occasional crackle from the fireplace and the muted sounds of the castle beyond the door. The sense of watchfulness was not one of tension but of readiness, a shared commitment to protect the peace of the room for as long as they could.

When Clara finally leaned back in her chair, it was with the easy posture of someone who had settled into her role completely. She would be here tomorrow, and the day after that, and for as many days as it took. There was no counting down, no tallying hours until Ben's return. There was only the present, and the work of guarding it. The two women exchanged a final glance before the quiet took over entirely — a look that said everything words could not. They would manage, because they must. And that was the end of it.

The last of the day's light clung to the horizon, bleeding into the low clouds that promised rain before morning. Ben moved slowly along the outer wall, each step deliberate on the worn stone path that had been walked by generations before him. His palm traced the rough surface of the parapet, the grit and coolness grounding him in the reality of this place — this fortress that was both home and shield. Above the city, the scent of damp earth and sea drifted in on the wind, carrying with it the faintest echo of the harbour bells.

He stopped near the first corner tower, letting his gaze fall over the rooftops of Copenhagen. The city seemed still from this height, as though the bustle of the streets had been folded away for the night. But he knew better. Somewhere out there, a camera waited, a headline already half-written. The quiet was not a guarantee, only a pause before the next intrusion. He breathed deeply, not to calm himself, but to memorise the balance between peace and vigilance that this moment offered.

The north gate drew him onward. Its iron hinges, blackened with age, were as much a part of the castle's history as the royal seal. Ben rested his hand against the thick timber, feeling the faint vibration of the wind through the wood. Beyond it, the road wound toward the heart of the city, where lights flickered in the gathering dark. This was the line between the safety of the walls and the uncertainty beyond.

He had walked these walls countless times, but tonight the air carried a weight that had nothing to do with weather. Every step was an acknowledgment that he would soon be on the other side, away from these stones, away from Isla and the twins, away from the life that had been carefully shielded from the outside world. Leaving now was not surrender — it was strategy, shaped with the precision of a move made in full knowledge of its cost.

As he reached the far corner, the view opened wider. The harbour spread out like a silvered sheet, its surface broken only by the shifting silhouettes of moored boats. Somewhere among those docks, rumours had already begun to swirl. Copenhagen was loyal, yes, but even loyalty had limits when tested by hunger for a story. The air tasted faintly of salt, and it caught in his throat in a way that made him think of departures too many times past.

The stones beneath his hand told their own story. Pitted, cracked, yet still holding firm after centuries of storms, they were the castle's quiet promise of endurance. He thought of Isla's face earlier that evening, of the unshaken resolve in her voice when she told him again to go. She was not asking; she was directing, just as he would have done if their positions were reversed. That certainty steadied him now more than any plan.

Pausing under one of the wall's narrow watchpoints, he looked down at the gardens below. Even in the dimming light, the shapes of the hedges were clear — precise, intentional, maintained by hands that understood the value of order. He envied their simplicity. The hedges did not wonder what tomorrow would bring; they stood where they were told to stand. People, he thought, were far less cooperative.

From this height, the sound of the city was muted. He could almost believe it slept, though he knew it never truly did. Somewhere, a street vendor was packing away the last of the day's trade. Somewhere else, a conversation was turning toward speculation about the King's family. He wondered if the one who had betrayed them thought of him now, and whether they understood the damage they had done — or if the coins in their pocket were enough to quiet any remorse.

At the northernmost stretch, he stopped again, this time leaning against the wall, letting the cool stone press into his shoulder. The weight in his chest was not fear but calculation. Every move he made from this point forward had to be exact. There was no margin for error, no space for second-guessing. Protection meant precision, and precision meant stepping away before the danger could close in completely.

The rain began as a fine mist, carried sideways by the wind. He did not move to avoid it. Instead, he let it settle into his hair, dampen his collar, and bead along the back of his hands. It was an honest thing, rain — no agenda, no eyes watching from behind a lens. He wished he could keep such simplicity around his family, shield them from the manufactured storms that human ambition could conjure.

He thought briefly of the cottage in Kent, of the narrow lane that would lead him there and the garden where the air would smell of grass instead of salt. In Kent, the walls were not stone but hedgerows, and they held their own kind of privacy. He wondered how long it would take before he missed the sight of Copenhagen's skyline at night, before the absence of this view became another quiet ache to carry.

A faint light flickered near the east gate — not a threat, just one of the outer lamps catching in the damp air. Still, his eyes followed it, trained to notice even the smallest change in his surroundings. Sørensen's lessons over the years had become habit: observe everything, assume nothing, prepare for both. The truth of those words was carved deeper than any fear could reach.

Ben pushed away from the wall, turning back toward the keep. His footsteps were measured, the sound swallowed quickly by the wet stone. There was no need to look over his shoulder; the city would still be there tomorrow, and the day after that, waiting for his return. The question was whether it would wait quietly.

As he neared the courtyard, the scent of woodsmoke drifted up from the kitchens. It was a reminder that life inside the walls carried on regardless of plans or departures. Children still laughed in the hallways, meals were still prepared, and fires were still lit against the chill. That constancy was its own kind of defence, one the outside world could never fully penetrate.

Crossing the threshold back into the main keep, he let the door close behind him with a muted thud. The walk along the walls had not changed his mind — it had only sharpened the edge of his resolve. Leaving was not retreat. It was a blade drawn in defence of what mattered most, and it would be wielded without hesitation when the time came.

The lamp on Ben's desk burned low, casting its light in a narrow pool across the polished wood. Outside, the night pressed against the window, its quiet deepened by the slow patter of rain. He sat with the pen balanced between his fingers, the paper before him untouched for several minutes as he searched for the words that would not betray the truth. This was not a letter of departure, nor was it a confession. It was a promise, drawn carefully from the part of himself that still believed in coming home whole.

He began without flourish, writing Isla's name as he always did — without titles, without ornament. The ink moved steadily, the sentences plain but weighted with what he could not bring himself to say aloud. He told her that the days apart would be counted, not wasted, and that his absence was not abandonment but a shield raised in her defence. Every line was measured, each one designed to hold its strength long after his voice could no longer fill the room.

When the page was full, he set the pen aside and read it once through. There were no goodbyes, only the unshakable assertion that he would return when it was safe. He folded the sheet once, pressing the crease firmly, then reached for the envelope. The seal was applied without ceremony, but the moment his thumb left the wax, a weight settled in his chest. It was done. The letter would wait for her, quietly, until either his return or her need for it outweighed her patience.

He stood and crossed to the far side of the study, where the bottom drawer of the desk kept its most guarded possessions. Sliding it open, he placed the envelope beside the worn album of Kent, the same one he had shown Casper and Maria. His fingers lingered on the edge of the paper, unwilling to let go as if his grip could anchor him to the life he was preparing to leave. When at last he released it, the sound of it settling in the drawer was far louder in his mind than it was in the room.

The stillness broke when he sat back heavily in his chair, elbows on his knees, and let the strain in his chest unravel into open grief. There was no dignity in holding it back; Isla would not have wanted him to. The thought of her alone with the twins — their small hands, their soft breath against her skin — tore through him with the same sharpness as the knowledge that he would miss their first smiles, perhaps their first words. The air between them in these next weeks would be measured in miles and in silence.

His breathing slowed, but the ache did not fade. It deepened when the door to the study opened without a knock. Emil Søren Ravn Harvick stood there, eight years old and watchful in the half-light. The boy did not speak at first, only lingered near the threshold, his small hands curling into fists at his sides. There was something brittle in his posture, a quiet stiffness that Ben recognized too late for comfort.

Emil stepped forward, his voice low and flat when it came. He asked if Ben was leaving, though it was not really a question. The answer was already there in the packed bags, in the hush of the castle corridors, in the way no one quite met his eyes today. What came next was harder. Emil asked why it mattered so much to protect everyone else when it seemed no one had thought to protect him.

Ben's reply caught in his throat. Emil's eyes — so much older than his years — did not waver as he said that the twins had her, Casper had them all, Maria had the comfort of her promise, and Isla had every glance, every word, every touch that spoke of love. But he, Emil, had nothing. No goodnight hug, no I love you, no proof that his place here was more than an obligation. His voice did not shake, but each word landed with a weight that Ben could feel in his chest.

Emil said it plainly: maybe it would be better if he went back into the foster system. At least there, someone might choose him and mean it. The sting of it was sharper than any accusation Ben had faced in his life. This was not rebellion. This was truth, raw and unadorned, and it left no room for defence. For a moment, all Ben could do was sit in the silence Emil had left hanging between them.

Ben reached out, but Emil stepped back. The boy's expression did not change, though his jaw tightened as if to keep something from spilling out. Ben told him he was wrong about not being loved, but even as the words left his mouth, he knew they were not enough. Love, to a child, was not measured in statements but in proof — in moments and gestures and time given freely. Emil had been watching the proof given to others, and in that watching, had counted his own absence from it.

The study seemed smaller, the walls closer. Ben thought of the letter in the drawer, the one written for Isla, and felt the sharp contrast of its presence against the absence Emil was describing. There were no sealed envelopes for this boy, no hidden promises waiting to be found. The truth was uncomfortably clear: while the castle had been holding the world at bay, it had also, unintentionally, been holding Emil at a distance.

Ben rose from his chair and closed the space between them, moving slowly enough for Emil to step away if he wished. The boy did not. When Ben knelt, it was not the gesture of a king but of a man who had failed someone without meaning to. He told Emil that leaving now would not fix what had been neglected, but that coming back would. The words were quiet, and though they did not erase the hurt, they carried the one thing Ben could offer in that moment — intention.

Emil did not answer. He only nodded once, the smallest motion, and stepped past Ben toward the door. Before he reached it, he paused, his back still to the room. In the stillness, Ben thought he might say something more, but Emil simply continued on, the soft tread of his steps fading into the corridor.

Alone again, Ben returned to the desk. His hand hovered over the drawer where Isla's letter lay, but he did not open it. There was another letter to be written now, one not born of strategy or caution, but of recognition. The ink would dry quickly, but the work of proving it would take far longer. And this time, he thought, it would not be left hidden in a drawer.

Emil lay awake in his bed, staring at the shadowed ceiling, his thoughts running in restless circles. He had not spoken since the kitchen meeting, not even when Maria had tried to coax a smile from him in the hallway. Now, with the castle hushed around him, the silence became a weight he could no longer carry. He reached for the phone on his nightstand, his small fingers curling around it as he considered the number he had memorized weeks ago — Judge Algren's direct line. If anyone could make the arrangements, it would be him. Emil's chest tightened at the thought, not from fear but from a weary certainty that maybe life would be better somewhere else.

Down the corridor, Ben had been pacing the length of his chamber, unable to settle despite the hour. The sound of a floorboard creaking in Emil's room caught his attention, faint but out of place at this time of night.

He moved quietly, pausing just outside the half-closed door, the glow of the bedside lamp casting a narrow line across the hallway carpet. Ben stepped inside, his voice low but steady. "Couldn't sleep?" he asked. Emil didn't answer right away, his eyes fixed on the phone in his hand. When he finally spoke, the words were clipped. "I was going to call Judge Algren. I want to go back into the foster system."

The admission landed with more weight than Ben had expected. He closed the door gently, crossing to sit at the edge of the bed. "You think that's what you need?" he asked, careful not to sound defensive. Emil's gaze didn't waver. "Nobody here notices me anymore. The twins get all the attention, Casper gets the rest, and I… I'm just here." The words carried no malice, only the dull ache of feeling invisible. Ben let the moment stretch, knowing that rushing his reply would only push the boy further away.

When he finally stood, Ben didn't offer an answer. Instead, he told Emil to wait, his voice even but not dismissive. He left the room and walked the short distance to where Sørensen was making his final security checks for the night. The older man straightened when he saw Ben approaching, sensing from the younger man's expression that this was not about the departure plan. "It's Emil," Ben began, his voice pitched low. "He wants to call Algren and go back into the foster system. Says he feels invisible. I need to know what to do."

Sørensen leaned against the wall, folding his arms across his chest, his brow furrowing in thought. "Invisible is a dangerous place for a child to live," he said at last. "You can't order him to stay. That'll make him run in his mind, even if his feet never leave. But you can show him there's space for him that no one else can fill." His eyes met Ben's with the weight of a shared understanding — this wasn't about strategy or protection from the outside. It was about repairing something from within before it broke entirely.

Ben nodded slowly, his mind already moving through possibilities. "What if I took him with us?" he asked. "The cottage can hold eight easily. He'd have his own space, and maybe getting away from here — from all of this — would give him a chance to breathe." Sørensen didn't answer right away. His eyes drifted toward the darkened windows, his expression unreadable. "It's a risk," he said finally, "but not for the reasons you think. Sometimes, when you take a hurt child into a new place, the hurt comes with him. But if you're ready to carry it with him, maybe that's exactly what he needs."

The weight of the decision settled on Ben's shoulders, heavier than the departure itself. He had thought of Kent as an escape route, a pause before the next move, but now it could also be a place of repair. The question was whether Emil would see it that way — or whether he had already decided that no place under Ben's care could be home. The thought gnawed at him, but there was no time for hesitation. The clock was moving.

Midnight struck with the soft chime of the castle's old clock tower, the sound rolling through the halls like a measured heartbeat. Ben returned to his chamber, the window drawn open to the night air. From where he stood, he could see the lanterns flickering along the path that led to the gates, their glow swaying in the breeze. In five days, those lights would burn without him. He imagined the gates closed behind him, the lanterns still standing watch over a home he would not see again for weeks.

He drew a long breath, the cool air filling his lungs, carrying the faint scent of damp stone and distant rain. This was the quiet before the storm, a pause so thin it could shatter at the first footstep on gravel. Behind him, the fire in the grate had burned low, casting the room in amber shadows. The stillness wrapped around him, but it brought no comfort. Instead, it sharpened his focus, fixing every detail in place — the weight of the curtains, the angle of the light on the floorboards, the distant murmur of the guard's voices below.

Ben let his gaze follow the line of the lanterns to where they disappeared beyond the north wall. Somewhere out there, the city was sleeping, unaware of the decisions being made within these walls. The countdown had begun, each hour a step toward an inevitability that could no longer be delayed or undone. There would be no turning it back. The plan was set. The players were in position. And yet, a single boy's future — Emil's — hung in the balance alongside everything else.

In the stillness, he realised that the two paths ahead were not separate after all. Leaving and staying were both acts of protection; the difference was in who was being shielded, and from what. Emil's hurt could not be left behind like a forgotten suitcase. If Ben carried him to Kent, it would be with the understanding that the journey was not about escape, but about building something that might survive the return.

He turned from the window, his decision beginning to take shape. There would be more to discuss — with Isla, with Emil, with Sørensen — but the choice was leaning into the only direction that felt like it kept faith with the boy. He would not let Emil slip quietly into someone else's care, not when the boy had already been passed between too many hands. Kent might not be a cure, but it could be a start.

The fire cracked softly in the hearth, and the castle seemed to exhale around him. The night was far from over, and neither was the work. But for the first time in hours, Ben felt a thread of resolve tighten in his chest. He would carry Emil's hurt if he had to, and he would carry it all the way to Kent. In five days, they would leave together — and when they returned, it would be as more than what they were tonight.

The castle was deep in its slumber when Ben returned to Emil's room. The lamp was still on, casting a soft circle of light over the boy's small frame. Emil was not asleep. He lay on his side with the phone clutched loosely in one hand, his gaze fixed on nothing in particular.

Ben paused at the door, noting how much smaller the boy looked when curled into himself. There had been too many nights like this, nights when the weight of feeling unwanted had pulled Emil into a quiet corner where no one else could reach him. Tonight, Ben decided, that corner would not be left to grow darker.

Crossing the room, Ben sat on the edge of the bed, the old mattress dipping under his weight. Emil turned his head slightly, just enough to see that it was Ben and not someone coming to scold him for being awake. "I've been thinking," Ben began, his tone measured, "and I have an idea. But I need you to hear me out before you say anything." Emil blinked, cautious, his fingers tightening around the phone. Ben reached over, gently setting it on the nightstand. "You said you want to go back into the system. I'm not going to tell you that's wrong or that you can't feel that way. But before you make that call, I want to give you another choice."

Emil pushed himself up onto one elbow, his brow furrowing in suspicion. "What choice?" he asked, his voice quiet but edged. Ben met his eyes without hesitation. "Come with us to Kent," he said plainly. "We'll be gone for a while. The cottage has enough room for all of us. You'd have your own bed, your own space, and time away from everything that's making you feel invisible here." He didn't overpromise. "It won't fix everything overnight, but it'll be somewhere new. Somewhere you can breathe."

The boy studied him for a long moment, as though weighing the truth behind the words. "Why?" Emil finally asked. "Why do you even care now? You've been busy with the twins, with Casper, with… everything else." The bluntness cut, but Ben didn't flinch. "Because you're part of this family too," he replied, steady. "And I've been failing at showing you that. I can't change the last few weeks, but I can change the days ahead. I'm asking you to come with me so we can start doing that right."

Emil looked down at his hands, his fingers curling into the blanket. "And if I say no?" Ben leaned forward slightly. "Then I'll still make sure you're safe. But I'd rather you were safe with me. You've had enough people walk away from you in your life. I don't want to be one of them." The words hung between them, not as a plea but as a promise — firm, deliberate, and without conditions.

The silence stretched, broken only by the faint hum of the heater. Emil's mind ran through images he didn't speak aloud — the quiet loneliness of the foster homes, the awkwardness of being the new boy over and over, the way no one ever stayed long enough to become permanent. Kent was unknown, but unknown was not automatically bad. Still, trust did not come easily to him anymore. "Would I get to do anything there?" he asked finally. "Or just sit in a room while everyone else lives their lives?"

Ben smiled faintly, the corner of his mouth lifting. "You'd do what everyone else does. We'll explore the village, you can help me in the orchard, there's a library down the road… and yes, we'll kick a football around. You won't be on the sidelines." He leaned back slightly. "But only if you choose it. I'm not forcing you into another life you didn't ask for."

Emil's eyes narrowed slightly, testing for the smallest crack in Ben's sincerity. "And what if you get busy again? Forget I'm there?" The question was sharper than his voice, almost a challenge. Ben's answer came without pause. "Then you tell me. Loudly, if you have to. I'm not perfect, but I can listen. And I can make sure you're never invisible again."

For the first time that night, something in Emil's expression shifted — not trust, not yet, but the faintest sign that the wall between them had weakened. He sat up fully, drawing his knees to his chest. "If I go… can I take my books?" Ben's relief was quiet but undeniable. "All of them," he said. "And we'll find you more when we get there."

The boy considered this, his gaze drifting to the phone on the nightstand. He reached out, not for the device, but to click off the lamp, leaving them in the dim light of the hall spilling through the door. "I'll think about it," he murmured. It wasn't a yes, but it wasn't the rejection Ben had feared. Sometimes, the space between was the best you could hope for — and from there, it could grow.

Ben stood, resting a hand lightly on the blanket near Emil's leg. "That's all I'm asking," he said. "Just think about it." He turned toward the door, pausing only once to glance back. Emil had already settled against the pillow, his eyes open but softer than before. The phone remained untouched.

Back in his own chamber, Ben let the quiet settle around him again. The lanterns outside still burned, their light a steady reminder that the clock was moving. In five days, the decision would be made one way or the other. But tonight, there was the faintest hope that Emil might be at his side when the gates opened.

Morning broke slowly over Rosenshavn Castle, the pale spring light filtering through low clouds and brushing the stone walls with a muted glow. In the kitchen, the first signs of the day were quiet — the clink of cups, the low hum of the kettle, and the soft tread of Sørensen's boots as he stepped inside. He had no intention of drawing attention to himself. Watching was an art, and he had mastered it years ago, both in service to the crown and in the quieter work of understanding the people under his care. Today, that work was focused entirely on Emil.

The boy arrived late for breakfast, his hair tousled and his steps dragging just enough to suggest he had not slept deeply. Sørensen, standing near the doorway with his coffee, took in every detail without appearing to look. Emil didn't rush to join the others. Instead, he hovered by the counter, pouring himself a glass of juice before sliding into a seat at the far end of the table. It was the kind of seating choice that told a story — close enough to be present, far enough to feel apart.

Ben, already halfway through his toast, didn't press him. That was wise, Sørensen thought. Pushing a boy in Emil's frame of mind would only send him retreating further. Instead, Ben let the conversation at the table flow as normal, letting Emil absorb it from his chosen distance. Maria and Casper chattered about the cottage in Kent, listing what they planned to bring, their voices rising with excitement. Sørensen noticed that Emil's spoon stilled briefly over his cereal when Maria mentioned sharing bedtime stories there.

When breakfast was done, Emil lingered. Not to help — though he rinsed his bowl and glass without being asked — but to drift toward the window that overlooked the castle's rear gardens. Sørensen moved quietly to stand near the sideboard, close enough to catch the boy's reflection in the glass. Emil's gaze followed a pair of gardeners crossing toward the orchard, their voices lost in the wind. His expression was unreadable, but there was no mistaking the way his shoulders eased, if only for a moment, as he watched the open space.

The rest of the morning unfolded in its usual rhythm. Isla, resting with the twins in the nursery, sent Maria and Casper to the library for their lessons. Ben retreated to his study to write letters that would never see the public eye. Emil, however, did not vanish into his room as he often did. Instead, he followed the others into the library, taking a seat at the long oak table without a word. Sørensen slipped into a chair in the corner, a book in his hands that he never really read.

From behind the veil of pages, Sørensen observed. Emil kept his eyes on the text in front of him but turned his head slightly when Casper began describing the pond near the Kent cottage. Maria mentioned that the air there smelled different — softer, fresher, with the scent of apples in bloom. Emil's pencil paused mid-word. He didn't look up, didn't speak, but Sørensen knew enough to recognise when someone was listening harder than they meant to.

At midday, Sørensen watched again as Emil trailed the others into the dining room. This time, he didn't sit at the far end. He took a seat two chairs closer, within easy reach of the breadbasket and the conversation. The change was subtle, the kind that most would overlook, but Sørensen noted it with the same precision he would have marked a shift in an enemy's movement. Proximity was a choice, and today Emil was edging closer.

The afternoon brought a break in the weather, and the children spilled into the courtyard for fresh air. Sørensen kept to the shadow of the archway, watching as Emil remained near the wall at first, his hands stuffed into his pockets. It wasn't until Casper kicked a ball in his direction — casual, almost careless — that Emil's head came up. He hesitated, then gave the ball a light kick back. It rolled only a few feet, but it was enough to make Casper grin and send it toward him again. This time, Emil kicked it harder.

For ten minutes, Sørensen saw something rare: Emil engaged, moving, even smiling faintly when Maria joined in. He didn't take over the game, but he didn't excuse himself either. It was not yet belonging, but it was movement toward it. And movement, Sørensen knew, could build into momentum if nurtured.

When the game ended, the boy lingered outside instead of fleeing back indoors. He wandered toward the edge of the gardens, pausing near the old apple tree. Sørensen followed at a distance, careful not to intrude. Emil reached up to touch one of the low branches, running his fingers over the rough bark. It was the smallest of gestures, but it held the weight of curiosity — the kind that imagined something beyond the walls.

Inside again, Sørensen caught Ben in the corridor. "He's listening," Sørensen murmured, keeping his voice low. "Not ready to say yes, but he's leaning. Don't push him." Ben nodded, the faint crease between his brows easing slightly. It was all he needed for now — a reason to keep the door open.

By evening, the house had settled into its familiar quiet. Emil joined the others in the sitting room without prompting, claiming a chair off to the side but well within the circle of lamplight. He listened as Maria read aloud, his gaze fixed on the fire. Sørensen, standing by the mantel, saw the way his eyes flicked toward Ben at certain moments, as if weighing whether the offer to come along might truly hold.

When bedtime came, Emil didn't vanish into sullen silence. He offered a brief goodnight to Maria and Casper — nothing dramatic, nothing loud, but present enough to notice. Sørensen marked it down in his own quiet ledger. The boy was not retreating further. He was inching forward, testing the ground.

Later, alone in his own room, Sørensen reviewed the day in his mind. Emil's movements were small, but they told a story as clear as any report. He was considering Kent. Not yet committed, but the seed had been planted. All that remained was to give it light, and time, and the freedom to choose without pressure.

Tomorrow, Sørensen decided, would bring another chance to watch. And if the boy gave him even one more sign, no matter how small, then the choice might not be so far away.

The morning began with a damp mist curling over the castle grounds, softening the outlines of the towers and muting the colours of the garden below. Emil sat at the far end of the courtyard steps, his chin resting in his hands, watching the drizzle bead along the stone. He was not waiting for anyone in particular, but when Sørensen appeared from the north gate with his usual deliberate stride, Emil's head came up. The man carried no urgency in his step, only the quiet authority that had long made the children of Rosenshavn feel both safe and seen. Without invitation, Emil fell into step beside him as they crossed toward the stables.

It was not conversation that drew them together at first, but the rhythm of the patrol. Sørensen greeted the groundskeepers, checked the gates, inspected the toolshed lock, and Emil mirrored each action in smaller ways, glancing up at the man now and then as if confirming that he was keeping the pace correctly.

Maria, skipping along the other side of her father, offered occasional commentary about the rose beds or the new nesting swallows under the eaves. Emil listened but said little, though Sørensen could feel the boy's presence tightening closer with each turn of the path.

By the time they reached the south wall, the mist had thinned and the wind off the city carried the faint tang of salt from the distant harbour. Emil stopped, hands in his pockets, looking outward as though measuring the world beyond the stone. Sørensen, sensing the pause, waited beside him. When the boy finally spoke, it was without preamble. "Would you adopt me?" The words were flat, unadorned, but heavy enough to still the air between them.

Sørensen turned to look at him fully, one eyebrow lifting, the corner of his mouth tugging upward into a slow, genuine smile. "I would love to," he said simply. "But you belong to Ben." The answer was honest without being final, a door left half-open. Emil gave the smallest of nods, his gaze dropping to the gravel underfoot, and then resumed walking. Maria glanced between them, sensing something important but choosing not to interrupt.

Later, in the armoury, Ben passed by the open door and caught the low murmur of voices. Emil was talking again — really talking, not offering one-word replies. His tone was lighter, more fluid, and it was directed entirely at Sørensen. They were discussing crossbow maintenance, of all things, with Emil asking about range and accuracy. Ben paused just beyond sight, one hand braced against the doorframe, listening to the easy cadence between them. It was a kind of comfort the boy had never shown him.

The realisation tightened something in Ben's chest. It was not jealousy, but an awareness of absence — a father-shaped space Emil was filling with someone else. Sørensen had earned the boy's trust by sheer constancy: being there every morning, taking him along without question, making no promises he could not keep. Ben knew that kind of steadiness was what Emil craved, perhaps more than the safety of the castle walls themselves.

In the library that afternoon, Ben found Emil reading at one of the smaller desks. Sørensen sat a few chairs away, sharpening a penknife while Maria sketched in her notebook. It looked, for a moment, like a small, separate household inside the castle — its own unspoken unit. Ben crossed to the table, placing a hand lightly on Emil's shoulder. The boy stiffened but did not pull away. "I'll need to speak with Isla," Ben said quietly, glancing toward Sørensen as he spoke. There was no need to explain what about; the man's slight nod said he understood.

That evening, Ben brought it up to Isla in their private sitting room. She listened without interrupting, her expression a mixture of sympathy and concern. "If Emil feels safest with Sørensen, then that's where he should be for now," she said at last. "It doesn't take away from your place in his life. But you can't force him to see you as the father he needs right now." Ben knew she was right, but hearing it still carried its sting.

The conversation weighed on him as he made his rounds before bed. In the nursery, the twins slept undisturbed, their tiny breaths steady in the lamplight. Across the hall, he found Emil's door half-open. Inside, the boy was kneeling beside his bed, packing away a handful of marbles into a small pouch. "You'd like Kent?" Ben asked softly. Emil shrugged without looking up. "Maybe. Be nice to get away." The answer was neither rejection nor acceptance — just a window left cracked for possibility.

Sørensen appeared behind Ben, leaning against the doorframe with the ease of a man who belonged anywhere he stood. "We'll make sure he's ready," he said quietly. Emil glanced up at that, his eyes flicking between them, but said nothing. Still, there was no hostility in the look — only calculation, the kind a boy makes when measuring whether to trust one more step.

The next day, Sørensen took Maria and Emil on another patrol, this time looping through the market quarter outside the castle gates. Ben followed at a distance, blending into the foot traffic, and saw Emil walking closer to Sørensen than he ever had to him. They spoke in low tones, and more than once, Emil's laughter rose above the clatter of carts and the calls of merchants. It was an unfamiliar sound, unguarded and light.

Back at the castle, Ben and Sørensen met briefly in the map room. "If he comes to Kent," Sørensen said, "it shouldn't be as your responsibility alone. Let him feel like he's choosing both of us." Ben studied him for a moment before answering. "And if he chooses only you?" Sørensen's answer was immediate. "Then you still win, because he's safe."

That night, as lantern light traced long shadows across the courtyard, Ben sat alone in his study, the offer he had made to Emil now transformed into something larger. It was no longer just about taking the boy to Kent to shield him from the chaos; it was about giving him the stability he had been denied for too long. Whether that came through himself or through Sørensen, it could not be half-measures.

And somewhere down the hall, Emil lay awake, the idea of Kent taking shape in his mind. Not as a royal escape, not as part of Ben's world, but as a place where patrols might be quieter, trust might be earned without force, and a man who never broke his word might just be the father he had always wanted.

The morning light spilled into the sitting room in long, angled bands, cutting through the fine dust that hung in the still air. Isla sat at the writing desk by the balcony, a sheet of parchment before her, untouched but for the neat date at the top. She was not writing, not yet; instead, she watched the gardens below where Sørensen, Maria, and Emil moved along the gravel paths in easy formation. From this height, their shapes seemed like three points on a line that never broke. She noted how Emil's stride matched Sørensen's, how Maria's chatter kept pace without slowing them. The boy did not look back at the castle once.

She rested her chin on her hand, considering how quickly this bond had formed. Emil, who only weeks ago had moved through the halls like a shadow, was now carrying himself with a faint but visible confidence. That change had not come from Ben, nor from herself, though she had tried in small ways to draw him closer. It had come from Sørensen's steady, unflinching presence — the same quiet strength that had once made him seem formidable when Ben was a boy, now softened into something fatherly. Isla felt no jealousy in this observation, only clarity.

When Ben entered the room a few minutes later, she turned toward him and saw that same clarity already in his eyes. He came to stand beside her, leaning one shoulder against the desk, his gaze following the figures in the garden. For a long moment neither spoke. Finally, he said, "I'm not meant to be his father." The words were plain, almost weightless in tone, but Isla knew the cost of speaking them. She reached for his hand without looking away from the window.

"You're not failing him by seeing the truth," she replied quietly. "Sometimes the right place for a child isn't with the one who has the title, but with the one who holds their trust." She thought of her own children, the way a mother knows which arms they will seek in moments of fear. Emil had already chosen. It was simply a matter of honouring that choice before it hardened into resentment.

The rest of the day unfolded with a strange sense of acceleration, as if the decision had triggered a clock they could no longer slow. Meals passed in a blur of half-finished conversation, the business of preparing for departure overshadowed by the unspoken matter of Emil's future. Ben moved through his duties with precision, but Isla caught him glancing toward the courtyard more than once, tracking Emil's movements as though committing them to memory.

That evening, they found Sørensen in the armoury, inspecting a crate of equipment for the trip to Kent. Maria sat cross-legged on the floor beside him, polishing a small brass spyglass, while Emil carefully wound rope into tight coils. The sight could have been mistaken for an ordinary moment, but to Isla, it was the very picture of belonging. Ben stepped forward, clearing his throat gently, and when Sørensen looked up, he said, "We need to speak about Emil."

Sørensen set the rope aside, signalling Maria to take Emil into the corridor for a moment. When the door closed behind them, Ben spoke without hesitation. "He should be with you. Not just for this trip — for as long as he needs a home." There was no bitterness in his tone, no attempt to disguise the relief that came with the words. Isla saw something flicker across Sørensen's face then — not surprise, but the weight of being entrusted with a life.

"If that's what you believe is right, I won't refuse him," Sørensen said. His voice carried no hesitation, and Isla knew in that instant the decision was sealed. She had expected perhaps a pause, a request for time, but Sørensen accepted the responsibility as though he had been preparing for it all along. Ben nodded once, the finality of the exchange settling over them like the quiet after a storm.

Maria and Emil returned, their steps slowing as they sensed the change in the room. Emil looked between the adults, suspicion in his eyes. Ben crouched to meet his gaze and said, "If you want to stay with Sørensen, it's not temporary. It's your home now too." The boy didn't answer right away, but his glance toward Sørensen was telling — a look that sought confirmation rather than permission. Sørensen gave a small nod, and that was enough.

The hours after that felt almost suspended in air. Supper was eaten in a calm that bordered on solemnity, though there was no grief in it. Emil seemed lighter somehow, speaking a little more freely, even laughing when Maria teased him about his choice of dessert. Ben watched it all without regret, though there was a faint ache in knowing the boy's ease had not come from him.

Later, Isla found Ben alone in their chamber, fastening the last clasp on his travel case. She crossed the room, resting her hands on his shoulders, feeling the quiet strength there. "You did the right thing," she told him. "You gave him what he needed, even if it wasn't you." Ben exhaled slowly, the tension in his posture easing for the first time that day. "It's still family," he said. "Just not the way I thought it would be."

Outside, the castle settled into night. In the guest wing, Emil's laughter could be heard faintly through the open door of Sørensen's quarters, Maria's voice rising in playful protest as they argued over whose turn it was to set out clothes for the morning. It was the sound of a household finding its shape, even in the midst of uncertainty. Isla listened for a moment before drawing the curtains closed.

In the end, the decision had been less about removing Emil from their care and more about placing him where he was already rooted. The days ahead would move quickly now, the departure drawing close, but Isla felt a steadiness in knowing that one piece of the puzzle had settled into place. Emil would not be lost in the shuffle of royal duties or swallowed by the shadow of the twins' arrival. He had a home, and it was exactly where he wanted to be.

Ben stood at the window, looking out into the dark, the lanterns along the path glimmering in the mist. "We leave soon," he murmured. Isla joined him, their shoulders touching, both aware that the journey ahead would carry them farther from some ties and closer to others. And somewhere down the corridor, Emil was where he belonged — not just for now, but for as long as the man he had chosen could keep the promise.

The hour had slipped well past supper, yet no one in the east wing seemed ready to settle for the night. Ben had chosen this time deliberately, when the castle was quiet enough for words to carry weight without being interrupted. He found Emil in Sørensen's quarters, sitting on the edge of the bed with his shoulders slightly hunched, as though bracing himself for a conversation he did not want to have. Sørensen stood at the far side of the room, sorting a stack of folded shirts into a case, but his eyes lifted immediately to Ben's. There was no tension between them — only an unspoken understanding of what was about to take place.

Ben stepped forward, his pace measured, his voice low. "We should talk before I leave." Emil did not look up at first, but when he did, there was no anger in his expression, only a guarded weariness. Ben sat beside him, leaving enough space to keep the moment from feeling forced. "You'll be with Sørensen from now on," he said, the words delivered with a steadiness that surprised even himself. "Not because I don't want you here, but because I want you to have the father you've already found." Emil's eyes flickered toward Sørensen at that, and something in his posture shifted.

Sørensen crossed the room then, no longer pretending to busy himself. He knelt in front of Emil, his large hands resting gently on the boy's knees. "Come here, lad," he said softly, the gravel in his voice muted by warmth. Emil hesitated for only a breath before leaning forward, and then the embrace happened — not the stiff courtesy of an adult comforting a child, but the full, closing-around-you hold of someone who meant it. Emil pressed his face into Sørensen's chest, the fabric of his shirt darkening with the sudden release of tears that had been held far too long.

It was then that Sørensen felt the trembling — small at first, then stronger, until it became a quiet, shuddering cry that shook through Emil's frame. This was not the quick sob of a scraped knee, but the deep, hollow ache of months spent unseen. Sørensen tightened his arms, holding the boy as though anchoring him to the ground itself. There were no words in those first moments, because there didn't need to be. Only the steady heartbeat under Emil's ear, and the sure weight of hands that would not let go.

Maria had been standing just inside the doorway, watching silently, her small fingers curled around the edge of the frame. When she saw Emil's head bow deeper into her father's chest, she moved forward without hesitation. Climbing onto the bed, she leaned into the embrace, her arm slipping around Emil's shoulders until they were both encircled in the same sheltering hold. She kissed him lightly on the lips, not out of habit but with intention, and when she spoke, her voice carried the weight of a vow. "You are loved," she told him.

She didn't look away when she said it, and Emil didn't either. He met her gaze, searching for any sign of insincerity, and found none. She had said it in the way children do when they have never been taught to hide the truth — plainly, without conditions. Sørensen glanced at her briefly, recognising the strength in her small frame, and then returned his attention to Emil. "I love you, son," he said, the word given without hesitation or trial period. "I always will."

Something broke in Emil then, but it was not a breaking apart — it was the crack that lets in light. His arms tightened around Sørensen's neck, his voice muffled but clear enough to cut through the air. "I love you, Dad." The title was new on his tongue, but it landed with the certainty of something that had always been there, waiting. Sørensen closed his eyes briefly, feeling the weight of it settle into his chest. "I will not ignore you, Emil," he promised. "Not now, not ever."

Ben had remained silent throughout, watching the scene with a mix of quiet pride and a faint ache in his ribs. There was no jealousy in him — only the knowledge that this was the right shape for the boy's life. He stepped forward then, placing a hand on Emil's back. "You'll still see me," he said, "and you'll still be part of this family. But Sørensen is your father now." Emil gave a small nod, but did not release his hold on the man who had just claimed him without condition.

The room felt warmer after that, as though the air itself had taken on the promise that had been spoken. Maria leaned back slightly, her arm still resting across Emil's shoulders, and grinned at her father. "We're a bigger family now," she said simply. Sørensen chuckled low in his throat, kissing the top of her head before pressing his cheek briefly to Emil's hair. "A better one too," he replied.

They remained like that for some time, not speaking, each taking their share of the quiet. Ben eventually stepped back, content to let the moment hold without rushing it toward conclusion. He knew there would be days ahead when this scene would replay in his mind, but it would not be with regret. This was not a goodbye — it was a handing over, and in that handing over, something had been mended.

Outside, the lanterns along the castle walls flickered in the wind, their light catching on the glass of the corridor windows. In the courtyard, the night watch changed shifts, boots clicking against the stone, but the sound did not reach the three figures bound together on the bed. Inside, time had been allowed to stop long enough for the boy in the middle to believe, fully and without doubt, that he was wanted.

Maria finally slid down from the bed, stretching her arms above her head and announcing she was going to make hot chocolate. Emil remained where he was, his head still resting against Sørensen's chest, but there was no tension in his posture now. "We'll have plenty of that in Kent," Sørensen told him quietly. "And we'll have the space to make it just ours." Emil's small smile at those words was the first real one Ben had seen from him in weeks.

The promise had been made, and the promise would be kept. In the days that followed, they would indeed be in Kent — the three of them, plus Casper — a smaller circle within the larger family, but no less bound. And for Emil, the castle would no longer be the place where he felt invisible. It would be the place where he had found his father.

The hour had slipped well past supper, yet no one in the east wing seemed ready to settle for the night. Ben had chosen this time deliberately, when the castle was quiet enough for words to carry weight without being interrupted. He found Emil in Sørensen's quarters, sitting on the edge of the bed with his shoulders slightly hunched, as though bracing himself for a conversation he did not want to have. Sørensen stood at the far side of the room, sorting a stack of folded shirts into a case, but his eyes lifted immediately to Ben's. There was no tension between them — only an unspoken understanding of what was about to take place.

Ben stepped forward, his pace measured, his voice low. "We should talk before I leave." Emil did not look up at first, but when he did, there was no anger in his expression, only a guarded weariness. Ben sat beside him, leaving enough space to keep the moment from feeling forced. "You'll be with Sørensen from now on," he said, the words delivered with a steadiness that surprised even himself. "Not because I don't want you here, but because I want you to have the father you've already found." Emil's eyes flickered toward Sørensen at that, and something in his posture shifted.

Sørensen crossed the room then, no longer pretending to busy himself. He knelt in front of Emil, his large hands resting gently on the boy's knees. "Come here, lad," he said softly, the gravel in his voice muted by warmth. Emil hesitated for only a breath before leaning forward, and then the embrace happened — not the stiff courtesy of an adult comforting a child, but the full, closing-around-you hold of someone who meant it. Emil pressed his face into Sørensen's chest, the fabric of his shirt darkening with the sudden release of tears that had been held far too long.

It was then that Sørensen felt the trembling — small at first, then stronger, until it became a quiet, shuddering cry that shook through Emil's frame. This was not the quick sob of a scraped knee, but the deep, hollow ache of months spent unseen. Sørensen tightened his arms, holding the boy as though anchoring him to the ground itself. There were no words in those first moments, because there didn't need to be. Only the steady heartbeat under Emil's ear, and the sure weight of hands that would not let go.

Maria had been standing just inside the doorway, watching silently, her small fingers curled around the edge of the frame. When she saw Emil's head bow deeper into her father's chest, she moved forward without hesitation. Climbing onto the bed, she leaned into the embrace, her arm slipping around Emil's shoulders until they were both encircled in the same sheltering hold. She kissed him lightly on the lips, not out of habit but with intention, and when she spoke, her voice carried the weight of a vow. "You are loved," she told him.

She didn't look away when she said it, and Emil didn't either. He met her gaze, searching for any sign of insincerity, and found none. She had said it in the way children do when they have never been taught to hide the truth — plainly, without conditions. Sørensen glanced at her briefly, recognising the strength in her small frame, and then returned his attention to Emil. "I love you, son," he said, the word given without hesitation or trial period. "I always will."

Something broke in Emil then, but it was not a breaking apart — it was the crack that lets in light. His arms tightened around Sørensen's neck, his voice muffled but clear enough to cut through the air. "I love you, Dad." The title was new on his tongue, but it landed with the certainty of something that had always been there, waiting. Sørensen closed his eyes briefly, feeling the weight of it settle into his chest. "I will not ignore you, Emil," he promised. "Not now, not ever."

Ben had remained silent throughout, watching the scene with a mix of quiet pride and a faint ache in his ribs. There was no jealousy in him — only the knowledge that this was the right shape for the boy's life. He stepped forward then, placing a hand on Emil's back. "You'll still see me," he said, "and you'll still be part of this family. But Sørensen is your father now." Emil gave a small nod, but did not release his hold on the man who had just claimed him without condition.

The room felt warmer after that, as though the air itself had taken on the promise that had been spoken. Maria leaned back slightly, her arm still resting across Emil's shoulders, and grinned at her father. "We're a bigger family now," she said simply. Sørensen chuckled low in his throat, kissing the top of her head before pressing his cheek briefly to Emil's hair. "A better one too," he replied.

They remained like that for some time, not speaking, each taking their share of the quiet. Ben eventually stepped back, content to let the moment hold without rushing it toward conclusion. He knew there would be days ahead when this scene would replay in his mind, but it would not be with regret. This was not a goodbye — it was a handing over, and in that handing over, something had been mended.

Outside, the lanterns along the castle walls flickered in the wind, their light catching on the glass of the corridor windows. In the courtyard, the night watch changed shifts, boots clicking against the stone, but the sound did not reach the three figures bound together on the bed. Inside, time had been allowed to stop long enough for the boy in the middle to believe, fully and without doubt, that he was wanted.

Maria finally slid down from the bed, stretching her arms above her head and announcing she was going to make hot chocolate. Emil remained where he was, his head still resting against Sørensen's chest, but there was no tension in his posture now. "We'll have plenty of that in Kent," Sørensen told him quietly. "And we'll have the space to make it just ours." Emil's small smile at those words was the first real one Ben had seen from him in weeks.

The promise had been made, and the promise would be kept. In the days that followed, they would indeed be in Kent — the three of them, plus Casper — a smaller circle within the larger family, but no less bound. And for Emil, the castle would no longer be the place where he felt invisible. It would be the place where he had found his Dad.

CHAPTER 10: THE ROYAL JET TO GATWICK

The first light of the morning sat low and colourless, the kind of pale dawn that did not promise warmth but instead carried the stillness of a room where everyone had already spoken their piece the night before. The castle's private tarmac stretched ahead in muted grey, empty except for the waiting jet and a single luggage cart standing idle beside it. Ben moved with steady deliberation, not hurried, yet not lingering.

Every step was measured, not for ceremony but for control, a quiet statement to anyone watching—if anyone was watching—that there was nothing unusual here. Sørensen walked a half-pace behind him, the kind of positioning that looked accidental to the untrained eye but in truth was deliberate. His right hand hovered near Maria's shoulder, his left closer to Emil, as though his children's proximity anchored him in the moment. The four of them, plus Ben, cast long, thin shadows on the cold tarmac, shadows that converged toward the aircraft's open stairway.

No one spoke of their destination. The rule had been set before dawn—conversation would be ordinary, deliberate, and absolutely uninteresting to anyone who might be near enough to overhear. Casper, carrying a satchel slung across one shoulder, said something about whether the coffee service on board would have oat milk or just cream. Maria wanted to know if the luggage had been stowed yet. Emil asked why the clouds were moving so fast.

These were questions chosen carefully, simple enough to dissolve into the air without a trace of meaning. Ben answered each of them in turn, his voice calm and without weight, even as his mind ran through the exact order of events that would follow the moment they crossed into the cabin. Sørensen's gaze never settled on any one person for long; his eyes moved from shadow to shadow, corner to corner, scanning the hangar, the service road, the airport fence in the far distance. He had been a protector too long to believe in coincidences.

The pilot stood at the base of the stairs, cap pulled low, his stance relaxed but his eyes sharp. There was no handshake, no exchange of greetings. He simply stepped aside as Ben approached, his nod brief, almost mechanical. One by one they climbed the narrow steps, the hiss of the wind across the metal the only sound beyond their footsteps. Inside, the cabin lights glowed soft gold, the scent of coffee already present, mingling with the faint leather of the seats. The attendants were there, but they kept to the far end of the aisle, silent except for the muted clink of china being set in place. This was a departure meant to leave no impression, to be forgettable even to those within it.

Ben slid into a window seat without glancing outside. He had already looked at the horizon from the ground, memorising the way the castle walls met the edge of the sky. Sørensen settled across from him, setting his children between them, his large frame blocking them from view of the aisle. Casper took the seat behind Ben, leaning forward to speak in a low tone about the flight time to Gatwick.

Maria pressed her face briefly to the glass, then sat back, her hands folded neatly in her lap. Emil tapped his fingers against the armrest in an uneven rhythm, the only sign that he was aware this was no ordinary trip. The engines began their low hum, a vibration that seemed to move through the soles of their feet, steadying them even as the weight of why they were leaving pressed in from all sides.

There were no farewells at the edge of the runway, no waving figures to shrink into the distance. The castle would not watch them go, and they would not look back. That was the agreement. The fewer who knew, the safer the path ahead would be. Ben kept his eyes forward as the aircraft began to taxi, the cabin rocking gently with the turns. Sørensen leaned slightly toward him, speaking so low that even the hum of the engines might have swallowed the words if they had not been meant for Ben alone. "We stay quiet. Even in Kent." It was not a suggestion but a confirmation of what they both already understood.

Outside, the tarmac blurred into streaks of grey and white as the engines rose to a fuller roar. Maria's hand slipped into her father's without a word, and Emil stopped tapping. Ben felt the lift in his chest a fraction before the wheels left the ground, that subtle shift when the earth lets go. The city, the castle, the watchful eyes that might still be searching—all of it fell away into the patchwork below. The clouds swallowed them, and for a moment the world was only the muted rush of air over metal, the faint clink of a cup being placed on a saucer somewhere behind him, and the silent agreement that none of them were to speak of this journey as anything more than a routine trip.

The low rumble of the engines deepened, the sound threading through the still morning air, pulling their departure into motion. Ben's gaze shifted, almost against his will, toward the castle's upper east windows. Through the narrow glass, framed by the pale stone, Isla stood cradling the twins. Even at this distance, her stillness was unmistakable—shoulders drawn back, head tilted slightly forward, the kind of posture that belonged to someone holding themselves steady for the sake of another. One of the infants moved in her arms, a faint shifting of fabric, but she did not take her eyes from the aircraft. It was as though she were memorising its outline, committing the exact cut of its wings and the gleam of its body to the same part of her mind where she kept the sound of his voice.

He could not wave. The arrangement between them left no room for gestures that could be misread by anyone watching from the grounds below. Yet his eyes held hers across the expanse, a look that carried more than any signal could. She knew what this leaving meant. It was not a severing, not a retreat in shame, but a necessary step in keeping them all beyond reach of the claws that had begun to close. Still, necessity did not soften the sharp pull in his chest, nor the quiet ache in hers. He felt it in the way her chin lifted slightly, in the still curve of her mouth that refused to tremble.

Sørensen had paused at the base of the boarding steps, his stance wide, his head turning slowly from one side to the other. Decades of guarding royalty had trained his senses to read a scene not for what was visible, but for what was missing. The absence of movement near the service building. The peculiar stillness of a fuel truck that should have already been gone. The flicker of something metallic in the shadow of a hangar wall. He stored each detail in silence, only moving when he was certain the path was clear. His hand lifted slightly toward Ben, a gesture that was part signal, part reassurance, and then he turned to usher the others forward.

Maria and Emil followed close to their father, keeping their pace even as instructed. Casper lingered a step behind Ben, his head angled toward the windows as though trying to catch a glimpse of Isla himself. Ben did not tell him to look away. There was something in that connection—Isla watching them, Casper returning the watch—that felt like a thread running through all of them, invisible yet strong. The boarding steps creaked under their weight, each sound drawn into the deep hum of the engines.

At the top, Ben paused with one hand on the doorframe. He did not look directly toward Isla again, knowing the angle would hide her from view, but his mind carried the exact image of her face, the way the morning light had struck her hair and softened the edges of her figure. That image would remain with him long after the castle itself was nothing more than a shape on the horizon. No words passed between them—none were needed. The nod they had exchanged earlier was enough, weighted with the unspoken promise that they would close this distance again.

Inside, the warmth of the cabin pressed against the cold he had carried from the tarmac. Sørensen entered last, his eyes making a final sweep across the airfield before the door sealed shut. The sound was soft, but to Ben it marked the moment the choice became irreversible. The cabin seemed smaller now, as though the air inside had thickened with the reality of the journey ahead. He settled into his seat again, hands folded loosely, eyes fixed on nothing in particular while the pilot's voice murmured a confirmation to the crew.

Through the small oval of the window, the castle's towers still rose against the morning, their pale stone catching what little light the sky offered. The east wing, where Isla stood, became a single stroke in the larger shape, and then even that distinction began to blur. He kept his gaze on it until the aircraft's angle shifted and the towers fell from sight. In their place was only the open expanse of the airfield, the grey strip of runway waiting to take them further from home.

Sørensen leaned forward slightly, his voice low but steady. "They'll guard her like their own." It was not a reassurance meant to comfort—it was a fact stated with the certainty of a man who had chosen the right people for the task. Ben gave a single nod in reply, knowing that anything more would loosen the control he had fastened around himself. The hum of the engines deepened again, signalling the final taxi toward departure.

The others settled into their seats, each occupied with the small tasks of fastening belts or adjusting blankets. Only Casper continued to glance toward the windows, his brow furrowed slightly as though unwilling to let the castle slip entirely from view. Ben did not tell him to stop. Let him look. Let him remember the way it stood this morning, unshaken, with Isla inside holding the new lives they had both brought into the world.

As the aircraft rolled forward, the airstrip stretched endlessly ahead, its edges blurred by the low-lying mist. The sense of motion came first to the body, the faint pull against the seat, and then to the eye, as the ground began to slide away beneath them. Ben exhaled once, not in relief but in acknowledgment. The separation had begun, and it would not be bridged until the time was right.

The lift, when it came, was smooth, almost without resistance. The castle did not reappear; it was already behind them, hidden by distance and the curve of the earth. In its place, the clouds thickened, closing them in a pale shroud. Ben leaned back, eyes forward now, carrying with him the final image of Isla at the window, still as the stone around her, holding their children as if they were the anchor in a storm neither of them could yet see the end of.

The jet's cabin, though fitted with the finest materials, did not feel like a space for leisure. It was a vault in the air, its walls lined not with gold but with precaution. The curtains had been drawn the moment the door sealed, and any hint of daylight that managed to slip through was quickly redirected by a fold of heavy fabric. Here, there would be no silhouettes cast against the windows for a distant lens to capture, no casual glimpses of passengers that could be enlarged and passed around by those with nothing better to do than speculate. The air was warm and dry, but the atmosphere held the crispness of discipline, as though the very space had been trained to keep its occupants alert.

Casper and Maria sat at the small table between the forward seats, their card game unfolding in silence broken only by the faint shuffle of the deck. The movements were deliberate, unhurried, their expressions unreadable. Each child understood that sound carried in unexpected ways on a flight like this. They had been raised with an awareness that travel in their family was never simply about the destination—it was about how little could be revealed along the way. Still, now and then, Maria's mouth curved in a quick, fleeting smile before she masked it again, the joy of the game leaking through despite the seriousness of their surroundings.

Emil had claimed the seat beside Sørensen and had not moved since take-off. His gaze followed every adjustment of his father's posture, every reach toward the armrest, every glance toward the curtained window. It was as though he were memorising a sequence he might one day be required to perform himself. The boy's hands rested still in his lap, but his attention was unblinking, an inheritance of focus that Sørensen recognised but did not yet acknowledge aloud.

Sørensen himself was not a man to leave anything to chance. Even here, within the confines of a controlled environment, he lifted the secure sat-phone from the side pocket and tested its encryption link. The confirmation tone came back clean—still, he ran the check again. There were no indulgences for trust in his work. When he finally slipped the phone back into the compartment, it was not out of complacency but because he had calculated the window of need and found it sufficient for now. Messages sent from here would be brief, coded, and stripped of any detail that could betray position or purpose.

Across from him, Ben sat with the slim black case resting on his knees. His hands were steady as he ran his fingers over the edge, feeling for the recessed latch. The case was unmarked—deliberately so—but to him it carried a weight far beyond its size. Inside were the documents that mattered more than any title, any crown, any gesture of recognition. Pages that traced his blood through centuries, that placed him in the direct line of houses whose names still carried force in rooms where most people were not allowed to stand. Atop those documents, wrapped in an oilskin sleeve, was the item he would not entrust to anyone else: the DNA records that proved it beyond question.

The sound of the engines filled the pauses between movements, a steady reminder that they were no longer within reach of the castle walls. Ben's eyes lifted briefly toward the drawn curtain, but he did not move to part it. The discipline was ingrained—curiosity was not worth the cost of exposure. He shifted the case slightly, feeling the reassuring resistance of its lock, and then placed it on the table between his knees. It was not something to be opened idly, even here.

Maria glanced up from her cards long enough to study the case before returning to her hand. She said nothing, but her glance was not lost on Ben. The children had seen it before, in passing, always in moments like this—between departures and arrivals, when the air seemed thicker with unspoken truths. None of them had yet asked to see inside, and he had not yet decided when that request would be met with a yes.

Casper broke the silence, his voice no louder than the whisper of a page turning. "You'll tell us again?" The question did not need clarification; Ben knew what he meant. The story, the lineage, the reason for the precautions, the shape of the life they were both shielded from and bound to. Ben gave a small nod, not immediately, but in a way that promised the answer would come before the day's end. It was not a bedtime story, not something to be told when the mind was half-asleep—it was something to be received with full attention.

Sørensen leaned back, his eyes on Ben now. "We keep to the plan. No deviations." His voice was flat, but not unkind. It was a statement, not a suggestion. Ben's gaze held his for a moment before shifting to the case again. "No deviations," he agreed, the words carrying both assent and the recognition that plans could fracture under the wrong kind of pressure. Still, this plan was sound, and every mile between here and Gatwick would be guarded by it.

The minutes stretched in the cabin, not uncomfortably, but with the measured patience of people accustomed to travel under restraint. Emil shifted slightly in his seat, leaning just close enough to his father to speak without carrying his voice across the aisle. "We'll see it?" he asked. Sørensen's hand rested briefly on his son's shoulder before returning to the armrest. "In time," he said. The answer was enough to still the boy's curiosity for now.

Ben's mind moved ahead to the next steps—the landing, the transfer to Harrison's vehicle, the narrow lanes that would carry them into the county where no one asked questions they didn't want answered. He thought of the cottage behind the old house, its timber frame still weathered but solid, the smell of the wood when the door first opened after months without use. That thought steadied him, as though the place itself were a promise of protection.

The jet banked slightly, and the change in pitch pressed the sound of the engines deeper into the walls. The children continued their game. Sørensen glanced once more toward the phone compartment, but did not reach for it. Ben closed his hands over the black case, not to open it, but to feel its weight as a reminder of what this journey was meant to secure.

Beyond the drawn curtains, clouds moved past in a silence that matched the one inside. The air was steady, the course unchanged, the miles drawing them closer to the place where old truths could rest—at least for a while—beyond the reach of those who would twist them.

Once airborne, the sensation of movement began to dissolve into something almost unreal. The steady hum of the engines blurred into a low constant, a sound that neither rose nor fell, as though the jet had slipped into a realm between worlds. Below, the landscape was reduced to soft-toned abstractions, strips of green and grey bleeding into each other until they no longer carried names or histories. For Ben, there was comfort in that anonymity; here, above the clouds, there were no castle gates, no flashing lenses, no whispered rumours in the marketplace. Yet the same anonymity carried its own danger. They were invisible to the casual observer, yes—but their flight path, masked and coded though it was, still existed in the files of a few whose trust could never be taken for granted.

Sørensen did not treat this stretch of the journey as a reprieve. His movements were subtle, but constant—a slight lean forward to check the alignment of a seatbelt buckle, the slow turn of his head to measure the position of each passenger, the shift of his weight to test the stability of his stance in mild turbulence. His vigilance was not the restless pacing of a man unnerved, but the deliberate conditioning of one who had learned that trouble often appeared where no one expected it. His eyes drifted now and then toward the storage compartments overhead, his memory ticking through the sequence of their inspection before boarding.

Maria, seated just behind him, reached forward and rested a small hand on his shoulder. It was a simple gesture, but it anchored him in a way even he did not dismiss. Sørensen glanced back long enough to meet her eyes and gave the faintest nod before returning to his silent watch. She had grown into the role of emotional compass without ever being asked, sensing when his mind needed grounding. Her touch did not distract him from his vigilance—it steadied it, reminding him that his purpose was not simply to guard against threats, but to safeguard the lives that depended on him.

The children, for their part, seemed entirely unfazed by the travel. Casper continued to shuffle his cards, Emil leaned back in his seat with arms folded, and Maria—between her quiet reassurances to her father—occasionally joined in the game when the deal passed to her. Their calm was a performance learned over years of journeys where drawing attention was not an option. The illusion of ease was as important as the reality of control, and they wore it as naturally as other children might wear excitement.

Maria had taken on another responsibility in the quiet moments between turns: ensuring her promise to Casper and Emil was kept. She moved easily between the two boys, never allowing either to feel eclipsed by the other. A hand on a shoulder here, a small smile there, an unspoken check that each felt seen. It was not a matter of fairness in her mind, but of balance; their bond as siblings—though shaped by adoption and circumstance—had to be maintained in the same way her father maintained the cabin's security. She understood, perhaps instinctively, that love was not simply declared, it was demonstrated in repetition.

Ben watched this with the faintest trace of a smile, though it never fully reached his lips. It was a private recognition, one that he allowed himself only when certain it would not be mistaken for distraction. He saw in Maria the quiet leadership that came without ceremony, and in Casper and Emil the rare gift of siblings who accepted one another without competition. It struck him that in this family, bonds were often strengthened in motion, in the liminal spaces between where they had been and where they were going.

The flight maintained its steady rhythm, but Ben's mind moved ahead to the descent, to the delicate shift from protected airspace to the watchful, if unsuspecting, ground. Each phase of travel brought with it a different calculation of exposure, and while the anonymity of altitude was a shield, it was not an unbreakable one. There were still points along the route where a well-placed camera or a persistent mind could draw lines between departure and arrival. Those lines could not be erased, only obscured, and for that, every detail had to hold.

Sørensen's gaze swept the cabin again, pausing this time on Ben. There was no exchange of words, only a mutual awareness that this part of the journey was about endurance, not action. The fewer movements, the fewer deviations, the smaller the target they became. It was a philosophy they had both learned in different arenas, one that now bound them together in purpose.

Casper's voice, low but deliberate, drew Ben's attention back to the present. "How long until we're there?" The boy asked it not out of impatience, but as a measure of time left to prepare. Ben gave him the truth without embellishment—just under two hours. The answer was met with a nod, as though Casper were ticking the information into some mental schedule of his own.

Maria leaned back into her seat, one hand still resting lightly on her father's shoulder. She did not need to look at Ben to know he had seen the way she moved between her brothers. It was enough that she had noticed his stillness when he watched them. She understood that in their world, approval was often given in the absence of correction.

Emil's gaze shifted to the curtain-drawn windows, his mind clearly tracing the unseen path below them. He had not yet learned the details of the routes, but he knew that every trip carried a logic—one that kept them safe. That logic was invisible to the untrained eye, but to those within their circle, it was as tangible as the locks on the case Ben carried.

The air in the cabin was kept cool, a deliberate measure against fatigue. Ben felt its clarity in his lungs, though he knew the weight in his chest came from elsewhere. Every mile that carried them closer to Kent was a mile further from the twins, from Isla's watchful gaze, from the fragile shield that distance itself created. It was a paradox he could not escape: safety meant separation, and separation was the one thing they had always worked to avoid.

Outside, clouds continued to drift past, their forms shifting in slow procession. The world beneath remained blurred, nameless, unclaimed in their sight. Inside, the illusion of calm held—maintained by vigilance, sustained by trust, and bound by the unspoken agreement that anonymity was both their mask and their weapon.

The pitch of the engines shifted almost imperceptibly, a subtle deepening of tone that only those accustomed to long hours in the air would notice. To Ben, it was the signal that they were leaving the anonymity of altitude and re-entering a world where every movement could be traced, measured, and—if luck faltered—followed. Beyond the drawn curtains, the faintest tilt of the cabin suggested their path angling westward, the unseen line between Denmark and England narrowing with each passing minute. His mind moved ahead of the aircraft, sketching the curve of the roads in Kent, the bend past the library's weathered brick, the lane bordered by hedges that shielded the gate to the old property.

Sørensen leaned forward in his seat, the angle of his body speaking to a shift in focus. With his voice kept low, he addressed Maria and Emil, who sat across from him with the attentive stillness of children who had learned that quiet was its own form of protection. "When we land," he began, his tone calm but carrying an unmistakable weight, "there are rules. You do not run ahead. You do not break from my side. You do not speak to anyone you do not know—no matter how friendly they appear." His eyes moved between them, ensuring the words settled not just in their hearing, but in their understanding.

Maria gave a single nod, her gaze steady. She had heard this before, in other places and under different circumstances, but repetition had never dulled its seriousness. Emil mirrored her movement, his smaller frame leaning forward slightly, as though the act of listening required his whole body. Neither child needed to be told the reasons behind these rules. They understood instinctively that their world carried layers unseen by those outside it, and that breaking a rule—even a simple one—could peel back a layer better left in place.

Casper, seated just behind them, caught Sørensen's glance and offered a faint smile of reassurance. He had already taken the same instructions to heart in earlier travels and now watched over the younger ones with the quiet authority of an elder sibling. His role was not to speak for them, but to make sure the shape of the rules stayed intact when Sørensen's eyes were elsewhere.

Ben, watching the exchange from his seat, felt the familiar tightening in his chest that came with this final approach. The coastline ahead was not yet visible, but he could feel its presence in the steady change of the cabin's rhythm. Soon, the anonymity of flight would give way to the exposure of arrival. Even here, with every precaution in place, there was no such thing as complete invisibility. They would be seen, even if only in passing, and every glance had the potential to linger in the wrong memory.

The hum of the engines deepened further, and Ben imagined the Channel waters below—grey, restless, and cold under a March wind. Somewhere beneath those waves ran the invisible boundary between the world he had left that morning and the one he was returning to now. It was not simply a change in geography; it was the crossing from one version of himself to another. In Denmark, he was King in silence. Here, he was the boy from Kent who had once vanished and now returned under the cover of necessity.

Sørensen, satisfied with the children's attention, sat back but did not relax. His gaze swept the length of the cabin once more, his hand brushing against the secure sat-phone as if to confirm its presence. The descent checklist would be brief, but his mental preparations were longer. He was entering a land where his authority carried no formal weight, but where his loyalty to Ben carried all the force of a sworn oath. That was enough to keep his senses sharpened.

Maria, still seated opposite her father, reached for Emil's hand. It was not a gesture born of fear but of solidarity—a silent pact between siblings that whatever lay beyond the aircraft's door, they would face it as they always had: together, in step, without hesitation. Emil's grip tightened in return, his small fingers curling with surprising firmness around hers.

Ben's eyes shifted to the slim black case resting beside him. Inside, the documents and DNA records lay precisely as he had packed them—untouched since their inspection before departure. He had carried them across borders before, but never with the same awareness that the truths they contained might soon need to be wielded, not merely preserved. This journey was not simply about refuge. It was about readiness.

The flight attendants, trained to move without drawing notice, began securing the cabin. Each latch, each checked buckle, each whispered reminder to remain seated formed part of a choreography designed to appear routine. The more ordinary their arrival looked, the more easily it would be swallowed by the day's greater noise.

Casper leaned slightly toward the window, though the curtain allowed only the faintest sliver of grey light to pass through. He seemed to take comfort in knowing the ground was near, even if he could not yet see it. For him, England was a place of familiarity, of remembered streets and voices. For Ben, it was that and something more: the ground where truths had once been uncovered, and where—if pushed—more could be revealed.

As the jet began its gradual drop through the cloud layer, the cabin's light shifted. The muted daylight filtered in with a different weight now, thicker, tinged with the hue of sea and shore. In that change, there was an unspoken recognition among them: the crossing was nearly complete. Soon, the routines of flight would end, and the rules of the ground would take hold.

Sørensen's voice, calm but edged with finality, broke the silence one last time. "When the wheels touch down," he said, looking directly at each of the children in turn, "you follow me. No questions. No exceptions." The nods he received were not hurried, not distracted—they were deliberate, the silent acknowledgment that the crossing of the Channel was not simply a journey, but a shift into a different kind of vigilance.

The wheels met the tarmac with a muted thrum, a smoothness that might have gone unnoticed by anyone not counting the seconds to arrival. For Ben, the moment carried a weight far beyond the mechanics of descent. It was the quiet confirmation that the first part of the plan had held—no delays, no unexpected company in the sky, no last-minute diversions. Yet the landing was not relief. It was the opening move of a controlled retreat, and the very act of stepping onto English soil meant entering a field where every sound, every shadow, and every glance could matter.

The pilot, professional and wordless, guided the jet away from the central bustle of the main terminal. The aircraft rolled along the outer taxiway, past service trucks and fuel lines, until the private terminal came into view—a cluster of low buildings set apart, discreet but hardly invisible. Instead of pulling toward the obvious entry, the jet angled toward the farthest edge of the compound, where a black vehicle waited under the washed-out light of a clouded afternoon.

Harrison stood beside it, the open space around him giving no shelter but making any approach immediately visible. His posture, to the untrained eye, could have passed for casual— one hand in his coat pocket, the other resting on the vehicle's roof—but the slow, precise sweep of his gaze over the perimeter betrayed the same brand of vigilance Sørensen carried. He was not waiting idly. He was measuring the air, the lines of sight, and the small movements at the far edges of the scene.

The aircraft slowed to a halt, its engines settling into a steady idle. No service crew appeared, no luggage carts approached. The absence was deliberate, arranged ahead of time so that the jet could be unloaded without curious eyes or wandering questions. Even at airports, people noticed when something broke the rhythm of the ordinary. The key was to make the arrival look like something too mundane to bother watching.

Sørensen rose first, checking the cabin's exit before signalling to the others. His children followed his movement with instinctive precision, stepping into place without the need for verbal instruction. Ben gathered the black case from beside his seat, the motion fluid and practised, the handle gripped not just for possession but for control. It was the one item he would not entrust to anyone else—not here, not now, not ever.

As they stepped down the narrow boarding stairs, the cool English air wrapped around them, damp and carrying the faint tang of jet fuel. Ben resisted the urge to look toward the terminal windows. Even if they were too far for anyone to make out his face, he had no interest in leaving traces for someone to piece together later. His eyes stayed on the car, on Harrison, and on the small stretch of ground between the aircraft and the safety of closed doors.

Harrison's greeting, when they reached him, was not a handshake or an embrace. It was a single, almost imperceptible nod, the kind exchanged between men who understood the value of conserving words. He opened the rear door with one hand while his other motioned Sørensen to move his family in first. There would be time for formalities later, but not here, not while the air still held the echo of the engines.

The luggage followed in a single, efficient sequence—two cases lifted directly from the hold by Sørensen himself, another by Harrison, and the remainder by Ben and Casper. No one called for help. No one broke the rhythm with unnecessary movement. What came out of the jet went straight into the vehicle, the transition so seamless it could have been mistaken for a well-rehearsed drill.

Once the last bag was stowed, Harrison closed the boot and gave a brief glance toward the pilot. The man in the cockpit returned the look with a short dip of his head before beginning the process of turning the aircraft for departure. That was another layer of the arrangement—the jet would not remain on the ground any longer than absolutely necessary. Lingering in one place only invited questions.

Inside the vehicle, the air was warm, the scent faintly of leather and something sharper—Harrison's choice of aftershave, unchanged since Ben's earliest memories of him. Ben slid in beside Sørensen's children, keeping the black case on his lap, his eyes still scanning the glass for movement beyond. Harrison took the driver's seat without a word, checking the mirrors not once but twice before shifting into gear.

The tyres rolled across the narrow service lane that led away from the terminal, bypassing the usual checkpoints entirely. Every turn had been planned, every clearance granted hours earlier under discreet codes known only to the few involved. Still, Harrison's gaze flicked to the rearview mirror at every stretch of open road, as if daring anyone to follow.

Sørensen, seated in the front passenger seat, finally allowed himself to settle back, though his hand remained near the inside pocket where his documents and sidearm rested. His eyes met Harrison's briefly in a silent exchange of acknowledgement. Different roles, same responsibility.

For Ben, the act of leaving the airfield was not victory—it was merely the passing of one threshold to the next. Here, on these familiar roads, the stakes did not diminish. They changed shape, trading the anonymity of strangers for the scrutiny of those who might think they knew him. The county was close now, but closeness did not mean safety.

The black vehicle merged onto the outer road, the airport falling away behind them, swallowed by the grey horizon. Harrison's voice came at last, low and even, cutting through the silence. "We keep to the back roads," he said, eyes still forward. "Less chance of being noticed. And if anyone asks, you were never here." Ben did not need to answer. The truth of it was already understood.

Harrison stepped forward from the shadow of the black vehicle, his pace unhurried but deliberate, every movement measured as if the space between them were a final checkpoint. The damp air clung to his coat, carrying the muted hum of distant engines, yet his eyes stayed fixed on Ben with the same level scrutiny he had given him when Ben was barely taller than the wheel arch of his old Land Rover. There was no rush toward embrace, no exaggerated display of reunion. Instead, the moment distilled into a single clasp—Harrison's hand closing firmly over Ben's, not as a greeting to be witnessed but as a confirmation that they were exactly where they had planned to be, and that both understood the stakes without speaking them aloud.

The grip was unshakable, steady but not theatrical, the kind of handshake that locked more than palms. It was a transaction of trust, an acknowledgment that the same man who had guarded Ben's anonymity for decades was now guarding his passage. Harrison had always been economical with gestures, preferring the plain weight of reliability over any outward show. Ben returned the clasp in equal measure, a signal that neither time nor distance had diluted what they had built together—an alliance born in the quiet spaces of Kent, far from courtrooms and councils, when a young boy with unasked questions found his first true confidant.

Sørensen observed from a pace behind, his gaze shifting between the two men with a soldier's instinct to read body language before words. He noted the lack of hesitation in either movement, the way both seemed to occupy the same rhythm without needing to agree upon it first. This was not the polite civility of acquaintances. It was the calm exchange of men who had rehearsed loyalty over years, long before the current urgency. In his silence, Sørensen granted his approval—not as a man handing over responsibility, but as one recognising that it had never been in doubt.

Their words came only after the clasp released, each syllable pared down to its function. "Back roads," Harrison said, eyes flicking toward the distant line of the service road. "Gateside by dusk. No detours." Ben gave a single nod, his reply equally clipped. "Documents are ready. Black case stays with me." There was no elaboration, no pleasantries inserted to soften the exchange. The language of their meeting was the same as it had always been—direct, unornamented, and designed to leave no trail in memory beyond the essential facts.

It was this economy of language that had made Harrison such a fixture in Ben's guarded history. When Ben was a boy of four, still piecing together fragments of truth about his life, Harrison had been twenty-seven, already seasoned by the kind of quiet responsibilities that left no medals and no public recognition. In those early years, Harrison had been the one to teach him which questions could be asked aloud and which must be locked away until the right ears could hear them. That discipline had not faded with time; if anything, it had sharpened into a tool as valuable as any map or code.

Maria and Emil stood near the open door of the vehicle, their eyes shifting between the men as if catching the shape of a ritual they didn't fully understand but instinctively respected. Casper, kept still and let the exchange run its course. Harrison's gaze swept over them briefly, assessing without intruding, before returning to Ben as if to confirm that their presence was not only known but accounted for in the plan ahead.

Sørensen's approval was not given lightly, yet here it came in the form of a small nod, almost imperceptible but enough for Harrison to register. It was an unspoken clearance between two men who understood the thin margin between caution and overreach. Both were guardians in their own right—one by blood-tied loyalty, the other by a lifetime of earned trust—and in this moment, their responsibilities overlapped without conflict.

The air between them held the unbroken thread of years past. Ben remembered afternoons in Kent when Harrison's guidance came not in long speeches but in the quiet demonstration of how to remain unnoticed—how to enter a room without shifting the air, how to leave without leaving a shadow. Those lessons now informed every step of their movement, and in this handshake, those years compressed into the present, informing each choice they would make from this point forward.

Harrison was not a man who lingered over introductions. Once the essentials were spoken, he gestured toward the open rear door of the vehicle, his arm moving in a way that balanced courtesy with urgency. Ben moved toward it without hesitation, the black case still in his grasp, knowing that the sooner they were inside, the sooner the controlled part of their retreat could resume. The handshake had been enough; the rest would be carried in the road ahead.

In the final glance before stepping in, Ben caught the faintest trace of a smile on Harrison's face—not one meant for comfort, but the kind that acknowledged the scale of what they were undertaking. It was as if Harrison were saying, without saying at all, that the weight of this journey was not Ben's alone to carry. Sørensen noticed it too, though he kept his thoughts to himself, allowing the moment to pass into the quiet rhythm of departure.

When Harrison closed the door behind them, it was with a sound that felt almost ceremonial—the dull click of metal that sealed them away from the open air and any prying eyes that might have lingered at the edges of the terminal. The handshake had done its work; the rest was now in motion.

The hum of the tyres against the damp tarmac was steady, a low rhythm that threaded through the quiet of the vehicle's interior. Harrison's hands rested with ease on the wheel, but Ben knew the calm was deceptive; each turn, each downshift, was calculated, chosen for its ability to keep them unseen. The road unfurled ahead in a narrow ribbon, lined with hedgerows so thick they seemed to hold the darkness in place. Even without looking, Harrison knew each curve, each hidden junction. It was not the efficiency of a navigator, but the instinct of a man whose memory of these routes had been sharpened over decades.

From the rear seat, Ben allowed his gaze to drift beyond the glass, letting familiar shapes rise from the night. The skeletal outline of an old oak stood where it always had, its branches still arching over the lane like the frame of an unspoken welcome. He remembered walking this stretch as a boy, carrying books too heavy for his small arms, the air always heavy with the scent of wet earth. Now, those same scents drifted faintly through the sealed cabin whenever Harrison lowered a window at a bend. Sørensen sat beside him, silent but watchful, his eyes occasionally cutting to the side mirrors, checking for lights that did not belong.

The villages slipped by in near silence. Here and there, a lamplight glowed behind curtained windows, casting amber pools on stone walls that had stood since before any of them were born. Ben caught the shapes of old shopfronts—some boarded, some brightened with fresh paint—and felt the strange compression of time, how the streets could remain and yet be utterly altered. He traced the bend of each corner as though testing his own memory against reality, and in most cases, the match was exact. The years had not erased this place; they had only worn its edges smooth.

Harrison drove as though the road itself were an ally. He slowed before blind turns not out of caution, but because he knew precisely where they lay. He skirted the main road into town, diverting instead through a narrow lane that ran between two rows of cottages. Here, the hedges brushed close enough to the windows that Ben could have reached out and touched them if the glass were down. These were not roads for strangers, nor for those in a hurry; they were the old veins of Kent, carrying life where the world was least inclined to look.

In the dim light of the dashboard, Sørensen's profile was cut in clean lines, his posture relaxed yet anchored. His children were a contrast to his stillness. Maria leaned lightly against Emil, her head tilted just enough that her hair brushed his shoulder. Casper sat opposite them, his eyes half-lidded, though Ben suspected he was more awake than he let on. Travel had its own rhythm, and the children had learned it early—when to talk, when to sleep, and when to let the grown-ups hold the silence.

Ben's eyes moved to the right, tracing the low stone wall that marked the edge of the lane. Beyond it, fields stretched toward the horizon, their boundaries lost to shadow. Once, he had run across those fields, feeling the ground soften underfoot after rain, the smell of crushed grass heavy in his lungs. The image flickered and then gave way to the present—the hum of the engine, the muted creak of the suspension as Harrison took another turn. There was comfort in the continuity of place, even when the man returning to it was no longer the boy who had left.

Occasionally, a car would pass in the opposite direction, its headlights sweeping momentarily across the interior of their own vehicle before vanishing into the dark. Harrison's gaze never followed them for long. He kept his attention forward, measuring distance not by miles but by instinct. He knew how many turns lay between them and the safety of the cottage, how many seconds each junction should take. His driving was an exercise in precision, as if the roads themselves had been designed for this kind of passage.

The air inside the car was warm, but not stifling. The faint scent of coffee lingered from the flask Sørensen had brought aboard the jet, mingling with the subtle trace of leather from the seats. It was the kind of environment meant to dull the sense of movement, to make the journey feel less like an escape and more like a return. Ben leaned back slightly, his hand resting on the black case at his side. He did not grip it tightly, but he never let it leave his reach.

Every so often, Harrison would offer a short update without taking his eyes from the road. "Two miles to the turn," or "Railway crossing ahead." These fragments broke the silence without disrupting it, markers in a journey where too much conversation could draw attention to the wrong things. Ben responded with brief acknowledgements, his voice low enough that it barely carried beyond the front seats. The children, half-asleep, did not stir.

The deeper they moved into Kent, the more the roads seemed to fold inward, narrowing between hedges and walls until the outside world was reduced to a corridor of green and stone. Ben knew they were close when he saw the faint outline of the church spire in the distance—not as a landmark to approach, but as a marker to avoid. Harrison turned away from it without hesitation, steering them toward a road that no map would have considered the most direct.

Sørensen shifted slightly, adjusting his seat so he could see ahead more clearly. His watch ticked softly in the quiet, each second a reminder that their arrival was approaching. He knew, as Ben did, that these final minutes were the most vulnerable. If someone had followed them from Gatwick, this was where they would choose to close the distance. Yet the road behind them remained empty, their only companions the pale streak of sunlight and the hum of the engine.

A familiar bend appeared, the kind that tilted the car just enough to signal the change in terrain. Beyond it lay the last stretch before the property. Ben recognised the curve instantly, his memory supplying the feel of cycling around it as a boy, the tyres skidding just slightly on loose gravel. Now, the same bend felt like a threshold, one that divided the long miles of travel from the sanctuary ahead.

The hedgerows began to part, revealing the faint outline of a gate in the distance. Harrison slowed, the vehicle gliding forward with the same controlled pace it had carried all along. No words were needed; everyone in the car understood that they were at the edge of something both known and guarded. The cottage lay just beyond, unseen for now, but waiting in the same silence that had accompanied them from the start.

The approach to the old property came with a gradual slowing, as if the very air in this part of Kent required a gentler pace. Harrison guided the vehicle off the main road, tyres crunching softly over the thin layer of gravel that marked the start of the drive. Ahead, the outline of the house emerged from the sunset, its warm brickwork catching the faint spill of the headlights. Time had left its mark in softened edges and weathered tones, yet the structure stood with the quiet dignity of something built to endure. Ben felt the familiar tightening in his chest, not of fear but of recognition, as though the walls themselves might remember him.

The gardens lay trimmed and ordered, every hedge shaped, every bed free of weeds. The caretaker's hand was evident in the precision, but also in the restraint—nothing overdone, nothing too proud. It was care without vanity, the kind that tended to a place for the sake of preservation rather than display. Even at dusk, Ben could see the paths laid in clean lines across the lawn, their edges defined by pale stones that caught the passing light. The air here smelled of damp earth and clipped grass, the scents exactly as he remembered from boyhood summers.

Beyond the house, the faint shape of the cottage waited, half-hidden behind the screen of trees. The thick trunks and dense branches acted as a natural barrier, a shield against the view from the road. It was a clever arrangement, one that had kept the smaller building out of casual sight for generations. Ben knew its rooms by memory—the creak of the floor near the kitchen door, the narrow staircase that turned twice before opening onto the upper landing. That cottage had been his sanctuary once, and now it would be again, at least for as long as the world could be kept at bay.

Harrison eased the car to a stop just shy of the main house's front steps, choosing a position where the vehicle could be turned quickly if needed. Sørensen was already moving before the engine had gone quiet, his door opening in one swift motion. He stepped out with the measured precision of a man who knew every second mattered, his eyes scanning the perimeter in slow, deliberate sweeps. The faint crunch of his boots on the gravel was the only sound as he moved toward the treeline, checking the slightly dark spaces between the hedges and the gate.

Inside the car, the others waited without prompting. Years of travel under Sørensen's watch had taught them the unspoken rule: no one moves until given the word. Emil leaned forward slightly, watching his father's figure pass in and out of shadow. Maria sat back, her gaze fixed on the cottage beyond the trees, though she said nothing. Casper shifted once, then stilled, his hands resting loosely on his knees. The atmosphere held a quiet tension, not born of fear but of readiness.

Sørensen's return was as wordless as his departure. He opened the rear passenger door, standing back just enough for Ben to step out first. The air outside was cooler than it had been on the road, carrying the faint hint of rain. Ben's shoes met the gravel with a muted crunch, the sound oddly grounding after hours of muted cabin noise. He looked up at the house again, this time seeing it not just as it was, but as it had been—the summer evenings with windows open, the scent of baking drifting out from the kitchen, the sound of a clock ticking somewhere deep inside.

The front door remained closed, but light glowed faintly through the edges of the curtains. The caretaker had prepared the space, leaving a welcome that was understated but unmistakable. Harrison joined Ben on the gravel, his voice low as he gave a brief report on the property. "Caretaker's been in every week. No signs of anyone near the cottage." It was said without embellishment, but the reassurance was clear. Ben nodded once, acknowledging the information without comment.

Maria and Emil followed, their steps soft, instinctively matching the mood of the place. Emil glanced toward the trees, trying to catch a better view of the cottage, but the dense foliage allowed only the suggestion of its outline. Maria kept her eyes on the path ahead, her attention split between her footing and the shifting expressions on her father's face. Casper came last, moving with the steady, deliberate pace that Sørensen insisted upon whenever they were in a new—or in this case, renewed—setting.

The gravel path curved away from the main house toward the gate that led into the cottage's enclosure. Here, the air seemed heavier, the quiet deeper. It was not the silence of neglect, but of protection, the kind that absorbed sound and movement rather than letting them escape. Ben felt the familiar pull of that space, remembering the times he had come here as a boy to escape the noise of the larger house. Now, it would serve a different purpose, though the comfort it offered was the same.

Sørensen moved ahead, unlocking the gate with a key that turned smoothly, proof that the caretaker had kept it in use. The hinges made only the faintest sound as the gate swung open, revealing the narrow path that ran between the trees to the cottage door. For a moment, no one spoke, as though crossing that threshold required a pause in acknowledgment of what it meant to be here again. Then Harrison gestured for them to move, and the small procession began down the path.

Ben's eyes adjusted quickly to the dim light beneath the branches. The ground here was firm, the path well kept despite the shield of trees above. Small details came back to him—the smooth stone by the step where he used to sit, the narrow window in the upper gable that caught the morning sun. It was all still here, unchanged and waiting, as if the years since his last visit had been a mere handful of days. At the door, Sørensen paused once more.

The key turned without resistance, the tumblers aligning with the same easy precision they had years before. When the door swung inward, a cool breath of air drifted out, carrying with it the faint mingling of cedar and stone. It was a scent both grounding and ancient, the kind that seemed to belong to the walls themselves rather than to any single object inside. Ben paused at the threshold, taking in the stillness before stepping forward. Behind him, Sørensen waited, his posture as controlled as if entering a secure post. Harrison held back with the children, giving Ben the first right to cross into the space that had once been his own.

The interior offered no surprises, yet that in itself was startling. The worn wooden floors still bore the same scuffs in the same places, each one a small record of movement long past. To the left, the small hearth gave off a steady glow, its fire already lit in quiet welcome. The warmth reached into the room in slow, deliberate waves, as if easing the chill from the long journey. Harrison had seen to it that the flame burned clean and steady, the wood stacked neatly to the side in readiness for the days ahead. The air within the room felt settled, as though it had been waiting for a specific moment and now recognised that it had arrived.

Books lined the shelves in a familiar, almost defiant order. Their spines showed the wear of years but stood upright, unbowed, as if preserving not just words but the very shape of Ben's younger self who had once pulled them down to read by the lamplight. He could picture himself seated at the old oak table in the corner, a lamp casting its pool of light over pages, the sound of wind against the windows beyond. Here, memory and present overlapped so neatly that for a moment, the gap between them seemed irrelevant. Sørensen moved past without slowing, beginning the sweep that would take him through each room in turn.

The inspection was deliberate, without a wasted step. Sørensen entered the small kitchen first, checking the latch on the back door, the hinges on the windows, and the placement of the curtains. He opened cupboards not for their contents but for signs that someone else might have been there—an object out of place, a jar set at the wrong angle. Satisfied, he moved toward the sitting room, testing the weight of the floorboards as he went. Harrison leaned casually against the doorframe, but his eyes followed Sørensen's every move, alert to any unspoken cue.

Ben crossed to the small alcove where a table had been set with deliberate simplicity. At its centre stood the Braun Coffee Percolator, its chrome catching the firelight in muted gleams. Beside it, the sealed bag of coffee grounds gave off a faint aroma through the packaging, rich and unspoiled. A small tin of powdered creamer sat unopened, the seal intact, a sign that Harrison had chosen items that would keep without refrigeration. The precision of this readiness was not lost on Ben; in such matters, the smallest oversights could become the sharpest liabilities.

In the adjoining hallway, the creak of a floorboard signalled Sørensen's return from the first room check. He stepped into view and gave a short nod, neither rushed nor hesitant. "Clear," he said, his tone the kind that closed a subject rather than invited further discussion. He moved toward the narrow staircase without waiting for acknowledgment, the boards carrying his weight in a steady rhythm. Maria stood with her back to the wall, watching him pass, while Emil peered up the staircase as if trying to guess what lay beyond.

The second floor held no more complexity than the first. Four small bedrooms, each with a double bed neatly made, their blankets pulled tight, the corners folded with a precision that spoke of disciplined hands. And one bathroom. Sørensen opened each window briefly to test the hinges and ensure no swelling in the wood had made them stick. He ran his palm along the frames, as if reading the grain for hidden flaws. When he returned, it was without haste, but with the quiet assurance of a man satisfied with his work.

Ben, still by the hearth, poured water into the percolator's reservoir, measuring it with the familiarity of habit. The act was unremarkable in itself, yet it carried the weight of normalcy—a deliberate choice to engage with something mundane, even in the midst of caution. The soft hum of the percolator soon joined the room's sounds, blending with the low crackle of the fire. Maria drifted closer, drawn by the smell of coffee beginning to rise, her steps as quiet as if she were afraid to disrupt the atmosphere.

Outside the windows, the trees stood in unmoving ranks, their branches holding the stillness of a night that had not yet surrendered to wind. Harrison stepped to one of the panes, checking the angle of the curtains to ensure nothing of the interior was visible from the lane beyond. "We'll need to keep these drawn," he said quietly, without turning. His voice was neither warning nor suggestion, but the stating of a fact. Ben gave a brief nod, eyes still on the fire.

Casper, who had lingered by the doorway since entering, finally stepped inside fully, his gaze travelling along the bookshelves before settling on the table. He took the seat opposite the percolator, resting his arms on the surface without speaking. There was no impatience in his manner, only the stillness of someone who understood that arrivals were not complete until the space was claimed in more than just presence. Sørensen returned to stand behind him, one hand on the back of the chair, his stance relaxed but his eyes still active.

When the coffee was ready, Ben poured it into two cups, the first for Sørensen, the second for Harrison. Neither man needed sugar, and the creamer stayed in its tin. The first sip was taken in silence, the heat of the drink carrying an unspoken reassurance through the room. It was a ritual that confirmed the space as theirs again—not through ownership, but through use. The walls seemed to settle further with each quiet exchange, the fire holding its steady glow.

In the kitchen, Maria found a fresh extra large pizza on the counter with a note, likely left by the caretaker to Harrison. For our buddy Benedict, with love, Adrian. Maria lifted the slices carefully. Emil fetched plates without being asked, setting them on the table beside the cups. The meal was simple as it was complete. No one spoke of the road ahead or the reason for their arrival. This was the moment for grounding, not planning.

Sørensen, at last, allowed himself to lean back in his chair. His eyes softened, though his posture remained disciplined. "Secure," he repeated quietly, as if the word itself had weight enough to hold the walls in place. Harrison glanced toward Ben, and for the first time since Gatwick, the faintest curve of a smile crossed his face. It was not relief exactly, but recognition—a shared understanding that this was the safest they would be for now.

Ben took in the room once more, his gaze tracing the lines of shelves, the curve of the hearth, the simple table with its modest meal. Nothing here had changed, and that was the gift. In a world that had shifted beneath his feet more times than he could count, this place had remained fixed, unshaken. The thought anchored him in a way no fortress or title could. Here, he was not the figure the press wanted to chase, nor the name the dynasties feared. Here, he was simply home.

The morning air held the faint dampness of the Kent countryside, the sort that clung to the skin without chill. Harrison kept to Ben's right as they followed the narrow path toward the village, their steps measured and unhurried, each movement calculated to draw no notice. The hour was early enough that only the milkman's van rolled through the lanes, and even he passed without more than a nod. Ben carried nothing in his hands, his coat buttoned to the top, the collar turned against a breeze that had begun to stir. Ahead, the library's modest brick front emerged between hedgerows, unchanged in its proportions, its door still painted the deep green of his memory.

Harrison reached the door first, pausing only to glance down the street before stepping aside for Ben to enter. The scent inside was precisely as it had been years before—a mixture of paper, polished wood, and the faint sweetness of beeswax on the floors. Light fell through high windows in narrow shafts, touching the dust motes in slow spirals. The librarian stood behind the counter, arranging returns in neat stacks, her hands moving with the economy of someone who had performed this ritual for decades. When she looked up, her eyes settled on Ben with the steadiness of recognition, though her expression betrayed no surprise.

She did not speak his name. Instead, she closed the ledger gently, as if marking the end of a page, and came forward without haste. There was no handshake, no outward sign of greeting that could be misread by a passing witness. Her voice, when it came, was warm but even. "Do you still read the history shelves in the back corner?" she asked, as though the last fifteen years had been no more than an afternoon's gap. The words landed with quiet precision, a kindness layered with intent. It was not merely a question—it was a declaration that here, nothing had altered, and no story would be told beyond these walls.

Ben allowed the faintest lift at the corner of his mouth, an answer without formality. "I do," he replied, the syllables low enough to remain between them. Harrison moved toward the periodicals rack, his posture casual but his attention fixed on the room. The librarian gestured toward the far corner, her hand passing over the worn spines of books that had been there longer than either of them would admit aloud. Ben followed, feeling the slight give of the floorboards he had once crossed so many times in younger years, each one carrying him deeper into a space untouched by the noise of the world outside.

The history corner looked as it always had: narrow shelves packed tightly with hardbacks, their faded jackets showing the wear of many readings. A single table stood beside the window, its surface marked with the faint impressions of old ink and the press of elbows leaning over maps. Ben let his fingers trace along the familiar line of titles—chronicles of royal houses, naval histories, the endless volumes of county records. It was here, at this very table, that he had first found the trail of his own lineage, piecing together names from half-forgotten registries. The memory settled over him like a well-worn coat.

From her post at the desk, the librarian returned to her work without looking over again, her restraint as deliberate as her welcome had been. She had always known when to allow quiet to stand unbroken, and now was no exception. Harrison, having satisfied himself with a slow circuit of the room, stopped near the door to the corner alcove, giving Ben the space to move freely yet never stepping so far that the distance could not be closed in an instant. The weight of their unspoken understanding was a constant presence, an invisible line holding the room in balance.

Ben drew a single volume from the shelf—its binding loose, the lettering on the spine nearly erased. He set it on the table, opening it to the map that had once captured his attention for hours on end. It showed the old boundaries of the county, the divisions of land and title that had long since been redrawn. His thumb rested on the name that had first stirred suspicion in him as a boy, the one link that had led him into the web of discovery. Harrison, from where he stood, saw the map but asked nothing.

The librarian's movements were soundless now, her presence almost absorbed into the stillness. She knew better than to intrude on the weight of memory. Her earlier question had been enough, a simple recognition offered without prying. In this place, words were never currency to be spent carelessly. Ben closed the book after a few moments, sliding it back into its space with the care of one returning a trusted tool.

When he returned to the counter, she met his gaze directly. "They're just where you left them," she said quietly, meaning far more than the arrangement of books. He inclined his head, accepting the statement without answer. Harrison opened the door, letting in a slice of morning light that fell across the wooden floor.

They stepped outside together, the air cooler than when they had entered, as if the village itself wished to keep them moving. Behind them, the door closed with its familiar latch, the sound a promise that nothing of this encounter would find its way into any other ear. The library, like the woman who kept it, would remain what it had always been: a keeper of silence, and of truths too valuable to be shared without consent.

Ben did not look back as they walked toward the cottage, but he carried the certainty that in this one corner of the world, his past was safe. In a time when every movement could be catalogued, analysed, and turned into speculation, the librarian's memory was not a threat—it was a shield. And for now, that was enough.

The cottage might have been modest in size, but to Sørensen it was a fortress in miniature. Each morning began the same way: curtains drawn back just far enough to give him a clear view of the lane without revealing movement inside, his gaze sweeping from hedge to gatepost, lingering on every car that passed. He stood in silence as the village stirred, committing each sound to memory—the metallic clatter of the milk van, the measured pace of a postman on the gravel, the distant whine of a tractor starting in a far field. These were harmless noises now, but Sørensen's mind worked in contingencies, always considering what they might mask. To him, safety was not a reaction to danger; it was a structure built brick by brick, in the quiet moments before threat became visible.

The children had learned, without instruction, to move within that structure. Maria and Emil understood that games never carried them beyond the garden wall, and that voices carried farther than they thought in the still air. Even their laughter—bright as it was—seemed to fall into an unspoken rhythm, softening when they sensed his attention turning toward them. He never barked orders, nor did he hover; his presence was enough, a silent signal that boundaries existed and would be enforced without debate. Ben watched from time to time, recognising the discipline in Sørensen's methods. It was not the cold discipline of fear, but the ordered calm of a man who had spent his life making certain that those under his care reached the end of each day unscathed.

Every window in the cottage had been assessed by the second morning. Sørensen moved through each room with the patience of someone repairing a clock, noting the angles of view, the height from the ground, and the points from which an unseen approach could be made. He measured these in his head, as naturally as another man might recall the distance from door to stove. Escape routes were mapped not in panic but in preparation, each one rehearsed quietly in his mind. Even the children's sleeping quarters were considered—two points of exit, one direct and one concealed, because in his experience, the second path was often the one that saved lives.

Ben understood the necessity of this vigilance, though it contrasted sharply with the stillness he sought in Kent. He had come here for the anonymity the village afforded, yet he knew that anonymity could be shattered in seconds if someone chose to look too closely. Sørensen's watchfulness allowed him to move through his own tasks—visiting the library, walking the familiar roads—without the weight of constant self-surveillance. It was a division of labour born from trust: Ben would remain the visible man, Sørensen the unseen guard. In that balance, they found a way to breathe.

It was not unusual to find Sørensen standing in the garden long after dusk, his posture easy but his eyes tracking every flicker of movement beyond the hedge. Lights in the neighbouring cottages were catalogued, their patterns noted: when they came on, when they went dark, when they stayed burning later than usual. The habits of others mattered to him, for any change in rhythm could mean something had shifted in the wider circle of safety. He stored these observations as another man might keep ledgers, each entry precise, ready to be recalled without hesitation.

The children, for all their youth, were never excluded from this quiet schooling. Maria had inherited her father's sharpness of eye, often pointing out the make and colour of vehicles that passed more than once in a day. Emil, younger but equally observant, learned to distinguish between the idle curiosity of passersby and the lingering glance that suggested something more deliberate. Sørensen did not praise these observations overtly; he simply acknowledged them with a small nod, as though they were no more than part of the natural order.

Inside, his vigilance was subtler but no less thorough. Every latch was tested, every hinge listened to, every lock turned twice before night fell. The children knew not to touch the doors without permission after dusk, not because they feared what lay outside, but because they respected the ritual. Even the small act of closing curtains was performed with deliberate care, making certain no shape or shadow could be traced from the lane. It was in these details that Sørensen believed safety was maintained—not through force, but through the discipline of habit.

Ben, watching all of this, found himself recalling their earliest years together, when Sørensen had been chief of security at the castle. Back then, his manner had been harder, the lines of command more sharply drawn. Yet here in Kent, the hardness had softened into something more enduring: a quiet guardianship that asked for no thanks and drew no attention to itself. He was no less formidable now than he had been in those early days; the difference lay in how his vigilance wove itself into the life of the household without disturbing its rhythms.

Harrison, too, recognised the value of Sørensen's methods. On his visits to the cottage, he would exchange only the briefest of notes on local movement—vehicles that didn't belong, strangers lingering too long in the village shop—before leaving the rest to him. There was no overlap, no question of who held responsibility in which space. In that unspoken division, there was efficiency, and in efficiency, there was security.

As the days passed, Sørensen's vigilance never slackened. Even in moments of quiet—when coffee steamed gently in the percolator, or when Maria read aloud from one of Ben's old books—his eyes would flick toward the window at the faintest noise. It was not a paranoia that ruled him, but the lived understanding that peace was something you guarded, not something you assumed. In his world, the measure of safety was not in the absence of threat, but in the readiness to meet it before it could touch the people you loved.

And love, though he rarely spoke the word, was the core of his watch. It was why he checked the garden gate twice before bed, why he memorised the sound of every footstep on the lane, why his children never once felt the edge of fear even when caution ran high. To them, his vigilance was not a burden but a constant, as much a part of life as the turning of the seasons.

In Kent, where the world seemed to move at half its usual speed, it might have been tempting to relax, to believe in the illusion of distance from trouble. But Sørensen did not believe in illusions. The stillness here was a gift, and like any gift worth keeping, it was one that required guarding. That was his role, and he carried it with the same steadiness he had carried every duty before.

When the night deepened and the last lights in the village went dark, Sørensen would stand one final time at the kitchen window, his reflection faint in the glass. Beyond the hedge, the road lay empty, the only sound the wind moving through the trees. Satisfied, he would turn away, closing the latch with a quiet click. It was a simple act, almost invisible in its routine, but to him, it was the last lock on the day, the final seal on another safe passage through time.

The introductions began without ceremony, as though each meeting were no more than the natural crossing of paths in a small county. Harrison never announced names in a formal way; instead, he let Ben recognise faces or recall half-remembered voices from his boyhood. The butcher, still working behind the same counter where Ben had bought penny sweets, greeted him with no more than a nod and the brief tightening of the eyes that marked recognition. The exchange was wordless, but the understanding behind it was clear: nothing of what passed through this village left its borders. Sørensen, standing slightly behind, studied the man's manner and added him silently to the growing roster of trusted contacts.

Some of these allies were people Ben had known since before he understood what the word "royal" meant. There was the woman who had once kept the flower stall in the Saturday market, now older, her hands lined but steady as she adjusted the blooms in a vase on her front step. She greeted Harrison first, then Ben, with the same warmth she had offered a ten-year-old boy selecting roses for his mother. No mention was made of the castle, the titles, or the headlines; here, he was still the boy from Kent. Sørensen's eyes lingered on her a moment longer, registering that such loyalty, born of decades, could not be bought or faked.

The tradespeople were another layer entirely—men and women whose work tied them to the property in ways that made discretion second nature. The caretaker, who had tended the main house gardens since Ben's grandparents lived there, arrived in a battered truck with tools rattling in the back. His greeting was a simple, "Evening, sir," pitched low and without flourish. Sørensen caught the way his gaze flicked toward the tree line and back again, a habit of checking the edges before settling to conversation. That, too, went into his ledger of allies.

Harrison's method in these introductions was deliberate. He never lingered too long in one place, never allowed a conversation to drift toward speculation. Each meeting was brief enough to appear incidental, yet long enough to reaffirm bonds that had been quietly sustained over years. For Ben, it was a reminder that while some ties to Kent had frayed with time, others had been quietly strengthened by distance. For Sørensen, it was a practical assessment of the network that would surround them in the weeks ahead.

A handful of faces were unfamiliar to Ben—new shopkeepers, a mechanic who had taken over his father's garage, a young couple running the bakery. Each received Harrison's subtle endorsement in the form of a single phrase or glance. Ben followed his lead, offering polite greetings but nothing that might betray the reason for his return. Sørensen, though outwardly casual, watched closely, noting the tone of each reply, the way eyes met or avoided his. Allies, in his experience, were measured as much by what they did not say as by what they spoke aloud.

There was an unspoken order to these connections. Some would be the first to notice if strangers appeared in the village. Others could arrange for supplies or services without leaving a trail in the usual channels. A few, Harrison hinted, still owed favours to Ben's family from years past—debts repaid not in coin, but in silence when it mattered most. Sørensen absorbed these details without interrupting, his mind assembling them into the framework of a defensive perimeter that extended beyond the cottage walls.

By the week's end, the network felt less like a collection of acquaintances and more like a living shield. Every shopfront, every set of eyes behind a counter, every casual wave from across the lane carried the quiet weight of protection. Ben knew that in another world, such vigilance might feel oppressive, but here it was the currency of belonging. These people were not guarding him because he was a king; they were guarding him because he was theirs. Sørensen understood the value of that distinction better than most.

The final introduction came at dusk, in the back corner of the small pub that had stood for as long as either man could remember. Harrison brought them to a table where an older man sat with a half-finished pint, his weathered hands folded neatly in front of him. The exchange lasted less than five minutes, yet Sørensen caught the subtle weight of what passed between them—a quiet agreement, a reaffirmation of an old promise. No signatures, no oaths, just the knowledge that when called upon, these people would act without hesitation or question.

When they left the pub, the air was cool and damp, carrying the faint scent of rain. Harrison walked a few paces ahead, giving them space to absorb the evening's work. Ben glanced at Sørensen, who met his look with the faintest of nods. No words were needed; the ledger was full, the names recorded in a mind that forgot nothing. In the stillness of the village night, they knew that for now, the ground beneath them was secure.

Night settled over Kent with a damp stillness that muffled even the rustle of the hedgerows. Inside the cottage, the air was warm from the small hearth, the firelight flickering against the worn wooden table where maps, handwritten lists, and coded notes lay scattered. To anyone without context, the arrangement would look haphazard, an untidy collection of unrelated scraps. But between Harrison, Ben, and Sørensen, every page, every folded corner, and every underlined mark had meaning. These were the bones of a strategy meant to keep them unseen while ensuring their presence here could not be erased or overlooked. The fire popped quietly, a reminder that they were not far from the open world outside.

Ben leaned forward, elbows resting on the table, eyes scanning the notes as Harrison spoke in the low, deliberate tone of someone accustomed to delivering instructions in public without ever sounding like he was giving orders. "The trick," Harrison said, tapping one list with his forefinger, "is to be visible just enough that no one thinks you're hiding. Disappear entirely, and they'll start asking questions. Appear too much, and you'll give them something to follow." Sørensen nodded once, his gaze steady, already turning the words into action in his mind. His years in security had taught him that the best cover was often the one that looked almost careless.

The children had been kept away from the table at first, told to tidy their things and prepare for bed. But Emil, unwilling to retreat before having his say, leaned against the doorway with his arms folded, watching the adults with a mix of curiosity and quiet concern. "Will we see the castle again soon?" he asked finally, the question hanging in the air longer than it should. Ben looked at him for a moment, his reply measured. "Yes," he said simply, the word carrying the weight of a promise that would not be broken. There was no embellishment, no false comfort—only the certainty that they would go home.

Maria, ever the careful keeper of her word, took Casper's hand and told him she would sleep in his room so he would not feel alone. The boy accepted this without question, a small nod sealing the agreement between them. It was these quiet bonds, these subtle assurances between siblings, that Ben trusted more than any plan on paper. They moved to the narrow staircase, Maria glancing back once toward the table before disappearing into the upper rooms. Emil lingered a little longer before slipping away to join his father later, as was his habit when the night felt uncertain.

Once the cottage had grown still except for the crackle of the fire, Harrison unfolded a larger county map and spread it flat, smoothing its creases with the side of his hand. Small markings in pencil dotted the lanes and village corners—some indicating allies, others potential blind spots in the network. Ben traced one route with his finger, noting how it curved away from the main roads and cut through a cluster of back fields. "That's the one I'd use," he murmured, more to himself than anyone else. Sørensen's eyes followed the path and committed it to memory without comment.

They spoke sparingly, their voices low enough that even if a passerby stood outside the window, only the indistinct murmur of conversation would be heard. Harrison outlined the quiet watch patterns already in place—who would be near the library on certain mornings, who would keep an eye on the post office, and which shopkeepers could be relied upon to notice strangers without looking like they were watching. It was a delicate balance, one that required every participant to act as though nothing at all was happening. In Kent, such understatement was an art form.

The lists were then reshuffled, with Harrison sliding one toward Sørensen—a coded ledger of names and trades, each with a notation that meant something only to them. "This is for you," he said simply, "in case I can't get to you in time." Sørensen took it without hesitation, folding the paper neatly and slipping it into his inside jacket pocket. He did not need to read it now; he would remember it exactly as it appeared on the table. His mind had been trained to store such things as if they were etched in stone.

Ben kept his attention on the smaller slips of paper—supply lists, contact points, timings for discreet deliveries. Some were in Harrison's precise handwriting, others in Sørensen's neat block print, and a few in Ben's own script from earlier in the day. They represented layers of preparation built on years of quiet practice. These were not new methods; they were refinements of what had been done before, shaped to fit the present threat. Ben recognised in them the same principles Sørensen had taught him as a younger man: never overcomplicate what works, and never let complacency take root.

The fire burned lower, throwing softer light on the table as the conversation shifted from immediate routes to longer-term contingencies. Harrison spoke of the weather patterns that could be used to their advantage—fog in the mornings, rain in the late afternoons, and the darker pockets of the lanes after dusk. Sørensen added observations about the terrain around the cottage, where the trees could conceal movement and where the open ground would require caution. They discussed these things as though they were talking about nothing more than the garden or the state of the roof, their tone casual to the point of misdirection.

At one point, Ben leaned back in his chair, letting the discussion flow between the two men while he studied their expressions. Harrison's eyes carried the calm focus of someone who had been here before, who understood the rhythms of waiting and watching.

Sørensen's jaw remained set, his presence steady and unyielding, as though nothing could shake his watch. Between them, Ben realised, was the shield he needed to keep his family safe—one built not from force, but from patience and loyalty.

When the plans were finalised for the night, the maps were folded away, the notes gathered and tucked into a small tin box that Harrison placed inside the locked cupboard by the hearth. There would be no trace left on the table, no sign that anything more than an evening of conversation had taken place. To an outsider, the room would appear untouched, the fire simply the comfort of a quiet night in a country cottage. But those seated around the table knew that every detail had been decided, every path marked, and every name weighed.

Ben rose first, taking a moment to glance toward the staircase where Emil waited in the shadows, a blanket wrapped around his shoulders. Without a word, the boy followed him into the small bedroom, climbing into the double bed waiting for his dad. Ben pulled the covers over him, feeling the familiar weight of Sørensen son's head against his shoulder for a moment. It was a silent exchange of reassurance—the kind that required no explanation.

Sørensen stayed behind in the main room for a few minutes longer, standing at the window with the curtain pulled just enough to see the lane beyond. Harrison joined him briefly, their words too low to carry, before Sørensen gave a short nod and stepped back. The curtain fell into place, the lock on the door clicked softly, and the fire's glow became the only light in the room. Outside, the county slept without knowing—or perhaps fully knowing—that a quiet watch had been set over one of its own.

Upstairs, the stillness was broken only by the faint murmur of the wind outside. Maria's voice, soft and patient, carried from the next room as she spoke to Casper, promising again that she would be there when he woke. Her words were unhurried, the kind that settled deep enough to be believed without question. Emil's breathing slowed beside Ben, the day's travel and the weight of unspoken worry fading into the steady rhythm of sleep.

When the house was finally silent, Ben went to his own room and allowed himself the briefest moment of ease. The network in Kent was awake, the strategy laid out, and the first night of their quiet exile had passed without disturbance. Tomorrow would bring its own set of movements and precautions, but for now, the plan held. In this place, for this moment, they were safe.

The darkness that settled over the county had a different weight than the nights at Rosenshavn. Here, the stillness was not born of the sea's lull or the hush of castle walls, but of an older quiet—one that belonged to hedgerows, ancient trees, and lanes that knew the tread of few after sundown. Ben lay awake in the narrow bed, his eyes adjusting to the shadows that formed along the ceiling, tracing the familiar shapes of the cottage roof beams. It was not unease that kept him from sleep, but a sharpened awareness, a sense that each breath, each muted sound, belonged to a fragile balance they could not afford to disturb.

From the porch, Sørensen's slow, deliberate steps could be heard at intervals, the boards creaking under his weight as he made his rounds. The faint, narrow glow of his flashlight cut briefly across the garden gate, pausing there before sweeping back toward the lane. He was a figure cut from vigilance itself—methodical, patient, unwilling to yield even to the pull of fatigue. Inside, the fire had died to embers, its warmth barely reaching the far corners of the room, leaving the air cool enough to keep one alert.

Harrison emerged from the shadows by the boundary fence just before midnight, his voice carrying softly as he approached the porch. There was no need for formalities between the two men; their exchange was little more than a hand signal and a few quiet words. "I'll take it from here," Harrison said, the tone matter-of-fact rather than suggestive. "You get some rest." Sørensen hesitated only a moment, scanning the lane one last time before stepping back through the door. It was the kind of concession only trust could allow.

Inside, the cottage was still. The floorboards gave a muted groan beneath Sørensen's boots as he crossed the main room, pausing to check the latch on the front door before heading to the small bedroom where Emil slept. The boy stirred as his father lay down beside him, shifting closer instinctively, his head finding its place against Sørensen's shoulder. In that small movement, the tension drained from the man's frame, his breathing easing into a slower rhythm. The role of protector did not vanish in sleep, but it softened, becoming less a guard's watch and more a father's presence.

Ben listened to these movements without turning, recognising the comfort in knowing where each person was. It was part of the discipline Sørensen had instilled in him over the years—an awareness of placement, sound, and timing. The children were secure, the doors locked, and Harrison was outside walking the boundaries with the same patience and caution that marked every step of their plan. For now, the world beyond the lane did not exist. The cottage was their fortress, built not from stone, but from discretion.

The lane itself lay in near-complete darkness, broken only by the sweep of Harrison's flashlight as he moved along the hedgerows. He checked the sightlines from the drive, paused at the bend near the back field, and then retraced his steps with the quiet ease of someone who had walked this ground in every season. He did not expect trouble tonight—few would wander this way without reason—but habits formed over decades were not discarded simply because the hour was late.

Inside, Ben's thoughts shifted between the past and the present. The very bed in which he now lay had been his as a boy during summers in Kent, the cottage a retreat where days were spent in books and quiet discovery rather than the demands of a castle. Those years had taught him the value of places like this—unremarkable to the casual eye, yet carrying the strength of history and familiarity. It was why he trusted it now to shield his family while the world's gaze turned in other directions.

The wind pressed lightly against the cottage walls, carrying with it the scent of damp earth and the distant tang of wood smoke from another home further down the lane. Such scents belonged here, unchanged across decades, binding the present moment to the memory of every other night spent under this roof. Ben let his mind trace those connections, allowing them to knit the day's careful movements into the deeper fabric of his life. This was no random hiding place—it was part of his foundation.

From upstairs, a faint murmur of Maria's voice could be heard as she reassured Casper once more before sleep took hold. She spoke in the same quiet, even tone she had used earlier, repeating her promise without altering a word. The boy's breathing steadied in response, the sound drifting into the gentle cadence of rest. It was small, domestic, and ordinary—yet in a situation like this, it was also strategic. Rested children meant fewer questions, fewer risks, and a steadier day ahead.

Harrison's steps passed the porch again, the beam of his light briefly touching the windows before moving on. Ben could picture the expression on his old friend's face even without seeing it—the watchfulness, the readiness to act if the need arose. It was a comfort, knowing that the same man who had once looked out for him as a boy was now ensuring the safety of his children. The years between had changed them both, but not the bond formed in those early days.

Gradually, the small sounds of movement faded until the night settled into its deepest quiet. The only remaining noise was the faint shift of embers in the hearth and the occasional sigh from the timbers of the cottage as they adjusted to the cool air. Ben closed his eyes, letting the rhythm of these sounds settle into him, knowing they marked a night passing without alarm. The first stage of their stay was holding exactly as planned.

Yet beneath that calm, he remained aware of the fragility of their position. One wrong conversation, one unguarded moment, and the veil could slip. It was the same awareness that had shaped his life since taking the quiet throne in Denmark—an understanding that safety was never permanent, only maintained through vigilance. Tonight had gone without incident, but tomorrow would demand the same level of control.

The cottage seemed to breathe with them, its old timbers and stone walls absorbing the presence of its occupants as though they had never left. This was the advantage of returning to a place that had already kept its secrets for generations: it knew how to hold them. Ben turned once more toward the sound of Emil's steady breathing from the next room, letting the comfort of it anchor him in the moment.

Outside, the night deepened further, the last trace of moon slipping behind clouds. Harrison's patrol moved to the far side of the property, beyond the reach of sight from the cottage windows. Inside, no one stirred. The plan—layered, deliberate, and cautious—remained intact. For tonight, Kent was theirs alone.

The morning arrived without haste, the county unfolding itself in slow layers of pale light and damp air that clung to the hedgerows. From the cottage windows, Ben could see the narrow lane glistening faintly from the night's dew, the same lane he had walked as a boy on errands for his grandmother. There was a comfort in how unchanged it all felt, as though the years between then and now had been folded neatly away. Here, there was no need for ceremony or the cautious posturing that life at Rosenshavn demanded. The county did not greet him with applause; it greeted him with silence—and that silence was more protective than any public declaration could ever be.

By the time he stepped outside, the air carried the faint scent of wood smoke from a hearth somewhere beyond the bend. Sørensen was already on the porch, coffee in hand, his gaze sweeping the road as naturally as breathing. Harrison stood beside the car, leaning casually against the door, but his eyes tracked every movement within the periphery. The rhythm of this place was slower than Copenhagen, yet beneath that ease lay a vigilance that matched their own. It was in the way curtains shifted slightly as neighbours caught sight of them, and in the way those curtains closed again without a word.

The county's unwritten code was as old as its oldest families: a man's business was his own unless he chose to share it. Here, there would be no loose talk in the village shop, no whispers carried on the wind to London or Copenhagen. Those who had known Ben as a boy remembered the way he treated every villager—by first name, without distinction of wealth or station—and those memories weighed more than any rumour. In their eyes, he was still the boy who ran messages for the librarian, mowed the parish garden in summer, and repaired bicycles for pocket change. That boy had earned their trust, and trust here was not something to be sold.

Sørensen seemed to recognise the invisible shield around them, though he did not let it dull his watchfulness. As they walked into the village that morning, his eyes moved from doorway to rooftop, noting faces and movements, mapping the flow of the day. Yet he did so without tension, as if aware that the danger would not come from within these borders. Danger, if it came, would come from beyond, carried in by someone who did not understand what it meant to belong here.

Harrison's role in this was both practical and symbolic. He greeted those they passed with the ease of a man whose presence needed no explanation, and in doing so, he absorbed the attention that might otherwise have turned to Ben. A nod here, a brief exchange about the weather there—it was enough to keep their passing ordinary. The fewer details noticed, the fewer details that could be carried elsewhere. The village understood this rhythm instinctively, and it fell into step without the need for instruction.

The librarian was among the first to see them that day, standing just outside the library door to let in the morning air. Her eyes met Ben's with the same look she had given him when he was ten: direct, unhurried, and without surprise.

She did not ask about the castle or the children or the headlines that might eventually reach her. Instead, she mentioned that a new book on the history of Kent had come in, and that it was in the same section he used to frequent. It was an offering wrapped in normalcy, a reminder that here he was not a king, not a curiosity, but simply a reader returning to familiar shelves.

Maria and Casper followed a few paces behind, the boy's small hand anchored in hers as they crossed the square. They drew glances, but only the kind given to children who might belong to anyone—a visiting cousin, perhaps, or a neighbour's grandchild. Emil walked at his father's side, his expression open but alert, taking in the village with quiet curiosity. The locals, for their part, offered smiles but no questions. They did not need answers to protect someone they considered one of their own.

In the small shop, the exchange was just as seamless. Ben paid for bread, cheese, and tea for Sørensen without being asked for his name or residence. The shopkeeper's only comment was about the quality of the morning's milk delivery, a piece of harmless conversation that served as a buffer against anything more pointed. Transactions here were not opportunities for gossip; they were moments to affirm the ordinary, which in this case was the most extraordinary protection they could have hoped for.

Walking back along the lane, Ben could feel the subtle way the county folded itself around them. It was not the overt guard of palace gates or security details—it was the quiet acknowledgment of shared history, the kind that made one's presence unremarkable even when it might have been cause for spectacle elsewhere. It was, in its own way, the most effective security system he had ever known.

Sørensen commented on it only once, in the low tone of someone observing a truth rather than offering an opinion. "They know," he said, "and they're not going to tell." There was no need to elaborate. Ben understood that this was not just about secrecy; it was about allegiance. The people here had chosen long ago where their loyalty lay, and that decision did not waver simply because the stakes had changed.

Harrison, walking ahead, turned back just enough to catch Ben's eye. The look was one of quiet reassurance—confirmation that their presence here was not only safe, but reinforced by an unspoken pact. Whatever might come from the outside world, Kent would not be the source of the breach. That knowledge settled over Ben like a second skin, easing the tension that had shadowed him since their departure from Denmark.

Back at the cottage, the sense of safety deepened. The children moved freely between the rooms, their voices carrying through the open door without the sharp edge of caution. Sørensen allowed Emil to step out into the garden unaccompanied for the first time since their arrival, though he kept him in sight. Small freedoms returned quickly here, the kind that would have been impossible in the public spaces of Copenhagen.

Ben found himself lingering on the porch, watching the way the light shifted across the hedgerows. The view was unchanged from his boyhood, and in that familiarity lay a profound relief. This was not a temporary hiding place—it was a return to something elemental, something that existed beyond the reach of politics or scandal. Here, he was not defined by what he ruled or what others wanted from him, but by who he had always been.

The county's protection was not a service he could request; it was a gift freely given, built over years of shared moments that outsiders would never understand. That gift came with no conditions, no whispered debts to be repaid. It was simply the way of things in a place that valued loyalty over spectacle. And as the day settled into its quiet rhythm, Ben knew that for as long as they remained here, the world outside would find no entry point.

Evening would come soon enough, bringing with it the necessary rituals of security and watchfulness. But for now, the county held them in its quiet embrace, each villager playing their part in keeping him untouchable. In this place, he was not the King of Denmark. He was not the subject of rumours or headlines. He was a neighbour, a friend, and the boy the county had never stopped claiming as its own. And in that role, he was safer than any title could ever make him.

CHAPTER 11: THE KING OF QUIET

The light in the cottage breaks softly, filtering through the lace-trimmed curtains in a muted glow that neither demands attention nor disturbs the peace. Ben has claimed the corner armchair, his posture unhurried, the open book resting across his knee as though it had been there for hours. The scent of fresh coffee drifts from the kitchen, warm and earthy, joining the faint crackle from the hearth. Sørensen sits at the small table, methodically sharpening a pencil over a folded sheet of paper, each rotation slow and deliberate. The radio, sitting in its usual place on the shelf, remains untouched. In Kent, they are afforded the luxury of beginning the day without the intrusion of headlines.

This absence of outside noise is not laziness, nor is it a refusal to face the truth—it is a deliberate act of preservation. The papers have been left stacked by the door, their folded edges crisp, unbroken. If Ben wished, he could reach for them and read what Denmark has decided to make of him that morning. But the decision not to is part of the strategy, a quiet refusal to allow strangers' narratives to dictate the rhythm of the day. The world can shout from a distance; here, they answer only when they choose.

The lane beyond the hedge remains still. There is no traffic at this hour, no curious faces peering from behind net curtains. It is the kind of silence that settles into the bones, different from the high-ceilinged quiet of Rosenshavn. This is a county stillness, born of routine and shared understanding, the sort that does not need to be earned—only respected. Ben recognises it instantly; it is the same atmosphere he knew as a boy when his world was smaller and his days belonged to himself.

Sørensen glances toward the window but not in alarm. His movements are part of the natural order of things now, the constant awareness that has been trained into him over decades. His pencil is set down, the shavings swept neatly into the palm of his hand before being tipped into a small bin by the table. He does not ask Ben what he is reading; he already knows it will be something that demands thought, not distraction.

The children remain upstairs for now, the muffled sound of their steps above a soft reminder that not every moment here must be guarded. Maria has likely woken first, as she always does, and is coaxing the others into the day with the same gentle persistence she uses to win at card games. Ben listens to the faint rhythm of their movement, a reminder that even in exile there is a normality worth keeping intact.

He turns a page, the paper whispering under his fingers, and for a moment allows himself to absorb the words fully. Here, reading is not just an act of learning but of anchoring—an opportunity to root himself in something other than the shifting sands of public perception. The story he holds belongs only to him until he chooses otherwise. This, too, is part of holding ground without confrontation.

From the kitchen, the sound of the percolator deepens as the coffee reaches its strength. Sørensen pours two mugs, one for himself, one for Ben, without asking if it is wanted. The gesture is routine, the kind of silent understanding that years of trust produce. When the cup is placed within reach, Ben closes the book long enough to wrap his hands around the heat. No words are exchanged; they are not needed.

It is in these moments, Ben knows, that the most important decisions are often made—not in boardrooms, not in throne rooms, but in the still hours when no one is looking. The world might expect a statement, a public rebuttal, or some grand assertion of control. Instead, the day begins with coffee, with sharpened pencils, with the will to remain untouched by noise until the time is right.

The newspapers by the door remain unread, the radio unwound, the phone silent. Outside forces may believe they can dictate pace and reaction, but Kent's quiet is not easily breached. Ben has learned that sometimes the strongest move is not to move at all, letting the tide exhaust itself before stepping forward. In the meantime, the fire crackles on, the coffee cools slowly, and the book waits patiently for the next page to turn.

The morning air in Kent is sharp with the scent of grass still damp from the night, the kind of air that clears the mind before the day has had time to gather its noise. Ben has chosen the garden as the day's classroom, not because the cottage lacks space inside, but because here the world feels wider without being exposed. Maria, Casper, and Emil sit at a small wooden table under the apple tree, their notebooks spread open, pencils at the ready. A light breeze tugs at the edges of the pages, carrying with it the hum of bees from the far hedgerow. It is a place where learning becomes less about duty and more about discovery, where the lessons can take root in ways that walls sometimes cannot hold.

He begins with numbers, weaving them into stories so that they carry more weight than figures alone. Maria's sums are precise, her handwriting neat and deliberate, while Casper tests himself by working ahead, glancing now and then at Emil as if to compare speed without saying so. Emil, though the youngest of the three, shows the same determined concentration Ben remembers in himself as a boy—eyes narrowed, brow furrowed, determined to prove the answer right. Ben never hurries them. Each pause is a space for thought, and in those spaces, the children learn more than the numbers themselves.

When the sums are done, the lesson slides effortlessly into the history of Kent, a subject Ben can speak on without notes. He tells them of the roads that once served horse-drawn coaches, of the old market days when the county green filled with voices, and of the orchards that once stretched far beyond the hedgerows they see now. The children listen closely, not because they are told to, but because the past is spoken here as if it still breathes. Ben gestures toward the far field, explaining how certain rows in the soil still follow patterns laid down centuries ago, the kind of detail most passers-by would overlook.

Nature, too, finds its place in the morning's curriculum. A robin lands near the table, tilting its head as if assessing the new gathering, and Ben uses it as a lesson in observation. "Watch its movements," he says, voice low, "you'll learn more from its pauses than its hops." Maria sketches it quickly in the corner of her notebook, while Emil counts the beats between its movements. Casper, more interested in the shape of the apple blossoms above, stretches to touch one without breaking it from its stem. In this garden, there are no wrong answers—only different ways of seeing the same thing.

Sørensen stands at the edge of the hedgerow, hands loosely clasped behind his back, a silent sentry to the scene. His eyes sweep the lane beyond, but his presence does not intrude. It is a habit he has carried for years: protecting without overshadowing, guarding without casting a shadow over what should be free. Every so often, his gaze shifts to the children, and though he says nothing, there is an unmistakable pride in the way he watches them work.

Ben continues the lesson with quiet patience, shifting from spoken history to written exercises, ensuring each child has a chance to share what they have learned. Maria's account of the robin's movements is sharp and observant, Casper's description of the apple blossoms is filled with detail, and Emil's recounting of the soil's patterns is exact, his numbers matching the land. Ben praises each in turn, never favouring one over the other, the approval measured but sincere.

The sun has risen higher by the time the first part of the lesson is complete, casting dappled light through the apple branches. The air is warmer now, though the freshness lingers, and the garden seems to draw the sound of their voices into its quiet rhythm. Here, the outside world—its noise, its rumours, its demands—cannot intrude. The lesson belongs to them alone, bound by the trust that Kent has always given and that Ben now passes on in return.

By the time the children close their notebooks, the garden has become more than a classroom—it is a place where memory and knowledge take shape together. The laughter that follows the end of the lesson feels earned, a natural echo to the stillness that began the day. And in that space between instruction and play, Ben knows he has given them something that cannot be taken by headlines or speculation: the certainty that learning is not a performance, but a quiet act of strength.

The afternoons in Kent carry a different kind of weight. Where the mornings belong to lessons and quiet observation, the afternoons are claimed by discipline—Sørensen's domain. The old soldier wastes no time with warm greetings or idle conversation; his training sessions begin the moment Ben steps into the open space behind the cottage. Here, the ground is uneven enough to challenge balance, yet open enough to see any approach from a distance. Sørensen prefers it this way. The first drills are always physical: footwork, stance, controlled bursts of movement designed to keep muscles warm and reflexes sharp. Ben meets each instruction without hesitation, moving as if every step were calculated to within an inch.

There is no leniency in Sørensen's tone, no concession to the fact that this is Kent and not a field post in hostile territory. "Again," he says, when a movement is a fraction too slow. "Faster," when the timing feels measured rather than instinctive. Ben accepts it without complaint. In these sessions, he is not a king, not a figure to be guarded, but a student—one who understands that skill without practice fades into vulnerability. The repetition is unrelenting: pivot, strike, block, retreat, advance. It is a rhythm as precise as any clock, and Sørensen ensures it does not falter.

The children sit on the steps of the cottage, their play set aside in favour of silent fascination. Maria's eyes track every shift in Ben's stance, as if memorising the logic behind each movement. Casper leans forward, elbows on knees, drawn to the speed and sharpness of the exchanges. Emil, perched between them, watches his father's every command, his small frame mirroring the stances in miniature. Sørensen notices, though he does not acknowledge it aloud; observation, he knows, is the first step to mastery.

The drills progress into close-contact exercises, where timing becomes as critical as strength. Sørensen pushes Ben hard, their movements a blur of defensive holds and counter-manoeuvres. Each shift in position is tested and retested until Sørensen is satisfied that Ben could repeat it without thought in the dark. Sweat beads along Ben's brow, yet his breathing remains steady. He has trained like this for years, but each session in Kent feels sharper, stripped of distraction. The stakes here are quieter, yet no less real.

There are no spectators beyond the children, but Sørensen trains as if an enemy might step through the hedgerow at any moment. It is not paranoia—it is preparation. He reminds Ben, between movements, that comfort breeds complacency, and complacency is the first crack in any defence. Ben listens, the words absorbed as much as the physical drills. Trusting Sørensen's judgement is as natural to him now as breathing.

When the drills shift to weapons training, the tools are simple—wooden staffs, dulled blades, items that will leave bruises rather than wounds. Yet the discipline remains absolute. Every strike must land where intended; every defence must hold. Sørensen's movements are deceptively smooth for a man his age, his precision honed by decades of service. Ben matches him, not with youthful arrogance, but with the controlled respect of someone who knows that skill is not measured in brute force, but in the ability to outlast.

The children begin to whisper guesses about who might win if the drills became a true contest, though none dare say it loud enough for Sørensen to hear. Maria predicts Ben would win through endurance, Casper insists Sørensen would take the upper hand through sheer experience, and Emil refuses to choose between them at all. Their debate becomes background noise to the steady sound of strikes and steps on the grass.

By the time Sørensen calls an end to the session, the sun is leaning westward, the long shadows of the apple trees stretching across the training ground. Ben wipes his brow with the back of his hand, but there is no exhaustion in his movements—only the quiet satisfaction that comes from a task done thoroughly. Sørensen offers no praise, yet his nod at the end carries more weight than any words. The children rush forward, Maria and Casper peppering Ben with questions about specific moves, while Emil simply takes his father's hand, content to walk back toward the cottage in silence.

In Kent, where the lanes are calm and the nights are still, it might be easy to forget that danger can appear without warning. Sørensen ensures that none of them do. His training is as much about vigilance as it is about skill, and in the unbroken routine of these afternoons, Ben finds a discipline that sharpens more than his body—it clears his mind. In this way, Kent is not just a refuge; it is a proving ground.

The post that morning is delivered not by the usual knock of a postal carrier, but by the steady tread of Harrison's boots on the garden path. He carries no more than a small bundle in one hand, yet it is the single envelope at the top that matters. Its cream paper is familiar, its edges neatly pressed, the handwriting across its front unmistakably Isla's. Harrison does not speak as he passes it to Ben, only giving the faintest nod, as though acknowledging that whatever it contains will weigh more than its appearance suggests. The cottage kitchen is still warm with the scent of coffee, but in that moment, the air changes.

Ben does not open it immediately. He sits at the end of the table, turning the envelope once in his hands, feeling the slight impression of the ink beneath his fingertips. Around him, the morning routine carries on—Maria slicing bread for the younger boys, Sørensen checking the latches on the back door, the quiet scrape of chairs on the worn floorboards. Only when he is certain the children are settled does he slide a finger under the seal. The sound of paper tearing is soft, but it carries.

The letter is short—fewer than a dozen lines—but its economy only makes it heavier. Isla's script flows as it always has, but there is no indulgence in description, no pleasantries to soften the message. They're getting louder. Three words that speak to a truth he does not need explained. The media in Denmark is circling, the falsehoods swelling louder than the facts, and whatever silence he has kept will soon be tested. She does not elaborate, does not name sources or repeat the nonsense that others may be printing. She knows he will understand without detail.

He reads it again, his eyes steady, not betraying the shift he feels inside. When he folds the paper, his movements are slow, precise, as though returning it to its envelope might somehow keep the words contained. He places it on the table beside his coffee but does not touch either again. There is no visible reaction, no outward sign that the letter has altered the course of his day, yet a change settles into his posture—a narrowing of the shoulders, a weight in the way his hands now rest against the wood.

Sørensen notices. He has known Ben long enough to see the difference, to read the silence as clearly as any sentence. He says nothing before the children, but when Maria leaves the table to take Emil outside, his eyes meet Ben's across the room. The question is silent, the answer already understood. The letter has brought news they both expected, but the certainty of its arrival shifts the ground beneath them all the same.

Harrison remains leaning against the doorframe, watching with the same quiet alertness. He knows better than to ask, and he does not need to—he has lived in this county long enough to recognise when trouble is approaching from beyond its borders. His role is to keep it there. The lines around his mouth deepen, the expression of a man already thinking three steps ahead.

Ben does not speak of it again that morning. He does not show the letter to Sørensen, nor does he leave it in plain view. Instead, he tucks it into the inside pocket of his jacket, as if the fabric could muffle the echo of its words. The rest of the day proceeds as if nothing has changed—the children's lessons continue, the coffee is poured, the tools for repair are brought out into the garden—but beneath it all, the letter remains. It is a quiet warning, a reminder that even here, with hedgerows for walls and neighbours who keep their own counsel, the hunt can find its way across the sea.

And yet, Kent still holds. The air beyond the cottage windows is calm, the lanes empty, the county keeping its silence as it always has. For now, the sound of the hunt is distant, carried only in ink and paper. But Ben knows the way of such things. Distance is never enough for long.

The bundle of newspapers had been sitting untouched on the low table since Harrison left them there at first light, a habit born from the knowledge that most of what lay inside was poison dressed as news. Ben had ignored them for hours, focusing instead on the day's lessons and the deliberate calm of their cottage life. Yet the longer they sat, the more they seemed to demand attention—not to be believed, but to be examined. In the end, he pulled the top paper free, shaking it out across his knee. The scent of ink and pulp was sharp, its texture rough against his hands, but the print itself was what cut deepest.

The photographs came first—grainy, distant shots of him in places he had never stood, and of Isla with expressions cropped and stolen from other moments entirely. They had been paired with headlines in bold type, the kind designed to catch a passer-by's eye on a crowded street. His name was not used in full—never that—but the insinuations were heavy enough to make the connection obvious to anyone already following the rumours. He traced the edges of one image with his thumb, noting the subtle warping of perspective that told him it had been altered.

Sørensen, standing at the other end of the table, said nothing until Ben slid one of the pages toward him. The older man's eyes moved over the print with slow precision, reading each line not for its claims but for its intent. The corners of his mouth did not move, but the tightening of his jaw was visible, a sign Ben had seen countless times in the years they had known each other. It was not anger, not yet. It was the calculation that came before.

The articles themselves were built on half-truths and pure invention. One suggested that Ben had abandoned Denmark for luxury abroad; another claimed Isla had taken the twins to a private island. There were mentions of money changing hands, of supposed feuds with unnamed relatives, of whispered betrayals in the highest circles. The lies were constructed with the precision of someone who understood that the most effective untruths are those laced with enough familiarity to seem possible.

He read each paragraph slowly, not because he doubted the venom inside, but because he wanted to understand the method behind it. The sentences were short, the language charged, each one shaped to provoke rather than inform. He knew these tactics—had seen them used before on others—and he could almost hear the voices of the editors deciding which fabrication would sell the most copies. To them, the truth was irrelevant. The story was the commodity.

Sørensen finished his reading and folded the paper in half with deliberate care, as though handling something that could stain his hands. "You see the pattern," he said quietly, his voice carrying the weight of experience rather than outrage. Ben nodded. There was no need for them to discuss the details further; they both knew the damage such words could do if left unchecked. But they also knew that reacting too quickly would be its own kind of trap.

Ben set the papers aside, stacking them neatly rather than discarding them. They were evidence now—not to be argued with in public, but to be kept, dissected, and filed away for the day when they might need to be countered with precision. In Kent, among those who mattered, the lies would find no purchase. But beyond the hedgerows, the world was being taught to see a version of him that did not exist.

The weight of it settled on him not as fear, but as a cold clarity. These were not simply falsehoods meant to fill pages; they were pieces in a larger game, one in which the players could strike from a distance without ever showing their faces. And in that game, patience was as powerful as any public denial. He would wait. He would choose the moment. And when it came, it would not be in the form of a rebuttal—it would be something far more decisive.

The air in Kent carried no trace of the headlines that stained the papers stacked in the cottage. Life moved with its usual rhythm, the kind that could not be altered by foreign noise. When Ben stepped into the county grocer, the shop bell chimed as it always had, and the owner greeted him with the same unhurried smile he had worn since Ben was a boy buying bread rolls with coins from his pocket. There was no probing glance, no veiled question—only the exchange of goods and the familiar, unspoken understanding that here, he was simply Ben.

Along the high street, neighbours raised their hands in quiet waves, the sort that acknowledged his presence without demanding conversation. They did not crowd him, did not linger to fish for details. If they had read the stories, they gave no sign, and that absence was more powerful than any public defence. These were people who had watched him grow, who had seen him return again and again, and who measured truth not by what was printed in a distant city, but by the weight of years lived side by side.

At the library, the old brass handle was cool under his hand, the door swinging open with the same slight resistance it always had. Inside, the librarian looked up from her desk and smiled—not the polite courtesy offered to strangers, but the warm, almost conspiratorial smile of someone who had already decided that nothing in print could alter her opinion of him. She reached under the counter and placed a hardbound volume atop the stack he was borrowing, her voice light as she said, "You'll need this one too." No explanation was offered, and none was required.

The postmistress, who had known him since he first learned to write his name, slipped his letters into his hand without looking twice at the return addresses. The butcher, wiping his hands on a cloth, asked after the weather in Denmark but made no mention of what had been written there. Even the children in the lane treated him as they always had, running past with laughter, their games interrupted only long enough to wave. In this place, the world's storms broke harmlessly against the walls of habit and history.

Sørensen noticed it too. Walking beside Ben, he observed the glances, the nods, the subtle shifts in body language that spoke of quiet allegiance. He knew a community's stance could be measured by the smallest details—the angle of a smile, the absence of hesitation in a handshake. Here, every gesture was an affirmation that nothing had changed. They would not turn him away, not in whispers, not in action, and certainly not because of words written by people who had never set foot in this county.

The strength of Kent was not in loud declarations or public campaigns. It was in the consistency of its people, in the way they treated truth as something built over decades, not something purchased in an afternoon. Foreign papers could print whatever they liked, but the county's opinion was already set in stone. For them, loyalty was not a performance—it was a reflex.

When Ben returned to the cottage that evening, the silence of the lane behind him felt different. It was not isolation; it was insulation. The world might be clawing at the gates elsewhere, but here, the walls were made of memory and trust. The county had chosen its side long ago, and no headline—no matter how loud—was going to move it.

The introductions took place on an afternoon when the clouds were high and the air carried the faint scent of turned soil from the fields. Harrison, who seemed to know every family within twenty miles, brought the children to a neighbouring farm where four others, close in age to Maria, Casper, and Emil, were already waiting. There were no formalities, no stiff politeness—only the natural curiosity of youth sizing one another up. Within minutes, the reserve melted, replaced by the easy grins and quick exchanges that signal the start of something lasting.

Trust, in this part of Kent, was not given lightly, but with children it came more readily. The unspoken rule of the county—that certain matters were not to be repeated beyond its borders—seemed to settle into the newcomers without the need for explanation.

The four farm children did not ask why their new companions had come, nor did they seem concerned with who Ben was beyond being Maria, Casper, and Emil's guardian. The bond was built instead on the shared joy of running through tall grass, the excitement of exploring old stone walls, and the satisfaction of finding a friend who simply understood.

Their afternoons soon took on a pattern. After lessons in the garden or quiet reading indoors, the children would race across the hedgerow paths to meet, their voices carrying on the wind. They played with the kind of energy that left the air charged, games shifting fluidly from football to hide-and-seek among the barns. Mud-streaked boots and grass-stained knees became their common uniform, and none of them cared about the state of their clothes so long as the game continued until the sun began to dip.

From a distance, Ben and Sørensen would watch. Sørensen's arms were often folded, but the tightness in his posture eased when he saw Emil laughing without reserve. Ben, too, seemed lighter in those moments, as though the presence of new friends was restoring something his own boyhood had once enjoyed here. It was not merely companionship—it was the reaffirmation that safety could exist even in the company of others, that the children could live without the constant weight of caution pressing on their shoulders.

On more than one occasion, Maria took it upon herself to keep the group balanced, making sure that neither Casper nor Emil felt left out when the games paired off into smaller teams. Her instinct for fairness came as naturally as her quick smile, and the farm children, recognising her quiet authority, followed her lead without question. This was not leadership forced; it was the kind earned in small, everyday choices.

Casper, who could sometimes be reserved with strangers, found himself laughing more openly with these new companions. They did not push him to speak when he did not wish to, but when he did, they listened. Emil, for his part, thrived in the freedom of these afternoons, his bond with his father's watchful presence always visible in the way he would glance back toward the hedgerows before running off again. It was as though he needed that silent nod of permission before letting himself disappear into the fold of laughter.

The adults of the farms seemed equally at ease with the arrangement. They knew who the visitors were—of course they did—but their treatment never shifted to accommodate that knowledge. The children were left to be children, without the burden of lineage or the intrusion of whispered speculation. In Kent, that was the greatest kindness anyone could offer, and it was given freely.

By the time the sky deepened into evening, the games would wind down naturally. Footsteps slowed, voices softened, and the walk back to the cottage was filled with the comfortable quiet of shared fatigue. Ben would often glance toward the fields they had just crossed, the faint figures of the other children waving from the distance. In those moments, the weight of what waited beyond the county's borders seemed to lessen, replaced by the simple truth that here, bonds could be formed without calculation, and trust could grow without fear.

The library smelled of paper and polish, the same scent that had marked Ben's boyhood visits, and stepping through its door always brought a subtle shift in his posture. It was here that the noise of the world could never breach. The librarian was behind the counter, sorting a neat stack of returns, her hands moving with the same unhurried precision he remembered. When she looked up and saw him, her expression softened in a way that no headline or whispered rumour could touch. She did not ask how he had been or remark on the stories spreading beyond the county. Instead, she greeted him with a warmth that belonged to a time before such things mattered.

Her fondness was not born of royal titles or public intrigue. It was rooted in the sight of the boy who once appeared at her desk with a tower of books, barely tall enough to see over the counter, and yet determined to take home more than most adults could read in a month. She had known then that his mind was not like the others—restless, curious, unwilling to stop at the boundaries of a page. That knowledge had never left her, and it coloured the way she saw him now: not as a king, but as the same boy whose hunger for truth had shaped him into the man standing before her.

The years had not dulled her respect for his intelligence. She had seen it first-hand when he reorganised her catalogue at the age of eleven, convinced he could make it more efficient—and rightfully so. She had smiled then, indulging his quiet confidence, and watched in secret satisfaction as his system proved itself over time. To her, his intelligence was not something to parade, but something to be safeguarded from those who might exploit it. That, too, was part of her loyalty.

They spoke quietly, voices kept low in the familiar privacy of the library's hushed air. "My door is always open," she told him, not as an offer but as a standing truth. It was the same phrase she had given him years ago, when his world had begun to shift under the weight of discovery, and she had meant it with every fibre of her being. In the way of Kent, it was a promise made once and never broken.

She remembered the day he first came to her with the realisation of who he was—not in the grand sense of bloodlines and titles, but in the quiet, personal sense of identity. She had seen the conflict in his eyes, the mixture of wonder and unease, and she had sworn then to keep it to herself. That vow had never wavered. Even now, with the outside world straining to learn what she had known for so long, she held it tighter than ever.

There was a pause in their conversation as she reached for another stack of books, sliding them onto the counter for him to carry. It was a small, familiar ritual, one they had repeated countless times before. He took them without needing to be asked, balancing them with the same care he had shown as a boy, and for a moment it was as if no years had passed at all. The act was simple, but it bound them to the memory of a shared history that existed far beyond the reach of rumour.

Her protection of his name was not an act of defiance against the press; it was an act of love. She understood that his truth was his to reveal, not theirs to seize. And so she had kept her promise silently, as she had kept countless others in this quiet corner of the county. In her mind, he was still "the boy who never left," even if life had taken him far beyond these walls.

When she stepped out from behind the counter, it was not to shake his hand, but to embrace him. The hug was not rushed or formal—it was the same kind she had given him on days when he was small and carrying more books than sense, the kind that assured him he was safe. He leaned into it just enough to let her know it was welcome. There was no hesitation in the gesture, only the instinct of two people who had known each other long enough to skip over the need for explanation.

She called him by the name that mattered most to her—the boy who never left. There was no title in her voice, no trace of deference to the crown. It was spoken with affection, the same affection that had been there long before any claim to dynasties or the scrutiny of strangers. In her eyes, that name meant more than anything the newspapers could print.

Around them, the library remained still, the muted rustle of pages filling the air. To anyone passing by, it was nothing more than a quiet exchange between an old acquaintance and a trusted friend. But for Ben, it was a reminder that there were still places where he could exist without the burden of explanation, and still people who saw him for who he truly was. And for the librarian, it was the reassurance that the boy she had once known had never really gone—he had simply grown taller.

The market street of Kent carried its usual rhythm, with the faint clink of coins, the sliding of paper bags across wooden counters, and the low murmur of conversations that never strayed beyond what mattered to the day. Ben stepped into the greengrocer's shop first, holding the door long enough for Maria, Casper, and Emil to follow. The bell above the frame gave its polite chime, and the shopkeeper—broad-shouldered, apron tied tight—nodded once in greeting. There was no pause, no startled glance, and no mention of anything beyond the morning's apples and the freshness of the bread delivered that dawn. The silence was deliberate, a kindness honed over years.

At the butcher's, Sørensen lingered at the display case while Ben spoke with the owner about the week's cuts, their exchange woven into the pattern of old familiarity. It was a conversation that would sound unremarkable to any passing ear—how lean the beef was this week, whether the sausages had been made with the old seasoning or the new. Yet beneath the surface was the quiet assurance that both men understood more than they said. They had known each other long enough to communicate without ever naming the truth they both carried.

Every shop along the lane seemed to follow the same unspoken script. At the bakery, Maria's eyes wandered over the iced buns while Casper pointed out the loaf he wanted for breakfast. The baker's wife wrapped it in brown paper, tying the string in a neat bow before placing it in Ben's hands. She asked no questions, not about where they had been, not about the letters in the papers, not even about the steady trickle of outsiders who sometimes came to look for him. It was not willful ignorance—it was the discipline of trust.

The grocer across from the post office offered him the same treatment. "Morning, lad," he said, just as he had when Ben was small enough to stand on tiptoe to see the jars of sweets. The term lad carried no irony now, no sting of reminder that the boy had become a man and a king besides. Here, titles were as useless as umbrellas in summer. The only measure of worth was the history between neighbours, and by that measure, Ben was priceless.

What struck him most was how seamless it all felt. No eyes lingered too long, no voice dipped into whispers when he passed. The people of Kent understood that silence could be as protective as any wall, and they wielded it with the precision of craftsmen. They had learned long ago that the fewer words given to strangers, the fewer threads there were to pull.

Sørensen noticed it too, though he said nothing. He had been in enough places where curiosity led to trouble, where even the friendliest shopkeeper might let slip a detail for the price of a pint. Kent was different. Each interaction was a deliberate act of guardianship, a reinforcement of the invisible boundary that kept the outside world at bay.

There was no formal agreement binding these shopkeepers to Ben's protection. No meetings had been called, no oaths sworn. It was something older than that—an inheritance of loyalty passed down through years of shared history. They had known him as a boy who carried groceries for elderly neighbours without being asked, who repaired a broken bicycle chain for a stranger in the rain, who never took more than his fair share from the sweet jar. That boy had not been forgotten.

At the newsagent's, the proof of that loyalty was most evident. Bundles of newspapers sat stacked in neat piles, their headlines bold with the latest lies from Denmark. Yet when Ben stepped inside, the shopkeeper's hand moved without thought, sliding a plain paper over the top. The papers were still for sale, but no one here would be caught pressing them into his hands. He did not need reminding of what the world beyond Kent was saying.

The children noticed it in their own way. Maria observed how no one stared at them too long, how even a smile seemed to be given with care. Casper liked the way the shopkeepers treated them as though they had always belonged here, never asking where they came from or how long they might stay. Emil, who was more attuned to Sørensen's quiet vigilance, understood that this was more than politeness—it was protection.

Ben carried the parcels back toward the cottage, his steps unhurried. The weight in his arms was nothing compared to the weight he felt lifting in his mind. Each shop, each exchange, each familiar nod had reinforced the truth: Kent did not need to be told to protect its own. It already did so instinctively. Here, the outside world could batter itself against the walls of rumour, and still, the centre would hold.

In this county, silence was not the absence of speech—it was the presence of loyalty. It was an unshakable, unrecorded pact that stretched from the shopfront to the lane, from the library to the market, and it was as binding as any law Ben had ever known. And so, with every door that closed softly behind him, he stepped deeper into the safety of that unbroken trust.

The afternoon light slanted across the lane as Ben stepped out alone, letting his feet find their own course along the roads that had once been the boundaries of his boyhood world. The air here carried a texture he could not quite describe—soft, steady, and untouched by the urgency that haunted cities. He passed the same weathered fences, the same hedgerows bent under their own weight, and felt the quiet recognition of places that had known him long before the weight of a crown bent his shoulders. Kent did not look at him and see a ruler; it saw a boy who had once run along these lanes with muddy shoes and a pocket full of marbles.

The first stop was the library, not out of obligation but instinct. Its front steps creaked under his weight, just as they had when he was small enough to hop up two at a time. Through the glass, he could see the faint outline of the history shelves in the far corner, the place he had first learned to lose himself in the pages of lives long past. Back then, the books had been a doorway into worlds he could not touch; now they stood as proof that his own world had grown large enough to be written about. Yet here, no one hurried to remind him of that.

From the library, his steps carried him toward the old school. The building's brickwork was unchanged, though the paint on the doors had shifted shades over the years. He paused at the gate, letting the quiet hum of the place wash over him. He could almost hear the echo of the bell that once called them in from recess, the shuffle of boots against the worn wooden floors. The blacktop still bore the faint outlines of chalk games played decades ago, their borders weathered but not erased. Time had touched this place gently.

He moved on to the pond at the county's edge, the same stretch of water where he had once spent long afternoons skipping stones with boys whose names he still remembered. The surface mirrored the sky, unbroken save for the occasional ripple of a duck cutting across its stillness. As a boy, he had thought of the pond as the edge of the world. Now, it felt like the centre—an anchor point that reminded him that before the titles and the scrutiny, there had been something simpler and more enduring.

These places did not ask anything of him. They did not measure him by his reach or his responsibilities. Here, he was not a symbol, not a target, not a man carrying the silence of seven dynasties in his keeping. He was simply Benedict—the boy who borrowed too many books, who learned to run faster than the rain, who once carved his initials into the low fence near the post office and thought it might last forever.

Every turn in the lane brought a memory forward. The narrow bend where he had fallen from his bicycle, scraping his knee but refusing to cry. The corner shop where he once spent his last penny on a boiled sweet for a friend. The field where he had hidden from a summer storm under the thickest oak he could find. None of these moments appeared in the public record, yet they defined him more than any speech or decree ever could.

As he walked, he noticed how Kent itself seemed to conspire in keeping these memories intact. No one stopped him for photographs. No one asked him to recount his story. They allowed him to move through his own past in peace, as though they understood that a man's roots were not for public display. This restraint, so natural to them, was a shield stronger than any guard detail.

Sørensen, watching from a distance, recognised the significance of the walk. He had seen men lose themselves when the world's definition of them replaced their own. Ben was not one of those men, not here, not in the county that had shaped him. Each landmark was a thread in the weave of his identity, a reminder that no matter how wide his reach, it began here.

The walk ended where it had begun, at the cottage tucked behind the old house. The sight of its modest walls after so many steps felt like coming home twice over—once to the shelter it now provided, and once to the life that had first taught him what safety meant. Inside, the others were waiting, unaware of the full weight of the path he had taken. It was not a burden he needed to share. The meaning was his alone, and Kent, as always, understood.

In the stillness that followed, Ben realised that memory was not just a record of what had been. It was a guardrail, a quiet strength that kept him steady when the world tried to redraw his outline. And in Kent, that outline remained exactly as it had been carved—true, familiar, and entirely his own.

The first embrace came without ceremony. Ben had stepped into the small greengrocer's to fetch a basket of apples when the shopkeeper's wife appeared from behind the counter, arms outstretched, her smile as steady as it had been decades before. She folded him into her arms with a firmness that was neither hurried nor cautious, as though the years since his boyhood had been no more than a pause between visits. There was no talk of Denmark, no mention of headlines—only the quiet certainty of welcome. In that moment, the world outside the county ceased to exist.

Along the high street, the pattern repeated itself. An elderly neighbour, stooped now with age, reached for him in the doorway of the bakery, patting his back in the same rhythm she once used to dust flour from her apron when he had come by for a roll as a boy. A postman, whose rounds had brought him past Ben's childhood home a thousand times, stepped down from his bicycle just to clasp him by the shoulder, the greeting unbroken by years apart. These gestures were not performances; they were habits, unchanged by the passage of time or the arrival of titles.

Each embrace carried a weight that could not be measured. It was not pity, nor obligation, but recognition—an understanding that the man standing before them was the same boy who once raced them to the end of the lane or carried groceries for neighbours without being asked. They did not see the figure that the papers tried to paint; they saw the boy who belonged to them, and to whom they, in some unspoken way, belonged as well.

The hugs were different from the stiff, guarded greetings he had grown used to in official life. There was no choreography here, no calculation of angles for a photographer's lens. Arms were thrown around him without hesitation, holding him with the familiarity of someone who had every right to do so. He returned each one without reservation, the warmth of those moments sinking deeper than any words could.

Sørensen observed the exchanges with a quiet respect. He understood that these were more than casual gestures—they were a form of protection. Every person who embraced Ben in public was making a statement to any outsider watching: He is ours. In Kent, that meant something. It meant that gossip had no foothold, that outsiders would have to push through more than rumour to reach him.

Some embraces came with laughter, others with the brief squeeze of someone too moved to speak. A butcher grinned as he wrapped an arm around Ben, telling him he still owed him a favour for mending a fence when he was twelve. A seamstress in the square hugged him and whispered, "Don't let them change you," before stepping back to straighten her scarf. Each one gave him something intangible, but no less real than the apples or bread he carried home.

The librarian's embrace was the last of the day, and perhaps the most telling. She greeted him at the library's side door, as she had when he was a boy arriving before the official opening. Her hug lingered, her hands pressed against his shoulders as if to reassure herself that he was not just a memory she had conjured. When she stepped back, she said only, "You've not grown out of your place here," and turned to unlock the door. He followed her inside, knowing she was right.

By the time Ben returned to the cottage, the scent of cedar and coffee in the air, he carried with him more than the goods he had collected along the way. He carried the reaffirmation that Kent had not shifted in its loyalty. The embraces had said as much without needing to voice it: no matter what the outside world decided to print, they knew who he was, and they would stand by it.

That night, as he sat by the hearth with Sørensen, the memory of those hugs settled over him like the warmth of the fire. They were reminders that he did not need to defend himself here; his defence was already woven into the fabric of the county. In Kent, truth did not require proclamation—it was felt, and it was held, in arms that had known him all his life.

The words came without ceremony, spoken across the small kitchen table where the teapot sat between them. Harrison leaned back in his chair, his eyes steady, his tone unshaken. "You're safe here," he said, not as comfort but as fact. There was no theatrics in his delivery, no attempt to dramatise the statement. It was the kind of truth a man only spoke when he had weighed it against every possible circumstance and found no need for qualification.

Ben did not answer immediately. He simply watched Harrison pour the tea, the steam rising between them like a veil. Safety, he knew, was never absolute, but here it was different. In Kent, safety was not granted by gates or guards—it was rooted in people. It was a county's instinct to shield its own, and though outsiders might not understand it, Ben had lived it once before. The protection here did not waver with titles or politics; it was born of familiarity, of years when he was simply the boy down the lane.

Sørensen, standing by the counter, listened without interrupting. He had spent enough of his life calculating risks to know when a statement was more than wishful thinking. Harrison's confidence came not from ignorance of danger but from a knowledge of the ground, the people, and the history they shared. It was a promise underwritten by decades of tested loyalty, and in Sørensen's eyes, it carried more weight than any security detail Denmark could assemble.

Harrison went on, his voice low but certain. "If someone comes asking questions, they'll get what they always get—directions to the next county and nothing else. If they press harder, they'll find doors shut before they've finished knocking. We've done it before. We'll do it again." His words were measured, not boastful. It was not about hostility toward strangers; it was about preserving what mattered, and in this county, Ben mattered.

Ben thought of the morning greetings in the shops, the librarian's quiet nod, the unbroken trust in every handshake and embrace. They were not performances for his benefit—they were part of the fabric here. Kent had its own kind of code, unspoken but ironclad. Those who lived within its bounds understood that some truths were not for sharing, and some names were not for passing along.

The sound of rain began to patter against the window, soft at first and then steadier, as though sealing the walls of the cottage in a curtain of privacy. Ben felt the weight in his shoulders ease, not in complacency but in recognition. This was what it meant to be among people who did not need to be convinced of his worth. They already knew it, and they guarded it as they would their own.

Sørensen set a mug of tea in front of him, a silent acknowledgement that he too trusted the strength of this place. But he caught Ben's eye for a moment, the faintest flicker of caution there. Safety here was real, but it did not mean they would grow careless. That was the balance—trust in the county, but never in chance.

Harrison lifted his cup, taking a long sip before speaking again. "You'll hear the noise from outside," he said. "It'll get louder. Let it. It doesn't cross the county line unless we allow it." There was no challenge in his words, no need to convince—just the quiet assurance of a man who had already decided how things would be. Ben nodded once, not in gratitude but in agreement. In this corner of England, the noise could rage on forever, and still, it would not reach him.

From the front porch of the cottage, Sørensen stood as he always did—feet planted, shoulders squared, eyes fixed beyond the neat line of hedgerows that marked the property's boundary. His gaze travelled further than the gravel lane and the bend in the road; it searched the horizon as if reading a book whose pages only he could turn. The quiet here was real, but it was never complete. In the stillness, he sensed the faint tremors of a world beyond Kent, one that had not forgotten Benedict's name.

The morning air carried the damp scent of the rain from the night before, but it also carried the sound of a distant radio—static, then muffled voices, the tell-tale rhythm of news bulletins. Sørensen didn't need to hear the words to understand their shape. He knew the pattern of stories the same way a seasoned fisherman knows the pull of the tide. Headlines rose and fell like swells, each one circling back to the same point: the King who would not speak.

Inside, Ben sat at the small table, the day's first cup of coffee untouched in front of him. He listened without appearing to, catching the way Sørensen's boots shifted on the porch boards, the subtle scrape that meant his mentor had stopped pacing and was now locked in thought. Ben understood that stillness—it was the moment before a conclusion, the gathering of threads before they were tied into a single knot.

When Sørensen stepped back inside, he didn't sit. Instead, he remained by the doorway, one hand braced against the frame. "They'll keep at it," he said simply, his voice carrying the same certainty as a weather forecast. "Doesn't matter if it's truth or not—they'll run the cycle until something else distracts them. Question is whether you give them a reason to keep looking, or let them tire themselves out." His words were stripped of emotion, but not of weight.

Ben nodded, though his eyes remained on the map spread across the table. Every day here in Kent was another day of quiet advantage, another day to plan without interference. But he knew the luxury of time could not be mistaken for permanence. The longer he remained silent, the more speculation would grow. The challenge lay in choosing the moment when silence became strategy, and not weakness.

Outside, the wind shifted, carrying with it the faint rumble of distant traffic—a reminder that while Kent felt like an island, it was still connected to the greater whole. Sørensen's vigilance was a constant, but even he could not stand against the inevitability of change forever. His eyes returned to the lane, tracking the curve where any unexpected visitor would first appear.

"Another clear day," he said, though both of them understood that the forecast he was reading was not about the weather at all. Ben leaned back in his chair, the coffee still cooling between his hands. "Clear," he agreed. But in his mind, he was already watching the same horizon Sørensen saw, measuring the distance between calm and the first ripple of disturbance.

The orchard lay just beyond the hedgerow, where the grass grew uneven in the shadow of the old apple trees. It was here, in the shelter of branches twisted by years of wind, that the children gathered. Maria had brought a tin of biscuits wrapped in a tea towel, while one of the local boys carried a glass bottle of lemonade under his arm as if it were treasure. They sat in a loose circle on the flattened grass, sunlight dappling their hair through the shifting leaves.

It began innocently enough—one of the farm boys asking, between mouthfuls, whether "the newspapers really meant anything." Maria's eyes had flickered towards Casper and Emil before answering, a pause so deliberate it made the others fall quiet. Then, in the way that only children could, the subject turned from a question into a pact. They agreed, without prompting, that there were things they would not repeat. Not to their parents. Not to teachers. Not to anyone.

The terms were simple: the castle, the titles, and anything that could lead an outsider to Ben's door would remain unspoken. No games of pretend with real names, no teasing about "royal" things in public. It was to be their secret in full, kept as tightly as the knots they would tie in the twine around the biscuit tin. There was no ceremony, no grand declaration—only the unshakable seriousness that comes when a child recognises the weight of trust placed in them.

Maria poured the lemonade into mismatched mugs, each child holding theirs with both hands as if it were part of the ritual. The toast was clumsy but heartfelt: to keeping their word, to protecting what mattered, to never letting the noise from elsewhere reach the orchard. They clinked mugs, the sharp sound cutting briefly through the hum of bees in the clover, then drank in unison.

Casper, never one for speeches, simply placed the last biscuit in the centre of their circle and said, "We save this one. For when we've kept the promise." The others nodded without question, as though he had just declared an unbreakable law. Even Emil, usually restless, sat still, the gravity of the moment pulling him into its orbit.

The laughter that followed was lighter, the tension melting into games of chase around the orchard. Yet beneath the play, the pact held. Each child knew instinctively that what they had agreed upon was not to be undone. It was more than secrecy—it was loyalty in its purest form, untainted by politics or gain.

From a distance, Sørensen watched them, unseen behind the hedgerow. He recognised the shape of what they were doing, even if the language was different from the oaths he had sworn in his own life. These were not soldiers, and yet they understood the first lesson of his trade: trust is earned, and once earned, it must be guarded. He let them be, knowing that such bonds, once formed in the honesty of childhood, often outlasted the noise of the adult world.

The air cooled steadily as the light withdrew from the sky, drawing long shadows across the lawn and softening the outlines of the hedgerows. Ben settled into the old wooden chair on the porch, its familiar creak answering his weight. Sørensen took the seat beside him, leaning back with the kind of measured ease that came only when every perimeter had been checked twice. Harrison remained standing for a time, one hand in his pocket, his eyes following the last curve of the sun as it dipped behind the distant trees. The countryside carried its own quiet music— the faint rustle of leaves in a slow wind, the intermittent chirp of crickets, and the far-off call of an owl announcing its presence.

No words passed at first. It was a silence of choice, not of awkwardness. Ben let his gaze wander to the gate at the end of the drive, where the gravel shimmered faintly under the silver light. Somewhere beyond, the county moved at its own unhurried pace, indifferent to the storms gathering in other places. Sørensen shifted in his chair, the movement small, almost imperceptible, yet enough for Ben to sense the enduring readiness that lived in him. Harrison finally lowered himself onto the steps, resting his forearms on his knees, head bent slightly forward as if he were listening for something beyond the reach of hearing.

They did not discuss strategy. No plans were drawn, no urgent whispers exchanged. Tonight, stillness was the point—the deliberate act of allowing the day to close without burdening it with tomorrow's demands. The owl called again, nearer now, and Ben followed the sound until it vanished into the fields. It reminded him of the nights in his boyhood when this porch had been the safe edge of his world, a place where nothing beyond the fence could touch him. That memory pressed close, not as nostalgia but as reassurance that the space still held.

The wooden boards beneath their feet retained a trace of the day's warmth, though the breeze carried the scent of cool earth and the faint tang of woodsmoke from a neighbouring farm. Harrison leaned back on his hands, his shoulders easing under the weight of nothing immediate to guard against. Sørensen remained upright, eyes half-lidded but far from sleep, scanning the treeline out of habit more than necessity. Ben knew he would never entirely stop, just as he himself would never stop thinking three moves ahead, even in moments of rest.

Somewhere inside the cottage, a lamp flickered on, casting a soft amber glow through the curtains. The children's muffled voices reached them in fragments—laughter, a shuffle of footsteps, the scrape of a chair across the floor. Ben let the sound settle around him, drawing in the truth of it: they were here, they were safe, and for this evening at least, the world could be kept at bay. He did not need to explain that truth to either man beside him. It was understood in the same way they understood the value of silence—that sometimes the most important work was to do nothing at all.

The weight of the day lifted in the way only Kent could manage—without ceremony, without announcement, but with the quiet certainty of a place that refused to let the world's noise in. Ben sat by the window in the cottage's small front room, the lamplight framing him in a pool of gold, the curtains drawn just enough to let in the silver outline of the hedgerows. His thoughts were his own, unprompted by questions, untouched by the demands that would follow if he were anywhere else. No voice here asked him to justify his presence. No hand here reached to strip away the silence. In this county, his absence from Denmark's stage was not a scandal—it was a given.

The seven dynasties he carried in the quiet vault of his mind remained undisturbed, guarded not by a wall of speech but by the stronger shield of refusal. In Kent, no one asked about lineage or titles; they already knew and had long since decided that those truths belonged to him alone. It was not ignorance—it was the discipline of people who understood that some things are not to be handled like gossip in a shop queue. The respect was palpable, not as a performance, but as the natural order here. In this way, the county formed its own crown around him, though it was never visible and never needed to be.

To be the King of Quiet was not to retreat from responsibility, but to understand that power was not always in the spoken word. It lived in the pauses, in the restraint, in the choosing of when and how to be heard. Each day spent here was another act of deliberate inaction—strategic, controlled, and as necessary as any declaration. Sørensen knew it too; he never pressed, never urged Ben to break the stillness unless the time demanded. Harrison understood as well, his every move reinforcing the invisible perimeter that allowed silence to exist without threat.

Outside, the county road lay in its usual peace, disturbed only by the occasional passing of a neighbour's car, each driver lifting a hand in the same understated greeting they had given him since boyhood. The message was the same now as it had been then: you belong here, and no one can take that from you. There was no deference to title, no bending of posture as he passed; the respect here came without bowing, without ceremony. They valued the man before the monarch, the boy before the king, the neighbour before the headline.

The cottage air carried the scent of the evening's fire, its embers still warm in the hearth. From the back room came the faint sound of the children's breathing, steady in sleep, untouched by the urgency that waited in Denmark's headlines. Ben closed his eyes briefly, committing the sound to memory. It was proof enough that the strategy was working. The dynasties could wait; the speeches could wait. The silence here was not just a reprieve—it was an asset, a resource as valuable as any alliance or claim.

When he opened his eyes, the lamplight had deepened into the darker tones of night. He reached for the book on the table but did not open it, letting his gaze rest instead on the unbroken space between the curtain's edge and the window frame. Beyond it, the county slept, its quiet unshaken, its loyalty unbought. Here, the world could not dictate the pace of his breath or the weight of his thoughts. Here, he was not compelled to be the King of Denmark. He was the King of Quiet, and in this role—unseen, unprovoked, unchallenged—he might hold the truest power of all.

CHAPTER 12: THE DIGITAL GHOST

The cottage study was dim but not dark, lit by the low amber glow of a desk lamp whose light spilled only as far as the papers immediately beneath it. The rest of the room held its shadows close, as though the walls themselves had agreed to keep secrets. Ben stood at the far end, his weight balanced on the heel of one boot, watching Sørensen kneel to lift the loose plank from the corner of the floor.

The air beneath smelled faintly of cedar and time, a sealed pocket that had been left undisturbed for over a decade. Sørensen's hand found the small steel lockbox, and he raised it without a word. The key was unnecessary; both men knew the combination by touch, each number turned with deliberate care, the quiet click of the tumblers sounding like the first move in a match already set in motion.

The lock released, and inside lay the encrypted drive—its black casing unmarked, its surface dull under the lamp. Ben took it without ceremony, as though picking up a pen, yet there was nothing casual about the way his fingers closed around it. He carried it to the desk, the drive's weight more psychological than physical, as if the years since its last use had pressed into its circuitry. Thirteen years ago, it had been a weapon wielded by a boy who understood more about systems and networks than most seasoned technicians. Now, it returned to the hands of a man who carried not only that skill but also the full gravity of responsibility for his family's safety.

Sørensen remained standing behind him, arms folded, eyes fixed on the slow, deliberate movements of the startup sequence. No one spoke as the first password prompt appeared, its blinking cursor waiting like a challenge. Ben's hands did not hesitate; muscle memory guided each keystroke, the rhythm precise and unbroken. The first lock fell, then the second, each revealing deeper layers until the vault opened fully—a cascade of dormant code and operational frameworks, untouched yet still alive. It was like breathing life into something that had only been sleeping, though the air it drew now felt heavier, less playful, edged with purpose.

The glow from the monitor lit the side of Ben's face, sharp against the surrounding darkness. He scrolled through the embedded subroutines, fingers tracing over lines of logic that had once been born out of late nights in the back room of Rosenshavn Castle. The original "Stink Bomb" had been clever, disruptive, and impossible to trace—but this was different. This was the kind of work that left no digital shadow, no echo for even the most persistent adversary to follow. The protocols were still sound, but thirteen years had given him new tools, new tricks, and a colder understanding of what such a system could do when applied without hesitation.

A knock, soft and deliberate, came from the study door. Sørensen crossed the room, opening it just enough to admit the Librarian. She entered without speaking, her steps quiet, her presence calm but resolute. She closed the door behind her, turning the lock in a way that made it sound less like securing a room and more like sealing an agreement.

She did not ask what they were doing; she already knew. Her role in this was as old as the operation itself—supply the records, feed the names, keep the outside world guessing. She carried a small notebook, its cover worn, the pages inside holding details only she could have gathered without drawing attention.

Ben looked up briefly, their eyes meeting with the familiarity of long trust. She approached the desk, setting the notebook down beside the keyboard. Her voice was steady, almost casual, when she said she would be ready whenever he called for the first wave of information. He nodded, then turned back to the screen. That was the way it had always been between them—clear understanding without wasted words. She knew that her public role in the village required complete innocence, that any hint of involvement could fracture the protective ring that Kent had quietly maintained around him for years.

The Librarian took a seat in the corner, her hands folded neatly over her notebook. She watched the scrolling code with the kind of interest one reserves for a familiar play seen after many seasons, the plot known but the performance fresh. Every so often, her eyes shifted to Sørensen, reading his stance, gauging the unspoken tempo of the room. When she finally spoke again, it was to remark on a shipment schedule, disguised in such a way that an outsider might think she was talking about library returns. Ben caught the reference instantly, adjusting his timelines in response.

Outside the study, the cottage remained in its usual evening quiet. The children were in their rooms, the Braun coffee maker in the kitchen ticking softly as it's percolation came to a halt. The blackout perimeter was already in place—Kent's own silence sealing the outer wall. What they were building here would not simply disrupt the eyes and ears of the world; it would erase the trail entirely, making it seem as though Ben had stepped out of reality itself. The digital and the physical would fold over one another, each strengthening the other until nothing could penetrate.

Ben leaned back for a moment, his hands resting on the edge of the desk. He thought of the last time he had run Sovereign Burn, of the electric rush it had given him then. But that had been a boy's thrill, an experiment in control and defiance. This was no thrill. This was the sharpening of a blade, the setting of a trap designed not to snap shut loudly but to remain unseen, its prey only realising its mistake when retreat was impossible. His jaw tightened, not from doubt, but from the knowledge that this time, once engaged, there would be no half-measures.

Sørensen stepped forward, placing a folded sheet of paper on the desk beside the notebook. It held a list of confirmed safe contacts—those who could move within the county without question and who would act on instruction without hesitation. The Librarian added two more names in her careful script, neither of which Ben questioned. Trust here was binary: absolute or nonexistent. He glanced over the list once, then tucked it beneath the keyboard.

The keystrokes began again, faster now, the build sequence taking shape. Old code was stripped and replaced, firewalls doubled, redundancies layered. Ben's hands moved with a precision that bordered on artistry, each command a note in a composition only he could hear. The Librarian observed quietly, making mental notes of which data points she would prepare and how she would deliver them without leaving a fingerprint. Sørensen shifted his stance, leaning slightly closer to the desk, scanning the progress bar as though counting down to a launch.

When the first diagnostic completed, the system reported a perfect pass—no leaks, no vulnerabilities. Ben allowed himself a slow exhale. The Librarian closed her notebook, a small but deliberate movement, as though sealing her part of the preparation. She would play her role to perfection, her public ignorance a shield no amount of investigation could breach.

"Ready," Ben said simply, his eyes still fixed on the screen. It was not an announcement, not a signal to begin—only a confirmation that the ghost was awake again. In the corner, the Librarian gave the faintest nod, and Sørensen stepped back into the shadows of the study, his silence as steady as the operation itself. Outside, the wind shifted in the hedgerows, carrying away the last trace of the old dust from beneath the floorboards. What replaced it was something far less tangible, and far more dangerous.

The diagnostic window faded, leaving behind the clean slate of the command shell. Ben's hands resumed their rhythm without pause, the screen filling with the skeletal framework of a system that no longer bore the raw edges of its youth. Sovereign Burn's original architecture had been a razor in a child's grasp—sharp, effective, but unpredictable in its bite. Now, under his deliberate shaping, it became a scalpel. Every subroutine was examined, trimmed, or replaced outright, the dead weight of outdated code discarded without sentiment. He wasn't here to reminisce. He was here to refine a weapon into something untraceable and precise.

Sørensen shifted slightly, the soft creak of the floorboards under his boots the only sound to break the steady clatter of keys. His eyes stayed fixed on the screen, noting every alteration with a soldier's attention to detail. Where once his role in this had been the imposing figure standing watch, now it was the quiet sentinel ensuring no corner of the build carried risk. He wasn't watching for enemies outside the cottage; he was watching for the invisible ones—weaknesses buried so deep they could be exploited before the system's first strike.

Ben layered in a new command sequence, the cursor blinking in time with the narrowed focus in his eyes. The pulse cycle—once an even, predictable rhythm—was reshaped into something erratic to outside observers but perfectly patterned beneath the surface. In precise intervals, it would reach out, touch the signal paths of nearby satellites, and withdraw again before anyone could confirm it had been there. The interference would register as a momentary disruption, blamed on weather, solar flares, or the natural imperfections of aging equipment. Each pulse left no residue, only absence.

The Librarian had moved closer, her gaze following the structure as it unfolded on the screen. She didn't ask questions; she didn't need to. She saw the careful way Ben tied the new protocols into the old foundation, weaving modern algorithms into lines of code she remembered watching him write thirteen years ago. Her mind mapped the patterns not for replication but for understanding—enough to know when to step in with the right information at the right moment. She could feed this system with whispers that looked like static to anyone else.

With each keystroke, Ben tightened the safeguards, triple-locking every gate before linking it to the next. Access paths branched and vanished in loops, forcing any intruder to chase false corridors until they lost the trail entirely. Sovereign Burn had been a fortress before; now it was a labyrinth. No two maps of it would ever match, not even the one in Ben's own head. Sørensen approved of the redundancy—it was a soldier's kind of thinking, the same principle that ensured escape routes doubled back on themselves in unfamiliar terrain.

The core protocols came next, built in layers so thin and fast that they could slip between surveillance scans unnoticed. Ben adjusted their tempo to ride the edge of detectability, moving just beneath the range where automated systems flagged irregularities. It was a game of shadows, and he was playing with the confidence of someone who knew both the rules and how to bend them until they broke. Every so often, his lips moved silently as he counted cycles in his head, checking them against the unspoken rhythm he'd created over years of practice.

Sørensen leaned in closer, his hand resting lightly on the back of Ben's chair. "No vulnerabilities," he murmured—not as an observation but as an order. Ben answered with a curt nod, his focus unbroken. The screen now displayed a cascade of green checks beside each compiled segment, the system confirming what both men already knew: there were no cracks to exploit, no misplaced keystrokes to betray them. The architecture was sound, but it was more than that—it was alive in a way only a builder could feel.

A single line of text appeared at the bottom of the screen: Designation required. Ben typed the name slowly, deliberately, each letter a quiet acknowledgment of what this build had become. Stink Bomb 2.0. It was the only time the name would exist in open view. With a final tap, he locked it away, buried so deep in the system's inner shell that it might as well have been carved into stone at the bottom of the sea. Even if someone managed to take apart the shell, they would never find the heart.

The Librarian exhaled softly, her fingers tightening around her closed notebook. She understood the significance of that act. Naming something gave it identity; sealing that name in the dark gave it protection. In her own way, she would protect it too—not by touching the system, but by guarding its edges, keeping the human channels free from contamination. No misplaced word in the wrong ear, no detail allowed to drift beyond the circle that had already been chosen.

Ben moved to the next phase, linking the disruption cycle to the county's blackout perimeter. When engaged, the cottage and its surrounding ten miles would effectively vanish from electronic maps. GPS signals would skew, communications would jitter and drop, and surveillance feeds would loop in on themselves until they displayed nothing but still frames. To anyone outside, it would look like Kent was simply having a quiet day—a small place too unremarkable to notice.

Sørensen studied the readout, his finger tracing a line of data that marked the system's first projected sweep. "It'll hold," he said quietly. Ben didn't answer, but his eyes flicked toward the clock on the wall. They didn't need to speak to know what the next step would be. The system wasn't just ready to defend—it was ready to send a message, one that would travel without origin, without trace, and without the faintest suggestion of permission.

The Librarian broke the silence only once, reminding Ben of the timelines they'd discussed. Her words were wrapped in the same casual tone she might use when asking about a shipment of new books. Ben acknowledged her with a glance, already adjusting the intervals in the system's cycle to match her intelligence. She had given him the edge before; she would do it again.

The screens shifted, lines of code freezing into their final state. Ben leaned back, his fingers finally still. The hum of the system filled the space where conversation might have been, a low, steady presence that promised it was awake and watching. Stink Bomb 2.0 was no longer an idea or a plan—it was a living barrier, a moving shadow that could smother the reach of any enemy before they even realised they were being watched in return.

"Good," Sørensen said simply, stepping back to let the machine breathe. The Librarian closed her notebook for the last time that night, her eyes moving between the two men with the quiet satisfaction of someone who knew they had just witnessed the first movement in a piece that would not end until it had played out entirely on their terms. Outside, the cottage walls held steady, and beyond them, Kent slept without knowing it was already under the guard of a ghost.

The system's pulse counter ticked down from the corner of the main monitor, each digit changing in measured, deliberate rhythm. Ben's eyes remained fixed on the display, tracking not only the numbers but the invisible chain of processes that were waiting to engage. The first wave would be subtle—a sweep so precise it would draw no immediate suspicion, a warm-up of the machine's strength before the strike reached full amplitude. At ten o'clock sharp, the cursor blinked, waiting for his hand to start the cycle. Sørensen gave a single nod, his approval as unembellished as the act itself.

Outside, Kent's streets were already quiet, the occasional passing car carrying the familiar, unhurried pace of a place untroubled by the noise of the larger world. The cottage windows reflected nothing but the lamplight within, concealing the silent coordination that filled the room.

The Librarian had moved to the far desk, her role now reduced to silent observation, her earlier intelligence work already woven into the fabric of the operation. Harrison had taken position in the garage, waiting for the signal to begin his perimeter run. No one else in the county would see them work, and even fewer would ever understand what had just been set in motion.

The final keystroke fell without ceremony. The system accepted it instantly, the hum of its core deepening by a fraction—barely audible to human ears, yet distinct to those who knew what to listen for. Invisible threads unspooled from the command centre, snaking outward in carefully calculated paths. No physical structure shifted, no streetlamp dimmed, no alarm sounded, but the effect was absolute. In the space of a breath, the air above Kent lost its reach.

Mobile networks in the ten-mile radius folded in on themselves, their signals severed mid-transmission. The towers still stood against the night sky, their lights blinking steadily as if nothing had changed. Birds still roosted in their frames, unaware that the electronic pulse beneath them had gone still. It was not destruction—it was suspension. The difference mattered. The blackout was surgical, slicing neatly through the targeted frequency bands and leaving everything else untouched. Power remained. Water flowed. Radios, wired lines, and purely local systems continued unhindered.

Locals, as always, adapted with ease. In the nearest farmhouse, a teenager frowned at his phone before tossing it onto the kitchen counter, deciding the interruption wasn't worth the trouble of complaint. At the corner shop, a pair of old men in flat caps joked about the "ghost in the wires" as they continued their game of dominoes. No panic. No questions that couldn't be laughed away. Kent had seen stranger things, and those who lived here understood that some silences were worth keeping.

Outsiders, however, were met with a wall they could neither see nor climb. A news freelancer attempting to send an email from the edge of the county found his screen locked in an endless loop of sending.... A government vehicle passing along the B-road lost its navigation feed entirely, the display freezing on a location marker that might as well have been painted on glass. The drivers swore under their breath, turned around, and left, never once suspecting the precision that had severed them from their destination.

Harrison's headlights cut a narrow path through the darkness as he guided the black vehicle toward the county's perimeter. At each checkpoint—a bend in the road, a rise in the land—he slowed, checked the small handheld scanner resting in the cup holder, and moved on. The device, tuned to Ben's own specifications, measured the strength and reach of the blackout field. Each reading matched the numbers exactly. At the ten-mile mark, the signal resumed as suddenly as it had vanished, clean and uncorrupted. The border was perfect.

Back at the cottage, Sørensen stood at the window, watching for the sweep of Harrison's return lights. He trusted the readings, but trust did not replace verification. When Harrison's vehicle finally appeared on the lane, he stepped outside to meet it, boots crunching on the gravel. The two men exchanged no unnecessary words—only the brief nod of confirmation that meant the perimeter was holding exactly as planned.

Ben remained at the console, reviewing the silent ripple of the network map as it adapted to the blackout. To the outside world, the missing signals appeared as a series of coincidental failures—minor blips in an otherwise functioning grid. They would not last long enough to trigger automated recovery systems, nor would they be frequent enough to suggest deliberate interference. It was an operation designed to live in the grey space between suspicion and proof, feeding on the complacency of those who dismissed anomalies as inevitable.

The Librarian leaned closer to see the shifting patterns, her gaze narrowing at the faint echoes on the outer edge of the sweep. "Residual ping," she murmured. Ben acknowledged her observation with a quick series of adjustments, sealing the leak before it could register beyond the cottage walls. She didn't ask what it had been—knowing it had been handled was enough. Her role was not to master the machine but to recognise when it required the hand of its maker.

By 10:37, the system's rhythm was steady, the blackout a living, breathing boundary around the county. Harrison remained on standby, ready to test the field again at Ben's signal, while Sørensen returned to the table to mark the successful activation in his logbook. The act of writing it down seemed almost ceremonial—proof that even a ghost could leave a record for those meant to find it.

Ben allowed himself a brief moment to step away from the screen, pouring a cup of coffee before returning to the console. His eyes did not leave the map. He knew this was only the first wave; the blackout was a shield, not a weapon. The strike, when it came, would be aimed far beyond Kent's borders, but the shield had to be flawless first. Sovereign Burn's teeth would stay hidden until there was no choice but to bare them.

Outside, the county continued to move in its slow, untroubled rhythm. Inside, the ghost in the wires stood ready, watching the edges of its reach with patient, silent intent. The perimeter was sealed. The air was still. The clock on the wall ticked toward midnight, when the second wave would test just how deep this silence could go.

The shift from ground control to orbital interference was deliberate, executed without a single break in the system's steady hum. Ben's hands moved across the console with the same precision he used when handling fragile glass, each command layered so it left no fingerprint. On the main screen, satellite paths arced in thin white lines, converging in points above Kent like threads in a loom. These were the eyes that governments and corporations trusted to watch the earth without blinking. Tonight, they would see only what Ben allowed.

A stored library of high-resolution aerial images waited in the system's hidden archive, each one carefully selected for clarity and lack of identifying movement. Farm animals frozen mid-step in a field, cars parked neatly in drives, clouds drifting lazily above the coastline—ordinary scenes captured in the glow of a summer morning. As the satellites' scheduled passes drew near, Ben queued the loop, aligning each image with the current orbital angle so that not even a cloud's shadow would appear misplaced.

The transition, when it came, was invisible to the operators on the receiving end. Their screens continued to show a living county, free of movement but entirely believable. No vehicles appeared where they should not, no gatherings drew attention, no unusual patterns suggested something worth a closer look. The illusion was perfect in its ordinariness. Those who were looking for movement would see none, and those looking for stillness would find it exactly where they expected.

Within each image, however, was a whisper—one pixel in every thousand altered in a precise sequence, invisible to the untrained eye. This was Ben's watermark, a cipher that mapped the image's origin and the time it had been fed into the loop. It was a code only he and Sørensen could read, a way of knowing which images had been intercepted, altered, and returned. If any leak occurred, they would know exactly when and where it had happened, and which watcher had been fed the lie.

Sørensen stood at his shoulder, arms folded, his gaze not on the monitor but on the subtle changes in Ben's expression. He knew the rhythm of this work—how each stage built upon the last, how each quiet victory here meant another layer of safety outside. "Feeds are stable," Ben said, his voice low enough not to break the concentration in the room. Sørensen didn't answer; his nod was enough.

Harrison, still in the garage, ran his own sweep of the county's visible skies. Through a pair of binoculars, he tracked the faint glint of a passing satellite as it caught the moonlight, utterly unaware that its camera was now blind. He reported back over the secure channel, the faint crackle of static underlining his words. "Nothing on the ground. Nothing in the air. Looks clean."

The Librarian shifted in her seat, glancing between the satellite paths on one screen and the local mapping grids on another. "They'll assume it's a compression error if they notice the pixel shift," she murmured. Ben almost smiled. She was right—these agencies had seen minor glitches before. What they would not suspect was that the so-called error was alive, adapting, and watching them in return.

By eleven o'clock, the system had intercepted and replaced every active aerial feed targeting the county. Commercial mapping services updated their tiles with Ben's loops, the timestamps adjusted to match the expected refresh intervals.

Government reconnaissance satellites received the same treatment, their data streams patched at the point of downlink. Even private weather satellites, harmless to the operation, were given edited views—not out of necessity, but to ensure that nothing in the sky escaped his reach.

This was the shield's second layer: the blackout on the ground meant no signals could escape, and the blackout in the air meant no one could watch. Together, they formed a dome of controlled perception. Inside it, Kent moved at its own pace, untethered from the scrutiny of those who would twist its reality into a weapon.

Ben leaned back for the first time in hours, stretching his fingers before returning them to the keys. His eyes flicked to the countdown in the corner of the screen—thirty-seven minutes until the satellites shifted into their next orbits. The loop would have to adapt on the fly, replacing each view again before the moment passed. It was a constant dance between timing and precision, one mistake enough to reveal the truth beneath the illusion.

The first orbital shift passed without incident, the images swapping in mid-stream without a flicker on the receiving end. Ben's watermark pattern rotated to a new sequence, the altered pixels shifting like a heartbeat. To anyone else, the county was unchanged. To Ben, it was a message in plain sight, proof that the sky itself had been bent to his will.

By the time the second shift completed, Sørensen had moved to the porch, scanning the quiet hedgerows. It wasn't the satellites he was worried about—it was the possibility that someone might come in person to do what their machines could not. But as the wind moved through the trees and the lane remained empty, he allowed himself the rare comfort of knowing that every approach, from above or below, was under their control.

Ben closed the satellite control module at precisely 11:52, locking it behind layers of encryption. The loops would continue to run on their own, updating and adjusting without human oversight until he called them down. He took a slow sip of coffee, his eyes still fixed on the dim glow of the screen. Outside, Kent slept beneath an artificial sky that no one but him could see.

The last of the satellite feeds locked into its loop, Ben shifted his focus from the sky to the ground. The blackout had been established, but it was the terrain that would decide whether a breach could slip through unnoticed. From a steel cabinet under the desk, he withdrew a rolled bundle tied with string—archival county maps that had been hidden since the last time Sovereign Burn was activated. The paper was thick, slightly brittle at the edges, the ink faded in places but still precise. These maps predated the era of constant digital updating; they showed the land as it truly was, without the overlays and simplifications of online charts.

He spread the first sheet across the table, weighting the corners with empty mugs to hold it flat. Sørensen leaned over his shoulder, already scanning for vantage points and choke zones. The blackout radius, calculated in the preceding hours, was sketched in a neat circle with Ben's fountain pen. From there, he began marking secondary arcs, blind corners where even a determined observer would lose sight of the lane.

The old county hedgerows and copses of oak became more than landmarks; they were assets. Ben traced routes that used these natural barriers as shields, ensuring that no direct line of sight could be established toward the cottage. Narrow lanes that dipped between earthen banks became escape channels, while certain rises in the ground—harmless to the untrained eye—were flagged as watch points to be avoided during movement.

Sørensen committed each segment to memory with the same focus he had once reserved for military briefings. Every blind corner, every detour, every crossing point that could be used to mask an approach was studied until it felt instinctive. When Ben spoke of a particular lane or bend, Sørensen could already picture its camber and the way the light fell across it at different times of day.

As each sheet was completed, Ben made annotations in the margin—small, deliberate marks that would mean nothing to anyone else. They were not just navigational notes but cues for action: where to slow, where to cut the lights, where to listen before moving. These were not escape plans born of fear, but of calculated readiness.

The Librarian, seated quietly at the far end of the table, occasionally brought forward an older survey sheet, her fingertips brushing across the paper with the care one might give to a rare book. "This field's been fenced off since before you left," she noted, pointing to a green patch near the western boundary. Ben adjusted the mark accordingly, shifting the safe route to avoid it entirely. Her memory was as much a part of the plan as the ink and paper.

Once the mapping was complete, Ben gathered the sheets into a single stack. There would be no chance for them to fall into the wrong hands. One by one, he fed them into the small iron stove in the corner. The flames curled eagerly around the edges, consuming the county's secrets with a quiet crackle. The smell of scorched paper filled the room, mingling with the faint aroma of coffee and cedar from the hearth.

Sørensen stood by the open window, watching as Ben emptied the stove's tray into a small tin. The ash was still warm when he carried it outside, scattering it into the wind beyond the garden wall. In moments, the fragments were gone—drifting invisibly over the hedgerows and fields they had just charted. The routes now existed only in the minds of the three people in the room.

Harrison arrived at the back door just as the last embers faded. He didn't ask what had been burned; he only glanced at Ben's expression and understood that the ground was now as shielded as the air above. "It's clean," Ben said, answering the question that had not been asked. Harrison nodded once and stepped inside, shaking the cold from his coat.

Ben rolled his shoulders, the tension of hours at the desk settling into the muscles of his back. This was the third layer of the shield—first the signal silence, then the blinded sky, now the mapped and controlled ground. Each was designed not only to protect but to mislead, to funnel any attempt at intrusion into paths that would yield nothing.

At the table, Sørensen turned the pen slowly between his fingers, his mind replaying the newly memorised routes. He could walk them blind if needed, counting the steps between one turning and the next. It was not enough to know the land—he had to inhabit it, to move through it like someone who belonged there, unseen and unquestioned.

The Librarian rose, smoothing her skirt, her eyes still on the stove where the maps had been reduced to nothing. "You've made Kent disappear without erasing it," she said quietly. Ben's mouth lifted at one corner, but he said nothing. The compliment was not for vanity—it was recognition of craft, and in this game, craft was survival.

By the time the last ash had settled beyond the wall, the county's defensive shell was complete in three dimensions. Kent was no longer simply a place—it was a fortress disguised as open countryside, invisible to the world beyond its hedgerows. The lines on the map had vanished, but their meaning would live in the minds of those who needed them, ready to be recalled at a moment's notice.

In the cottage, the fire settled into a steady glow, casting its light across the table where only the mugs remained. Outside, the wind carried the remnants of paper across fields that now existed only in memory, and for the first time that night, Ben allowed himself the smallest exhale. The land was ready.

The blackout lines had been drawn in the air, across the maps, and into the memory of those trusted to walk them. Now the next layer of defence took form—control of every item that crossed the perimeter. Harrison accepted the role without question. He had handled such duties before, but never with this degree of precision. In the war of shadows Ben and Sørensen were waging, supplies were not merely provisions; they were controlled variables in a carefully balanced equation.

Every crate of food, every jerrycan of petrol, every length of rope or packet of screws came through his hands alone. The system was designed so that even if one link faltered, no unvetted goods could reach the cottage. Deliveries came through trusted suppliers whose loyalty was as generational as the county itself. Names and faces were known, habits observed, and the knowledge that they were supplying Ben was kept silent under the weight of unspoken understanding.

Harrison's drop points shifted each night like pieces on a chessboard. Sometimes he left the van in a barn owned by an old friend, walking the last mile on foot under the cover of hedgerows. Other nights, he drove down to the disused mill by the river, where the black water hid any hint of movement from the lane. No pattern was ever repeated in succession, ensuring that even an unseen watcher could never predict the next handoff.

To the casual eye of the county, Harrison's comings and goings were routine. He was the man who fixed gates, fetched tools, and ran errands between farms. His absence was never remarked upon; his return, never questioned. In Kent, familiarity bred not curiosity but trust, and it was that trust that kept the shield in place.

Crossing the blackout boundary was a ritual in itself. As soon as he passed the invisible line where the mobile signals returned, Harrison switched devices, using an old, battered handset that contained only the numbers of the suppliers. No messages were stored. No calls lasted longer than necessary. If anyone tried to track the handset, they would find only a string of perfectly ordinary purchases—nothing to suggest the walls being built behind him.

Each item was inspected before it left the supplier's hands. Harrison's eye for detail caught the smallest irregularities—a seal fractionally misaligned, a label newer than the box it was stuck to. Anything suspect was refused without explanation, replaced with something verifiably clean. It was a dance of logistics and instinct, honed by years of knowing what could be hidden in the seams of a package.

The deliveries themselves were stripped of excess. Plastic was burned, paper pulped, tins flattened and buried in compost heaps across the county. No trail was left for anyone to follow—not even a bin of discarded packaging that could be picked through by someone with enough time and malice. The goods entered the cottage as if they had materialised from the earth itself.

Harrison rarely spoke of his routes, even to Ben. It was not secrecy between friends, but the awareness that in a siege, the fewer who carried a detail, the safer the whole became. Sørensen respected the silence. In his view, an operation's integrity depended as much on the discipline of the quiet as on the precision of the active work.

The trust placed in Harrison was complete, but it was not blind. Ben kept a secondary ledger, not to monitor him but to ensure that if something happened—if Harrison was delayed, intercepted, or worse—the network could adapt without a break in the chain. Sovereign Burn demanded redundancy as much as it demanded stealth.

There were nights when the drop came in foul weather, when rain turned the lanes into channels of mud and wind lashed through the trees. Those were the nights Harrison valued most. No one followed in a storm, not when the county roads could vanish under water in minutes. In such moments, the weather itself became part of the shield.

The cottage door would open soundlessly at the prearranged hour, and Harrison would step inside with his cargo, the scent of rain clinging to his coat. The goods would be unpacked in silence, each item placed exactly where it belonged before the paper records were burned and the rest stored. By the time the fire in the hearth settled, the outside world's connection to the delivery had been erased.

The county understood without being told. They saw him in the shops, at the fuel station, or leaning on a fence post to speak with a neighbour, and they knew these were not idle errands. It was the same way they had once watched a boy named Benedict carry books home under his arm—there was more to it than appeared, and that was enough to keep their questions quiet.

In the war of invisibility, Harrison's supply chain was more than sustenance. It was the artery through which the operation's heartbeat continued, carrying not only what they needed to live, but the assurance that each day behind the blackout line could be met without stepping into the light. His van might have looked like any tradesman's, but within its quiet engine and shifting routes lay one of the most important shields in Sovereign Burn's design.

By the time dawn crept over the fields, Harrison would already be back on his rounds, empty van, clean tyres, no trace of the night's work left on the road. The county remained as it always was—green, quiet, and loyal. And beyond its hedgerows, the blackout held.

The rain outside tapped against the window like a muted metronome, pacing the lesson as Ben adjusted the screen's glow to the lowest setting. Casper leaned forward in the chair beside him, his elbows pressed into the desk, eyes locked on the lines of code that scrolled past. There was no play-acting in this teaching; Ben did not sugar-coat the process for a younger mind. He moved deliberately, each keystroke carrying the weight of intent, and let Casper watch in complete silence before explaining the logic behind it.

"This," Ben said quietly, "is not for amusement. It is for defence." The boy nodded without breaking focus. His fingers itched to touch the keyboard, but he kept them still, understanding the unspoken rule that before action came observation. On the screen, Ben mapped a flood test—packets surging and dissipating in controlled waves that would leave no trace once withdrawn. Casper followed the sequences in his head, recognising the rhythm even before the command executed.

Ben's hand moved to the next panel, where the masking protocols lived. He explained the difference between erasing a trail and never leaving one in the first place. Casper listened without blinking, grasping the subtlety—that one was reaction, the other was prevention. "We build it clean," Ben said, "so it looks like it was never touched. You can't follow what was never there." The boy's eyes lit not from mischief, but from comprehension, as though a curtain had been pulled back on an entirely different way of thinking.

Trace scrubbing came next, demonstrated with the precision of a craftsman sanding a fine edge. Ben triggered a dummy trace from an outside network, then erased it in layers until not even the server logs would show a blip of its existence. He leaned back slightly, letting Casper process the sequence. The boy's lips moved without sound, replaying the steps in his mind. Sørensen stood in the doorway, watching, not to interrupt, but to measure how quickly the boy was absorbing the lesson.

Casper asked his first question only after Ben closed the dummy operation: "If it's this clean, how would anyone even know we're here?" Ben met his gaze. "They wouldn't. That's the point. Protection doesn't always mean fighting—it can mean erasing the fight before it starts." The answer settled over him with the gravity of responsibility, and Casper sat straighter, the weight of the work beginning to root itself in his posture.

From there, Ben introduced the masking overlays—the virtual false walls that misdirected would-be intrusions into dead-end loops. Casper followed every switch, understanding the principle as much as the execution: keep them chasing shadows until they lose the trail entirely. The boy smiled faintly when the final loop closed and the network map went dark except for the heartbeat of their secure channel. It was the quiet satisfaction of seeing a door locked and bolted against the night.

Ben let him type his first command at the end of the lesson, a minor pulse loop designed to mask their local IP without altering any live data. The keystrokes were hesitant at first, then grew more certain as the lines responded exactly as intended. When the confirmation ping came through, Casper exhaled as though he had been holding his breath the entire time. Ben did not offer praise; he simply nodded, the way Sørensen had always done for him when the work was done well.

The lesson ended not with ceremony but with the closing of the laptop, the click of the lock sliding into place, and the return of the room to its dim stillness. Outside, the rain had stopped, replaced by the deep quiet of the county night. Casper rose from the chair, still replaying the movements in his mind, already aware that what he had learned could never be written down, never spoken aloud beyond these walls.

Ben followed him to the door, placing a hand on his shoulder. "It's not just knowing how to do it," he said, "it's knowing when—and why." Casper nodded again, his face serious beyond his years. In that moment, the boy understood that he had not merely been shown how to build a digital wall; he had been given the keys to a fortress.

Sørensen stepped aside as they left the study, his expression unreadable but his approval evident in the slight incline of his head. The boy passed him without a word, heading toward the kitchen where the faint smell of Harrison's late-night coffee still lingered. Ben lingered a moment longer, his fingers brushing over the locked case on the desk, aware that this was the beginning of a legacy—not in titles, but in the quiet skills that kept their family safe.

The cottage returned to its usual rhythm. Harrison came in through the side door with a crate of supplies, boots muddy from another trip beyond the blackout line. He glanced toward the study but didn't ask questions. In this house, everyone knew the value of letting the important things go unspoken.

Upstairs, Casper climbed into bed without the restless shifting of a boy unsettled by his thoughts. His breathing steadied quickly, but Ben knew his mind was still turning, tracing the sequences again and again until they became part of him. This was how it had begun for Ben all those years ago, under Sørensen's watchful eye, in another small room lit by a single lamp.

In Kent, the world outside might grow louder, but within the blackout's reach, the knowledge was passing quietly from one generation to the next. Casper's first lesson was complete. The next would come when he was ready, and not a moment sooner.

The study door closed behind Casper, but the work inside the cottage did not stop with him. In the soft lamplight of the front room, Maria and Emil sat across from Sørensen, the table between them bare except for a folded map of the village and a small, well-sharpened pencil. This was their turn—not to learn the machinery of firewalls and packet floods, but the slower, quieter craft of watching. Sørensen's lessons carried no flourish; he explained in few words and long pauses, letting them piece together meaning without prompting. The rules were simple: notice everything, speak of nothing, and always report back.

Maria leaned forward first, tracing her fingertip along the lanes and alleyways they knew from countless afternoons. "This one," she murmured, pointing to the narrow cut behind the grocer's, "is where strangers will stand if they're waiting without wanting to be seen." Sørensen did not nod or smile, but his eyes flicked toward her with the smallest mark of approval. Emil, seated upright beside her, followed with his own note—two unfamiliar cars spotted near the post office on consecutive mornings. He spoke with the same measured calm he had seen in his father during field work, never rushing to the end of a sentence.

The map became their silent ledger. Each mark, each half-sketched arrow, represented a moment when something or someone had stepped outside the rhythm of the village. Sørensen showed them how to group these observations, drawing connections between details that might otherwise appear harmless—a man lingering by the bus stop too long, a delivery van taking the same back street twice in one day. To the casual eye, it was coincidence. To the trained one, it was a pattern in the making.

Afternoons became their reconnaissance hours. Maria took the high street, blending into the normal flow of shoppers, greeting neighbours with the ease of someone born to the county. Emil kept to the quieter routes—the bridle path by the old orchard, the gravel lane running behind the school—places where unfamiliar faces stood out more starkly. Each carried the quiet confidence of knowing their presence raised no suspicion; they were just children moving through their own village, a truth no outsider would challenge.

Their eyes grew sharper. Maria noticed which window blinds shifted slightly when she passed, and which shopkeepers' glances lingered toward the end of the lane. Emil learned to remember number plates without writing them down, committing them to the same mental storehouse where he kept fishing knots and fire drill steps. They never spoke of these findings aloud until the cottage door was shut and Sørensen was seated before them, his focus as unbroken as the first day he had trained Ben.

In the evenings, their reports took shape in the smallest details—a change in the way the butcher's boy carried his deliveries, a man in a dark coat returning to the same bench three afternoons in a row. Sørensen asked for no theories, only facts. "Patterns tell their own story," he reminded them, "if you let them." His voice carried the same low steadiness that had once taught Ben to trust his instincts above all else.

Ben listened from the kitchen doorway more often than not, saying little but taking in everything. He recognised in Maria the same quick-reading eye that could pick out an anomaly from a crowd in seconds, and in Emil the patience to follow a lead without rushing it. It was a pairing Sørensen had clearly anticipated—one to gather the moment, the other to wait for the proof. Together, they formed a net far finer than brute force surveillance.

By the second week, the operation was running on two fronts: Casper's digital barricades humming unseen in the background, and Maria and Emil's field reports giving shape to the shadows moving through Kent. Neither side worked alone; each reinforced the other. A flagged van in Emil's notes could be cross-checked against the digital logs Casper kept hidden, and a stranger spotted by Maria might explain a spike in foreign IP activity. The lattice of defence tightened with every small, unassuming step.

The village itself seemed to shelter them further the more they worked. Shopkeepers glanced a moment longer when the children passed, as if aware of their purpose but content to pretend otherwise. Neighbours waved from porches, their faces carrying the unspoken promise that they too were watching. Whether the children knew it or not, they were not only learning from Sørensen—they were teaching the county how to stay vigilant without drawing attention.

When night fell, Maria and Emil sat side by side by the hearth, their feet tucked beneath them, listening as Sørensen closed the map for the day. No congratulations were offered; that was not his way. But in the pause before he rose, the weight of his approval filled the room more surely than any praise could. The children exchanged a brief glance—one of quiet pride, the kind that would never need to be spoken aloud.

They were not just helping; they were part of the wall being built around this place, each brick set by observation, memory, and silence. Ben knew the value of such work better than anyone. Thirteen years ago, he had been in their place, walking these same streets under Sørensen's instruction, learning that the greatest defences often looked like nothing at all. Now, watching his own children and Sørensen's boy take up that same mantle, he felt the strange, steady assurance that the operation was no longer his alone to bear.

The lamp was turned down, the map tucked away, and the cottage returned to its nightly stillness. Outside, the village slept, unaware of the threads being woven through its quiet lanes. Inside, Maria and Emil had already begun to think about tomorrow's watch—where to stand, what to note, and how to blend in until they were invisible. In this work, invisibility was victory.

By the second night, the work of the cottage shifted from building defences to sending a message. The study's curtains were drawn tight, the lamps turned low, and the quiet tap of keys filled the air like a clock ticking toward an unseen hour. Ben leaned forward, the glow of the monitor casting a pale light across his face, while Sørensen stood just behind, arms folded, watching each line of code compile. No words were wasted; the plan had been shaped earlier, and now it was only a matter of execution. At 11:47 p.m., the final command was entered. There was no flourish, no confirmation sound—only the subtle, invisible ripple of the first warning leaving the safety of Kent and finding its targets across the continent.

The recipients were not chosen at random. Each had, in the past month, placed Ben's name in print or online—some in speculation, others in malice. Political columnists, society pages, tabloid reporters, even freelance bloggers who prided themselves on "inside knowledge." Their inboxes became the landing points for something they could neither source nor ignore. The subject line was empty. The body contained only three words, spaced on a single line, each given the gravity of a closing bell: Leave him alone.

No threats. No claims of power. No attachments or signatures. Just the quiet, absolute certainty that whoever had sent it knew exactly where to find them, and could do so again. The simplicity of it was its edge—there was nothing to trace but the knowledge it left behind. Ben knew from experience that it would unsettle far more than any rant or insult ever could. Silence, properly delivered, carried the kind of weight noise never achieved.

Across Europe, screens lit up in kitchens, offices, and late-night cafés. Some journalists stared for a long time before moving their cursor to delete, as though by erasing it they could erase the fact of having received it. Others shut their laptops altogether, the unspoken question curling in the back of their minds: How did they find me? In a few newsrooms, the message was whispered about in hallways but never discussed in official channels. Admitting you had been warned was almost as damning as the warning itself.

Harrison, seated in the corner of the room with a second terminal, monitored the delivery confirmations without comment. He had seen such tactics before, though never with this kind of reach. Each time a delivery was marked as complete, he added a silent tick to his mental ledger. There were no bounces. No undeliverables. Every intended recipient had been reached. He closed the terminal with the slow care of a man putting away a weapon.

Casper, seated cross-legged on the floor, watched the process with wide-eyed fascination. He did not ask how the messages had been sent or why the trail could not be followed. Those lessons would come later.

For now, he simply absorbed the truth that a single, well-timed act could speak louder than any argument. Maria and Emil, returning from their evening watch, slipped into the room in time to hear Sørensen's quiet assessment: "They'll think twice now." The tone made it clear that thinking twice was the entire point.

In some offices, the warning was met with stubborn pride. A few journalists typed Ben's name into new drafts out of defiance, only to find themselves pausing at the first paragraph, wondering if the story was worth the unease gnawing at them. Others quietly pulled pending articles, citing "editorial redirection" as their excuse. In the space of a few hours, the public conversation around Ben began to thin—not vanish, but slow, the way a stream narrows when something blocks its flow upstream.

Ben did not watch the coverage change in real time; he trusted the effect. The warning had not been crafted for immediate headlines or applause—it had been set loose to work quietly, shifting the ground under the feet of those who thought they could name him without consequence. The less they said, the more space he had to move without shadow. He leaned back in his chair, the faintest thread of relief crossing his features, though it did not stay long.

Sørensen glanced at the clock and then at the dark window beyond the curtains. "First step's done," he said, not as a declaration, but as a marker in the ongoing work. They both knew the warning was only as strong as the next move. That was the rhythm of such operations: act, wait, watch, and be ready to act again before the other side regained its footing. Ben gave a short nod, already mapping the next phase in his mind.

Outside, the county slept as if nothing had changed. Inside the cottage, the quiet hum of the hard drives filled the air. Somewhere beyond the blackout boundary, in offices and apartments across Europe, men and women lay awake staring at their ceilings, turning over the same thought: He found me once. He could do it again. In that thought alone, the operation had succeeded. The first warning was not a shot—it was the sound of a door closing, and the knowledge that it would only open if Ben chose it to.

Harrison moved without drawing notice, speaking only to those who had long since proven themselves in matters of loyalty and silence. He did not knock on unfamiliar doors or explain more than was necessary. Instead, he walked the lanes and the quiet rows of shops, pausing briefly in each to pass on the same careful message: eyes open, doors closed to strangers. It was not framed as an order, but as a reminder of what they had always done for their own. The people of Kent did not require long explanations. They had seen enough over the years to know that certain moments demanded a deeper stillness.

The librarian understood before Harrison finished speaking. She folded her hands on the counter and gave a single nod, her expression unreadable to anyone who might be watching. In her mind, the old rules came back into focus—what was seen in the county stayed in the county. She did not ask who was behind the renewed vigilance. She had no need. For her, it was the same as it had been when Ben was a boy: you did not let strangers wander freely when the air carried that kind of weight.

Shopkeepers followed the same unspoken rhythm. A man stocking shelves near the back of his grocer's stall simply turned the lock on the front door after Harrison left, not to shut out customers, but to choose carefully who stepped inside. The few who were allowed entry were met with the same cheerful greetings as always, though there was a watchfulness behind the words. The change was so subtle that an outsider might not have noticed, but anyone raised in Kent would have recognised the shift immediately.

Neighbours who tended to their gardens along the main lane adjusted their routines without comment. Tools were set down earlier in the evening. Walks were taken in pairs instead of alone. Windows that had stood open in the afternoons were closed and latched by dusk. No one announced the pattern, yet the pattern took hold. Each movement was both ordinary and deliberate, the quiet weaving of a net across the county's narrow roads and footpaths.

At the post office, a clerk who had known Ben since childhood made a point of sorting all county-bound letters by hand, ensuring no unfamiliar sender passed unnoticed. She had done this once before, years ago, when word had spread of someone asking too many questions about "the boy from the big house." Back then, it had been enough to keep trouble from taking root. This time, the stakes were higher, but the principles were the same.

For those who had never left Kent, the county's high alert did not feel like a disruption. It was simply an intensification of what they already knew to do when protecting their own. Outsiders often misunderstood the county's stillness, taking it for inaction. In truth, stillness here was an active state, a way of making the ground unsteady beneath the feet of anyone who did not belong. To move too loudly or too quickly in such a place was to announce yourself in all the wrong ways.

Harrison returned to the cottage before nightfall, his work done for the day. He reported the readiness of the county in plain terms—shopkeepers alert, neighbours watchful, the librarian fully aware and standing by. Sørensen listened without interruption, nodding only when the picture was complete. Ben, seated in the corner, heard every detail without shifting in his chair. He knew that what Harrison had set in motion was not just precaution; it was the quiet tightening of a circle that had no beginning and no end.

The county was now an extension of the blackout. What the satellites could not see and the networks could not reach, the people themselves would protect. A stranger might still walk into Kent, but they would feel the weight of eyes on them from the moment their foot touched the lane. Conversations would pause as they passed. Smiles would be polite, but they would not be invitations. And when they left, as strangers always did, they would take with them nothing but the sense that something here was not to be touched.

In the cottage's small kitchen, the lamps burned low as Harrison's words settled over the room. Outside, the county's night lay heavy and absolute, every hedge and lane drawn into a quiet defence. No sign would be posted at the borders, no public statement made, but the truth was as solid as stone: Kent had closed itself to the world, and it would not open again until Ben chose to let it.

Sørensen began the test without preamble, his fingers moving over the keys with the same certainty as a man checking the locks on his own home. The first simulated breach was simple—an open probe disguised as a weather data request. In less than a second, the system blocked it, sending the signal into a dead loop that would keep the requesting device chasing its own tail until the operator shut it down. Ben did not even glance away from his own terminal; he knew the response times, and this one was faster than the original build had ever achieved.

The second attempt was more aggressive. Sørensen masked his location through a chain of international relays, a tactic designed to confuse lesser systems. Sovereign Burn's rebuilt core treated it as if it were a child's riddle, tracing the route backward in near real time, stripping away each layer until the true source sat exposed on the screen. The coordinates appeared with a slow, deliberate blink, the way an old typewriter keys out a word—more a statement than a notification. Ben leaned forward slightly, reading the origin and nodding to himself.

From there, the drills escalated. Sørensen launched a flood of packet requests, a tactic meant to overwhelm most defensive firewalls. Instead of blocking them outright, Sovereign Burn absorbed them, scattered their contents, then sent them back wrapped in a harmless echo that would register as ordinary traffic to the sender. "It's learning," Sørensen observed under his breath, though they both knew that the learning was the result of years of buried refinements Ben had never stopped making in his head.

The fourth breach was the one Sørensen most wanted to test—a deep infiltration attempt that mimicked the methods used by professional intelligence agencies. This was no longer play-acting; it was the sort of strike they might one day face for real. The system reacted without hesitation, isolating the incoming signal, mapping its path, and then sealing it off so completely it was as if the attempt had never happened. And yet, the log recorded everything—IP chains, timestamps, device signatures—all stored in an encrypted vault only Ben could access.

"Run it again," Ben said quietly, not because he doubted the result, but because he wanted to see the rhythm of the system under repeated stress. Sørensen obliged, firing off variations on the same deep strike, each masked differently. None made it past the outer gate. The screens showed no signs of strain, no lag in processing. Sovereign Burn absorbed each wave like a shoreline accustomed to the sea, letting the force break against it and wash away.

Between drills, Ben adjusted small parameters in the code—tiny corrections that seemed insignificant to an outsider, but to him, each was the difference between a defence that reacted and one that anticipated. The system was no longer a simple barricade; it was a living map of their perimeter, aware of its own vulnerabilities and adjusting to close them before they could be exploited. Sørensen watched the way Ben's hands moved, recognising the blend of instinct and calculation that had made the first Stink Bomb such an unshakable tool all those years ago.

When the final test ended, the logbook showed a perfect defence record. Every breach had been stopped, every source traced, every trace filed away for later use. Ben leaned back, satisfied, and closed the encrypted vault with a single keystroke. "That's enough for now," he said, though they both knew the system would keep running in the background, ever watchful. Testing was just confirmation; the real operation had already begun.

Outside, the county lay in the same deep quiet as the night before. No one beyond their circle would ever know that the air above and the lines below had been turned into a wall, and that every hand that reached toward it had been marked. The defences were more than ready—they were waiting.

Ben did not shut the system down after the tests. Instead, he shifted its focus, laying down the first of the false trails with the precision of a cartographer drawing maps for an enemy who would never realise the ground had been altered beneath them. Each trail began with a believable point of entry—a forgotten substation on the edge of the county, a dormant municipal server in a neighbouring district—then wound outward through layers of fabricated traffic. To the pursuer, it would look like genuine activity, complete with time-stamped access logs and simulated user habits.

Sørensen watched from across the desk, arms folded, saying nothing while Ben worked. He understood this was not simply a matter of hiding; it was about giving the hunter something to chase, something convincing enough to hold their attention while the real ground stayed untouched. The brilliance of the method lay in its plausibility—every destination was a location that might, in theory, conceal something worth finding, and yet each was nothing more than an echo in a hollow room.

One of the first decoys led to an empty warehouse in Dover, its ownership records tracing back to a defunct import company dissolved over a decade ago. Another pointed toward an abandoned barn in the Midlands, complete with falsified CCTV archives showing grainy, looped footage of shadows moving in the rafters. An offshore server farm in Iceland rounded out the trio, its virtual doors open just wide enough to tempt a deeper search before sealing without warning, leaving the intruder holding nothing but their own reflected signal.

The system scattered these trails like seeds in the wind, each one buried under layers of harmless data so that no two chases would lead the same way twice. If a pursuer returned to retrace their steps, they would find the trail altered, the signs rearranged, as if the landscape itself had shifted overnight. It was a game designed not to frustrate outright, but to exhaust—slowly, methodically, until the chaser began to doubt their own competence.

Harrison entered briefly, placing a sealed envelope on the desk without breaking the flow of Ben's work. He did not ask what was happening; he did not need to. One glance at the scrolling lines of code, the coordinates, and the ghosted server names told him enough. The county's safety was being built not only on what outsiders could not see, but on what they were meant to see and believe.

As each false trail settled into the network, Ben checked and rechecked their triggers. Some were timed to go cold within hours, others left to hum quietly for weeks before collapsing into digital silence. A few were designed as loops, leading a determined pursuer back to the very first point of entry, ensuring that they would never quite realise they had been running in circles.

Sørensen leaned forward at last, studying one of the plotted routes. "And if they're clever enough to spot the trap?" Ben's answer was immediate: "Then they're already where I want them to be." The words carried no bravado, only the certainty of a man who had played this game before and won. In the quiet of the study, the false trails settled into place, invisible walls shaping the battlefield before the enemy even realised there was one.

By the fourth day, the change is visible not in what is printed, but in what is not. The headlines that once carried his name shrink to sidebars, then vanish altogether. Without fresh images, without the oxygen of gossip, the story loses its heat. In newsrooms across Europe, editors eye the metrics—clicks dropping, interest waning—and quietly move on to scandals that promise easier returns. What was once a feeding frenzy becomes a dry well. The machine that thrives on constant movement cannot tolerate stillness, and Ben has made sure stillness is all it can see.

Sørensen watches the shift with the satisfaction of a man who has seen sieges crumble, not through force, but through starvation. He knows this is not permanent; curiosity can always flare again. But for now, the front lines have gone quiet. The enemy is looking elsewhere, chasing easier prey. The operation has not merely hidden Ben—it has made him too costly to pursue. Each failed inquiry, each unanswered call, is a subtle reinforcement of the wall they have built.

Those who try to push through find themselves walking in circles. Investigators feed satellite coordinates into their systems and are met with the same sunlit country lanes, day after day. Photographers attempt to call sources in the county, only to find the lines dead or the conversations drifting back to mundane pleasantries. Even the most determined tabloid stringers can extract nothing beyond mentions of the weather, the lambing season, and the state of the hedgerows. The tone is polite but final: there is nothing here for you.

In the cottage, Ben works without the rush of victory. He does not allow the quiet to lull him into complacency; instead, he uses it as space to refine the system, tightening threads, reinforcing locks. Each delay in the outside narrative is another opportunity to strengthen the inside perimeter. Harrison's updates from the village confirm what Ben already suspects—the county has absorbed the blackout into its own rhythm, making the absence of intrusion feel as natural as the turning of the seasons.

The Librarian plays her part with the ease of long practice, noting which strangers come through town, what questions they ask, and how quickly they leave when given nothing to feed on. She reports her observations in passing, never lingering on the subject, allowing them to be folded into the larger intelligence net without attracting attention. Every thread is kept taut, every hand in the county still holding the line.

By week's end, the shift is complete. In the eyes of the outside world, Ben is no longer a figure in the present tense—he is a rumour, a past curiosity, a story that failed to keep pace with the news cycle. This, he knows, is the moment of greatest advantage. Not when they are chasing him, but when they have convinced themselves he is no longer worth the effort. It is here, in this carefully cultivated void, that the real work can begin.

Each night, the kitchen becomes the command post, the glow of the single overhead lamp pooling over maps, notes, and the day's quietly gathered intelligence. The sound of the kettle is the only intrusion, steam curling between them as they settle into the rhythm of review. Ben speaks sparingly, his words clipped to the essentials, while Sørensen works the pencil over the logbook with precise, unhurried strokes. Harrison reports in low tones, relaying movements seen on the roads, shifts in shop chatter, and subtle changes in the pattern of who comes and goes from the county's edges.

The children, though younger, are not dismissed from the table. Maria notes an unfamiliar car that idled near the lane before reversing away. Emil reports two strangers walking the high path who turned back after seeing the hedgerow gate closed. Casper offers his tally of the day's system pings, marking each failed intrusion attempt in his own neatly ruled column. The details, small as they are, form the living pulse of the operation—every beat recorded, every anomaly considered.

Trust here is absolute, but it is not blind. The circle has been shaped through years of proving and re-proving loyalty, through trials where hesitation could have been costly. No one beyond this table is given the full design; even allies in the county see only the part they are meant to hold. The strength lies not in the number of hands on the wheel, but in the certainty that every hand knows its place.

Harrison glances toward the windows more often than the others, his habit of checking the perimeter ingrained so deeply it has become part of his breathing. Sørensen, catching the movement, shifts the conversation toward tomorrow's adjustments—how the routes will change, where Harrison will collect the next delivery, and which boundary points require a new pass. The discussion is layered, the flow seamless, each decision shaped to keep them three moves ahead of any outside attempt to close in.

The children listen more than they speak, but their presence is part of the structure. This is not just a defence for the present—it is training for the future, the slow transfer of understanding that cannot be rushed. Ben watches them without comment, recognising the subtle way they absorb the discipline, learning that vigilance is not an act of fear, but of responsibility.

When the logbook is closed and the kettle rinsed, no summary is spoken aloud. They leave the table with the same understanding they brought into it: that the circle holds because it is kept small, because trust here is currency too valuable to spend freely. Outside these walls, the blackout hums on, the false trails hold steady, and the county sleeps in unknowing protection.

By the time the last lamp is extinguished, the day's weight has already been folded into their quiet machinery. There is no celebration, no expression of triumph—only the calm of knowing that tonight, like the night before, the line has held. And in Kent, that is enough.

The kitchen has long since gone dark, the others settled into the kind of deep, unbroken sleep that only a secure night can bring. Ben remains in the study, the lamplight casting a tight circle over the desk where the laptop hums in near silence. Lines of code march across the screen, layered in complex structures that would seem meaningless to anyone without the exact key to their sequence. His hands move without hesitation, recalling patterns first built over a decade ago, now sharpened and hardened by years of quiet refinement. This is not a flourish to intimidate—it is a seal, an unseen mark of ownership over the battlefield no outsider will ever realise they've entered.

The message takes form in the deepest fold of Sovereign Burn's architecture, a place so deeply nested it exists beyond the reach of casual probes or brute-force attacks. It is tethered to an activation sequence so precise that even an experienced adversary would not know they were triggering it until it was too late. If you reach this, you've already lost. The words appear on his screen only long enough for him to verify their exact placement before they are buried again beneath encrypted layers, invisible to any scan, dormant until the precise moment they are meant to surface.

Sørensen's steps sound faintly in the hall—just a check-in, no intrusion. He doesn't ask what Ben is working on; he has learned that some safeguards work best when they remain unspoken. He merely pauses at the doorway, the unlit hall behind him casting his frame in silhouette, before giving a single nod and turning away. The understanding passes without words: this final stroke is not for now, but for when the operation reaches its last stand.

Ben knows the psychology of such a find. By the time an intruder sees those words, their access will be collapsing around them. Servers will have purged, decoys will have multiplied, and every trace of their intrusion will have been redirected to dead-end systems designed to devour their time. The message is not just a declaration of defeat—it is the confirmation that they have been manoeuvred into a place where no retaliation is possible.

The cursor blinks on the final line, a steady pulse like a quiet heartbeat. He locks the file, re-engages the full encryption cycle, and watches as the command-line confirms the burial of the code into the system's core. There is no flourish, no moment of satisfaction—just the steady certainty of having closed another door against the world outside.

When the last process completes, he shuts the laptop with the care of one sealing a vault. The study returns to stillness, save for the faint ticking of the clock on the far wall. Outside, the blackout holds, the skies above Kent still showing nothing but looped images of quiet lanes and sleeping fields. Somewhere far beyond the county, journalists and their employers still scratch at the edges of the story, unaware that the game has already been fixed against them.

Ben leaves the study without looking back. The code will wait, patient and hidden, for a day that may never come. But if it does, those who find it will understand instantly and completely—there is no way forward from here. The field has already been lost.

By the fifth night, the operation is no longer an active effort but a living presence, woven into the quiet fabric of Kent like a second atmosphere. The blackout hums without interruption, its patterns so seamless they feel as if they have always existed. The satellite loops continue to show the same empty lanes and soft clouds drifting over green fields, while the networks beyond the county's reach remain choked in silence. Ben no longer needs to monitor every line of code; Sovereign Burn breathes on its own now, precise and unyielding, as much a part of this place as the stone walls and hedgerows.

To the people of Kent, his absence from public view is neither strange nor concerning. They sense his presence in the way the librarian keeps the back corner shelf dusted, in the extra loaf of bread left at the cottage gate, in the way no one lingers near the lane unless they belong. The unspoken understanding binds them as tightly as any contract: he is here, and that is all that matters. To speak of it would be to invite what they have all agreed must never come.

Beyond the blackout, the absence begins to gnaw. Editors and investigators who once filled their columns with speculation now have nothing to print. No sightings, no whispers, not even a hint of movement. The name "Benedict" fades from their rosters, not from lack of interest, but from the quiet dread of chasing a shadow that may turn and find them. The warning sent days earlier still lingers in their minds, an echo they cannot shake.

Sørensen remarks one evening, while checking the perimeter maps, that it feels like living inside a sealed vault—one with windows that show only what they choose to be seen. Harrison agrees, though his words are softer, noting that sometimes the most powerful position is to be absent from the board entirely. Ben says nothing, but his eyes show that he understands perfectly. This silence is not retreat—it is control.

Casper watches his father with a growing comprehension that this, too, is part of the lesson. Power is not always loud or visible; sometimes it is the ability to remain unseen while shaping the course of events from a position no one can touch. Maria and Emil carry their own share of that understanding, their vigilance in the village becoming as natural as breathing. Together, they are the eyes and ears of a man the world thinks has disappeared.

The night air in Kent is heavy with the scent of damp earth and woodsmoke, carrying no trace of the digital fortress that now shields it. In the study, the encrypted drive is locked away once more, its routines cycling in silence, ready to adjust at the smallest command. The house sleeps under its watch, every heartbeat within it protected by walls far higher than any stone could build.

By the time the first frost of morning glistens on the hedges, Ben is already awake, standing at the window with a mug of coffee, the fields stretching beyond him in perfect stillness. Somewhere out there, the world still wonders if he has vanished. In truth, he is closer than they could ever imagine—present in every blocked signal, every dead trail, every looped image. He is the Digital Ghost, and in this silence, his hold is absolute.

CHAPTER 13: THE LETTER TO THE EDITOR

The morning light settled upon the small cottage in Kent with the patience of an old friend, streaming through the single-paned, wood-framed window and falling across the desk where Benedict sat in absolute stillness. Outside, the narrow lane was silent except for the distant call of a blackbird somewhere among the hedgerows, and within the room, there was no sound save for the soft hiss of the fire in the grate.

The desk itself was stripped to essentials—no clutter, no idle distractions—only the thick sheaf of cream paper laid square before him, the uncapped fountain pen whose polished barrel gleamed faintly, and the neatly stacked folders containing the proof of his ancestry. These were not decorative keepsakes. They were evidence, each sheet a fragment of history, bound together not merely to tell a story, but to settle a truth that could no longer remain unspoken.

Benedict's right hand hovered over the first page for longer than he expected, the familiar weight of the pen pressing into his fingers like a silent reminder of the consequence behind every stroke. He had written letters before—letters of courtesy, of condolence, of command—but never one quite like this.

This was not an exchange between equals, nor an attempt to persuade. It was a statement for the record, sharpened to the form of a blade and set to cut through the noise that had been building since his name first began to slip between the cracks of guarded silence. He was not here to beg for peace. He was here to make it known that the line between private life and public curiosity was fixed in law, and that any trespass upon it would not be forgiven.

The cottage itself felt like part of the letter—its thick walls holding back the world, its oak beams carrying the weight of generations past. This was the same desk where, years ago, he had first read the genealogical documents Isla had found, the same seat where he had pieced together the truth of who he was and why it had been hidden for so long.

Now, those same truths would be placed into words not for the sake of his own understanding, but for the sake of warning others never to mistake his silence for weakness. He did not intend to send this letter as one might send news to a casual acquaintance. He intended it as a permanent record, something that would outlast the day's rumours and tomorrow's headlines.

Outside, the air was bright and clean, but Benedict kept his gaze on the page. The first words formed with deliberate pressure, the ink flowing evenly in dark, decisive lines. He began not with his name, not with titles, but with the subject of the letter itself—his children. They were the reason for the tone, the weight, the refusal to yield.

Every paragraph would be constructed with their safety in mind, their right to live without intrusion, their right to have the kind of childhood he had lost far too early. He knew the men and women who would read these words, the kind who called themselves journalists but carried cameras instead of conscience. They would need to understand that this was not simply a polite request to leave his family alone; it was a legal demand with the full backing of every court that mattered.

He paused after the first sentence, his eyes narrowing as he measured its force. It was too easy for such documents to sound like mere protest if not drafted with precision. He needed this letter to feel like the closing of a door that no amount of knocking could reopen. The language had to be exact—cold enough to remove doubt, clear enough to stand in a courtroom without alteration. This was not for the gossip column. This was for the files that mattered when the law was called to stand between what was right and what was merely wanted. It was the difference between a man asking for his peace and a king declaring it.

The pen moved again, slow and deliberate. Every sentence he wrote was followed by a moment of stillness, as though he were listening for flaws in the cadence. He refused to give them a single careless word that could be twisted into weakness. He knew the reach of the modern press—their skill at distorting context, their appetite for scandal. He had no interest in feeding them. This letter would be the opposite of what they hoped for: a wall of words so solid that even the most persistent could find no way through it without breaking the law. There would be no poetic indulgence here, no colourful phrasing to tempt misquotation. Every line would be a matter of fact.

The fire gave a soft crack, and Benedict's eyes lifted briefly toward the sound before returning to the paper. The stillness of the room was a kind of armour in itself, the absence of interruption allowing each thought to be placed exactly where it belonged. There was a rhythm to the act of writing that he had always found grounding, but today it carried a sharper edge. Each stroke of the pen was a reminder that once these words were set down, there would be no taking them back. They would belong to the record, unchanging and unchallengeable. That was precisely what he wanted.

The light shifted across the desk as the sun rose higher, and with it came the slow build of momentum. Paragraph by paragraph, the letter began to take shape, the structure firming under his hand. He had begun with the children, moved to the legal framework, and would now advance to the consequences of violation. This was where the tone would harden fully, leaving no trace of doubt that the protection of his family was not negotiable. In law, as in life, boundaries were meaningless if not enforced. He intended to enforce them without hesitation.

At times, he thought of the people who might one day read this letter without ever having met him—the archivists, the court officials, the occasional historian looking for the truth behind the quiet years of his reign. He imagined their eyes following the lines of ink, recognising in the precision of the words the nature of the man who wrote them. It did not matter whether they admired him. It mattered only that they understood him. That understanding was the strongest defence against misinterpretation.

The pen slowed as he reached the end of the page, his thoughts already moving toward the next. He turned the sheet over, sliding it neatly beneath the stack, and began again. This was a process he refused to rush. Every page was to be weighed, measured, and balanced against the one before it. The tone could not waver. The facts could not bend. This was the foundation upon which the rest of the letter would stand, and if the first strokes were anything less than exact, the entire structure would falter.

Somewhere in the back of his mind, he could hear Sørensen's voice from years ago, reminding him that the first impression in any negotiation—or confrontation—was the one that lingered longest. Sørensen had taught him many things, but one lesson stood above the rest: speak only when ready, and when you do, make certain it cannot be undone. That philosophy now guided every mark on the page, every measured pause, every choice to cut a phrase that might weaken the message.

When the paragraph reached its natural close, Benedict allowed himself a moment to lean back, the pen resting against his thumb and forefinger. He studied the ink drying on the page, the dark sheen catching the light before settling into permanence. There was no flourish in his handwriting, no attempt to impress with style. It was neat, deliberate, and unadorned—just as it should be. The content was the weapon, not the script.

He knew the letter would be read by the editor first, but it would not stop there. It would be examined by legal teams, debated in boardrooms, and—if anyone were foolish enough to test him—presented in court. That knowledge was both a weight and a comfort. He did not need to imagine the outcome. He had already decided it. This was not an invitation to negotiate. This was the first and final word.

The stack of blank paper seemed smaller now, though only one page had been written. That was the nature of such work—each line carried the mass of ten, each sentence demanding the focus of a full argument. He reached for the pen again, feeling the familiar readiness return to his grip. The next page awaited, and with it, the next step in securing the boundary between his family and the world that would happily consume them for profit.

By the time the first three pages lay complete, the light had shifted again, falling more squarely across the desk. The ink was dry, the words unmovable. Benedict sat for a moment longer, eyes steady on the letter as though committing its exact phrasing to memory. He had no illusions about the people he was addressing. They would not be deterred by politeness. They would be deterred only by the certainty that crossing him would cost them far more than they could afford to lose.

In that quiet, with the pages before him and the world held at bay by the cottage walls, Benedict allowed himself the faintest exhale. It was not satisfaction—there was still far more to write before the letter was complete—but it was a beginning. And beginnings, as he well knew, were the most important strokes of all.

The letter's second paragraph began without flourish, the ink pressed deep into the fibres of the page as though to anchor each word beyond dispute. Benedict addressed the editor by name, not out of familiarity, but out of precision. This was not a generic statement meant to drift among piles of unanswered correspondence. It was a directed, deliberate message aimed squarely at the man whose publication would either respect the boundaries set forth or suffer the full measure of consequence. Each sentence was shaped to carry weight in two courts at once—the court of public opinion and the court of law. There would be no room for misreading.

From the outset, Benedict rejected any language that could soften the impact. There were no metaphors, no suggestive turns of phrase, nothing that could be reinterpreted as negotiation. It was all statement and statute, built line by line to close every possible gap a dishonest mind might seek to slip through. The editor would see the name at the top of the page, read the direct salutation, and feel the unmistakable certainty that this was not written for amusement. It was written for enforcement. The air in the room seemed to thicken as the words took form, the page gaining an unspoken authority with each deliberate stroke.

The opening made it clear that this was not simply a matter of preference or personal request—it was a declaration underpinned by the protections of UK, Danish, and international law. Benedict knew that an editor who thrived on speculation would instinctively look for loopholes, but he gave none. The language was explicit: any unauthorised photography, filming, or fabrication of information regarding his family would result in immediate legal action. He wrote it not as a threat, but as a promise backed by the full reach of his resources. There was nothing performative here, no bravado for the sake of appearance. It was the kind of certainty that unsettled even seasoned professionals.

Each sentence was read back silently before moving on to the next, not for rhythm or beauty, but for legal precision. He knew that once this letter left his desk, it would be dissected by lawyers, editors, and perhaps even judges, line by line, looking for any flaw. There would be none. He had learned from past conflicts that the first impression in such matters must strike like a gavel—swift, unambiguous, and final. The tone had to be unyielding without veering into rage, firm without inviting mockery. This was the fine balance he maintained in every stroke, the discipline of a man who had spent years building walls no intruder could climb.

As the pen moved steadily, Benedict considered the man who would first lay eyes on this page. He imagined the editor's expression shifting from curiosity to discomfort as the message unfolded. This was not a celebrity's demand for privacy written in the polite tones of a publicist. This was a sovereign's legal position, crafted to eliminate doubt about his willingness to act. The man reading it would understand within the first few lines that this was not correspondence to be tested, nor was it one that could be buried in a drawer and ignored. It was the sort of document that insisted on acknowledgment.

The letter spoke in absolutes. Words like "shall," "will," and "without exception" appeared in deliberate measure, chosen for their inability to be twisted into softer terms. Benedict refused to offer anything conditional. Conditional language was a door left open, and once open, it would be stepped through. He knew the habits of journalists who had long since forgotten the weight of truth. They worked in half-truths and insinuations, shaping perception rather than presenting fact. Against that, only the steel of clear, enforceable language could stand.

He leaned slightly forward as he worked, his eyes fixed on the lines he was forming, the movement of the pen steady and without hesitation. There was an order to the construction: first the statement of law, then the definition of violation, followed by the description of consequence. This was how such letters were built—not as appeals to morality, but as the framework for action. In time, if tested, this page would become part of the evidence. It would stand beside affidavits and court filings, a foundation that could not be shaken by argument or opinion.

Each paragraph seemed to carry its own momentum, ending with a point sharp enough to leave the reader holding his breath for the next. Benedict made certain that no section could be lifted and quoted without carrying its full meaning. Too many public statements had been gutted in the press by selective quotation. He refused to allow that here. Every sentence was constructed to be self-defending, carrying its context within itself, impossible to separate from its intended weight.

At intervals, he paused—not for inspiration, but to re-read with the eyes of an opponent. What loophole would they see? What ambiguity would they exploit? Each time he found a phrase that might, under strain, bend in meaning, he rewrote it with the cold patience of a man filing the edges of a blade. This was not a race to the signature. This was a meticulous act of fortification, and the letter would leave his hands only when every possible breach had been sealed.

The tone remained steady throughout—unflinching, measured, and resolute. There was no rise in volume, no shift into the emotional. Anger would weaken the piece; sentiment would make it vulnerable. Instead, there was the slow tightening of grip, paragraph upon paragraph, until the reader was left with no doubt as to the seriousness of what they were holding. This was not a man's opinion—it was a sovereign's decree masked in the polite form of correspondence.

Somewhere beyond the walls of the cottage, the world carried on with its noise and demands. But here, in this quiet, Benedict was building something that would outlast the day's distractions. It was a shield fashioned from law, precedent, and the authority he had long been careful to keep in reserve. In the wrong hands, authority was wasted on performance. In his, it was a tool meant for exact application, and today it was being applied with deliberate care.

The paragraphs grew longer, the flow uninterrupted by hesitation. When his pen lifted from the page, it was only to draw breath and assess the balance between what had been said and what remained. Each new line was anchored by the one before it, building a rhythm that was less about style and more about inevitability. By the time the first page of this section neared its close, the tone had been set beyond reversal. The reader had been walked from polite acknowledgment to absolute boundary without once being given a place to step aside.

He imagined the letter arriving at its destination, the envelope bearing nothing but the necessary return address and the weight of expectation inside. There would be no mistaking the intent. By the time the editor finished reading the first section of the letter, the message would have already been received in full. The rest would be reinforcement—details, statutes, and the undeniable reality of what defiance would cost.

This was not merely about protecting his family from prying eyes. It was about drawing a legal perimeter around the life he had built, a line that could not be crossed without consequence. In a world where too many believed titles came with forfeited privacy, Benedict was making clear that his was not a title to be exploited. It was, in fact, the reason such exploitation would not be tolerated. The tone had been set, and from here, the rest of the letter would carry that same unwavering force to its final word.

Benedict did not waste the next paragraph on pleasantries. The first line cut directly into the heart of the matter, its weight drawn not from emotion but from law. He cited the protections granted under the constitutional and statutory frameworks of both the United Kingdom and Denmark, the dual shields under which his life was guarded. Yet this was not an academic recital. He did not scatter statutes like loose stones for the reader to pick through. Instead, he threaded them through a living warning, each law bound to a specific act of violation. The crimes were named plainly—defamation of character, unlawful photographing of minors, intrusion upon private life—each framed as both a moral trespass and a legal one. There was no comfort for the reader in vagueness. Every offence came with its consequence.

The language was deliberate, its force amplified by clarity. He wrote of defamation not as a hypothetical, but as an offence already anticipated. False statements, he declared, whether through headline, broadcast, or whispered rumour, would be treated as calculated harm, no matter the guise of "journalistic duty" used to excuse them.

Unlawful photographing of his children, especially, was marked as an act beyond repair—an automatic trigger for litigation, immediate and without negotiation. He made it known that in such cases, damages would not be token amounts for the sake of formality; they would be pursued with an aggressiveness designed to bankrupt offenders. The intent was plain: to leave no one wondering whether the cost of intrusion was worth the prize.

The reference to Danish law was woven not as an afterthought, but as a declaration of jurisdictional reach. Benedict reminded the reader that in Denmark, the right to privacy was not merely an expectation—it was codified protection. He cited provisions that shielded the dignity of the private individual, regardless of public standing, making it clear that his residence within Danish borders placed him under a legal canopy far broader than the UK press often acknowledged. The message was unmistakable: any breach committed against him in one jurisdiction would follow the violator into another.

He built the framework like a strategist reinforcing the walls of a fortress. Each paragraph closed the gap on potential escape routes. Intrusion upon private life, he wrote, would not be judged by the trespasser's intent, but by the impact upon those intruded upon. Telephoto lenses, hidden microphones, or the calculated loitering of so-called "freelancers" outside his home would be recorded, documented, and answered through legal channels. There would be no tolerance for claims of artistic pursuit or public interest. Public interest, he stated, ended where his children began.

The tone of the writing shifted slightly here—not to soften, but to sharpen. He described the photographing of minors without consent as not merely an ethical failing, but as a grave violation under the laws of multiple nations. Such acts, he reminded, were recognised internationally as infringements upon the most vulnerable, carrying both civil and criminal implications. The phrasing left no space for the reader to imagine that these were idle threats. This was the voice of a man prepared to pursue offenders until the last legal avenue was exhausted.

Benedict was careful to point out that his status as a sovereign did not diminish these protections—it reinforced them. Those who imagined that holding a royal title meant forfeiting private rights would find themselves dangerously misinformed. The very laws that bound him to the responsibilities of his position also safeguarded his family against exploitation. It was not a contradiction; it was the balance upon which the entire framework of his life rested. To cross that boundary was not merely to offend him personally—it was to violate the legal order he was sworn to uphold.

His pen moved with unbroken rhythm, each new sentence locking into the structure like a stone fitted to its neighbour. The British legal tradition, he wrote, recognised the sanctity of private life, and its courts had a long history of penalising those who sought to dismantle it for profit. Likewise, the Danish courts would act with equal resolve, their judgments carrying weight across borders through treaties and international enforcement mechanisms. These were not idle citations—they were advance notice of the battlefield upon which any intruder would find themselves standing.

As the page filled, Benedict allowed the warning to settle into the deeper recesses of the reader's mind. He made no attempt to dazzle with rhetoric; the words stood on the strength of their certainty. He spoke of calculated litigation, not as a blunt instrument swung wildly, but as a finely honed blade drawn only when warranted—and when drawn, never sheathed until the matter was resolved in full. To test that resolve, he implied, would be to invite a conflict that could not be quietly walked away from.

He reminded the editor that the law was not a passive shield—it could be wielded with precision. Any journalist or photographer who crossed the line would find themselves entangled not only in civil suits but, where applicable, in criminal proceedings as well. Evidence would be gathered with the same meticulous care with which he now crafted this letter. And when presented, it would carry the same unshakable tone: that of a man who did not bend under pressure, who did not bluff, and who did not retreat.

There was no hiding the fact that Benedict's resolve came from experience. He had seen what reckless reporting could do—not only to reputations, but to the safety and well-being of families. This was why his warning carried the weight of personal history. He was not writing in theory; he was drawing a line from past harm to future prevention, ensuring that those who might consider overstepping it would think twice. The law, in his hands, was not a tool for revenge, but for deterrence. And in that, it was at its most dangerous.

The structure of his argument allowed no opportunity for sympathy to sway judgment. Those who violated these boundaries would receive no leniency in the name of misunderstanding. Ignorance of the law, he reminded, was no defence. Those who chose to work in the field of media carried the responsibility of knowing the limits of their craft, and to cross those limits was not a mistake—it was a choice. Choices carried consequences, and he was prepared to see those consequences carried out in full measure.

Every line returned to the central principle: privacy was not negotiable. It was not an indulgence granted at the whim of the press, nor a courtesy that could be withdrawn at will. It was a right, protected in writing by nations, enforced by courts, and defended by those with the means to do so. Benedict's life, his marriage, and his children existed within that protected space. To breach it was not only to challenge him—it was to challenge the laws that governed civilised society itself.

As he wrote, he could almost feel the document crystallising into something that would one day be cited in court filings. He saw it being read aloud, each word landing with the force of a verdict. The letter was no longer merely a communication—it was becoming a pre-emptive strike, one that would force its recipients to consider the cost of their actions before committing them. It was, in its own right, a line of defence as tangible as the walls of the castle he had left behind in Denmark.

The legal groundwork was now laid, each provision and protection set firmly in place. All that remained was to build upon it, to move from the statement of rights into the illustration of consequences. And in that next stage, Benedict would ensure that the editor—and anyone else who read these words—would understand that what had been written here was not a request for privacy. It was a demand backed by the full measure of law, readiness, and resolve.

Benedict shifted the weight of the letter from law to consequence, the ink now carrying the sharpness of a drawn blade. There was no turn of phrase to soften the blow, no diplomatic flourish to ease the sting. He addressed them—the photographers with long lenses, the editors who approved the shots, the freelance hunters who prowled for a cheque in exchange for stolen moments—directly and without flinching. Every word carried the quiet certainty of a man who had made peace with his willingness to destroy those who tested him. They were to know, without a shadow of doubt, that once the gate of his patience was forced open, there would be no closing it again.

The first consequence he described was financial, but it was not the token fine some papers paid from petty cash as the cost of doing business. No, his litigation would be measured in sums designed to strip not only the profit from their hands, but the very structure of their livelihood. A single lawsuit could freeze accounts, dismantle operations, and sell their offices piece by piece to cover judgments. The loss would not be a slap on the wrist; it would be a severing of the hand that reached for what was not theirs. This was not vengeance—it was deterrence at its most surgical.

He likened the press to predators who, for too long, had mistaken the lack of retaliation for weakness. That illusion would end here. A predator who oversteps into his territory, he wrote, must not expect to retreat unscathed. He would meet them in courtrooms on both sides of the Channel, his legal reach stretching across borders, prepared to drag the fight into every jurisdiction where the law favoured his claim. They would learn that this was not the prey they thought they were circling—it was a sovereign with claws.

The letter was explicit in its refusal to negotiate with offenders. Those who crossed the boundary would find no backroom settlements, no polite agreements to remove the offending material in exchange for silence. By the time they received the first notice of legal action, he assured them, it would already be too late to bargain. This was not about money alone—it was about principle, about making an example so potent that others would think twice before taking the same risk. In his words, a single case could stand as a warning to an entire industry.

He allowed the warning to reach beyond individuals to the corporations that enabled them. Editors, publishers, and media executives were not exempt from liability simply because they had not held the camera themselves. In law, he reminded, those who ordered or authorised the unlawful act bore the same responsibility as those who carried it out. Their signatures on contracts, their approvals of layouts, and their distribution of images would all serve as evidence against them. If they thought their titles or their distance from the field would shield them, they were mistaken.

The metaphor of the locked gate returned here, not as poetry but as a truth carried in steel. He explained that his patience was finite, and its barrier was fortified not by words alone, but by preparation. Every approach to his family had been noted, every appearance of an unfamiliar face near his home recorded. The moment the gate was forced—be it by intrusion, defamation, or theft of image—the barrier would not merely open; it would collapse entirely, allowing his full legal force to sweep through without restraint. Those who caused that collapse would bear the weight of everything that followed.

Benedict wrote with a clarity that stripped even the bravest of fools of their illusions. This was not a man posturing for the page; this was a man writing from readiness. He was not warning them because he feared them—he was warning them so that when the reckoning came, they could not plead ignorance. He wanted them to understand that the silence they had mistaken for indifference was, in fact, the stillness of someone choosing his moment. And once chosen, there would be no reversal.

He spoke of past encounters with those who had underestimated him, carefully omitting names but making the outcomes clear. Some had lost jobs, others careers; a few had watched their companies dissolve under the strain of prolonged legal battles. In each case, he had acted quietly, without spectacle, allowing the ruin to unfold in the slow, methodical way that left no room for counterattack. This, he promised, would be no different. The absence of noise was not the absence of action—it was the sound of inevitability drawing closer.

The tone did not waver as he addressed the freelancers, those who often considered themselves untouchable due to their lack of affiliation with major outlets. He reminded them that in the eyes of the law, independence was not immunity. If anything, it left them more vulnerable, with no corporate resources to shield them from the cost of their mistakes. Their names would appear on the filings, their assets would be the first seized, and their reputations would carry the scar long after the judgment was paid.

Benedict was unafraid to make the warning personal. He wrote that anyone who targeted his wife, his children, or any member of his extended household would face not only legal retribution but the permanent mark of public condemnation. Their names, once dragged into the court record, would remain searchable long after their careers had ended. No publisher, he suggested, would risk employing someone with such a stain on their history. The act of intrusion would become the gravestone of their professional life.

He reminded the reader that these measures were not theoretical. His position, his resources, and his network of legal advisors made him fully capable of executing every threat written here. This was not an idle display of authority; it was the formal notification of a man who had both the will and the means to act. There was no bluff to call—only the certainty of consequence.

The letter moved toward its close without losing any of its weight. The warning was now layered—legal, financial, and reputational—designed to reach every aspect of a potential offender's life. There was nowhere to retreat that would not carry the echo of this letter, nowhere to hide from the knowledge that they had been warned in advance. The responsibility, he made clear, would rest entirely on their own shoulders.

Benedict made no apology for the severity of his stance. Those who preyed upon others, he wrote, deserved no comfort from the thought that they might be forgiven. Forgiveness was a luxury reserved for those who recognised their error before harm was done. For predators, the only path forward was to face the consequences they had invited upon themselves. He would not meet them halfway. He would meet them in court.

The closing paragraph of this section was as blunt as the first. He told them plainly: this letter would stand as evidence in any future litigation, proof that they had been given fair warning. No editor, no photographer, no opportunist would be able to claim surprise. If they crossed the line, they would do so with the knowledge that the gate had been opened—and that once it was open, it would never close again.

Benedict made it plain within the body of his writing that the letter was never to be mistaken for an interview. This was not the careful conversation of two men seated across from one another, exchanging thoughts over the course of an afternoon. It was not a feature article, ripe for editorial colour or the soft edges of narrative licence. It was a formal document, conceived and written for the express purpose of drawing a line in black ink. Those who read it in newsrooms would feel the hard edge of its purpose; those who read it in court would recognise it as a deliberate record of position and warning.

He explained that interviews, by nature, allowed for interpretation. A reporter might hear an answer and, with or without malice, frame it within their own understanding or their own agenda. That risk did not exist here. The letter offered no space for opinion, no conversational tone that could be twisted into something it was not. Every sentence was deliberate, weighed against the potential for misrepresentation, and locked into place so firmly that even the most cunning of editors would find no room to slip their own intent between the lines.

The separation, Benedict knew, had to be clearly defined for anyone who might later claim that the contents of the interview and the letter were one and the same. The letter was the wall— cold, immovable, and complete. The interview would be the gate—closed to the world and opened for a single man alone. In the letter, he made certain that this metaphor, while unspoken, would be understood in practice. There could be no overlap. What one contained, the other would never hold.

Carl Winston's name appeared only once in the text, positioned carefully in a way that removed it from any suggestion of endorsement. He was not mentioned as a friend or confidant, though both were true; instead, he was referenced as the sole individual granted access to an entirely separate and private discussion. That single mention was enough to signal that Carl's role was different—exclusive, trusted, and entirely outside the reach of the wider press.

This distinction mattered because Benedict had no interest in leaving a door ajar for others to claim equal access. Too many in his position had fallen into that trap—granting one interview, then finding themselves cornered by others who argued for the same treatment under the guise of fairness. There would be no fairness here, because there was no equality of trust. Carl Winston was not chosen out of convenience, but out of history. That history was earned over years, not in the heat of scandal.

Benedict recalled, even as he wrote, the first time Carl had been invited to the cottage. It was twelve years ago, when the truth of his lineage had been fresh and fragile, and Carl had carried a recorder the size of his hand, speaking less than he listened. That interview had never been leaked, never repeated, and never even hinted at in passing conversation. It was the silence afterward, the unbroken trust, that proved Carl worthy of a second visit. This was not sentiment—it was proof of character.

He allowed the letter to draw a bright line around Carl's role without handing the public enough detail to follow him. The location of the meeting would remain undisclosed, just as it had the first time. The mode of transport—a private vehicle—would be known only to the driver, and even that driver would know nothing of the conversation once Carl stepped inside the cottage. Every element of the arrangement was designed to protect not only Benedict's privacy, but Carl's integrity as a journalist who could not be compelled to reveal what he had learned.

In his own mind, Benedict likened the coming interview to a conversation held in a locked vault. What passed between the two men would remain sealed, not because of any formal agreement on paper, but because both understood the rarity of absolute trust in their professions. The letter, however, was the opposite—open for all to read, dissect, and interpret within the limits of the law. The duality was intentional: one piece to stand as a public declaration, the other to exist as a private exchange immune to public consumption.

He wrote with care to ensure that the separation would be legally binding in spirit, if not in statute. Should anyone attempt to argue that Carl's knowledge, gleaned in privacy, could be used in the same way as the printed letter, they would face a solid wall of refusal. The court would see the letter for what it was—a fixed, controlled document—and the interview for what it was not—public property. That legal clarity was not left to implication; it was implied, reinforced, and underlined by omission.

The discipline required to maintain such boundaries was not new to Benedict. In his life, the keeping of secrets had been less an occasional necessity and more a daily practice. Some information was never meant to be shared broadly, and once given to the wrong ears, it could not be reclaimed. He approached this interview with the same caution he had learned in other, more dangerous circumstances—offer only what you are prepared to defend, and offer it only to the one person capable of carrying it without harm.

The trust in Carl Winston was not blind. It was measured against the reality that, even in the most controlled settings, words could take on a life of their own. Yet, history had proven Carl's discretion, and in this case, discretion was the lifeblood of the entire arrangement. If the letter was a fortress built of stone, the interview would be the single key to the inner chamber, held only by the man who had proven he would never sell it.

Benedict did not dwell on sentiment in these lines. There was no warm reminiscence of shared meals or fond recollections of old conversations. Trust, in this case, was not romanticised—it was treated as a currency more valuable than gold. Carl had earned it once, and now he was being given the chance to prove, again, that it had not tarnished with time. The letter existed in part to make that exclusivity visible to the world without revealing a single word of what might later be said in private.

He reminded the reader, indirectly, that the separation served both men equally. For Benedict, it protected the integrity of his stance; for Carl, it preserved his position as a journalist who had never broken the confidence of a source. To blend the two—the public letter and the private interview—would strip both of their power. Keeping them apart allowed each to serve its own purpose without compromise.

As the section of the letter drew to its close, Benedict returned once more to the image of boundaries. The wall of the letter was high, unbroken, and visible to all. The gate of the interview was narrow, locked, and opened only for one. There was no way for the reader to mistake the two, no path by which they could claim passage without his consent. This was how it would remain. The wall was for the world; the gate was for Carl Winston, and no one else.

The fountain pen lay in its rest, the final line of ink drying against the crisp surface of the paper, while Benedict reached for the old landline telephone that sat in the far corner of the room. It was an instrument that had served this cottage for decades, its cream-coloured casing dulled by time, its coiled cord slightly twisted from years of casual use.

When he lifted the receiver, the weight of it felt different from the sleek, hollow devices of the modern age. There was substance to it—an anchor in the hand, as though every call made upon it had been deliberate. He placed his finger into the worn groove of the first digit, turned the rotary, and listened to the gentle clicking return. The hum on the line carried a faint static, the sound of an older world that had never quite left.

When Carl Winston's voice came through, it was as though no time had passed at all. It was not loud, not rehearsed—simply steady, the way it had always been. That voice had once carried him through a conversation that changed the course of his private life twelve years ago, and it held the same unwavering timbre now. Benedict did not waste time on pleasantries. The warmth was there, tucked into the corners of each word, but the brevity was intentional. They had spoken too many times before to clutter this one with the unnecessary. This was not a social call. It was an arrangement, and both men understood it.

He told Carl the day. He told him the hour. The words were few, but the weight behind them was understood in full. There was no need to elaborate on why the meeting was necessary or what might be discussed; that would be for the moment they sat across from one another. For now, the only thing that mattered was that Carl knew when to arrive. There would be a car, a driver who would speak to no one, and a route chosen not for speed, but for invisibility. These were not instructions Carl needed to question.

Carl's acceptance came in a single word—acknowledged. There was no flourish, no suggestion of excitement or curiosity. That was one of the reasons Benedict trusted him. Too many would have asked for details, pressed for some hint of what was to come, or betrayed their own eagerness to hold a story before it was ready to be told. Carl had never been one of them. His discipline was not born of caution alone, but of a kind of respect that was rare in his profession. He understood that information carried too soon was as dangerous as a match struck in a dry field.

The memory of their first arrangement was as sharp in Benedict's mind as if it had taken place the day before. Twelve years ago, the stakes had been different, but the necessity for privacy had been no less urgent. Back then, Carl had arrived without a word to anyone, carrying a modest recorder and a notepad, using both sparingly. He had left the cottage with exactly what had been agreed upon, nothing more, nothing less. In the years that followed, not once had he spoken of it—not to colleagues, not to friends, not even to those who might have been close enough to guess. That silence had built a trust that could not be bought.

Benedict knew that Carl's line of work had changed since then. The world of journalism had grown harsher, faster, and far less forgiving. The rise of digital platforms had bred a generation of writers more concerned with being first than being correct. In that climate, Carl had remained an outlier—measured, patient, unwilling to trade his integrity for speed. That was why Benedict had picked up the phone now. He did not have to sift through options, weighing one against another. There was only one name to call.

As they spoke, there was a mutual understanding that neither man needed to voice. The nature of this meeting would be the same as it had always been: private, protected, and without any trace left for others to find. Benedict did not have to instruct Carl to leave his mobile phone behind or to ensure that no one followed him. Carl had taken such precautions before, and he would do so again without being asked. This was muscle memory between them—habits formed through necessity and refined through repetition.

Benedict leaned back slightly in the chair, the receiver still pressed to his ear, and allowed himself the smallest measure of ease. It was not relief—there was too much still to be done for that—but there was a steadiness that came from knowing the next step was in the hands of someone who would not fail him. The sound of Carl's voice carried that assurance, the way a well-built bridge carries weight without strain. It did not matter that the world outside was restless and unpredictable; within this call, there was control.

They spoke for only a few minutes more, the kind of measured conversation that could be replayed in full from memory alone. No extraneous words, no conversational detours—only what was needed to confirm the plan. In the final moments, Benedict repeated the day and time, as much for habit as for certainty. Carl affirmed it once more, his tone unchanged, his confidence unshaken. Then came the soft click of the receiver being replaced in its cradle, the sound of the call ending without any trace of farewell.

Benedict sat for a moment longer, the receiver still warm in his hand. He studied the faint dust along the cord and the small crack in the casing near the base, marks of an object that had served long past its expected life. There was something fitting in that—how certain tools, like certain friendships, endured not because they were flawless, but because they were reliable. This call had been exactly what it needed to be, no more, no less.

Outside, the day carried on without interruption. Somewhere, beyond the hedgerows and the narrow roads that led away from the cottage, Carl Winston was continuing with his own work, already making quiet arrangements to be where he needed to be. There would be no trail to follow, no whispered mention of the meeting to come. It would happen the way all important things did—without the world knowing until it was over.

Benedict rose from the chair and replaced the receiver gently, the base settling with the soft thud of wood meeting wood. He glanced at the letter still lying on the desk, the ink now fully dry, and felt the weight of the two tasks before him. The letter was for the public, for those who needed to be warned. The call was for the private, for the one man who would be allowed to hear the rest. In that separation lay the strength of the entire plan.

It struck him, as he looked once more at the paper, that the call had been the easier part. Words written for the world to see required a precision that could not be recalled once sent. The conversation with Carl, by contrast, could shift and breathe when they sat together, adapting to the moment. But each had its place, and each would be carried out without compromise. That balance was what had kept him intact for so many years.

He moved the letter to one side, clearing a small space on the desk for the preparations that would follow. There was still much to arrange—the vehicle, the timing, the layers of security that would ensure Carl's arrival and departure went unseen. But the foundation had been laid. The call had been made. In the quiet that followed, Benedict allowed himself a final thought before moving on: in a world full of shifting loyalties, there were still a few constants. Carl Winston was one of them.

As the weight of the receiver left his hand, Benedict remained seated, letting the hum of the past rise unbidden. The call had ended in moments, but the echo it stirred was twelve years deep, reaching back to a day when the air in this cottage carried the same quiet gravity. He could see it clearly: the narrow desk between them, its surface bare except for the modest digital recorder set at the centre like a silent referee. Carl Winston had sat opposite him then, pen poised but seldom used, his focus unbroken from the first question to the final answer. Nothing about that day had felt hurried, and nothing about it had been careless.

It had been a winter afternoon, the kind where the light faded early and the chill pressed itself against the glass. They had brewed coffee—not tea, never tea—and set it on the far side of the desk, untouched for most of the meeting. Carl had explained, briefly, that his purpose was not to extract drama but to record the truth exactly as it was given. He had meant it, too; Benedict could tell by the absence of those leading inflections so many journalists use when they are hoping to pull a sensational thread. Carl had no appetite for embellishment. He preferred the clean line of fact over the jagged edge of speculation.

Benedict remembered the precision with which he had spoken that day. Every word chosen, every phrase tested in the space between thought and voice. There had been things he could not say—not yet, perhaps not ever—but what he did share was delivered without disguise. Carl had matched that honesty with discipline, capturing only what was offered, never straying into the shadows where trust would have been broken. By the end of the interview, there had been no doubt in either man's mind that this was a professional bond unlike any other.

When the recorder had clicked off, there was no flurry of gathering papers or rush to the door. Instead, they had sat for a while longer, the way men do when they are both measuring the worth of what has just taken place. Carl had closed his notepad without looking at it, as though the act itself signified that nothing more needed to be written. That gesture had stayed with Benedict—simple, almost casual, yet it carried the finality of a sealed agreement. The understanding between them did not require signatures or witnesses.

In the weeks that followed, Benedict had waited for the world to twist his words, for headlines to emerge that bore his name but none of his truth. It never happened. When the piece appeared, it was plain, exact, and untouched by the fever of gossip. Carl had resisted the urge—if he had even felt it—to dress the story in anything other than the fabric of reality. That alone had set him apart in a time when most journalists, even the respectable ones, could not resist polishing their work until the truth wore an unfamiliar face.

That first meeting had been arranged under circumstances that were precarious, though far less hostile than they were now. Even then, Benedict had been cautious, testing every path to the cottage for signs of intrusion. Carl had respected the need for discretion, arriving without escort, without equipment that could broadcast his location, and leaving without leaving a trace. It was not the kind of thing one could ask of just anyone; it required a temperament rare enough to be trusted with silence.

The recorder itself had been unremarkable—a compact device, silver and black, with a single red light that glowed steadily when active. Yet in that small object lay the preservation of a moment that could have easily been corrupted by the wrong hands. When the interview was done, Carl had handed the recorder back across the desk without so much as glancing at the files. It had been Benedict who reviewed the contents, confirming the integrity of the record before transferring a copy. That gesture had confirmed what was already evident: Carl was there to listen, not to own.

Over the years, that recording had become a kind of touchstone for Benedict. On the rare occasions when doubt pressed too heavily on him—when the noise of the outside world threatened to drown the steady voice within—he would return to it, not to hear himself, but to remember the clarity of that exchange. In Carl's measured questions and the unbroken chain of truth in his answers, there was proof that such conversations could still exist in a time when they were almost extinct.

The contrast between then and now was stark. Twelve years ago, the media had still held pockets of restraint; there were still corners of the profession where ethics had not been traded for reach. Now, the predators were faster, more aggressive, less concerned with being right than with being first. Benedict knew that for Carl to have survived in that climate without bending to it was no small feat. It meant his principles were not simply professional—they were personal, and therefore unshakable.

As the memory unfolded in his mind, Benedict could almost smell the faint tang of the coffee cooling untouched between them. He remembered the muted ticking of the clock on the wall, the way it seemed to pace their exchange without ever rushing it. Those details, small as they were, formed the frame around the image of that day. They were reminders that truth, like trust, was not built in grand moments, but in the accumulation of smaller ones, each honoured without compromise.

He considered, briefly, the possibility that Carl might have changed since then. Twelve years is a long time in any profession, and journalism was more corrosive than most. But the call they had just shared told him otherwise. The same steadiness was there, the same refusal to press for what was not offered. If anything, the years had tempered it, turning discipline into instinct. That was why this meeting would work as the last had—because neither man had drifted from the place they began.

In truth, Benedict had never stopped trusting Carl. The gap of years between their meetings had not been filled with suspicion or doubt; it had simply been the natural distance that time and circumstance impose. That trust was not blind. It was measured, tested, and found intact. The call they had just concluded was a renewal of that original agreement, unspoken but binding nonetheless.

The recorder they would use this time would be different—newer, perhaps quieter in its mechanics—but its role would remain the same. It would be the silent witness to a conversation not meant for public hearing until Benedict allowed it. In that way, it was as much a participant as either man, bound by the same rules of accuracy and restraint.

The memory of that earlier day did more than remind him of Carl's worth; it anchored him in the knowledge that this was not the first time he had walked this path. The stakes were higher now, the consequences sharper, but the structure was familiar. He had done this before, and he could do it again. That certainty was a rare gift in times such as these.

By the time Benedict rose from the chair, the memory had settled into place—not as nostalgia, but as preparation. The past was not there to comfort him; it was there to sharpen his understanding of the present. He moved to the desk, laid his hand on the letter once more, and allowed himself the smallest of acknowledgements: twelve years ago, this had worked. Twelve years later, it would again.

Sørensen had not moved from his place in the far corner of the room since Benedict began writing. His arms remained folded across his chest, his posture as steady as the oak beam he leaned against. Years in security had trained him to read a room not by what was happening in it, but by what could happen if discipline failed. His eyes followed the pen without interruption, watching each deliberate curve and stroke as though he were tracking the slow assembly of a weapon. He did not need to ask what the letter contained; he could feel it in the weight of the silence.

When the final sentence of the page settled into place, Sørensen's gaze did not waver. He was no stranger to declarations like this. He had delivered them himself, though rarely on paper. His were spoken in doorways, in the shadowed corners of airport terminals, in the measured steps between a car and a building where the air seemed too still. But there was something about the way Benedict chose his words, how they carried not just warning but certainty, that told him this was a different kind of weapon. It would not be fired once and discarded; it would be kept, sharpened, and used again if needed.

The faintest curve of a smile tugged at the corners of his mouth, but it was not amusement. It was recognition. He had seen Benedict at his most unpredictable—at ten years old, dismantling an electronic lock in half the time it took a trained professional, then smiling as though it were a game. He had seen him at his most measured—standing before a room of people who doubted him and leaving them with nothing to say. This was the latter. Controlled, deliberate, built to last. It was the side of Benedict that Sørensen trusted most.

He had always known that if Benedict ever turned his full attention to the press, it would not be with the wild retaliation of a man provoked, but with the quiet, unavoidable force of one who knew exactly where to strike. What Sørensen approved of now was not the sharpness of the blade, but the steadiness of the hand holding it. Rage burned quickly and left ash. Control burned slowly and left a scar. That was what the letter would do—it would mark anyone foolish enough to ignore it.

The nod he gave was subtle, almost imperceptible, but Benedict saw it. It was the kind of acknowledgment they had exchanged for years, one that carried no excess movement, no need for words. In that single gesture was the full weight of their understanding: this was the right move, at the right time, and with the right level of restraint. They had spent too many years navigating threats together for either of them to mistake the importance of that balance.

In the years since they met, Sørensen had not often allowed himself the luxury of visible approval. His role had been to challenge, to test, to make certain that Benedict's instincts were more than just quick—they had to be correct. But in this moment, the quiet approval was deliberate. It was a signal not just of trust, but of alignment. When they left for the meeting with Carl Winston, there would be no need to question whether they were on the same page. They already were.

His mind was already mapping the space where the meeting would take place, recalling the angles of entry, the distances to cover, the places a man could stand without being seen. That was his way of approving—by preparing to guard the truth as fiercely as Benedict was preparing to speak it. He would not interfere with the conversation, but he would be close enough that his presence alone would remind Carl, and anyone else who might be tempted, that no breach of trust would go unanswered.

The trust he held for Carl was not without measure. He remembered the first meeting twelve years ago as clearly as Benedict did. He had been there too, standing not far from where he stood now, watching a man ask questions without circling like a vulture. That had been enough to earn Carl a place in the narrow space between guardedness and openness that Benedict allowed few to enter. Even so, Sørensen would be there again—because trust was not the absence of vigilance.

The approval in his nod was layered. It was for the letter's edge, yes, but also for Benedict's ability to hold that edge without letting it cut in the wrong direction. He had seen men ruin themselves by speaking too quickly, by letting anger dictate their choice of words. This letter had none of that. Every sentence was clean, every point anchored in law, every warning reinforced by the weight of certainty. It was the kind of document that left no space for argument without making its author appear the aggressor. That was skill.

In a way, Sørensen saw the letter as an extension of the very training he had given Benedict years ago—self-defence, not assault. Strike only when struck, but strike in such a way that the other party does not wish to repeat the encounter. It was the same principle whether the weapon was a hand, a word, or a page. And Benedict had learned it well enough to apply it without hesitation.

The approval did not soften his expression. His face remained as it always did in these moments—composed, slightly stern, with the eyes doing most of the speaking. To anyone else, it might have looked as though he was withholding judgment, but Benedict knew better. That look meant the foundation was solid, that the course was set, and that nothing in the plan needed correction.

Sørensen shifted his weight slightly, not out of restlessness, but to mark the close of his silent appraisal. He let his arms drop to his sides, the fold breaking as naturally as it had formed. The moment of judgment had passed. Now it was a matter of execution—making certain that the meeting with Carl unfolded exactly as intended, without interference from the outside world.

In that brief movement, Benedict caught the final note of the approval he had already seen in the nod. It was not just that the letter was worthy of being sent—it was that Sørensen trusted him to handle whatever storm it might stir. That was a different kind of trust, one that did not come from words or plans, but from years of watching a man's actions and finding them consistently sound.

The room held its silence a moment longer, as though allowing both men to fix the shape of it in their minds before the next step. The letter lay finished on the desk, the pen set aside, and the weight of what it would do already beginning to settle in the air. Sørensen stepped forward just enough to stand parallel to Benedict, his presence now beside him rather than across the room. It was a quiet reminder that whatever came of this, they would face it together, as they always had.

When Benedict glanced at him one last time before folding the letter, the approval was still there—unchanged, unspoken, but entirely clear. The message had been written with precision, but it would be delivered with presence. And Sørensen's presence was as much a part of its strength as the words themselves.

The door to the cottage eased open without a knock, the hinges barely making a sound. Harrison stepped inside carrying the pot as though it were the only weapon worth bringing into the room. The aroma of the coffee reached them before his voice did, thick and dark, the kind of scent that made the air feel heavier in the chest. He did not ask who wanted it. In this circle, the answer was always the same. Tea had no place here, and never would. He crossed the small stretch of floor between the door and the table with the unhurried certainty of a man who belonged in the room.

Benedict did not look up from the paper, but the slight pause in his pen stroke was enough to acknowledge Harrison's arrival. Harrison filled his mug without comment, the stream of coffee catching the light for a moment before disappearing into the dark surface of the cup. Sørensen's mug was next, though his nod of thanks was almost as brief as Benedict's pause. There was no chatter, no casual remark about the weather or the day—just the quiet act of pouring and the subtle understanding that coffee was part of the work itself.

The scent settled into the room like another layer of presence, grounding the moment in something tangible. It was a scent that had followed them through countless late nights and early mornings, through planning sessions in shadowed rooms and silent hours in safe houses. Harrison brewed it the same way every time, strong enough to stand on its own, without sugar, without compromise. It was a drink for men who did not need softening at the edges.

Benedict lifted the mug without shifting his focus from the page, the steam curling across his face like a passing thought. The first sip was measured, not for temperature but for effect. The caffeine did not jolt him—it sharpened him. The deliberate pace of his writing tightened further, each word finding its place with greater precision. He did not waste letters, any more than he would waste a move in a fight. Harrison, watching from the edge of the table, saw it happening the way a sailor sees the wind fill a sail—quietly, steadily, without the need for fanfare.

Harrison had been there for most of the storms in Benedict's life. He had stood on the edges of family conflicts, legal battles, and moments when the public had leaned too close. He knew the difference between the times Benedict wrote quickly, pouring out a flood of thought that would later need refining, and the times—like now—when the words came slowly, each one weighed before it was set down. This pace meant the outcome would be decisive. Harrison had seen it too many times to doubt it.

Sørensen accepted his coffee with the same silent ease as the rest, though his eyes remained on Benedict. He understood what Harrison understood: coffee was not here to keep them awake; it was here to keep them still, to hold them in the kind of focus where no movement was wasted. The air was thick with it now, and the letter seemed to draw from that strength. Harrison leaned back slightly, letting his own cup warm his hands, content to let the silence do the rest.

There was a certain ritual to these moments, one they never spoke about but always followed. Harrison brought the coffee when the work required clarity. He brewed it himself, never leaving it to chance or to someone else's hand. The act was as much about consistency as it was about taste. When the mugs were full, the room seemed to settle. The edges of thought aligned, the pace found its rhythm, and what needed to be done was done without the distraction of hunger, thirst, or fatigue.

Benedict's eyes did not leave the paper, but Harrison could see the shift in his posture. Shoulders squared just slightly, the lines of his back set in that way they always did when a plan had moved from thought to certainty. Harrison knew that the coffee was not the cause—it was simply part of the environment that allowed such precision to surface. In the years they had known each other, he had come to think of coffee as an unspoken ally in these matters, one that had its own place in their unshakable routines.

The quiet was not oppressive. It was the kind of quiet that held weight, where the scrape of a chair leg or the soft set-down of a mug was magnified in meaning. Harrison never tried to fill it. He understood that when Benedict wrote like this, the noise in his mind was already being turned into something solid. His role was to keep the physical space as steady as the mental one. Coffee was part of that stability, a simple constant in a room where everything else might shift with the turn of a page.

The pot sat within reach, still half full, ready for another pour when the first round was gone. Harrison did not ask if anyone wanted more—he would see the empty mugs when it was time. This was not service, not in the formal sense. It was participation. His presence in the room, his hand on the pot, his quiet watch over the mugs, was his way of being part of what was being built on the page. He did not need to read the words to know their weight.

As the minutes passed, the steam rising from Benedict's cup thinned, but the pen did not slow. Harrison refilled it without prompting, his movement as seamless as a change in the weather. The flow of coffee matched the flow of ink, each sustaining the other. He had seen letters written under duress, scribbled with the shaking hand of a man under pressure. This was not that. This was the work of someone in full control, building something that would stand long after the coffee cooled.

Sørensen caught Harrison's eye once, a brief exchange that needed no words. It was the look of two men who had both stood guard over this process before, each in his own way. Harrison guarded the moment with the steady ritual of coffee; Sørensen guarded it with the silent readiness of a man who would act without hesitation. Between the two of them, Benedict was surrounded by the kind of support that allowed him to write without looking up.

When the pot finally emptied, Harrison set it aside and folded his hands around his own mug. The coffee was as strong in the last pour as it had been in the first—another point of consistency he never compromised. He took a slow sip, his eyes still moving between Benedict's hand and the edges of the room. The letter was nearing completion. He could see it in the way Benedict's pen returned to the inkwell less often, the lines tightening as they approached the end.

Harrison thought about the times he had watched Benedict fight in other arenas—on the street, in courtrooms, in closed rooms where the words spoken would never reach the public. Those battles had their own pace, but this one had something different in it.

This was pre-emptive, not reactive. It was the difference between blocking a blow and making sure the other man never raised his hand in the first place. The coffee was not a weapon, but it was part of the armour, and Harrison had brought it for exactly that reason.

The moment felt complete when Benedict finally set the pen down and reached for his cup again, lifting it with the unthinking ease of a man whose focus had not once broken. Harrison took a final sip of his own and allowed himself the faint satisfaction of knowing the coffee had done its part. Whatever storm this letter might stir, they would meet it on their own terms—and the world would not be ready for it.

The first draft sat before him like an open challenge, black ink cutting into the paper with more force than grace. Benedict read it through once, then again, his eyes narrowing slightly at the turns of phrase that no longer satisfied him. He did not hesitate to strike a line straight through entire sentences, letting the blunt edge of the nib dig a furrow into the paper. This was no time for sentiment, no room for the indulgence of leaving words untouched out of pride. Sørensen had told him long ago that the first draft was the skeleton—necessary, but not yet strong enough to stand on its own.

He reached for a fresh page without shifting in his chair, the smooth pull of the paper from the stack accompanied by the faint rustle that filled the otherwise still air. His handwriting was slower now, deliberate in its formation, each word weighed against the one before it. The goal was not beauty; it was precision. In this kind of letter, there was no such thing as a harmless word. Every syllable had the potential to strengthen or weaken the case, and Benedict would not give an enemy the satisfaction of finding a loose thread to pull.

The pen scratched steadily, the sound almost hypnotic in its persistence. A small pile of discarded sheets began to gather on the left corner of the desk, each one a casualty of his unwillingness to settle for "good enough." He knew the habits of journalists too well—how they would seize on the smallest ambiguity, twist it, and claim authority over the meaning. This letter was not going to give them that opening. If it could not survive being read aloud in a court of law without amendment, it did not belong on the page.

Certain phrases demanded more than a single rewrite. He circled them, crossed them out, rewrote them, then circled them again until the wording felt immovable. It was not simply about the immediate audience; it was about permanence. If someone dug this letter out fifty years from now, it should still hold the same force, the same unshakable structure. Sørensen's voice echoed in his head—A letter like this should be able to stand as its own witness. That was the standard, and Benedict intended to meet it without compromise.

He tested the clauses for balance, pairing legal inevitability with personal authority. It was not enough to state the law; he had to own it, to write in such a way that even a reader unfamiliar with the statutes would feel the weight of them.

The letter needed to read like a door slammed shut—not angrily, but with the finality of one that would never open again. Benedict leaned back for a moment, scanning the paragraph he had just finished, and allowed himself a single nod before leaning forward to continue.

Each revision tightened the flow. Redundant words vanished, replaced by cleaner, harder phrasing. Adjectives were pared back to the essential, verbs chosen with the same care one might use in selecting weapons. He was not building an argument that begged to be heard; he was building a statement that demanded to be obeyed. There was no softness here, no gap for interpretation. If the reader was not sure what he meant by the end of the first page, they had not been paying attention.

The discarded drafts now covered the corner of the desk like fallen leaves, each one a record of his refusal to settle. He kept the rejected pages in view as a reminder that effort mattered, that words should be earned, not simply written. Harrison glanced at the growing stack once, then looked away, knowing better than to comment. This was Benedict's process, and interrupting it would be like stepping into a sparring match uninvited.

Benedict worked through the final paragraphs with an intensity that narrowed the room to the desk, the pen, and the sound of his own breath. He wrote as though each word would be weighed against him in some future trial—and perhaps it would. That was the point. A letter of this nature was not a passing communication; it was a fixed piece of armour, built to withstand repeated blows without denting. Sørensen had taught him to think like this, to anticipate not only the first strike but the second, the third, and the unseen one that might come years later.

At one point, he paused to rewrite an entire sentence simply because the cadence of the words was off. It was not enough for the meaning to be exact; the rhythm mattered too. In court, a line delivered with the wrong pacing could sound uncertain, and uncertainty was poison. He adjusted the sequence of clauses until they fell in the right order, then read them under his breath, listening for the way the consonants hit, the way the line carried weight. Only when it felt unshakable did he move on.

Harrison poured another round of coffee without a word, the sound of the liquid filling the mugs barely registering in Benedict's mind. He sipped without looking up, his attention fixed on the sentence he had just completed. The caffeine was doing its work, keeping his thoughts sharp as the hours passed. Outside, the light shifted, but inside the pace did not change. Draft followed draft, each one more refined, more precise than the last.

When the revisions reached the closing paragraph, Benedict slowed even further. The ending was not simply the final line; it was the lock on the door. Everything before it would be judged by the strength of that close. He tightened it until there was no excess, no kindness mistaken for hesitation. It was a warning, pure and final, and it carried the weight of a man who intended to be taken seriously. The ink settled into the fibres of the page as if it belonged there.

Sørensen moved closer, standing just behind him now, his shadow falling across the desk. He did not read over Benedict's shoulder—he did not need to. He could feel from the posture, from the steady, even hand, that the letter was nearing completion. When Benedict finished the final stroke of the final word, he set the pen down with the same care he might give to sheathing a blade.

The room seemed to exhale with him. The pile of discarded drafts sat to one side, the finished letter alone in the centre. There was no need to compare them; the difference was obvious in every line. The early drafts had been the work of a man sharpening his tools. The final draft was the work of a man who now held them ready in his hands.

Benedict read it through once more, silently, his eyes moving with deliberate care. No word stumbled, no phrase faltered. It was clean, hard, and impossible to misinterpret. He knew that once it left this room, it would have a life of its own—and he was ready for it to stand on its own legs, unshaken. Sørensen gave a single nod when Benedict slid the pen aside. Approval did not need to be spoken.

Harrison took the empty coffee mug from the desk and set it aside, as though clearing the last obstacle between the letter and its journey. Benedict sat back, his shoulders easing for the first time since he had begun. The work was done, the words locked into place. What came next would be action—and the letter was ready to meet it.

The cottage took on a different character as the preparations began, the comfortable warmth of its daily life slowly replaced by a sharper, more deliberate atmosphere. Harrison moved with quiet efficiency, checking each lock twice, turning the latches until they clicked with certainty. He pulled the curtains tight over the small windows, leaving no gap for a passing glance. In this place, even the smallest breach could turn trust into a liability, and no one here was willing to allow that.

Sørensen's work was different, his tall frame filling the doorway as he stepped outside to walk the perimeter. He moved with the same deliberate pace he had used in the days when guarding Benedict meant scanning every rooftop, every shadow, every street corner. Though the cottage stood on a quiet lane in Kent, the habit was too ingrained to abandon. He checked the treeline, the gravel path, even the angle of the parked car, ensuring no sightline offered an uninvited view of the meeting place.

Inside, Harrison cleared the table in the main room, moving every object that did not belong. The surface would hold only what was essential: the recorder, polished and tested earlier that morning; a second set of notes, handwritten and clipped neatly; and a single sealed envelope containing Benedict's terms for publication. He placed each item with the precision of someone setting tools for surgery, every placement intentional, every angle deliberate.

The envelope itself seemed to carry weight beyond its paper and ink. It was thick enough to resist a careless bend, sealed with the kind of press that would show tampering instantly. The terms inside were final, not open to negotiation, and their presence on the table was a silent contract between Benedict and Carl before a word was spoken. Harrison placed it to the right of the recorder, close enough for Benedict to reach, but not within anyone else's casual grasp.

In the kitchen, the faint aroma of coffee lingered from earlier, but even that felt sharper now, stripped of its leisurely pace. Harrison poured a fresh pot and left it warming on the side counter, two clean mugs placed neatly beside it. Hospitality had its place in this meeting, but it would be measured and deliberate, the same as everything else. In this cottage today, even the smallest detail mattered.

Sørensen returned from his circuit without a word, the slight narrowing of his eyes signalling that all was secure. He closed the front door firmly behind him and took his place near the window, standing just far enough back to avoid casting a shadow on the curtain. From here, he could see the approach without being seen. It was a habit from years of guarding, and one Benedict trusted without question.

Benedict himself had not moved from the desk in the corner, though his hands were still now, the pen laid aside. He was reading through the letter again, not because he doubted it, but because the act of reviewing steadied him for what was coming. Every meeting of this nature had its own rhythm, and part of his role was to match it from the first moment Carl stepped inside. The cottage might be theirs, but in these hours, it would also be a stage.

The air inside had shifted—subtle, but undeniable. Where earlier there had been the easy quiet of a lived-in space, now there was the measured stillness of a room about to be entered by someone carrying purpose. The familiar creak of the floorboards under Harrison's step sounded different now, the sound sharper in the close air. Even the clock on the wall seemed to tick more deliberately, marking time as though counting down to the arrival.

On the far shelf, Harrison had placed a small tray with fresh paper and a sharpened pencil, a courtesy for Carl should he wish to take his own notes. It was not an invitation to record beyond the agreed means, but it was a gesture of respect—a sign that Carl's role here was not simply as a guest, but as a participant in something permanent. Nothing in this room would happen by chance, and nothing would be done without intent.

Sørensen moved to check the back door, his steps silent over the old wood. The latch was firm, the hinges quiet. He allowed himself a brief glance at Benedict before returning to his post, a silent confirmation that the room was now secure on all sides. No one would approach this cottage unseen, not today.

Benedict rose then, stepping away from the desk to join Harrison at the table. He picked up the recorder, turned it over in his hands, and placed it exactly in the centre of the cleared space. The second set of notes remained stacked neatly beside it, the envelope unmoved. He did not speak, and neither did they. There was no need. Each of them understood their role here without the exchange of a single word.

In the corner, Harrison adjusted the chair where Carl would sit, pulling it out just enough to be an unspoken welcome without undermining the formal gravity of the meeting. It was a small gesture, but it carried weight; even in matters of control, there was room for courtesy. The arrangement of the chairs meant Benedict would sit with his back to the window, the light falling toward him, while Carl faced inward, away from distraction.

The cottage seemed to breathe with them, its walls absorbing the quiet anticipation. Outside, the wind moved faintly through the hedges, carrying no sound of approach yet. Inside, the only motion came from the three men—each one steady, each one deliberate. The stage was set, the tools in place, the air holding its breath.

Harrison poured himself a small measure of coffee and drank it in silence, eyes on the table as though guarding it. Sørensen's gaze never left the window. Benedict rested one hand lightly on the sealed envelope, not in possession but in readiness. This was no longer simply a home. For the hours ahead, it was a chamber of record—a place where truth would be spoken, documented, and sealed against the meddling of anyone beyond its walls. When Carl arrived, nothing would need to be explained. The room itself would tell him everything.

The sound of tyres over gravel broke the stillness long before the black saloon came into view. Sørensen, already at his post near the window, tracked its slow approach with the quiet focus of a man who never trusted anything until it was inside the gate. Harrison moved to the front door without a word, his hand resting loosely on the latch as though he had been expecting the knock for years, not minutes. Benedict remained seated, his gaze steady on the table, knowing the moment would play out exactly as planned.

The vehicle rolled to a stop in the narrow space beside the hedgerow. The driver, dressed in plain black, stepped out first, scanning the lane before opening the rear door. From within emerged Carl Winston, his movement unhurried, as if stepping into an environment where haste was a kind of offence. The same weathered satchel hung from his shoulder, the leather worn smooth where his hand had rested countless times before. His coat bore the faint creases of years of service in unpredictable weather, and its weight seemed as much a part of him as his own frame.

Sørensen's eyes flicked briefly to Benedict, the smallest nod confirming all was well. The man outside was exactly who they expected. The door opened, and Harrison stepped aside, allowing Carl to cross the threshold without the jolt of an unnecessary greeting. Here, familiarity was not measured by words, but by the absence of them. Carl removed his hat as he entered, the gesture neither rushed nor theatrical, and placed it gently on the narrow table near the wall.

Benedict rose then, the chair sliding back with a sound that belonged to the room. The two men faced each other, no handshake, no clasped arms—only the kind of nod reserved for those who had already proven themselves. Carl's eyes carried no flicker of curiosity about the details of the letter; he understood that it existed apart from him. His work here would be to document, not to shape, and that restraint was why he had been invited at all.

The air in the cottage did not change at Carl's arrival—it had already been waiting for him. He stepped into it as though stepping into a sealed archive, aware that every word spoken from this point on would be weighted, deliberate, and permanent. Harrison gestured toward the chair opposite Benedict's place at the table. Carl sat without hesitation, placing the satchel at his feet and unfastening the single brass clasp with the precision of a man who kept his tools in order.

From the satchel emerged a notebook, its pages lined with a clean, narrow script, and a pen that bore the faint scratches of long service. Carl placed them neatly before him, then glanced toward the recorder on the table. His eyes met Benedict's briefly, a silent request for permission. Benedict answered with a slow nod. There would be no hidden devices here, no second-hand accounts twisted by unseen hands. This meeting was as controlled as a trial.

Sørensen closed the door quietly and remained standing near the wall, his position neither looming nor casual. He was not here to intimidate Carl—he didn't need to. His presence was a fact, one that any man with sense would respect without instruction. Carl did not so much as glance toward him; he understood the rules of this kind of room.

Harrison poured coffee into the two waiting mugs, placing one in front of Benedict and one in front of Carl. The steam rose in thin spirals, carrying with it the grounded aroma that seemed to settle the air further. Carl accepted the mug with a slight inclination of the head but did not drink immediately. His attention was fixed on Benedict, his hands resting lightly on the table's edge, ready but not eager.

Benedict took the envelope from beside the recorder and set it squarely in the centre of the table. He did not slide it across. That movement would come later, when the letter was ready to leave this room in Carl's care. For now, its position was symbolic—a reminder that what was to be discussed would live beyond this meeting, but only under the terms set forth within. Carl's eyes lingered on it for a fraction of a second before returning to Benedict's face.

The first words exchanged were not the beginning of the interview. They were acknowledgements, measured and free of ceremony. Benedict thanked him for coming under the agreed conditions. Carl replied with the same assurance he had given twelve years ago: no one would hear of this meeting from his lips except in the exact form it was meant to be told. The exchange was simple, and it was binding.

Outside, the lane remained silent, the vehicle still parked where it had stopped. The driver, unseen from within, would remain in place until called. In the cottage, the air held steady, not tense but purposeful. Every movement—the turning of a page in Carl's notebook, the faint click as he adjusted his pen—seemed amplified in the close quiet.

Benedict leaned forward slightly, resting his forearms on the table. He studied Carl the way one studies an instrument before playing—knowing its sound, but needing to feel the weight of it again. Carl waited without prompting, understanding that in this space, the rhythm was Benedict's alone to set. There was no rush, no filler conversation to warm the air. The work would begin when it was meant to.

The smell of fresh coffee mingled with the faint scent of paper and ink, grounding the moment in its physical reality. These were not the sterile surroundings of a press office, nor the staged backdrop of a televised interview. This was a private chamber, a place where words would be crafted with the same care as a legal testament. And in truth, that was exactly what it was.

Carl adjusted his chair slightly, leaning forward enough to signal readiness without breaking the stillness. Benedict's eyes held his for a long moment, reading the man across from him the way others might read the letter already written. In that quiet exchange, the purpose of this meeting was sealed. The letter might have teeth, but this conversation would give it a voice.

It was Sørensen, not Benedict, who broke the silence at last. His deep voice carried no edge, only the factual weight of a man stating that the room was secure. That single confirmation closed the invisible door between this space and the outside world. From here on, every word spoken would stay inside these walls until it was carried out under the strict terms already waiting in the sealed envelope.

Carl reached for his pen, not to write yet, but to hold. Benedict took a measured breath. The meeting had not officially begun, but its gravity was already in the room. They both knew that when it did, there would be no turning back.

The recorder sat in the centre of the table like a silent arbiter, its small red light still dark. Benedict's hand hovered near it, not ready to press the button just yet. His eyes fixed on Carl, the weight of the moment building in the stillness between them. This was not a casual conversation to be revisited or amended later. This was a covenant. He made it clear from the outset that once this device captured his words, they would live exactly as spoken—unaltered, final, and immune to the erosion of time. There would be no return, no gentle second attempt to temper his meaning.

Carl listened without interruption, his expression steady. His years in journalism had trained him to wait through silences, but this was something more—an understanding that the man across from him was drawing a line that no one would cross twice.

The very act of being here was a rare concession, one granted only because Carl had already proven himself as a custodian of truth. His earlier interview, twelve years past, remained unblemished in Benedict's mind, an unbroken chain of trust from that day to this one.

Benedict leaned back slightly, as if to give Carl space to reconsider, though he already knew the answer. He wanted the man to feel the gravity of this agreement not as a weight forced upon him, but as one willingly carried. "There will be no second interview," Benedict said, each word measured, the kind that could be read in a court transcript without losing force. "Once you leave here, that is the record. It stands, unchallenged, as the truth."

Carl's reply was as simple as it was certain. "I understand." His voice did not carry the bravado of a man seeking to prove himself; it was the quiet acceptance of someone who had been entrusted with something that could never be taken back. He did not ask for clarifications, nor did he seek exceptions. The agreement was complete in that single exchange, bound not by ink or signature, but by the spoken word and the character of the men who spoke it.

Sørensen shifted slightly near the wall, his eyes moving between them with the quiet satisfaction of a witness to a pact made without loopholes. He knew the rules of such things. In his own work, trust was a currency rarer than gold, and once spent, it could never be regained. This, he understood, was Benedict's version of a contract—no less binding for lacking paper.

Harrison, refilling Carl's mug, paused long enough to meet his gaze, a silent acknowledgement passing between them. Though Harrison had no role in the content of the interview, he understood its permanence. His presence here was not just service, but solidarity. Every person in this room knew what was at stake—not just the integrity of Benedict's words, but the security of the family they were meant to shield.

Benedict's hand rested on the recorder now, his fingers brushing against its worn edge. He remembered the first time he had used it, the faint static hum it made when the tape began to spin. It was the same device, kept in working order through years of disuse, a small relic of the last time he had opened his life to anyone beyond the family. The familiarity of its weight grounded him, reminding him that nothing here was improvised. Every element had been chosen with intent.

Before pressing the button, he spoke once more—not for Carl's benefit, but for his own clarity. "When this starts, it does not stop. There will be no cuts, no omissions. If you misquote me, it will be deliberate, and it will end our agreement. Permanently." His tone carried no heat, no sharpness, only the kind of certainty that comes from knowing one's boundaries with absolute precision.

Carl nodded, his pen poised but unmoving. He had no intention of interrupting the flow once it began. His role here was to witness and preserve, not to steer. For all his years in the industry, he had rarely been in a room where the story itself was given the dignity of dictating its own form. Most stories, he knew, were wrestled into the shape an editor wanted. This one would resist such treatment, and he would not be the man to break it.

Sørensen's eyes narrowed slightly, reading every movement, every inflection. He was not looking for deceit—he already trusted Carl's loyalty—but for the subtle signs that indicated readiness. He saw no hesitation, no restless flicker of the gaze. Carl was here for the truth, not for the headline. That was enough.

The coffee between them cooled slowly, steam thinning as the moment drew nearer. Harrison set the pot back on the stove without looking over, as if by unspoken agreement that the room must be undisturbed now. Outside, the world carried on in ignorance—pedestrians passing in the village, the occasional car humming down the lane—but within these walls, time had narrowed to a point.

Benedict's thumb hovered over the button, then pulled back just a fraction. "I want you to remember something, Carl," he said, his voice lowering slightly. "This isn't just for me. It's for them. Every word I speak will be theirs to carry, long after I'm gone. If you ever doubt the weight of this, remember whose names you'll be protecting."

Carl's jaw set in a quiet line of resolve. "I'll remember." There was no embellishment, no grand oath-making gesture. It was the kind of promise that relied on the history between them, not on theatrics.

The pause that followed was deliberate, a final stillness before movement. Then, without further ceremony, Benedict pressed the button. The recorder clicked, its small red light blinking to life. The faint hum of its mechanism filled the silence, a sound both ordinary and irreversible.

Sørensen's posture shifted almost imperceptibly, the signal that the room was now sealed in more than one sense. Whatever passed between these walls from this moment forward would live here until the time came for it to step into the world exactly as it was spoken.

Benedict's first words into the recorder were not introductions, nor were they polite acknowledgements. They were the opening of a truth long held under lock, now spoken under the strictest of conditions. The one-time privilege had begun.

The faint mechanical hum of the recorder settled into the air like a presence of its own, the small red light blinking in unbroken rhythm. Benedict leaned forward slightly, his elbows resting on the solid oak table, the paper before him untouched for now.

He did not begin with titles, honours, or the kind of ceremonial preamble that the press would expect. He began with his name—spoken slowly, clearly, in the way one reclaims what has been borrowed too long by strangers. It was not a plea for recognition; it was a declaration of ownership. His name belonged to him, not to headlines, and certainly not to speculation.

Carl's pen did not move at first. He knew these opening moments carried more weight than any line he could draft. The words came with a steadiness that reminded him of walking through an old cathedral—not for prayer, but for the echo of steps on stone, each one deliberate and certain. This was not a confession, nor an unveiling of hidden scandal. It was the setting of the record straight, the cementing of a truth long misrepresented, and Carl understood instinctively that his role was to guard it in its purest form.

Benedict spoke without rushing, his cadence unwavering. Every syllable was measured as though he were laying bricks, ensuring each one was level and secure before moving to the next. He did not alter his tone to provoke, nor did he sweeten it to disarm. There was no theatre in his delivery. This was a man speaking to another man, not to an audience, and certainly not to the faceless, uninvited presence of the press.

Midway through a pause, Benedict reached to the side and lifted a small, leather-bound folder from the table. He slid it across to Carl without flourish, as though passing along something mundane. But when Carl opened it, the stillness of his breath betrayed the significance. Inside was a single photograph—Benedict himself, taken only weeks earlier, candid and unposed. It was the kind of image the public would claw for, the kind tabloids would pay fortunes to possess.

"This is yours," Benedict said plainly. "Not for print. Not for sale. Yours, because you've earned it." The simplicity of the statement struck Carl harder than any elaborate gesture could have. In an age where images were traded like currency, this was a gift without a price tag—a trust freely given but impossible to replace if broken.

Carl closed the folder carefully, the weight of the moment making even that simple action deliberate. His fingers lingered on the leather cover before he slid it into his satchel, as though sealing it away from the possibility of temptation. The knowledge that no one else would ever see that image, that it would remain his alone, was more than a token of friendship; it was proof that his restraint over the years had not gone unnoticed.

Benedict resumed speaking as though no interruption had occurred, his voice steady in the quiet. "This is not for them," he said, and Carl understood "them" to mean the entire machinery of those who fed off distortion. "This is for the record. It will not be twisted, it will not be spliced, and it will not be reworded to suit a headline. You will keep it as it is."

Carl's response was nothing more than a small nod, but Benedict caught it, storing it away as confirmation. They both knew there was no need for elaborate assurances. The proof of loyalty was already sealed in the satchel. This was not a transaction—it was an exchange between men who understood the fragility of trust in a world built to shatter it.

Sørensen shifted his stance slightly, though his gaze remained fixed on the two at the table. He had seen negotiations of far higher stakes in his life, yet he recognised the particular significance of this one. The red light on the recorder might have been small, but it signified something irreversible. What began here would not be undone, and Sørensen, for all his quiet watchfulness, respected that this was between Benedict and Carl alone.

The rhythm of Benedict's speech resumed, a steady layering of statements, clarifications, and affirmations. He moved from personal truth into the broader scope of principle, making it clear that what applied to him applied to his family, and that any breach against one would be treated as a breach against all. The legal firmness in his tone left no room for misinterpretation, yet it carried no overt hostility—it was the certainty of a man who had already decided what lines could never be crossed.

Carl noted the precision of each phrase. This was not a man speaking off the cuff; every word had been pre-assembled in thought, if not on paper. There were no wasted sentences, no tangents to trim. For a journalist accustomed to sifting through hours of speech for the few clean lines worth keeping, it was almost unsettling to find every one of them already honed to readiness.

The coffee on the table cooled between them, untouched now. Harrison, sensing the change in the air, did not approach to refill the mugs. Even he understood that the clink of ceramic would be too much interruption for a moment like this. The recorder's hum was the only sound beyond the voice of the man speaking.

Benedict's hands never fidgeted. He did not lean back, did not shift unnecessarily in his chair. His stillness mirrored the content of his words—fixed, deliberate, and unwilling to yield. Even his pauses seemed calculated, giving each point time to settle before he moved to the next. Carl could almost imagine these recordings being played decades from now, the voice carrying the same steadiness long after both men were gone.

When he touched briefly on the matter of the photograph again, it was only to reaffirm its purpose. "That's not leverage. It's not a bargaining chip. It's yours, because friends don't trade in the currency of betrayal." The statement hung in the air like a promise and a warning in equal measure.

Carl sat back slightly, allowing himself a breath. He knew he would leave here with more than an interview. This recording, when it left Benedict's hands, would carry an invisible seal—one not recognised by any court, yet stronger than any legal binding. It was a seal forged from years of patience, trust, and an unbroken thread of truth.

The red light blinked on, steady and constant, as if marking the pulse of the room itself. What had begun as a single act—the pressing of a button—was now something far larger. It was the beginning of the one version of events that would matter, told once, told right, and never told again.

When the recorder was switched off and the hum of its motor faded into silence, Benedict reached for the sheaf of paper waiting on the far side of the table. The interview had been a separate act entirely, yet its gravity lingered in the air, guiding the precision of what he was about to do. He read the opening lines again, not because he doubted them, but because they deserved the final inspection of a man unwilling to leave a single mark of ink to chance.

The letter was more than words on a page. It was a position statement, a boundary line, and a declaration of rights wrapped into one document. He read each sentence aloud under his breath, measuring the weight of each phrase as though he were testing the balance of a sword. The pen rested ready beside him, but he did not reach for it until every clause and comma felt immovable.

Sørensen remained at his quiet post near the window, eyes steady on the road beyond. His presence was a reminder that while words could strike, there were still moments when force might be required. Yet here, in this act of sealing the letter, Benedict was wielding something more enduring than physical strength. He was fixing his stance in permanent record, ensuring it could not be bent by misquotation or erased by denial.

Carl said nothing. He knew his part of the day's work was done, and anything more would disrupt the careful stillness in the room. He simply watched as Benedict's gaze scanned line after line, the same way a craftsman studies the blade he has forged, running his eyes over every contour for imperfections invisible to all but himself.

Harrison placed a fresh cup of coffee within reach, though Benedict barely acknowledged it. The steam curled upward in silence, but his attention did not break. Every line he reread confirmed the purpose with which it had been written: this was not a letter designed to provoke a fight—it was designed to end one before it began.

When he finally took up the pen, there was no hesitation. The signature was written in full, each letter of his name clear, deliberate, and complete. No initials, no shorthand. It was the mark of a man taking ownership not only of his words but of the consequences they would carry. The scratch of the nib across the paper was the only sound in the room, sharp and final.

He set the pen aside and let the ink rest a moment before sliding the sheets together with a single, smooth motion. The envelope was already prepared, its paper thick enough to endure handling without folding or fraying. He placed the letter inside, aligning it so that it would arrive exactly as it had left—uncreased, unmarked, and uncompromised.

The seal was pressed into place with the weight of his palm. It was not wax, but a reinforced adhesive that would tear the paper before it allowed the flap to be lifted. This was not an envelope meant for idle opening. Its contents would be read only by the eyes for which it was intended, and only when it reached them by the trusted path he had already chosen.

Benedict wrote the recipient's name in precise strokes—Editor, London Time—the ink as unshaken as his resolve. There was no return address. The absence was deliberate. This letter was not an invitation for correspondence; it was a one-way delivery of terms that required no reply.

He placed the envelope flat upon the table, resting his hand over it for a moment as though feeling the weight of what it contained. It was not the paper he felt—it was the inevitability of its effect. Like a blade laid flat, it would cut only when moved, and when moved, it would cut cleanly where intended.

Sørensen stepped forward, his shadow falling across the table. "It will get there," he said quietly, his voice more promise than reassurance. He knew who would deliver it, and the chain of trust between here and the editor's desk would be unbroken.

Benedict slid the envelope toward him. "By hand. No post. No messenger I haven't known for years." It was not a request, and Sørensen understood it as an order. The fewer hands between the seal and its destination, the more certain its contents would remain untampered.

Carl finally rose from his chair, watching as the envelope was secured inside a leather folio. He knew he would never see it again, but he also knew that the next time he opened a paper and read those words in print, they would be unchanged from the moment they left this table. That certainty was rare, and he valued it as much as the interview itself.

The envelope left the cottage in Sørensen's possession, the door closing softly behind him. The sound was final without being loud, the kind of ending that signalled not closure, but the beginning of a controlled outcome. Benedict remained at the table for a moment longer, looking at the empty space where it had been.

Only then did he reach for the cooling coffee, taking the first sip since it had been poured. The bitterness was grounding, a reminder that while this chapter of the day was finished, its consequences were still in motion. Somewhere between here and London, the blade he had forged in ink was on its way to being drawn.

Benedict rose from his chair, the last echoes of conversation still faint in the air, and crossed the short space to where Carl stood. There was no handshake between them, no formal nod of parting; instead, Ben placed both arms around his friend in an embrace that spoke without words. It was a rare gesture from him, one given only when the bond was deeper than circumstance. Carl returned it without hesitation, his leather satchel pressed against Ben's shoulder in the closeness of it.

They lingered in that moment, both aware that the roads of their lives might not cross again for years, perhaps not at all. The weight of that truth was not mournful, but it was felt. There were things each of them still needed to do—duties that did not bend for the sake of reunion. Carl had his pen and his discipline; Benedict had a kingdom, however quiet, that would not defend itself without him.

When they parted, Carl gave the kind of nod that marked the end of a chapter, not the end of a friendship. "Until then," he said simply, voice low enough to keep the words between them. Ben answered with a faint smile, his eyes holding the steadiness of a man who does not speak farewell lightly. There was no need to explain further; everything that could be said had already been said, and the rest would live in their mutual silence.

Sørensen held the door for Carl, his broad frame a shield against the weather outside. The rain had strengthened to a steady percussion, drops spattering against the hood of Carl's coat as he stepped into the waiting vehicle. The door shut with a muted thud, and in that instant, the cottage seemed to reclaim its own quiet. The car eased away without a headlight flare, disappearing into the curve of the lane that led toward the main road.

Inside, the coffee mugs sat empty on the table, the faint rings at their bases marking where the heat had met wood. Harrison gathered them without a word, the soft clink of ceramic in his hands the only sound to accompany Carl's absence. The scent of coffee still lingered faintly, mixing with the faint smoke from the fire that had settled low into glowing embers.

Benedict returned to his chair but did not sit immediately. He rested his hand on the table's edge, letting the absence of voices sink into the space between them. The walls seemed to breathe again, the stillness wrapping around him like a familiar coat. This was not relief—it was recalibration. The letter had been the first strike in a sequence, and he knew better than to confuse a beginning with an ending.

When he did sit, it was with his gaze fixed not on the fire, but on the window where rain streaked the glass in silver lines. Each drop seemed deliberate, as though marking time until the moment his words would appear in print. He could see London in his mind's eye, the bustling offices of the paper, the editor's measured reading of each sentence. Somewhere in that imagined scene, the first ripple of his warning would form.

Sørensen stepped back into the room, his boots leaving faint marks on the rug from the damp outside. "On his way," he said, his tone carrying the certainty of a man who did not need to explain how he knew. Benedict gave a single nod. He had trusted Sørensen with more than a letter before, and each time the trust had been returned in full.

Harrison placed the mugs into the basin with a soft rattle, then returned to tend the fire. The sound of the poker stirring the embers was as steady as a clock hand moving, slow and sure. Sparks rose briefly, then faded back into the orange heart of the logs. It was the sound of a house returning to itself, reclaiming its rhythms after the disruption of company.

Ben leaned back at last, his hands folded loosely in his lap. There was no relaxation in his posture, only a readiness that had settled deeper into him now that the letter was no longer in his keeping. The act of writing had been one kind of labour; the act of letting it go was another. He knew the real contest would not begin until his words met the eyes of those they were meant for.

The rain outside softened, its rhythm shifting to something lighter, as though the weather itself had decided to wait. The air in the cottage was warm, the kind of warmth that comes from more than just fire—there was the weight of decision in it, the heat of a move already made but not yet answered. Benedict could feel the stillness as a taut string, ready to sound.

He thought of the editor, of the moment that envelope would be opened and the first line read. He imagined the pause, the flicker of understanding, and the awareness that this was not a letter to be filed and forgotten. It was a line drawn with such precision that to cross it would be to step knowingly into peril. That was exactly as he intended.

Carl's departure had not emptied the room; it had cleared it. Now, the table bore only what mattered—a stack of notes, a cooling fire, and the lingering scent of black coffee. Benedict regarded them all as markers in a larger plan, pieces that would be remembered when the day came to explain how it began.

He rose once more to close the curtains, shutting out the sight of the rain. Whatever happened next would happen beyond those windows, beyond the reach of the quiet he was preserving here. The cottage was his stronghold, and for now, it remained intact. The battle outside could wait its turn.

The fire sank lower, the last threads of flame curling inward. Harrison let them be. Benedict remained at the table, the chair angled slightly toward the door as though he might rise at any moment. The night ahead was long, but he had no intention of wasting it. The letter was already in motion. The world just didn't know it yet.

CHAPTER 14: KENDRICK SPEAKS

The Castle's communications chamber was never built for show. It was a narrow, oak-lined room at the heart of Rosenshavn, where antique maps clung to the walls as if guarding centuries of quiet negotiations. Among the relics were devices that belonged to no museum, discreet instruments chosen not for pomp but for precision. Kendrick — Ken, as everyone in Copenhagen called him — sat at the head of the polished table, his hands resting on the armrests as though they belonged there by law rather than vanity. He had agreed to this broadcast not because he was pressured, but because the hour had come where silence was no longer a defence. Outside these walls, questions had been hammering against the gates for weeks. Tonight, the hammer would strike the anvil instead.

A bank of lights hummed faintly, the only hint that technology was awake in this room of history. Two cameras, sleek and patient, waited at fixed angles. Behind them, no audience sat, no press corps jostled for position. This was not a stage. It was a message chamber, and Ken was the only voice permitted to speak. When the feed went live, it would reach the offices of editors who had been demanding clarity, to embassies that had been speculating in whispers, and to citizens far beyond Denmark who had never once heard his full name. But they would hear it now. Calm. Cold. Legal. The way truth was meant to be delivered.

Copenhagen's people had not asked for this spectacle. In truth, they had resisted it. When photographers tried to lurk near the Castle gates, the citizens themselves became the wall. Families stepped forward in the streets, forming a living barricade, sending journalists back with empty notebooks and bitter expressions. This was not by command; it was by loyalty. Ken had spent decades walking their markets, helping mend a child's bicycle chain, or spending a Sunday afternoon at the soccer field, running until sweat dampened his shirt just as it did the shirts of the other players. He was never the man in the crown. He was the man in the goal net, laughing when the youngest players outmanoeuvred him.

The soccer field sat a good walk from the Castle, out beyond the cobbled lanes where the city's oldest bakeries still worked through dawn. Ken went there without entourage or announcement. It was not called a pitch here, nor would he ever call it football — the word carried none of the rhythm of what they played. It was soccer, and that was enough. On warm days, his attire was as plain as the next man's: a faded t-shirt, shorts, worn-in trainers. On colder days, he layered up like anyone else, a scarf thrown haphazardly around his neck, a jacket zipped against the wind. If there was a role to play, it was simply being part of the game.

Inside the chamber tonight, those same people were in his thoughts. Not as subjects. Not as a public to be placated. They were, to him, the same as family. He had stood shoulder-to-shoulder with them in joy and in hardship. He had watched their children grow from toddlers clinging to their parents' legs into confident teens racing down the field after a soccer ball. They, in return, had shielded his family from the sharp edge of gossip and intrusion. It was an unspoken pact, the kind that needed no parchment to bind it.

The tension tonight was not in Ken's body. His posture was steady, his hands motionless save for the occasional tapping of a finger against the table. The real tension was outside these walls, in the restless minds of those who believed they deserved to know what had been kept from them. He had always believed that a man's worth was measured by what he gave to his people, not what he revealed to strangers. Yet, he understood the mechanics of law and power. There were times when privacy had to yield to declaration.

Ken's mind wandered briefly to the cost of this night. Once the words left his mouth, they would not return to silence. His declaration would reach those who had never stepped foot in Denmark, never spoken to a Dane, never understood why this country guarded its own so fiercely. It would stir those with no personal stake to begin imagining that they had one. In the hours that followed, the press would spin, the analysts would dissect, and the neighbours across seas would debate. But none of that changed the fact that this moment was his choice, not theirs.

Across the table, a small digital clock ticked toward the scheduled start. The broadcast was timed to hit prime viewing in Copenhagen and late evening in London, catching the early afternoon cycle in North America. The networks had been notified — not invited, not consulted, simply told that a feed would arrive. No credentials would be issued, no questions answered. The message would be one-way, as final as an engraved seal.

In a small alcove behind him, an aide adjusted the backup transmitter. The hum of electronics joined the softer sound of a kettle in the distant kitchen — coffee, of course, not tea. Tea had never crossed Ken's lips willingly, and he did not trust anyone who thought it a proper drink. Coffee was the only liquid fit to keep the mind sharp in moments like this. It was a running jest among his closest friends that if Denmark ever ran out of coffee beans, the Castle itself would be evacuated.

Outside, the evening air hung heavy with the weight of expectation. The citizens still gathered at the outer gates, not to protest but to hold the line against intrusion. They stood there in quiet resolve, some with hands in pockets, others chatting casually, but all with the same message in their presence: no one enters without our say. It was not theatrical; it was protection. Ken knew they did this not because of his title, but because of the years he had spent proving that titles meant nothing without respect.

As the cameras powered on, the lights adjusted, bathing the room in a soft, steady glow. Shadows retreated into the corners, leaving only Ken in clear focus. It was as though the Castle itself had leaned in to listen, aware that history was about to be spoken within its walls. Somewhere in another room, the twins likely stirred, their infant noises muffled by layers of stone. Life went on in the Castle as it always had — children playing, meals being prepared, doors opening and closing. Tonight's words would not interrupt that rhythm, only ripple out beyond it.

Ken's gaze dropped briefly to the notes before him. They were sparse — a name, a date, a legal citation or two. He had no intention of reading from a script. The people would see his eyes, hear his voice, and understand that this was not a prepared performance but a deliberate act. When he spoke, it would be with the precision of a man trained to choose his words like an archer selects arrows.

A deep breath filled his chest, and he exhaled slowly. No crown waited for him to put on. No robe lay over the chair. His authority did not require props. The map-lined walls, the hum of the lights, the readiness of the cameras — that was the stage. And when the red light blinked on, the truth would no longer be something whispered in Copenhagen's alleyways. It would be known everywhere the signal reached.

The door to the chamber closed with a muted click, sealing out the faint noises of the Castle. In the stillness, Ken could almost hear the years behind him — the quiet conversations, the hard decisions, the times when leadership meant holding back as much as stepping forward. Tonight was different. Tonight was not about holding back.

The technician gave a brief nod, fingers poised over the control board. In the seconds before the feed would open, Ken let his gaze travel once more over the antique maps. Borders shifted on those parchments over centuries, lines redrawn by hands long gone. He wondered, fleetingly, what lines tonight's words might shift. Then the red light blinked to life.

Ken leaned forward, hands resting on the polished wood. Somewhere, across oceans, televisions flickered on, streams loaded, and living rooms went silent. This was not the moment they had been promised by rumour or imagined by gossip. This was the moment they would remember for what it truly was — the man they called Ken, speaking not as an image, but as himself.

It had been a long climb toward this moment, and Ken felt every step of it in his chest. Oscar's arrest for treason, now one month and two weeks behind them, had sent a tremor through every quiet corridor of the Castle. Those who once called themselves friends now kept their distance, as if loyalty had turned contagious and dangerous all at once. Ken had not looked for this fight, yet it had landed squarely in his hands, and the more the outside world pressed for an explanation, the more he knew they would receive it only on his terms.

Evening shadows stretched across the Castle courtyard, though Ken hardly noticed them. He had spent those past weeks navigating half-whispered inquiries, measured warnings from political allies, and the kind of press demands that arrived with claws hidden beneath polite phrasing. Copenhagen could weather the noise—they always had—but Ken understood that silence could be its own liability. If a statement had to be made, it would be sharp as a blade and as unshakable as law itself.

Inside the communications chamber, the quiet seemed almost unnatural. The air was still, the hum of the equipment constant but muted, and in that stillness Ken measured the cost of each word he intended to say. Every sentence would have weight. Every pause would mean something. The cameras would be live to every corner of the world, and there would be no pulling back what was spoken. This would be final, binding, and without loopholes.

Messages from abroad had been piling up on his desk, each more pointed than the last. Some came wrapped in false concern, others in thinly veiled threats. Ken had ignored most of them. He refused to let foreign interests dictate what was said in Copenhagen's name. No outsider would tell him how to handle the truth about his family, and certainly not about Benedict. The choice to speak would remain his alone, and tonight it would be exercised in full.

He leaned back in his chair, recalling how Sørensen had handled such matters in years past. The man was far away now, in Kent, England, keeping watch over Ben and the three children. It was where they needed to be—out of reach, shielded by the walls of the small hidden cottage, and spared the uproar building in Denmark. Ken could almost picture them: Ben keeping the older children busy, Sørensen never letting the yard go unguarded, and the laughter of Maria and Emil mingling with Casper's eager questions. They were safe there. Safe, and waiting.

The decision to speak had not come from impulse. It had been forged in the long days after Oscar's sentencing, when Ken walked the city streets and heard the citizens' voices rise above the media's noise. Copenhagen's people had no patience for traitors, and no tolerance for those who betrayed one of their own. They were not royal subjects; they were neighbours, teammates, coffee-drinking friends who joined Ken for a game of soccer on the city field when time allowed. In their loyalty, he found the resolve to answer the world directly.

"What I say tonight," Ken thought, "must leave no space for misinterpretation." That was the point. Not ceremony. Not theatre. Just the unvarnished truth, shaped into words that no court or commentator could twist. He had no intention of dressing the moment in royal imagery or sentimental flourishes. His authority would come from the weight of law and the certainty of his position, nothing more and nothing less.

The Castle staff had grown accustomed to his pace in these tense weeks. They did not hover or intrude, but they moved with quiet efficiency around him, preparing the chamber without the need for repeated instruction. Every light was tested, every feed connected, every contingency accounted for. When Ken entered, there would be no fumbling, no hesitation. It was a discipline learned over years of keeping the Castle's public voice steady even under strain.

Ken had seen the faces of those who underestimated him before. They often mistook his composure for hesitation, his directness for simplicity. That mistake would not survive tonight's broadcast. There was no victory in the thought—only the understanding that, once spoken, the truth would change the shape of what the world expected from Denmark and from him.

The air in the chamber felt cooler now, as if the walls themselves understood the weight of the hour. Ken rose from his seat at the side table, the faint creak of the chair marking the end of his planning and the beginning of action. In the quiet, he let his mind settle on the people who mattered most: Isla with the twins, Ben holding his ground in Kent, and the citizens who trusted him to speak for their city. They would hear his voice not as a ruler, but as one of them.

The last days had been heavy with waiting, but Ken knew that hesitation could not be allowed to breed uncertainty. If others saw silence as weakness, they would move against it. That was why his decision was not only to speak, but to speak decisively, in a way that shut every door that could lead to further doubt. Once the broadcast began, it would not stop until every necessary word had been spoken.

He paced once along the length of the table, then back again, each step firm but measured. This was the point from which the rest of the story would move, and he would not allow it to falter. Across the city, people would pause in their homes, their cafés, their late-night walks, and they would hear not the voice of a distant ruler but of a man who lived among them, trusted them, and would protect them.

Somewhere in Kent, Ben would be listening, too. Ken hoped the words would reach him as intended—not as pressure, not as command, but as a reminder that the bond between them did not break with distance. This was for Ben's sake as much as for Denmark's, for the security of the family and the clarity of the truth.

Ken stopped at the edge of the camera frame, hands resting on the table's polished wood. Soon the red light would blink to life, and there would be no sound but his own voice carried across continents. The decision had been made. The terms were his. The moment was here.

The broadcast opened without ceremony, no musical introduction, no soft-spoken announcer offering polite context. Ken stepped into the frame, shoulders square, eyes locked on the lens, and spoke with the weight of a man who had already decided that his words would leave no room for dispute. "You wanted truth. You got it. Now back off." The sound cut through the air like a blade, the silence that followed so stark it seemed to press in on the walls. Those in the control room barely breathed, knowing that what came next would reshape the conversation in every newsroom across the world.

The pause was not hesitation—it was the calculated stillness of a man who understood timing. Ken allowed the weight of those first words to settle, to travel into the homes, cafés, and offices where television screens and live feeds glowed. Then, with no shift in tone, no softening of expression, he delivered the truth in its purest, most unyielding form: "Benedict Adrian Harvick of House Rosenshavn is the reigning King of Denmark. This is not symbolic. This is not emotional. It is legal." The syllables landed with the precision of a legal ruling, because that was exactly what it was.

Across the globe, television anchors glanced down at their notes and then back up to their cameras, as if uncertain whether they had heard him correctly. Teleprompters stalled. Producers signalled frantically off-camera. In one London studio, a veteran anchor actually removed her earpiece, convinced there had been a technical error. But there was no mistake, and there was no mishearing. Ken had just placed the truth in the open, where it could never be pulled back.

The statement was not a flourish of royal imagery or romantic language; it was the cold, sharp confirmation of a fact long hidden under layers of secrecy. Those who had speculated now had their answer, though few could have anticipated its delivery in such stark, uncompromising terms. It was as if Ken had driven a stake through the heart of every rumour, ensuring that none could rise again without facing the weight of proof.

In homes across Copenhagen, there was no shock—only the steady nods of those who had always known. The people had never needed a press release to tell them who Benedict was. They had seen him among them for years, moving without guards through markets, playing soccer with their children, speaking to them not as a ruler but as a neighbour. For them, the statement was not revelation; it was confirmation, a public acknowledgment of a truth they had guarded for him out of loyalty.

Far beyond Denmark, however, the reaction was far less settled. In capitals where royal titles were weighed against political advantage, conversations erupted in hurried whispers and sharp demands for clarification. Legal advisors were summoned, press officers scrambled to draft statements, and in some cases, emergency meetings were called before Ken had even finished speaking. His words had detonated in the corridors of power with a force no one could ignore.

The cameras in the broadcast room caught none of this; they remained fixed on Ken's face, on the set of his jaw and the steady calm in his voice. He knew the chaos his words would create. In fact, he was counting on it. To speak softly here would have been to invite challenge. By speaking plainly and without adornment, he had made his declaration unassailable. The truth, stated as law, could not be softened or doubted.

For Benedict, listening from Kent, there would be no surprise either. He had known this day was coming, even if the exact timing had been Ken's alone to decide. Sitting in the quiet of the cottage with Sørensen and the children, he would hear those words and understand the shield they were meant to be. Public recognition meant public accountability, and with it came a degree of protection that secrecy could no longer provide.

The world might now recognise him as King, but Benedict knew that title had never changed the man he was. He had ruled without a crown for years, and he would continue to do so, whether in the calm of Rosenshavn Castle or in the quiet lanes of Kent. But the difference now was that his name was no longer a whisper among the few who dared to speak it. It was a headline. It was a fact. And it was permanent.

Ken did not linger on the point. There was no repetition, no attempt to reframe the statement for clarity. Once was enough. Any more would have sounded like defence, and Ken had nothing to defend. The declaration had been made in full, and the world would have to adjust to it on his terms. Those who thought they could push for more would soon learn otherwise.

In the control room, the producer glanced at the clock, then back to Ken, waiting for the signal to cut to the next prepared segment. It did not come. Ken remained in place, gaze unbroken, as if daring anyone watching to look away. The moment was not for theatre—it was for memory. He wanted the image fixed in their minds: the man who spoke the truth and did not flinch.

The pause stretched again, not in awkwardness, but in dominance. He was showing the world that he would speak when he wished and stop when he wished, on no one else's schedule. Every second of silence carried the same message as his words: Benedict was King, and Copenhagen would stand with him. Anyone who thought to challenge that would be met with a wall of resolve.

Finally, Ken gave a single nod to the unseen crew, signalling the close of that first, most crucial part of the broadcast. But the air in the room had changed. This was no longer the Castle's private chamber. It was the stage from which the world had been reminded that Denmark's crown was not for negotiation. It was inherited, lawful, and untouchable.

In living rooms, cafés, newsrooms, and offices, the ripple of Ken's words began to spread. They would be replayed, analysed, dissected, and misquoted within hours. But it would make no difference. The truth, once spoken, could not be withdrawn, and Ken had given it in the only form it could survive—stripped of artifice, secured in law, and broadcast to all.

The feed faded to black for a moment, and the control room prepared for the next segment. But Ken knew the most important part had already happened. The truth was out. The lines had been drawn. And there was no turning back.

Ken did not lean forward, did not gesture, did not invite debate. His posture alone was its own declaration. "By Danish law and the statutes of succession recognised by the House of Rosenshavn, Benedict Adrian Harvick is the reigning King of Denmark." The words were not amplified by theatrics; they were carried instead on the gravity of documented fact. "The claim is not ceremonial. It is not symbolic. It is lawful." Behind him, resting on a stand of black oak, were the documents—bound in deep green leather, stamped with gold seals—that had been signed, witnessed, and preserved for decades.

He spoke of the House's succession rights as though they were common knowledge, a quiet reminder that those who should have known them already did. Centuries-old decrees, reaffirmed across generations, left no ambiguity in the order of inheritance. Benedict's position was neither granted as favour nor voted upon in council; it was born into him, in bloodline and in binding law. Every legal scholar who had reviewed the case, from Copenhagen to Aarhus, had reached the same conclusion. The right was his from birth, unshaken by distance, silence, or time.

Ken turned one page of the legal ledger, his voice still even. "Every name in the succession has been documented against the established statutes. Each witness in the chain is recorded. The bloodline is traced without break." He tapped the page, not for the cameras, but for his own certainty. "No challenge exists that can stand against this evidence." To those watching at home, the statement was clear—what had been bound by law could not be undone by gossip, envy, or foreign opinion.

Genealogical charts, some centuries old, had been examined alongside modern records with clinical precision. The House archivists had worked with historians and legal analysts, ensuring each link in the chain was indisputable. The research had gone further still—DNA analysis from accredited labs matched each generational claim, erasing the possibility of fraud. "DNA does not lie," Ken said, the phrase falling like the final line of a verdict. No courtroom could improve upon its certainty.

In Copenhagen, the archivists themselves were watching the broadcast in their dim-lit offices, the smell of old parchment and leather bindings clinging to the air. They knew every inch of the documentation Ken held. They had handled it with gloved hands, had compared signatures against centuries of letters and decrees, had spent nights verifying ink age under forensic light. This moment was as much theirs as it was his—years of meticulous record-keeping distilled into a single public affirmation.

Across the Atlantic, in the newsrooms of New York and Toronto, the reaction was sharper. Legal commentators scrambled to keep up with the citations Ken delivered, their own background notes suddenly insufficient. The story was no longer about rumours of a quiet king in Copenhagen; it was about a lawful monarch whose claim had withstood every test the law could devise. And with each paragraph of statute and genealogical proof Ken recited, the foundation beneath that claim grew more unshakable.

Ken spoke of the House succession rights as more than tradition—they were an unbroken mechanism of governance, recognised by the Danish constitution and respected by international treaty. "There is no appeal," he said without raising his voice. "The law is complete. The decision binding." The phrasing was deliberate, a nod to the fact that this was not the announcement of a change, but the formal acknowledgment of an order that had already been in force for years.

In Kent, Benedict sat with Sørensen and the children, the television casting its muted glow across the room. He heard every word, his jaw set in the quiet way Ken had once teased him for—an expression that looked passive until you saw the steel in it. He knew these were not just facts being read into the air; they were armour being fitted around him, piece by piece. With the law publicly laid bare, anyone seeking to challenge his position would find themselves standing against the full weight of Denmark's own statutes.

Ken allowed the camera to linger on the documents, though the fine print was unreadable through the lens. What mattered was that the seals were visible—the red wax pressed under the House crest, the signatures in deep black ink. These were not props. They were the physical proof of the words he spoke, and even those who disliked the message could not deny their authenticity.

Legal recognition, Ken reminded them, was not about popularity. Monarchs had been crowned in times of unrest, had ruled despite opposition, because the law did not bend to sentiment. In Denmark, the House of Rosenshavn's succession was insulated from political interference. It was written into the law that the crown could not be taken by vote, sale, or foreign decree. That protection was not symbolic—it was the shield under which Benedict's reign had already stood for years without the world's awareness.

Ken gave no space for doubt to settle. Each point was anchored to a law, each law supported by evidence, each piece of evidence backed by multiple confirmations. This was not storytelling; it was litigation conducted in public view, and the verdict had already been delivered before the cameras had been switched on. Anyone still questioning the legitimacy of Benedict's rule would find themselves without legal standing before they could even reach a court.

In Copenhagen's public squares, televisions in shop windows carried the broadcast live. People stopped mid-step to listen, not because they were uncertain of the truth, but because they recognised the precision of Ken's delivery. They had trusted him for years to speak only when the moment mattered, and his presence on the screen meant the matter was beyond doubt.

Ken's tone never shifted, but the structure of his words built an undeniable momentum. This was not a plea for acceptance; it was an audit of fact, laid out in perfect sequence. The audience was not being asked to agree—they were being informed of what already was. That distinction was everything. By removing opinion, Ken removed the possibility of argument.

The final lines of the statement settled like stone. "This succession is not under question. It is not open to review. It is affirmed by the laws of Denmark and bound to the House of Rosenshavn. It has been so for years." He closed the ledger, the soft thud of its binding loud enough for the microphones to catch. It was the sound of a door locking, and it would not be opened again.

The camera did not cut immediately. Ken held his gaze steady for another moment, letting the image imprint itself across every screen. The law had spoken, and the law, unlike rumour, could not be undone.

Ken let the weight of the previous declaration settle before turning the page to a chart that was older than the building they sat in. "The bloodline of Benedict Adrian Harvick is pure," he said, his tone free of flourish, "and it carries the documented descent from His Majesty King Béla the Third of Hungary." The camera caught the genealogical map beside him, the sweeping lines of ink showing centuries of connection. "Through the R-S660 Y-DNA group, his lineage is proven. Through the R-M222 marker, he is linked directly to the ancient Uí Néill Dynasty of Ireland." The names alone were enough to make anchors in foreign studios pause, unsure whether to treat them as history lessons or breaking news.

He did not speak of these markers as curiosities, as some in the modern world might when discussing genealogy. Ken spoke of them as legal artefacts, genetic seals upon a royal charter. These were not hypothetical claims; the R-S660 and R-M222 markers were matched in multiple accredited laboratories, cross-checked, and archived in the national genealogical registry. "These markers are recognised by the governing bodies of hereditary law," he added, turning a page to reveal the certificates. "There is no doubt in their authenticity. None."

The camera did not linger on his face now, but on the scroll-like chart that listed centuries of royal houses—each line descending, unbroken, until it reached the name Benedict Adrian Harvick. Ken's hand rested lightly on that name as though marking a point on a map. "These connections are not symbolic. They are active and binding under the succession laws of each respective dynasty." The phrasing left no ambiguity: this was not a theoretical family tree. This was a living claim.

Ken then named them, one by one, as the press scribbled furiously. "The House of Árpád, Hungary. The House of Uí Néill, Ireland. The House of Dunkeld, Scotland. The House of Wessex, England. The House of Capet, France. The House of Oldenburg, Denmark. The House of Wettin, Saxony." With each name, he paused just long enough for the weight to settle. "Seven houses," he said at last, "each bound to him by blood and by law."

The effect was immediate, even in silence. Across living rooms and office foyers, people exchanged glances—not because they doubted the claim, but because they understood the magnitude. To be king of one realm was power. To be the rightful heir to seven was something the modern age was not prepared to process. This was not a matter of romantic fiction or academic theory; it was the blunt presentation of a reality most nations had quietly believed was impossible.

Ken's voice remained steady, refusing to let the drama of the moment distort the clarity of fact. "If he were to choose—if he were to claim the rights afforded to him—Benedict Adrian Harvick could stand as sovereign under the law of all seven thrones. Not as an intruder. Not as a pretender. As the rightful and lawful heir." The distinction between could and would was deliberate, giving no promise yet leaving the path in plain sight.

In Kent, where the late-afternoon light slanted through the window, Sørensen glanced at Benedict as the list was read. The children, sitting close enough to touch their dad's sleeve, were too young to fully grasp the scope, but they understood the sound of their dad's name spoken in this way. Benedict said nothing, only folded his arms and watched, the stillness in his posture the same as it had been when Ken spoke in private counsel.

Back in the broadcast chamber, Ken spoke of the records that made such a declaration possible. They were not museum pieces, though they were treated with equal reverence. Bound charters from France, preserved parchments from Ireland, coronation records from Hungary—all aligned to the same bloodline, each carrying seals that had not been broken in centuries. Where there were gaps in history, they had been filled with forensic genetic proof, signed off by independent verification bodies.

Ken knew his words would not stay within Denmark's borders. In France, the House of Capet's descendants would be listening with forensic interest. In Hungary, archivists would recognise the names and dates as their own heritage. In Ireland, the claim to the Uí Néill name carried more than ceremonial pride; it carried centuries of tribal and monarchical authority. These were not empty titles. Each one carried weight in law, in custom, and in the inherited memory of their people.

He explained that the succession laws of each house, though varied in detail, all recognised the principle of bloodline primacy. "Where law confirms lineage, lineage confirms sovereignty," Ken said. "No act of parliament or council can extinguish that right without violating its own founding statute." The meaning was sharp: if Benedict chose to claim, no legislative body could deny him without dismantling its own legal foundation.

This, Ken reminded the world, was not a challenge. It was not a threat. It was a statement of position—one that had existed long before cameras and microphones were turned on. "The crown does not ask for permission to be worn," he said, his tone still measured. "It rests where the law has placed it."

In the newsrooms that had speculated for years on the whispers of a hidden Danish king, there was now an abrupt pivot. This was no longer a story about Denmark alone. It was about the stability of monarchies across Europe and the question of what would happen if one man, legally entitled, decided to step forward into all his claims. Ken's phrasing left that possibility alive in every viewer's mind.

The pause before his closing words was deliberate, a final measure to let the enormity settle. "Seven thrones," he said, the syllables measured. "Seven crowns. One man." The camera caught the faintest movement in his eyes—not triumph, not challenge, but certainty. This was not a boast. It was the architecture of law, unshaken and immovable, laid bare for the world to see.

The broadcast did not cut away quickly. The producers, sensing the weight of the moment, let the image linger—Ken seated before centuries of proof, his hand resting lightly on the chart that ended with Benedict's name. The world could debate the meaning for months, years even, but the facts would remain as they had always been: Benedict Adrian Harvick, by law and by blood, was already more than a king of Denmark. He was the rightful heir to seven thrones.

The cameras did not flinch as Ken shifted his weight and straightened the stack of papers before him, though everyone watching knew the words that followed would be heavier than any prepared script. He set the first sheet aside untouched, speaking without looking down, his voice deep and deliberate. "Benedict was born in the United Kingdom," he began, letting the syllables settle like a stone in still water. "Raised there until the age of ten. No castles. No servants. No titles." It was a statement meant to pull him from the pedestal the press kept building beneath him, to remind them that behind the surname and the seal, there was once only a boy who ran down narrow streets and climbed trees for no reason other than he could.

He did not offer the name of the town, the county, or the county, and for a very good reason. The law bound him. So did loyalty. "There is more to be said about his origins," Ken continued, "but there are things I will not disclose. That is my right, and it is his safety." Even those in the room, the technicians and aides who had heard him speak a thousand times before, knew not to break the rhythm with a cough or a shuffle. Somewhere in that unnamed corner of the UK, there were people who would guard Ben with their own lives if needed. They had done so since his first steps, and they were doing so now.

Ken knew the temptation to pry would grow after this broadcast, but he also knew the steel that lived in those who loved Ben from the beginning. "You will not find him," Ken said plainly. "Not without the consent of those who have known him far longer than any of you." He spoke of them not as a community, but as a fortress — one without walls, without gates, yet impossible to breach. There was no registry, no public record, no casual mention that could be pieced together. What they held was not just affection; it was an unspoken vow.

The reporters who had been hoping for a slip — a single word that could be turned into a headline — found themselves instead facing a man who spoke like a locked safe. His pauses were not hesitations but barriers, shutting down the path before it began. "It is enough for you to know he was born on British soil," Ken said, "and it is enough for you to understand he will not take the crown of the House of Windsor." He leaned forward then, the faintest shadow of a smile crossing his face. "He will not because he will not need to."

The refusal to take the Windsor crown was not a rejection of heritage but a choice made from kinship. Ben and the current king were cousins by blood, and more than that, friends who did not compete for thrones. Ken spoke of it as one might describe an unshakable truth. "A crown," he said, "is not the only thing that proves a man's worth." Yet he never strayed into sentiment. Every line had the weight of finality, a reminder that what he left unsaid was as deliberate as what he chose to reveal.

He allowed himself a moment to touch on Ben's deeper lineage — the kind that went far beyond the UK. "His ancestry traces through Hungary, to the House of Árpád," Ken declared, the syllables of that ancient name resonating in the chamber. "That line carries through to Denmark, to the House of Rosenshavn, where it remains unbroken." He did not linger on the romance of it, but rather on the precision, as if he were reciting coordinates. It was history as fact, not folklore.

What he did not mention — and would never mention — was the thread between that history and the place Ben now walked unseen. To name it would be to betray him, and Ken would sooner take the full brunt of public fury than speak a syllable of it. "Some truths are not for public record," he said, eyes narrowing as if to punctuate the point. The words were not an evasion but a warning: stop asking.

Those who knew Ken understood that his restraint was not weakness. It was control. Every answer was designed to close more doors than it opened, to turn curiosity into exhaustion. "I will not speak of his home," Ken repeated, "and it is not because I lack the right words, but because the world has no right to them." The silence that followed was not empty; it was loaded with the knowledge that even the most skilled investigator would find nothing to work with here.

Beyond the cameras, in a place that had no need for guards or walls, Ben lived without the trappings that now threatened to consume him elsewhere. Ken knew that to describe it, even in passing, would draw the wrong eyes. Those who lived there knew the stakes. They were not subjects. They were not witnesses. They were guardians in plain sight. And they did not break.

As Ken spoke, there were likely those who thought they could lure him into revealing more — perhaps with a sympathetic question, perhaps with a feigned misunderstanding. But they would be disappointed. He did not wander off-script because the script was in his head, burned in by the memory of every oath he had ever sworn.

He made it clear that the decision to share anything further about Ben's birthplace would never be his. "If Benedict chooses to speak of it, that will be his choice," Ken said. "Until then, the matter is closed." The phrase "the matter is closed" was not a metaphor. It was an iron lock slammed shut.

It was not just a defence of Ben's privacy; it was a defence of an entire way of life — the idea that some things, even in an age of instant information, could remain untouched. The irony was that those closest to Ben did not see themselves as guarding a king; they saw themselves as looking out for the boy they had always known.

Ken's gaze did not soften as he concluded. "He is where he needs to be," he said. "And you will not be the ones to decide otherwise." The last sentence was delivered without flourish, yet it landed with the same weight as a verdict. Cameras caught the stillness in the room, the unspoken understanding that no follow-up question would cross that line.

There would be speculation, of course — endless, fruitless speculation. But Ken had given them nothing they could use, and that was the point. Every answer had been a shield. Every omission had been armour. And as the broadcast continued, the world was left to face an uncomfortable truth: not all crowns can be hunted, and not all kings can be found.

The words never reach the broadcast, yet they find their way into print within hours, carried in black ink across the world. Ken does not dress them in sentiment or excuse. "Benedict is my stepson," he states, the phrase clipped, precise, and deliberate. It is the kind of truth that needs no embroidery, no pause for interpretation. Those listening in the private room understand instantly that this admission will ripple far beyond Denmark's borders, not because it changes Ben's standing, but because it reveals the depth of choice behind Ken's loyalty.

He does not speak as though he has surrendered a claim; rather, he speaks as though he has claimed something greater. "He is not of my DNA," Ken continues, "but he is of my life." The phrasing is sharp enough to cut through any doubt the public might harbour. It is a statement designed to survive the slow decay of rumours, the way only truths spoken without apology can endure. He does not look to the side for reassurance, nor does he measure the room's reaction. The weight of his voice is the only measure he needs.

Ken names Annemarie next, his tone neither elevated nor softened, but steady. "His mother is Annemarie, my wife." He lets that rest without the embellishment of adjectives or the parade of family history. He knows the temptation will be for people to dig — to weigh her role against his, to question the lines of influence — but Ken's delivery leaves no such openings. She is Ben's mother. He is her husband. Those are the facts. Everything else is private.

The journalists who later transcribe these words for the morning editions will note how unflinching they sound. In a world used to carefully curated phrases and rehearsed sentiment, Ken's flat presentation is almost jarring. There is no stagecraft here, only the sound of a man stating what is and refusing to elaborate beyond the boundaries he has set. He makes no appeal to the emotions of the crowd. He does not ask for approval.

In the days to come, headlines will strip the delivery of its tone, boiling it down to the barest summary: Stepfather claims King as son. Yet those who were present in the room will know that what Ken offered was not a claim but a statement of fact that had already been lived for years. The words did not create the bond; they only described it for those who had never seen it in practice.

Ken does not linger on the legalities, but the implication is clear — there is no requirement for blood to bind a family. His guardianship of Ben has never been contested, never been diminished by the absence of shared DNA. In his eyes, and in the eyes of those within the Castle walls, family is not defined by the chart of lineage but by the constancy of presence.

The truth, in many ways, is more unshakable than if Ben had been his biological son. The choice to stay, to defend, to mentor — these are deliberate acts. Ken had not inherited Ben by birthright; he had chosen him by conviction. And choice, as those who live by it know, is often stronger than obligation.

There is a reason Ken avoids romanticising this truth for the press. To dress it in sentiment would invite them to dissect it, to twist it into a narrative of charity or pity. He does not see it that way, and he will not let them write it that way. This is not about what he has done for Ben; it is about the life they have built as equals in loyalty, even if unequal in years.

In the room, no one misses the subtle steel in his eyes when he says, "I hold for him the same responsibility I would for any son born to me." There is no tremor in the statement. The weight behind it suggests that any who would harm Ben — in word, in act, or in rumour — would answer to him without hesitation. It is as much a warning as it is an affirmation.

Annemarie's name is given only once, but it lands with the quiet gravity of respect. Ken does not speak for her; he does not tell her part of the story. He simply recognises her as the link between them, the point from which their paths became shared. It is a form of acknowledgement that does not require flourish to be understood.

The headlines that follow will inevitably cut these nuances, choosing instead the blunt, marketable truth. Yet within the Castle, and among those who have seen Ken and Ben together, the printed words will barely scratch the surface of what they know. It is not the title of "stepson" that defines their bond, but the years of quiet moments — conversations on walks, silent understandings in meetings, the kind of trust that does not have to be declared to be real.

Ken has always been careful to frame his loyalty to Ben as permanent, not conditional. The world may see their connection as unusual, perhaps even fragile without the anchor of shared ancestry, but Ken knows better. He knows that bonds built by decision, by shared trials, and by deliberate loyalty are often harder to break than those held together by blood alone.

It is a reality that confounds the curiosity of the press. They are trained to look for fracture points — to find where bonds might weaken under pressure. Ken leaves them nothing. The more they search for a tension that isn't there, the more they expose the limits of their own understanding.

And so, the quiet revelation becomes something larger than intended. In trying to define Ben's place by genealogy, the public is instead confronted by a truth that genealogy cannot measure. Bloodlines may trace thrones, but choice defines who will guard them.

Ken does not retract his words, nor does he attempt to expand upon them after the fact. What has been said is final. The pages of the morning papers will carry it across the world, but they will never carry the full meaning. That is reserved for the few who live it, and for the one young man who knows exactly how much was left unsaid for his sake.

Ken's description of Rosenshavn Castle never leans toward grandeur for the sake of it. He does not feed the imagination of those who think a castle must be a place of gold-tipped corridors and guarded thrones. Instead, he speaks plainly, as if describing any family home. "It is where we live," he says, the words carrying no air of spectacle. "Not where we display ourselves." In his voice is the unspoken understanding that the Castle is not a relic for public consumption but a living, breathing household where the daily rhythm is measured not by court announcements, but by the sound of footsteps on familiar floors.

He does not deny the Castle's history. Its stone walls carry the weight of centuries, the kind of age that gives a building authority even without its inhabitants. Yet, to Ken, its greatest significance is not in its lineage but in the life it shelters now. It is the place where Ben and Isla's young family has begun, where the cries of newborn twins echo through the same halls that once heard the measured discussions of monarchs. For Ken, that is its truest legacy — continuity not of titles, but of life.

The Castle's exterior, with its towers and narrow windows, still draws curious eyes from the city below, but Ken is careful to keep its gates from becoming a parade ground. "We are not here to be stared at," he remarks, a reminder to those who think the family owes them open corridors and public chambers. Copenhagen respects this boundary; the citizens have never been ones to treat Rosenshavn as anything other than the family's home.

Inside, rooms are arranged not for ceremony but for comfort. The great hall, which could easily host royal audiences, is far more often used for family meals or late-night conversations by the fire. Children play on the rugs, scattering wooden blocks and toys without thought to the space's formality. The tapestries remain on the walls, not as props for history tours, but as part of the household's fabric — background to a life being lived in the present.

The arrival of the twins has shifted the atmosphere entirely. The first royal births in this bloodline to remain entirely within Danish borders have brought an air of quiet celebration to the household. Ken speaks of it without flourish, but there is pride in his tone. "They were born here, and they will grow here." It is a sentence that needs no embellishment; the simple fact carries more weight than any proclamation could.

In the nursery, sunlight filters through narrow windows in the morning, falling across cradles carved decades ago but polished anew for their small occupants. Isla, despite the demands of caring for two infants, has insisted on maintaining the room's warmth — soft fabrics, gentle colours, and no sense of grandeur that might make the space feel less like a child's refuge.

Ken notes that the Castle's rhythm has changed since the twins' arrival. Nights are punctuated by the predictable cries of hunger, mornings by the shuffle of footsteps as the household adjusts to its newest members. Yet, there is no complaint in his description, only the acknowledgment that life here is now measured in a different way — by feedings, lullabies, and the moments of rare quiet when both children sleep at once.

There are no royal nannies in stiff uniforms, no ceremonial nurses standing in attendance. Isla and Ben have chosen to keep their children's care within the family, helped only by those they trust implicitly. "We do not pass our children to strangers," Ken remarks, a statement that reads as both tradition and protection. In the Castle, trust is currency, and it is never spent lightly.

The Castle grounds remain as much a private refuge as the interior. Gardens are tended not for spectacle but for use, growing herbs and vegetables alongside the flowers. In the warmer months, children — both of the Castle and from nearby homes in Copenhagen — run barefoot across the grass. It is not unusual to see Ben among them, chasing a ball or laughing at a missed catch, blending into the life of the community without the formality that titles might suggest.

Ken points out that this blending of roles — king in title, neighbour in practice — is deliberate. Rosenshavn's strength lies not in separating itself from the city but in remaining part of it. The Castle is not a fortress against the world but a home within it. The gates may be guarded, but they are not closed to those who come with goodwill.

It is this openness, carefully balanced against the need for privacy, that has allowed Rosenshavn to remain what it is: a place of life rather than display. Ken does not invite the public into the private wings, nor does he hide behind layers of formality. He walks through the markets, speaks to neighbours, and joins games on the soccer field. In this way, the Castle extends into the city without losing its own identity.

The birth of the twins has tightened this bond with Copenhagen. News of their arrival spread quickly, but unlike the rest of the world, the city has respected the family's wish for privacy. There are no camera lenses pressed against the gates, no reporters lurking in alleyways. The citizens themselves ensure it, driving away anyone who oversteps. To Ken, this loyalty is the truest form of protection the family could have.

It is a loyalty born not from obligation, but from years of shared life. Ken has played soccer on the same fields, shopped in the same markets, sat in the same cafés. Ben and Isla have done the same, never holding themselves apart from those who share their streets. In return, the people of Copenhagen guard their privacy as fiercely as the Castle's own walls.

Ken does not need to say that this protection extends to the twins. The city has already claimed them as its own, not in title, but in affection. They are not simply royal children; they are Copenhagen's children. And so, the Castle remains a place where they can grow without the constant scrutiny that follows most heirs from birth.

Rosenshavn, as Ken describes it, is not the kind of castle found in storybooks. It is not defined by its towers or its history, though it has both. It is defined by the lives it holds, the bonds it shelters, and the quiet understanding between those within and those beyond its gates. For Ken, that is all it needs to be — and all it will ever be.

The morning in Marden held the kind of stillness that comes only before the first footstep on the street, when the air is heavy with unspoken thought and the distant hum of the waking world. Ben sat across from the journalist at a small, square table tucked near the far window of a quiet tea room. The scent of roasted coffee drifted between them, clinging to the polished wood, while the steam from the journalist's tea curled into the space like a ribbon too thin to catch. Outside, a fog lay low over the rooftops, the county hidden in its own silence.

There had been no formal summons, no publicised interview. This meeting was born of a choice — Ben's choice — and that alone set it apart from the feeding frenzy of press calls that had swarmed since the first newspaper carried the truth. Ken had given his address to the world in the Castle, but this was different. This was Ben, unshielded by anyone else's voice, asking the question himself. It was not for a headline, not for a prepared statement. It was for his own understanding.

The journalist, a seasoned man from the London Times with a face lined more by observation than by age, seemed almost reluctant to meet Ben's gaze at first. He stirred his tea with unnecessary care, as though buying time before answering the question that had been laid before him like a gauntlet. "Why," Ben had asked, "is the world so obsessed with me as a young king? What is it they truly want to know, and why?" The query hung in the air, heavy enough to silence even the clink of the teaspoon against porcelain.

Ben had grown accustomed to being the unspoken centre of speculation. The years of anonymity in Denmark had been deliberate, a choice shaped by quiet counsel and a shared belief in the sanctity of family life. Foreign interference was not a phantom to him; it was a tangible force, one that could arrive in the form of a reporter's pen as easily as it could in the form of political pressure. He had seen enough of both to know the difference between curiosity and intrusion.

The journalist leaned back, his expression measured. "People don't see you," he said finally, "they see what you represent. A crown without a throne, a title that doesn't need to be worn to exist. To them, you are the embodiment of something they believe they've lost — authenticity. And that frightens as much as it fascinates." His voice carried no malice, only the bluntness of one who had witnessed too much theatre in public life to believe in coincidence.

Ben listened without movement, his hands resting on the table, one thumb brushing against the rim of his coffee cup. He had heard versions of this answer before, usually dressed in softer language or veiled in political flattery. This, however, was stripped of embellishment, the truth laid bare. It was not about him as a person; it was about the story others could tell through him.

He had kept silent for a reason — a dozen reasons, in truth — but at the core was the belief that Denmark's stability depended on the quiet strength of its leadership, not on the spectacle of its history. Foreign governments, particularly the UK and North America, were skilled in making noise out of silence. They thrived on a narrative they could bend, a headline they could sharpen into a weapon. To feed them information was to invite interference.

Until the leak.

The newspaper in Copenhagen had changed everything, not because the truth had never been told, but because it had been told without his consent, stripped of the context that kept it from becoming a weapon. The traitor's name would not pass his lips in this conversation. This was not a morning for vengeance. It was a morning for clarity.

"I never wanted the story told this way," Ben said quietly, his voice carrying the weight of withheld years. "But now that it's out, I want to know — do they seek to understand me, or do they seek to own the narrative?" It was a question for the journalist, but it was also one for himself, a line drawn in the space between public identity and private life.

The journalist considered this, his eyes narrowing slightly as if testing the shape of the truth before speaking it. "Some will try to understand," he said at last, "but most will try to own it. It's what they do. They'll make you a symbol, and once you're a symbol, they'll claim pieces of you until there's nothing left to belong to yourself."

The words were neither accusation nor warning; they were a statement of fact. Ben knew it already, but hearing it spoken aloud in the quiet of that tea room made it heavier. Symbols could not choose how they were interpreted. They could only choose whether to exist in the public eye or to remain in the shadows, knowing that both choices carried their own cost.

The coffee had cooled in his cup, untouched for several minutes. Ben took a sip now, letting the bitterness settle on his tongue, a taste that grounded him in the present moment. Outside, the fog was lifting, revealing the faint outlines of shopfronts and cobblestones. In the shifting light, the county felt both exposed and protected, much like himself.

He thought of Kent, of the people who had known him since before he could speak, people who would never trade his trust for a handful of currency. They had been his shield in ways the world could not see, their silence more valuable than any public declaration of loyalty. They understood that there were truths worth keeping, not because they were forbidden, but because they were sacred.

The journalist broke the silence. "You could refuse them all, you know. No interviews. No stories. Let them wonder." It was said with the half-smile of someone who knew that mystery often carried more weight than revelation.

Ben set his cup down, his gaze steady. "Wonder is safer than intrusion," he replied. "But the problem with silence is that it can be filled by anyone who wants to speak in your place." The statement was not for the journalist's benefit; it was the truth he had lived under for years.

The fog outside continued to thin, the day making its way into the streets of Marden. Inside the tea room, the air remained heavy with the scent of coffee and the lingering question of how much of himself he was willing to give to the world. This was not the day to decide, but it was the day to acknowledge that the decision would come. And when it did, it would be on his terms, or not at all.

Ken stood before the cameras with the same measured calm that had carried him through the earlier statements, yet the air around him felt different now. The previous sections of his address had been about facts — verifiable, unshakable — but this part cut deeper. It was not a matter of ancestry or titles; it was about betrayal. His words were deliberate, each one chosen with the precision of a man who understood the gravity of public record. He named no one, gave no direct trail for the curious to follow, yet the weight behind his voice told the world that this was no casual incident.

He began with the simple truth: the one who leaked Benedict's identity had once stood close enough to the family to be considered part of its inner circle. This was not the act of a stranger. It was the act of someone who had shared their table, walked freely through the Castle without suspicion, and been trusted implicitly. Trust, Ken knew, was not something you rebuilt once it had been traded away. It was a structure — and once dismantled, it could not be reconstructed from the same pieces.

The motive was as old as human frailty. Desperation, Ken explained, had driven this person to seek money. The kind of desperation that blinds reason, that convinces the mind that the smallest betrayal will go unnoticed if the reward is large enough. They had sold the truth — a truth protected for years — to the highest bidder. And in doing so, they had placed not only Ben but the entire household in the crosshairs of an international media storm.

His tone never shifted into anger. Anger would have been a release, and Ken was not offering release. Instead, he spoke with the calm of inevitability, the kind of composure that carried more weight than any raised voice could. This was a public record, and public records were not for venting. They were for ensuring that the truth could not be rewritten later.

He reminded the public that in Denmark, treason was not an abstract notion reserved for political conspiracies. It was a living crime, one that could be committed as easily through a whispered secret as through the theft of state property. The betrayal had been tried in court, and the verdict had been delivered without hesitation. Forty years in prison — a sentence that reflected both the severity of the act and the permanence of the damage it had caused.

The name of the traitor remained unspoken, but it did not need to be spoken. In Copenhagen, those who had followed the trial already knew it. The city's people were not strangers to loyalty, nor to the swift cutting-off of those who broke it. The man was gone now, locked behind stone walls and iron bars, and his absence was a wound that would never quite heal.

Ken made it clear that the punishment was not born of vengeance. The law had spoken, and the law had been applied. But beneath that legal clarity lay the personal cost, the understanding that someone who had been considered family had, for the sake of currency, thrown away years of trust. That was a debt no prison sentence could repay.

He paused for a moment, allowing the silence to sit heavy in the room, the kind of silence that made the listeners lean forward, even in their living rooms. It was a silence meant to be felt, not just heard — a reminder that betrayal was not a word to be tossed lightly.

The media would no doubt run their own stories, Ken knew. They would speculate on motives, dig for interviews with anyone who had ever known the traitor, and try to find some narrative that would make it more palatable. But here, before the nation, the truth was recorded plainly: the act had been committed, the cost was irreparable, and the sentence was just.

In the weeks since the arrest, life at Rosenshavn Castle had continued, but not unchanged. Doors that had once been open to trusted friends were now closed. Conversations that had once been held freely were now measured. The family had learned again — as they had so many times before — that openness carried its own risks, and that the line between friend and foe could be thinner than a breath.

Ken closed the segment of his address with a final statement, one that carried no legal weight but spoke volumes in tone: "Loyalty is not bought with coins, and once sold, it cannot be bought back." The cameras caught the set of his jaw, the quiet steel in his eyes. He had said all that needed saying, and no more.

The reaction across the city was immediate. Citizens who had long defended the family's privacy took the news as a personal offense. In the coffee shops and markets of Copenhagen, the conversation turned from curiosity about Ben's lineage to outrage at the betrayal. The people of the city had always been protective of their own, and now they felt that the violation was against them as much as against the Castle.

For Ben, hearing Ken's words from a distance was both painful and necessary. In Kent, surrounded by those who would shield him from the noise, he could feel the closing of a chapter he had never wanted to write. The betrayal was out in the open now, stripped of speculation and presented as fact. The law had spoken. The nation had heard. And the family, though bruised, would endure.

But there was one truth that neither the cameras nor the newspapers could carry: trust, once broken, changes the very air between people. It makes the familiar strange, the once-safe unpredictable. And for all the legal justice that had been done, that change would remain. Forever.

The low stone walls of the cottage garden stood like a quiet sentinel between Ben and the noise of the outside world. In the stillness of an English spring morning, there was little to betray that the man walking among the budding rosebushes was at the centre of a storm stretching across continents. He had chosen this place for its silence, for the way the hills folded inward and muffled the wind, for the way the lanes narrowed until strangers thought twice before wandering through. Here, the air carried the faint scent of damp earth and woodsmoke — scents that spoke of safety. Yet safety, he knew, was never a given.

Inside the cottage, Uncle Sørensen moved with the quiet discipline of a man who had once commanded entire security teams without ever raising his voice. His eyes scanned each window, each latch, each curtain's edge. Though the pace was unhurried, nothing escaped him. Sørensen had been more than a guard for years now; he was family, and his presence here was not ceremonial. The air between the two men was easy, filled with the unspoken language of shared trust and long history.

The children — Casper, Maria, and Emil — were gathered around the wide oak table, the surface scattered with books and coloured pencils. They chattered about things only they found urgent: who could draw the tallest tower, which page in a book was the most interesting, whether the neighbour's cat was brave enough to cross the fence. Their energy filled the room, softening the edges of the day. None of them thought about cooking; meals here were the work of capable adult hands, and Sørensen kept a careful eye to ensure little fingers stayed away from stove and knife.

Across the Channel, in Denmark, the twins remained in Isla's care under security measures more rigorous than any the family had ever known. Their lives now unfolded inside a protected bubble, guarded from the outside world by both walls and people. Ben's decision to remain away was not explained in statements or speeches, but those who knew the currents of such matters understood the implication. He had removed himself from the immediate line of fire, not to flee, but to shield.

The journalist from the London Times arrived without ceremony, stepping into the kitchen like an old acquaintance rather than a stranger. He carried the quiet, alert manner of a man who knew his news was not for casual ears. After setting down his cup of tea on the worn wooden counter, he leaned in slightly, lowering his voice. "There's been another leak," he said. The words were steady, but the weight in them was unmistakable.

Ben listened without interrupting, his hands loosely clasped before him. The journalist continued, explaining that this time the source was not from Copenhagen, nor anyone within the Castle walls. It was a passerby from Brighton, someone who had been driving through the countryside of Kent and recognised him by chance. Whether by vanity, recklessness, or the same greed that had driven the first betrayal, they had passed the sighting along. The story was already taking shape in backrooms and editorial meetings.

There was no anger in Ben's response, only the quiet firmness of a man who had long ago learned the limits of outrage. "People talk," he said at last, "but not everyone listens to the right people." He understood the difference between gossip and proof, between rumour and danger. But in a world where whispers could turn into headlines overnight, the distinction was no comfort.

That afternoon, he asked to meet with several locals — men and women who had known him since childhood. The gathering took place in the county hall, the old timbers overhead arching like the ribs of a ship. No speeches were made, no chairs arranged in rows. They stood in a loose circle, the kind that invited honesty without performance. Ben told them what had happened, how another piece of his quiet had been chipped away by someone he had never met.

The reaction was swift, almost instinctive. Kent was not a place that welcomed intrusion. Here, neighbours watched out for one another, and a familiar face was not easily mistaken for a stranger. The locals assured him that nothing in their power would allow unwanted eyes or ears to pierce the calm of the valley. "You've been ours since you were small," one woman said, her voice carrying the certainty of truth. "We keep our own."

Sørensen stood at the edge of the gathering, listening but silent. He knew these people well enough to trust their word. They were not guards in uniform, but their vigilance was no less effective. In a place where everyone knew the bend of the road and the sound of a neighbour's footstep, it would be nearly impossible for an outsider to go unnoticed.

Back at the cottage, as dusk folded itself over the garden, Ben sat at the kitchen table with Sørensen. Between them, no more needed to be said. The plan was simple — remain in place, stay quiet, and let the people of Kent do what they did best: protect their own. It was a defence not found in statutes or treaties, but in the fierce loyalty of a small community that had already chosen its side.

The children returned to their books and drawings, the scrape of pencil on paper a small, steady sound in the warm room. Outside, the wind shifted, carrying with it the faint clang of the church bell from the next county. It was the kind of sound that spoke of time passing without hurry, of lives lived at their own pace, regardless of the storms beyond the hedgerows.

Ben knew the leak would stir trouble in the days to come. It would feed the papers and draw questions from places far beyond the reach of Kent's narrow roads. But here, within these walls and under these skies, the trouble could not reach him without first passing through the steadfast hearts of those who had known him not as a king, but as a boy.

In Kent, where the hedgerows pressed close to the narrow lanes, Uncle Sørensen's presence was as deliberate as it was reassuring. He did not stand in the background like an idle guest; his very position in the cottage was part of a design Ben had not needed to explain. This was no exile of leisure. Every movement, every placement of a chair near a window, every glance through the lace curtain, was rooted in decades of knowing how to protect without drawing a crowd. Sørensen had once been the Castle's strictest chief of security, a man whose word was followed without delay. Now, in this quieter chapter, the same precision served a family, not an institution.

Ben had always known that Sørensen's loyalty was not earned easily. In their earliest years together, when Ben was still learning the boundaries of trust, Sørensen was a wall of formality. Commands were given, rules laid down, no questions invited. But time has a way of working on even the hardest edges, and the boy had found the cracks — moments of humour, small acts of kindness returned with sincerity. From there, the man who once barked orders softened into something rarer: a guardian whose care was personal, not just professional.

At the cottage, Sørensen handled the rhythm of each day as if guarding a fortress. He kept the children's laughter from spilling too far into the lane where curious ears might pause. He checked the locks before the lamps were lit and again before the last candle was snuffed out. His calm manner allowed Ben to think without distraction, to weigh his next steps without the tension of wondering who might be watching from the shadows.

News of the second leak had already shifted his posture from watchful to fully alert. When he heard of the passerby from Brighton, his mind moved quickly through possibilities — not just the risk of another photograph or whispered remark, but the chain of attention it could set off. His duty was not only to shield Ben from danger but also to preserve his state of mind. A rattled man makes different choices than a steady one, and in these days, every choice counted.

Harrison entered the picture as naturally as a gust through an open door. Word of the leak had travelled to him through the same network of locals who had been quietly watching since Ben first arrived. Sørensen met him just beyond the garden wall, the two men speaking in the low, even tones of those who have no need for dramatics. Harrison, as ever, offered no questions about the deeper matters; he simply said, "I'll keep watch, same as before."

The memory of their last arrival here hung between them. That night, Harrison had stood outside long after the lamps went dark, leaning against the low stone wall with the patience of a man who knew that presence alone could turn away trouble. It was the same now. No formal guardhouse, no uniforms — just two men who understood their roles without needing them spelled out.

Ben watched from the kitchen window as Harrison took up his place along the edge of the lane. The man's posture was easy, even casual to an untrained eye, but Sørensen recognised the small cues: the way Harrison scanned the rise of the road, the measured steps that kept him from becoming a fixture in one spot. He was not merely looking for a face; he was studying the patterns, noting what belonged and what didn't.

Inside, Sørensen maintained his own perimeter. His respect for Harrison's presence did not mean he stepped back from his duties. Rather, he adjusted the layers of protection, blending the local's familiarity with the discipline of a trained operative. The two approaches wove together into a net that would be hard for any intruder to slip through unnoticed.

The children remained blissfully unaware of the details. To them, Harrison was simply another familiar face who sometimes brought stories from the lane or a stray dog needing a scratch behind the ears. The stability of their days depended on this careful separation of what was seen and what was left unsaid. Sørensen was determined to keep it that way.

As dusk stretched over the cottage, Sørensen stepped onto the back step, leaning on the frame as he watched Harrison in the distance. There was no need to call out. Both men knew their positions, knew the weight of the task, and knew that tonight — like so many nights before — their success would be measured not in action taken, but in trouble that never reached the door.

Ken leaned forward slightly as the cameras shifted their focus, his voice steady and even. There would be no flourish here, no attempt to dress the matter in theatrical airs. "Oscar's arrest," he began, "was not a question of hurt feelings or personal grudges. It was a matter of law. And when the law is clear, there is no place for hesitation." The words landed without a tremor. There was no need for him to raise his tone; the truth itself was heavy enough to be heard.

The charge of treason had not been drafted overnight. Ken detailed how months of careful observation, corroborated statements, and physical evidence had been weighed before the decision was made. The conclusion, when it came, was not born of rumour but of fact. To do nothing would have been to gamble with the safety of a household that was already under more scrutiny than it had ever known.

In the heart of those facts lay the most dangerous truth — Oscar's actions had been deliberate, not careless. Information of the kind he leaked did not slip by accident; it was passed hand-to-hand, knowingly, with the awareness of its value and its consequences. In doing so, he had placed the security of the Castle, and the lives of those within it, on a precarious edge.

Ken spoke with the precision of a man who understood the weight of every word. He outlined the legal steps that followed: the warrant signed by Judge Eldrin, the arrest carried out without resistance, the formal reading of charges in Copenhagen's court. It had been an unshakable process, rooted in the very laws designed to shield the monarchy from internal sabotage.

The public, hearing this for the first time in such clarity, might have imagined that personal loyalties had clouded the decision. Ken allowed no such misinterpretation. "This was not a choice between friendship and duty," he stated plainly. "It was a choice between the survival of the throne and the dismantling of it. And I will not preside over its destruction."

Treason, in Denmark's history, was not a word flung about carelessly. Ken reminded the audience that it carried the highest legal consequences, and with them, the deepest cultural condemnation. To betray the Crown was to sever oneself from the community entirely. There was no road back, no quiet forgiveness whispered in corridors.

The courtroom had been filled that day, not with a crowd of strangers, but with faces that once dined together, celebrated together, and trusted each other without question. It was a cruel kind of justice to strip away that bond, but justice it remained. The evidence, when presented, spoke without need for embellishment.

Oscar's sentence — forty years in the city jail of Copenhagen — was not designed to send a message to the world. It was designed to ensure that he would never again have the opportunity to endanger what had been entrusted to the family. The term was severe because the breach was irreparable.

Ken allowed no sympathy to colour his account. He did not indulge in speculation about why Oscar had done what he had. The whispers of financial desperation were not denied, but neither were they offered as an excuse. "We all face moments of choice," he said, "and we are all judged by the choice we make. His was the wrong one."

The danger extended beyond the leak itself. In exposing Ben's identity to those who had no right to it, Oscar had opened the door to interference from abroad. The political weight of that revelation could not be measured in headlines alone. It was the kind of information that shifted alliances, that redrew lines of influence without a single formal meeting.

Ken did not pretend that the fallout was over. "We are still living with the consequences," he admitted, though the admission was not weakness. It was simply fact. The heightened security, the guarded communications, the necessary separation of family members — all of it traced back to that one betrayal.

In the weeks since the sentencing, Ken had heard the questions: Was forty years too harsh? Could Oscar not be rehabilitated? He dismissed them with the quiet authority of someone who understood the cost of leniency in matters of state security. "You cannot rebuild a wall with the same stone that caused it to crumble," he said, letting the thought rest without further defence.

For Ben, the wound was both political and personal. Here was a man who had once walked freely through the Castle halls, who had been welcomed into moments of private joy, who had sat with the children as they played. Now, he was spoken of in the same breath as those who sought to dismantle the very family he had called his own.

Ken closed the matter with a tone that allowed no further debate. "The law was followed. Justice was served. The throne stands." And with that, he let the subject drop, knowing the facts would stand long after the noise of speculation faded.

Ken's tone shifted, if only slightly, when he spoke her name. Freja-Marie. It was not a political name, nor one destined to rattle off a herald's tongue. It was a family name, spoken in kitchens and gardens, not in state halls. At just thirteen months old, she had no knowledge of lines of succession or the weight of royal history. She knew only the warmth of her mother's arms, the sound of her dad's voice, and the familiar patterns of the Castle that had become her world.

He made no attempt to dress her existence in ceremonial importance. Freja-Marie was not in line to the throne before Thomas, nor before Ben and Isla's newborn twins. That was the fact. But there was a different kind of place for her — one that did not depend on titles or decrees. She was the visible thread that wove together the life Ken had before the storm with the life he was determined to protect after it.

In speaking of her, Ken was not addressing the court of public opinion; he was speaking to the people who understood family not as a legal arrangement but as a living, breathing network of care. Those who knew that a home was more than stone walls and signatures, that the bonds forged in laughter and trust were worth guarding as fiercely as any throne.

Freja-Marie had been born after years of quiet hope, in a home that had already seen its share of trials. She was the child who had turned the sound of the Castle into something gentler — a place where the echo of hurried footsteps could be interrupted by the sudden giggle of a toddler playing in the corridor. She had no crown, yet somehow her presence felt like a reign of her own.

Ken did not look at her as a symbol of political continuity. She was a reminder that even in households bound by duty, life could grow in the spaces untouched by politics. That reminder was as important to him as any public declaration he had made that day. It was the reason he had fought so hard to keep the family's private life sealed against the noise outside.

Those watching from abroad might have dismissed the mention of a one-year-old as an attempt to humanize a public figure. But those who knew Ken — truly knew him — understood that it was not strategy. It was truth. The safety of Freja-Marie was tied directly to the safety of everyone in Rosenshavn Castle. If one fell, all would be exposed.

Her relationship with Ben was not one of half-sibling formality. Ben had been there in her first weeks, a quiet guardian who made her laugh in the way only he could. He had taken her on slow walks around the Castle grounds, pointing out birds and clouds as if she could understand. And when the twins were born, it was Freja-Marie who reached for them first, her small hands eager to hold what she instinctively knew were part of her.

Annemarie's role as her mother, and Ken's as her dad, was never up for debate — but neither was the understanding that Freja-Marie belonged to all of them in spirit. She was as much Ben's little sister as she was Ken's daughter. In that sense, she stood as a quiet testament to the blended life they had built.

Ken had never explained this to the public before. There had been no need. But on this day, with the world's attention fixed on the Castle, he chose to let them see a fragment of the truth. Not the kind that altered laws or claimed thrones, but the kind that reminded people of what those thrones were meant to protect in the first place.

The decision to mention her was deliberate. In naming her, he anchored the conversation back to the family's core — away from the noise of treason, succession, and international headlines. She was the living proof that there was more at stake than political advantage.

Freja-Marie would grow up without remembering the day her name was spoken in the same breath as these revelations. But one day, she would read it. And when she did, Ken wanted her to know that she had been part of the reason he stood so firmly now. She was part of the home he refused to let crumble.

There was no fanfare in how he closed this part of the address. "She is my daughter," he said simply. The weight of that claim was not in the words themselves, but in the unspoken vow behind them — that her safety, and the safety of all his children, would remain the measure of every decision he made.

For those who listened closely, the mention of Freja-Marie did more than soften the moment. It placed everything else — the arrests, the declarations, the risks — into their true frame. This was not about ruling over millions. It was about protecting the few who made those millions matter.

Ken's voice settled back into its previous rhythm as he moved on, but the image lingered. Somewhere beyond the cameras and the noise, a little girl was likely reaching for a toy, unaware that her dad had just named her in front of the world — not as a royal, but as the heart of the family he was fighting to keep whole.

Ken's eyes narrowed ever so slightly as he approached the end of his address. The tone of calm authority that had carried through the earlier sections of his speech remained, but there was a weight now, a gravity that settled over each word. This was no closing pleasantry meant to round out a broadcast. It was the part that would be quoted, repeated, dissected, and carried across every border within hours. He was about to remove any doubt that might still linger in the minds of those watching, both friends and adversaries alike.

He spoke without raising his voice. "Let this be understood," he began, his gaze never straying from the camera's lens. "Any nation, any person, or any entity that seeks to undermine Benedict Adrian Harvick or Isla Harvick's rule — directly or indirectly — will face full legal consequences." There was no rhetorical flourish, no room for interpretation. It was plain language delivered in a tone that stripped away the possibility of misunderstanding.

The pause that followed was deliberate. Ken knew that silence could be louder than any phrase, and in that brief stillness, the words took root. He allowed them to settle like stone, each syllable anchoring itself in the minds of those who might have considered Denmark an easy target in its quiet approach to governance. That illusion, if it still existed, had just been dismantled.

He made it clear through his delivery that this was not the indulgent bluster of a man defending pride. It was an oath spoken by someone with both the legal reach and the personal resolve to see it carried out. Denmark's laws were not ornamental, and Ken's influence within them was not symbolic. He did not make promises lightly, and those who knew him understood that he never threatened without the means to act.

Observers abroad might have been tempted to dismiss the statement as political theatre, a calculated performance for the home audience. But they would have been mistaken. There was no audience Ken catered to. This warning was aimed with precision — toward intelligence agencies, corporate boards, political operatives, and media powers who had quietly measured what they could take.

For years, Denmark had been underestimated, its royal house considered ceremonial, its leadership viewed as cautious. Ken had allowed that perception to persist because it served the family's need for privacy. But in the wake of recent leaks and betrayal, that protective invisibility had been breached. This warning was the rebuilding of the wall — higher, stronger, and with teeth along the top.

Ken leaned forward slightly, not toward the camera, but as if closing the physical distance between himself and those he meant to reach. "We will not be provoked," he continued. "But make no mistake — if you strike, we will answer. And our answer will be final." The shift in his voice was subtle but unmistakable, a move from measured statement to unshakable declaration.

In the Castle's communications room, the staff remained utterly still. Even those who had heard Ken at his most unfiltered could feel the edge in his tone now. It was not born of anger; it was born of resolve. There was nothing reactive in him at this moment. He was not defending against a blow — he was fortifying before it could come.

For the people of Copenhagen, watching from their homes, cafés, and shopfronts, the warning was not alarming. It was a reassurance. They knew Ken, knew his refusal to posture, and understood that if he had reached the point of speaking so plainly, the threat to the family — and by extension, to the stability of their daily lives — was real enough to warrant it.

Internationally, the reaction would be less uniform. Some would see the statement as a challenge, a line drawn that could be tested. Others would recognize it for what it was: a signal that Denmark's leadership was prepared to act decisively, without the slow, hesitant manoeuvres of traditional diplomacy. It was not aggression; it was the prevention of chaos.

Ken closed this part of his address without softening the message. There was no sudden smile, no return to lighter matters. "Consider yourselves informed," he said, and that was all. No further clarification, no invitation for questions. His warning was a sealed document — final, binding, and irrevocable.

When the cameras shut off, the air in the room held the same taut stillness as during the pause in his speech. It was the silence that follows the setting of a cornerstone, a foundation upon which everything else in the coming days would be built. The statement would not fade; it would be replayed and remembered. And that was the point.

Outside the Castle walls, the people of Copenhagen did what they always did when Ken spoke with this kind of clarity. They closed ranks. Neighbours looked out for one another a little more closely. Conversations in markets and courtyards circled back to what had been said, and the unspoken agreement was clear — Denmark's strength was not just in its leadership, but in the unity of its people.

In England, where Ben and Uncle Sørensen remained with the children, the warning carried across in real time. Sørensen said nothing, but his eyes lingered on the screen long after Ken's image had faded. Ben caught the glance and understood without a word that the old security chief approved. It was not often Sørensen nodded at a political move, but this one was different. It was not politics. It was protection.

The warning would stand as the closing frame of the day's declaration, the final note in a broadcast that had named a king, laid bare a betrayal, and reasserted the quiet strength of a family determined to endure. Anyone listening closely would know that Ken's words were not meant for the curious. They were meant for the ambitious — the ones who might imagine that Denmark was still a small stage on which they could play their games.

And in that single, unyielding moment, Ken had made certain they would think twice before stepping onto it.

The broadcast ended without ceremony, the last image of Ken frozen in the minds of all who had been watching. Across continents, newsrooms erupted into movement. Phones rang before anchors could remove their earpieces, producers barked orders, and legal analysts were summoned from late dinners to comment on what had just been declared. In some offices, the sound of Ken's warning still lingered in replay, looping as editors hunted for the most powerful stills. The world had been handed the truth, and now it would decide how to carry it.

In Kent, the stillness was different. Ben sat at the long wooden table in the cottage kitchen, the steam from his coffee rising in lazy spirals as the quiet pressed in. Uncle Sørensen sat opposite him, his hands folded over his own mug, eyes watching but not intruding. They had both listened without interruption from the first word to the last. Neither had needed to speak; Ken's voice had filled the room with something heavier than conversation could carry.

Those who lived in the village, the ones who had known Ben since he was small enough to hide behind their knees, had listened too. They had no questions for him afterward. Instead, one by one, they appeared at the cottage gate, not to pry but to reassure. "We've got you," they told him, with the quiet conviction of people who understood loyalty without conditions. It was not a pledge made for show — it was the truth of their nature.

The journalist from the London Times, seated a few chairs down from Ben, broke the silence with measured words. He carried news — good news, in its way. They had found the man behind the latest attempt to distort Ben's story, the one who had tried to pass a fabrication to the public as truth. The journalist called it a "fluff piece," but the tone in his voice left no doubt it had been meant to harm.

Ben's brow furrowed as he listened, his hands tightening around the warm porcelain of his cup. The journalist explained that the story had been sold to the National Enquirer, dressed up as scandal, with not a thread of it rooted in fact. "We traced it," he said, "and the man's name is in police hands." There was a satisfaction in his voice, but no triumph. Lies, once told, could not be untold — but they could be stopped from spreading.

The journalist continued, explaining that his connections inside the Enquirer's circle had confirmed the falsehood before it went to print. The man responsible had been picked up for questioning, and formal charges were being processed. "By morning," he assured Ben, "you'll know the outcome. But I'd wager you'll be hearing the word 'arrested.'" It was as much a promise as an update, and Ben nodded once, absorbing it without flourish.

Back in the kitchen, the air was warmer now, the kind of warmth that comes from people and not just the stove. Sørensen reached for the coffee pot, topping up Ben's cup without asking, the simple act carrying all the familiarity of years spent together. Dern leaned against the counter, his own coffee in hand, watching the scene with the quiet patience of someone who understood the weight of the day.

Coffee was the common ground here. It wasn't ceremony, just habit. Ben had never taken to tea, not as a boy and certainly not now, and he found a kindred spirit in Dern's preference for the same. Even Harrison, standing just outside the kitchen door, sipping from a heavy ceramic mug, favoured coffee over the village's traditional tea. They might be in Kent, but the rhythm in the cottage tonight felt like Copenhagen — brisk, steady, and awake.

Sørensen spoke at last, his voice low but even. "Ken did right." It was not a comment meant to spark discussion, merely a truth he wanted voiced aloud. Ben met his gaze, offering only the faintest of nods in return. They both understood that rightness did not make the situation less dangerous, only clearer.

The cottage itself seemed to listen, its walls holding the murmur of the conversation and the faint crackle from the fireplace. Outside, the lane was empty, save for the occasional shadow of a neighbour passing by on their way home. Protection here did not come from visible guards or cameras; it came from watchful eyes and the unspoken promise that no harm would pass unchallenged.

Ben's thoughts wandered briefly to Copenhagen, to Isla and the twins, secure within the Castle's quiet perimeter. He knew they would have watched as well, Isla holding the babies close while Ken's words carried across the airwaves. The distance between them was measured not in miles but in the knowledge that for now, this separation kept them all safer.

The journalist stood, placing a folded piece of paper on the table in front of Ben. "That's the name," he said simply. "In case you want it." Ben didn't unfold it. The name mattered less than the fact that it would no longer be in circulation, whispering lies into the ears of those willing to believe them.

As the night deepened, the kitchen filled with the soft sounds of cups being set down, chairs shifting against the floorboards, and the occasional breath of wind against the windows. No one spoke of what tomorrow might bring. For now, the silence was enough — not the heavy silence of uncertainty, but the settled kind that comes after a decisive stand has been taken.

Outside, Kent remained still, the narrow lanes leading away from the cottage disappearing into the dark. Somewhere beyond them, the world was already reacting to Ken's broadcast. But here, the only movement was the slow drift of steam rising from fresh coffee, curling into the air before fading away.

It was in that quiet, among friends who needed no persuasion, that Ben let the tension in his shoulders ease. The fight was far from over, but for tonight, it was held at bay. And in the silence after, the truth had room to breathe.

The news arrived before midnight, delivered not with ceremony but in the steady voice of the London Times journalist. The man who had peddled the so-called puff piece in the UK had been arrested and charged — not simply with spreading lies, but with defamation of character. It was a charge that carried weight, and Ben took the news in silence, the relief tempered by the reality that such battles would never fully cease. The journalist's eyes held the faint satisfaction of a man who had fought for truth and won a round, even if the war was ongoing.

Across the table, Dern leaned back in his chair, the curve of a grin forming before he spoke. He had been listening quietly, but now that the matter was settled, his attention shifted. "So… Copenhagen," he said, his tone somewhere between curiosity and mischief. Ben looked up, one eyebrow raised, not yet aware of what Sørensen had planned. It was Sørensen who leaned forward, the corners of his mouth twitching as if the thought had amused him for hours before he voiced it aloud.

"Full month. All expenses paid," Sørensen said, his words slow and deliberate, as if dropping stones into still water. "You come to the Castle. Not as a guest. As family." The statement hung in the air for a moment before Dern laughed outright, his hand hitting the table. "Family? You realise you're offering me a front-row seat to all the chaos, don't you?" His voice carried a warmth that cut through the day's heavier shadows.

Ben chuckled, the tension in his shoulders easing as he imagined the sight. "Chaos doesn't even begin to cover it," he said. "We're talking about the full tour — thunder-farts in the hallways, midair soccer-farts on the field, diaper bombs that would make you question the laws of physics." His tone had shifted now, the earlier gravity giving way to humour, and even the journalist cracked a smile.

Sørensen was already picturing it in his mind. "You'll eat better than you ever have in your life," he said, the gleam in his eyes betraying a hint of wicked fun. "But I'll warn you — you'll probably leave heavier than you came. Thirty, maybe forty pounds if you take seconds at every meal. And believe me, you'll want seconds." Dern's grin widened, the image of himself lumbering home fattened and happy clearly not unwelcome.

"Running on the soccer field won't save you either," Ben added. "We'll make sure you're too busy laughing to burn anything off. And if you feel the need to let something slip mid-run, well, no one's going to stop you." The room broke into low laughter, the kind that settles deep and lingers, and for a moment, the heaviness of the past weeks was forgotten.

The offer wasn't a polite courtesy; it was genuine. In Copenhagen, the Castle was not the cold, gilded fortress outsiders imagined. It was a living, breathing household where play and responsibility shared the same walls. Dern would see it all — the kitchen's warmth in the mornings, the sound of children's feet on polished floors, the muffled roars of laughter when an ill-timed fart disrupted a chess game.

Sørensen leaned back, satisfied with the reaction. "You'll see the truth of it," he said. "No staged photographs. No formal dinners where everyone's afraid to breathe. You'll see how we really live — doors open, voices loud, and the occasional soccer ball knocking something over it shouldn't." Dern seemed to savour the idea, his gaze distant for a moment as if already picturing himself there.

"Thunder-farts, pull-up diaper bombs…" Dern began, shaking his head. "I might need to pack more than clothes. Maybe armour." Ben laughed, his eyes bright. "You'll adapt. Or you won't. Either way, you'll remember it." There was truth in the words — life at Rosenshavn Castle wasn't polished for guests. It was lived, fully and unapologetically, and those who stepped inside either embraced it or found themselves overwhelmed.

Harrison, who had been leaning against the doorway listening, finally spoke. "You'll be fine," he said with a smirk. "Just don't try to outrun the smell after a midair soccer-fart. That's a rookie mistake." The table erupted again, the sound spilling into the kitchen like sunlight. It was the first time in weeks the laughter had felt entirely unforced.

Ben knew, in a quiet corner of his mind, that this was how resilience took shape — not in grand speeches or sweeping gestures, but in the willingness to laugh even when the world beyond the door was watching too closely. The invitation to Dern wasn't just about offering hospitality. It was about drawing someone into the fold, showing them that life, for all its strains, could still be lived loudly and without apology.

Dern took a slow sip of his coffee, letting the moment settle. "One month," he said at last. "Fine. But if I come back weighing forty pounds more, I'm blaming you." Ben smiled. "Blame me all you want," he replied. "Just don't pretend you didn't enjoy every second of it."

Outside, the wind carried faint scents of the countryside through the open window, mingling with the rich aroma of coffee in the room. The night beyond Kent was still, but inside the cottage, it felt as though the day had ended on something more than survival. It had ended on the promise of laughter yet to come.

The silence after was no longer the same. It carried with it the weight of truth, yes, but also the promise of absurdity, companionship, and the unfiltered joy of living as one's self. And for Ben, that balance — between the gravitas of the day and the ridiculousness of a thunder-fart on a soccer field — was exactly what kept life whole.

CHAPTER 15: RETURN OF THE KING

Harrison's message came without a stamp of urgency, without any grand announcement, just a few simple words sent in his familiar, steady manner. Ben read it once, then again, his expression unchanged save for the faint lift in his brow. Sørensen, leaning back in his chair, glanced at it over Ben's shoulder, the movement so casual it might have been mistaken for disinterest, though nothing in his gaze was ever casual. "That it?" Sørensen asked. "That's it," Ben replied, folding the paper in half with deliberate precision. There was no need for more. A signal from Harrison meant only one thing — the road home was clear. The three children, already restless in their own quiet way, picked up on the shift in the room. Maria and Emil, Sørensen's adopted pair, exchanged a quick look. Casper, Ben's boy, was the first to speak. "We're going back?" Ben's nod was small, but the smile that followed was enough.

Maria crossed the room without hesitation, her bare feet making a soft patter against the polished wood. "Does that mean we'll see the castle before dark?" she asked, her voice carrying more excitement than she tried to hide. Emil stood beside her, hands shoved deep in his pockets, pretending not to care though his eyes gave him away. "We're going to win this time," he said, as though the castle gates themselves were part of a competition only he understood. Casper smirked, tilting his head. "You wish. I'm faster than both of you." Ben allowed them their chatter, letting the familiar argument carry through the air. It was the sound of normalcy, of something steady in a world that had felt far too unpredictable in recent weeks.

Sørensen pushed himself to his feet with the quiet authority of a man who didn't need to raise his voice to be obeyed. "Pack light," he said to the children. "And keep it tight. No fuss." The command was simple, and they knew better than to test it. Maria was the first to run for her room, Emil on her heels, the two of them muttering about what they could and couldn't fit in their bags. Casper lingered by Ben's chair, looking up at him with the weight of an unspoken question. "You'll tell me if we're in trouble, right?" Ben's hand rested briefly on the boy's shoulder — not a hug, not an indulgence, but an acknowledgment. "If we were in trouble, we wouldn't be going home," he said, his tone leaving no room for doubt.

The room settled into a rhythm of movement. Bags were pulled from under beds, shirts folded and refolded, shoes checked for laces and stray pebbles. Tobias, watching from the doorway, took in the familiar sight of Sørensen's quiet efficiency paired with Ben's unspoken readiness. There was no over-preparation, no unnecessary caution, just the assurance of two men who had done this before, in far less comfortable circumstances. "Feels like an old op," Sørensen muttered, half to himself, as he ran a hand along the zipper of his duffel. Ben gave a short laugh. "Let's hope it doesn't end like one."

When the children reappeared, their excitement had crystallised into a more controlled energy, the kind they reserved for moments that truly mattered. Maria carried her bag with both hands, the weight clearly testing her, but she refused help. Emil wore his backpack slung low, determined to appear older than he was. Casper had packed with ruthless precision, a skill Ben had taught him without meaning to. "Ready?" Ben asked. Three heads nodded at once. Sørensen gave the smallest of approving grunts, his version of a full salute.

Ben took the folded message from his pocket one last time before sliding it into his jacket. Harrison's words weren't elaborate. They never were. But there was an understanding between them that went back years — back before titles and castles, before the eyes of the outside world could follow. Harrison didn't deal in false alarms, and he didn't send for Ben without reason. "He's sure?" Sørensen asked, not because he doubted, but because protocol demanded the question. "He's sure," Ben said, and that was the end of it.

The children were herded toward the door, their voices lowering now that departure felt imminent. Outside, the sky stretched wide and unbroken, the kind of blue that promised a clean flight. Tobias followed, careful not to speak over the moment. It wasn't his place to explain what needed no explaining. Some departures are best understood by the sound of footsteps, the shift of a bag's weight on a shoulder, and the faint, steady thud of a heart finally set on the way home.

The hangar was a wash of pale light spilling out onto the black tarmac, the shadows of the jet stretching long and sharp under the glare. Its engines idled in a low, even hum, as though aware that this was no hurried departure. Sørensen walked with the same quiet readiness that had marked every journey he had ever taken with Ben, his eyes shifting over every approach and corner, not from suspicion, but from the discipline that never left him. Ben's stride was straight, forward, and without the pause of a man torn between leaving and staying. It was not a night for farewells, and he allowed none to linger in his mind.

Michael Dern followed a step or two behind, his suitcase rolling smoothly over the hangar floor. He was not here as a reporter looking for flaws to exploit, nor as a stranger invited to inspect the family. Ben had made that clear from the first conversation — he was here as a guest, treated as family, and afforded the courtesy that Castle tradition demanded. In Denmark, you did not scold your guests, you did not put them on trial in your home, and you certainly did not make them feel unwelcome. Michael had been offered a month-long, all-expenses-paid stay, and he was taking it exactly as intended: as a rare opportunity to see the truth of a household everyone claimed to know but none truly understood.

"You travel light for a month," Ben remarked, glancing at the single piece of luggage. His voice carried no judgement, only curiosity. "I've learned the less you carry, the less you lose," Michael replied, his eyes following the silver fuselage of the jet. "Besides, I'm still on vacation, aren't I?" "That depends," Sørensen said, one corner of his mouth tightening into something close to a smile. "If you consider being trapped in a castle with forty children a holiday, then yes. You are on vacation." Michael gave a short laugh. "I've interviewed foreign ministers in war zones, Sørensen. I think I can survive forty children."

Ben's pace slowed just enough to match theirs. "I'm not asking you to survive them. I'm asking you to see them. That's the point of all this. Too many people think they know who we are. I want you to write something that makes them realise they don't." Michael nodded slowly. "The truth, then. Not a puff piece. Not an attack."

"Exactly," Ben said, the word carrying the weight of an agreement. "When you write it — if you write it — you share it with us first. Kendrick will read it before it ever reaches your editor. That's not censorship. That's respect. And if it stands as truth, he'll approve it without a single change." "That's fair," Michael agreed. "You're giving me the story of a lifetime, whether you realise it or not."

Sørensen shifted his bag onto the narrow conveyor leading into the jet's hold. "You'll be writing about more than just the man who sits on the throne. You'll be writing about the people who keep him standing. Don't forget them." "I won't," Michael said, and there was no pretence in his tone. The boarding stairs clanged faintly underfoot as they climbed, the cool night air carrying the faint scent of aviation fuel. Ben paused at the top, letting the others step inside before him, a quiet habit formed from years of ensuring that those with him were settled first. Once aboard, he turned into the narrow aisle, the familiar interior of the Royal Jet wrapping around him like a second home.

Michael found his seat without needing direction, his reporter's eyes already measuring the details of the cabin. "You really travel without ceremony," he said quietly, almost to himself.

Ben caught the remark. "Ceremony wastes time. People like to dress travel in gold, but the point is not how you leave — it's that you arrive." Sørensen lowered himself into the seat opposite Ben, his movements deliberate and without haste. "And this time, arrival matters more than speed."

Michael buckled in, leaning back with a faint smile. "Then I suppose I should put my pen away until we land." "No," Ben said, shaking his head. "Keep it in your hand. Truth doesn't wait for you to be comfortable."

Michael sat angled slightly toward the aisle, watching the subtle exchanges between Ben and Sørensen with the trained eye of a man who had spent half his life noticing what others overlooked. It was the silence that told him most — the measured glances, the near-invisible shifts in posture, the way a hand rested on the arm of a seat without urgency, signalling reassurance more than command. He recognised the mutual discipline of men who had worked in places where noise meant exposure and exposure meant risk. This was not theatre, not the polished artifice of staged diplomacy; it was the quiet certainty of those who had long since discarded spectacle.

It was easy to forget that Ben was a king at all. The trappings were absent here: no royal crests stitched in gold, no entourage of aides bustling at his elbows, no sense that the cabin was anything more than a travelling council chamber. Michael felt less like a member of the press and more like a witness at a private gathering. The air itself carried a weight — not oppressive, but deliberate — as if every word spoken within these walls would be remembered, even if never repeated.

"So," Michael began, leaning back with the tone of a man breaking ice rather than shattering it, "what exactly am I walking into when we land? The schedule sounded… vague." From across the aisle, Sørensen's eyes flickered with faint amusement. "Vague is polite," he replied. "You're walking into a castle with more children than some villages have residents."

Ben looked up from the notes on his lap, a faint grin tugging at the edge of his mouth. "And that's before you count the staff's children." "Children aren't a problem," Michael said lightly. Casper, sitting forward in his seat just behind Michael, leaned over the armrest with the conspiratorial air of someone delivering a classified warning. "Have they told you about Thunder-Fart yet?"

Michael blinked. "Thunder… what?" Maria, two seats over, nodded gravely. "Thunder-Fart. If you hear it, move. It's always followed by a Diaper Bomb." Michael glanced from one child to another, half-expecting this to be some elaborate joke. "You're telling me this is a… standard occurrence?"

Emil leaned forward, lowering his voice as though they were discussing espionage rather than bodily functions. "And there's the Roasting Games. That's when you roast someone — but be ready, because they'll roast you back." Ben shook his head slowly, though his eyes betrayed amusement. "You're doing a fine job of preparing him, aren't you?"

"We're doing him a favour," Maria said matter-of-factly. "You don't want to be standing in the wrong place at the wrong time. Especially at dinner. Some kids eat more than their stomachs can hold. And when that happens…" She let the sentence trail off with a deliberate shiver. Michael laughed, more at their delivery than the content. "I'm beginning to wonder if this was all part of a plan to keep visitors away."

Sørensen adjusted in his seat, his expression unreadable. "No. This is just the truth. You said that's what you came for, didn't you?" Michael met his gaze evenly. "I did. And if this is the truth, then I'll take it exactly as it is. Thunder-Fart, Diaper Bombs, and all." Ben leaned back, satisfied. "Good. Because once you step inside, you're family. And in our family, nobody gets a warning twice."

The hum of the engines was steady and unbroken, a sound that seemed to smooth the edges of every thought, lending the cabin a strange calm that belonged only to flight. Ben sat in his seat with his hands folded loosely, his posture neither guarded nor entirely relaxed, the sort of composure he wore when a matter of importance was being spoken of. Across from him, Michael sat with a notebook open on his lap, though no pen moved upon it yet. Sørensen occupied the seat to Ben's right, angled just enough that his eyes could measure both men at once, a habit so ingrained it felt less like vigilance and more like breathing. The cabin lights were warm against the dim blue beyond the windows, and for a moment the three of them seemed to inhabit their own private council in the sky, cut off from the world below.

Ben began without preamble, his voice carrying the even weight of a man who had explained such things before but never quite in the same way twice. He spoke of Rosenshavn Castle not as a fortress or symbol but as a living, breathing home, full of routines that owed nothing to ceremony. He told Michael that within those walls, children did not hold back their laughter because of royal blood, that games were not halted for the arrival of dignitaries, and that the air often carried the scent of cooking or the chaos of a practical joke far more often than the polished formality outsiders imagined. "You'll see it for yourself," Ben said, leaning back, "and when you do, you'll understand that what we are is far less than a legend and far more than a family."

Michael listened with the intent stillness of someone who knew that every sentence deserved to be weighed before being set down. He asked if there were any limits to what he might write, and Ben answered without hesitation that there was only one — truth. "Not the kind people want to hear because it flatters them, and not the kind that sells because it stirs outrage," Ben said. "The truth as it is. If you see us stumble, you write it. If you see us do something worth respect, you write that too. But you will not dress it in the clothes the world expects us to wear."

Sørensen's gaze shifted slightly, the faintest tilt of his head showing his approval. He had heard Ben make agreements before, but he knew this was different. Michael was not a passing acquaintance nor a man who had come looking for the story others would have chased. He was here because Ben had asked, and that was no small thing. "And if I write something that cuts too close?" Michael asked after a moment, his pen now in hand though still resting on the page. "Then you'll show it to Ken before it leaves your desk," Ben replied. "If he says it stands, it stands. If he says it waits, it waits. That is the rule, and it will not be bent."

Michael gave a slow nod, the kind that carried both agreement and the quiet weight of a promise. He understood that what Ben was offering was not control over the narrative in the way politicians demanded it, but a safeguard — not for Ben's pride, but for the family's safety. Outside those castle walls, even the most harmless detail could be twisted into something unrecognizable, and Michael had seen enough of the press to know that damage was rarely undone once the ink was dry.

Ben leaned forward, his elbows resting on his knees, and let the cabin fall into a brief silence before continuing. "You'll hear things," he said, his voice lower now, almost conversational. "About the games the children play, the jokes they make, the chaos they cause. Some of it will sound ridiculous to anyone who hasn't lived it — Thunderfart games, diaper bombs, roasting matches where you give as good as you get. They're part of the fabric here. No one pretends otherwise." Michael gave a faint smile, already picturing the kind of scenes Ben was describing. "And I'm supposed to put that in the article?" he asked. "If it's true," Ben said simply, "then yes. Let the world see that royalty is still human."

Sørensen let out a low sound — something between a chuckle and a breath — as though recalling a memory best left unnamed. "You'll want to keep your wits about you," he said, finally speaking. "The children will size you up faster than you think. They'll decide if you're a target before the end of your first meal. If you're lucky, they'll roast you for sport. If you're not, well… you might be in the wrong place when someone's stomach gives up." Michael laughed, but there was a flicker of caution in his eyes, the way a man laughs when he knows a warning might carry more truth than jest.

The conversation turned, as it always did on such flights, toward what awaited them on the ground. Michael asked about the first moments he would spend in the castle, and Ben described them without embellishment — the warmth of greetings that required no pomp, the way people moved in and out of rooms without knocking, the sound of children's footsteps carrying from one end of the hall to the other. "It won't feel like you've stepped into a palace," Ben said. "It'll feel like you've stepped into a place you've always known, but can't quite remember until you're there."

Michael's pen began to move at last, but not quickly. He wrote in short, deliberate bursts, pausing between each to look up at Ben or Sørensen, as though making sure he hadn't missed the weight behind a word or the shadow behind a pause. The hum of the engines filled those silences, and no one felt the need to break them unnecessarily. The journey was not long, but it was long enough for trust to take root in the way it only could when shared over distance and time.

Ben studied Michael for a moment, his eyes narrowing slightly in thought. "There will come a day," he said, "when the world will know more than it should. When that happens, I need to know you'll remember what you've seen and not just what you've heard. That you'll write the truth, not the noise." Michael looked up from his page, meeting Ben's gaze with steady assurance. "Then you've asked the right man," he said.

The conversation eased after that, moving in and out of lighter topics, but the shape of the agreement had been set. Outside, the night stretched endless and dark, the only movement the slow drift of clouds beneath the wings. Inside, the three men sat in a quiet balance, the unspoken understanding between them as steady as the engines carrying them forward.

By the time the flight began its slow descent, Michael had written little more than a page, but each line was anchored in something real. He closed his notebook as the seatbelt sign came on, glancing once more at Ben, who gave a short, knowing nod. Sørensen had already shifted his focus to the landing, his eyes scanning for anything unusual, but the set of his shoulders was easy. Whatever came next, they were arriving prepared — and with that, the quiet council of the skies ended as it had begun, without ceremony, but with purpose.

The descent began with the first break in the clouds, the muted glow of the Danish coastline slowly emerging beneath them like a memory recalled in pieces. The Royal Jet moved with unhurried precision, its nose tilting toward Copenhagen as the cabin lights dimmed to allow the outside view its full command. The sea below was calm, its surface shifting between silver and slate as the late light caught and released it in soft waves. Ben leaned slightly toward the window, though not enough for the movement to draw attention, his eyes tracing the familiar landmarks that were still just beyond clarity. For him, this approach was not simply geography. It was recognition, the return to a ground that did not just belong to him, but to which he belonged in equal measure.

Sørensen, seated with the same upright posture he had maintained since takeoff, shifted forward just enough to rest his forearms on his knees. His gaze was not fixed on the horizon alone, but on every movement in the air and on the ground — the shadow of a vessel cutting through the water below, the pattern of headlights along the coast roads, the spacing of aircraft lights in the distance. Years of security work had trained him to catalogue without appearing to stare, and even now, on a journey home, the habit was unbroken. To his left, Michael observed this quiet vigilance, recognising it for what it was — the measure of a man who prepared for trouble even when none was expected.

"It looks calmer than when we left," Michael said at last, his voice low enough to be contained in the space between them. Ben's mouth curved in the faintest of acknowledgments. "The city hides its noise well from the air," he replied. "It won't look this calm when we land." Michael let the answer rest, understanding that Ben was not speaking of traffic or weather, but of the lives and obligations that waited beyond the tarmac.

The coastline stretched wider in the window now, the shapes of harbours and breakwaters becoming clearer with each passing second. Ben's eyes moved from one to the next, as though ticking through a mental list, confirming each was as it should be. The hum of the engines was a steady counterpoint to his thoughts, a sound that spoke of control, of a journey measured in deliberate steps rather than rushed leaps. He had been away for weeks, but it felt longer. Every return carried its own weight, and this one bore more than most.

"I take it this isn't just another arrival," Michael said, his pen tapping once against the edge of his notebook. "No," Ben answered, his gaze still forward. "It's reclaiming what's mine. Not for the sake of possession, but for the sake of standing where I'm meant to stand." There was no arrogance in the words, only a certainty that left no room for question.

Sørensen glanced at Ben, catching the edge of the statement with an expression that was almost approval. "It's also about showing you haven't gone soft," he added, the corner of his mouth lifting just enough to make the comment half-teasing, half-truth. Ben let out a quiet breath that might have been a laugh. "Anyone who thinks that can test it for themselves," he said.

The light over Copenhagen was softer than in most cities, as if the air itself conspired to temper the edges. The sea's reflection carried that softness inland, tinting rooftops and spires in a way that could almost make one believe in stillness. But Ben knew better. Beneath that surface calm, the city was in motion, and word of his return would move faster than the aircraft on which he rode.

Michael studied him for a moment before speaking again. "You really feel it, don't you? The city, I mean." Ben turned slightly toward him, his eyes narrowing with quiet amusement. "Feel it? I know it. The pulse changes when you've been away. You can hear it the moment you step off the plane, if you've lived with it long enough."

"That's not something you can fake," Michael said, more to himself than to either of the men. "And it's not something you can explain to someone who hasn't felt it," Ben replied. "They'll think it's poetry or nostalgia. It isn't. It's connection." His tone made it clear that this was not sentimentality, but fact.

The first sweep of the city's outer districts came into view, rows of buildings and streets knitting together in the fading light. Sørensen's attention remained divided between the window and the muted radio chatter filtering through his earpiece, the latter carrying updates from the ground team that would meet them on arrival. His nods were small, his responses quieter still, but they told Ben all he needed to know — the reception was in place, the routes were clear, and no irregularities had been reported.

"You'll have a car waiting?" Michael asked, his curiosity slipping through the professional reserve he'd maintained so far. "Two," Sørensen answered without looking away from the window. "And a third that no one will see unless it's needed." Michael nodded slowly, storing the detail away without writing it down.

The Royal Jet began its final banking turn, the sea now on one side and the lights of the city stretching wide on the other. Ben leaned back in his seat, his posture one of a man ready to rise the moment the wheels touched down. Michael glanced at him again, seeing in that stillness the same readiness he had observed earlier between him and Sørensen — an ease with the unknown, not because it lacked danger, but because they had already calculated its shape.

The city grew larger in the windows, the details sharpening until individual buildings stood out. Ben's gaze held steady, not searching for any one thing, but taking in the whole. This was not just an approach. It was a statement. His return was not something he announced, but it would be known all the same.

As the landing gear extended with a muted shudder, the hum of the engines deepened, carrying with it the inevitability of arrival. The tarmac lights below glowed like a runway of stars pulled down to earth, guiding them in without fanfare. For Ben, the moment the wheels would meet the ground was already alive in his mind — the shift from flight to presence, from being away to being exactly where he was meant to be.

The approach to Rosenshavn Castle was neither marked by sirens nor the rigid stance of ceremonial guards. Instead, the road that wound toward the great iron gates felt more like a lane leading home than an entry to royal grounds. The hedgerows on either side were green and full, the kind that seemed to grow more confidently in the presence of long summers and familiar footsteps. The air was scented faintly with the salt from the nearby sea, mixing with the smell of damp earth after rain. Ben sat back, eyes taking in the view through the car window, not with the detachment of a man returning to duty, but with the quiet recognition of someone coming back to his rightful place.

The gates themselves stood open, their weight held easily by the hinges as though they had been waiting all this time. No lined-up guards in crisp uniforms filled the view; instead, the first figures to appear were neighbours — men and women whose coats were buttoned against the wind, faces breaking into genuine smiles as the car rolled closer. One man raised his hand in a slow wave, his expression carrying no formality, only the welcome reserved for someone long considered one of their own. It was this, more than any title or possession, that grounded Ben in the moment.

Clusters of children stood just beyond the gates, their soccer balls tucked under arms or balanced against their hips. They had the restless energy of those who had been counting the days until they could resume their games on the castle lawn, certain now that the time had come. One boy nudged another with his elbow, pointing toward the car, his grin so wide it seemed to threaten the corners of his face. A girl in a thick scarf stamped her feet against the cold, clearly torn between holding her ground and racing forward to greet the returning figure.

Sørensen's eyes scanned the gathered faces, but there was no edge to his scrutiny. Here, the familiar outweighed the unpredictable, and even his protective instincts seemed to soften in the presence of so much ordinary warmth. "Same as we left it," he said quietly, his voice pitched so that only Ben could hear. Ben's mouth lifted at one corner. "Better," he replied. "They've been waiting."

Michael, seated behind them, leaned slightly toward the window, his notebook forgotten in his lap. "They know you," he said, his tone carrying both observation and curiosity. "They know who you are to them," Ben corrected. "That's not the same thing as knowing a king. They've lived with me, not beneath me." Michael nodded slowly, considering the difference.

The car eased through the gates at a crawl, the tyres crunching lightly over the gravel. Children stepped aside just far enough to let them pass, their faces pressed to the glass as though trying to catch every detail. One boy called out, "Are we playing tonight?" and his friends broke into laughter. Ben leaned slightly toward the window, lifting his hand in a casual wave. "If you're ready," he called back, his voice carrying easily through the narrow gap Sørensen had rolled down.

The courtyard stretched out ahead, framed by the castle's familiar stone walls and tall windows glowing with warm light. The castle did not stand like a fortress in this moment; it opened itself in welcome, its doors already ajar, the faint sounds of movement within spilling into the air. Ben could see figures passing in the entrance hall, some already making their way toward the steps, their pace quickening at the sight of the car.

"This is not what I expected," Michael admitted, his eyes still fixed on the scene beyond the glass. "I thought there would be more ceremony." Sørensen gave a short laugh. "That's because you're used to people who need it. Here, we don't put on a show for someone who's been part of the table for years." Michael looked at Ben with a small smile. "You've built something different here." Ben shook his head lightly. "No, we've kept it different."

The car came to a gentle stop before the main steps, the engine idling low. Ben stepped out first, the cold air meeting him with the same bracing sharpness it always had. Before his feet had reached the second step, a group of the children had closed in, their voices overlapping in greetings and hurried questions. "Did you bring anything back?" "When are we playing?" "Is Michael going to play too?" Michael blinked at the sudden shift of attention toward him. "I suppose that depends on the rules," he said, drawing a chorus of grins.

Sørensen lingered a step behind, his hands in his coat pockets, watching as neighbours and children alike moved in close without hesitation. There was no need for distance here, no sense of separation between the castle's residents and those who lived beyond its walls. The stone steps, worn smooth over years, had held the same gatherings in every season — in summer for long, slow evenings of laughter, and in winter for quick conversations before retreating inside.

A woman from the village stepped forward, her scarf wound high around her chin, and clasped Ben's hand in both of hers. "Good to have you back," she said warmly. Ben nodded, his grip firm but not lingering. "Good to be back." There was no exchange of titles, no bow or curtsey. Just the words of neighbours who knew the worth of presence over presentation.

As the children darted toward the side lawn, soccer balls bouncing against the ground, Ben caught Michael watching them with interest. "They're going to invite you into that game whether you like it or not," Ben said. Michael chuckled. "Then I'll just have to like it." Sørensen raised an eyebrow. "You say that now. Wait until the first tackle."

The doors to the castle stood open now, the light from within spilling across the gravel like a path. Ben glanced toward them only briefly before turning back to the gathering outside. This was part of the arrival, too — not stepping straight inside, but standing in the cold long enough to exchange a few words, to hear the latest small news from those who had kept watch in his absence.

The evening air seemed to hold the sounds more clearly — the laughter of children on the lawn, the low murmur of neighbours catching up with one another, the faint creak of the castle's old hinges when the wind caught the door. For all the weight of titles and obligations, this was the truest form of welcome Ben knew. No ceremony. No staged photographs. Just the shared understanding that he was back, and that was enough.

When at last they turned toward the doors, Sørensen cast one last glance over his shoulder, not out of caution but out of habit. The gates stood as they had when they arrived — open, unguarded, a picture of trust that belonged to this place alone. And as the castle closed around them, the sounds of the courtyard faded, replaced by the warmth of home.

The great doors closed behind Ben with the softened thud of well-oiled hinges, shutting out the night air and the faint chatter still drifting from the courtyard. Warmth wrapped around him instantly, the kind that had nothing to do with the steady hum of the castle's heating and everything to do with the life within its walls. The air carried the gentle scent of fresh linens and something faintly sweet — perhaps tea cooling on a nearby table — but it was the sight before him that claimed his focus entirely. Isla stood in the centre of the hall, framed by the muted gold of lamplight, one of the twins resting against her shoulder in quiet contentment. The other lay in a bassinet close by, the curve of their small cheek rising and falling with the rhythm of sleep.

For a moment, Ben simply looked at her. It was not hesitation but the gathering of memory, the mental stitching together of all the days that had passed without this sight. Isla's smile was steady, unforced, carrying none of the tension he had feared to find in her. She met his eyes without urgency, her expression saying more than any rush of words could — that all had been managed, that no burden had bent her, that the household and the heart of it had stood unshaken.

When he crossed the remaining steps to her, his hands went to her shoulders first, not in formality but in silent greeting, the pressure of his fingers communicating the relief that refused to be spoken. She shifted the child slightly so that his arms could encircle both of them, and in that instant, the world beyond the castle's walls receded entirely. The embrace was unhurried, without the awkward stiffness of someone mindful of an audience, and heavy with the quiet weight of separation brought to its end.

Ben felt the dampness gather in his eyes before he even realised the tears had formed. It was not grief or exhaustion but the sudden release of a strain he had carried since the day he left. The moment the first tear slipped free, Isla's thumb brushed it away, her other hand still supporting the tiny figure between them. "You're here now," she said softly, not as reassurance but as a fact that needed no embellishment. He nodded, his throat tightening against any answer.

He kissed her then, without counting the seconds or measuring the moment. It was the kiss of two people for whom time had been an enemy and was now, for a brief stretch, a friend again. When they parted, it was only enough to allow their eyes to meet. Hers held that unshaken steadiness, but he saw the flicker of emotion there too — the relief, the welcome, the shared understanding that nothing else in the day mattered as much as this reunion.

Sørensen, still near the doorway, remained silent but watchful, the hint of a smile tugging at one corner of his mouth. He knew better than to intrude, yet his presence carried its own warmth, a quiet reminder that family was not measured solely in bloodlines. He inclined his head slightly when Ben glanced his way, an unspoken exchange that all was as it should be.

Michael, standing a step behind, had the sense to remain in the periphery, his notebook held loosely at his side. He made no move to write, understanding that some moments did not belong to ink until much later. Instead, he allowed himself the role of observer, quietly noting the absence of spectacle in what was, by any measure, a deeply significant homecoming.

The baby in Isla's arms stirred slightly, a small sound escaping before settling again into the curve of her shoulder. Ben reached to stroke the child's back, his palm moving with the careful touch of someone conscious of how new life demanded gentleness. His other hand found Isla's again, their fingers locking with the ease of a bond that had weathered far more than distance.

Across the hall, the soft creak of the bassinet signalled the other twin's wakefulness. Isla shifted, guiding Ben toward it. He knelt without hesitation, resting his forearms on the edge and gazing down at the tiny features framed by the blanket. "Hello there," he murmured, his voice quieter than the room required, as if instinct itself demanded that kind of reverence. The child's eyes fluttered open briefly, unfocused but searching, before closing again in the trust of sleep.

When Ben stood again, Isla's hand lingered against his chest for a moment longer than necessary. "They've grown," he said simply, the words carrying more awe than surprise. "Every day," she replied, her voice warmed with the quiet pride of a mother who had kept watch in his absence. "And they've been waiting for you."

He looked at her then, truly seeing the measure of what she had carried — not just the children, but the endless cadence of the household, the constancy of a queen whose reign was measured not in decrees but in steadfast care. "You've done more than I could have asked," he said, his voice thick. She shook her head lightly. "I've done what we both promised. We hold this place together."

The sound of distant laughter from the corridor beyond reminded them that the castle did not pause for reunions, however significant. Life here was built on the intertwining of moments — solemn and light-hearted, private and shared. But for now, the bustle could wait at the edges while they reclaimed this space between them.

Ben brushed one last kiss against her temple, then turned his attention back to the child in her arms. "You've kept them safe," he said, though it was as much a statement to himself as to her. Isla smiled again, her eyes glistening now too. "We've all kept each other safe."

In the glow of that hall, with the soft sounds of the twins' breathing and the unspoken comfort of being in each other's reach again, the walls of Rosenshavn felt less like stone and more like shelter. And for the first time in weeks, Ben let the weight slip fully from his shoulders, content to stand exactly where he was.

The room was warm in a way that had nothing to do with the fire in the hearth. It was the kind of warmth that came from familiar sounds — the soft creak of a rocking chair, the muffled cooing of a child, the quiet shifting of blankets that had been folded and unfolded a dozen times today. Ben stepped into that space with measured steps, though his pace betrayed the pull in his chest. The bassinet stood just ahead, draped with the soft weave Isla favoured, the pale fabric catching the lamplight. Two small bundles lay within, each with their own slow rhythm of breathing, each existing in their own small, perfect world.

He had seen them before, of course. At birth, he had held them for the first time with the mixture of awe and disbelief that only comes once. But this moment was different. This was not the sterile light of the delivery room or the hurried introductions that follow. This was home. This was the place where days had passed without him, where their lives had begun to weave into the life of the household in ways he had missed. He felt the absence in that realisation, but it was softened by the fact that he was here now, standing close enough to touch.

Isla moved aside slightly, reading the thought in his eyes before he could voice it. She lifted the first twin with practiced care, the tiny body curling instinctively toward her warmth, then toward his. He took the child as if the motion had been rehearsed for years, his arms adjusting without thought, his hands fitting into the shape of the task as if they had always known it. The small head nestled under his chin, and he could feel the faint hum of breath against his chest.

It was not a grand gesture, not a reunion meant for watching eyes. The twins were too young to know the difference between hours and days, between presence and absence, yet something in the way their fingers flexed against his coat seemed to mark the moment all the same. He inhaled, and with it came the faint, comforting scent of home — not just soap and fabric, but the scent of the place and the people who had kept it for him.

The second twin was still dozing, though Isla shifted them gently so he could reach. Ben brushed his fingers along the small hand that had worked its way free of the blanket, marvelling at how the grip closed almost immediately around his index finger. It was a grasp without awareness, yet it carried a kind of trust that made his chest tighten. He thought of all the decisions, all the steps taken and avoided, that had been made for the sake of preserving that trust.

He sat down then, still holding the first twin, his posture instinctively protective. Isla passed the second to him once they stirred, and soon both were resting in the crook of each arm. The weight was light, yet it anchored him more than anything else could have. He studied their features — the small shifts of expression, the slow blink of unfocused eyes, the way their breathing fell into an unintentional harmony. Every detail was a reminder that life had gone on here, quietly and steadily, while he was away.

Sørensen lingered in the doorway, leaning slightly against the frame. He said nothing, but the softening in his eyes betrayed a rare tenderness. He had guarded Ben for years, had stood in the way of threats, had planned for outcomes others could not imagine. Yet even he understood that this moment was one no shield or strategy could provide.

Michael, too, remained on the edge of the scene, his hands still, his notebook forgotten. There would be time enough to record the political weight of Ben's return, the undercurrents of the family's position, the stories that would travel beyond the castle walls. But this, he seemed to know instinctively, was not a story for the world. This was for the family alone.

The twins shifted in his arms, one sighing softly, the other making a small sound of protest before settling again. Ben rocked them gently, his movements unhurried, content to let the world narrow to the space between his arms. The conversations of the day, the plans yet to be made, even the unease that had trailed him home — all of it receded into a distant hum.

He looked up at Isla, who watched from the side with a smile that was both proud and knowing. "They've grown," he said quietly, echoing the words from earlier but with a different weight now that he could feel it in the steadiness of their limbs, in the way they fit against him. She nodded, her eyes bright. "Every day. And they've been waiting for you."

He lowered his head slightly, brushing his lips against the soft hair of the child closest to him. The gesture was instinctive, a seal on a promise he had made long before their birth. When he finally looked up again, the room seemed somehow smaller, not in size but in focus, the walls drawn close around the four of them as if to hold the moment in place.

Even the faint sounds from elsewhere in the castle — the distant clink of dishes being set, the muffled chatter of children in another room — seemed to fall away. For now, this was the centre of the world, and Ben let himself believe, if only for these minutes, that nothing could intrude.

He shifted the twins slightly, mindful of their comfort, and glanced once more at Isla. "We'll keep them safe," he said, not as a plan but as an unbreakable fact. She reached out, her fingers brushing his before resting lightly on one of the children. "We already are," she replied.

And in that warm, lamplit space, with the quiet rhythm of their breathing filling the room, Ben allowed the weight of his absence to be replaced by the solidity of his presence. Whatever came next, whatever waited outside these walls, could remain there for now. Here, in this moment, he was exactly where he was meant to be.

The dining room at Rosenshavn Castle glowed under the soft light of its chandeliers, the long oak table set without pretension. There were no place cards, no stiff arrangements that separated one from another — only chairs filled as people wandered in, each carrying their own laughter, their own threads of conversation from other rooms. Michael took his seat without ceremony, noting the ease with which the household moved from one topic to the next, the rhythm of a place where formality was not an obligation. Plates were passed, hands reached across the table without hesitation, and the air was warm with the smell of roasted meat, fresh bread, and the faint sweetness of something baking in the kitchen.

Ben sat midway down the table, leaning back slightly in his chair, his gaze alternating between Isla beside him and the children scattered along the benches. He did not preside over the meal in the manner of a king — there was no tapping of glasses for silence, no grand address. Instead, he was part of the conversation, one voice among many, sometimes teasing, sometimes listening, always attentive. Michael watched how easily people addressed him by name, without hesitation or pause, as though "Ben" was the only title worth using here.

Sørensen, seated opposite Michael, was a steady presence. His eyes scanned the room with habitual awareness, yet there was a softness to his expression that matched the laughter in the air. Every so often, he would lean toward the children nearest to him, responding to a question or chuckling at a whispered joke. He did not interrupt their flow, nor did he correct their exaggerations — he let them talk, knowing that in this house, their voices were part of the music of the evening.

Michael kept his notepad near his plate but used it sparingly. This was not the moment to collect sharp quotes or weave narrative hooks; this was a moment to absorb. He understood instinctively that what made this place remarkable could not be caught in a single sentence. It was in the way someone poured another's drink without being asked, in the way the younger children leaned on the older ones without a word, in the way laughter seemed to ripple rather than burst, spreading naturally from one end of the table to the other.

The talk moved easily between practical matters — the schedule for the next day, the arrival of a delivery for the kitchen — and the absurdities that kept the household from ever becoming too serious. Someone mentioned the infamous "Thunder-Fart" games, earning groans from the older children and grins from the younger. A few seats down, a mock argument began about who was responsible for a particularly memorable "Diaper Bomb" incident last month, and though the details were not for delicate ears, the laughter that followed was enough to make Michael smile into his glass.

Every so often, Ben would glance toward Michael, as if to say, This is what I meant. He had spoken on the jet about the truth of this place, about its refusal to conform to the expectations of royal life. Now, Michael saw it for himself — not through staged introductions or curated moments, but in the unpolished reality of an ordinary meal. Here, rank was irrelevant, and affection was the only measure that mattered.

Even the twins made their presence known, though they remained in their bassinets at the far end of the room under Isla's watchful eye. From time to time, someone would rise to check on them, returning with a whispered report or a gentle laugh at a half-awake expression. It was clear to Michael that no one here saw them as burdens to be managed — they were simply part of the life of the table, included without question.

The meal stretched on, not because the courses were elaborate, but because no one seemed eager to leave. Stories were exchanged in overlapping threads — tales of misadventures on the football field, kitchen experiments gone wrong, and the occasional retelling of moments so ridiculous that even the reteller could barely get through them without laughing. The air was thick with the kind of warmth that could not be manufactured, and Michael knew it was this feeling, more than any event or headline, that would define his time here.

By the time plates were cleared, the room had taken on the quiet hum of contentment. Some moved to the sitting room, others to the kitchens to help tidy up. A few children lingered at the table, heads propped on their arms, fighting the pull of sleep. Michael remained where he was for a moment longer, letting the rhythm of the household sink in.

It occurred to him that much of what he had witnessed tonight would never appear in print. He could describe the food, the laughter, the relaxed conversations, but those were only the surface. The truth was deeper — a truth built on years of trust, of shared history, of people who knew each other's flaws as well as their strengths and chose to stay anyway. That was not the kind of thing that could be captured in a headline.

Ben passed him on the way to check on the twins, pausing to place a hand on his shoulder. It was a small gesture, but it carried weight — a silent acknowledgement that Michael understood more now than he had that afternoon. Michael nodded, returning the look without words. He had come here to write the truth, and tonight, he had begun to find it.

When he finally rose from the table, the room was nearly empty. The fire had burned low, casting soft shadows along the stone walls. Michael glanced at his notepad, still open beside his plate, and wrote only one line before closing it again: Warmth outweighs title. It was not much, but it was enough for now.

Ken's study was lit only by the desk lamp, its soft glow pooling over the neat stack of correspondence beside his right hand. The scent of old leather and polished oak lingered in the air, a quiet reminder that this was a room where decisions were made without spectacle. Michael stood across from him, notes in hand, his outline prepared with the precision of someone who understood the stakes. He did not pitch it like a journalist in search of an angle, nor like a courtier seeking favour. Instead, he spoke plainly — a story of truth, drawn from what he had seen, with no intent to embellish or wound.

Ken listened without interruption, his gaze steady, his posture relaxed but unreadable. Now and then, he shifted in his chair, not out of impatience but in the way of a man who had learned to read more from tone than from words. Michael's account was structured without flourish, shaped by the understanding that this house did not need defending so much as it needed representing with accuracy. There was no eagerness in his delivery, no attempt to oversell. He simply laid out the bones of the work: portraits of family life as it truly unfolded, moments both dignified and unguarded, the kind of truths that lived between public record and private memory.

When Michael finished, the silence that followed was measured, not awkward. Ken leaned back in his chair, hands folded loosely in his lap, eyes narrowing slightly in consideration. He let the weight of the words settle, as if testing them for balance. The faint ticking of the mantel clock was the only sound between them. At last, he drew a breath, leaning forward so that the lamplight caught the edge of his expression — not stern, not indulgent, but deliberate. He gave a single nod, small yet absolute, the kind of gesture that carried both approval and command.

"This will be shared with the family first," Ken said at last, his voice even, the tone leaving no room for misunderstanding. "Every word, every page, before the press sees a single line." It was not a request, but it was not a challenge either. It was a condition — one rooted not in distrust, but in the firm belief that the truth, once spoken, belonged to those who lived it before it could be released to those who merely read it.

Michael met the gaze without hesitation, giving a slight nod of his own. "Agreed," he replied simply. There was no need for negotiation; the boundary was fair and, in his view, necessary. He understood that trust, once broken in a place like this, could never be fully restored. This was not the kind of access one could regain through apologies or corrections.

Ken reached for a glass of water on his desk, taking a slow sip before setting it down again. "Then you'll have what you need," he said, and though his voice was calm, there was a finality to the words. He did not speak of credentials or permissions. Approval had been given — and that, in this household, was the only clearance that mattered.

Michael tucked his notes back into his folder, not with the air of someone retreating from a challenge, but with the satisfaction of a man whose work had been set on solid ground. He had come into this room knowing that Ken's judgement would be exacting. Now, leaving it, he carried not only approval but the weight of the responsibility that came with it. The story was his to tell — but only because it had been entrusted to him.

He stepped into the corridor outside, the muted sounds of the household filtering in from the far end of the hall. Somewhere, laughter rose briefly before fading into the softer tones of evening conversation. Michael paused, glancing back toward the study door now closed behind him. The agreement was simple, yet in its simplicity lay the unspoken promise that the truth he would write would belong to them first. And that was precisely how it should be.

The sound travelled differently here, not in the jarring bursts of cameras or the press of strangers, but in the steady undercurrent of familiarity. Word of Ben's return had already drifted ahead of him, carried along the winding streets of Copenhagen like a warm breeze that needed no formal announcement. It moved through bakeries and corner shops, between neighbours passing on bicycles, in the voices of parents leaning down to whisper something into their children's ears. It was not a spectacle; it was the quiet hum of recognition that reached people before the gates were even in sight.

As they drew closer to the heart of the city, Sørensen glanced out the window, his sharp eyes catching the way faces shifted when they recognised the man beside him. It was never loud — never the pointed glare of curiosity — but instead the unmistakable change that came when a familiar figure returned. Hands lifted in casual waves, not as subjects greeting a king, but as friends acknowledging someone they had missed. It was, Ben thought, the kind of reception that could never be staged because it grew only from years of genuine presence.

Children, with footballs tucked under their arms and hair wild from play, called out his name between bursts of laughter. Some ran alongside the car for a few steps, their feet slapping the cobblestones in uneven rhythm before darting back to their games. There was no formal line of greeters here, no choreography of flags and speeches. Instead, there was life continuing exactly as it had before — only now with the subtle brightness that came from seeing someone they cared for returned to his rightful place.

Ben watched from his seat, not leaning forward to wave, not breaking the moment by forcing his presence into it. He understood the value of letting it exist as it was — a natural, unforced welcome. The city did not need him to make a grand show of acknowledgment; it only needed him to be here. That was enough. The cobblestones rolled beneath them, the street narrowing in the familiar way it did near the older quarters, where every window held a story and every door had once been passed through in friendship.

Michael Dern sat quietly, taking it all in, his pen unmoving for the moment. He had expected more distance between royalty and the public, some invisible line that would keep them apart. But here, he saw no such thing. The greetings were not rehearsed, and the people did not bow. They grinned. They shouted jokes across the street. They called for him the same way they would call for a neighbour's son who had been away too long. Michael realised this was the sort of truth that would dismantle the most stubborn misconceptions — and it needed no embellishment.

Sørensen, still scanning the walkways out of long habit, caught sight of a shopkeeper stepping outside with a loaf of bread under one arm and a small cloth bag in the other. The man raised the bag in Ben's direction, a wordless gift, and then simply set it on the shop bench without approaching. Sørensen noted the gesture but said nothing. This was not the first time Ben's return had prompted such quiet offerings — tokens left without ceremony, the kind that spoke more loudly than any speech could.

The hum of conversation followed them the rest of the way, not rising to a roar, but never fading either. It wrapped around the car like a familiar song, one that shifted in tone as they neared the gates of Rosenshavn Castle. There, the neighbours who had been waiting did not crowd forward or demand attention. They stood where they were, greeting him with nods, smiles, and the occasional shouted remark about football games or shared plans for the weekend. It was not the language of subjects to their monarch. It was the language of home.

Ben exhaled slowly, feeling the knot of travel loosen in his chest. This was not about being seen as a ruler or even as a public figure. It was about returning to the space where his presence meant something personal. He let the moment stretch, storing it in memory for the days ahead when the world beyond these walls would inevitably intrude again. But for now, here in the gentle roar without a stage, he belonged — and the city knew it.

It was not spoken as a speech, nor written as a declaration for the public to dissect. Instead, Ben's decision was given in measured words to those whose counsel and loyalty had been proven over the years. He told them plainly that Denmark was enough — that no other throne, no matter how firmly his bloodline entitled him to it, was worth the cost of stretching his reach. The weight of heritage was not a crown to him, but a responsibility, and responsibility meant knowing when to refuse as much as when to accept.

Sørensen, listening from his usual place at Ben's side, understood before the sentence was finished. There had been opportunities before — whispers from foreign courts, discreet letters slipped through diplomatic channels, half-promises of power in places where his family's name had not been spoken aloud in decades. Each offer had carried its own allure, but each had also demanded a price that was not worth paying. Now, Ben was making it clear to all that such offers would find no welcome here.

Michael Dern wrote nothing during this exchange, his pen still beside his notepad. This was not the kind of statement to be taken down like a press quote. It was the foundation of a man's rule, the kind of resolve that could be undone by a careless headline if misrepresented. He simply listened, committing the tone, the certainty, to memory, knowing that when it appeared in his work it would be framed with the precision it deserved.

Ben's refusal was not born of disinterest in his ancestry; it was rooted in the belief that loyalty to one's own people outweighed ambition for more. To rule beyond Denmark would be to scatter the focus that had kept his home safe. He had no intention of leaving his family to the mercy of divided duties. Denmark was where his children would grow, where their names would be spoken with familiarity rather than formality, and where the bonds between ruler and citizen were not strained by distance.

There were, of course, those who bristled at his stance. Allies abroad wondered quietly if his rejection was an insult; rivals muttered that it was fear disguised as contentment. But Ben knew that power without peace was not power at all — it was a trap. He would not trade the stability of his home for the uncertain prestige of foreign crowns.

Sørensen's approval came in the form of silence, the rare kind that carried weight rather than absence. It was the silence of a man who knew that a decision had been made in full awareness of its consequences, and that it would stand. That quiet understanding between them was more binding than any signed agreement.

In the end, Ben's message reached further than the walls of the Castle. It travelled quietly, as such things always did, through the careful conversations of those who had been present when he spoke it. The world beyond might still speculate, but those closest to him now understood that Denmark was not the beginning of a larger conquest. It was the whole of it. And in that choice, there was strength.

The sun was only beginning to tilt westward when the first ball was kicked across the lawn, its spin catching in the short grass before rolling straight into a cluster of waiting feet. There was no whistle, no official signal — the game began the same way it always had, with someone shouting a name and everyone else pretending not to hear until the ball came flying at them.

The older children darted ahead, weaving in and out with nimble steps, while the younger ones ran with all the grace of a collapsing clothesline, arms flailing but faces lit with pure glee. Michael Dern stood to one side, notebook forgotten in his jacket pocket, watching the first few minutes unfold like a story no outsider could have scripted.

Ben was in the thick of it before Michael had even seen him move, his long strides carrying him through the fray with a deliberate ease that spoke of practice. Sørensen stayed close to the edges, not playing but not distant either, the occasional chuckle slipping from him when someone made an especially wild kick. The match had the chaos of a marketplace and the joy of a festival, but there was a rhythm under it — an unspoken understanding of when to push, when to fall back, and when to make space for someone smaller to have their moment. Michael saw it in how Ben eased the ball toward Maria's feet, pretending to fumble so she could score, and in the way Emil leapt forward to block Casper's shot, both boys laughing too hard to care that the ball veered off course.

Then came the first "incident" — the kind that, Michael would later learn, was not just expected but practically celebrated. A particularly excited dash from Lukas ended with a sudden pause, a comical widening of eyes, and a sound that could have been mistaken for a distant motorbike if not for the way the children immediately collapsed in laughter. The ball was abandoned for a moment as Lukas doubled over in mock agony, claiming loudly that his own thunderfart had cost him the winning goal. Ben clapped him on the back with a grin, while Sørensen called out that the wind could have carried the ball over the net if Lukas had timed it better. Michael caught himself laughing too, the sound surprising him with its lack of restraint.

As the match went on, the field became a moving patchwork of small rivalries and temporary alliances. Every missed kick was met with exaggerated groans, every goal with cheers loud enough to draw the attention of a few neighbours who leaned on the gate to watch. There was no scoreboard, but there was memory — players kept track of who had "won" in past matches, and no one forgot the creative reasons offered for losing. A sudden shout from Peter Emil about a "phantom goal" sent half the field into debate, while the other half used the distraction to take the ball and score. Michael noticed that no one truly minded; the rules were more suggestion than law here.

What struck him most was the way even the smallest children had a place in the chaos. Little Maja, barely tall enough to see over the ball, was lifted high by her brother Mathias after she managed to make contact for the first time that day. On the opposite end, Valdemar was fending off two determined attackers with a look of exaggerated concentration, his hair sticking up like he'd just rolled out of bed. The sheer inclusivity of it — the way every age and skill level was folded into the same game — felt like a statement in itself.

Michael made a mental note, though he didn't pull out his pen just yet. This wasn't the kind of scene you could record in fragments; it had to be absorbed whole, with the sounds, the smells, the weight of the laughter. He could see now why Ben had insisted he write the truth about this family. It wasn't in the titles or the history books — it was here, in a lawn game named for an unapologetic bodily function, played without self-consciousness in the shadow of a royal castle.

When the final kick sent the ball skidding toward the hedge, there was no official end called, only the gradual dispersing of players toward the water table, where pitchers of juice and stacks of mismatched cups waited. Shirts were grass-stained, knees were dusty, and no one seemed to care. Ben's hair was damp from the effort, his smile easy and unguarded. Sørensen finally stepped forward to join the group, handing Lukas a towel and muttering something that made the boy burst into fresh laughter. Michael stood a little apart, committing the picture to memory before he ever let his pen touch the page.

The night air had taken on a slight chill by the time everyone gathered in the main lounge, the fire in the hearth throwing a soft amber glow across the circle of chairs and sofas. Ben had shed the last trace of formality, his sleeves rolled, his posture loose, ready for the evening's particular tradition — the Roasting Games. It was a Castle ritual known to unsettle the uninitiated, though never out of cruelty. The aim was precision, not meanness, and those who could land a line that made everyone laugh without wounding pride were considered masters of the art. Michael Dern sat on the edge of his seat, notebook closed, having been told firmly by Sørensen that "if you're scribbling, you're not playing."

The first volley came from Maria, whose innocent expression disguised a wit far sharper than her years. "Casper," she began sweetly, "you run like you're still holding the football from earlier, afraid someone will take it away." Casper, grinning, leaned back and replied without pause, "And you laugh like you're trying to convince us you understood the joke." The room erupted, and the circle tightened as everyone realised the game had begun in earnest. Michael noted the lack of hesitation; no one here paused to check if their words would be taken wrong — trust was the currency, and it was plentiful.

Ben was drawn into the fray by Emil, who fixed his gaze on the King with exaggerated seriousness. "Uncle Ben," Emil said, "for a man who says he doesn't like losing, you sure did let me score this afternoon." Ben's eyes narrowed playfully. "That wasn't charity, Emil. That was strategy — I wanted to see if you'd trip over your own victory dance." Even Sørensen chuckled at that, shaking his head as Emil pretended to be deeply wounded. The rhythm of the roasts was quick, like a ball passed in rapid succession, and the warmth in the room had less to do with the fire than with the shared history between these people.

When Sørensen's turn came, the children fell silent with a mix of respect and anticipation. He folded his arms, surveying the group as though choosing his target with military precision. "Michael," he said at last, "you've been here two days and haven't yet tried the pickled herring. I'm beginning to think you're not committed." Michael laughed, unoffended. "If commitment means eating something that looks like it swam here on its own, I'm happy to be accused." The exchange earned him a ripple of approval — a guest who could volley back was welcome indeed.

The roasts moved around the circle like a well-rehearsed play. Ava teased Lars about his tendency to "talk like a rule book," only for Lars to counter that Ava "collects shoes the way most people collect excuses." Even the younger children joined in with wide-eyed daring, knowing they'd be met with affection no matter how sharp their attempts. The game had a strange kind of equality; here, titles dissolved, ages blurred, and quick thinking was the only crown that mattered.

Michael found himself targeted more than once, each remark testing his readiness. Ben suggested he "writes slower than Sørensen checks a perimeter," while Clara observed that "for a journalist, he's very quiet — maybe he's saving all his words for an article that will get him banished." Michael returned each jab with ease, surprising himself at how quickly he'd fallen into the rhythm. "Banished?" he said to Clara. "If I survive another night of your tea, I'll have earned citizenship." The laughter that followed felt like acceptance.

By the time the fire had burned down to a steady bed of coals, the roasts had grown gentler, more wrapped in shared jokes than pointed barbs. Some players leaned back, content to watch rather than participate, while others seemed energised by the chance to squeeze in one last remark before the night closed. Michael, sipping from a mug of something warm and spiced, realised that what he had witnessed wasn't simply a game — it was a measure of belonging. Here, you didn't get roasted unless you were one of them.

The corridors of Rosenshavn were hushed now, their familiar creaks and sighs softened under the weight of the late hour. Most of the household had long since retired, the last embers in the main lounge smouldering behind the closed doors. Ben walked the length of the hall with the slow, unhurried step of a man who knew every inch of it without needing light. Sørensen was already in the smaller study, a lamp casting a warm circle on the polished table between two armchairs. The air carried the scent of oak and the faint tang of the drink waiting beside each seat. This was their place — not claimed by title or ceremony, but by habit.

Ben sank into the chair opposite him, loosening his shoulders as the glass was placed within reach. The first sip carried the quiet comfort of familiarity, that deep burn followed by a softness that coaxed the muscles into ease. For a moment, they didn't speak. It wasn't necessary; the silence between them was never empty. Sørensen's gaze was steady, the sort of look that took in every detail without revealing what he kept. Ben mirrored it, the two of them settling into the old rhythm that had been forged in operations where a single glance had been enough to communicate what needed to be done.

"You read the terrain before you even stepped off that plane," Sørensen said at last, his tone more observation than compliment. Ben gave a slight nod. "It's the same ground, Sørensen, but the winds feel different. I can't quite decide if that's me or the air itself." The older man leaned back, swirling his drink, considering this without rushing to answer. "Both," he said finally. "The city knows you're back. And you — you know you can't stay away forever, no matter what the distance buys you."

They spoke then of the journey, tracing its steps not as a timeline but as a series of moments where instinct had ruled over plan. The boarding of the Royal Jet, the quiet exchange of glances, the way Michael Dern had settled in without needing to be told the rules. Each part had been carried out with precision, but now, in this stillness, they could acknowledge the weight of it without the armour they wore in motion. Ben found himself smiling at the thought of Michael trying to keep pace with the children's games — both the football and the roasts — and Sørensen's mouth twitched in the way it always did when amusement was tucked behind restraint.

The conversation turned to old operations, the kind that were never written down but lived in the muscle memory of those who had walked them together. They recalled the night in Aarhus when the route had changed mid-step, forcing them into an alley neither had scouted, and the time in Odense when a distraction of exactly four minutes had made the difference between success and discovery. Ben spoke of these with the ease of a man remembering a shared language, and Sørensen listened, occasionally adding a detail that shifted the whole picture in retrospect.

But even in the warmth of the drink and the comfort of the room, Sørensen's edge never dulled. "Vigilance never sleeps, Ben," he said, the words quiet but firm. "You can let it rest tonight, but only tonight. Tomorrow, the air will carry news, and you'll need to decide what to do with it." Ben accepted this without protest, knowing it was not a warning but a truth. In the years they had known each other, such truths had been offered sparingly and always without room for argument.

They fell into a companionable quiet, the kind where the clock's measured ticking seemed to underscore rather than interrupt. Ben traced the rim of his glass with one finger, thinking not of the weight of leadership but of the steadiness of the man across from him. In Sørensen's presence, he was never just a King, never just a man with decisions pressing in on all sides. He was simply Ben, the younger friend who had once made the old soldier laugh in spite of himself.

It was Sørensen who broke the silence again, his voice lighter now. "You softened me, you know. I wasn't always this pleasant." Ben's laugh was quiet but full. "Pleasant is stretching it. But I'll take credit for you being less of a bulldog." Sørensen grunted, the corner of his mouth turning upward. "You're still the only one who ever got away with calling me that."

The night deepened around them, the lamp's glow the only defiance against the shadows gathering at the edges of the room. They spoke of the family — of Isla's quiet strength, of the children's unshakable bond, of the way the Castle seemed to hold them all in a kind of living embrace. Sørensen's tone softened when he mentioned Maria and Emil, and Ben recognised in it the same depth he felt for Casper. Family, for both of them, had been built as much by choice as by blood.

Ben finished his drink and set the glass down with care, the weight of the day easing fully from his shoulders. "Tomorrow will be its own storm," he said, more to the fire than to his companion. "But tonight — tonight is ours." Sørensen inclined his head, the gesture both agreement and benediction. No more words were needed.

When Ben finally rose to leave, the older man did not stand but watched him go with the steady eyes of a guard who was also, unshakably, a friend. The kind of friend who knew when to let the watch rest, if only for a few hours. The door closed softly behind him, leaving the study in its pool of quiet light, the echo of their conversation lingering like the last warmth of the glass in Ben's hand.

The lamps in the hallway cast a soft spill of light that reached just far enough to mark the edges of the window alcove where Ben stood. The glass beneath his fingertips was cool, holding the faint vibration of wind that moved along the outer walls. Beyond it, the grounds stretched into the night, silvered in places where the moon caught the frost-tipped grass. It was late, but not the sort of late that urged sleep. This was the hour where stillness carried its own weight — a measured pause between the day that had ended and the one that had yet to begin.

He rested one hand against the wooden frame, the familiar grain worn smooth from years of such moments. No strategy occupied his mind, no quiet tally of who had moved where or what message had been sent. The silence outside was matched by the quiet within, as though the walls themselves understood that this night belonged to rest. His breath fogged faintly on the pane, vanishing almost as soon as it appeared, as though even the air was careful not to disturb him.

From here, the castle grounds took on their own rhythm. The distant treeline shifted gently under the push of the wind, and the gravel paths reflected thin ribbons of light from the wall lamps. Somewhere near the far gate, a watchman's slow patrol could be guessed at by the faint crunch of boots on stone. Ben's eyes followed the invisible path of that sound until it faded again into the dark. Every detail spoke of order without tension — a place secure not because it was guarded, but because it was loved.

The study behind him was dim but warm, the fire reduced to a slow pulse of embers. It had been hours since his conversation with Sørensen, yet the weight of that talk still lingered in the edges of his thoughts. He could still hear the low cadence of the older man's voice, steady as the man himself, reminding him that vigilance might rest for a night but would always return with the morning. There was comfort in that truth, just as there was comfort in the knowledge that his family slept safely under this roof.

He leaned his shoulder lightly against the frame, eyes still fixed on the sweep of the lawns. From here, the stone benches near the south wall were just visible, pale against the shadowed hedges. In daylight, that space would be loud with children's games and easy laughter, but now it was still, claimed only by the night air. The thought drew a faint smile to his mouth, not the kind shown in public but the one reserved for these private recollections.

The twins were asleep upstairs, their breaths rising and falling in rhythm no one could measure except a parent who had been away too long. He had held them earlier, felt the weight of them settle into his arms with the ease of belonging. Now, as he stood here, he thought of their faces — one already frowning in dreams, the other with that faint half-smile that seemed to run in the family. This, he thought, was the truest measure of return. Not the crossing of borders or the recognition of neighbours, but the simple knowledge of where the people you love are when night falls.

The quiet was occasionally broken by the muted creak of old timbers, sounds he knew so well they barely registered as sound at all. A faint draft found its way along the floor, and he shifted slightly, drawing the edges of the curtain just enough to soften it. The fabric moved against his fingers, heavy and worn in a way that spoke of years, not months. In this house, nothing was merely kept — it was kept until it carried memory in its very weight.

A fox crossed the farthest edge of the lawn, its movement fluid and unhurried, a streak of pale fur barely visible against the shadows. Ben followed its path until it disappeared near the garden wall, and the quiet resumed. It felt right that even the wildlife here moved with a sense of belonging. No one and nothing in this place was hurried unless they chose to be.

His thoughts wandered briefly to Michael Dern, likely in his guest room now, making the kind of notes that could only be written while memory was still warm. Ben knew there would be a truth in those pages that no staged audience or public statement could ever match. The journalist would see the cracks and the colour, the unvarnished heart of the place — and that was exactly what Ben wanted the world to understand.

The window glass reflected him faintly now, catching the outline of his face, the set of his shoulders. He studied the shape without judgement, as though meeting his own gaze across a distance. Here, there was no crown, no staging, no distance between what he carried inside and what was seen. In this quiet, he was simply Ben — son, husband, father, friend. That was enough.

He exhaled slowly, letting his shoulders drop the last fraction they held from habit. The night outside did not demand anything of him, and the room behind him did not press for his return. This moment, suspended between the two, was its own kind of peace. He thought of it as a bookmark — not the end of a chapter, but a marked place he could return to when the next storm inevitably rose.

The moon had shifted slightly, its light brushing the nearer trees with a colder silver. Time was passing, though it did not feel as though it was slipping away. It was simply moving in step with him, willing to hold pace rather than rush ahead. That, he thought, was the gift of nights like this — they asked nothing and gave quietly in return.

Eventually, he stepped back from the window, not because the moment had ended but because it was time to let it rest. The curtain fell into place with a soft sigh, the kind only old fabric makes. He took one last look at the line where the grounds met the dark, and then turned toward the steady warmth of the room.

Crossing the floor, his hand brushed the back of the armchair by the fire. The embers glowed faintly, enough to hint at heat but not enough to reach the air. Tomorrow, the fire would be built fresh, the day would begin with its own demands, and he would meet them. But tonight, this was enough — to stand, to breathe, to be home without needing to hold the weight of anything more.

He left the study with the same measured pace he had carried in, closing the door with a soft click. The hallway waited, quiet and empty, and as he walked toward his room, the silence walked with him. In the privacy of that walk, the truth was simple: he was home, and for now, that was enough.

CHAPTER 16: THE FINAL HEIRS

Ben stood in the Castle's private nursery, the lamplight falling in a golden spill across the soft wool blanket that cradled Hannah in the crook of his left arm. She was asleep, her breath no louder than the whisper of curtains at a half-opened window. Frederick, settled in his right, blinked at the light with the slow, deliberate gaze of a newborn learning to map the world. Their warmth pressed through his shirt, a steady reminder that nothing in his life, not even the titles he carried, was heavier than the small, living weight of these two. They were impossibly small and yet impossibly vast — heirs not to one name, but to all that came before it, the sort of legacy that could fill rooms long after a voice was gone.

The names had been chosen with care that went far beyond sentiment. Ben had carried them in his mind for months, weighing each syllable like a craftsman testing the balance of a blade. Hannah — not simply a sweet sound, but a thread to the women in his family whose quiet strength had kept history intact. Frederick — a nod to kingship without the crown's parade, chosen because it would anchor the boy in the same truth Ben had clung to: that real power lay in the doing, not the showing. He had learned the lesson young, and now, standing here, he was passing it on before either child could walk or speak.

From the window seat, Isla watched him. Her hair was pulled back, not out of vanity but so nothing would shadow her eyes, eyes sharp enough to see the flicker of thought crossing his face even when his mouth said nothing. She knew him well enough to read the language of his silences, to know when his mind had travelled to Kent, to the old rooms, the old roads, the boyhood he had left but never truly shed. In her stillness, she made a frame for the scene — the man who never asked for this life, holding the future of it without flinching.

The nursery itself was hushed, not the brittle quiet of formality, but the living quiet of a day that would be remembered without needing to be marked on a calendar. The fire in the grate had been reduced to a bed of embers, casting a steady heat across the room. The scent of freshly laundered cotton drifted from the stack of folded cloths on the low dresser. Somewhere below, the sounds of the Castle carried — the faint thud of a closing door, the muted laugh of one of the kitchen staff — but here, the world had narrowed to the span of his arms.

Hannah stirred against him, the subtle stretch of a tiny arm pushing through the blanket. He shifted her slightly, the motion so instinctive that it felt as though his body had been waiting years to remember it. Frederick's eyes tracked the motion, his small brow furrowing in what Ben liked to imagine was concentration, though it might only have been the reflex of newborn puzzlement. Still, in those few seconds, the boy looked like someone already weighing the measure of his surroundings.

"Names are promises," Ben said, the words low enough that they would not wake the sleeping half of his arms. "You'll find out what yours means in time." He wasn't speaking for anyone else to hear, but Isla caught it. She leaned back, letting the rhythm of his voice fill the space between them, because she knew that to Ben, speaking aloud was the first step in setting a truth into motion.

Outside the window, dusk settled over the gardens, the sky sliding from pale gold into the muted blue that always made the Castle seem larger. Somewhere in the hedgerows, the first of the evening birds called, the sound carrying up and into the stone walls as if to mark the hour. Ben didn't move. He had the sense — not rare for him — that moments like this were the real measure of a reign, that all the declarations in the world meant less than the feel of a child's weight in your hands when the world was quiet enough to hear your own thoughts.

In the corner, the cradle stood waiting. It had been made by a craftsman from a village far north, a man who had taken three weeks to carve the curves and joints until they moved without a sound. Ben had run his hands over it earlier, feeling the smoothness where the grain had been coaxed rather than forced into shape. The thought that the twins would one day outgrow it already struck him as strange, almost unwelcome. For now, they fit exactly where they were, and so did he.

Casper's photograph sat on the shelf just above the cradle. The boy was already part of the family, his adoption complete in both law and heart. Ben had made sure the papers were not only signed but delivered into a record that would never be misplaced. Casper's grin, caught mid-laugh in that photo, reminded him that legacies could be built as much by choice as by blood. It had been his decision to bring the boy into their name, and in doing so, he had altered the shape of what Rosenshavn would mean in the years ahead.

The thought that Kendrick would soon step down lingered like the slow fade of an echo. It was not a shock — they had spoken of it often enough — but the finality of it pressed against the edges of this moment. When it happened, there would be no parade, no gilded speeches. Ben would take the place set before him as he always had: quietly, with no need to prove anything to anyone. Isla would be there, not as an ornament, but as the equal who had stood in every shadow with him and never once asked to trade it for light.

He adjusted his hold, glancing once more at each of the twins as if to assure himself they were still as they had been a heartbeat ago. Hannah's hand curled against his chest, a small anchor in the weave of his shirt. Frederick's breathing had settled into a slow, even rhythm. These were not just his children; they were the last word in a sentence written by generations before him, the answer to questions he had been asked since he was old enough to understand what was expected of him.

"They think this is over," he said finally, his voice pitched so low that only Isla caught the words. Her gaze met his without question. He shifted his weight, the twins balanced like two halves of a single truth, and finished the thought: "But it hasn't even begun." The words hung in the air, not as a threat, but as the sort of promise a man makes when he knows exactly what's at stake and has no intention of turning from it.

And then, as if nothing had been said at all, the nursery settled back into its steady hum. The fire hissed softly. The night drew in close. And in the shelter of the Castle's oldest walls, the man who had never wanted the crown held it in the form of two sleeping heirs, each carrying a name that would not be forgotten.

Casper Arthur Bille Rosenshavn walked into the nursery with the kind of steady step that belonged to someone who knew exactly where he was going. There was no pause at the threshold, no nervous glance to see if he had been noticed or permitted. This was not the tentative walk of a guest. It was the quiet stride of someone who understood, even without the formalities, that this was his place. His arrival did not shift the air; it simply folded into the moment as though he had been part of it all along.

The adoption had been completed without ceremony, in a muted office where pens clicked and papers slid across a polished table under the eyes of officials who, for all their professionalism, could never fully grasp the meaning of what they witnessed. They saw names being signed, legal phrases stamped in black ink, but they did not hear the years of unspoken promises that had led here. For Ben, those papers were not a beginning. They were a conclusion to something that had been true long before law had caught up.

It was an act of making public what had been private for years, an acknowledgment of a bond that had never needed witnesses to be real. In Ben's mind, there was no "before" and "after" — only the quiet truth that the boy had been his from the moment he decided he would be. The Castle had known it, the staff had known it, and most importantly, Casper himself had known it. The surname he now carried was not a gift. It was an inheritance of belonging, signed into permanence.

He came to stand beside Ben without looking at the twins first, though their small faces and slow movements caught the light like tiny mirrors. His eyes found Ben's instead, holding them for a moment that spoke more clearly than words. The look said, I was already yours, and Ben returned it with one of those rare nods that carried a lifetime's worth of acknowledgment. In that glance, they settled it between them without need for explanation.

Ben shifted slightly, so that Casper could see Hannah and Frederick from where he stood, not as strangers, but as the siblings he had been given — not by chance, not by law, but by the deliberate decision of a man who did not collect people like possessions, but kept them like family. Casper leaned forward a fraction, taking them in with the careful study of someone cataloguing a detail for later. He didn't reach out. He didn't need to.

Isla, still seated by the window, watched the scene without interrupting. She had been there when Casper first came into their lives, when the boy had been smaller, quieter, guarded in ways that children should never have to be. She knew the work it had taken to earn his trust, the patience required to chip away at the walls he'd built without ever demanding they come down all at once. Seeing him now, standing so easily at Ben's side, she understood the full weight of this moment in a way the papers could never convey.

Casper's gaze flicked once to the cradle in the corner, then back to Ben, as if confirming for himself that there was enough space in this room — and in this life — for all three of them. It was not jealousy that moved in his expression, but something closer to cautious relief. Ben caught it, read it, and gave the boy the briefest squeeze on the shoulder. It was not a hug. It was a mark of acknowledgment, a signal that nothing had been replaced or diminished.

The boy's chin lifted slightly at the touch, his spine straightening in the subtle way of someone whose presence had just been reaffirmed. He had been at the Castle long enough to know that words like family and home were lived before they were spoken, proven before they were claimed. In that instant, the truth was proven again. He was not an addition. He was part of the foundation.

Ben's memory flickered briefly to the day he had first met Casper, the guarded expression the boy had worn like armour, the way he had measured every word before speaking. He thought of how Sørensen had warmed to him almost immediately, the former chief of security recognising in the boy the same quiet resilience he had once seen in Ben himself. That shared understanding had done more to settle Casper here than any signed decree ever could.

"Come on," Ben said quietly, angling his stance so Casper could see the twins better. His tone was not instructive, not coaxing, but an invitation given without conditions. Casper stepped closer, close enough to see Hannah's hand shift in her sleep, Frederick's eyelids fluttering with dreams too small to hold. He didn't smile, not outwardly, but there was a change in his face that spoke of acceptance — not just of them, but of what their presence meant for him.

The nursery held them in a kind of balanced silence, the fire's low crackle filling in what the three of them didn't need to say aloud. It was not the hush of fragility, but the pause of something settling into place. For all the grandeur of the Castle's walls, for all the names and histories that pressed in from every corridor, the only legacy that mattered right now was the one contained in the space between a man, a boy, and two sleeping children.

Ben adjusted his hold on the twins, the motion deliberate, and glanced down at Casper again. "Your place isn't changing," he said, not as reassurance, but as fact. Casper gave the smallest of nods in reply, the kind that didn't need to be seen by anyone else to have meaning. They both knew the truth already — the words were just the final stone laid on a foundation that had been years in the making.

For the first time since he'd entered the room, Casper looked fully at Hannah and Frederick, and something in his gaze softened. Not a breaking down, but an opening up. Ben saw it and said nothing. Moments like these were not meant to be narrated or framed. They were meant to be kept.

The boy stepped back finally, giving one last glance at Ben before turning toward the door. He left without ceremony, without the stiffness of someone excusing themselves from a place where they didn't belong. He left as someone who knew he could return at any time and find his place exactly as he had left it. That was the quiet privilege of belonging — it didn't need to be claimed twice.

When the door closed behind him, the nursery settled again. Ben breathed in the steady rhythm of the twins, his thoughts lingering on the unspoken exchange. Casper had not needed the name to belong. But now that he carried it, the truth of his place here could never be argued, by anyone, ever again.

The main hall of the Castle had a way of swallowing sound, as though its vaulted ceiling and polished stone had learned over centuries to keep certain moments preserved in quiet. It was here that Kendrick chose to speak, his voice carrying not with volume, but with the deliberate weight of a man who knew his words would not need to be repeated. There was no lectern, no arrangement of flowers, no ceremonial robe or sash. The absence of display was intentional.

He stood in the centre of the hall, the long tables cleared, the great windows open to the muted afternoon light. His eyes passed over the gathered staff — not counting them, but meeting them — and he began. The words were simple, stripped of decoration, free of the long-winded flourishes that often accompany such moments. He told them what they already suspected: that his time as the Castle's head was ending, and that it was ending by his own hand.

There was no tremor in his voice, no hesitation in his phrasing. Each sentence was shaped to be understood exactly as it was spoken, leaving no room for interpretation, no open door for rumours to slip through. In a house where history lived in every beam and tile, Kendrick knew the dangers of ambiguity. Clarity was the only safeguard.

He did not frame it as a resignation, nor as a retirement. It was simply a step aside, taken not out of weakness or defeat, but out of the quiet certainty that the one taking his place would carry the name forward without fracture. The room absorbed the statement like stone absorbs heat — slowly, steadily, without any outward reaction.

When he spoke Ben's name, it was not announced as a successor. It was acknowledged as an inevitability. Kendrick did not raise a hand toward him, did not invite him forward, for such gestures belonged to staged ceremonies, not to truths that had already been lived. Ben, standing toward the side, felt the weight of the moment not in the sound of his own name, but in the stillness that followed it.

Kendrick's eyes lingered on him for a fraction of a second longer than on anyone else, a wordless exchange that carried more meaning than the speech itself. It was not a passing of power in the theatrical sense. It was a recognition of what had already been in motion. The formalities, after all, were for those who needed convincing.

The staff stood in silence. No one shifted, no one whispered. The quiet was not awkward, but respectful — the kind of silence that comes when an ending is recognised for what it is. Kendrick allowed it to sit in the air for a moment before giving the smallest of nods, signalling that there was nothing more to be said.

Ben felt the gaze of the room turn toward him without any formal prompt. He did not step forward, did not raise his voice. This was Kendrick's moment to close, and Ben's to inherit in silence. The exchange was not a transaction to be observed, but a current that everyone present could feel moving beneath the surface.

In that quiet, Kendrick stepped slightly aside — not toward the shadows, not toward a doorway, but simply out of the centre. It was enough. It said without words that the reins had been placed where they belonged. The moment did not need to be marked by applause or proclamations. Its finality was in its simplicity.

Sørensen, watching from the far end of the hall, understood it better than most. He had seen such transitions in other halls, under other banners, and he knew that the loudest ones were often the least enduring. This, however, was different. It would last because it had been prepared for without fanfare.

Kendrick's hands remained at his sides, his posture unchanged, his expression calm. There was no trace of regret, no shadow of reluctance. If anything, there was a faint sense of relief — the quiet exhale of a man who had carried something heavy for a long time and now set it down knowing it would be guarded.

Ben met his eyes once more, offering the smallest tilt of his head in acknowledgment. It was not thanks, not in the ordinary sense. It was something older, something closer to the way soldiers exchange recognition on a field without ever speaking a word. Kendrick returned it with equal restraint.

The room began to stir again, the quiet folding back into the hum of Castle life. Staff moved with the same steady rhythm as before, but something had shifted — not in the way the halls were walked, but in the knowledge of who now carried the name at the top. It was understood without being stated again.

Kendrick left the hall without any procession, walking at his usual pace, neither slower nor faster than on any other day. Ben remained where he was, the moment settling into him like a stone dropped into deep water, its ripples too slow to see but certain to reach every corner of the Castle in time.

When the last of the light from the windows drew long across the floor, Ben finally moved, not toward the centre where Kendrick had stood, but toward the hallway leading back to the nursery. He knew the true weight of the reins he had just been handed — and he knew where his first steps should take him.

The hall had not changed in appearance, yet the moment Kendrick stepped aside, something in the air shifted. Ben did not stride forward, did not call for attention, and made no effort to claim the space. Instead, he moved with quiet certainty into the place left open, his pace unhurried, his presence unannounced. It was a transition so seamless that anyone arriving at that precise instant might not realise it had taken place at all.

No banners were lowered, no symbols exchanged. The absence of ceremony was not an oversight, but a deliberate choice, one that matched the reality of the moment. Power here was not transferred through spectacle. It was assumed, as naturally as water finding its level. Those who had served in the Castle long enough recognised the shift without needing it spoken aloud.

There was no applause. There were no cries of allegiance. Instead, the silence deepened, becoming a presence of its own. The staff's eyes turned to Ben in unison — not searching, not questioning, but acknowledging. The man they had known as a neighbour, a confidant, and sometimes even a co-conspirator in their lighter moments was now the one whose final word would settle any dispute.

Ben did not change his expression, nor did he try to mask the fact that he felt the weight of their attention. He simply accepted it. This was not about earning authority. That had already been done in countless, unrecorded moments — in his willingness to listen, in his refusal to stand above them, in the quiet way he remembered names and details others forgot.

Sørensen, standing near the far wall, gave the smallest nod, a gesture so subtle it could have been mistaken for nothing more than an adjustment of posture. But Ben saw it. That nod carried a history of battles fought without weapons, of operations completed without recognition, of loyalties earned without demand.

The air in the hall seemed tighter now, not with tension, but with cohesion. It was the same room, yet under his presence, it carried a different shape, as though invisible lines had drawn themselves from every corner toward the place where he stood. The staff felt it too. Even without ceremony, there was no mistaking who held the reins.

Ben's hands remained loose at his sides. He did not take up any symbol of office, did not hold a staff, did not wear a crown. These were trappings he neither needed nor wanted. The truth of his position lay not in objects but in the collective recognition of those before him. That recognition was already complete.

In the hush, he let his eyes sweep across the hall. He did not linger on any one face, yet he met every gaze. It was not a challenge, not a test — merely an acknowledgment. It was his way of saying, I see you, and I am here. In return, they gave him their stillness, a form of acceptance older and more binding than applause.

Kendrick had already stepped back into the edges of the gathering, blending into the periphery with the ease of a man who no longer sought the centre. There was no awkwardness between them, no trace of tension. The change had been made, and both men accepted it as something inevitable, not negotiable.

No one took notes, no one recorded the moment. There would be no official photograph to mark the transition. In years to come, the memory would exist only in the recollections of those who had been there — and in the way Castle life would subtly shift from this day forward.

Ben spoke no words to mark the moment, for words would have been unnecessary. Everything that needed to be said had been spoken long before, in quieter settings, in smaller rooms, where trust was built not through declarations but through action. This was simply the moment that trust took its final shape.

The hall did not resume its noise all at once. Instead, the silence loosened slowly, as though each person needed to adjust to the new alignment. When the first sounds of movement returned — footsteps on the stone floor, the soft closing of a distant door — they carried no urgency. Life in the Castle was continuing, as it always did.

Ben's presence in the centre was brief. He did not linger there as though staking a claim. Instead, after allowing the weight of the shift to settle into the bones of the room, he began to move toward the side corridor, the one that would take him back to the nursery. There, his role was different, yet just as binding.

Those who watched him go knew that nothing outward had changed — yet everything had. The quiet passing of the role was done. No signatures, no speeches, no scripted displays. And yet, in the absence of all that, the truth of it was undeniable. The Castle had a new centre now, and it was a man who had taken it without asking, because it had always been his to take.

Isla's hand came to rest against the small of his back with the familiarity of someone who had done so a hundred times before and would do so a hundred more. It was not a possessive gesture, nor one meant to reassure in front of others; it was a steadying point, a single, silent acknowledgement that she was exactly where she was meant to be. She had seen him face storms that had nothing to do with weather, and she knew the weight he carried now was heavier than any crown.

Her posture was naturally straight, as if she had been born to stand in such moments, though there was no performance in it. She did not need to work at presence — it followed her, not because of titles, but because of the unshakable calm that lived in her. She stood beside him without flinching at the eyes upon them, her own gaze meeting each one without invitation yet without fear.

Ben felt her touch more than the attention of the room. The voices and movement around them faded into the periphery, but that hand at his back anchored him in a way nothing else could. He did not look at her, nor did he need to. Their connection was an unbroken line that needed no reinforcement from sight or speech.

There was no attempt between them to play to the room. They did not turn to exchange staged smiles, nor did they arrange themselves for the view of those who might be watching. Isla's presence beside him was not part of the presentation; it was part of the foundation. Together they formed a single, unyielding line in the centre of the hall, and the people around them instinctively respected its boundary.

Ben knew she understood the cost of this day in a way few others could. He had not told her every detail of what had brought them here, but she had pieced together enough over the years to know that leadership was rarely about the moments others celebrated. It was about the quiet toll it took behind closed doors. And she was ready to bear her share of it, not as a burden, but as a choice.

When the hall seemed to settle into a quieter rhythm, her touch did not shift. It was not a fleeting contact meant to be seen and then withdrawn. It stayed — a quiet insistence that no matter what eyes followed them or what thoughts stirred in the minds of those present, the two of them were united in more than appearance.

The respect in the room deepened, though no one spoke of it. Those who worked in the Castle understood that strength here did not need to roar; it could stand silent and still and command as much attention as any grand declaration. And in that stillness, Ben and Isla made their point without uttering a single word.

A glance passed between them — brief, almost imperceptible — but it held more meaning than a roomful of speeches. In it was the promise that they would weather what came next, whether it arrived as a storm or as a calm. Theirs was not a union built on shared titles, but on shared resolve.

She had been his anchor in private moments when no one else had been watching, and now, in this most public of transitions, she remained so without altering a thing. To Isla, there was no difference between the man who stood in this hall and the one who laughed with her over tea in the quiet hours before dawn.

The people closest to them — Kendrick, Sørensen, a handful of staff who had known them longest — understood that the strength in this moment did not come from the transfer of authority alone. It came from the way they stood together, not leaning into each other for support, but holding the same line, shoulder to shoulder.

Ben did not need to announce her role in what was to come. The way she stood beside him, her head high, her hand steady, said more than any title could. She was not his shadow, nor his echo. She was the other half of the decision, the equal weight to his own.

As the hall began to disperse, their stance did not change. They allowed the motion of others to flow around them, moving only when they chose to, not when prompted by the shifting crowd. The line they formed was invisible, yet every person who passed respected it, curving their steps so as not to cross it.

When they finally turned toward the corridor that would lead back to the nursery, her hand slipped from his back only so she could take his hand instead. It was a natural exchange, a continuation rather than a release. The hall had seen them as a united front; the nursery would see them as a united family.

And in the unspoken agreement that had carried them through the day, they walked away without needing the room to understand them. They did not seek understanding. Respect was enough — and respect they had, in full.

The Castle might now have a new king, but in truth, it had always had them both.

Ben leaned toward her in a movement so subtle it could have been mistaken for a shift in balance, a breath drawn in the quiet after a long moment of standing. It was not the sort of gesture one would notice unless watching for the fine details — and almost no one here would have thought to watch him in that way. The room's focus was on the title now in his keeping, but Isla's attention had never been on titles. She caught the faint incline of his head, the way his shoulder brushed hers as if in passing, though he did not pass at all.

His voice was barely above the air, meant for no one but her. "They think this is over. But it hasn't even begun." The words came without weight in tone, yet with a density that settled between them like a stone placed deliberately in the foundation of something new. They were not spoken in warning, nor in reassurance — but in certainty. The kind of certainty that does not need proof.

The sentence hung there, sealed, as if it were a message placed in an envelope they both knew would not be opened for some time. There was no need to unwrap it yet; the meaning was already theirs, tucked into the shared space between thought and spoken word. Around them, the room moved as it had been moving — shifting bodies, quiet conversations, footsteps against the stone floor — but for the two of them, the moment slowed.

Isla's eyes did not flicker, her expression not shifting so much as a degree. Yet in the breath she drew, there was the faintest sharpness, the smallest adjustment that betrayed the depth of her understanding. She knew what he meant. She knew this was not the close of a chapter, nor the laying down of arms after a long campaign. This was the opening of something larger, something heavier.

They did not need to speak of it further here. The hall was not the place for what would come next, nor was this the time to weigh aloud the shape of their future moves. The strength of their partnership lay partly in knowing which words belonged to the world, and which belonged to only them. This one was for them alone.

Ben's gaze did not wander, though it might have appeared to on the surface. He let it travel across the hall in a way that suggested observation, yet in truth he was measuring the space, noting who was where, noting which faces carried the gleam of curiosity and which carried the stillness of loyalty. He had spent years reading people this way, and Isla had learned enough from him to see it too.

Their silence was not empty. It was the same kind of silence that had carried them through past challenges, a silence in which entire conversations unfolded without a sound. She stood close enough to feel the rhythm of his breathing, steady and unhurried, even as she recognised the calculation working beneath it.

He had made his statement without making a scene, and that was what unsettled those who did not yet know him well. A man who could step into a place of power without announcing himself was a man who would not play by predictable rules. That unpredictability was not recklessness — it was strategy. Isla knew it, and she matched it.

Some in the hall would believe his arrival marked the end of a long uncertainty, the drawing of a final line under questions that had been whispered in kitchens and corridors. But Ben knew, and Isla knew, that this was not an end. It was a beginning disguised as closure. They understood that the most decisive moments rarely arrived with a trumpet blast. They arrived like this — softly, almost invisibly — so that only those who needed to know saw them coming.

Her eyes shifted once, deliberately, toward Kendrick. He was still near enough to hear them if they had spoken aloud, but far enough that the whisper had passed unnoticed. Kendrick's expression was unreadable, and Isla knew he would not press for meaning. He was a man who understood the value of letting some things remain between two people.

When Ben straightened again, it was with the same unhurried grace he had shown all day. There was no tell-tale sign of what had just been shared, no tightening of his jaw, no flicker in his eyes. It was as if the whisper had never happened — at least to anyone who was not Isla. Yet to her, it rang as clearly as if he had spoken it at full volume.

The hall's noise washed back into their awareness, a tide they had briefly stepped out of. Isla adjusted her stance, the shift almost imperceptible, but it aligned her just slightly closer to him. It was a move of instinct, the kind that came from knowing that what lay ahead would require not only public unity, but private readiness.

Ben felt the change and, without looking at her, allowed the corner of his mouth to soften just slightly. Not a smile. Just an acknowledgement. He knew she understood. And knowing she understood was enough.

Around them, the day continued in its expected fashion. But in the space between that whisper and their next step, a different day had begun — one no one else in that room yet realised had started.

The nursery did not welcome them with ceremony, only with the soft weight of familiar sounds — the quiet rustle of blankets, the faint patter of small feet against polished wood, the muted hum of voices too young to know the weight of the day. The air in here was warmer, calmer, carrying with it the scent of clean linen and the faint sweetness of milk. Ben stepped in first, his arms already filled, one hand cradling Hannah's sleeping form, the other arm wrapped around Frederick's small body, whose head rested contentedly against his chest. Behind him, Isla's presence lingered at the doorway for a heartbeat, her gaze sweeping over the room as if to make certain it was unchanged.

Casper was already there, seated in the armchair nearest the hearth as though it had been waiting for him. He rose without hesitation, crossing the short space between them with an ease that needed no invitation. His hand reached for Hannah's blanket, not to pull it back, not to claim her, but simply to touch the edge — the quiet acknowledgement of one sibling to another. Then, without prompting, he shifted close enough that his knee brushed Ben's leg, positioning himself so that both twins were within his reach.

There was no choreography to it, no instruction given about who would sit where, who would hold which child, or who would stand apart. The shape of the moment formed naturally, like water filling the curves of its own vessel. Ben sat with them, drawing Casper in against his side, the three of them forming a single, unbroken line. No one in that room would have been able to point to where blood ended and adoption began — the thought itself would have felt out of place here.

The twins, in their newness, seemed unaware of the gaze that lingered on them. Hannah's breathing was deep and even, her small mouth forming the faintest pout as she shifted in her sleep. Frederick's eyes were open, though heavy with the pull of rest, and every so often they flicked toward the movement of his brother's hand near him. The contact between them was simple, instinctive, and without the need for meaning to be assigned by anyone watching.

Casper, older by years yet bound by something deeper than time, did not speak. He didn't need to. His quiet nearness was its own declaration, one that spoke more clearly than any formal vow or legal document. Ben, aware of the unspoken strength in that silence, let it remain unbroken. There was a certain peace in knowing that the truest bonds did not require performance — they were simply lived.

In that stillness, Ben allowed himself to see them without the frames others might place around their faces. Not as heirs, not as names to be inked on family trees, but as children — his children — each carrying the same claim upon his heart. The world beyond these walls would one day ask them to bear more than their own lives, to carry histories and futures in equal measure. But here, in the quiet shelter of the nursery, they were only themselves.

Isla moved to stand behind them, her hand brushing lightly across Ben's shoulder as she passed. She stopped at his other side, her gaze falling on all three with a steadiness that matched his own. It was not an act of possession, nor of protection, but of recognition. The family before her was whole, not because of law, nor lineage, but because they had chosen each other long before this day.

The fire cracked softly in the hearth, a small reminder that life beyond these walls was still moving — that the air outside might be colder, harsher, and filled with expectation. But here, in this moment, no such weight pressed upon them. They could exist as they were, without explanation or defence, bound by something no title could define.

The moment lingered, unhurried, as if the very walls understood the need to hold it intact for as long as possible. Ben shifted slightly to adjust Frederick's position, careful not to disturb Hannah's sleep, and in doing so, pressed his knee more firmly against Casper's. The boy did not move away. Instead, he leaned into the space offered, closing the small gap until they were shoulder to shoulder.

It was a quiet claim, that closeness — one that said I belong here without ever demanding to be heard. Ben, who had spent his life reading between the lines of words left unsaid, understood it perfectly.

It began with the faintest shift of movement at the edges of the nursery, a quiet ripple that spread without spoken instruction. One by one, the staff stepped closer, their footsteps muted on the thick carpet, their approach measured yet certain. There was no line to form, no formal greeting to prepare, yet each of them seemed to understand they were part of something that would never repeat in exactly the same way again. The air warmed with the subtle hum of their presence, carrying the scent of polish from the hall and the faint aroma of fresh bread drifting from the kitchens below.

The first to draw near were those who had known Ben since before the Castle recognised him as its quiet ruler — the older stewards, the housekeepers who had seen him race through corridors as a boy, the gardeners who remembered the sound of his laughter carried across the lawns. Their nods were slow, deliberate, and laced with an understated pride that required no words to explain. In their eyes was the recognition of a journey watched from its uncertain beginning to its unshakable present.

Behind them came the younger staff, those newer to Rosenshavn's rhythm but quick to learn its unspoken rules. They moved with a natural respect, as though drawn into the gravity of the moment by instinct alone. Their glances were not questioning; they did not need the history recited to them to feel its weight. In their faces was a quiet pledge — that this was as much theirs to protect as it was his to bear.

No one reached out to shake hands or offer embraces. Instead, the tribute came in smaller, more telling gestures: a slight bow of the head, a smile held just long enough to be seen, a murmured "Sir" or "Your Majesty" uttered in a tone that carried neither formality nor familiarity, but a balance of both. The space between them was filled with the kind of silence that spoke volumes — a silence that carried respect, loyalty, and something gentler still.

From his chair, Ben let the moment unfold without interruption, without trying to break it with words of thanks or attempts to lighten its gravity. He met each gaze, acknowledging every face, his own expression steady yet softened by the presence of his family around him. Hannah shifted in his arm, her small sound drawing smiles from those nearest, while Frederick's half-lidded stare seemed to rest briefly on each figure in turn, as though memorising them.

Isla stood slightly behind him now, her presence aligning with theirs — not as Queen in the ceremonial sense, but as the quiet centre from which this household drew much of its steadiness. Her eyes moved over the gathered staff in the same way Ben's did: with recognition, with appreciation, and with the certainty that what was being given here was real.

There was no applause, no grand declaration to close the moment. When the staff eventually stepped back, they did so with the unhurried ease of people confident that the connection had been made. The room felt different when they left — not lighter, but fuller — carrying the unshakable assurance that the bonds within these walls could not be dictated by title alone.

It began without any official bulletin, without the glare of cameras or the stiff announcement of a press office. Instead, the first signs travelled in ways only Copenhagen seemed to manage — through the pause in a shopkeeper's hands as she wrapped bread for a regular, through the murmured exchange between two old friends leaning on their bicycles outside a flower stall, through the flicker of recognition that passed between strangers when Ben's name surfaced mid-conversation. These were not rumours; they were acknowledgements, carried not on headlines but on the familiar warmth of shared knowledge.

In the market squares, where crates of vegetables leaned against tables and the air held the scent of earth and salt from the harbour, people spoke his name as though tasting a truth they had long expected. There was no need for speculation, no sharp turn toward intrigue — only the gentle certainty of a city that knew its people as well as its own streets. To them, the shift at Rosenshavn Castle was not a distant political movement. It was the return of someone they had watched grow into his place without ever demanding it.

Cafés caught the rhythm next, their conversations rising and folding over cups of strong coffee and plates of smørrebrød. Here, the news slipped into the background hum, not disrupting the day but colouring it. A waiter, passing between tables, caught a single line from a customer — "He's back." — and carried it silently with him to the next room, as though it were a small gift not yet ready to be unwrapped.

In the narrow streets where cobblestones had been worn smooth by centuries of footsteps, the atmosphere took on a quieter current. Neighbours greeting each other did so with an extra glance, a slight tilt of the head, as if confirming they were both aware of the same truth. There was no urgency in it; the city had always been patient with such things. The knowledge itself was enough.

For those who had known him personally — the shopkeepers, the ferry operators, the men who stacked chairs at the end of the waterfront day — the news carried a different weight. This was not just about titles or duties. It was about the friend who had stood beside them in simpler times, who had listened without pretense, who had treated their stories as worth keeping. And so, the return of the King was not the return of authority, but the return of a familiar presence they trusted without question.

By the time the Castle would make any formal statement, the city had already decided the matter for itself. No banners were needed, no public cheers summoned. The acceptance was already woven into the day, like the scent of baking bread or the sound of gulls along the quay — unspoken, undeniable, and entirely theirs.

The nursery light was softened by the drawn curtains, turning the air into a muted glow that made every detail sharper in its stillness. Hannah's fingers had found the edge of Ben's jacket, the tiny knuckles curling tight as though the fabric itself was the line between her and the rest of the world. It was not a reflexive grasp; it was a hold with intent, the sort that seemed to say she already knew where safety lay. The weight of her in his arm was nothing, yet it was everything — the kind of weight a man carried for the rest of his life without once setting it down.

Frederick stirred against him, the faintest murmur in his half-sleep, shifting until his cheek found the centre of Ben's chest. It was a movement so slight that it might have gone unnoticed, but Ben felt the trust in it as clearly as a spoken vow. The boy's breathing evened, falling into the same rhythm as his own, and in that quiet tether there was an understanding that could never be taught in words. It was something inherited not by blood alone, but by the example of how a man chose to stand in the world.

Ben did not think of crowns or duty in that moment. The titles could wait, the obligations could circle elsewhere for a while. Here, with one child in each arm, there was only the knowledge that whatever the world demanded of him, it would have to pass through this point first. This was the claim they laid upon him — not as heirs to a throne, but as the only voices that could ever command him without needing to speak.

He had held them both in the delivery room, still damp from the hour they were born, but this felt different. Then, they had been new. Now, they were his. The change was not in the law or the bloodline, but in the bond that had settled between them in these early weeks — a bond that did not negotiate, did not bend. He had not asked for their claim; they had simply taken it, and he had let them.

Isla watched from the low chair by the window, her hands folded in her lap, her gaze fixed not on him but on the line formed by the three of them together. She did not need to move closer to be part of it; her presence was already in the way the children stilled when he entered the room, in the way Hannah's fist tightened whenever she sensed the air change. She understood, without the need for discussion, that this was not a moment to intrude upon — it was one to witness.

The nursery carried the faint scent of warmed milk and clean cotton, the understated comforts of early life. Somewhere in the distance, the Castle's walls held the low murmur of movement — the staff going about their tasks, the occasional muted clang of metal from the kitchens — but none of it reached here with any urgency. This was a room removed from the day's pace, as if time had accepted its own need to pause.

Ben's thoughts turned, not to the day's duties, but to the years ahead. These two would grow into a life that would be watched, measured, and often judged. That was the reality of their names. But here, now, they knew nothing of it. Their claim on him was not for what he represented to others, but for what he was to them — a constant figure, unshaken, who would meet the world head-on so they would not have to face it alone until they were ready.

Hannah's grip had loosened slightly, the weight of her hand now resting against his chest instead of pulling at his jacket. Frederick had slipped deeper into sleep, the small rise and fall of his shoulders syncing perfectly with his own breath. It was a rhythm Ben wanted to hold onto, even knowing it would change as they grew. One day, their hands would be too large for this, their shoulders too broad to fit into the crook of his arm. But the claim would remain.

Outside, the city might still be murmuring about his return, and the Castle might still be adjusting to the shift in its leadership, but none of that reached them here. In this small, warm space, the balance of the world was set by two children who had no idea how much power they already held.

Ben knew what this meant. They would inherit more than the names Hannah and Frederick Rosenshavn. They would inherit the way he stood against the pressures that came with those names. They would learn, not from lectures or proclamations, but from watching how he carried himself when the ground shifted under his feet. And they would remember, always, that he had never once put them down when the world called for him.

He shifted his hold slightly, bringing them both closer, and for a moment allowed himself the selfish thought of wanting this to last forever — the stillness, the unbroken trust, the quiet weight of two names that would one day carry their own history. But for now, they were simply his children, and that was enough.

He would defend that truth against anyone who thought to diminish it, against anything that threatened to make them forget who they were outside of titles. The claim they had on him was absolute, and he welcomed it. This was not a duty. This was the one part of his life that was his entirely by choice.

The twins, even in sleep, seemed to sense the solidity of his resolve. Hannah's fingers twitched once against his shirt, Frederick's breath warmed the fabric over his heart, and in the quiet hum of the nursery, Ben knew there was no place in the world more immovable than where he stood now.

It was not a crown that anchored him. It was this — the quiet claim of two small lives, holding him as tightly as he would hold them, now and for every day that followed.

Casper moved without instruction, his steps measured, placing himself a breath's distance ahead of the cradle where the twins rested. It was not posturing, not the over-eagerness of a child eager to prove himself, but something instinctive. His stance was angled just enough to give him full sight of the door, while his shoulder stayed close enough to the crib to block a straight reach. Ben recognised the formation instantly — the subtle forward lean, the relaxed but ready placement of feet — and it struck him not as learned behaviour, but as something absorbed quietly, the way a tree takes in light without knowing it is growing.

The boy's face did not shift into the false sharpness some use to mask uncertainty. Instead, his gaze swept the room once and returned to rest in a still, unblinking watch. There was no sign of strain in the posture, no awkwardness in the weight he placed on his heels. It was a stance that Sørensen had carried for years — one that said, You may look, but you will not pass without meeting me first. And in that moment, Ben saw not a child playing at defence, but the quiet emergence of someone who had already decided where he stood in this family.

Ben did not speak. Words would have diluted the meaning of what was taking shape in front of him. Instead, he shifted his own stance, the twins balanced in his arms, and let his eyes find Casper's. It was a meeting held longer than casual acknowledgement would allow. There was no smile exchanged, no nod, just the unbroken recognition between two people who understood that protection was not a task — it was a way of being.

In that silence, Ben felt something settle, as if a thread had been tied between them without needing to be pulled taut. It was not a moment of inheritance, nor of command. It was something older than either of those — the unspoken pact of those who would put themselves between danger and the people they loved, not because they were told to, but because they could not imagine any other way to stand.

Casper's fingers brushed the edge of the crib, a small, steady touch that seemed almost incidental. But Ben saw it for what it was — a point of contact, an anchor for the silent promise he was making. He did not have to look down at the twins to know they were the centre of that promise. He could see it in the way the boy's shoulders had squared, in the way he had placed himself where he could be the first to meet whatever crossed that threshold.

There were no oaths spoken, no vows repeated after an elder. The boy's age would have made such formality absurd, but the absence of words made the vow stronger. This was not the kind of promise that faded once a room emptied or an audience moved on. This was the kind that stayed, embedded so deep it became part of muscle and reflex. Ben had lived by such promises. He knew their permanence.

The quiet stretched, but it was not uncomfortable. It was the kind of pause that clarified rather than stalled. Ben gave the faintest incline of his head, the kind that said, I see it, and I accept it. Casper's eyes narrowed just slightly, not in challenge, but in understanding that the acknowledgement meant the pact was now mutual. What was promised one way was now returned the other.

From the corner of the room, Isla watched without breaking the moment. She knew better than to intrude, just as she knew what this meant for all three of them. There were battles she and Ben would fight together, but there were others that would fall to the lines drawn between the men of this family — regardless of age. This was one of them.

Casper shifted his weight only when the moment had fully sealed. It was a fractional move, the kind a sentry makes when adjusting for comfort without giving up his ground. His eyes returned to the door, but Ben knew the connection between them hadn't lessened. It would not.

In the years to come, that stance would change. It would grow taller, broader, steadier. But the shape of it would remain exactly the same as it was now — a quiet wall, an unshakable line. And long after this day was spoken of, if it was ever spoken of at all, the pact would still hold.

Ben felt the twins shift slightly in his arms, their small warmth pressed against him. He glanced once more at the boy ahead of them, knowing this moment would never need to be repeated for it to last. It was already written into the way they stood in that room, into the air they breathed between them.

In another life, or under another roof, such a moment might have been marked with ceremony. Here, it was enough that it had happened. Enough that both of them knew it, without telling a soul.

Casper remained in place, his shadow falling over the crib. And though no one in the room spoke it aloud, every person who saw him then — whether in that moment or years later in memory — would know exactly what he had said without saying a single word.

Kendrick stepped in close, his movement quiet enough that it drew no notice from the few staff still lingering at the edge of the hall. His shadow met Ben's, and for a moment, they stood as they had a hundred times before — mentor and student, neither making a show of it. When he spoke, his voice was low, each word carrying the weight of a man who had never wasted breath on things that did not matter. There was no preamble, no clearing of the throat. Just the clean edge of sentences shaped by years of command.

"You'll find that the rules they hand you in writing are worth less than the ones no one tells you," Kendrick said, his tone flat, unbothered by whether the thought sounded heavy or not. "The written rules are for them. The real ones are for you. Keep your own list short. Keep it yours." Ben didn't answer. His eyes stayed on Kendrick's, reading what was between the words — that the hardest part of the role would never be public decisions, but the private lines he refused to cross.

Kendrick's gaze didn't drift. "They'll come at you in ways you expect and in ways you don't. Don't waste time on the first. Save it for the second." The advice was not coated in reassurance, nor in warning. It was simply given, like a tool passed from one hand to another. Ben felt its weight settle instantly — the kind of truth that wouldn't fade no matter how much time passed between hearing and using it.

Neither man moved to close the distance further. This was not the kind of exchange that asked for a clasped hand or a held shoulder. It lived in the space between them, where understanding had been built brick by brick over years of knowing each other's limits. Kendrick had stepped down as cleanly as he had taken up the role years ago, and in that clarity, there was no room for sentiment dressed as formality.

"You've already been doing the work," Kendrick added, his voice tightening slightly. "Now you'll just do it with fewer people thinking they can tell you no." It might have sounded like a compliment if it weren't delivered with the same tone he used to point out a loose hinge or an unsecured gate. Ben almost smiled, but the weight of the day kept the expression behind his eyes.

The pause that followed was deliberate. Kendrick wasn't searching for words — he was letting the ones already spoken find their place. Ben let the silence hold, knowing from experience that rushing it would mean missing something. Sure enough, Kendrick's final words came without warning. "You don't need them to like you. Just make sure they never doubt you." That was it. No explanation, no story to wrap around it.

When Kendrick stepped back, it was with the quiet finality of a man who had given exactly what he intended and nothing more. Ben didn't move to stop him, nor did he offer thanks. Both knew gratitude was built into the very fact that the conversation had taken place at all.

Kendrick's retreat was slow, unhurried. He didn't glance back, didn't wait for any sign of approval. And Ben didn't give one. Their connection didn't need such gestures. It lived in the memory of long winters, guarded corridors, and decisions made when no one else was awake to see them.

The space Kendrick left behind didn't feel like absence. It felt like the moment after a door had been locked — the kind of security that came from knowing the man before you had cleared the ground and left it solid beneath your feet. Ben adjusted his stance slightly, feeling the truth of that in the floor under him.

Even in stepping away, Kendrick had managed to leave something behind — not as a weight to carry, but as a reminder of the steel woven into the job. It wasn't advice meant to comfort. It was advice meant to last. And Ben knew it would.

By mid-morning, the order had been given without the sound of a command. The gates swung shut with the ease of a long-rehearsed motion, their iron weight meeting stone with a finality that could be felt through the courtyard floor. It was not an act of secrecy; the Castle had no need to hide. Instead, it was the deliberate drawing of a boundary — a declaration that the day belonged wholly to those within. Ben had not asked for silence, but silence came all the same, settling over the grounds with the same precision as the lock sliding into place.

Inside, the movement of people was unhurried, the steps of staff and family softened by the knowledge that the next knock at the gate would not come until they allowed it. There was an ease to their passing in and out of the halls, a rare kind of stillness that did not need guarding because the line had already been drawn. Those closest to the family understood the privilege of this pause. There was no schedule to keep, no summons to answer, no audience to prepare for — only the uninterrupted rhythm of the Castle breathing on its own.

Beyond the gates, the city did not press. The people of Copenhagen, familiar with the Castle's rare days of solitude, did not mistake the closure for absence. They could feel its presence even from the streets below, the tall iron keeping its vigil as firmly as any watchman. Shopkeepers in the market stalls spoke of it with casual acceptance, their tones reflecting a quiet respect that required no embellishment. Those who might have been tempted to test the boundary chose otherwise, as if some shared understanding kept curiosity in check.

The gates themselves stood as more than a barrier. To those outside, they were a message — that the King's time was not a commodity to be taken or demanded. The weight of that message was not in any posted guard or official decree, but in the simple fact that no one challenged it. That respect had been earned over years, in moments far smaller than a public speech and far quieter than any parade.

Within the walls, children's voices carried in bursts through open windows, drifting into the garden where Isla walked slowly with the twins. Casper trailed ahead on the path, a sentry without orders, his eyes catching movement before it reached the hedgerows. It was the kind of safety only a closed gate could provide — one where the sounds of life could spill into the air without fear of being cut short.

Ben moved between rooms without the weight of being watched, his steps unhurried as he crossed thresholds that usually demanded precision. The day felt different, not for the absence of the outside world, but for the presence of something rare inside: uninterrupted time. Conversations could be finished. Decisions could be made without the pull of a waiting car or the press of an appointment. Even the air in the great hall seemed to hold a steadier temperature, as though the walls themselves knew they were not to be disturbed.

By the time afternoon settled in, the closed gates had taken on the feel of ritual. No one needed to check their position, no one needed to guard them. They simply were — unyielding in the face of the city, soft in the shelter they provided to those within. The Castle had been many things over its long life, but today it was a harbour, holding steady against the tide of the world just beyond its iron frame.

The plan is not announced, yet it hangs in the air like a scent one cannot name but instantly recognises. Ben moves through the room with the unhurried pace of someone appearing at ease, yet every glance carries calculation. His eyes measure doorways, trace the angles of light through the tall windows, and pause on certain faces longer than courtesy requires. It is not suspicion — it is assessment. Those who have worked beside him long enough know the signs. This is the way he thinks when the next move has already taken root in his mind.

Isla catches it first, not through words, but through the shift in his breathing when he stops beside her chair. She has seen this before, in moments when everyone else thought they were at rest but he was already planning the next step. She says nothing, allowing him to hold his silence, because she understands that the weight of a plan too soon spoken can be enough to break it. Instead, she matches his quiet, her stillness a kind of assent.

Around them, the Castle carries on as if unaware. Footsteps pass in the hallway, the faint clink of porcelain sounds from the kitchens, and a distant laugh drifts from the nursery. Yet for all the movement, there is a contained centre in the room where Ben stands. Those who notice him there — Sørensen, Kendrick, even the older members of staff — feel the pull of something unseen. It is not tension. It is momentum gathering quietly, waiting for the moment when the door will open and the plan will step through.

Ben does not look at Isla when he finally moves, but she knows it is not because he has forgotten her presence. It is because she is already part of the plan, stitched into it without the need for confirmation. Her role, like his, will be clear when the time comes. For now, they hold it between them — an unspoken pact that needs no signature, no witness, only the shared understanding that when the first step is taken, they will take it together.

Evening settles over Rosenshavn without the clang of carriage gates or the shuffle of unfamiliar feet in the corridor. The absence of guests is deliberate, not a matter of scheduling but of choice. Soft pools of light spill across the polished floors, the lamps trimmed low so the Castle feels less like a seat of rule and more like a home. Outside, the grounds are quiet, the breeze carrying only the faintest movement of branches, a sound too subtle to disturb the stillness within. Tonight, there is no court to observe, no audience to address, no polite exchanges to weather — only the rare possession of their own hours.

The private dining room, tucked in the west wing where the windows frame the last stretch of sunset, holds a table smaller than most in the Castle. Its surface is laid without grandeur, the silver modest, the plates chosen for their familiarity rather than display. The family gathers without the rigid formality that public life demands. There is no order of seating dictated by title; instead, chairs scrape across the floor in the easy disorder of those who need no arrangement to define their places.

Conversation begins in low voices, not hushed for secrecy but softened by the calm of the day's end. The rhythm is slow, each exchange stretching without the need to be filled. Between words, there is the steady clink of cutlery, the faint scent of baked bread cooling at the edge of the table, and the occasional small noise from the nursery beyond the closed door. Ben does not lead the conversation, nor does he withdraw from it. He listens, responds, and lets the flow move as it will.

The children's presence shapes the table's mood more than any decision could. Hannah, cradled in Isla's arm, stirs once before settling again. Frederick rests in a bassinet pulled close to Ben's chair, his breathing even, his small hands shifting now and then. Casper sits upright, content with the rare closeness of a meal uninterrupted by schedules or interruptions from outside the Castle walls. In his posture there is a quiet pride — not in the food, but in belonging to this circle without question.

It is not a celebration in the way the outside world might expect. There are no toasts, no rehearsed words marking the day's significance. Instead, it is a claiming — of the right to gather in peace, to eat without performance, to close the day on their own terms. The room holds a warmth that does not come from the lamps, but from the shared understanding that such nights are rare, and must be kept when they arrive. Even Kendrick, seated near the corner with a glass in hand, lets the silence stretch comfortably between his few remarks, his presence more a watchful guard than an active participant.

Ben looks once around the table, not in inspection but in quiet acknowledgement. This, more than any hall or title, is where his rule begins and is measured. The absence of outsiders is not a withdrawal from duty, but an assertion that the crown — silent though it may be — does not strip him of the right to keep a space untouched by public reach. He does not need to say it aloud; the truth is written in the very air of the room.

When the last plates are cleared, no one rises immediately. They remain in their chairs, the conversation drifting in unhurried turns, the hours uncounted. Outside, the city waits, the world waits, but tonight, the Castle does not open its gates to them. Tonight belongs only to those already within.

The Castle is at its quietest when the last lamps are lowered, the corridors empty but for the faint echo of a door settling into its frame. In the master room, the stillness feels earned, a rare thing held without fear of losing it. Ben stands near the tall window, its panes reflecting a fractured view of the city lights beyond the closed gates. Hannah is asleep in the crook of his arm, her breath warm against the fold of his sleeve. Her weight is slight, yet the presence she carries is unshakable — as if she already knows she has been born into a story that will not let her slip into the shadows.

The night air presses faintly against the glass, the kind that carries the scent of the city without its noise. Frederick lies in the crib, one arm raised above his head in the unguarded sprawl of deep sleep. The dim light catches the curve of his cheek, the rise and fall of his chest in a rhythm that soothes even as it sharpens Ben's sense of what lies ahead. He watches both children in turn, measuring not the hours behind him but the road that has just begun to stretch forward.

Isla leans against the bedpost, her gaze fixed on him rather than the view outside. She does not move, does not speak, because she knows that some silences are too precise to disturb. She reads the set of his shoulders, the way his fingers adjust fractionally on Hannah's blanket, the almost imperceptible pause before his eyes lift from the sleeping child to the horizon. It is not the posture of a man at rest. It is the stance of one about to move.

Beyond the walls, the city lights flicker in the distance, scattered across the dark like points on a map yet to be drawn. Each one feels like a reminder — of those watching, of those waiting, of those who will not wait quietly for long. The gates are closed for now, but Ben knows there will come a day when they will open not at his choosing, but because the world will demand it. That day does not trouble him; it simply exists, waiting in its place.

He shifts his hold on Hannah, careful not to wake her, and lets his gaze settle fully on the night. There is no part of him that believes in pauses as an end; pauses are only breaths before the next turn. Isla's presence behind him is not an anchor holding him in place, but the steady weight that ensures when he steps forward, it will be with full measure. She has seen this look before, in smaller moments, in quieter fights — and she knows this one will not be small.

When the thought comes, it is without hesitation, without the need to be shaped into anything more. His voice is low, meant for no one else's ear, not even for the child in his arms. "It begins here." The words are not spoken with hope, nor with the uncertainty of what-ifs. They are an acknowledgement of a starting point that cannot be reversed. The sound of them does not linger in the room; it settles deep, like a weight dropped into still water, unseen but unmistakable.

In the pause that follows, Ben keeps his eyes on the dark line of the horizon, as if by holding it in his sight he can hold everything beyond it at bay until the moment he chooses to move. Hannah shifts slightly, her small hand pressing into his chest, a gesture that tightens his grip by instinct rather than thought. Frederick stirs in the crib, but does not wake. Isla remains still, her breathing the only sound in the room besides the faint hum of the city outside.

The master room holds the same truth as the hall earlier that day — that power does not always arrive with noise. Sometimes it is a quiet claim, spoken to no one but oneself, marking the line where the before ends and the after begins. Tonight, that line has been drawn. The rest will follow.

EPILOGUE – THE LINE BEFORE THE STORM

The Castle had settled into the kind of quiet that follows not peace, but the careful folding away of a day that will not be repeated. Outside the gates, Copenhagen still breathed with its easy rhythm, but the air beyond the walls felt heavier, as though the city itself was bracing for something it could not name. Inside, Ben walked the length of the main hall with measured steps, his eyes not on the marble beneath him, but on the long shadow cast ahead. Each sound — the muted echo of his boots, the subtle hum of the lights — marked the close of one chapter, even as the next began to stir.

In the private study, a single envelope lay on the desk. It had arrived without herald, slipped into the Castle by hands neither clumsy nor careless. Ben had already read it twice, each line a thread tied to the seven royal houses whose names had mocked his in closed rooms for far too long. The paper held no threats, no direct challenges, only the kind of veiled language nobles had used for centuries to disguise disdain. He knew their tone. He knew their game. And this time, he would not play it on their terms.

Isla stepped into the room without knocking, her presence a steady line in the shifting haze of the day. She glanced at the envelope but did not reach for it. She didn't have to. Whatever was written there, she already understood it was no longer just paper — it was the last stone in a wall that had been building for years. She crossed to him and rested her hand against his shoulder, not in comfort, but in solidarity.

The city outside might have thought this was the end. The world beyond Denmark might have believed that today's quiet marked the close of a private drama. But Ben knew better. The world already had his name, and the mistake they were making was assuming that knowing it meant they knew the man who carried it. They didn't. Not yet.

On the far wall, the old map of Europe stretched under soft light. His gaze traced borders that had shifted over centuries, kingdoms that had risen and collapsed, houses that had claimed permanence only to vanish in the turn of a decade. He saw the names of the seven who still sat on their thrones as if the centuries owed them fealty. He thought of the lines of their faces, the careless curl of their words in meetings they assumed he would never attend.

Sørensen entered without announcement, his expression unchanged from the years Ben had first known him — the same eyes that had measured threats with precision, the same shoulders that carried more than armour. He looked once at the map, then at Ben, and gave the smallest nod. It was not permission. It was confirmation.

Beyond the walls, reporters still lingered at a respectful distance, their long lenses catching shadows at windows, their questions hanging in the air like fishing lines waiting for a bite. They had their story: the young King, the new heirs, the quiet shift in the Castle's hierarchy. What they didn't have was the ending — and Ben intended to make sure they wouldn't write it before he did.

Casper passed the study door on his way to the nursery. He didn't speak, but his glance inside was enough to tell Ben that even the boy had caught the change in the air. The twins were still too young to sense it, but in time they would know exactly what this night meant. It was the point where their father stopped avoiding the game and began reshaping the board.

Ben folded the letter once more and set it aside, his hands steady. There was no rush. The kind of move he was preparing for required patience, the deliberate pace of a man who knew every step would be measured for years to come. When he finally made it, there would be no mistaking it for anything else.

The House of Windsor would be left untouched. They had no part in the insults that had built this moment. But the others — the seven whose whispers had turned into open derision — would learn that silence from Rosenshavn was never surrender. It was calculation.

In the corridor beyond, Isla's footsteps faded toward the nursery, the soft rhythm reminding him what the stakes truly were. This was not about crowns for the sake of crowns. It was about clearing a path for the ones who would inherit a Europe worth inheriting.

Sørensen lingered in the doorway a moment longer, then asked the only question that mattered: "When?" Ben's answer was as quiet as it was final. "When they've convinced themselves I won't."

The study lights dimmed as he left, the envelope still on the desk, the map on the wall casting its quiet challenge. In the dark, Europe waited, unaware that its comfortable order was already counted in weeks.

From the high windows of Rosenshavn, the city looked almost still, its streets glinting under the lamps, its roofs gathering the soft weight of night. Ben stood at the glass, his reflection overlaying the skyline, the face the world now knew set against the city he had claimed as his own.

He did not smile, did not speak. The silence was its own declaration. And somewhere beyond the walls, in the palaces of seven royal houses, the faintest tremor had already begun.

The scent of polished wood and faint smoke from the hearth hung in the study long after the fire had faded. Ben crossed to the desk again, not to read the letter, but to rest his hand upon it — the way one might pause over a weapon, testing its weight before use. He had never needed bluster, never needed to raise his voice to be heard. The ones who mattered always listened, and the ones who didn't… learned.

A faint wind rattled against the high panes of the window, carrying the city's night sounds up to the Castle walls. Somewhere far below, the late trams slid along their rails, and the quiet laughter of a street still alive at midnight drifted upward. It was a reminder that life went on outside these gates, indifferent to the politics of palaces — until those politics came for them.

Ben allowed himself one last look at the map before extinguishing the lamp. Seven names. Seven crowns. Seven lines of power that thought themselves untouchable. By the time his work was done, they would understand the difference between position and authority. One could be inherited. The other had to be earned — or taken.

In the corridor, his reflection followed him, fractured in the old glass of the Castle windows. He thought of the paths he had walked to reach this point: the streets of Kent, the libraries of his youth, the quiet discoveries that had rewritten everything he thought he knew about himself. None of it had been wasted. Every moment had been preparation, whether he had known it at the time or not.

The Castle doors locked behind him with the deep, slow thud that always reminded him of closing a vault. Tonight, it was more than security — it was a seal. When they opened again, the first steps toward his endgame would already be in motion.

The End Game

The study door closed with a sound that felt less like wood against wood and more like the final turn of a lock on an argument that had dragged on for generations. Ben stood alone in the dim light, the desk before him cleared of all but a single folded sheet. It was not a treaty, not a plea — just the names of seven royal houses, written in his hand with the precision of a man who knew he would not have to write them again. They had played their game across decades, baiting, mocking, underestimating. Tonight, the board was cleared.

He did not pace. He did not sit. Instead, he reached for the heavy chair at the head of the desk and pulled it back without ceremony, lowering himself into it with the quiet confidence of someone who had already won. The world outside believed in the noise of victory — speeches, banners, applause. But victory, real victory, was the silence that followed the last move. He looked down at the paper again, his lips barely moving as he spoke the words that would never be forgotten in the rooms that mattered: "Check mate."

The lamplight cut a sharp line across his face as he leaned back, the weight of the moment settling not on his shoulders but in the air itself. Europe had been playing this match since before his birth, but they had never expected the opponent who played without their rules, without their weaknesses. He had not come to join their game. He had come to end it. The House of Windsor remained untouched — not from mercy, but because they had not crossed him. The others had. And now they would feel the full consequence of mistaking his silence for absence.

Through the tall windows, the city of Copenhagen glowed in the distance, unaware of the precision with which its King had just redrawn the lines of power. Tomorrow, the whispers would begin — not the frantic guesswork of rumour, but the sharp, measured conversations of those who knew enough to be concerned. The pieces on the board had not merely been moved. They had been removed.

Ben rested both hands flat on the desk, the polished wood warm beneath his palms. He had taken everything they thought they could protect, not through force, but through inevitability. There was nothing left to bargain over. Only the understanding that from this night forward, they answered to him. It was not arrogance. It was the simple truth of the board, and the game they had already lost.